HANDBOOK OF

Modeling High-Frequency Data in Finance

Wiley Handbooks in

FINANCIAL ENGINEERING AND ECONOMETRICS

Advisory Editor

Ruey S. Tsay
The University of Chicago Booth School of Business, USA

The dynamic and interaction between financial markets around the world have changed dramatically under economic globalization. In addition, advances in communication and data collection have changed the way information is processed and used. In this new era, financial instruments have become increasingly sophisticated and their impacts are far-reaching. The recent financial (credit) crisis is a vivid example of the new challenges we face and continue to face in this information age. Analytical skills and ability to extract useful information from mass data, to comprehend the complexity of financial instruments, and to assess the financial risk involved become a necessity for economists, financial managers, and risk management professionals. To master such skills and ability, knowledge from computer science, economics, finance, mathematics and statistics is essential. As such, financial engineering is cross-disciplinary, and its theory and applications advance rapidly.

The goal of this Handbook Series is to provide a one-stop source for students, researchers, and practitioners to learn the knowledge and analytical skills they need to face today's challenges in financial markets. The Series intends to introduce systematically recent developments in different areas of financial engineering and econometrics. The coverage will be broad and thorough with balance in theory and applications. Each volume will be edited by leading researchers and practitioners in the area and covers state-of-the-art methods and theory of the selected topic.

Published Wiley Handbooks in Financial Engineering and Econometrics

Viens, Mariani, and Florescu · *Handbook of Modeling High-Frequency Data in Finance*

Forthcoming Wiley Handbooks in Financial Engineering and Econometrics

Bali and Engle · *Handbook of Asset Pricing*
Bauwens, Hafner, and Laurent · *Handbook of Volatility Models and Their Applications*
Brandimarte · *Handbook of Monte Carlo Simulation*
Chan and Wong · *Handbook of Financial Risk Management*
Cruz, Peters, and Shevchenko · *Handbook of Operational Risk*
Sarno, James, and Marsh · *Handbook of Exchange Rates*
Szylar · *Handbook of Market Risk*

HANDBOOK OF

Modeling High-Frequency Data in Finance

Edited by

FREDERI G. VIENS
MARIA C. MARIANI
IONUŢ FLORESCU

WILEY
A JOHN WILEY & SONS, INC., PUBLICATION

Published by John Wiley & Sons, Inc., Hoboken, New Jersey
Published simultaneously in Canada

Library of Congress Cataloging-in-Publication Data:

Viens, Frederi G., 1969–
Handbook of modeling high-frequency data in finance / Frederi G. Viens, Maria C. Mariani, Ionuţ Florescu. — 1
p. cm. — (Wiley handbooks in financial engineering and econometrics ; 4)
Includes index.
ISBN 978-0-470-87688-6 (hardback)
1. Finance–Econometric models. I. Mariani, Maria C. II. Florescu, Ionuţ, 1973– III. Title.
HG106.V54 2011
332.01′5193–dc23
2011038022

Printed in the United States of America

10 9 8 7 6 5 4 3 2 1

Contents

Preface

This handbook is a collection of articles that describe current empirical and analytical work on data sampled with high frequency in the financial industry.

In today's world, many fields are confronted with increasingly large amounts of data. Financial data sampled with high frequency is no exception. These staggering amounts of data pose special challenges to the world of finance, as traditional models and information technology tools can be poorly suited to grapple with their size and complexity. Probabilistic modeling and statistical data analysis attempt to discover order from apparent disorder; this volume may serve as a guide to various new systematic approaches on how to implement these quantitative activities with high-frequency financial data.

The volume is split into three distinct parts. The first part is dedicated to empirical work with high frequency data. Starting the handbook this way is consistent with the first type of activity that is typically undertaken when faced with data: to look for its stylized features. The book's second part is a transition between empirical and theoretical topics and focuses on properties of long memory, also known as *long range dependence*. Models for stock and index data with this type of dependence at the level of squared returns, for instance, are coming into the mainstream; in high frequency finance, the range of dependence can be exacerbated, making long memory an important subject of investigation. The third and last part of the volume presents new analytical and simulation results proposed to make rigorous sense of some of the difficult modeling questions posed by high frequency data in finance. Sophisticated mathematical tools are used, including stochastic calculus, control theory, Fourier analysis, jump processes, and integro-differential methods.

The editors express their deepest gratitude to all the contributors for their talent and labor in bringing together this handbook, to the many anonymous referees who helped the contributors perfect their works, and to Wiley for making the publication a reality.

Frederi Viens
Maria C. Mariani
Ionuţ Florescu

Washington, DC, El Paso, TX, and Hoboken, NJ
April 1, 2011

Contributors

Peter C. Anselmo, New Mexico Institute of Mining and Technology, Socorro, NM

Ernest Barany, Department of Mathematical Sciences, New Mexico State University, Las Cruces, NM

Maria Pia Beccar Varela, Department of Mathematical Sciences, University of Texas at El Paso, El Paso, TX

Dragos Bozdog, Department of Mathematical Sciences, Stevens Institute of Technology, Hoboken, NJ

Alexandra Chronopoulou, INRIA, Nancy, France

Germán Creamer, Howe School and School of Systems and Enterprises, Stevens Institute of Technology, Hoboken, NJ

José E. Figueroa-Lòpez, Department of Statistics, Purdue University, West Lafayette, IN

Ionuţ Florescu, Department of Mathematical Sciences, Stevens Institute of Technology, Hoboken, NJ

Eric Hillebrand, Department of Economics, Louisiana State University, Baton Rouge, LA

Alec N. Kercheval, Department of Mathematics, Florida State University, Tallahassee, FL

Khaldoun Khashanah, Department of Mathematical Sciences, Stevens Institute of Technology, Hoboken, NJ

Steven R. Lancette, Department of Statistics, Purdue University, West Lafayette, IN

Kiseop Lee, Department of Mathematics, University of Louisville, Louisville, KY; Graduate Department of Financial Engineering, Ajou University, Suwon, South Korea

Yang Liu, Department of Mathematics, Florida State University, Tallahassee, FL

Maria Elvira Mancino, Department of Mathematics for Decisions, University of Firenze, Italy

Maria C. Mariani, Department of Mathematical Sciences, University of Texas at El Paso, El Paso, TX

Yanhui Mi, Department of Statistics, Purdue University, West Lafayette, IN

Emmanuel K. Ncheuguim, Department of Mathematical Sciences, New Mexico State University, Las Cruces, NM

Hongwei Qiu, Department of Mathematical Sciences, Stevens Institute of Technology, Hoboken, NJ

Cristian Pasarica, Stevens Institute of Technology, Hoboken, NJ

Marc Salas, New Mexico State University, Las Cruces, NM

Simona Sanfelici, Department of Economics, University of Parma, Italy

Ambar N. Sengupta, Department of Mathematics, Louisiana State University, Baton Rouge, LA

Indranil Sengupta, Department of Mathematical Sciences, University of Texas at El Paso, El Paso, TX

Carlos A. Ulibarri, New Mexico Institute of Mining and Technology, Socorro, NM

Jim Wang, Department of Mathematical Sciences, Stevens Institute of Technology, Hoboken, NJ

Junyue Xu, Department of Economics, Louisiana State University, Baton Rouge, LA

PART ONE

Analysis of Empirical Data

CHAPTER ONE

Estimation of NIG and VG Models for High Frequency Financial Data

JOSÉ E. FIGUEROA-LÓPEZ and
STEVEN R. LANCETTE
Department of Statistics, Purdue University, West Lafayette, IN

KISEOP LEE
Department of Mathematics, University of Louisville, Louisville, KY;
Graduate Department of Financial Engineering,
Ajou University, Suwon, South Korea

YANHUI MI
Department of Statistics, Purdue University, West Lafayette, IN

1.1 Introduction

Driven by the necessity to incorporate the observed stylized features of asset prices, continuous-time stochastic modeling has taken a predominant role in the financial literature over the past two decades. Most of the proposed models are particular cases of a stochastic volatility component driven by a Wiener process superposed with a pure-jump component accounting for the

Handbook of Modeling High-Frequency Data in Finance, First Edition.
Edited by Frederi G. Viens, Maria C. Mariani, and Ionuţ Florescu.

discrete arrival of major influential information. Accurate approximation of the complex phenomenon of trading is certainly attained with such a general model. However, accuracy comes with a high cost in the form of hard estimation and implementation issues as well as overparameterized models. In practice, and certainly for the purpose motivating the task of modeling in the first place, a parsimonious model with relatively few parameters is desirable. With this motivation in mind, *parametric* exponential Lévy models (ELM) are one of the most tractable and successful alternatives to both stochastic volatility models and more general Itô semimartingale models with jumps.

The literature of geometric Lévy models is quite extensive (see Cont & Tankov (2004) for a review). Owing to their appealing interpretation and tractability in this work, we concentrate on two of the most popular classes: the variance-gamma (VG) and normal inverse Gaussian (NIG) models proposed by Carr *et al.* (1998) and Barndorff-Nielsen (1998), respectively. In the "symmetric case" (which is a reasonable assumption for equity prices), both models require only one additional parameter, κ, compared to the two-parameter geometric Brownian motion (also called the *Black–Scholes model*). This additional parameter can be interpreted as the percentage excess kurtosis relative to the normal distribution and, hence, this parameter is mainly in charge of the tail thickness of the log return distribution. In other words, this parameter will determine the frequency of "excessively" large positive or negative returns. Both models are pure-jump models with *infinite jump activity* (i.e., a model with infinitely many jumps during any finite time interval $[0, T]$). Nevertheless, one of the parameters, denoted by σ, controls the variability of the log returns and, thus, it can be interpreted as the volatility of the price process.

Numerous empirical studies have shown that certain parametric ELM, including the VG and the NIG models, are able to fit *daily returns* extremely well using standard estimation methods such as maximum likelihood estimators (MLE) or method of moment estimators (MME) (c.f. Eberlein & Keller (1995); Eberlein & Özkan (2003); Carr *et al.* (1998); Barndorff-Nielsen (1998); Kou & Wang (2004); Carr *et al.* (2002); Seneta (2004); Behr & Pötter (2009), Ramezani & Zeng (2007), and others). On the other hand, in spite of their current importance, very few papers have considered intraday data. One of our main motivations in this work is to analyze whether pure Lévy models can still work well to fit the statistical properties of log returns at the intraday level.

As essentially any other model, a Lévy model will have limitations when working with very high frequency transaction data and, hence, the question is rather to determine the scales where a Lévy model is a good probabilistic approximation of the underlying (extremely complex and stochastic) trading process. We propose to assess the suitability of the Lévy model by analyzing the signature plots of the point estimates at different sampling frequencies. It is plausible that an apparent stability of the point estimates for certain ranges of sampling frequencies provides evidence of the adequacy of the Lévy model at those scales. An earlier work along these lines is Eberlein & Özkan (2003), where this stability was empirically investigated using hyperbolic Lévy models and MLE (based on hourly data). Concretely, one of the main points therein was to estimate the model's parameters from daily mid-day log returns[1] and, then, measure the distance between the empirical density based on hourly returns and the 1-h density implied by the estimated parameters. It is found that this distance is approximately minimal among any other implied densities. In other words, if $f_\delta(\cdot;\theta_{\mathrm{d}}^*)$ denotes the implied density of X_δ when using the parameters θ_{d}^* estimated from daily mid-day returns and if $f_{\mathrm{h}}^*(\cdot)$ denotes the empirical density based on hourly returns, then the distance between $f_\delta(\cdot;\theta_{\mathrm{d}}^*)$ and f_{h}^* is minimal when δ is approximately 1 h. Such a property was termed the *time consistency of Lévy processes*.

In this chapter, we further investigate the consistency of ELM for a wide rage of intraday frequencies using intraday data of the US equity market. Although natural differences due to sampling variation are to be expected, our empirical results under both models exhibit some very interesting common features across the different stocks we analyzed. We find that the estimator of the volatility parameter σ is quite stable for sampling frequencies as short as 20 min or less. For higher frequencies, the volatility estimates exhibit an abrupt tendency to increase (see Fig. 1.6 below), presumably due to microstructure effects. In contrast, the kurtosis estimator is more sensitive to microstructure effects and a certain degree of stability is achieved only for mid-range frequencies of 1 h and more (see Fig. 1.6 below). For higher frequencies, the kurtosis decreases abruptly. In fact, opposite to the smooth signature plot of σ at those scales, the kurtosis estimates consistently change by more than half when going from hourly to 30-min log returns. Again, this phenomenon is presumably due to microstructure effects since the effect of an unaccounted continuous component will be expected to diminish when the sampling frequency increases.

One of the main motivations of Lévy models is that log returns follow ideal conditions for statistical inference in that case; namely, under a Lévy model the log returns at any frequency are independent with a common distribution. Owing to this fact, it is arguable that it might be preferable to use a parsimonious model for which efficient estimation is feasible, rather than a very accurate model for which estimation errors will be intrinsically large. This is similar to the so-called model selection problem of statistics where a model with a high number of parameters typically enjoys a small mis-specification error but suffers from a high estimation variance due to the large number of parameters to estimate.

An intrinsic assumption discussed above is that standard estimation methods are indeed efficient in this high frequency data setting. This is, however, an overstatement (typically overlooked in the literature) since the population distribution of high frequency sample data coming from a true Lévy model depends on the sampling frequency itself and, in spite of having more data, high frequency data does not necessarily imply better estimation results. Hence, another motivation for this work is to analyze the performance of the two most common estimators, namely the method of moments estimators (MME) and the

[1]These returns are derived from prices recorded in the middle of the trading session. The idea behind the choice of these prices is to avoid the typically high volatility at the opening and closing of the trading session.

MLE, when dealing with high frequency data. As an additional contribution of this analysis, we also propose a simple novel numerical scheme for computing the MME. On the other hand, given the inaccessibility of closed forms for the MLE, we apply an unconstrained optimization scheme (Powell's method) to find them numerically.

By Monte Carlo simulations, we discover the surprising fact that neither high frequency sampling nor MLE reduces the estimation error of the volatility parameter in a significant way. In other words, estimating the volatility parameter based on, say, daily observations has similar performance to doing the same based on, say, 5-min observations. On the other hand, the estimation error of the parameter controlling the kurtosis of the model can be significantly reduced by using MLE or intraday data. Another conclusion is that the VG MLE is numerically unstable when working with ultra-high frequency data while both the VG MME and the NIG MLE work quite well for almost any frequency.

The remainder of this chapter is organized as follows. In Section 1.2, we review the properties of the NIG and VG models. Section 1.3 introduces a simple and novel method to compute the moment estimators for the VG and the NIG distributions and also briefly describes the estimation method of maximum likelihood. Section 1.4 presents the finite-sample performance of the moment estimators and the MLE via simulations. In Section 1.5, we present our empirical results using high frequency transaction data from the US equity market. The data was obtained from the NYSE TAQ database of 2005 trades via Wharton's WRDS system. For the sake of clarity and space, we only present the results for Intel and defer a full analysis of other stocks for a future publication. We finish with a section of conclusions and further recommendations.

1.2 The Statistical Models

1.2.1 GENERALITIES OF EXPONENTIAL LÉVY MODELS

Before introducing the specific models we consider in this chapter, let us briefly motivate the application of Lévy processes in financial modeling. We refer the reader to the monographs of Cont & Tankov (2004) and Sato (1999) or the recent review papers Figueroa-López (2011) and Tankov (2011) for further information. Exponential (or Geometric) Lévy models are arguably the most natural generalization of the geometric Brownian motion intrinsic in the Black–Scholes option pricing model. A geometric Brownian motion (also called *Black–Scholes model*) postulates the following conditions about the price process $(S_t)_{t\geq 0}$ of a risky asset:

(1) The (log) return on the asset over a time period $[t, t+h]$ of length h, that is,

$$R_{t,t+h} := \log \frac{S_{t+h}}{S_t}$$

is Gaussian with mean μh and variance $\sigma^2 h$ (independent of t);

(2) Log returns on disjoint time periods are mutually independent;

(3) The price path $t \to S_t$ is continuous; that is, $\mathbb{P}(S_u \to S_t, \text{ as } u \to t, \ \forall\, t) = 1$.

The previous assumptions can equivalently be stated in terms of the so-called log return process $(X_t)_t$, denoted henceforth as

$$X_t := \log \frac{S_t}{S_0}.$$

Indeed, assumption (1) is equivalent to ask that the increment $X_{t+h} - X_t$ of the process X over $[t, t+h]$ is Gaussian with mean μh and variance $\sigma^2 h$. Assumption (2) simply means that the increments of X over disjoint periods of time are independent. Finally, the last condition is tantamount to asking that X has continuous paths. Note that we can represent a general geometric Brownian motion in the form

$$S_t = S_0 e^{\sigma W_t + \mu t},$$

where $(W_t)_{t \geq 0}$ is the Wiener process. In the context of the above Black–Scholes model, a Wiener process can be defined as the log return process of a price process satisfying the Black–Scholes conditions (1)–(3) with $\mu = 0$ and $\sigma^2 = 1$.

As it turns out, assumptions (1)–(3) above are all controversial and believed not to hold true especially at the intraday level (see Cont (2001) for a concise description of the most important features of financial data). The empirical distributions of log returns exhibit much heavier tails and higher kurtosis than a Gaussian distribution does and this phenomenon is accentuated when the frequency of returns increases. Independence is also questionable since, for example, absolute log returns typically exhibit slowly decaying serial correlation. In other words, high volatility events tend to cluster across time. Of course, continuity is just a convenient limiting abstraction to describe the high trading activity of liquid assets. In spite of its shortcomings, geometric Brownian motion could arguably be a suitable model to describe low frequency returns but not high frequency returns.

An ELM attempts to relax the assumptions of the Black–Scholes model in a parsimonious manner. Indeed, a natural first step is to relax the Gaussian character of log returns by replacing it with an unspecified distribution as follows:

(1′) The (log) return on the asset over a time period of length h has distribution F_h, depending only on the time span h.

This innocuous (still desirable) change turns out to be inconsistent with condition (3) above in the sense that (2) and (3) together with (1′) imply (1). Hence, we ought to relax (3) as well if we want to keep (1′). The following is a natural compromise:

(3′) The paths $t \to S_t$ exhibit only discontinuities of first kind (jump discontinuities).

Summarizing, an exponential Lévy model for the price process $(S_t)_{t\geq 0}$ of a risky asset satisfies conditions (1′), (2), and (3′). In the following section, we concentrate on two important and popular types of exponential Lévy models.

1.2.2 VARIANCE-GAMMA AND NORMAL INVERSE GAUSSIAN MODELS

The VG and NIG Lévy models were proposed in Carr *et al.* (1998) and Barndorff-Nielsen (1998), respectively, to describe the log return process $X_t := \log S_t/S_0$ of a financial asset. Both models can be seen as a Wiener process with drift that is time-deformed by an independent random clock. That is, (X_t) has the representation

$$X_t = \sigma W(\tau(t)) + \theta\tau(t) + bt, \tag{1.1}$$

where $\sigma > 0, \theta, b \in \mathbb{R}$ are given constants, W is Wiener process, and τ is a suitable independent subordinator (nondecreasing Lévy process) such that

$$\mathbb{E}\tau(t) = t, \quad \text{and} \quad \mathrm{Var}(\tau(t)) = \kappa t.$$

In the VG model, $\tau(t)$ is Gamma distributed with scale parameter $\beta := \kappa$ and shape parameter $\alpha := t/\kappa$, while in the NIG model $\tau(t)$ follows an inverse Gaussian distribution with mean $\mu = 1$ and shape parameter $\lambda = 1/(t\kappa)$. In the formulation (Eq. 1.1), τ plays the role of a random clock aimed at incorporating variations in business activity through time.

The parameters of the model have the following interpretation (see Eqs. (1.6) and (1.17) below).

1. σ dictates the overall variability of the log returns of the asset. In the symmetric case ($\theta = 0$), σ^2 is the variance of the log returns per unit time.
2. κ controls the kurtosis or tail heaviness of the log returns. In the symmetric case ($\theta = 0$), κ is the percentage excess kurtosis of log returns relative to the normal distribution multiplied by the time span.
3. b is a drift component in calendar time.
4. θ is a drift component in business time and controls the skewness of log returns.

The VG can be written as the difference of two Gamma Lévy processes

$$X_t = X_t^+ - X_t^- + bt, \tag{1.2}$$

where X^+ and X^- are independent Gamma Lévy processes with respective parameters

$$\alpha^+ = \alpha^- = \frac{1}{\kappa}, \quad \beta\pm := \frac{\sqrt{\theta^2\kappa^2 + 2\sigma^2\kappa} \pm \theta\kappa}{2}.$$

One can see X^+ (respectively X^-) in Equation (1.2) as the upward (respectively downward) movements in the asset's log return.

Under both models, the marginal density of X_t (which translates into the density of a log return over a time span t) is known in closed form. In the VG model, the probability density of X_t is given by

$$p_t(x) = \frac{\sqrt{2}e^{\frac{\theta(x-bt)}{\sigma^2}}}{\sigma\sqrt{\pi}\kappa^{\frac{t}{\kappa}}\Gamma(\frac{t}{\kappa})}\left(\frac{|x-bt|}{\sqrt{\frac{2\sigma^2}{\kappa}+\theta^2}}\right)^{\frac{t}{\kappa}-\frac{1}{2}} K_{\frac{t}{\kappa}-\frac{1}{2}}\left(\frac{|x-bt|\sqrt{\frac{2\sigma^2}{\kappa}+\theta^2}}{\sigma^2}\right), \tag{1.3}$$

where K is the modified Bessel function of the second kind (c.f. Carr *et al.* (1998)). The NIG model has marginal densities of the form

$$p_t(x) = \frac{te^{\frac{t}{\kappa}+\frac{\theta(x-bt)}{\sigma^2}}}{\pi}\left(\frac{(x-bt)^2+\frac{t^2\sigma^2}{\kappa}}{\frac{\theta^2}{\kappa\sigma^2}+\frac{1}{\kappa^2}}\right)^{-\frac{1}{2}} K_1\left(\frac{\sqrt{(x-bt)^2+\frac{t^2\sigma^2}{\kappa}}\sqrt{\frac{\sigma^2}{\kappa}+\theta^2}}{\sigma^2}\right). \tag{1.4}$$

Throughout the chapter, we assume that the log return process $\{X_t\}_{t\geq 0}$ is sampled during a *fixed time interval* $[0, T]$ at evenly spaced times $t_i = i\delta_n$, $i = 1, \ldots, n$, where $\delta_n = T/n$. This sampling scheme is sometimes called *calendar time sampling* (Oomen, 2006). Under the assumption of independence and stationarity of the increments of X (conditions (1') and (2) in Section 1.2.1), we have at our disposal a random sample

$$\Delta_i^n := \Delta_i^n X := X_{i\delta_n} - X_{(i-1)\delta_n}, \quad i = 1, \ldots, n, \tag{1.5}$$

of size n of the distribution $f_{\delta_n}(\cdot) := f_{\delta_n}(\cdot; \sigma, \theta, \kappa, b)$ of X_{δ_n}. Note that, in this context, a larger sample size n does not necessarily entail a greater amount of useful information about the parameters of the model. This is, in fact, one of the key questions in this chapter: Does the statistical performance of standard parametric methods improve under high frequency observations? We address this issue by simulation experiments in Section 1.4. For now, we introduce the statistical methods used in this chapter.

1.3 Parametric Estimation Methods

In this part, we review the most used parametric estimation methods: the method of moments and maximum likelihood. We also present a new computational method to find the moment estimators of the considered models. It is worth pointing out that both methods are known to be consistent under mild conditions if the number of observations at a *fixed* frequency (say, daily or hourly) are independent.

1.3.1 METHOD OF MOMENT ESTIMATORS

In principle, the method of moments is a simple estimation method that can be applied to a wide range of parametric models. Also, the MME are commonly used as initial points of numerical schemes used to find MLE, which are typically considered to be more efficient. Another appealing property of moment estimators is that they are known to be robust against possible dependence between log returns since their consistency is only a consequence of stationarity and ergodicitity conditions of the log returns. In this section, we introduce a new method to compute the MME for the VG and NIG models.

Let us start with the VG model. The mean and first three central moments of a VG model are given in closed form as follows (Cont & Tankov (2003), pp. 32 & 117):

$$\begin{aligned}
\mu_1(X_\delta) &:= \mathbb{E}(X_\delta) = (\theta + b)\delta, \\
\mu_2(X_\delta) &:= \mathrm{Var}(X_\delta) = (\sigma^2 + \theta^2\kappa)\delta, \\
\mu_3(X_\delta) &:= \mathbb{E}(X_\delta - \mathbb{E}X_\delta)^3 = (3\sigma^2\theta\kappa + 2\theta^3\kappa^2)\delta, \\
\mu_4(X_\delta) &:= \mathbb{E}(X_\delta - \mathbb{E}X_\delta)^4 = (3\sigma^4\kappa + 12\sigma^2\theta^2\kappa^2 + 6\theta^4\kappa^3)\delta + 3\mu_2(X_\delta)^2.
\end{aligned} \tag{1.6}$$

The MME is obtained by solving the system of equations resulting from substituting the central moments of X_{δ_n} in Equation 1.6 by their corresponding sample estimators:

$$\hat{\mu}_{k,n} := \frac{1}{n}\sum_{i=1}^{n}\left(\Delta_i^n - \bar{\Delta}^{(n)}\right)^k, \quad k \geq 2, \tag{1.7}$$

where Δ_i^n is given as in Equation 1.5 and $\bar{\Delta}^{(n)} := \sum_{i=1}^n \Delta_i^n/n$. However, solving the system of equations that defines the MME is not straightforward and, in general, one will need to rely on a numerical solution of the system. We now describe a novel simple method for this purpose. The idea is to write the central moments in terms of the quantity $\mathcal{E} := \theta^2\kappa/\sigma^2$. Concretely, we have the equations

$$\mu_2(X_\delta) = \delta\sigma^2(1+\mathcal{E}), \quad \mu_3(X_\delta) = \delta\sigma^2\theta\kappa(3+2\mathcal{E}),$$
$$\frac{\mu_4(X_\delta)}{3\mu_2^2(X_\delta)} - 1 = \frac{\kappa}{\delta}\,\frac{1+4\mathcal{E}+2\mathcal{E}^2}{(1+\mathcal{E})^2}.$$

From these equations, it follows that

$$\frac{3\mu_3^2(X_\delta)}{\mu_2(X_\delta)\left(\mu_4(X_\delta) - 3\mu_2^2(X_\delta)\right)} = \frac{\mathcal{E}\,(3+2\mathcal{E})^2}{\left(1+4\mathcal{E}+2\mathcal{E}^2\right)(1+\mathcal{E})} := f(\mathcal{E}). \tag{1.8}$$

In spite of appearances, the above function $f(\mathcal{E})$ is a strictly increasing concave function from $(-1+2^{-1/2},\infty)$ to $(-\infty,2)$ and, hence, the solution of the corresponding sample equation can be found efficiently using numerical methods. It remains to estimate the left-hand side of Equation 1.8. To this end, note that the left-hand side term can be written as $3\mathrm{Skw}(X_\delta)^2/\mathrm{Krt}(X_\delta)$, where Skw and Krt represent the population skewness and kurtosis:

$$\mathrm{Skw}(X_\delta) := \frac{\mu_3(X_\delta)}{\mu_2(X_\delta)^{3/2}} \quad \text{and} \quad \mathrm{Krt}(X_\delta) := \frac{\mu_4(X_\delta)}{\mu_2(X_\delta)^2} - 3. \tag{1.9}$$

Finally, we just have to replace the population parameters by their empirical estimators:

$$\widehat{\mathrm{Var}}_n := \frac{1}{n-1}\sum_{i=1}^{n}\left(\Delta_i^n - \bar{\Delta}^n\right)^2, \quad \widehat{\mathrm{Skw}}_n := \frac{\hat{\mu}_{3,n}}{\hat{\mu}_{2,n}^{3/2}}, \quad \widehat{\mathrm{Krt}}_n := \frac{\hat{\mu}_{4,n}}{\hat{\mu}_{2,n}^{2}} - 3. \tag{1.10}$$

Summarizing, the MME can be computed via the following numerical scheme:

1. Find (numerically) the solution $\hat{\mathcal{E}}_n^*$ of the equation

$$f(\mathcal{E}) = \frac{3\,\widehat{\mathrm{Skw}}_n^{\,2}}{\widehat{\mathrm{Krt}}_n}; \tag{1.11}$$

2. Determine the MME using the following formulas:

$$\hat{\sigma}_n^2 := \frac{\widehat{\mathrm{Var}}_n}{\delta_n}\left(\frac{1}{1+\hat{\mathcal{E}}_n^*}\right), \quad \hat{\kappa}_n := \frac{\delta_n}{3}\,\widehat{\mathrm{Krt}}_n\left(\frac{(1+\hat{\mathcal{E}}_n^*)^2}{1+4\hat{\mathcal{E}}_n^*+2\hat{\mathcal{E}}_n^{*2}}\right), \tag{1.12}$$

$$\hat{\theta}_n := \frac{\hat{\mu}_{3,n}}{\delta_n\hat{\sigma}_n^2\hat{\kappa}_n}\left(\frac{1}{3+2\hat{\mathcal{E}}_n^*}\right), \quad \hat{b}_n := \frac{1}{\delta_n}\bar{\Delta}^n - \hat{\theta}_n = \frac{X_T}{T} - \hat{\theta}_n. \tag{1.13}$$

We note that the above estimators will exist if and only if Equation 1.11 admits a solution $\hat{\mathcal{E}}^* \in (-1+2^{-1/2},\infty)$, which is the case if and only if

$$\frac{3\,\widehat{\mathrm{Skw}}_n^{\,2}}{\widehat{\mathrm{Krt}}_n} < 2.$$

Furthermore, the MME estimator $\widehat{\kappa}_n$ will be positive only if the sample kurtosis $\widehat{\mathrm{Krt}}_n$ is positive. It turns out that in simulations this condition is sometimes violated for small-time horizons T and coarse sampling frequencies (say, daily or longer). For instance, using the parameter values (1) of Section 1.4.1 below and taking $T = 125$ days (half a year) and $\delta_n = 1$ day, about 80 simulations out of 1000 gave invalid $\hat{\kappa}$, while only 2 simulations result in invalid $\hat{\kappa}$ when $\delta_n = 1/2$ day.

Seneta (2004) proposes a simple approximation method built on the assumption that θ is typically small. In our context, Seneta's method is obtained by making the simplifying approximation $\hat{\mathcal{E}}_n^* \approx 0$ in the Equations 1.12 and 1.13, resulting in the following estimators:

$$\hat{\sigma}_n^2 := \frac{\widehat{\mathrm{Var}}_n}{\delta_n}, \quad \hat{\kappa}_n := \frac{\delta_n}{3}\widehat{\mathrm{Krt}}_n, \tag{1.14}$$

$$\hat{\theta}_n := \frac{\hat{\mu}_{3,n}}{3\delta_n \hat{\sigma}_n^2 \hat{\kappa}_n} = \frac{\widehat{\mathrm{Skw}}_n (\widehat{\mathrm{Var}}_n)^{1/2}}{\delta_n \widehat{\mathrm{Krt}}_n}, \quad \hat{b}_n := \frac{X_T}{T} - \hat{\theta}_n. \tag{1.15}$$

Note that the estimators (Eq. 1.14) are, in fact, the actual MME in the restricted symmetric model $\theta = 0$ and will indeed produce a good approximation of the MME estimators (Eqs. 1.12 and 1.13) whenever

$$\mathcal{Q}_n^* := \frac{3\,\widehat{\mathrm{Skw}}_n^2}{\widehat{\mathrm{Krt}}_n},$$

and, hence, $\hat{\mathcal{E}}_n^*$ is "very" small. This fact has been corroborated empirically by multiple studies using daily data as shown in Seneta (2004).

The formulas (Eqs. 1.14 and 1.15) have appealing interpretations as noted already by Carr *et al.* (1998). Namely, the parameter κ determines the percentage excess kurtosis in the log return distribution (i.e., a measure of the tail fatness compared to the normal distribution), σ dictates the overall volatility of the process, and θ determines the skewness. Interestingly, the estimator $\hat{\sigma}_n^2$ in Equation 1.14 can be written as

$$\hat{\sigma}_n^2 = \frac{1}{T - \delta_n} \sum_{i=1}^{n} \left(X_{i\delta_n} - X_{(i-1)\delta_n} - \frac{X_T}{n} \right)^2 = \frac{1}{T - \delta_n} \overline{RV}_n + O\left(\frac{1}{n}\right),$$

where $\overline{RV}_n$ is the well-known realized variance defined by

$$\overline{RV}_n := \sum_{i=1}^{n} \left(X_{i\delta_n} - X_{(i-1)\delta_n} \right)^2. \tag{1.16}$$

Let us finish this section by considering the NIG model. In this setting, the mean and first three central moments are given by Cont & Tankov (2003) (p. 117):

$$\begin{aligned}
\mu_1(X_\delta) &:= \mathbb{E}(X_\delta) = (\theta + b)\delta, \\
\mu_2(X_\delta) &:= \mathrm{Var}(X_\delta) = (\sigma^2 + \theta^2\kappa)\delta, \\
\mu_3(X_\delta) &:= \mathbb{E}(X_\delta - \mathbb{E}X_\delta)^3 = (3\sigma^2\theta\kappa + 3\theta^3\kappa^2)\delta, \\
\mu_4(X_\delta) &:= \mathbb{E}(X_\delta - \mathbb{E}X_\delta)^4 = (3\sigma^4\kappa + 18\sigma^2\theta^2\kappa^2 + 15\theta^4\kappa^3)\delta + 3\mu_2(X_\delta)^2.
\end{aligned} \tag{1.17}$$

Hence, the Equation 1.8 takes the simpler form

$$\frac{3\mu_3^2(X_\delta)}{\mu_2(X_\delta)\left(\mu_4(X_\delta) - 3\mu_2^2(X_\delta)\right)} = \frac{9\mathcal{E}}{5\mathcal{E}+1} := f(\mathcal{E}), \tag{1.18}$$

and the analogous equation (Eq. 1.11) can be solved in closed form as

$$\hat{\mathcal{E}}_n^* = \frac{\widehat{\mathrm{Skw}}_n^2}{3\,\widehat{\mathrm{Krt}}_n - 5\,\widehat{\mathrm{Skw}}_n^2}. \tag{1.19}$$

Then, the MME will be given by the following formulas:

$$\hat{\sigma}_n^2 := \frac{\widehat{\mathrm{Var}}_n}{\delta_n}\left(\frac{1}{1+\hat{\mathcal{E}}_n^*}\right), \quad \hat{\kappa}_n := \frac{\delta_n}{3}\,\widehat{\mathrm{Krt}}_n\left(\frac{1+\hat{\mathcal{E}}_n^*}{1+5\hat{\mathcal{E}}_n^*}\right), \tag{1.20}$$

$$\hat{\theta}_n := \frac{\hat{\mu}_{3,n}}{\delta_n\hat{\sigma}_n^2\hat{\kappa}_n}\left(\frac{1}{3+3\hat{\mathcal{E}}_n^*}\right), \quad \hat{b}_n := \frac{1}{\delta_n}\bar{\Delta}^n - \hat{\theta}_n = \frac{X_T}{T} - \hat{\theta}_n. \tag{1.21}$$

1.3.2 MAXIMUM LIKELIHOOD ESTIMATION

Maximum likelihood is one of the most widely used estimation methods, partly due to its theoretical efficiency when dealing with large samples. Given a random sample $\mathbf{x} = (x_1, \ldots, x_n)$ from a population distribution with density $f(\cdot|\theta)$ depending on a parameter $\theta = (\theta_1, \ldots, \theta_p)$, the method proposes to estimate θ with the value $\hat{\theta} = \hat{\theta}(\mathbf{x})$ that maximizes the so-called likelihood function

$$\mathcal{L}(\theta|\mathbf{x}) := \prod_{i=1}^{n} f(x_i|\theta).$$

When it exists, such a point estimate $\hat{\theta}(\mathbf{x})$ is called the *MLE* of θ.

In principle, under a Lévy model, the increments of the log return process X (which corresponds to the log returns of the price process S) are independent with common distribution, say $f_\delta(\cdot|\theta)$, where δ represents the time span of the increments. As was pointed out earlier, independence is questionable for very high frequency log returns, but given that, for a large sample, likelihood estimation is expected to be robust against small dependences between returns, we can still apply likelihood estimation. The question is again to determine the scales where both the Lévy model is a good approximation of the underlying process and the MLE are meaningful. As indicated in the introduction, it is plausible that the MLE's stability for certain range of sampling frequencies provides evidence of the adequacy of the Lévy model at those scales.

Another important issue is that, in general, the probability density f_δ is not known in a closed form or might be intractable. There are several approaches to deal with this issue such as numerically inverting the Fourier transform of f_δ via fast Fourier methods (Carr *et al.*, 2002) or approximating f_δ using small-time expansions (Figueroa-López & Houdré. 2009). In the present chapter, we do not explore these approaches since the probability densities of the VG and NIG models are known in closed forms. However, given the inaccessibility of closed expressions for the MLE, we apply an unconstrained optimization scheme to find them numerically (see below for more details).

1.4 Finite-Sample Performance via Simulations

1.4.1 PARAMETER VALUES

We consider two sets of parameter values:

1. $\sigma = \sqrt{6.447 \times 10^{-5}} = 0.0080$; $\kappa = 0.422$; $\theta = -1.5 \times 10^{-4}$; $b = 2.5750 \times 10^{-4}$;
2. $\sigma = 0.0127$; $\kappa = 0.2873$; $\theta = 1.3 \times 10^{-3}$; $b = -1.7 \times 10^{-3}$;

The first set of parameters (1) is motivated by the empirical study reported in Seneta (2004) (pp. 182) using the approximated MME introduced in Section 3.1 and daily returns of the Standard and Poor's 500 Index from 1977 to 1981. The second set of parameters (2) is motivated by our own empirical results below using MLE and daily returns of INTC during 2005. Throughout, the time unit is a day and, hence, for example, the estimated average rate of return per day of SP500 is

$$\mathbb{E}X(1) = \mathbb{E}\log\left(\frac{S_1}{S_0}\right) = \theta + b = 1.0750 \times 10^{-4} \approx 0.1\%,$$

or $0.00010750 \times 365 = 3.9\%$ per year.

1.4.2 RESULTS

Below, we illustrate the finite-sample performance of the MME and MLE for both the VG and NIG models. The MME is computed using the algorithms described in Section 1.3.1. The MLE was computed using an unconstrained Powell's method[2] started at the exact MME. We use the closed form expressions for the density functions (Eqs. 1.3 and 1.4) in order to evaluate the likelihood function.

1.4.2.1 Variance Gamma. We compute the sample mean and sample standard deviation of the VG MME and the VG MLE for different sampling frequencies. Concretely, the time span δ between consecutive observations is taken to be 1/36,1/18,1/12,1/6,1/3,1/2,1 (in days), which will correspond to 10, 20, 30 min, 1, 2, 3 h, and 1 day (assuming a trading period of 6 h per day).

[2]We employ a MATLAB implementation due to Giovani Tonel obtained through MATLAB Central (http://www.mathworks.com/matlabcentral/fileexchange/).

Figure 1.1 plots the sampling mean $\bar{\hat{\sigma}}_\delta$ and the bands $\bar{\hat{\sigma}}_\delta \pm \text{std}(\hat{\sigma}_\delta)$ against the different time spans δ as well as the corresponding graphs for κ, based on 100 simulations of the VG process on $[0, 3 * 252]$ (namely, three years) with the parameter values (1) above. Similarly, Fig. 1.2 shows the results corresponding to the parameter values (2) with a time horizon of $T = 252$ days and time spans $\delta = 10$, 20, and 30 min, and also, 1/6, 1/4, 1/3, 1/2, and 1 days, assuming this time a trading period of 6 h and 30 min per day and taking 200 simulations. These are our conclusions:

1. The MME for σ performs as well as the computationally more expensive MLE for all the relevant frequencies. Even though increasing the sampling frequency slightly reduces the standard error, the net gain is actually very small even for very high frequencies and, hence, does not justify the use of high frequency data to estimate σ.
2. The estimation for κ is quite different: Using either high frequency data or maximum likelihood estimation results in significant reductions of the standard error (by more than 4 times when using both).
3. The computation of the MLE presents numerical issues (easy to detect) for very high sampling frequencies (say, $\delta < 1/6$).
4. Disregarding the numerical issues and extrapolating the pattern of the graphs when $\delta \to 0$, we can conjecture that the MLE $\hat{\sigma}$ is not consistent when $\delta \to 0$ for a fixed time horizon T, while the MLE $\hat{\kappa}$ appears to be a consistent estimator for κ. Both of these points will be investigated in a future publication.

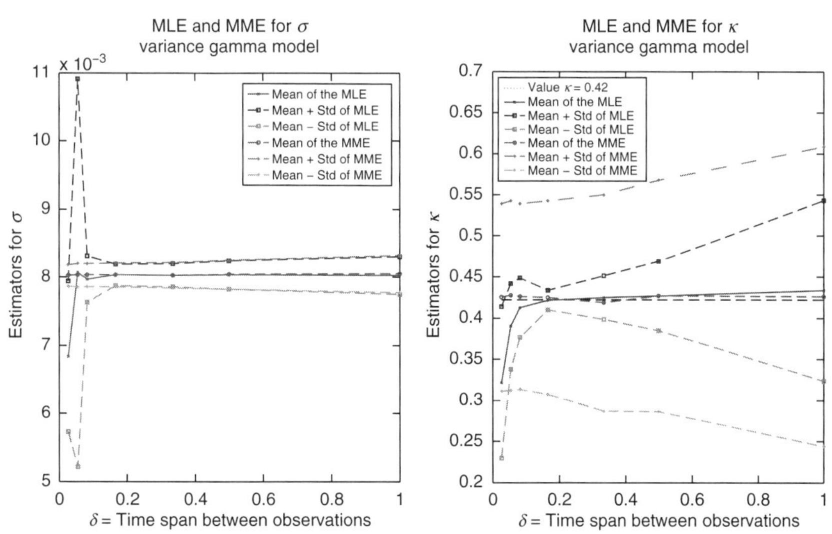

FIGURE 1.1 Sampling mean and standard error of the MME and MLE for the parameters σ and κ based on 100 simulations of the VG model with values $T = 252 \times 3$, $\sigma = \sqrt{6.447 \times 10^{-5}} = 0.0080$; $\kappa = 0.422$; $\theta = -1.5 \times 10^{-4}$; $b = 2.5750 \times 10^{-4}$.

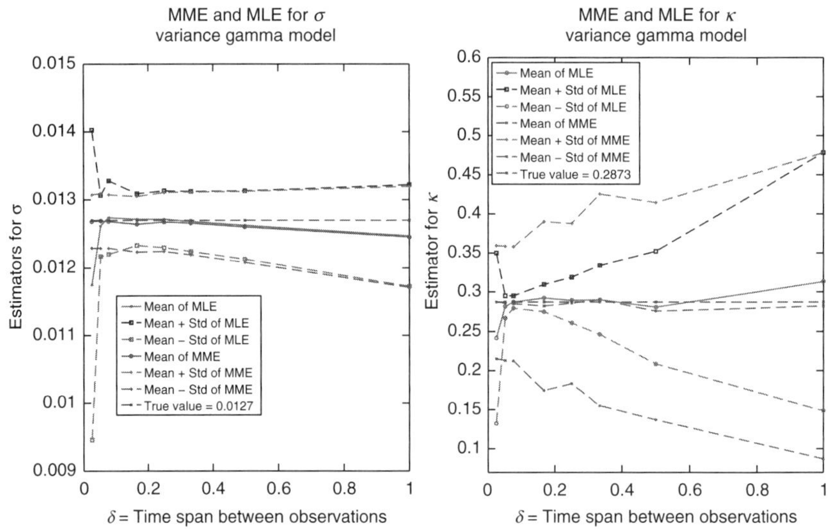

FIGURE 1.2 Sampling mean and standard error of the MME and MLE for the parameters σ and κ based on 200 simulations with values $T = 252, \sigma = 0.0127; \kappa = 0.2873; \theta = 1.3 \times 10^{-3}$; $b = -1.7 \times 10^{-3}$.

For completeness, we also illustrates in Fig. 1.3 the performance of the estimators for b and θ for the parameter values (2) based again on 200 simulations during $[0, 252]$ with time spans of 10, 20, and 30 min, and 1/6, 1/4, 1/3, 1/2, and 1 days. There seems to be some gain in efficiency when using MLE and higher sampling frequencies in both cases but the respective standard errors level off for δ small, suggesting that neither estimator is consistent for fixed time horizon. One surprising feature is that the MLE estimators in both cases do not seem to exhibit any numerical issues for very small δ in spite of being based on the same simulations as those used to obtain $\hat{\sigma}$ and $\hat{\kappa}$.

1.4.2.2 Normal Inverse Gaussian. We now show the estimation results for the NIG model. Here, we take sampling frequencies of 5, 10, 20, and 30 s, also 1, 5, 10, 20, and 30 min, as well as 1, 2, and 3 h, and finally 1 day (assuming a trading period of 6 h). Figure 1.4 plots the sampling mean $\bar{\hat{\sigma}}_\delta$ and bands $\bar{\hat{\sigma}}_\delta \pm \text{std}(\hat{\sigma}_\delta)$ against the different time spans δ and the corresponding graphs for κ, based on 100 simulations of the NIG process on $[0, 3 * 252]$ with the parameter values (1) above. The results are similar to those of the VG model. In the case of σ, neither MLE nor high frequency data seem to do better than standard moment estimators and daily data. For κ, the estimation error can be reduced as much as 4 times when using high frequency data and maximum likelihood estimation. The most striking conclusion is that the MLE for the NIG model does not show any numerical issues when dealing with very high frequency. Indeed, we are able to obtain results for even 5-s time spans (although the computational time increases significantly in this case).

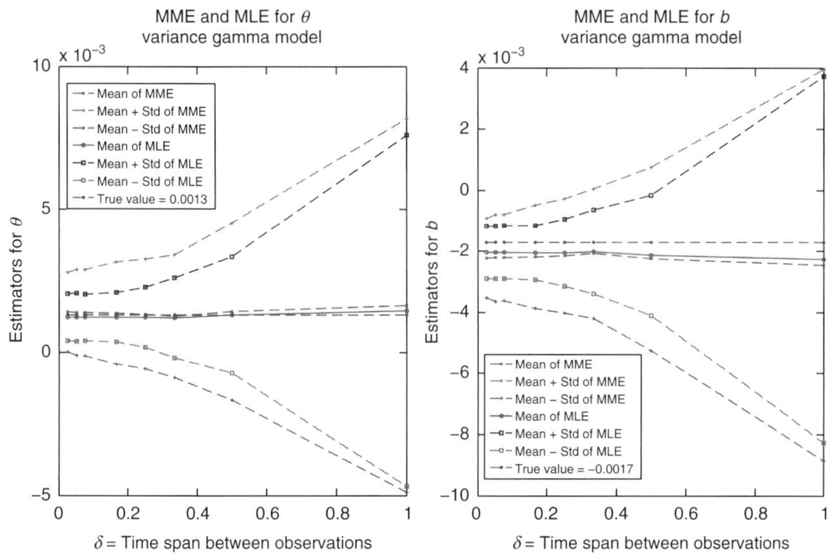

FIGURE 1.3 Sampling mean and standard error of the MME and MLE for the parameters θ and b based on 200 simulations with values $T = 252, \sigma = 0.0127; \kappa = 0.2873; \theta = 1.3 \times 10^{-3}$; $b = -1.7 \times 10^{-3}$.

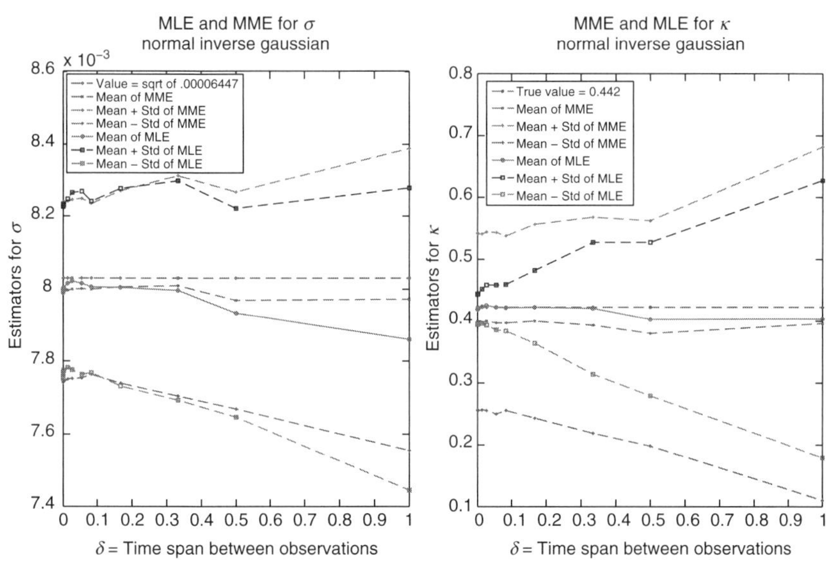

FIGURE 1.4 Sampling mean and standard error of the MME and MLE for the parameters σ and κ based on 100 simulations of the NIG model with values $T = 252 \times 3$, $\sigma = \sqrt{6.447 \times 10^{-5}} = 0.0080; \kappa = 0.422; \theta = -1.5 \times 10^{-4}; b = 2.5750 \times 10^{-4}$.

1.5 Empirical Results

1.5.1 THE DATA AND DATA PREPROCESSING

The data was obtained from the NYSE TAQ database of 2005 trades via Wharton's WRDS system. For the sake of clarity and space, we focus on the analysis of only one stock, even though other stocks were also analyzed for this study. We pick Intel (INTC) stock due to its high liquidity (based on the number of trades or ticks). The raw data was preprocessed as follows. Records of trades were kept if the TAQ field CORR indicated that the trade was "regular" (namely, it was not corrected, changed, signaled as cancelled, or signaled as an error). In addition, the condition field was use as a filter. Trades were kept if they were regular way trades, that is, trades that had no stated conditions (COND=" or COND='*'). A secondary filter was subsequently applied to eliminate some of the remaining incorrect trades. First, for each trading day, the empirical distribution of the absolute value of the first difference of prices was determined. Next, the 99.9th percentile of these daily absolute differences was obtained. Finally, a trade was eliminated if, in magnitude, the difference of the price from the prior price was at least twice the 99.9th percentile of that day's absolute differences and this difference was reversed on the following trade. Figure 1.5 illustrates the Intel stock prices before (a) and after processing (b).

1.5.2 MME AND MLE RESULTS

The exact and approximated MMEs described in Section 1.3.1 were applied to the log returns of the stocks at different frequencies ranging from 10 s to 1 day.

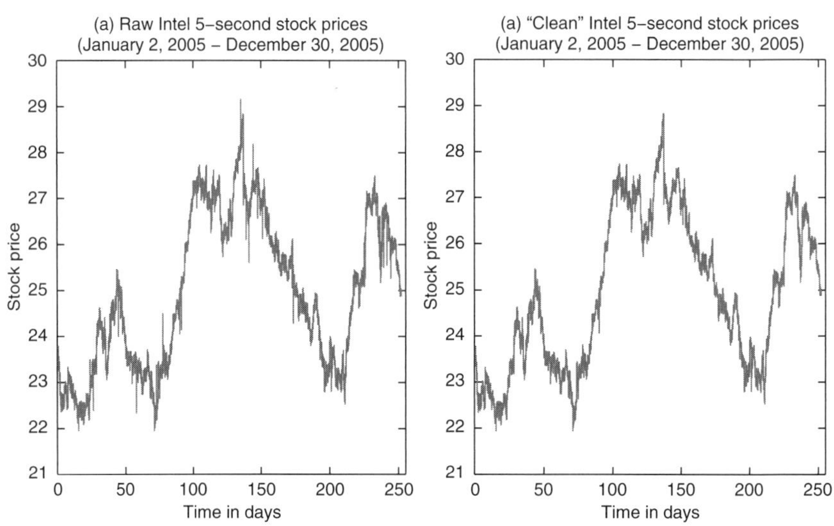

FIGURE 1.5 Intel stock prices during 2005 before and after preprocessing.

Subsequently, we apply the unconstrained Powell's optimization method to find the MLE estimator. In each case, the starting point for the optimization routine was set equal to the exact MME. Tables 1.1–1.4 show the estimation results under both models together with the log likelihood values using a time horizon of one year. Figure 1.6 shows the graphs of the NIG MLE and approximated NIG MME against the sampling frequency δ based on observations during $T = 1$ year, $T = 6$ months, and $T = 3$ months, respectively.

1.5.3 DISCUSSION OF EMPIRICAL RESULTS

In spite of certain natural differences due to sampling variation, the empirical results under both models exhibit some very interesting common features that we now summarize:

1. The estimation of σ is quite stable for "midrange" frequencies ($\delta \geq 20$ min), exhibiting a slight tendency to decrease when δ decreases from 1 day to 10 min, before showing a pronounce and clear tendency to increase for small time spans ($\delta = 10$ min and less). This increasing tendency is presumably due to the influence of microstructure effects.
2. The point estimators for κ are less stable than those for σ but still their values are relatively "consistent" for mid-range frequencies of 1 h and more. This consistency of $\hat{\kappa}$ abruptly changes when δ moves from 1/6 of a day to 30 min, at which point a reduction of about half is experienced under both models. To illustrate how unlikely such a behavior is in our models, we consider the simulation experiment of Fig. 1.2 and find out that in only

TABLE 1.1 INTC: VG MLE (Top), Exact VG MME (Middle), and Approximate VG MME (Bottom)

δ	20 min	30 min	1/6	1/4	1/3	1/2	1
$\hat{\kappa}$	0.0354	0.0542	0.1662	0.1724	0.2342	0.2098	0.2873
$\hat{\sigma}$	0.0115	0.0117	0.0120	0.0121	0.0123	0.0125	0.0127
$\hat{\theta}$	0.0010	0.0023	0.0019	0.0011	0.0020	0.0020	0.0013
$\hat{b}$	−0.0014	−0.0027	−0.0023	−0.0015	−0.0024	−0.0023	−0.0017
$\log \mathcal{L}$	2.2485e+4	1.4266e+4	6.0015e+3	3.7580e+3	2.6971e+3	1.6783e+3	745.8689
$\hat{\kappa}$	0.0571	0.0834	0.1839	0.1804	0.2694	0.1579	0.1383
$\hat{\sigma}$	0.0116	0.0119	0.0120	0.0121	0.0123	0.0124	0.0125
$\hat{\theta}$	0.0016	0.0010	0.0032	0.0019	0.0024	0.0028	0.0041
$\hat{b}$	−0.0020	−0.0014	−0.0036	−0.0022	−0.0028	−0.0032	−0.0045
$\log \mathcal{L}$	2.2438e+4	1.4243e+4	5.9946e+3	3.7578e+3	2.6966e+3	1.6780e+3	745.5981
$\hat{\kappa}$	0.0573	0.0835	0.1887	0.1819	0.2749	0.1603	0.1423
$\hat{\sigma}$	0.0116	0.0119	0.0121	0.0122	0.0124	0.0124	0.0126
$\hat{\theta}$	0.0016	0.0010	0.0031	0.0018	0.0024	0.0027	0.0040
$\hat{b}$	−0.0020	−0.0014	−0.0035	−0.0022	−0.0027	−0.0031	−0.0043
$\log \mathcal{L}$	2.2437e+4	1.4243e+4	5.9942e+3	3.7577e+3	2.6965e+3	1.6781e+3	745.6023

TABLE 1.2 INTC: VG MLE (Top), Exact VG MME (Middle), and Approximate VG MME (Bottom)

δ	10 s	20 s	30 s	1 min	5 min	10 min
$\hat{\kappa}$	0.0128	0.0112	0.0183	0.0354	0.0501	0.0191
$\hat{\sigma}$	0.0465	0.0300	0.0303	0.0293	0.0173	0.0120
$\hat{\theta}$	−0.0004	−0.0004	−0.0004	−0.0004	−0.0004	−0.0002
$\hat{b}$	0.0000	−0.0000	0.0000	0.0000	0.0000	−0.0002
$\log \mathcal{L}$	5.2980e+6	2.4338e+6	1.5115e+6	6.6256e+5	1.0540e+5	4.7949e+4
$\hat{\kappa}$	0.0010	0.0023	0.0052	0.0080	0.0153	0.0282
$\hat{\sigma}$	0.0169	0.0152	0.0145	0.0138	0.0125	0.0121
$\hat{\theta}$	−0.0001	0.0014	0.0025	−0.0040	−0.0013	0.0011
$\hat{b}$	−0.0003	−0.0018	−0.0029	0.0036	0.0009	−0.0015
$\log \mathcal{L}$	4.3254e+6	2.0063e+6	1.2823e+6	5.8998e+5	1.0203e+5	4.7897e+4
$\hat{\kappa}$	0.0010	0.0023	0.0052	0.0081	0.0153	0.0282
$\hat{\sigma}$	0.0169	0.0152	0.0145	0.0138	0.0125	0.0121
$\hat{\theta}$	−0.0001	0.0014	0.0025	−0.0040	−0.0013	0.0011
$\hat{b}$	−0.0003	−0.0018	−0.0029	0.0036	0.0009	−0.0015
$\log \mathcal{L}$	4.3254e+6	2.0063e+6	1.2823e+6	5.8987e+5	1.0203e+5	4.7897e+4

TABLE 1.3 INTC: NIG MLE (Top), Exact NIG MME (Middle), and Approx. NIG MME (Bottom)

δ	20 min	30 min	1/6	1/4	1/3	1/2	1
$\hat{\kappa}$	0.0557	0.0874	0.2621	0.2494	0.3412	0.2024	0.2159
$\hat{\sigma}$	0.0116	0.0118	0.0121	0.0122	0.0124	0.0124	0.0126
$\hat{\theta}$	0.0019	0.0017	0.0017	0.0012	0.0018	0.0019	0.0019
$\hat{b}$	−0.0022	−0.0021	−0.0021	−0.0016	−0.0022	−0.0023	−0.0022
$\log \mathcal{L}$	2.2498e+4	1.4274e+4	5.9988e+3	3.7575e+3	2.6969e+3	1.6777e+3	745.6436
$\hat{\kappa}$	0.0570	0.0833	0.1791	0.1789	0.2640	0.1554	0.1343
$\hat{\sigma}$	0.0116	0.0119	0.0120	0.0121	0.0123	0.0124	0.0125
$\hat{\theta}$	0.0016	0.0010	0.0033	0.0019	0.0025	0.0028	0.0042
$\hat{b}$	−0.0020	−0.0014	−0.0037	−0.0022	−0.0028	−0.0032	−0.0046
$\log \mathcal{L}$	2.2498e+4	1.4274e+4	5.9952e+3	3.7564e+3	2.6963e+3	1.6775e+3	745.5409
$\hat{\kappa}$	0.0573	0.0835	0.1887	0.1819	0.2749	0.1603	0.1423
$\hat{\sigma}$	0.0116	0.0119	0.0121	0.0122	0.0124	0.0124	0.0126
$\hat{\theta}$	0.0016	0.0010	0.0031	0.0018	0.0024	0.0027	0.0040
$\hat{b}$	−0.0020	−0.0014	−0.0035	−0.0022	−0.0027	−0.0031	−0.0043
$\log \mathcal{L}$	2.2498e+4	1.4274e+4	5.9957e+3	3.7563e+3	2.6964e+3	1.6776e+3	745.5465

1 out of the 200 simulations the exact MME estimator for κ increased by more than twice its value when δ goes from 30 min to 1/6 of a day (only 3 out 200 simulations showed an increment of more than 1.5). In none of the 200 simulation, the MLE estimator for κ increased more than 1.5 its value when δ goes from 30 min to 1/6 of a day. For the NIG model, using the

TABLE 1.4 **INTC: NIG MLE (Top), Exact NIG MME (Middle), and Approx. NIG MME (Bottom)**

δ	10 s	20 s	30 s	1 min	5 min	10 min
$\hat{\kappa}$	0.1349	0.0061	0.0012	0.0024	0.0125	0.0220
$\hat{\sigma}$	0.0341	0.0190	0.0149	0.0134	0.0119	0.0114
$\hat{\theta}$	−0.0002	0.0007	0.0086	0.0095	0.0042	0.0037
$\hat{b}$	−0.0000	−0.0009	−0.0088	−0.0097	−0.0044	−0.0038
$\log \mathcal{L}$	3.8974e+6	1.8740e+6	1.2188e+6	5.8072e+5	1.0206e+5	4.7957e+4
$\hat{\kappa}$	0.0003	0.0007	0.0012	0.0031	0.0157	0.0252
$\hat{\sigma}$	0.0194	0.0161	0.0148	0.0134	0.0119	0.0114
$\hat{\theta}$	0.0194	0.0187	0.0160	0.0134	0.0070	0.0042
$\hat{b}$	−0.0196	−0.0189	−0.0162	−0.0136	−0.0072	−0.0044
$\log \mathcal{L}$	3.8863e+6	1.8718e+6	1.2135e+6	5.7856e+5	1.0204e+5	4.7955e+4
$\hat{\kappa}$	0.0003	0.0007	0.0012	0.0031	0.0160	0.0255
$\hat{\sigma}$	0.0194	0.0161	0.0148	0.0134	0.0120	0.0114
$\hat{\theta}$	0.0194	0.0187	0.0159	0.0132	0.0069	0.0042
$\hat{b}$	−0.0196	−0.0188	−0.0161	−0.0134	−0.0070	−0.0044
$\log \mathcal{L}$	3.8863e+6	1.8718e+6	1.2135e+6	5.7850e+5	1.0204e+5	4.7955e+4

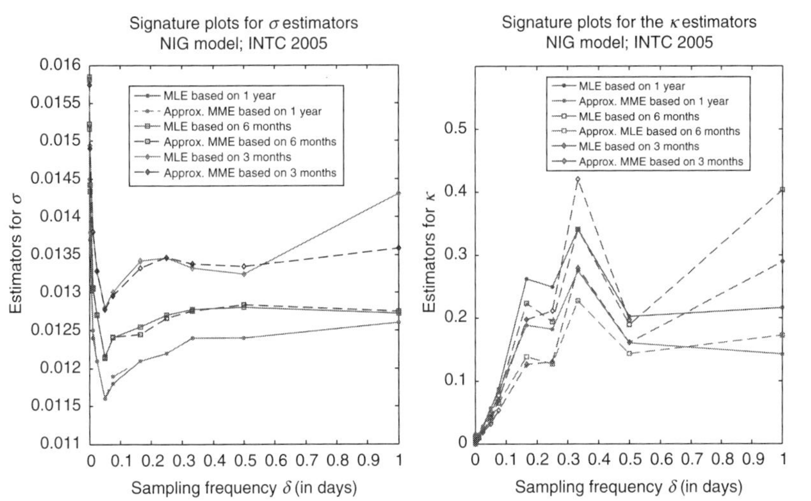

FIGURE 1.6 **Signature plots for the MLE and MME for σ under a NIG model based on different time horizons.**

simulations of Fig. 1.4, we found out that in only 3 out of 100 simulations the MME estimator for κ increased by more than 1.2 when δ goes from 30 min to 1/6 of a day (it never increased for more than 1.5). Such a jump in the empirical results could be interpreted as a consequence of microstructure effects.

3. According to our previous simulation analysis, the estimators for κ are more reliable when δ gets smaller. Hence, we recommend using the value of the estimator for δ as small as possible, but still in the range where we suspect that microstructure effects are relatively low. For instance, one can propose to take $\hat{\kappa} = 0.1662$ under the VG model (respectively $\hat{\kappa} = 0.2621$ under the NIG model), or alternatively, one could average the MLE estimators for $\delta > 1/2$.
4. Under both models, the estimators for κ show a certain tendency to decrease as δ gets very small (<30 min).
5. Given the higher sensitivity of κ to microstructure effects, one could use the values of this estimator to identify the range of frequencies where a Lévy model is adequate and microstructure effects are still low. In the case of INTC, one can recommend using a Lévy model to describe log returns higher than 1 h. As an illustration of the goodness of fit, Fig. 1.7 shows the empirical histograms of $\delta = 1/6$ returns against the fitted VG model and NIG model using maximum likelihood estimation. We also show the fitted Gaussian distributions in each case. Both models show very good fit. The graphs in log scale, useful to check the fit at the tails, are shown in Fig. 1.8.

1.6 Conclusion

Certain parametric classes of ELM have appealing features for modeling intraday financial data. In this chapter, we lean toward choosing a parsimonious model

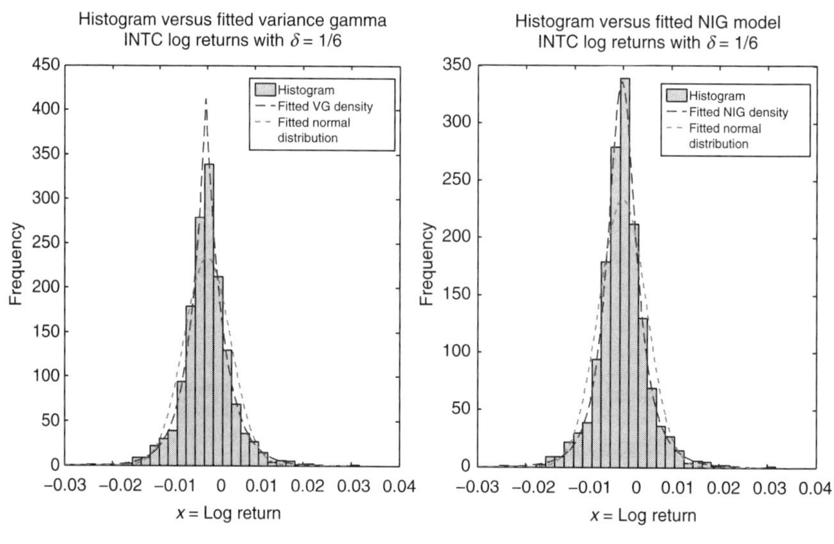

FIGURE 1.7 Histograms of INTC returns for $\delta = 1/6$ and the fitted VG and NIG models using maximum likelihood estimation.

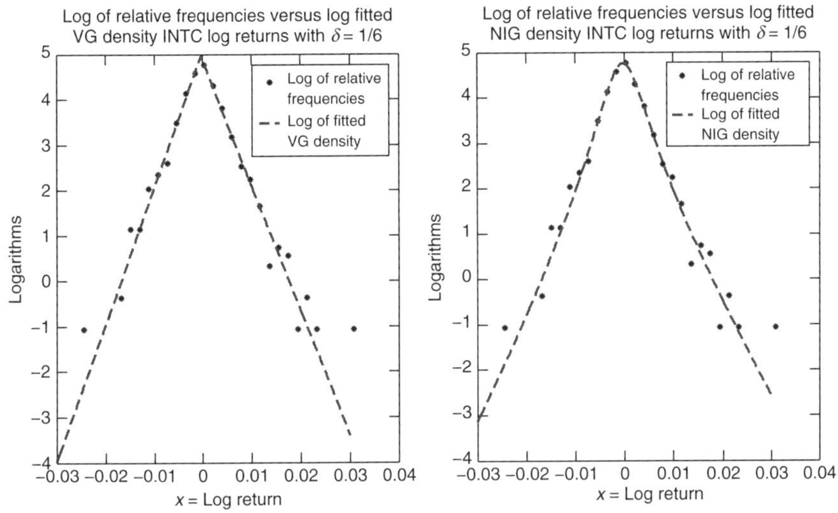

FIGURE 1.8 Logarithm of the histograms of INTC returns for $\delta = 1/6$ and the fitted VG and NIG models using maximum likelihood estimation.

with few parameters that has natural financial interpretation, rather than a complex overparameterized model. Even though, in principle, a complex model will provide a better fit of the observed empirical features of financial data, the intrinsically less accurate estimation or calibration of such a model might render it less useful in practice. By contrast, we consider here two simple and well-known models for the analysis of intraday data: the VG model of Carr *et al.* (1998) and the NIG model of Barndorff-Nielsen (1998). These models require one additional parameter, when compared to the two-parameter Black–Scholes model, that controls the tail thickness of the log return distribution.

As essentially any other model, a Lévy model will have limitations when working with very high frequency transaction data and, hence, in our opinion the real problem is to determine the sampling frequencies at which a specific Lévy model will be a "good" probabilistic approximation of the underlying trading process. In this chapter we put forward an intuitive statistical method to solve this problem. Concretely, we propose to assess the suitability of the Lévy model by analyzing the signature plots of statistical point estimates at different sampling frequencies. It is plausible that an apparent stability of the point estimates for certain ranges of sampling frequencies will provide evidence of the adequacy of the Lévy model at those scales. At least based on our preliminary empirical analysis, we find that a Lévy model seems a reasonable model for log returns as frequent as hourly and that the kurtosis estimate is a more sensitive indicator of microstructure effects in the data than the volatility estimate, which exhibits a very stable behavior for sampling time spans as small as 20 min.

We also studied the in-fill numerical performance of the two most widely used parametric estimators: the MME and the maximum likelihood estimation. We discover that neither high frequency sampling nor maximum likelihood estimation significantly reduces the estimation error of the volatility parameter of the model. Hence, we can "safely" estimate the volatility parameter using a simple moment estimator applied to daily closing prices. The estimation of the kurtosis parameter is quite different. In that case, using either high frequency data or maximum likelihood estimation can result in significant reductions of the standard error (by more than 4 times when using both). Both of these results appear to be new in the statistical literature of high frequency data.

The problem of finding the MLE based on very high frequency data remains a challenging numerical problem, even if closed form expressions are available as it is the case of the NIG and VG models. On the contrary, in this chapter, we propose a simple numerical method to find the MME of the NIG and VG models. Moment estimators are particularly appealing in the context of high frequency data since their consistency does not require independence between log returns but only stationarity and ergodicity conditions.

1.6.1 ACKNOWLEDGMENTS

The first author's research is partially supported by the NSF grant DMS-0906919. The third author's research is partially supported by WCU (World Class University) program through the National Research Foundation of Korea funded by the Ministry of Education, Science and Technology (R31-20007). The authors are grateful to Ionuţ Florescu and Frederi Viens for their help and many suggestions that improved the chapter considerably.

REFERENCES

Barndorff-Nielsen O. Processes of normal inverse Gaussian type. Finance Stochast 1998;2:41–68.

Behr A, Pötter U. Alternatives to the normal model of stock returns: Gaussian mixture, generalised logF and generalised hyperbolic models. Ann Finance 2009;5:49–68.

Carr P, Geman H, Madan D, Yor M. The fine structure of asset returns: an empirical investigation. J Bus 2002;75:305–332.

Carr P, Madan D, Chang E. The variance gamma process and option pricing. Eur Finance Rev 1998;2:79–105.

Cont R. Empirical properties of asset returns: stylized facts and statistical issues. Quant Finance 2001;1:223–236.

Cont R, Tankov P. Financial modelling with jump processes. Chapman & Hall, Boca Raton, Florida; 2004.

Eberlein E, Keller U. Hyperbolic distribution in finance. Bernoulli 1995;1:281–299.

Eberlein E, Ozkan F. Time consistency of Lévy processes. Quant Finance 2003;3:40–50.

Figueroa-López J. Jump-diffusion models driven by Lévy processes. Jin-Chuan Duan, James E Gentle, Wolfgang Hardle, editors. To appear in Handbook of Computational Finance. Springer; 2011.

Figueroa-López J, Houdré C. Small-time expansions for the transition distributions of Lévy processes. Stoch Proc Appl 2009;119:3862–3889.

Kou S, Wang H. Option pricing under a double exponential jump diffusion model. Manag Sci 2004;50:1178–1192.

Oomen R. Properties of realized variance under alternative sampling schemes. J Bus Econ Stat 2006;24:219–237.

Ramezani C, Zeng Y. Maximum likelihood estimation of the double exponential jump-diffusion process. Ann Finance 2007;3:487–507.

Sato K. Lévy processes and infinitely divisible distributions. Cambridge University Press, UK; 1999.

Seneta E. Fitting the variance-gamma model to financial data. J Appl Probab 2004;41A:177–187.

Tankov P. Pricing and hedging in exponential Lévy models: review of recent results. To appear in the Paris-Princeton Lecture Notes in Mathematical Finance, Springer-Verlag, Berlin, Heidelberg, Germany; 2011.

CHAPTER TWO

A Study of Persistence of Price Movement using High Frequency Financial Data

DRAGOS BOZDOG, IONUŢ FLORESCU, KHALDOUN KHASHANAH, and JIM WANG

Department of Mathematical Sciences, Stevens Institute of Technology, Hoboken, NJ

2.1 Introduction

When studying price dynamics, the price–volume relationship is one of the most studied in the field of finance. Perhaps the oldest model used to study this relationship is the work of Osborne (1959), who models the price as a diffusion process with its variance dependent on the quantity of transaction at that particular moment. Subsequent relevant work can be found in Karpoff (1987), Gallant *et al.* (1992), Bollerslev and Jubinski (1999), Lo and Wang (2003), and Sun (2003). In general, this line of work studies the relationship between volume and some measure of variability of the stock price (e.g., the absolute deviation, the volatility, etc.). Most of these articles use models in time; they are tested with low frequency data and the main conclusion is that the price of a specific equity exhibits larger variability in response to increased volume of trades. We also mention the autoregressive conditional duration (ACD) model

Handbook of Modeling High-Frequency Data in Finance, First Edition.
Edited by Frederi G. Viens, Maria C. Mariani, and Ionuţ Florescu.

of Engle and Russell (1998), which considers the time between trades as a variable related to both price and volume. In the current work, we examine the relationship between change in price and volume. We study the exception of the conclusion presented in the earlier literature. In our study we do not consider models in time but rather make the change in price dependent on the volume directly.

The old Wall Street adage that "it takes volume to move prices" is verified in this empirical study. Indeed, this relationship was studied using market microstructure models and it was generally found true (Admati and Pfleiderer, 1988; Foster and Viswanathan, 1990; Llorente *et al.*, 2002). The advent of electronic trading using high frequency data, the increase in the trading volume and the recent research in automatic liquidation of large orders may lead to inconsistencies and temporary contradictions of this statement. For short time periods during trading, we may encounter large price movements with small volume. However, if the claim is true then large price movements associated with small volume should be only temporary and the market should regain the momentum it had exhibited before the fleeting price movement.

This is the premise of the current study. We propose a methodology to detect outlying observations of the price–volume relationship. We may refer to these outliers as rare events in high frequency finance or rare microevents to distinguish them from rare events for low frequency sampled data. In our context, because of the joint price–volume distribution, we may encounter two types of outliers. The first type occurs when the volume of traded shares is small but is associated with large price movement. The second type occurs when the volume of traded shares is large coupled with small price movement. Of the two types of rare events, we are only interested in the first type. The second type is evidence of unusually high trading activity which is normally accompanied with public information release (a well-documented event as early as (Beaver, 1968)). We formulate the main objectives of this work as follows:

Objectives:

- Develop a method to detect rare events in real time where the movement of price is large with relatively small volume of shares traded.
- Analyze the price behavior *after* these rare events and study the probability of price recovery. What is the expected return if a trade is placed at the detected observation?

The second objective is of particular interest to us. Recent research (Alfonsi *et al.* 2007, Zhang *et al.* 2008) analyze ways of liquidating a large order by splitting it into smaller orders to be spread over a certain period of time. There are several available strategies to achieve this objective. However, all strategies make one or several assumptions about the dynamic or structure of the limit order book. One specific assumption seems to be common in the literature and that is to assume a degree of elasticity/plasticity of the limit orders, that is, the capability of the bid/ask orders to regain the previous levels after a large order has been executed. This elasticity degree is usually assumed as given but there are no methods which actually estimate the *current* nature of the market when the large order is executed, immediately *before* the liquidating strategy is being put into place. We believe that our second objective provides a way to estimate the current market conditions at the time when an outlying observation is detected. In particular, we believe that the frequency of these rare events relative to the market total trade volume sheds light about the current market condition as well as the particular equity being researched.

The chapter is structured as follows. In Section 2.2, we present the basic methodology for detecting and evaluating the rare events. Section 2.3 details results obtained applying the methodology to tick data collected over a period of five trading days in April, 2008. Section 2.4 presents the distribution of the trades and the rare events during the trading day. Section 2.5 presents conclusions drawn using our methodology.

2.2 Methodology

In this analysis, we use tick-by-tick data of 5369 equities traded on NYSE, NASDAQ, and AMEX for a five-day period. We need the most detailed possible dataset; however, since our discovery is limited to past trades we do not require the use of a more detailed level 2 order data. We perform model free statistical analysis on this multivariate dataset.

For any given equity in the dataset an observation represents a trade. Each trade records the price P of the transaction, the volume V of the shares traded and the time t at which the transaction takes place. In this study, we are primarily interested in large price movement with small volume, thus for *any* two observations in the dataset, we construct a four-dimensional random vector $(\Delta P, \Delta V, \Delta N, \Delta t)$. Here ΔP is the change in price, ΔV is the change in volume, ΔN is the number of trades, and Δt is the period of time all variables calculated between the two trades. The number of trades elapsed between two observations is a variable that may be calculated using the given dataset.

The reason for considering any pair of trades and not only consecutive trades is that in general the price movement occurs over several consecutive trades. The main object of our study is the conditional distribution:

$$h(\text{Max}(\Delta P) \mid \Delta V < V_0)$$

that is, the maximum price movement given the cumulative volume between two trades is less than a value V_0 specific to each equity. The study of this distribution will answer the specific questions asked in the beginning of this chapter.

2.2.1 JUSTIFICATION OF THE METHOD

2.2.1.1 Why Restricting the Distribution Conditional on V_0? According to our declared objective, we are interested in price movement corresponding to small volume. Therefore, by conditioning the distribution we are capable of providing answers while keeping the number of computations manageable.

2.2.1.2 Why Should V_0 be Constant in Time and Only Depend on the Equity? Indeed, this is a very important question. There is no reason for V_0 to be constant other than practical reasons. A valid objection is that the dynamics of the equity change in time. A time changing model is beyond the scope of the current study, though in this work we investigate several (fixed) levels of this parameter.

2.2.1.3 Why Not the More Traditional Approach of Price and Volume Evolution in Time? First the price evolution in time will not answer the questions asked. Furthermore, the volume of traded shares changes predictably during the day. In general, heightened trading activity may be observed at the beginning and the end of the trading day due to premarket trading activity, rebalancing of portfolio positions, and other factors. By tracking a window in volume we are unaffected by these changes in trading behavior. The net consequence is a change in time duration of the volume window which is irrelevant for our study.

2.2.2 SAMPLING METHOD—RARE EVENT DETECTION

Consider the current trade S_n for a certain equity. Construct the sequence of consecutive trades $S_k, S_{k+1}, \ldots, S_n$ and their associate volumes $V_k, V_{k+1}, \ldots, V_n$, such that $v_k + v_{k+1} + \cdots + v_n < V_0$. Then let

$$\Delta p_n = \max\{S_n - S_k, S_n - S_{k+1}, \ldots, S_n - S_{n-1}\}.$$

We repeat the process for every trade by calculating a corresponding maximum price movement within the last V_0 trades. Once we obtain these values for the entire sequence of trades, we detect the extreme observations by applying a simple "quantile type" rule. Namely, for a fixed level α we select all the observations in the set

$$Q_\alpha^+(x) = \{x : \text{Prob}(\Delta p < x) < \alpha \text{ or } \text{Prob}(\Delta p > x) > 1 - \alpha\}. \tag{2.1}$$

The probability above is approximated using the constructed histogram of maximum price movements. We note that the rule above is different than the traditional quantile definition which uses nonstrict inequalities. The modification above is imposed by the specific nature of the tick data under study (i.e., discrete data).

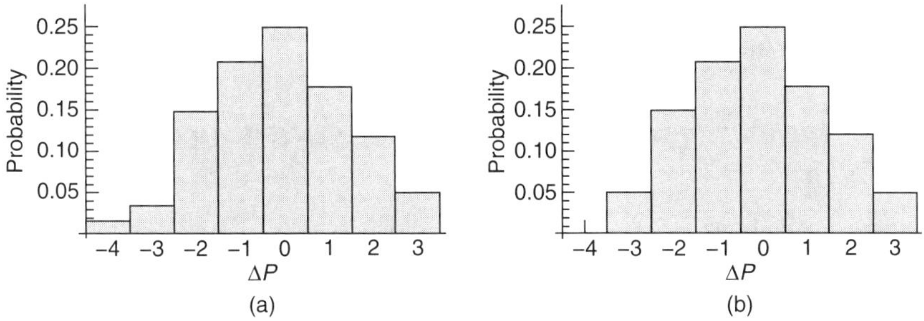

FIGURE 2.1 Two price change distributions. (a) Distribution with one interesting observation and (b) distribution lacking interesting observations.

For illustration consider the two distributions of the price change Δp(cents) in Fig. 2.1. Suppose we are interested in rare events that occur with probability $\alpha = 0.015$. The rule in Equation 2.1 will select the observations corresponding to $x = -4$ for distribution in Fig. 2.1a and no observation in Fig. 2.1b. A traditional quantile rule for any level $\alpha \leq 0.015$ no matter how small will indeed select the observations corresponding to $x = -4$ for the distribution in Fig. 2.1a, however, for the distribution in Fig. 2.1b will select all the observations at $x = -3$ and $x = 3$. Therefore, using a traditional quantile rule would force us to analyze points from distributions which lack extreme observations.

Note: Using rule (Eq. 2.1) with returns instead of change in price will be preferable in a trading environment. We use change in price (Δp) for clarity of exposition.

2.2.2.1 A Discussion About the Appropriateness of the Rule of Detecting Rare Events. Our rule is nonstandard and further discussion is necessary. We first note that because of the way Δp_n quantities are constructed they are not independent. Thus their histogram is only an approximation of the true probabilities of price movement. However, since we are only interested in extreme price movement, rule (Eq. 2.1) will identify candidate rare events which may or may not correspond to the true probability level α. We may have a better depiction of the true histogram of the price movement by considering nonoverlapping windows. There are two reasons why this is not feasible. First, by considering nonoverlapping windows, we may lose extreme price differences calculated using prices from these nonoverlapping windows. Second, in a previous study (Mariani *et al.*, 2009), the authors have shown that returns calculated from tick data exhibit long memory behavior. Thus, even by considering nonoverlapping windows one cannot guarantee that the observations are independent.

Furthermore, why do we use our rule and not a more traditional rule for detecting outliers such as 1.5*IQR rule or a parametric outlier test? A parametric detection rule does not make sense in our context since we do not want to hypothesize an underlying statistical model. The interquartile range (IQR) rule is useful for outlier detection not rare events. It is essentially equivalent with our rule since it uses quantiles but it is a very rigid rule. In general, it does not find outliers very often for fat tailed distributions (such as the ones under study here).

2.2.3 RARE EVENT ANALYSIS—CHOOSING THE OPTIMAL LEVEL α

After we obtain the rare event candidates, we need to develop a systematic methodology to evaluate them. According to our assumption the movement in price is abnormal and the equity should recover and reverse its momentum. We assume that a trade is placed at the time when a rare event is discovered. We consider a limited volume window (called the *after-event window*) and we analyze the price behavior (Fig. 2.2).

DEFINITION 2.1

We say that a favorable price movement occurs for a fixed rare event if either

the price level within the after-event window decreases below the event price level for at least one trade if the event was generated by a negative value for rule (Eq. 2.1)

the price level within the after-event window decreases below the event price level for at least one trade if the event was generated by a positive value for rule (Eq. 2.1)

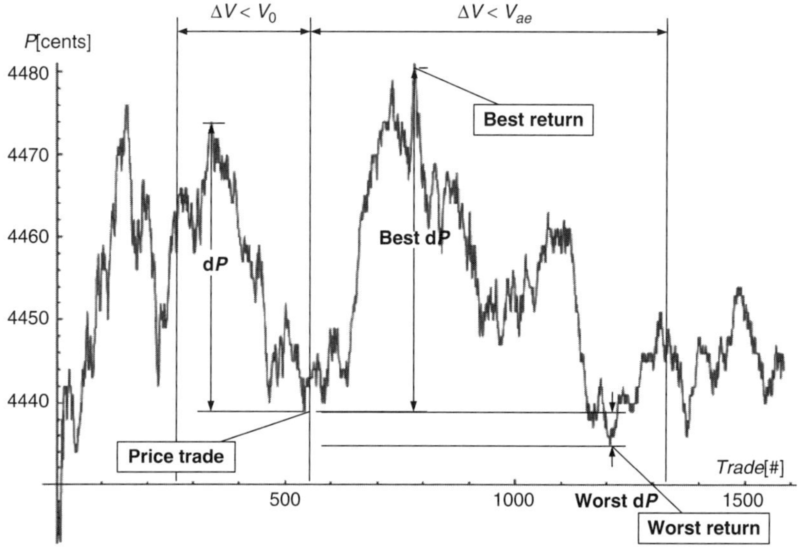

FIGURE 2.2 Visual depiction of the quantities used in the study.

This definition allows to estimate the probability of a favorable price movement for a specific level α. Specifically, if n is the total number of rare events detected by rule (Eq. 2.1) and k is the number of favorable price movements among them then the probability desired is simply k/n. As we shall see this definition allows the optimal selection of the level α. As the level α increases the events will stop being rare and just plain events.

Definition 2.1 does not allow the selection of the optimal volume window size V_0 or the optimal after-event window size. To investigate this selection, we consider the return on a trade. To this end, we consider the following strategy:

A trade is placed at every rare event, long or short, according to the sign of the quantile detected.

An after-event window size is fixed at the moment of the trade.

We close the position either during the after-event window if a favorable price movement takes place or at the last trade of the after-event window if a favorable price movement does not take place.

The return of such a strategy depends on the price at which the position is closed during the after-event window. To determine the optimal window size and optimal α level, we use the following trading strategy.

DEFINITION 2.2

> A position is opened at a point determined according to rule (1). The position is closed according to the following:
>
> If a favorable price movement takes place in the after-event window we close the position using the best return possible.
>
> If a favorable price movement does not take place within the after-event window we close the position using the worst return possible within the window.

For a certain level α and an after-event window size V_{ae} we calculate the expected return by averaging all the trade returns placed following the above strategy.

We note that we shall use the trading rule in Definition 2.2 only for determining optimal level α and window size. In practice, using back-testing and strategy calibration will determine a satisfactory favorable price movement and the position will be closed as soon as that level is reached.

2.2.4 MULTISCALE VOLUME CLASSIFICATION

Econometric analysis traditionally distinguishes between results obtained for highly traded stocks versus less frequently traded equities. Most of the studies are focused on what are called *large capitalization* equities which are defined as having market capitalizations larger than a specified cutoff. This definition is often vague, varies over the years and, more importantly, does not necessarily have direct relevance to trading patterns. For example, an equity traditionally classified as a large-cap stock may have a small average daily volume (ADV) and since the later is essential for us, we use a different nomenclature based directly on ADV. The results obtained for a highly liquid equity do not necessarily hold true for less liquid stocks even if both belong to the same capitalization class. Herein, we analyze the change in price from the volume perspective; therefore, we recognize the need for classifying equities into classes based on the average daily traded volume. We refer to this classification as the *multiscale volume classification*.

The histogram in Fig. 2.3 corresponds to the average daily trading volume (ADV) of the total universe of 5369 equities considered in this study.

The distribution of the ADV among the stocks is skewed to the right and our selection criterion follows certain features. As a preliminary step in our analysis, we need to eliminate all equities with ADV below 30,000 shares. The 30,000 volume cutoff value is not arbitrary, but it is found to be the minimum level required to perform our analysis. These stocks are grouped in class index 1 and are not used in any of the further analysis. The highest ADV values are concentrated around major indexes and large capitalization equities with more than 10 million shares traded daily. The three intermediary classes contain large, medium, and small ADV stocks. The resulting five classes in our multiscale volume classification are summarized in Table 2.1.

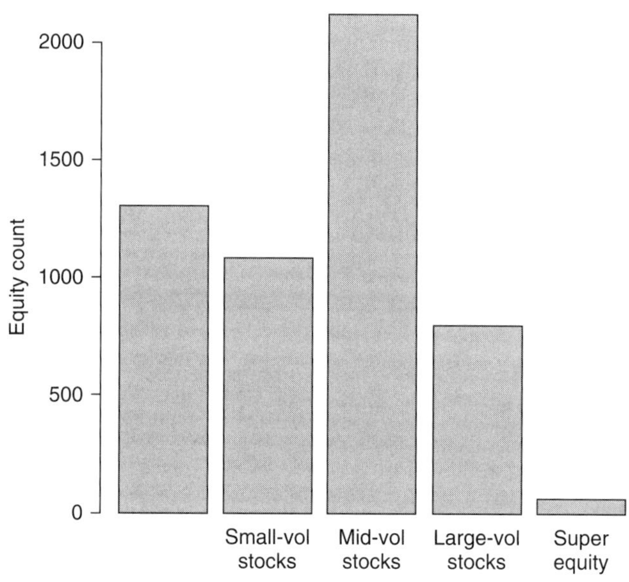

FIGURE 2.3 Average daily volume distribution.

TABLE 2.1 **Equities Partitioned into Five Classes**

	Class	Average Daily Volume (Shares)	Number Equities
1	—	$\text{ADV} \leq 30,000$	1305
2	Small-vol stocks	$30,000 < \text{ADV} \leq 100,000$	1088
3	Mid-vol stocks	$100,000 < \text{ADV} \leq 1,000,000$	2117
4	Large-vol stocks	$1,000,000 < \text{ADV} \leq 10,000,000$	799
5	Super equity	$10,000,000 < \text{ADV}$	60

2.3 Results

The methodology described in Section 2.2 is applied to all the equity data within a class in a homogeneous way. For this purpose, we combine all the outlying events detected according to rule (Eq. 2.1) within each class. Table 2.2 presents the probabilities of a favorable price movement according to Definition 2.1.

We note that to calculate the probability of favorable price movement as in Definition 2.1, we need to specify a level α for the detection rule, a volume level V_0 as well as an after-event volume size (V_{ae}). To analyze the optimal choices of these parameters, Table 2.2 presents the results obtained for a discrete set of parameters. Specifically, we look at $\alpha \in \{0.02, 0.015, 0.01, 0.005, 0.002, 0.0015, 0.001, 0.0005, 0.0002\}$, $V_0 \in \{3000, 5000, 10,000\}$, and $V_{ae} = k \times V_0$, where $k \in \{1, 2, 3\}$.

For a better visualization and interpretation of these numbers we construct probability surfaces for each class and we plot them with respect to the α level and volume V_{ae} in Fig. 2.4.

According to the Definition 2.1, we expect the probabilities to increase as the α level becomes more selective, as well as the size of the after-event window volume to increase. Indeed, we observe this behavior in Fig. 2.4, but it is remarkable that the surfaces are parallel and smooth. This seems to indicate that the probability has a similar behavior for each class. Furthermore, by using a simple translation in α and V_{ae}, we may be able to map each surface into another. This translation is very important because once we decide on a optimal level for one class it automatically translates into optimal levels for the other classes.

To determine the optimal level for each class, we calculate the expected return of trades according to the Definition 2.2. Specifically, for fixed levels of α and V_{ae}, we average all the returns within each class and present the results in Table 2.3. We also construct the corresponding surfaces in Fig. 2.5.

Unlike the probability plots, the surfaces in Fig. 2.5 have different curvatures. For each class surface, we identify the α level which produces maximum return for each V_{ae}. First, unlike the probability surfaces which were decreasing in α the return surfaces have a maximum for each V_{ae}. Remarkably, within each class the maximum return is obtained for the same α level regardless

TABLE 2.2 Probability (%) of Favorable Price Movement for Equity Classes for All Days

Class	α Level for Rule (Eq. 2.1)	$V_0 = 3000$ V_{ae} (shares)			$V_0 = 5000$ V_{ae} (shares)			$V_0 = 10,000$ V_{ae} (shares)		
		3000	6000	9000	5000	10,000	15,000	10,000	20,000	30,000
Small-vol stocks	0.02	84.13	88.97	91.05	89.00	92.68	94.06	93.80	95.73	96.36
	0.015	85.30	90.00	91.78	90.17	93.43	94.66	94.68	96.46	97.00
	0.01	86.68	91.23	92.66	91.83	94.62	95.68	95.02	96.83	97.30
	0.005	89.52	93.48	94.59	94.07	96.08	97.14	96.81	97.75	98.05
	0.002	92.68	95.59	96.63	96.33	98.16	98.82	98.22	98.57	98.75
	0.0015	93.72	96.03	96.86	95.53	97.65	98.82	98.77	99.08	99.08
	0.001	94.52	97.26	98.63	97.46	99.15	99.15	98.63	100.00	100.00
	0.0005	n.a.	n.a.	n.a.	n.a.	n.a.	n.a.	n.a.	n.a.	n.a.
	0.0002	n.a.	n.a.	n.a.	n.a.	n.a.	n.a.	n.a.	n.a.	n.a.
Mid-vol Stocks	0.02	78.48	84.82	87.54	83.39	88.28	90.35	88.84	92.15	93.40
	0.015	78.85	85.09	87.71	83.70	88.55	90.54	89.28	92.42	93.62
	0.01	79.35	85.43	88.03	84.58	89.23	91.17	90.05	93.06	94.12
	0.005	81.24	86.95	89.28	86.37	90.44	92.31	91.76	94.27	95.03
	0.002	84.65	89.32	91.20	89.70	92.82	94.34	94.08	96.11	96.56
	0.0015	85.82	90.42	92.12	90.96	93.58	94.96	94.78	96.45	96.81
	0.001	86.98	91.25	92.73	91.71	94.07	95.36	95.56	97.07	97.38
	0.0005	88.91	92.78	93.88	93.21	94.93	96.11	96.46	97.65	97.87
	0.0002	88.87	92.23	93.49	94.28	95.65	97.25	97.58	98.07	98.07
Large-vol Stocks	0.02	76.54	83.14	86.14	80.55	86.19	88.73	85.47	89.85	91.79
	0.015	76.82	83.36	86.29	80.99	86.49	88.99	85.80	90.12	92.04
	0.01	77.29	83.72	86.58	81.46	86.77	89.23	86.21	90.45	92.37
	0.005	78.31	84.46	87.06	82.40	87.49	89.78	86.99	91.09	92.90
	0.002	80.50	85.98	88.30	84.05	88.71	90.76	88.78	92.66	94.09
	0.0015	81.47	86.72	88.87	84.94	89.35	91.25	89.69	93.51	94.72
	0.001	82.69	87.74	89.82	86.20	90.32	92.17	91.26	94.52	95.43
	0.0005	85.42	89.62	91.58	89.28	92.55	94.09	93.05	95.49	96.18
	0.0002	88.23	92.01	93.64	92.67	95.17	96.27	95.17	96.66	96.93
Super equity	0.02	71.75	79.76	83.52	77.36	83.99	87.05	81.49	86.93	89.21
	0.015	72.36	80.43	84.09	77.46	84.03	87.12	81.83	87.23	89.59
	0.01	74.10	81.90	85.28	78.00	84.57	87.68	83.03	88.04	90.29
	0.005	74.87	82.73	86.07	78.72	85.24	88.12	83.73	88.32	90.64
	0.002	76.27	83.25	86.76	80.53	86.77	89.50	86.08	90.16	91.78
	0.0015	76.44	83.25	86.86	80.96	87.23	90.05	86.21	90.04	91.69
	0.001	77.59	84.50	88.15	82.60	88.32	90.60	86.96	90.77	92.29
	0.0005	79.40	86.06	88.76	84.36	89.57	91.37	87.22	90.43	92.09
	0.0002	81.59	87.91	90.11	84.97	89.64	91.97	91.41	93.43	94.95

Abbreviation: n.a., Not available.

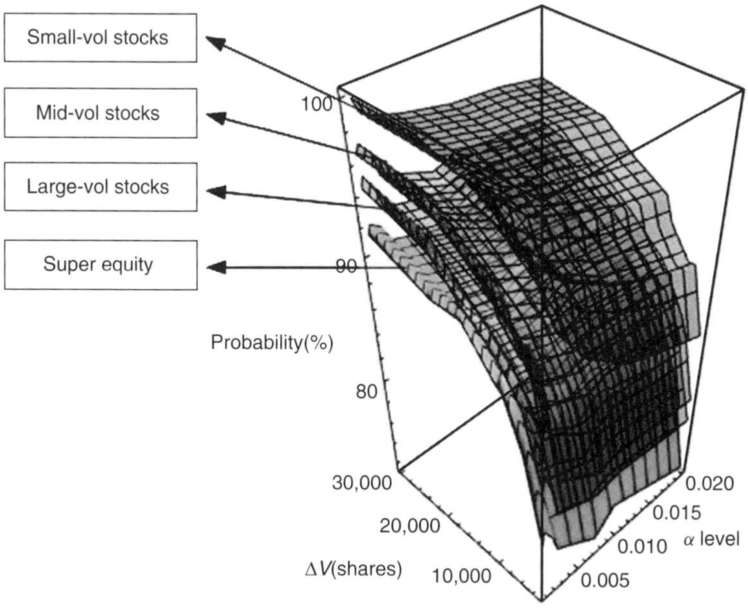

FIGURE 2.4 Probability surfaces for equity classes.

of the V_{ae} value. The corresponding α level is thus construed as optimal. The following list presents these values.

Class	Optimal Level α
Small-vol stocks	0.0025
Mid-vol stocks	0.0005
Large-vol stocks	0.0001
Super equity	<0.0001

The optimum α level is different for each surface and in general decreases as we consider larger ADV equities.

Once we have the optimal level α, we analyze the 3D plot in more detail to determine the optimal V_0 and V_{ae} levels. The numbers in Table 2.3 describe that in general the more we wait, the better the expected return. This, however, is an artifact because of the way we calculate the expected return (by taking the highest favorable value within the window). To calculate optimal values, we consider projections of the 3D plot in Figs. 2.6 and 2.7.

The analysis we need to perform is similar with a standard three way ANOVA. However, we avoid giving numerical values for the tests of interaction. The correlation between observations would cast a doubt on the validity of these numbers. Instead, we prefer a graphical depiction of the values.

TABLE 2.3 Expected Return (%) for Equity Classes for All Days

$$r = r_{\text{fav}} \cdot P + r_{\text{unfav}} \cdot (1 - P)$$

Class	α Level	$V_0 = 3000$			$V_0 = 5000$			$V_0 = 10{,}000$		
	for Rule	V_{ae} (shares)			V_{ae} (shares)			V_{ae} (shares)		
	(Eq. 2.1)	3000	6000	9000	5000	10,000	15,000	10,000	20,000	30,000
Small-vol	0.02	0.6119	0.8473	0.9963	0.8030	1.0562	1.2097	1.0696	1.3143	1.4380
stocks	0.015	0.6570	0.8976	1.0513	0.8507	1.1065	1.2626	1.1268	1.3781	1.5093
	0.01	0.7026	0.9620	1.1199	0.9189	1.1847	1.3475	1.1751	1.4485	1.5832
	0.005	0.7900	1.0784	1.2490	1.0585	1.3585	1.5390	1.2947	1.5884	1.7266
	0.002	0.8072	1.0755	1.2359	1.0108	1.2934	1.4649	1.2195	1.5165	1.6656
	0.0015	0.7844	1.0292	1.1670	0.9820	1.2802	1.4746	1.2184	1.5356	1.6997
	0.001	0.7030	0.9506	1.0579	0.9299	1.2352	1.3898	1.0963	1.5649	1.7453
	0.0005	n.a.	n.a.	n.a.	n.a.	n.a.	n.a.	n.a.	n.a.	n.a.
	0.0002	n.a.	n.a.	n.a.	n.a.	n.a.	n.a.	n.a.	n.a.	n.a.
Mid-vol	0.02	0.2396	0.3745	0.4643	0.3309	0.4821	0.5809	0.4685	0.6393	0.7437
stocks	0.015	0.2529	0.3916	0.4819	0.3467	0.5014	0.6008	0.4871	0.6587	0.7647
	0.01	0.2693	0.4118	0.5051	0.3719	0.5294	0.6302	0.5182	0.6922	0.8008
	0.005	0.3111	0.4633	0.5603	0.4218	0.5861	0.6927	0.5794	0.7587	0.8686
	0.002	0.3732	0.5348	0.6350	0.4931	0.6697	0.7832	0.6581	0.8441	0.9541
	0.0015	0.3949	0.5591	0.6626	0.5066	0.6835	0.7944	0.6652	0.8518	0.9622
	0.001	0.4034	0.5639	0.6694	0.5085	0.6856	0.7959	0.6706	0.8582	0.9665
	0.0005	0.3829	0.5345	0.6368	0.4720	0.6392	0.7454	0.6160	0.7962	0.8951
	0.0002	0.2988	0.4230	0.5112	0.4053	0.5548	0.6495	0.5240	0.6733	0.7506
Large-vol	0.02	0.0906	0.1385	0.1750	0.1171	0.1795	0.2263	0.1742	0.2596	0.3191
stocks	0.015	0.0953	0.1461	0.1840	0.1248	0.1904	0.2387	0.1830	0.2707	0.3312
	0.01	0.1039	0.1593	0.1992	0.1362	0.2056	0.2552	0.1963	0.2867	0.3490
	0.005	0.1198	0.1824	0.2263	0.1570	0.2317	0.2850	0.2191	0.3144	0.3777
	0.002	0.1458	0.2151	0.2619	0.1843	0.2643	0.3190	0.2533	0.3598	0.4256
	0.0015	0.1578	0.2291	0.2761	0.1956	0.2784	0.3335	0.2672	0.3764	0.4442
	0.001	0.1694	0.2418	0.2894	0.2117	0.2971	0.3547	0.2895	0.4011	0.4696
	0.0005	0.1978	0.2771	0.3274	0.2474	0.3367	0.3966	0.3234	0.4387	0.5091
	0.0002	0.2289	0.3189	0.3771	0.2742	0.3761	0.4386	0.3595	0.4821	0.5581
Super	0.02	0.0543	0.0721	0.0859	0.0666	0.0899	0.1081	0.0819	0.1130	0.1378
equity	0.015	0.0565	0.0762	0.0910	0.0659	0.0897	0.1072	0.0839	0.1178	0.1431
	0.01	0.0607	0.0828	0.0984	0.0646	0.0902	0.1083	0.0897	0.1272	0.1539
	0.005	0.0601	0.0833	0.1014	0.0636	0.0942	0.1143	0.0965	0.1334	0.1617
	0.002	0.0596	0.0829	0.1054	0.0708	0.1117	0.1343	0.1073	0.1508	0.1773
	0.0015	0.0615	0.0851	0.1092	0.0727	0.1167	0.1406	0.1149	0.1578	0.1865
	0.001	0.0659	0.0912	0.1172	0.0794	0.1263	0.1527	0.1175	0.1653	0.1942
	0.0005	0.0768	0.1111	0.1381	0.0811	0.1285	0.1555	0.1319	0.1807	0.2153
	0.0002	0.0881	0.1185	0.1502	0.0877	0.1436	0.1679	0.1490	0.1964	0.2470

Abbreviation: n.a., Not available.

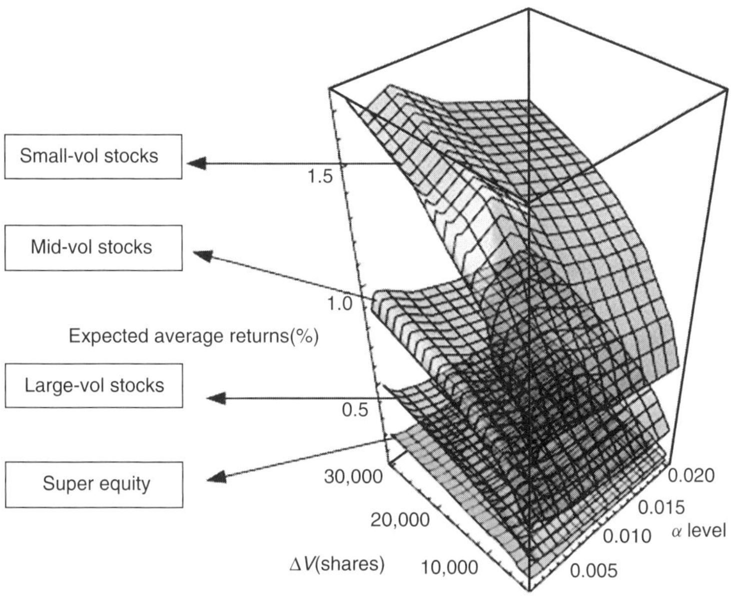

FIGURE 2.5 Expected return surfaces for stock classes.

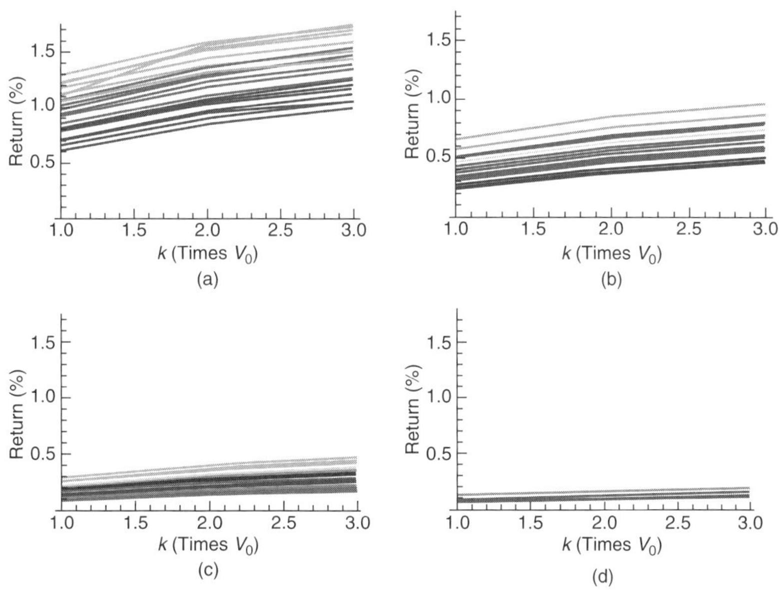

FIGURE 2.6 Sectional 2D plots of the surfaces in Figure 2.5 for each of the quantile levels considered. Each subfigure represents one surface from Figure 2.5. The x axis is the proportion of after-event window size with respect to the before-event window size, and lines of the same color represent the three original window sizes chosen (dark grey for $V_0 = 3000$, grey for $V_0 = 5000$, and light grey for $V_0 = 10{,}000$). (a) Small-cap stocks, (b) medium-cap stocks, (c) large-cap stocks, and (d) super equity.

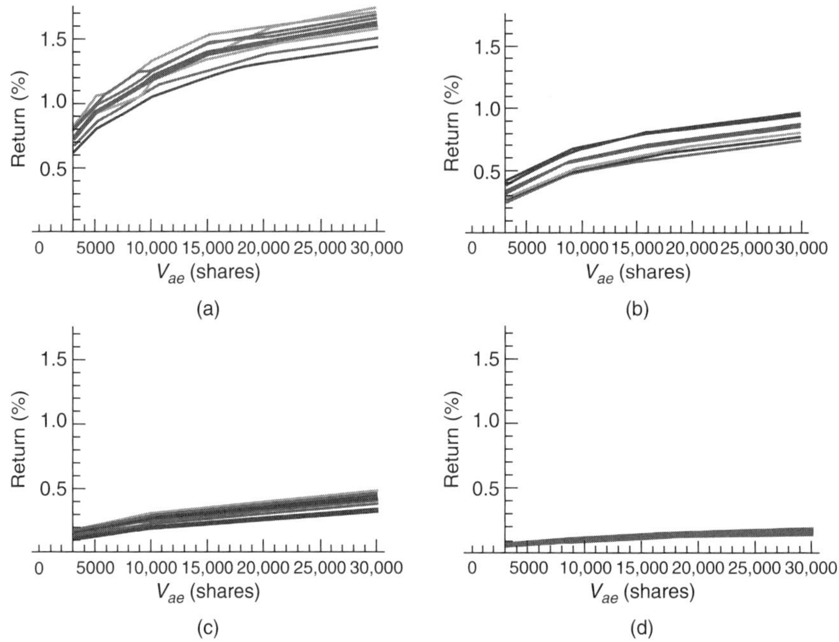

FIGURE 2.7 Sectional 2D plots of the surfaces in Figure 2.5 for each of the quantile levels considered. The x axis is the value of V_{ae} (in units of 100 shares). Each line represents a specific α level. The thicker grey line is an average of all the returns for all α levels. (a) Small stocks, (b) medium stocks, (c) large stocks, and (d) super equity.

In Fig. 2.6, we project the 3D plot onto the ratio V_{ae}/V_0. Each line represents a specific α level. With one exception the lines do not intersect. This means that there is little to no interaction between the α levels and the window sizes. Furthermore, using the same graphs we may determine if there is a significant increase in return as the ratio V_{ae}/V_0 increases.

From this Fig. 2.6, we deduce that for small and medium stocks, it may pay to wait longer (after-event window size two or three times larger than the original). In contrast for Large and especially for super large equity the expected return does not appear to increase significantly by enlarging the after-event window size (V_{ae}) with respect to the original window size V_0. In other words for highly traded stocks either the price bounces back very quickly or not at all.

Since the interaction was not found significant we proceed with Fig. 2.7 where we plot return versus V_{ae}. This figure provides an indication about the optimal after-event window size to use for each class of equity. Specifically, we look for points where the increase in return becomes negligible. Once again the lines are parallel (the level α factor and the windows size factor do not interact) thus, we look at the average return for all quantile levels (the thicker grey line in the image). Combining the results in Figs. 2.6 and 2.7, we may provide the following list of optimal values.

Class	Before-Event Window Size	After-Event Window Size
Small-vol stocks	5000	15,000
Mid-vol stocks	5000	15,000
Large-vol stocks	5000	10,000
Super equity	10,000	10,000

We emphasize that we give these values only as an example for these particular days and choice of classes. We observe that for small and medium volume stocks, it takes a longer after-event window for the price to recover. In contrast for the large volume stock and especially super-equity the price bounces back much faster.

2.4 Rare Events Distribution

In this section, we analyze time distribution of the rare events during the trading day. Recall that the way we define the rare events may be viewed as a quantile of the two dimensional price–volume distribution. Since most of the trades today are small, it is natural to ask: are these rare events just a percentage of the trades or are they concentrated at certain periods during the day?

First, we look at the distribution of trades within each minute for a full trading day. In Fig. 2.8, we present these distributions for small-, mid-, large-volume-, and super equity. They are constructed using the entire five days trading activity.

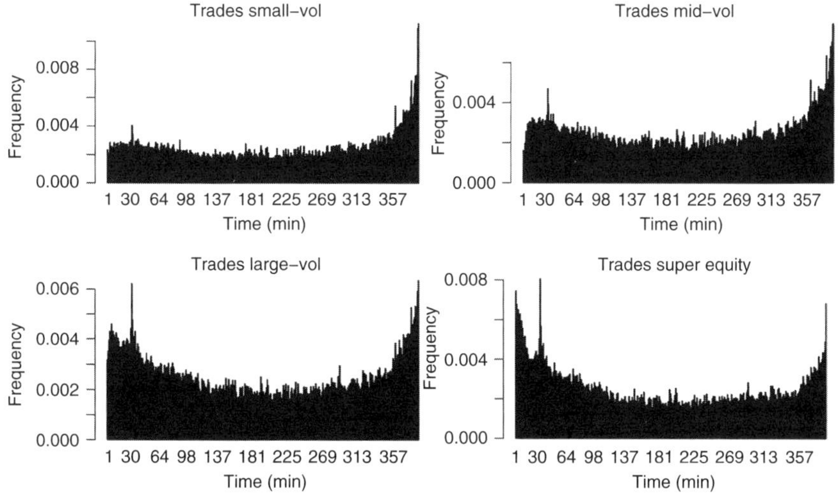

FIGURE 2.8 Distribution of trades during the day for small-, mid-, large-volume-, and super-equity classes.

The U-shape of these distributions is well documented in literature (Gerety and Mulherin, 1992) and (Foster and Viswanathan, 1993). However, in addition to these early studies, we note the presence of high trading activity around 30 min after the market opening. This spike becomes more prevalent for large volume and super equity. As already noted, the trading activity is increasing toward the end of market trading hours but again we see that early market activity compared to end market activity is stronger when looking at the large and super equity.

Next, we look at the rare events corresponding to the level $\alpha = 0.02$. We construct histograms for the rare events distribution during the day for each of the V_0 levels considered and for each equity class. Figure 2.9 presents these distributions. On each histogram, we also represent the corresponding percentage level (0.02) of trades with a light grey line.

We first note that if the distribution of rare events would occur at a percentage rate of the trades, then the rare events distribution during the day would have had to follow approximately the light grey line. From the Fig. 2.9, it is clear that the rare events do not follow the profile of the trades. Furthermore, they are concentrated in a region close to the opening.

Second, we note the similarity of these distributions for a specific equity class (small vol, mid vol, etc.). The skewness of the distributions decreases as V_0 increases and it is more significant for small and mid-vol stocks. This is easy to explain since this type of equities are more rarely traded and it takes a longer time period to detect the changes in equity using a 10,000 shares window versus a 3000 shares window.

Third, we remark the presence of a peak in the distribution of rare events during the day after about 30 min of trading across all classes. This does correspond to the previously observed peak in trading activity (Fig. 2.9) at about the same time. We hypothesize that the peak in rare events may be caused by the activation of various trading strategies after the stabilization of the market following the opening. Recall that the histogram presents the rare events detection for ALL equity within a class. This may be evidence of algorithmic trading starting at about the same time, reaching about the same conclusion, placing similar limit orders, and therefore pulling the market in the same direction with relatively little volume. We do underline, however, that this does not destabilize the market. This much is evident from the ensuing pattern of rare events which follows the same trend as before the spike.

Finally, we notice the presence of a significant number of rare events concentrated around noon for small- and mid-vol equity. This is not evident in the trades distribution (Fig. 2.9) and they correspond typically to the lowest level of volume traded during the day. We do not notice this concentration for the super-equity class. Somehow this period coincides with the end of lunch time (around 1:00 pm) during the real time and this may show increased trader activity after regrouping and using the information accumulated during lunch. This hypothesis may actually be strengthened by the absence of activity in the large and supper equity since the human factor is much less present in this type of equity (plus trading in these equities comes from around the globe; therefore, lunch time is meaningless).

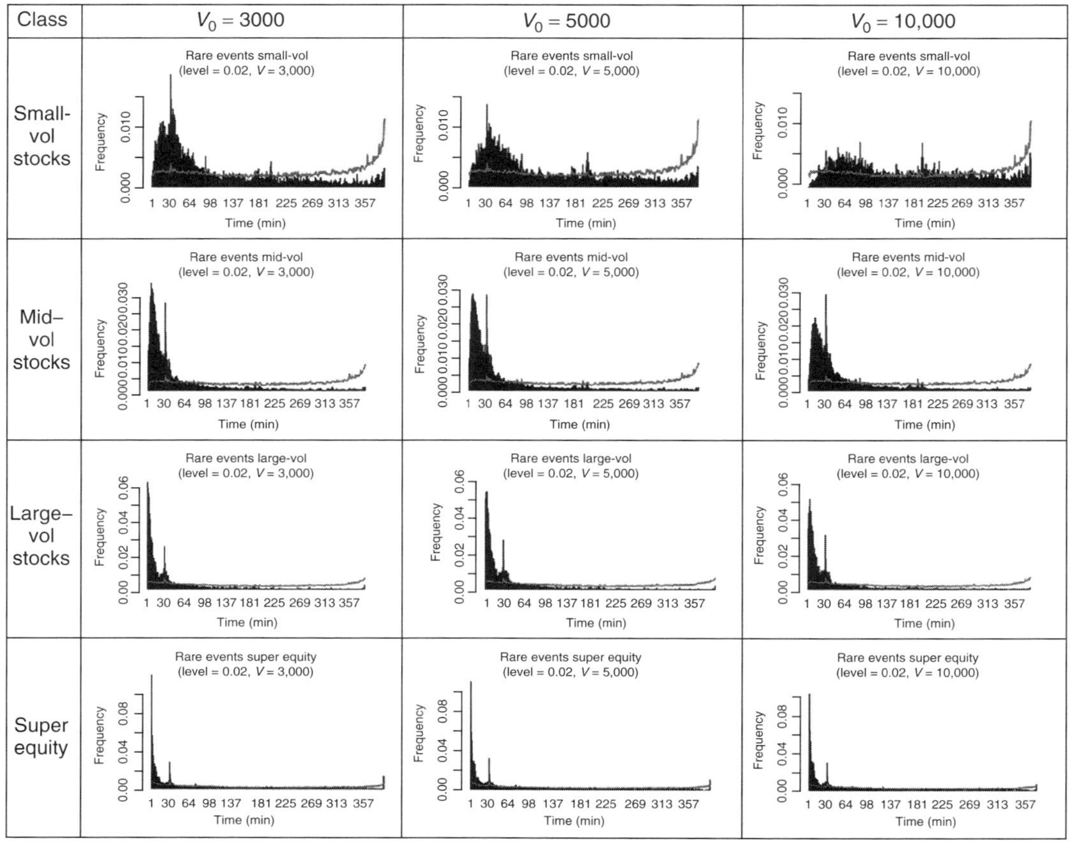

FIGURE 2.9 Distribution of rare events (level $\alpha = 0.02$) during the day for each type of equity and window volume considered.

If we look at the duration of time when the rare events are in excess of the light grey line, we find periods of about 90 min for small-vol class, 60 min for mid-vol class, 40 min for large-vol class, and about 35 min for super-equity class.

On the basis of the previous analysis of the probabilities for price reversal and the expected return of a trading rule and the rare event distribution, we note significant market inefficiencies for small and mid-vol classes and an increase in market efficiencies for the other two high volume classes. This is to be expected since higher volume means inefficiencies will disappear faster, but the histograms provide a time frame for the expected duration of these rare events in excess of the expectation.

In Fig. 2.10, we exemplify the rare events distribution for the optimum α level and V_0 determined in the prior analysis. This particularization for the optimal set provides a calibration method for optimal execution time and activation of a trading rule.

2.5 Conclusions

This chapter presents a simple methodology of detecting and evaluating unusual price movements defined as large change in price corresponding to small volume of trades. We classify these events as "rare" and we show that the behavior of the equity price in the neighborhood of a rare event exhibits an increase in the probability of price recovery. The use of an arbitrary trading rule designed to take advantage of this observation indicates that the returns associated with such

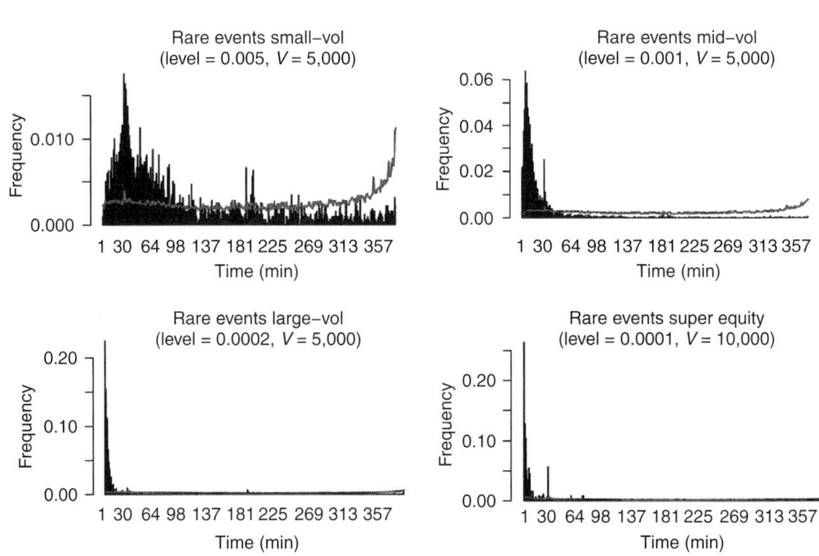

FIGURE 2.10 Rare events distribution relative to the frequency of the trade activity with optimal parameters determined in the analysis.

movements are significant. We therefore confirm the old Wall Street adage that "it takes volume to move prices" even in the presence of high frequency trading.

We present a way to calibrate and find optimal trading parameters for the specific trading strategy considered. The methods presented herein may be easily extended to any trading strategy based on rare events detection. The equity behavior is consistent throughout the equity classes considered in this work. The trading rule we consider provides positive returns when considering the entire universe of equities and neglecting transaction costs.

The classification of equity based on ADV allows us to draw more specific inference about the rebound behavior of the equity. We confirm that it takes a larger volume window to observe a rare event for super equity (e.g., SPY, JPM, MSFT, etc.) than for less traded equity. Furthermore, the price recovery after a rare event is much faster for highly traded stocks than for low volume stocks.

We look at the distribution of these rare events during the trading day. We show that they are not simply a percentage of the trades and we show that they accumulate at the beginning of the day. We observe an increase frequency around 30 min across equities and another at about the middle of the trading day for equity which is not traded very frequently. These may be explained and we formulate hypotheses about their appearance.

Essentially, the methodology we present measures the reaction of the market to abnormal price movements. Notably, a possible application of this methodology may involve the development of forensic tools for market trading activity. The delimitation between rare events and suspicious events is rather thin and additional market data regarding the origination of the trades recorded would be useful in identification of irregular trades.

REFERENCES

Admati AR, Pfleiderer P. A theory of intraday patterns: volume and price variability. Rev Financ Stud 1988;1(1):3–40.

Alfonsi A, Schied A, Schultz A. 2007. Optimal execution strategies in limit order books with general shape functions. http://www.citebase.org/abstract?id=oai:arXiv.org:0708.1756 (last accessed 2009).

Beaver WH. The information content of annual earnings announcements. Empirical research in accounting: selected studies; supplement to J Account Res 1968;6:67–92.

Bollerslev T, Jubinski D. Equity trading volume and volatility: latent information arrivals and common long-run dependencies. J Bus Econ Stat 1999;17:9–21.

Engle RF, Russell JR. Autoregressive conditional duration: a new model for irregularly spaced transaction data. Econometrica 1998;66:1127–1162.

Foster FD, Viswanathan S. A theory of the interday variations in volume, variance, and trading costs in securities markets. Rev Financ Stud 1990;3(4):593–624.

Foster FD, Viswanathan S. Variations in trading volume returns volatility and trading costs: evidence on recent price formation models. J Finance 1993;48(1):187–211.

Gallant AR, Rossi PE, Tauchen GE. Stock prices and volume. Rev Financ Stud 1992;5:199–242.

Gerety MS, Mulherin JH. Trading halts and market activity: an analysis of volume at the open and the close. J Finance 1992;47(5):1765–1784.

Karpoff J. The relation between price change and trading volume: a survey. J Financ Quant Anal 1987;22:109–126.

Llorente G, Michaely R, Saar G, Wang J. Dynamic volume-return relation of individual stocks. Rev Financ Stud 2002;15(4):1005–1047.

Lo, AW, Wang J. Trading Volume. Advances in economics and econometrics: theory and applications. Eighth World Congress, Volume II. Cambridge University Press; 2003, pp. 206–277.

Mariani MC, Florescu I, Beccar Varela MP, Ncheuguim E. Long correlations and Levy models applied to the study of memory effects in high frequency (tick) data, Physica A 2009;388(8):1659–1664.

Osborne MFM. Brownian motion in the stock market, Oper Res 1959;7(2):145–173.

Sun W. Relationship between trading volume and security prices and returns, MIT LIDS Technical Report 2638 February 2003, Area Exam, http://ssg.mit.edu/~waltsun/docs/AreaExamTR2638.pdf (last accessed 2009).

Zhang MY, Russell JR, Tsay RS. Determinants of bid and ask quotes and implications for the cost of trading. J Empir Finance 2008;15(4):656–678.

CHAPTER THREE

Using Boosting for Financial Analysis and Trading*

GERMÁN CREAMER

Howe School and School of Systems and Enterprises, Stevens Institute of Technology, Hoboken, NJ

3.1 Introduction

Quantitative evaluation of econometric models is usually done by evaluating the statistical significance of linear models. For example, previous studies on US securities (see the pioneering works of Altman (1968), Beaver (1966), and also see Altman (1974, 1989), Altman *et al.* (1998), Barr *et al.* (1994), Collins and Green (1982), Chen and Lee (1995), Clarke and McDonald (1992), Goudie and Meeks (1991), Hudson (1997), Lane *et al.* (1986), Hing-Ling (1987), Moyer (1977), Ohlson (1980), Pinches and Mingo (1973), Queen and Roll (1987), Rose and Giroux (1984), and Zavgren (1983) have used linear discriminant analysis or logistic regression for the prediction of financial distress, bankruptcy, and credit risk. This analysis is based on estimating the parameters of an underlying stochastic system, usually assumed to be a linear system.

One limitation of this methodology is that nonlinearities have to be incorporated manually. Another limitation is that the number of parameters that can be estimated reliably is limited by the amount of available data and is often very small.

*The author thanks the editors Ionuţ Fiorescu, Maria C. Mariani, and Frederi G. Viens for their valuable comments. The opinions presented are the exclusive responsibility of the author.

Handbook of Modeling High-Frequency Data in Finance, First Edition.
Edited by Frederi G. Viens, Maria C. Mariani, and Ionuţ Florescu.

By contrast, machine learning methods such as decision trees (Breiman *et al.*, 1984), boosting (Freund and Schapire, 1997), and support vector machines (Müller *et al.*, 1997) avoid the question of estimating the parameters of the underlying distribution and focus instead on making accurate predictions for some variables given others variables. Breiman (2001) contrasts these two approaches as the data-modeling culture and the algorithmic modeling culture. According to Breiman (2001), while most statisticians adhere to the data-modeling approach, people in other fields of science and engineering use the algorithmic modeling to construct predictors with superior accuracy. The main drawback of algorithmic modeling, according to Breiman, is that although the models are easy to generate, they are hard to interpret.

In this chapter, we review several applications of algorithmic modeling to planning and corporate performance evaluation and to forecast stock prices, cumulative abnormal return, and earnings surprises.

The rest of the chapter is organized as follows: Section 3.2 introduces the main methods used in this chapter; Section 3.3 presents the application of boosting to performance evaluation and the generation of balanced scorecards (BSCs); Section 3.4 shows how boosting can be applied to forecast earnings surprise and to algorithmic trading; and Section 3.5 presents the conclusions and recommendations.

3.2 Methods

In this section we introduce boosting and how it can be used to support the generation of BSCs.

3.2.1 BOOSTING

Adaboost is a general discriminative learning algorithm invented by Freund and Schapire (1997).

The basic idea of Adaboost is to repeatedly apply a simple learning algorithm, called the *weak* or *base* learner,[1] to different weightings of the same training set. In its simplest form, Adaboost is intended for binary prediction problems where the training set consists of pairs $(x_1, y_1), (x_2, y_2), \ldots, (x_m, y_m)$, x_i corresponds to the features of an example and $y_i \in \{-1, +1\}$ is the binary label to be predicted. A *weighting* of the training examples is an assignment of a nonnegative real value w_i to each example (x_i, y_i).

On iteration t of the boosting process, the weak learner is applied to the training sample with a set of weights $w_1^t, \ldots, w_m^t$ and produces a prediction rule h_t and a prediction score $F_t(x)$ that map x to $\{0, 1\}$ as follows:

$$F_0(x) \equiv 0$$

$$\text{for } t = 1, \ldots, T$$

[1]Intuitively, a weak learner is an algorithm with a performance at least slightly better than random guessing.

$$w_i^t = e^{-y_i F_{t-1}(x_i)}$$

Get h_t from *weak learner,*

$$\alpha_t = \frac{1}{2} \ln \left(\frac{\sum_{i:h_t(x_i)=1, y_i=1} w_i^t}{\sum_{i:h_t(x_i)=1, y_i=-1} w_i^t} \right)$$

$$F_{t+1} = F_t + \alpha_t h_t.$$

The requirement on the weak learner is for $h_t(x)$ to have a small but significant correlation with the example labels y when measured using the *current weighting of the examples*. After the rule h_t is generated, the example weights are changed so that the weak predictions $h_t(x)$ and the labels y are decorrelated. The weak learner is then called with the new weights over the training examples, and the process repeats. Finally, all the weak prediction rules are combined into a single *strong* rule using a weighted majority vote. The strong prediction rule learned by Adaboost is sign$(F(x))$. For an introduction to boosting, see Schapire (2002).

Friedman *et al.* (2000), followed by Collins *et al.* (2000) suggested a modification of Adaboost, called *Logitboost*. Logitboost can be interpreted as an algorithm for stepwise logistic regression. This modified version of Adaboost—known as *Logitboost*—assumes that the labels $y_i^{\prime}s$ were stochastically generated as a function of the $x_i^{\prime}s$. Then, it includes $F_{t-1}(x_i)$ in the logistic function to calculate the probability of y_i, and the exponents of the logistic functions become the weights of the training examples. The following formulation of Logitboost shows that the main difference with Adaboost is the logistic function of the weights w_i^t:

$$F_0(x) \equiv 0$$

for $t = 1, \ldots, T$

$$w_i^t = \frac{1}{1 + e^{-y_i F_{t-1}(x_i)}}$$

Get h_t from *weak learner*

$$\alpha_t = \frac{1}{2} \ln \left(\frac{\sum_{i:h_t(x_i)=1, y_i=1} w_i^t}{\sum_{i:h_t(x_i)=1, y_i=-1} w_i^t} \right)$$

$$F_{t+1} = F_t + \alpha_t h_t.$$

3.2.1.1 Alternating Decision Trees. One successful and popular way of using boosting is to combine it with decision tree learning as the base learning algorithm (Friedman *et al.*, 2000). We use boosting both to learn the decision rules constituting the tree and to combine these rules through a weighted majority vote. The form of the generated decision rules is called an *alternating decision tree* (ADT) (Freund and Mason, 1999). In ADTs, each node can be understood in isolation.

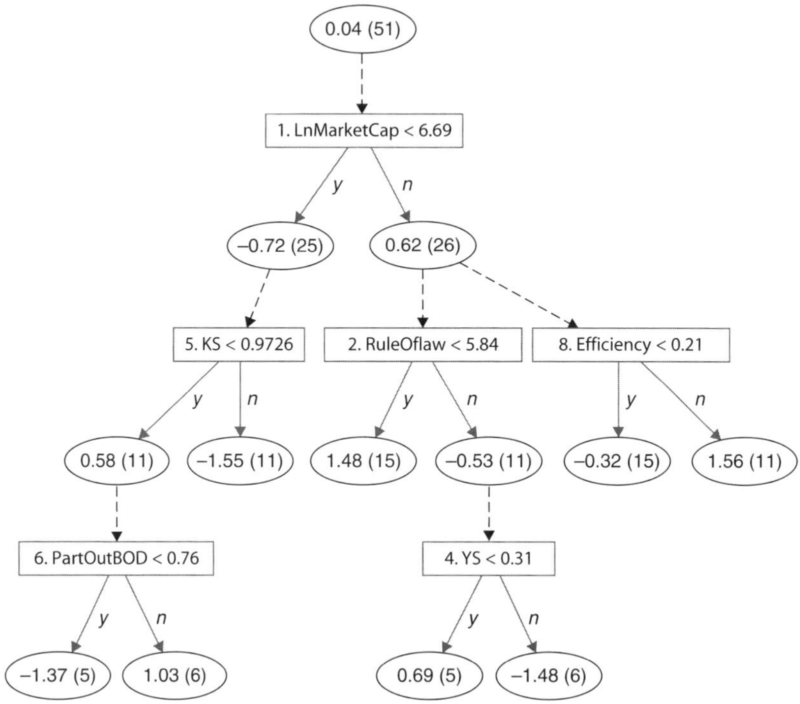

FIGURE 3.1 Representative ADT example from Creamer and Freund (2010b).

We explain the structure of ADTs using Fig. 3.1. The problem domain is corporate performance prediction, and the goal is to separate stocks with high and low values based on 17 different variables. The tree consists of alternating levels of ovals (*prediction nodes*) and rectangles (*splitter nodes*) (hence the word "alternating" in the name). The first number within the ovals defines contributions to the prediction score, and the second number (between parentheses) indicates the number of instances. In this example, positive contributions are evidence of high performance, while negative contributions are evidence of corporate financial problems. To evaluate the prediction for a particular company, we start at the top oval (0.04) and follow the arrows down. We follow *all* of the dotted arrows that emanate from prediction nodes, but we follow *only one* of the solid-line arrows emanating from a splitter node, corresponding to the answer (yes or no) to the condition stated in rectangle. We sum the values in all the prediction nodes that we reach. This sum represents the prediction score $F(x)$ above, and its sign is the final, or strong, prediction. For example, suppose we had a company for which LnMarketCap = 6, KS = 0.86 RuleOfLaw = 7.02, and PartOutBOD = 0.76. In this case, the prediction nodes that we reach in the tree are 0.042, −0.7181, 0.583, and 1.027. Summing gives a score of 0.9339, that is, a very confident indicator that the company has a high market value.

This example demonstrates how ADTs combine the contributions of many indicators to generate a prediction. The ADT in the figure was generated by Adaboost from training data. In Adaboost's terms, each prediction node represents a weak prediction rule, and at every boosting iteration, a new splitter node together with its two prediction nodes is added to the model. The splitter node can be attached to any previous prediction node, and not only leaf nodes, unless it already has a splitter node attached. Each prediction node is associated with a weight α that contributes to the prediction score of every example reaching it. The weak hypothesis $h(x)$ is 1 for every example reaching the prediction node and 0 for all others. The number in front of the conditions in the splitter nodes of Fig. 3.1 indicates the iteration number on which the node was added. In general, lower iteration numbers indicate that the decision rule is more important.

3.2.2 THE BOARD BALANCED SCORECARD

In response to the recent corporate scandals in the United States, several organizations and researchers have proposed corporate governance scorecards. Gompers *et al.* (2003) use 24 different provisions related to takeover defense and shareholder rights to create a governance index. They show that a trading strategy based on this index outperforms the market. Standard & Poor's Governance Services (2004) have developed a method that combines macro- and microvariables and uses qualitative and quantitative analysis.[2] The German Society of Financial Analysts (Stenger, 2004) has proposed a corporate governance scorecard for German corporations, which is based on a "Code of Best Practice" following the German law. The German Society of Financial Analysts and partially Standard & Poor's use a qualitative framework based on "best practices" and require a lengthy due diligence process for each company under study, while the Gompers approach is purely quantitative.

In a different line of research, Kaplan and Norton (1992) introduced the BSC as a management system that helps organizations define their vision and strategy and translate them into specific actions. The BSC provides feedback on internal business processes, performance, and market conditions in order to review the strategy and future plans (Kaplan and Norton, 1993, 1996a,b,c). Large US companies, such as General Electric and Federal Express, and nonprofit and public organizations have implemented the BSC approach (Ampuero *et al.*, 1998; Voelpel *et al.*, 2006).

The BSC suggests that an organization should be evaluated from four perspectives:

1. *The financial perspective* emphasizes the long-term objectives of the company in terms of revenue growth and productivity improvement. The financial goals should be the final goals for the other perspectives.
2. *The customer perspective* emphasizes the lifetime relationship and service delivery with clients.

[2] Even though the Standard & Poor's corporate governance scoring has been very successful in emerging markets, Standard & Poor's corporate governance services decided to withdraw from the US market in September 2005.

3. *The internal processes perspective* focuses on the use of clients' information to sell new products and services according to the clients' needs.
4. *The learning and growth perspective* is the foundation of the BSC. This perspective looks at the motivation, training, and capacity to innovate that employees need to have in order to implement the new strategies.

Different from the corporate governance scorecards presented at the beginning of this section, which emphasize corporate governance scoring, Kaplan and Nagel (2004) proposed the creation of a board BSC that includes corporate governance variables and is oriented to strategic planning at the board level.

The strategy of an organization, its main objectives, and its key business drivers define the indicators of the BSC. However, the choice of indicators is, in general, highly subjective and is often driven by the company management or industry practices. There are several proposals for more objective methods for quantifying board performance. Youngblood and Collins (2003) describe a method based on indicators using the multi-attribute utility theory. Clinton *et al.* (2002) base their method on the analytic hierarchy process. However, these methods still require a mix of quantitative measure and a qualitative evaluation by managers or experts. Creamer and Freund (2010b) propose a method that can partially automate the definition of the board BSC for US companies, thus, making the process of company evaluation more objective and more transparent. In this chapter, we expand and integrate the results of Creamer and Freund (2010a,b) and show how the boosting approach can be used for financial analysis and for performance evaluation through the BSC.

3.2.3 THE REPRESENTATIVE ADT ALGORITHM AND THE BALANCED SCORECARD

Boosting and ADTs have been criticized for their lack of clear interpretation and their instability, especially when there are samples' changes. Considering these problems, Creamer and Freund (2010b) propose an algorithm to calculate a representative ADT that extracts the common features among several trees. The representative ADT algorithm looks for the most frequent nodes among a set of ADTs with same positions, features, and thresholds. The selected nodes are ranked according to a rank coefficient obtained by the multiplication of the average iteration and the inverse of the frequency of nodes that share the same characteristics. A low value of this coefficient indicates that the node is more important because it is present in many nodes of the original set of ADTs and/or appears in the first iterations. The algorithm selects the most important nodes. In case the algorithm selects two nodes with the same position, the node with lower priority is put under the root.

The features and their relationship of the representative ADT is used to identify key business drivers, strategic objectives, and indicators of the BSC (Section 3.2.2). In the first step, the features and thresholds of the representative ADT become the indicators and targets of the BSC, respectively. If the representative ADT has several levels, then the relationship between the nodes also determines the relationship between the indicators of the BSC. In the second step, the indicators are transformed into objectives of the BSC and of the board strategy map. This step requires a dialog among managers, where the results of the representative ADTs are reviewed according to the priorities of senior management.

3.3 Performance Evaluation

This section briefly introduces the literature of executive compensation and corporate governance and their impact on performance. It also proposes how boosting can be used to recognize the optimal combination of these variables and semiautomate the generation of BSCs.

One of the main areas where the principal–agent conflict is expressed is in the compensation of the top executives of the firm. Before the 1970s, compensation was based mostly on salaries and bonuses that were linked to performance, but now most of the compensation is based on stock options. Jensen and Murphy (2004) calculate that the average total remuneration of CEOs from S&P500 firms has gone from $850,000 in 1970 to $9.4 million in 2002 (using 2002 constant dollars). The value of the options in the same period went from almost 0 to $4.4 million. Jensen and Murphy (1990a,b) as well as shareholder representatives suggested that executive compensation should include a larger options component. Compensations committees tend to grant stock options to CEOs and top managers since stock options are not debited as a cost to the firm. Jensen and Murphy (2004) recognize the excess of these compensations committees and propose instead that the cost of granting options is the opportunity cost of not selling these options in the market. The Sarbanes–Oxley Act of 2002 introduced important provisions for executive compensation, such as the prohibition of executive loans, and periods when insider trading is not allowed. The Financial Accounting Standards Board (FASB) and the Securities and Exchange Commission (SEC) complemented these rules requiring that if companies grant options to employees, those options should be registered in the financial statements as an expense for fiscal years beginning after June 15, 2005.

Several authors have studied the effect of altering the terms of executive stock options on performance (Brenner *et al.*, 2000) and as a reincentivization strategy (Acharya *et al.*, 2000). Firms with agency problems and with insider-dominated boards are more likely to reprice executive stock options (Chance *et al.*, 2000), while companies that have more outsiders as directors grant more compensation packages, such as equity-based compensation, to directors aligned with shareholders' interests (Ryan and Wiggins, 2004).

Jensen and Murphy (2004) indicate that the fundamental motivation to grant executive options, which is to align corporate and managerial goals, is not fulfilled by the current executive compensation policy. On the other hand, current research shows that some of the policies are at least partially effective.

Another major area where the principal–agent problem is evident is the insider ownership. According to Jensen and Meckling (1976), the separation of ownership and control is often seen as an opportunity for managers to accumulate wealth at the expense of shareholders (Berle and Means, 1932; Shleifer and Vishny, 1997). Ang *et al.* (2000), using a sample of small US companies, show how agency costs increase with a decrease in managerial ownership as proposed by Jensen and Meckling (1976). On the basis of the previous study by Weston (1979), who indicates that beyond board ownership of 20–30% a hostile bid cannot succeed, Morck *et al.* (1988) highlight the opposing effects of extensive insider ownership. On one hand, a high proportion of insider ownership has a positive impact on performance because of insiders' incentive alignment with other shareholders (convergence-of-interests hypothesis) (Jensen, 1993; Byrne, 1996; Crystal 1991). On the other hand, a high proportion of insider ownership has a negative impact on performance because of the insider's bargaining power that may lead managers to make self-interested decisions (entrenchment hypothesis) (Jensen and Meckling, 1976). Stulz (1988) finds—through a formal model—that the relationship between ownership and performance follows a roof-shaped curve where low levels of ownership improve performance, while high levels of ownership affects performance. McConnell and Servaes (1990) and Fuerst and Kang (2004) empirically confirm the implications of this model. Other studies show mixed results (Mikkelson and Ruback, 1985).

There is no theoretical support to indicate the optimal values of organizational variables such as insider ownership. Moreover, these variables may change from industry to industry and country to country. Therefore, an algorithm that would establish the appropriate values of corporate governance variables and the conditions under which executive options should be granted can potentially be used to align corporate and managerial interests and reduce the principal–agent conflict. In the following sections, we show how we used the boosting approach to generate a BSC.

3.3.1 CORPORATE GOVERNANCE AND PERFORMANCE ANALYSIS OF S&P500 COMPANIES

We applied the representative ADT algorithm (Section 3.2.3) proposed by Creamer and Freund (2010b) with stumps-averaged classifier trained using boosting to the companies that are part of the S&P500 index with available data from 1992 to 2004. The main sources of data for S&P500 companies were ExecuComp for executive compensation information and Compustat North America for accounting information. These two datasets are products of Standard & Poor's. We eliminated observations that did not have enough information to calculate Tobin's Q or incomplete executive compensation information.

We have selected the following accounting variables because of their predictive power and also as indirect indicators of corporate governance variables: the logarithm of market capitalization (LnMarketCap), long-term assets to sales ratio (KS) for its effect in the reduction of the agency conflict, debt to total assets ratio (DebtRatio) as a capital structure indicator, operating expenses to sales ratio (efficiency) as an efficiency or agency cost indicator, operating income to sales ratio (YS) as a market power proxy and to indicate cash available from operations, and capital expenditures to long-term assets ratio (IK) as a proxy for the relationship between growth and the possibility of investing in discretionary projects. A large IK ratio may indicate agency problems if managers are developing new projects that may increase their power, but do not add market value to the company. Region and sector are the indicators of the geographical area and industrial sector in which the company operates.[3]

We used Tobin's Q as the measure of performance.[4] Tobin's Q, as a measure of the value of intangibles of a firm, is the ratio of the market value of assets to the replacement cost of assets. This is a measure of the real value created by the management. A higher value of Tobin's Q indicates that more value has been added or there is an expectation of greater future cash flow. Any difference of Tobin's Q from one indicates that the market perceives that the value of total assets is different from the value to replace their physical assets. The value of internal organization, management quality, or expected agency costs is assumed to explain the difference. Values of Tobin's Q above one indicate that the market perceives the firm's internal organization as effective in leveraging company assets, while a Tobin's Q below one shows that the market expects high agency costs. We used as a proxy for Tobin's Q the ratio of book value of debt plus market value of common stocks, and preferred stocks to total assets.[5]

We also included insider ownership (T_Insider) and variables related to executive compensation for the top five senior managers. The variables of executive compensation are total compensation for officers (TotalCompExec) and CEOs (totalCompCEO); value of options for officers (OptionAllValExec), CEOs (TotalValOptCEO), and directors (OptionsDirectors); value of stock options for officers (OptionAllValExec); fees paid for attendance to board of directors meeting (TotalMeetingPay); annual cash paid to each director (PayDirectors); indicator variables to specify if directors are paid additional fees for attending board committee meetings (DcommFee); and annual number of shares granted to nonemployee directors (StockDirectors).[6]

We used the main features and thresholds of the representative ADT as indicators and targets of the board BSC, respectively. We restricted our analysis to the board BSC for the S&P500 companies, although we could use a similar methodology to develop the enterprise BSC and the executive BSC. We mostly concentrated on the financial perspective and the internal process perspective because these are the perspectives mainly affected by the corporate governance variables. We obtained the representative ADT when we included all variables (Fig. 3.2), and only the corporate governance variables (Fig. 3.3).

---

[3]Sectors of activity are by the Global Industry Classification Standard.

[4]Tobin's Q is the preferred indicator of performance in corporate governance studies (La-Porta *et al.* 2002).

[5]Several papers (Peterson and Peterson, 1996; Chun and Pruitt, 1994; Perfect and Wiles, 1994) indicate that this proxy is empirically close to the well-known proxy of Lindenberg and Ross (1981). For international stocks, the information to calculate the Lindenberg and Ross proxy is very limited.

[6]The discussion about the link between executive compensation and performance is very extensive and, in some cases, contradictory (Himmelberg *et al.*, 1999; Palia, 2001; Hillegeist and Peñalva, 2004).

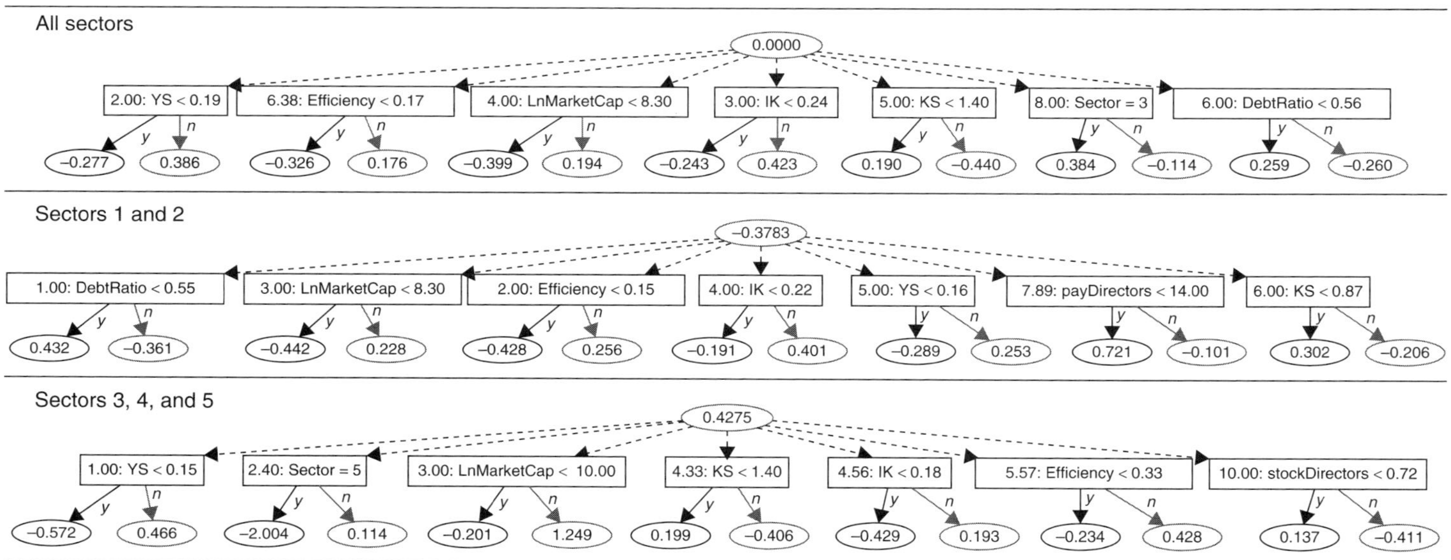

FIGURE 3.2 S&P500: representative ADTs with all variables by sectors. This figure includes representative ADTs when all variables are considered (top panel), sectors 1 and 2 (middle panel), and sectors 3, 4, and 5 (bottom panel). First number in each rectangle is the average iteration.

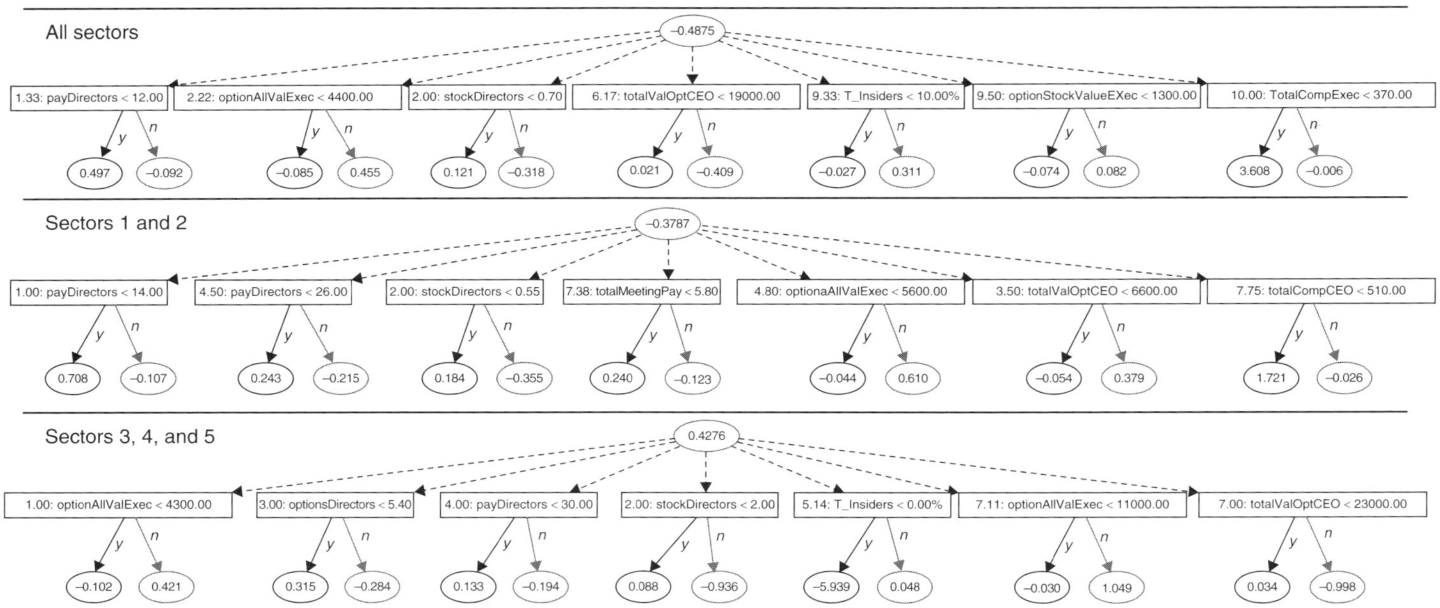

FIGURE 3.3 S&P500: representative ADTs with only corporate governance variables by sectors. This figure includes representative ADTs when all variables are considered (top panel), sectors 1 and 2 (middle panel), and sectors 3, 4, and 5 (bottom panel). First number in each rectangle is the average iteration.

3.3.1.1 Interpreting the S&P500 Representative ADTs with All Variables. The representative ADT for all variables has selected mostly accounting ratios. If the efficiency ratio (operating expenses/sales) (6.38 Efficiency) is below 0.17 in the top panel of Fig. 3.2, performance deteriorates. This counterintuitive result is explained because sectors 1 (energy and materials) and 2 (industrials and consumer discretionary)[7] are the sectors with the largest presence (52.2%) among the S&P500 companies, and a large proportion of these companies (84.5%) with an efficiency ratio below 0.17 have a low Tobin's Q or show poor performance. The representative ADT with all variables for these sectors (middle panel of Fig. 3.2) has an efficiency ratio (2. Efficiency) similar to that of the top panel of Fig. 3.2, while the representative ADT of sectors 3, 4, and 5 (bottom panel of Fig. 3.2) has an efficiency ratio (5.57. Efficiency) with a threshold of 0.33, which is a much higher value than observed in the previous two graphs. Considering that companies of sectors 1 and 2 are mostly of an industrial type or capital intensive, they may have higher fixed costs than the rest of the industries. So, if the operating expenses to sales ratio is too low, it may indicate that the operating expenses are not enough to cover an efficient level of operation, and performance deteriorates.

Different from the initial assumptions, there is no indication that in S&P500 companies (see top panel of Fig. 3.2), a large operating income to sales ratio (2. YS) or capital expenditures to long-term assets ratio (3. IK) may lead to corporate governance problems; even more, an IK above the mean improves results. However, the representative ADT establishes a limit to the long-term assets to sales ratio (5. KS). Companies that are in the top quartile according to the long-term assets to sales ratio show a lower performance than the rest of the companies.

The limitation of the ADTs of Fig. 3.2 is that the accounting variables dominate, even when we separate our sample between sectors (middle and bottom panels of Fig. 3.2). Companies of sectors 1 and 2 show only annual cash pay to directors (7.89. payDirectors) and companies of sectors 3, 4, and 5 show only stock shares granted to directors (10. stockDirectors) as relevant corporate governance variables.

In order to capture the effect of corporate governance variables, in the next section, we present a representative ADT that includes only these variables.

3.3.1.2 Interpreting the S&P500 Representative ADTs with Only Corporate Governance Variables. The representative ADT for all companies with only the corporate governance variables (top panel of Fig. 3.3) captures most of the variables (payDirectors, optionAllValExec, stockDirectors, and TotalValOptCEO) or rules associated with high corporate performance in all

[7] Energy includes energy equipment and services. Materials include chemical industries, construction materials, containers and packaging, metals and mining, and paper and forest products. Industrials include capital goods, commercial services and supplies, and transportation. Consumer discretionary includes automobiles and components; consumer durables and apparel; hotels, restaurants, and leisure; media; and retailing.

companies. This ADT suggests that the compensation policy should have a larger variable component granting more options to top officers (companies in the top quartile) (2.22. OptionAllValExec), with very broad limits for the value of the options to CEOs (companies in the fourth quartile) (6.17. totalValOptCEO) and a small cash payment to directors (companies in the first quartile) (1.33. payDirectors). Additionally, this ADT recommends that insider ownership should at least be 10% (9.33. T_Insiders). When we separate the representative ADTs by sectors of economic activity, the compensation policy varies. For sectors 1 and 2, the representative ADT (middle panel of Fig. 3.3) suggests a policy that grants very limited cash compensations to CEOs (companies in the first quartile) (7.75. totalCompCEO), and the rest of the compensation should largely be based on options (3.5. totalValOptCEO). For the top officers, the value of the options granted should also be high (companies in the fourth quartile) (4.8. OptionAllValExec). This ADT suggests that the compensation of directors should have a larger component of stocks (companies in the third quartile) (2. stockDirectors) and a smaller annual cash payment (less than the median) (1. and 4.5. payDirectors).

In the case of companies of sectors 3, 4, and 5, the representative ADT (bottom panel of Fig. 3.3) indicates that the compensation policy should have a larger amount of stocks (2. stockDirectors), cash payment to directors (4.4. payDirectors), and more options for top executives including the CEO (companies in the fourth quartile) than in the sectors 1 and 2 (1. OptionAllValExec). Additionally, the representative ADT shows that insiders ownership (5.14. T_Insiders) improves performance.

3.3.1.3 Designing the Board Balanced Scorecard. We include the variables that the representative ADTs selected for all companies (top panels of Figs. 3.2 and 3.3) in the board strategy map and in the board BSC suggested by Kaplan and Nagel (2004).

The board strategy map (Fig. 3.4) shows the interrelationship between the objectives of each perspective. An important element of the board strategy map and the board BSC is the perspective of "stakeholder" instead of "consumer" as was proposed in the original BSC. The reason to include the "stakeholder" perspective is that the stakeholders, such as shareholders and financial analysts, are the consumers or clients of the board of directors.

We have expanded the board strategy map proposed by Kaplan and Nagel (2004) to incorporate new objectives that were consistent with the main variables selected by the representative ADT. The new objectives that emerged are "balanced capital structure" in the financial perspective, "independent ownership structure" in the internal perspective, and "ensure corporate governance best practices" in the stakeholder perspective. The board BSC (Fig. 3.5) incorporates the new indicators and its targets according to the representative ADTs presented in Figs. 3.2 and 3.3. The indicators are the most important variables selected by the representative ADTs, and their targets are the threshold levels calculated for each variable.

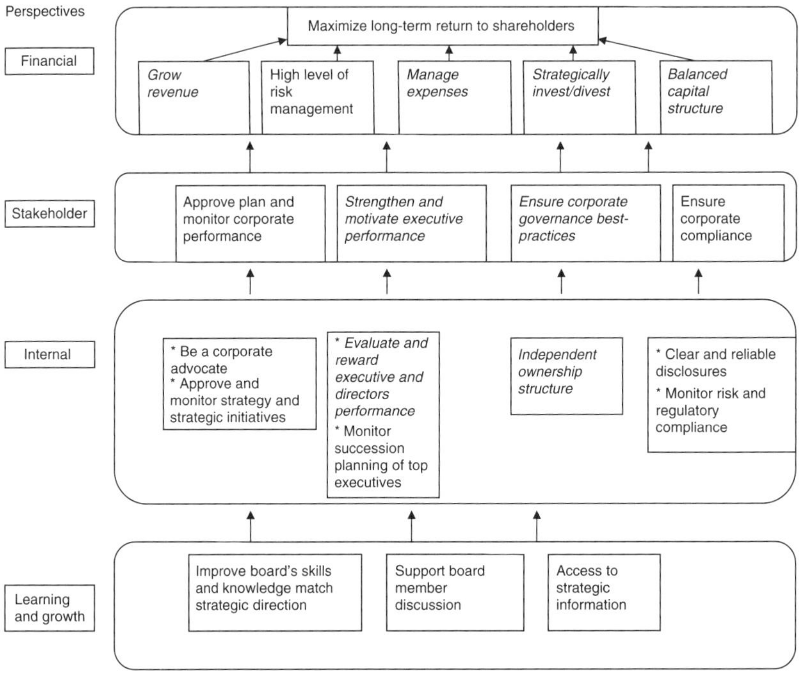

FIGURE 3.4 S&P500: representative board strategy map. This figure shows the causal relationship among corporate variables. Italics are the objectives selected or modified by representative ADTs. *Source:* Adapted from Kaplan and Nagel (2004) and Creamer and Freund (2010b).

3.4 Earnings Prediction and Algorithmic Trading

3.4.1 EARNINGS PREDICTION

Many of the recent bankruptcy scandals in publicly held US companies , such as Enron and WorldCom, are inextricably linked to a conflict of interest between shareholders (principals) and managers (agents). This conflict of interest is called the *principal–agent problem* in finance literature. The principal–agent problem stems from the tension between the interests of the investors in increasing the value of the company and the personal interests of the managers.

The principal–agent conflict has also led to the so-called "earnings game." CEOs' compensation depends on their stock options. So, top managers concentrate on the management of earnings and surprises. The Wall Street companies want to keep selling stocks. Thus, analysts try to maintain positive reviews of the companies.[8] Once a prediction is published, CEOs do whatever is necessary to

[8]In the last years, this situation is changing because of the new separation between research and investment banking.

Board's Strategic Objectives		Indicators	Target(s)	Scores		Owners
High-Level Objectives	Specific Objectives			Yes	No	
Financial:						
Maximize long-term total return shareholders	Grow revenues	Operating income/sales (YS)	<0.19	–0.277	0.386	Executive management
	Manage expenses	Operating expenses/sales (Efficiency ratio)	<0.17	–0.326	0.176	
	Strategically invest/divest	Long-term assets/sales (KS)	<1.4	0.19	–0.44	
		Capital expenditures/long-term assets (IK)	<0.24	–0.243	0.423	
	Balanced capital structure	Debt ratio	<0.56	0.259	–0.26	
Internal:						
Evaluate and reward directors' performance	Reduce fixed payment	Annual cash pay to directors (payDirectors)	<$12 K	0.497	–0.092	Compensation committee
	Limit options payment to directors	Number stocks granted to directors (stocksDirectors)	<700	0.121	–0.318	
		Total value options CEO's (totalValOptCEO)	<$19 M	0.021	–0.409	
Evaluate and reward executive's performance	Increase options payments to top officers	Value of all options to officers (optionAllValExec)	<$4.4 M	–0.085	0.455	
		Value stock options to officers (OptionStockValueExec)	<$1.3 M	–0.074	0.082	
		Total compensation officers (TotalCompExec)	<$370 K	3.608	–0.006	
Independent ownership struct.	Limit insiders' ownership	% insiders' ownership (T_Insiders)	<10%	–0.027	0.311	Governance committee

FIGURE 3.5 S&P500: representative Board Scorecard. The board scorecard assigns indicators to the objectives selected in the Board strategy map. The indicators of the financial perspective are from the representative ADT that includes all variables (Figure 3.2) and the indicators of the internal perspective are from the representative ADT that includes only the corporate governance variables (Figure 3.3). The targets come from the rectangle and the scores from the ovals of the representative ADTs. K is thousands and M is millions. *Source:* Adapted from Kaplan and Nagel (2004).

reach that prediction or boost the results above the analysts' prediction. CEOs play this game, even though a company may lose value in the long term, because it boosts the potential value of their stock options.

The Institutional Brokers' Estimate System (IBES) has collected the analysts' earnings forecast and their revisions since the early 1970s. Several other companies such as Zacks Investment Research and Thomson Financial[9] have also joined this effort and have extended the service to include other accounting indicators such as revenue announcements. These databases provide an estimation of markets expectations or market "consensus" about the future earnings announcement, which is a simple average of the market analysts' predictions. Investors very closely follow these consensus indicators to forecast and take their investment decisions. Another important use of this information is screening and ranking the analysts' according to their previous performance.

From the machine learning perspective, the existence of these financial databases offers a great opportunity to evaluate the capacity of several learning algorithms to search for new finance time-series patterns that may improve the current forecasts. From the finance industry perspective, small investors or large institutional investors in the international finance market do not have the capacity to conduct detailed investment research in every market that they invest. Therefore, machine learning methods can help them to process a large amount of existent data to forecast earnings surprises and cumulative abnormal return. Earnings surprise is the difference between actual quarterly earnings and consensus, while cumulative abnormal return is the return of a specific asset less the average return of all assets in its risk-level portfolio for each trading date. Dhar and Chou (2001) have already compared the predictive accuracy of tree-induction algorithms, neural networks, naive Bayesian learning, and genetic algorithms to classify the earnings surprise before announcement.

Creamer and Stolfo (2009) propose a link mining algorithm, CorpInterlock, that selects the largest strongly connected component of a social network and ranks its vertices using several indicators of distance and centrality. These indicators are merged with other relevant indicators in order to forecast new variables using a boosting algorithm. Creamer and Stolfo apply this link mining algorithm to integrate accounting variables of US companies with statistics of social networks of directors only (basic corporate interlock) and social networks of directors and analysts (extended corporate interlock) to forecast earnings surprises and cumulative abnormal returns. Link mining[10] is a set of techniques that uses different types of networks and their indicators to forecast or to model a linked domain.

CorpInterlock is implemented with Logitboost because it is a very flexible method and can analyze a large and diverse group of quantitative and qualitative variables. The boosting approach also generates a score with each prediction, which can be associated with the strength of the prediction. CorpInterlock implemented with Logitboost improves the prediction of earnings surprise in relation to the implementation of CorpInterlock with logistic regression.

[9]Thomson Financial acquired First Call, IBES, and StarMine.

[10]For a recent survey, see Getoor and Diehl (2005).

Creamer and Stolfo (2009) show that the basic and extended corporate interlocks have the properties of a "small-world" network. The "small-world" model was formalized by Watts (1999), Watts and Strogatz (1998), and Newman *et al.* (2001, 2002) based on the pioneering work of Milgram (1967), who shows how apparently distant people are connected by a very short chain of acquaintances.

The statistics of an extended corporate interlock, directors, and financial analysts, bring additional information to predict cumulative abnormal return. The relationship between analysts and directors improves cumulative abnormal return predictions during "bull" markets or during periods characterized by a great number of initial public offerings, mergers, and acquisitions. This role is less important in a "bear" market, especially after the Sarbanes–Oxley Act.

CorpInterlock is a flexible mechanism for increasing the explanatory power of social networks with the forecasting capability of machine learning algorithms, such as boosting. The capacity to improve the forecast of earnings surprises and abnormal return using a mixture of well-known economic indicators with social network variables also enriches the debate between the modern finance theory and behavioral finance to show how behavioral patterns can be recognized with a rigorous method of analysis and forecast.

3.4.2 ALGORITHMIC TRADING

The transformation of the major stock exchanges into electronic financial markets has encouraged the development of automated trading systems in order to process large amounts of information and make instantaneous investment decisions.

Automated trading systems have a long tradition on classical artificial intelligence approaches such as expert systems, fuzzy logic, neural networks, and genetic algorithms. Trippi and Turban (1990, 1993), Trippi and Lee (2000), Deboeck (1994), and Chorafas (1994) have reviewed these early systems. Goonatilake and Treleaven (1995) survey an application of the above methods to automated trading and several other business problems such as credit risk, direct marketing, fraud detection, and price forecasting.

Automated trading systems include a backtest or simulation module. In this respect, agent-based models could be useful to explore new ideas without risking any money.[11] The Santa Fe stock market model (Arthur *et al.*, 1997; LeBarone *et al.*, 1998; LeBaron, 2001) has inspired many other agent-based financial market models such as Ehrentreich (2002)'s, which is based on the Grossman and Stiglitz (1980) model. In the Santa Fe stock market, agents can classify and explore several forecasting rules that are built using genetic algorithms. Many of the models built in this perspective test the performance of agents or algorithms that have unique characteristics. For example, Lettau (1997) has built an agent-based financial market using simple agent benchmarks based on genetic algorithms, Gode and Sunder (1993) have developed a double auction market using random or zero intelligence traders, Arifovic (1996) has built a model

[11] For a survey of papers in the area of agent-based finance, see Lebaron (2000).

of the foreign exchange market using genetic algorithms, Routledge (2001) has extended the basic framework of Grossman and Stiglitz (1980) with agents that can learn using genetic algorithms, and Chan *et al.* (1999) and Chan (2001) have used the artificial market framework to explore the behavior of different trading approaches and their microstructure impact. The application of the Ising (1925) model to financial markets has led to several versions of the spin model where a sell position is a spin-up and a buy position is a spin-down. Prices are determined by the aggregation of traders' positions. Bornholdt (2001) modified this model introducing an antiferromagnetic coupling between the global magnetization and each spin, as well as a ferromagnetic coupling between the local neighborhood and each spin.

In recent years, financial data providers such as Reuters and Bloomberg are offering machine readable news that can be used by trading systems. In this line of research, Seo *et al.* (2004) and Decker *et al.* (1996) describe a multiagent portfolio management system that automatically classifies financial news. Thomas (2003) combines news classification with technical analysis indicators in order to generate new trading rules. Lavrenko *et al.* (2000) describe a system that recommends news stories that can affect market behavior. This is a special case of the activity monitoring task as suggested by Fawcett and Provost (1999). In a manner similar to fraud detection systems, activity monitoring generates alarms when an unusual event happens. These signals try to recognize when the trend of the market is positive and, therefore, can generate new trading signals. Wuthrich *et al.* (1998) and Cho *et al.* (1999) weight keywords based on their occurrences to predict the direction of major stock indices. Text classification and retrieval applied to finance is still an area underexplored in the literature. However, several investment banks and hedge funds are developing systems to automatically incorporate the impact of daily news into their trading systems.

Another important line of research is the use of learning algorithms to generate trading rules using technical analysis indicators. Technical analysis or technical trading strategies try to exploit statistically measurable short-term market opportunities, such as trend spotting and momentum, in individual industrial sectors (e.g., financial, pharmaceutical, etc.). In the 1960s and 1970s, researchers studied trading rules based on technical indicators and did not find them profitable (Alexander, 1961; Fama and Blume, 1970). These findings led Fama (1970) to dismiss technical analysis as a profitable technique and support the efficient market hypothesis. Part of the problem of the studies during the 1960s was the *ad hoc* specifications of the trading rules that led to spurious patterns in the data. Specification of rules retroactively may have led to biased studies. Allen and Karjalainen (1999) found profitable trading rules using genetic algorithms for the S&P500 with daily prices from 1928 to 1995. However, these rules were not consistently better than a buy-and-hold strategy in the out-of-sample test periods.

At present, many academics, banks, and hedge funds are exploring the application of machine learning methods to find patterns in financial time series. Lo *et al.* (2000), who used nonparametric kernel regression for technical pattern recognition of a large number of stocks for the period 1962–1996, found that technical indicators provide incremental information for investors comparing the unconditional empirical distribution of daily stock returns to the conditional distribution on specific technical indicators such as head and shoulders. Moody and Saffell (2001) found that a trading system using direct reinforcement learning outperforms a Q-trader for the asset allocation problem between the S&P500 and T-bill. Dempster and Romahi (2002) compared four methods for foreign exchange trading (reinforcement learning, genetic algorithms, Markov chain linear programming, and simple heuristic) and concluded that a combination of technical indicators leads to better performance than using only individual indicators. Dempster and Leemans (2006) reached a similar conclusion using adaptive reinforcement learning. Bates *et al.* (2003) used Watkin's Q-learning algorithm to maximize profits; these authors compared order flow and order book data and compared with technical trading rules. They concluded that using order flow and order book data was usually superior to trading on technical signal alone. LeBaron (1998) applied bootstrapping to capture arbitrage opportunities in the foreign exchange market and then used a neural network where its network architecture was determined through an evolutionary process. Finally, Towers and Burgess (2000) used principal components to capture arbitrage opportunities.

Creamer and Freund (2007, 2010a) follow the tradition of the papers in this section that use machine learning algorithms to find profitable trading strategies and also build completely automated trading systems. The authors use very well-known technical indicators such as moving averages or Bollinger bands. Therefore, the capacity to anticipate unexpected market movements is reduced because many other traders are expected to be trying to profit from the same indicators. However, the authors reduce this effect because the algorithms try to discover new trading rules using Logitboost instead of following the trading rules suggested by each indicator. The predictors may also improve if the technical indicators are transformed into more accurate ratios or if more informative indicators are selected, such as signals related to current news.

Creamer and Freund (2007) propose the constant rebalanced portfolio-technical analysis trading algorithm (CRP-TA) that combines intraday trading based on constant rebalanced portfolio (CRP) with daily price forecast based on technical analysis indicators. The algorithm was tested in the context of the Penn–Lehman Automated Trading Project (PLAT) competition (Kearns and Ortiz, 2003) and is based on three main ideas. The first idea is to use a combination of technical indicators to predict the daily trend of the stock. The combination is optimized using a boosting algorithm. The second idea is to use the CRPs (Algoet and Cover, 1988) within the day in order to take advantage of market volatility without increasing risk. The third idea is to use limit orders rather than market orders to minimize transaction costs. The algorithm was profitable during the PLAT competition, and after the competition, the authors enhanced it by including a market maker component. They show that the constantly rebalanced portfolio can improve if a classifier can anticipate the direction of the market: up, down, or no change. Additionally, transaction costs play a central role to raise performance. Instead of an automatic rebalance of the portfolio, the results of the PLAT competition indicate that if the CRP strategy is implemented only with limit orders, its results improve because of the rebates.

Creamer and Freund (2010a) propose a multistock automated trading system. The system is designed to trade stocks, and relies on a layered structure consisting of ADT, which is implemented with Logitboost, as the machine learning algorithm; an on-line learning utility; and a risk management overlay.[12] The system generates its own trading rules and weighs the suggestion of the different ADTs or experts to propose a trading position. Finally, the risk management layer can validate the trading signal when it exceeds a specified nonzero threshold and limit the use of a trading strategy when it is not profitable.

The expert weighting algorithm is tested with data of 100 randomly selected companies of the S&P500 index during the period 2003–2005. This algorithm generates excess returns during the test period. Every component of the trading algorithm is important to obtain positive abnormal returns, and brings some functionality that is complemented by the rest of the layers. We observe that even an efficient learning algorithm, such as boosting, still requires powerful control mechanisms in order to reduce unnecessary and unprofitable trades that increase transaction costs. Hence, the contribution of new predictive algorithms by the machine learning literature to finance still needs to be incorporated under a formal framework of risk management.

As part of the optimization of the trading system, Creamer and Freund (2010a) propose a method to simultaneously calculate the same features using different parameters, leaving the final feature selection to boosting. Many trader systems become very inefficient because they try all the parameters or are forced to select in advance parameters that are not adequate after a trading period. The above experiments show that the boosting approach is able to improve the predictive capacity when indicators are combined and aggregated as a single predictor. Even more, the combination of indicators of different stocks are demonstrated to be adequate in order to reduce the use of computational resources and still maintain an adequate predictive capacity.

3.5 Final Comments and Conclusions

This chapter has reviewed how several learning algorithms—mainly Adaboost, Logitboost, and link mining—that can be adapted to semiautomate two main corporate finance functions: strategic planning and trading. Both these activities require a significant amount of expensive corporate resources (highly trained financial analysts, traders, and computer equipment) that could be reduced if at least certain stages of the planning and trading processes are automated using machine learning algorithms.

This chapter has shown that learning algorithms can be applied to forecasting and automated trading in the following areas: (i) developing a link mining

[12]See Dempster and Leemans (2006) for a previous trading system using machine learning algorithms and a layered structure.

algorithm to integrate accounting and social network variables, (ii) identifying new predictive indicators using social networks of directors and analysts, (iii) exploring a trading strategy in a controlled competition, and (iv) developing a multistock automated trading system. Also, learning algorithms can be applied to strategic planning to semiautomate the generation of BSCs.

From the trading point of view, the development of electronic financial markets requires the development of efficient algorithms that can process significant amounts of diverse information and make extremely fast investment decisions. Economic models with leading indicators may predict prices. However, these indicators may not be profitable if they are not included in an efficient algorithm that is able to transform several indicators or a mixture of them into instantaneous trading signals.

From the planning point of view, the complexity of large organizations and the significant amount of data imply that those organizations that implement the most efficient methods to manage this information would have a competitive advantage. We revised an algorithm that ranked variables according to their level of importance in the ADTs and generated representative ADTs with the most important variables. Additionally, we showed how representative ADTs can be used as interpretative tools to evaluate the impact of corporate governance factors on performance and efficiency. Representative ADTs were particularly useful to understand the nonlinear relationship between the variables that affected performance and efficiency, as well as the most important indicators of the BSC. Additionally, the thresholds of the representative ADTs established targets or ranges of values of the indicators that managers could follow to improve corporate performance. With this combined tool, managers can concentrate on the most important strategic issues and delegate the calculation of the targets to a semiautomated planning system supported by Adaboost.

3.5.1 LIMITATIONS, RECOMMENDATIONS, AND FUTURE WORK

The finance literature is very suspicious of the so-called "nonparametric" methods[13] because of the risk of overfitting and the lack of parameters' estimation and interpretability of results. In relation to the first objection, overfitting in the case of boosting can be prevented using a validation set to select a number of iterations, and the value of other parameters that are associated with a reduction of the test error without overfitting. In relation to the second objection, lack of parameter estimation, and interpretability, boosting can be used as an interpretative method instead of a "black box" that simply forecasts without a clear understanding of the underlying rules. The use of boosting as an interpretative tool is possible because of the generation of a representative ADT where main variables are selected together with an ordered relationship.

Questions about algorithmic modeling are reasonable because of previous naive or straightforward applications of learning methods to the financial markets.

[13]This category includes numerical and machine learning methods that are data driven and are not based on formal statistical models.

Our experience in adapting boosting to finance problems is that a simple and straightforward application of boosting to finance does not bring a significant improvement in forecasting. There are other well-known methods used for finance problems, such as logistic regression, that have a similar performance to boosting. However, boosting can work with a mixture of quantitative and qualitative indicators, as well as with nonlinear time series. Furthermore, boosting can be used to understand the nonlinear relationship between the variables as mentioned above and can automatically select the best features.

The calibration of machine learning methods requires a significant amount of time. Creamer and Freund (2010b) proposed a method based on boosting that leads to an automatic selection of features and parameters. The application of this mechanism improved results and significantly reduced the time of adaptation of boosting to new problems. Boosting's predictions also depended of the quality and value of the indicators used. Hence, a direct application of boosting without the adequate calibration of the model or search for the best indicators may generate a very poor prediction. On the basis of this, Creamer and Stolfo (2009) also included new indicators to predict earnings surprises, such as social network statistics.

Additionally, boosting or other learning algorithms used to forecast time series may have predictive ability for only a certain period of time. However, the randomness and continuous change of the financial market may cause a trading strategy based on boosting or another predictor to become ineffective. Even though several hedge funds and investment banks are currently using learning algorithms to find trading strategies, they do not rely only on the learning algorithmic component. These funds or banks have strict risk management systems based on their practice and finance theory. This should be a standard requirement for any implementation of trading strategies using learning algorithms.

The automated trading system using boosting reviewed in this chapter could easily be adapted to other domains such as foreign exchange, fixed income, or the international equity market. Future research could be directed to evaluating the specific risk management mechanisms or alternative methods for selecting the most profitable trading strategies. Additionally, the comparison of boosting with other machine learning methods in different domains may provide a new light on the strengths and weaknesses of each method. For instance, the international market is much more volatile and exposed to many more risk factors than the US market. A trading system for the international equity market should be able to deal with these heterogeneous conditions.

A potential extension of this research is the application of boosting for portfolio selection using the Black–Litterman model (Black and Litterman, 1990, 1991). This model includes the subjective expectations of investors in a risk variance optimization model. An alternative line of research is to use the scores of boosting instead of the subjective expectations of the investors. Creamer (2010) has followed this approach combining the optimal predictive capability of boosting with a risk return optimization model.

Finally, this research can also be extended using boosting for the design of the enterprise BSC and by including other perspectives of those reviewed in this study.

Initially, the corporate governance variables did not seem to be very relevant to predicting corporate performance. However, when the results of these variables were interpreted together with the accounting variables using representative ADTs, the effect of corporate governance on performance became evident as the BSC demonstrated. A similar situation may happen with the variables of the other perspectives of the BSC. The recent cases of US bankruptcies have demonstrated that when companies are doing very well, corporate governance variables do not seem to be relevant. However, in moments of financial distress, corporate governance variables play a very important role in improving performance and efficiency. In this respect, another future direction for this research line is the evaluation of the abnormal return of two portfolios with top and bottom tier companies based on the suggestions of the representative ADTs and board BSC. Additionally, the combination of Adaboost and the BSC can be used as a semiautomated strategic planning system that continuously updates itself for board-level decisions of directors or for investment decisions of portfolio managers.

REFERENCES

Acharya VV, John K, Sundaram RK. On the optimality of resetting executive stock options. J Financ Econ 2000;57:65–101.

Alexander S. Price movements in speculative markets: trends or random walks. Ind Manag Rev 1961;2:7–26.

Algoet PH, Cover TM. Asymptotic optimality and asymptotic equipartition properties of log-optimum investment. Ann Probab 1988;16:876–898.

Allen F, Karjalainen R. Using genetic algorithms to find technical trading rules. J Financ Econ 1999;51:245–271.

Altman EI. Financial ratios, discriminant analysis and the prediction of corporate bankruptcy. J Finance 1968;23:589–609.

Altman EI. Evaluation of a company as a going concern. J Accountancy 1974;138:50–57.

Altman EI. Measuring corporate bond mortality and performance. J Finance 1989;54:909–922.

Altman EI, Caouette JB, Narayanan P. Credit-risk measurement and management: the ironic challenge in the next decade. Financ Anal J 1998;54:7–11.

Ampuero M, Goransson J, Scott J. Solving the measurement puzzle. How EVA and the balanced scorecard fit together. Perspect Bus Innov 1998; 45–52.

Ang J, Cole R, Lin JW. Agency costs and ownership structure. J Finance 2000;40:81–106.

Arifovic J. The behavior of the exchange rate in the genetic algorithm and experimental economies. J Polit Econ 1996;104:510–541.

Arthur WB, Holland JH, LeBaron B, Palmer R, Talyer P. Asset pricing under endogenous expectations in an artificial stock market. In: Arthur W., Durlauf S., Lane D., editors. The economy as an evolving complex system II. Reading, MA: Addison-Wesley; 1997. p 15–44.

Barr R, Seiford LM, Thomas F. Forecasting bank failure: a non-parametric frontier estimation approach. Rech Econ Louvain 1994;60:417–429.

Bates R, Dempster M, Romahi Y. Evolutionary reinforcement learning in FX order book and order flow analysis. Proceedings of the IEEE International conference on computational intelligence for financial engineering, Hong Kong, March 20–23, 2003. Hong Kong: IEEE; 2003. p 355–362.

Beaver W. Financial ratios as predictors of failure. J Account Res 1966;4:71–111.

Berle A, Means G. The modern corporation and private property. New York: Harcourt; 1932.

Black F, Litterman R. Asset allocation: combining investor views with market equilibrium. Fixed income research. Goldman Sachs & Co., New York; 1990.

Black F, Litterman R. Global asset allocation with equities, bonds, and currencies. Fixed income research, Goldman Sachs & Co., New York; 1991.

Bornholdt S. Expectation bubbles in a spin model of markets: intermittency from frustration across scales. Int J Mod Phys C 2001;12:667–674.

Breiman L. Statistical modeling: the two cultures. Stat Sci 2001;16:199–231.

Breiman L, Friedman JH, Olshen R, Stone C. Classification and regression trees. Belmont: Wadsworth and Brooks; 1984.

Brenner M, Sundaram RK, Yermack D. Altering the terms of executive stock options. J Financ Econ 2000;57:103–128.

Byrne JA. The best and worst boards. Bus Week 1996; 82–98.

Chan N, LeBaron B, Lo A, Poggio T. Agent-based models of financial markets: a comparison with experimental markets. Technical Report 124, MIT Artificial Markets Project, Cambridge, MA; 1999.

Chan T. Artificial markets and intelligent agents. PhD thesis, Massachusetts Institute of Technology, Cambridge, MA; 2001.

Chance DM, Kumar R, Todd RB. The 'repricing' of executive stock options. J Financ Econ 2000;57:129–154.

Chen K, Lee J. Accounting measures of business performance and Tobin's Q theory. J Account Audit Finance 1995;10:587–609.

Cho V, Wuthrich B, Zhang J. Text processing for classification. J Comput Intell Finance 1999;7:6–22.

Chorafas DN. Chaos theory in the financial markets. Chicago: Probus publishing; 1994.

Chung K, Pruitt SW. A simple approximation to Tobin's Q. Financ Manage 1994;23:70–74.

Clarke DG, McDonald JB. Generalized bankruptcy models applied to predicting consumer credit behavior. J Econ Bus 1992;44:47–62.

Clinton D, Webber S, Hassell J. Implementing the Balanced Scorecard using the analytic hierarchic process. Manag Account Q 2002;3:1–11.

Collins M, Schapire RE, Singer Y. Logistic regression, adaboost and Bregman distances. Mach Learn 2004;48:253–285.

Collins R, Green RD. Statistical methods for bankruptcy forecasting. J Econ Bus 1982;34:349–354.

Creamer G. Using link mining for investment decisions: extensions of the Black Litterman model. Paper presented at 2nd. Workshop on Information in Networks, NYU, New York; 2010.

Creamer G, Freund Y. A boosting approach for automated trading. J Trading 2007;2:84–95.

Creamer G, Freund Y. Automated trading with boosting and expert weighting. Quant Finance 2010a;10:401–420.

Creamer G, Freund Y. Learning a board balanced scorecard to improve corporate performance. Decis Support Syst 2010b;49:365–385.

Creamer G, Stolfo S. A link mining algorithm for earnings forecast and trading. Data Min Knowl Discov 2009;18:419–445.

Crystal G. In search of excess: the overcompensation of American executives. New York: W. W. Norton Company; 1991.

Deboeck GJ, editor.. Trading on the edge: neural, genetic, and fuzzy systems for chaotic financial markets. New York: John Wiley & Sons, Inc.; 1994.

Decker K, Sycara K, Zeng D. Designing a multi-agent portfolio management system. Proceedings of the AAAI workshop on internet information systems. AAI Press, Menlo Park, CA; 1996.

Dempster M, Leemans V. An automated FX trading system using adaptive reinforcement learning. Expert Systems with Applications (Special issue on financial engineering) 2006;30:534–552.

Dempster M, Romahi Y. Intraday FX trading: an evolutionary reinforcement learning approach. Proceedings of the Third International conference on intelligent data engineering and automated learning IDEAL 02, Manchester, UK, August 12–14, 2002, Volume 2412 of Lecture notes in computer science. Springer, London; 2002. p 347–358.

Dhar V, Chou D. A comparison of nonlinear methods for predicting earnings surprises and returns. IEEE Trans Neural Network 2001;12:907–921.

Ehrentreich N. The Santa Fe artificial stock market re-examined – suggested corrections. EconWPA, number: 0209001, Sep. 2002.

Fama E. Efficient capital markets: a review of theory and empirical work. J Finance 1970;25:383–417.

Fama E, Blume M. Filter rules and stock market trading. security prices: a supplement. J Bus 1970;39:226–241.

Fawcett T, Provost F. Activity monitoring: noticing interesting changes in behavior. Proceedings of the Fifth ACM SIGKDD International conference on knowledge discovery and data mining (KDD-99), San Diego, CA, USA, August 15–18, 1999. New York: ACM; 1999. p 53–62.

Freund Y, Mason L. The alternating decision tree learning algorithm. Machine learning: Proceedings of the Sixteenth International conference. San Francisco: Morgan Kaufmann Publishers Inc.; 1999. p 124–133.

Freund Y, Schapire RE. A decision-theoretic generalization of on-line learning and an application to boosting. J Comput Syst Sci 1997;55:119–139.

Friedman J, Hastie T, Tibshirani R. Additive logistic regression: a statistical view of boosting. Ann Stat 2000;38:337–374.

Fuerst O, Kang S. Corporate governance, expected operating performance and pricing. Corp Ownership Control 2004;1:13–30.

Getoor L, Diehl CP. Link mining: a survey. SIGKDD Explor 2005;7:3–12.

Gode DK, Sunder S. Allocative efficiency of markets with zero intelligence traders: market as a partial substitute for individual rationality. J Polit Econ 1993;101:119–137.

Gompers PA, Ishii JL, Metrick A. Corporate governance and equity prices. Q J Econ 2003;118:107–155.

Goonatilake S, Treleaven P, editors. Intelligence systems for finance and business. New York: John Wiley & Sons, Inc.; 1995.

Goudie AW, Meeks G. The exchange rate and company failure in a macro-micro model of the UK Company Sector. Econ J 1991;101:444–457.

Grossman S, Stiglitz J. On the impossibility of informationally efficient markets. Am Econ Rev 1980;70:393–408.

Hillegeist SA, Peñalva F. Stock option incentives and firm performance. IESE Research Papers D/535, IESE Business School; 2004. Available at http:// ideas.repec.org/p/ebg/iesewp/d-0535.html.

Himmelberg C, Hubbard G, Palia D. Understanding the determinants of managerial ownership and the link between ownership and performance. J Financ Econ 1999;53:353–384.

Hing-Ling AL. A five-state financial distress prediction model. J Account Res 1987;25:127–138.

Hudson J. Company bankruptcies and births matter. Appl Econ 1997;29:647–654.

Ising E. Beitrag zur theorie des ferromagnetismus. Z Phys 1925;31:253–258.

Jensen M. The modern industrial revolution, exit, and the failure of internal control systems. J Finance 1993;48:831–880.

Jensen M, Meckling WH. Theory of the firm: managerial behavior, agency costs and ownership structure. J Financ Econ 1976;3:305–360.

Jensen M, Murphy KJ. Performance pay and top management incentives. J Polit Econ 1990a;98:225–265.

Jensen M, Murphy KJ. CEO incentives: it's not how much you pay, but how. Harv Bus Rev 1990b;68:138–153.

Jensen M, Murphy KJ. Remuneration: where we've been, how we got to here, what are the problems,and how to fix them. Finance Working Paper 44/2004, European Corporate Governance Institute, Brussels, Belgium; 2004.

Kaplan RS, Nagel ME. Improving corporate governance with the balanced scorecard. Directors Monthly 2004; 16–20.

Kaplan RS, Norton DP. The balanced scorecard: measures that drive performance. Harv Bus Rev 1992;70:72–79.

Kaplan RS, Norton DP. Putting the balanced scorecard to work. Harv Bus Rev 1993;71:134–147.

Kaplan RS, Norton DP. Linking the balanced scorecard to strategy. Calif Manage Rev 1996a;49:53–79.

Kaplan RS, Norton DP, editors. The balanced scorecard. Boston: Harvard Business School Press; 1996b.

Kaplan RS, Norton DP. Using the balanced scorecard as a strategic management system. Harv Bus Rev 1996c;74:75–85.

Kearns M, Ortiz L. The Penn-Lehman automated trading project. IEEE Intell Syst 2003;18:22–31.

La-Porta R, de Silanes FL, Shleifer A, Vishny R. Investor protection and corporate valuation. J Finance 2002;57:1147–1170.

Lane W, Looney SW, Wansley JW. An application of the Cox proportional hazards model to bank failure. J Bank Finance 1986;10:511–531.

Lavrenko V, Schmill M, Lawrie D, Oglivie P, Jensen D, Allan J. Language models for financial news recommendation. Proceedings of the Ninth International conference on information and knowledge management, McLean, VA, November 6–11, 2000. New York: ACM; 2000. p 389–396.

LeBaron B. An evolutionary bootstrap method for selecting dynamic trading strategies. In: Refenes A-PN, Burgess A and Moody J, editors. Decision technologies for computational finance. Proceedings of the Fifth International conference computational finance. New York: Springer-Verlag; 1998. p 141–160.

LeBaron B. Agent based computational finance: suggested readings and early research. J Econ Dynam Contr 2000;24:679–702.

LeBaron B. Empirical regularities from interacting long and short memory investors in an agent-based financial market. IEEE Trans Evol Comput 2001;5:442–455.

LeBaron B, Arthur WB, Palmer R. The time series properties of an artificial stock market. J Econ Dynam Contr 1998;21:1487–1516.

Lettau M. Explaining the facts with adaptive agents: the case of mutual funds flows. J Econ Dynam Contr 1997;21:1117–1148.

Lindenberg E, Ross SA. Tobin's Q ratio and industrial organization. J Bus 1981;54:1–32.

Lo A, Mamaysky H, Wang J. Foundations of technical analysis: computational algorithms, statistical inference, and empirical implementation. J Finance 2000;4:1705–1765.

McConnell J, Servaes H. Additional evidence on equity ownership and corporate value. J Financ Econ 1990;27:595–612.

Mikkelson WH, Ruback R. An empirical analysis of the interim equity investment process. J Financ Econ 1985;14:523–553.

Milgram S. The small world problem. Psychol Today 1967;2:60–7.

Moody J, Saffell M. Learning to trade via direct reinforcement. IEEE Trans Neural Network 2001;12:875–889.

Morck R, Shleifer A, Vishny R. Management ownership and corporate performance: an empirical analysis. J Financ Econ 1988;20:293–316.

Moyer CR. Forecasting financial failure: a re-examination. Financ Manag 1977;6:11–16.

Müller KR, Smola AJ, Rätsch G, Schölkopf B, Kohlmorgen J, Vapnik V. Predicting time series with support vector machines. Proceedings of ICANN, Volume 1327. Springer, Berlin/Heidelberg; 1997. p 909–1004.

Newman M, Strogatz S, Watts D. Random graphs with arbitrary degree distributions and their applications. Phys Rev E 2001; 64.

Newman MEJ, Watts DJ, Strogatz SH. Random graph models of social networks. Proc Natl Acad Sci USA 2002;99:2566–2572.

Ohlson J. Financial ratios and the probabilistic prediction of bankruptcy. J Account Res 1980;18:1.

Palia D. The endogeneity of managerial compensation in firm valuation: a solution. Rev Financ Stud 2001;14:735–764.

Perfect SB, Wiles KW. Alternative construction of Tobin's Q: an empirical comparison. J Empir Financ 1994;1:313–341.

Peterson P, Peterson D. Company performance and measures of value added. Charlottesville, VA: The Research Foundation of the Institute of Chartered Financial Analysts; 1996.

Pinches G, Mingo K. A multivariate analysis of industrial bond ratings. J Finance 1973;28:1.

Queen M, Roll R. Firm mortality: using market indicators to predict survival. Financ Anal J 1987;43:9–26.

Rose PS, Giroux GA. Predicting corporate bankruptcy: an analytical and empirical evaluation. Rev Bus Econ Res 1984;19:1–12.

Routledge BR. Genetic algorithm learning to choose and use information. Macroecon Dyn 2001;5:303–325.

Ryan HJ, Wiggins RI. Who is in whose pocket? director compensation, board independence, and barriers to effective monitoring. J Financ Econ 2004;73:497–524.

Schapire RE. The boosting approach to machine learning: an overview. In MSRI Workshop on Nonlinear Estimation and Classification; 2002.

Seo YW, Giampapa J, Sycara K. Financial news analysis for intelligent portfolio management. Technical Report CMU-RI-TR-04-04, Robotics Institute, Carnegie Mellon University.

Shleifer A, Vishny R. A survey of corporate governance. J Finance 1997;2:737–783.

Stenger C. The corporate governance scorecard. Corp Govern Int Rev 2004;12:11–15.

Stulz R. Managerial control of voting rights. J Financ Econ 1988;20:25–59.

Standard & Poor's Governance Services. Standard & poor's corporate governance scores and evaluations; 2004.

Thomas JD. News and Trading Rules. PhD thesis, Carnegie Mellon University; 2003.

Towers N, Burgess AN. Implementing trading strategies for forecasting models. In: Abu-Mostafa YS, LeBaron B, Lo AW, Weigend AS, editors. Computational finance. Proceedings of the Sixth International conference on computational finance, New York, USA, January 6–9, 1999. Cambridge, MA: The MIT Press; 2000. p 313–325.

Trippi R, Lee J, editors. Foundations of investment system using artificial intelligence and web. New York: McGraw-Hill; 2000.

Trippi R, Turban E, editors. Investment management: decision support and expert systems. New York: Van Nostrand Reinhold; 1990.

Trippi R, Turban E. editors. Neural networks in finance and investing. Chicago: Probus publishing; 1993.

Voelpel S, Leibold M, Eckhoff R, Davenport T. The tyranny of the balanced scorecard in the innovation economy. JIntell Cap 2006;7:43–60.

Watts D. Networks, dynamics, and the small-world phenomenon. Am J Sociol 1999;105:493–527.

Watts D, Strogatz S. Collective dynamics of small world networks. Nature 1998;393:440–442.

Weston F. The tender takeover. Mergers Acquis 1979. 74–82.

Wuthrich B, Permunetilleke D, Leung S, Cho V, Zhang J, Lam W. Daily prediction of major stock indices from textual www data. Proceedings of the Fourth International conference on knowledge discovery and data mining, New York, August 27–31, 1998. New York: AAAI Press; 1998. p 364–368.

Youngblood A, Collins T. Addressing balanced scorecard trade-off issues between performance metrics using multi-attribute utility theory. Eng Manag J 2003;15:11–17.

Zavgren C. The prediction of corporate failure: the state of the art. J Account Lit 1983;2:1–37.

CHAPTER FOUR

Impact of Correlation Fluctuations on Securitized Structures

ERIC HILLEBRAND
Department of Economics, Louisiana State University, Baton Rouge, LA

AMBAR N. SENGUPTA
Department of Mathematics, Louisiana State University, Baton Rouge, LA

JUNYUE XU
Department of Economics, Louisiana State University, Baton Rouge, LA

4.1 Introduction

The financial crisis precipitated by the subprime mortgage fiasco has focused attention on the use of Gaussian copula methods in pricing and risk managing CDOs involving subprime mortgages. Gorton (2008) has analyzed the role of structured mortgage backed securities (MBS) vehicles in the subprime crisis.

In this chapter, we study, both theoretically and numerically, the Gaussian default modeling and its sensitivity to changes in default correlation over time. Our method avoids some typical pitfalls of using copulas over extended time

Handbook of Modeling High-Frequency Data in Finance, First Edition.
Edited by Frederi G. Viens, Maria C. Mariani, and Ionuţ Florescu.

periods by using the notion of *vintage* of a portfolio, rather than its age, an important distinction. In brief, we examine, at a fixed time, a sequence of portfolios that have been issued at different initiation times, hence of different *vintages*, in the past. The different vintages across time are connected through a serial correlation parameter, which we hold fixed for this study. An extensive study of vintage correlation is carried out in Hillebrand *et al*. (2010).

One concern about the simple Gaussian copula model of Li (2000), which assumes a default static correlation between different assets in the portfolio, is that the value of default correlation migrates over time (see Servigny and Renault, 2002; Das *et al*. 2006). To address this concern, Andersen and Sidenius (2005), Hull *et al*. (2009), and Berd *et al*. (2007) allow default correlation to vary. The dynamics of default correlation have important implications for risk management. As is shown by Andersen and Sidenius (2005), introducing dynamics into default correlation changes the loss distribution of CDO tranches. It is natural to ask then, how exactly default correlation dynamics affect the distribution of CDO tranche prices. It is of interest to know if the manner in which default correlation changes matters. We explore a model where the default correlation changes more smoothly than the simple regime switching scenario of Andersen and Sidenius (2005). We also study how tranche price distributions are affected when we introduce dynamics into both default correlation and the state variable.

As mentioned before, we consider MBS tranches of many subsequent vintages. Both the state variable and default correlation are assumed to be stochastic across vintages. We examine the impact of the dynamics of both the state variable and default correlation on tranche prices, as measured roughly through the expected value of cash flows. We also allow the smoothness of the change in default correlation to vary and inspect its impact on the tranche price distribution. We find that some of our results depend on the sensitivity of the tranche price to the change in default correlation, which in turn depends on the seniority of the MBS tranche. To study the impact of the change in default correlation, we slice the full investing spectrum of an MBS into a large number of thin tranches, which we refer to as *"high frequency" tranching*. The presence of such thin tranches in subprime MBS portfolios has been noted by Gorton (2008). Through a set of Monte Carlo simulations, we are able to study the impact of the dynamics of default correlation on the prices of such tranches.

This chapter is organized as follows: Section 4.2 describes a typical MBS vehicle and our models. We conduct a set of Monte Carlo simulations in Section 4.3 to examine the prices of a two-tranche MBS. We assume a regime-switching model for the default correlation and study the effects on the distribution of tranche prices. We then impose a more general logistic transition structure on the dynamics of default correlation. This model nests, as one limit point, the constant default correlation model and, as another limit point, the regime-switching default correlation model. In Section 4.4, we study an MBS with high frequency tranching. We numerically estimate the sensitivities of the tranche prices to a change in default correlation in a static model. We explore how dynamic default correlation affects the serial correlation and overall distributions of tranche prices.

4.2 Description of the Products and Models

The function of an MBS vehicle is to allocate capital from investors with a spectrum of risk tolerance to borrowers. Suppose there are investors labeled by interest rates $r_1 < \cdots < r_I$ that they seek, and there are borrowers whose risk levels qualify them for loan rates of $r'_1 < \cdots < r'_B$. An MBS portfolio pools together the funds from the investors and issues mortgage loans to the borrowers from this pool (of course, the same considerations apply to other asset-backed loans). More accurately, the interest rates r_i label *tranches* of the portfolio, which the investors may purchase. The allocation of risk of defaults in the loans to the different investors/tranches is a critically important task in the structuring of such an investment vehicle. An active market place in the securities (investments) would generate market-implied rates r_i, or, more precisely, *tranche prices*, but pricing any derivative product for such tranches would require a good model of the correlated default behavior of the mortgages. Errors in the modeling of such default behavior would show up either as arbitrage opportunities or, more seriously, as market instabilities. Copula models for default correlation have proved to be most useful in practice, despite serious theoretical drawbacks. More theoretically sound models may require a large number of parameters to be estimated, and each such parameter would itself be a source of possible error in risk management.

In this chapter, we consider V portfolios, issued at time instants

$$T_1 < T_2 < \cdots < T_V,$$

with the jth portfolio consisting of N mortgages. We assume, as an idealized situation, that each mortgage has a maturity of only one period. If the mortgage defaults during that period, all principal is lost. Otherwise, the mortgage receives full principal value at maturity. We construct two or more tranches of MBS from each portfolio of mortgages.

In principle, the labels T_v might indicate something other than time (geographic or industry sector, for instance). However, we will refer to v, as the *vintage* of the portfolio, and for the purpose of this chapter the vintage interpretation is more appropriate than are other interpretations of v. The performance of the MBS is examined at a certain time, say time T. The expected value of the cash flow received by each tranche of MBS of vintage v is calculated conditional on the information available at vintage v. This conditional expected value of cash flows can be regarded, in this simplified setup, as the price of the MBS.

The default behavior of mortgage i in the portfolio of vintage v is governed by a random variable $X_{v,i}$. If $X_{v,i}$ is below a threshold c_v, then mortgage i in vintage v has defaulted. Therefore, the default probability of a mortgage is

$$\mathbb{P}(X_{v,i} < c_v) = F_{v,i}(c_v), \tag{4.1}$$

where $F_{v,i}$ is the standard cumulative distribution function of $X_{v,i}$. There is no model yet.

In the one-factor Gaussian copula model, there are independent standard Gaussian variables Z_v and $\varepsilon_{v,1}, \ldots, \varepsilon_{v,N}$, such that

$$X_{v,j} = \sqrt{\rho_v} Z_v + \sqrt{1-\rho_v}\, \varepsilon_{v,j}. \tag{4.2}$$

Thus the assumption is that the variables $X_{v,j}$ are jointly Gaussian, with each being standard Gaussian, and have the following specific correlation structure:

$$\mathbb{E}[X_{v,i} X_{v,j}] = \rho_v \in [0, 1]. \tag{4.3}$$

Recall that for jointly Gaussian variables, each of mean 0, the joint distribution is completely determined by the pairwise covariances.

Following Anderson and Sidenius (2005), we will allow the possibility that the correlation parameter ρ_v is dependent on the stochastic state variable Z_v, and then take

$$X_{v,j} = \sqrt{\rho_v} Z_v + \kappa \varepsilon_{v,j} + m, \tag{4.4}$$

where κ and m are parameters that ensure $X_{v,j}$ has mean 0 and variance 1. Intuitively, Z_v can be viewed as a state variable that determines the conditional default probability for mortgages of vintage v. For these variables, we assume the following *serial correlation* behavior: the variables $Z_1, \ldots, Z_V$ are also jointly Gaussian with correlations

$$\mathbb{E}[Z_v Z_{v'}] = \phi^2_{v,v'} \in [0, 1], \tag{4.5}$$

where $\phi_{v,v'} \geq 0$.

In the case of continuous-time vintage $v \in [0, V]$, the process

$$v \mapsto Z_v$$

is Gaussian, with Z_v having mean 0 and variance 1 for each v. For instance, $Z_v = a(v) B_{b(v)}$, for a Brownian motion $v \mapsto B_v$, and $a(\cdot)$ and $b(\cdot)$ are suitable functions, which determine the correlation $\phi_{v,v'}$.

In this chapter, for simplicity, we always assume that Z_v follows an $AR(1)$ process of the form:

$$Z_v = \phi Z_{v-1} + \sqrt{1-\phi^2} u_v, \ \ v = 0, 1, \ldots, V \tag{4.6}$$

where Z_0 and u_v are all standard Gaussian variables.

Note that unlike the "traditional" use of the copula model, we do not apply the copula model to one portfolio over different time instants; instead we are considering *different portfolios* issued at different times (thereby of different vintages).

We have studied this model extensively in Hillebrand *et al.* (2010), the main results of which may be summarized as:

1. Default rates exhibit vintage correlation if and only if the state variable Z_v has serial correlation. Moreover, in the large portfolio limit, the vintage correlation approaches a limiting value determined by the magnitude of serial correlation and the value of default correlation.
2. Vintage correlation of default rates is positively correlated with serial correlation in the state variable Z_v.

In the present chapter, we explore situations where there may be stochastic fluctuation in the default correlation parameter ρ_v with respect to the vintage parameter v in particular, a transition between a high correlation regime and a low correlation regime. We then examine the impact on the tranche prices, as measured through the expected value of cash flows.

4.3 Impact of Dynamics of Default Correlation on Low-Frequency Tranches

4.3.1 CONSTANT DEFAULT CORRELATION

In this section, we study the impact of dynamics in the state variable on MBS tranche price distributions. For this purpose, we hold the default correlation constant and let the state variable vary across vintages.

We construct 2500 vintages by simulating one path of the state variables Z_v, where $v = 1, 2, \ldots, 2500$. For each vintage, we simulate a cohort of $N = 100$ homogeneous mortgages. Each mortgage has a principal of \$1. To reduce computational burden, these mortgages are assumed to have a life time of one period. A mortgage is assumed to receive no cash flow if a default event happens during its life time and to receive full principal otherwise.

From each cohort of mortgages, we construct 100 units of MBS. Each unit of the MBS has a principal of \$1. There are two tranches of our simplified MBS. The senior tranche consists of the top 50% of the face value of all mortgages created in each vintage. The equity tranche consists of the bottom 50%. The prices of each tranche of vintage v are simulated as the expected value of the cash flow received by each tranche conditional on the value of Z_v. The underlying procedure of the simulation is

1. A series of 2500 state variables Z_v is simulated with i.i.d standard Gaussian distribution.
2. For each Z_v, the default behavior of a cohort of $N = 100$ mortgages are simulated according to Equations 4.1 and 4.4. The unconditional default probability for each mortgage is fixed at 50% , meaning we keep c_v in Equation 4.1 fixed at 0. At this stage, we keep the default correlation parameter $\rho_v = 0.5$ constant. The cash flows received by each tranche of MBS at each vintage are calculated according to the simulated mortgage default behavior.

3. Step (2) is repeated 100,000 times, and the expected values of the cash flows received by each tranche of MBS for each vintage are estimated. These expected values can be viewed as the tranche prices.

Note that in our simulation, we only simulate one series of Z_v. This implies that the simulated series of prices follows one realization of the path of tranche prices observed at a later date T. Therefore, the unconditional distribution of these prices is comparable to the distribution of a series of observed historical prices of MBS of subsequent vintages. The histograms of tranche prices are shown in the first column of Fig. 4.1.

We then let Z_v be serially correlated according to Equation 4.6, where $\phi = 0.5$. The histogram of the simulated tranche prices in this case are shown in the second column of Fig. 4.1. Comparing the two columns of the figure, it appears that there is no significant difference in the two cases. This finding is verified by the Quantile–Quantile (QQ) plot of the price distributions shown in Fig. 4.2. In the first column of this figure, we display the QQ plot of the distribution of tranche prices when Z_v is not serially correlated against the tranche price distribution when Z_v is serially correlated. It can be seen from the figure

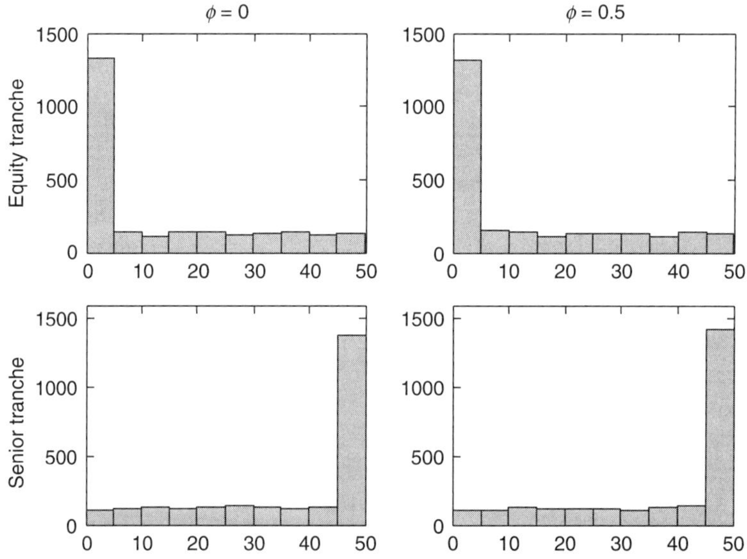

FIGURE 4.1 Histograms of tranche prices when Z_v has different values of serial correlation. In the figure, we plot the histogram of tranche prices across vintages. The tranche price is simulated as the expected value of cash flow received by a certain tranche of a certain vintage. In our simulations, we construct 2500 vintages, so there are 2500 prices for each tranche. In the first column, the state variable Z_v is white noise. In the second column, Z_v follows an $AR(1)$ process described in Equation 4.6 with $\phi = 0.5$. In both columns, $\rho_v = 0.5$ assumes to be constant across vintages. The unconditional default probability is assumed to be 50%. The dimension of the abscissa is Dollars. There are $100 nominal in each MBS, which in turn is divided into two equally sized tranches.

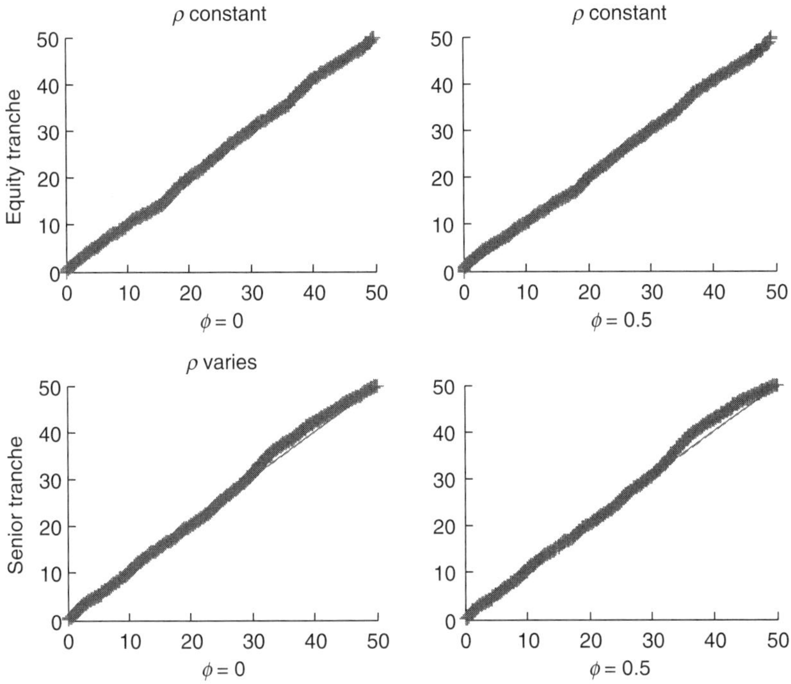

FIGURE 4.2 QQ Plot: $\phi = 0$ versus $\phi = 0.5$. In these figures, we display the quantile–quantile plot of tranche prices when Z_v has no serial correlation (horizontal axis) versus tranche prices when Z_v follows an $AR(1)$ process where the first order coefficient $\phi = 0.5$ (vertical axis). In the first column, the value of ρ_v is constant across all vintages. In the second column, the value of ρ_v varies across vintages according to Equation 4.7, where $\rho_l = 0.3$ and $\rho_u = 0.7$. The unconditional default probability is assumed to be 50%.

that the two distributions are very similar. This result indicates that the dynamics in Z_v do not affect the unconditional distribution of tranche prices.

4.3.2 REGIME-SWITCHING DEFAULT CORRELATION

We now allow the default correlation parameter ρ_v to vary stochastically across vintages. To model the dynamics of ρ_v, we follow Andersen and Sidenius (2005) and use a regime-switching model. Specifically, we set

$$\rho_v = \rho_l \cdot \mathbb{1}_{\{Z_v \geq Z^*\}} + \rho_u \cdot \mathbb{1}_{\{Z_v < Z^*\}}, \tag{4.7}$$

where $\rho_l = 0.3$, $\rho_u = 0.7$, and $Z^* = 0$. This means that the value of ρ_v assumes a lower value 0.3 when the state variable Z_v is positive and assumes a higher value 0.7 when the state variable is negative. This is consistent with the empirical finding that default correlation tends to be higher when the overall economy is in a bad state. Compared with our previous model, the mean of ρ_v remains the same. In doing this, we insulate the impact on default behavior caused by the dynamics of ρ_v from that caused by a change in the absolute level of ρ_v.

Note that the tranche price can be positively or negatively correlated with the value of default correlation according to the seniority of the tranche. (For example, Meng and Sengupta (2011) provide a detailed analysis of the sensitivities of tranche prices to change in default correlation.) This means that the dynamics of ρ_v described above have different impact on prices of different tranches. Since the price of a tranche is generally positively correlated with the value of Z_v, the dynamics of ρ_v exaggerate the effect of Z_v on tranches whose prices are negatively correlated with default correlation. For example, the price of a senior tranche is generally negatively correlated with the value of default correlation. When the value of Z_v is high, not only the conditional default probability is low but the default correlation is also low if ρ_v follows Equation 4.7. Thus in this case, a senior tranche benefits from a small ρ_v as well as a low conditional default probability. Similarly, the dynamics of ρ_v alleviate the effect of Z_v on tranches whose prices are positively correlated with default correlation. This may in turn affect the overall distribution of tranche prices.

Since ρ_v is now assumed to be a random variable that is dependent on Z_v, the state variable for each vintage, $X_{v,j}$ in Equation 4.2 no longer has an unconditional standard Gaussian distribution. In the model for the state variable in Equation 4.4, which we repeat here

$$X_{v,j} = \sqrt{\rho_v} Z_v + \kappa \varepsilon_{v,j} + m,$$

where Z_0 and $\varepsilon_{v,j}$ are standard Gaussian variables, we now use the parameters (Andersen and Sidenius, 2005)

$$\kappa = \sqrt{1 - \mathrm{Var}(\sqrt{\rho_v} Z_v)}, \tag{4.8}$$

and

$$m = -\mathbb{E}(\sqrt{\rho_v} Z_v). \tag{4.9}$$

The first and fourth columns in Fig. 4.3 compare the histograms of tranche prices in the case where ρ_v is constant and in the case where ρ_v varies according to Equation 4.7. As can be seen, for the senior tranche, when ρ_v varies, the likelihood of either receiving full payment or receiving nothing increases. In other words, the distribution of senior tranche prices has fatter tails when ρ_v varies than when it is constant. For the equity tranche however, the exact opposite happens. The likelihood of either getting full payment or receiving no payment decreases. These results are intuitive. Since the price of a senior tranche is negatively correlated with ρ_v, the dynamics of ρ_v, modeled by Equation 4.7, amplified the effect of Z_v on tranche prices, increasing the probabilities of either a very high or very low default rate. For the equity tranche, its price is positively correlated with default correlation. Thus, the assumed dynamics of default correlation alleviate the effect of Z_v, making the tranche less likely to receive either zero or full payment. These

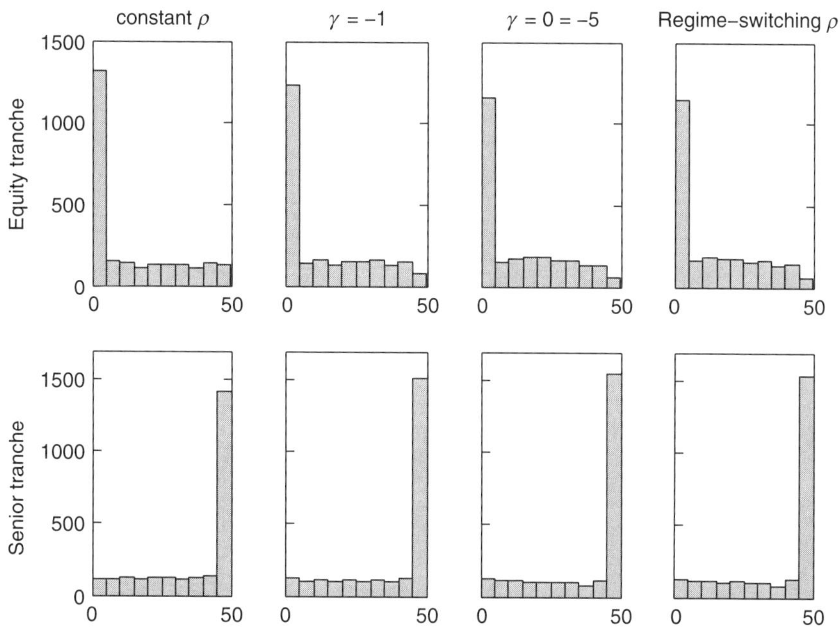

FIGURE 4.3 The histograms of tranche prices across vintages. The state variable Z_v is assumed to follow an $AR(1)$ process with the first order coefficient $\phi = 0.5$. The tranche price is simulated as the expected value of cash flow received by a certain tranche of a certain vintage. In our simulations, we construct 2500 vintages, so there are 2500 prices for each tranche. In the first column, the value of ρ_v is fixed at 0.5. In the second and third columns, the value of ρ_v is changing between 0.3 and 0.7 according to Equation 4.10. In the fourth column, the value of ρ_v assumes a regime-switching model specified by Equation 4.7, where $\rho_l = 0.3$, and $\rho_u = 0.7$. The unconditional default probability is assumed to be 50%.

findings are also supported by Fig. 4.4. In the third column of Fig. 4.4, we display the QQ plot of the distribution of tranche prices when ρ_v is constant against the distribution of tranche prices when ρ_v assumes a regime-switching model. It is clear from Fig. 4.4 that when ρ_v is stochastic relative to when ρ_v is constant, the equity tranche price has a distribution with thinner tails while the senior tranche price has a distribution of fatter tails. We also notice that the same can be concluded if Z_v does not have serial correlation. This can be seen from the first and fourth columns in Fig. 4.5 and the third column in Fig. 4.6, where we set Z_v to have no serial correlation.

Again, the dynamics of Z_v do not seem to affect the unconditional distribution of prices even when ρ_v is stochastic. This can be seen in Fig. 4.7. In the first column of the figure, we fix the autocorrelation parameter of Z_v to be 0, so Z_v is a series of white noises. In the second column, Z_v follows an $AR(1)$ process with $\phi = 0.5$. In both columns, we allow ρ_v to change according to Equation 4.7. Note that even though the state variable Z_v has different serial correlations, the distributions of tranche prices are almost identical between

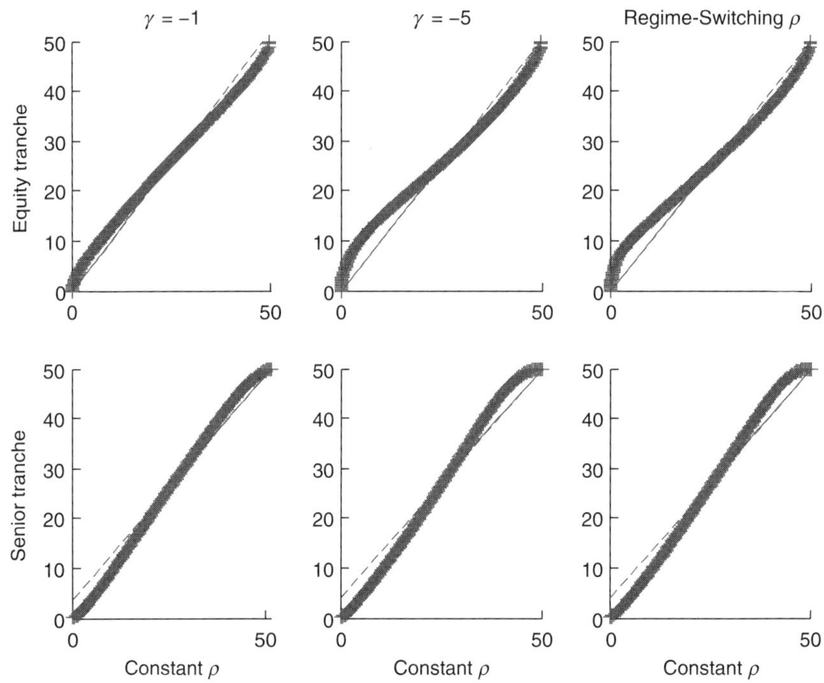

FIGURE 4.4 QQ Plot of constant ρ_v versus varying ρ_v. In these figures, we display the quantile–quantile plot of tranche prices when default correlation is constant versus tranche prices when default correlation is stochastic. In all figures, the horizontal axis denotes the case where ρ_v is constant. The vertical axis denotes the case where ρ_v varies across vintages. In the first column, the value of ρ_v has a logistic transition model according to Equation 4.10, where $\gamma = -1$. In the second column, the value of ρ_v has a logistic transition model according to Equation 4.10, where $\gamma = -5$. In the third column, the value of ρ_v has a regime-switching model and varies between 0.3 and 0.7 according to Equation 4.7. The state variable Z_v is assumed to follow an $AR(1)$ process where the first order coefficient $\phi = 0.5$. The unconditional default probability is assumed to be 50%.

the two columns. The QQ plot of the two distributions, which can be seen in the second column of Fig. 4.2, confirms that these two distributions are indeed the same. This is likely because of the fact that a change in serial correlation only affects the conditional distribution of Z_v but not its unconditional distribution. Therefore, only the conditional distribution of tranche prices changes while the unconditional distribution remains the same.

4.3.3 LOGISTIC TRANSITIONAL DEFAULT CORRELATION

A regime-switching model for ρ_v as described in the last section is intuitive, consistent with empirical findings, and allows efficient calibration to market prices. (Andersen and Sidenius, 2005.) However, it does have one major

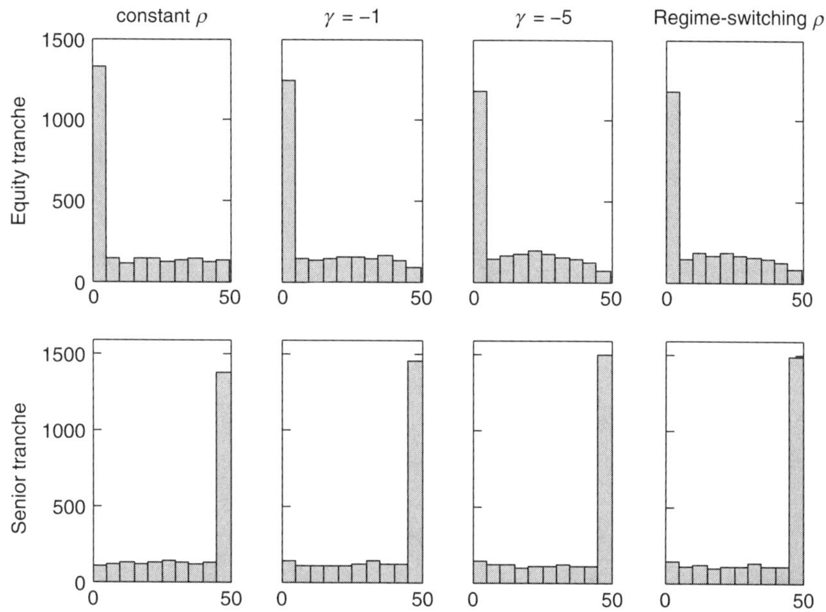

FIGURE 4.5 The histograms of tranche prices over vintages. The state variable Z_v is assumed to have no serial correlation. The tranche price is simulated as the expected value of cash flow received by a certain tranche of a certain vintage. In our simulations, we construct 2500 vintages, so there are 2500 prices for each tranche. In the first column, the value of ρ_v is fixed at 0.5. In the second and third columns, the value of ρ_v is changing between 0.3 and 0.7 according to Equation 4.10. In the fourth column, the value of ρ_v assumes a regime-switching model specified by Equation 4.7, where $\rho_l = 0.3$ and $\rho_u = 0.7$. The unconditional default probability is assumed to be 50%.

drawback in that the true default correlation is unlikely to assume just two values. To address this issue, we allow the default correlation parameter to change between two values "smoothly", meaning that ρ_v is a smooth function of Z_v. Specifically, we assume a logistic transition model for the default correlation parameter ρ_v,

$$\rho_v = \rho_l + (\rho_u - \rho_l)\frac{1}{1 + \exp(-\gamma(Z_v - c))}. \tag{4.10}$$

With this setup, ρ_v can take any values between ρ_l and ρ_u according to the value of Z_v. When the value of γ is negative, the value of ρ_v decreases smoothly toward ρ_l as Z_v increases. As Z_v decreases, ρ_v increases smoothly toward ρ_u. Note that γ determines the smoothness of the transition of ρ_v. The smaller the absolute value of γ, the smoother is the transition. For $\gamma \to -\infty$, this model converges to the regime-switching model described in the sections above. On the other hand, when γ is 0, it degenerates into the constant ρ_v model.

In our chapter, we fix $\rho_l = 0.3$, $\rho_u = 0.7$, and $c = 0$. Note that by using this specification, we manage to keep the mean value of $\rho_v = 0.5$. The relationship

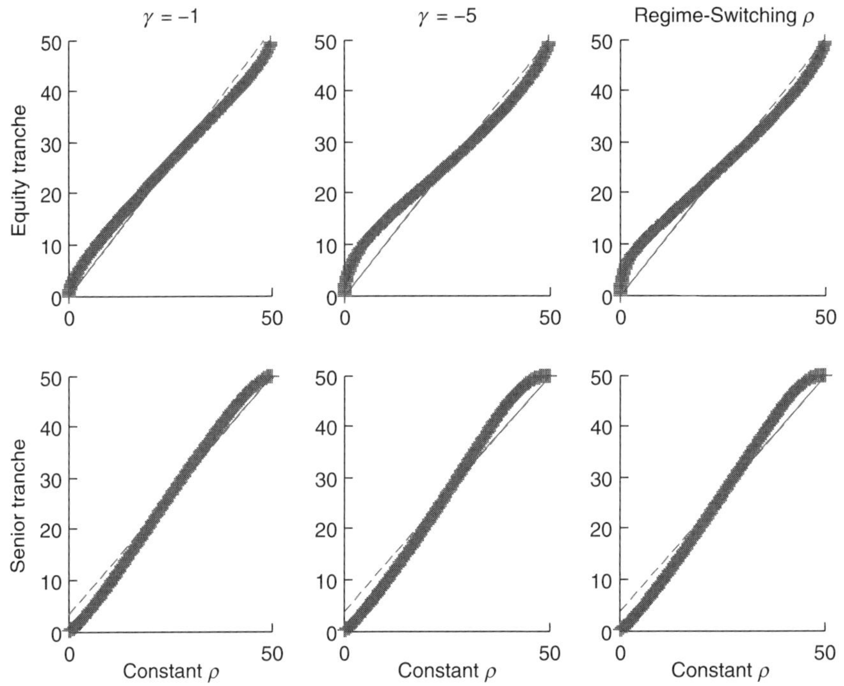

FIGURE 4.6 QQ plot of constant ρ_v versus varying ρ_v. In these figures, we display the quantile–quantile plot of tranche prices when default correlation is constant versus tranche prices when default correlation is stochastic. In all figures, the horizontal axis denotes the case where ρ_v is constant. The vertical axis denotes the case where ρ_v varies across vintages. In the first column, the value of ρ_v has a logistic transition model according to Equation 4.10, where $\gamma = -1$. In the second column, the value of ρ_v has a logistic transition model according to Equation 4.10, where $\gamma = -5$. In the third column, the value of ρ_v has a regime-switching model and varies between 0.3 and 0.7 according to Equation 4.7. The state variable Z_v is assumed to have no serial correlation. The unconditional default probability is assumed to be 50%.

between ρ_v and Z_v when $\gamma = -1, -5$ can be seen in Fig. 4.8. We follow the same steps as in Section 4.3.2 except that we replace the regime-switching model for ρ_v with the logistic transition model. We let Z_v follow an $AR(1)$ process according to Equation 4.6 with $\phi = 0.5$.

The histograms of the tranche prices are displayed in the second and third columns of Fig. 4.3. The QQ plots of the distributions of tranche prices when ρ_v assumes logistic transition models against the distribution of tranche prices when ρ_v is constant are displayed in the first and second columns of Fig. 4.4. As can be seen, compared with the case where ρ_v is constant, the equity tranche prices exhibit thinner tails while the senior tranche prices exhibit fatter tails. This is consistent with our findings in Section 4.3.2. Also note that the greater the absolute value of γ in Equation 4.10, or in other words, the less smooth the transition of ρ_v, the thinner the tails of the distribution of equity tranche prices, and the fatter the tails of the distribution of senior tranche prices. As the absolute

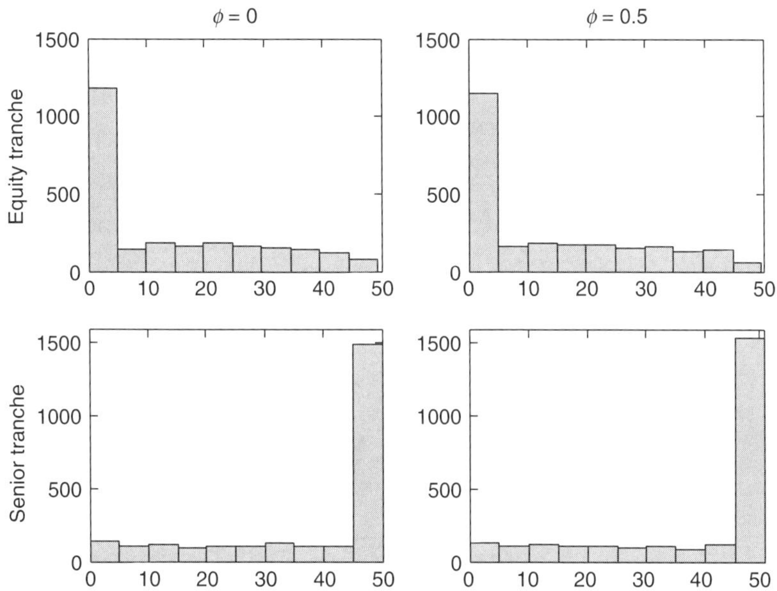

FIGURE 4.7 Histograms of tranche prices when Z_v has different values of serial correlation. In these figures, we plot the histogram of tranche prices across vintages. The tranche price is simulated as the expected value of cash flow received by a certain tranche of a certain vintage. In our simulations, we construct 2500 vintages, so there are 2500 prices for each tranche. In the first column, the state variable Z_v is white noise. In the second column, Z_v follows an $AR(1)$ process described in Equation 4.6 with $\phi = 0.5$. In both columns, ρ_v assumes a regime switching model as is described in Equation 4.7. The unconditional default probability is assumed to be 50%.

value of γ increases to infinity, the tranche prices converge in distribution to those when ρ_v follows a regime-switching model. As the absolute value of γ decreases to 0, the tranche prices converge in distribution to the those when ρ_v is constant.

We also consider the case where Z_v does not have serial correlation. The results are shown in the second and third columns of Fig. 4.5. Their QQ plots are shown in the first and second columns of Fig. 4.6. As can be seen, the pattern of the histograms of tranche prices when Z_v are white noise is very similar to the case where Z_v has serial correlation. This is also consistent with our findings in Section 4.3.2.

4.4 Impact of Dynamics of Default Correlation on High-Frequency Tranches

We study now the situation where the full risk spectrum for investors is subdivided into a large number of tranches each of thin width. We call such a situation *high frequency tranching*. As pointed out by Gorton (2008), subprime MBS portfolios included very thin tranches.

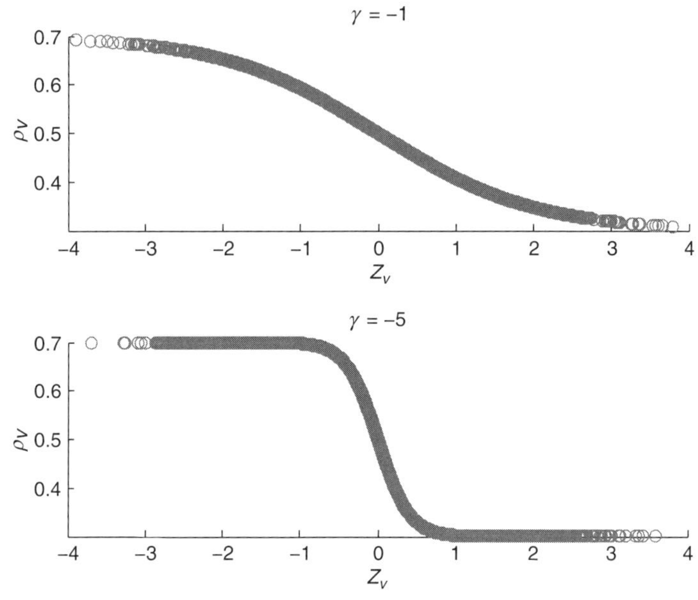

FIGURE 4.8 Relationship between ρ_v and Z_v. In this figure, 10,000 Z_v are generated with i.i.d standard Gaussian distribution. The corresponding values of ρ_v are calculated according to Equation 4.10, where $\rho_l = 0.3$, $\rho_u = 0.7$, and $c = 0$.

4.4.1 SENSITIVITY OF HIGH-FREQUENCY TRANCHE PRICES TO DEFAULT CORRELATION

As illustrated in the section above, imposing dynamics on default correlation has different effects on the price distribution of different tranches. This is because the sensitivity of tranche prices to a change in default correlation is different for each tranche. For example, holding everything else constant, the value of an equity tranche increases when default correlation increases, while the value of a senior tranche decreases.

Since the sensitivity of price with respect to default correlation of a tranche with arbitrary seniority and size is unclear, we cannot deduce from Section 4.3 the impact of the dynamics of default correlation on an arbitrary tranche. To better understand how a change in default correlation affects tranche prices, we slice each MBS portfolio into many thin tranches instead of just two tranches. We estimate numerically the prices of all these high frequency tranches of a fixed vintage for different values of default correlation. These prices can be used to calculate the price of any larger tranche that consists of a set of small tranches by simply summing up the prices of these smaller tranches.

Specifically, we slice each MBS into 100 equal-sized small tranches. Each tranche has a principal of \$1 at initiation. For different values of ρ_v, the expected values of cash flows received by these tranches are estimated using Monte Carlo

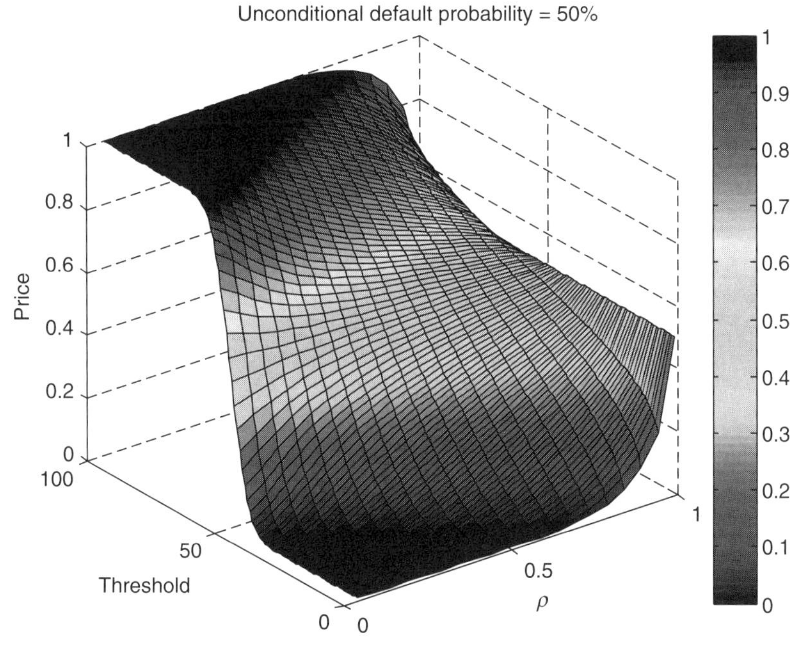

FIGURE 4.9 The sensitivity of tranche price to ρ.

simulation. Figure 4.9 shows the case where we fix the unconditional default probability at 50%. The figure shows that the prices of all the tranches of relatively high seniority decrease as ρ_v increases and the prices of tranches of relatively low seniority increase as ρ_v increases.

We also estimated the high-frequency tranche prices when the unconditional default probability assumes other values. These can be found in Fig. 4.10. In all cases, the tranche price is positively correlated with default correlation when the tranche seniority is below a certain level, which we call transition level. The tranche price is negatively correlated with default correlation when the seniority is above that level. The position of the transition level (its distance from the bottom tranche) is determined by the unconditional default probability. The higher the unconditional default probability, the higher is the transition level. In other words, the price as a function of seniority has a transition with locus at a certain threshold whose position is positively correlated with the value of unconditional default probability.

4.4.2 SENSITIVITY OF HIGH-FREQUENCY TRANCHE PRICES TO DYNAMIC DEFAULT CORRELATION

In Section 4.4.1, we have fixed the vintage v and analyzed the relationship between high-frequency tranche prices and default correlation in a static manner.

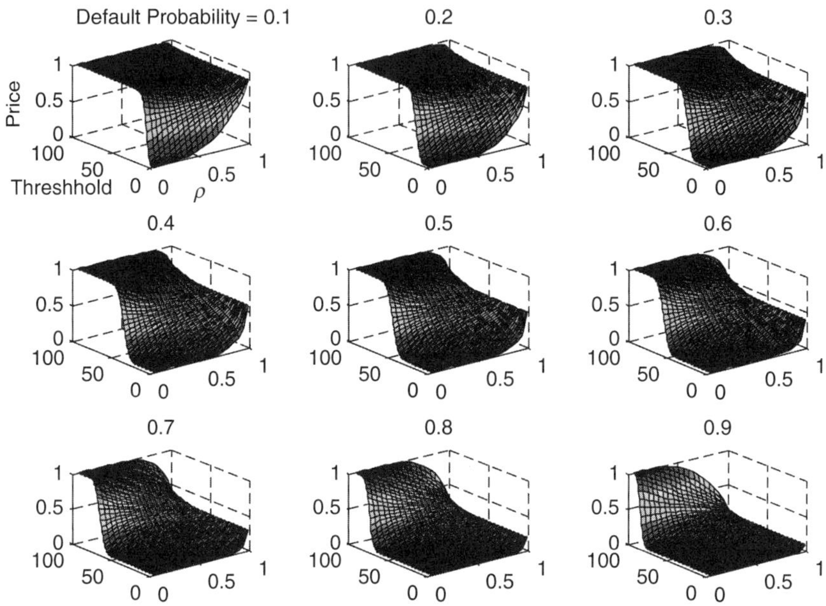

FIGURE 4.10 The sensitivity of tranche price to ρ.

Now we introduce the vintage dimension into the analysis extending results in Sections 4.3.1 and 4.3.2 to the case of 100 high-frequency tranches of MBS rather than just two tranches.

Again, we generate 2500 vintages of mortgages whose unconditional default probability is fixed at 50%. We assume the state variable Z_v to be serially correlated. We assume that Z_v follows an $AR(1)$ process described in Equation 4.6, where the $AR(1)$ coefficient $\phi = 0.5$. We first let the default correlation parameter $\rho_v = 0.5$. The expected values of the cash flow received by each tranche at each vintage $v = 1, 2, \ldots, 2500$ are estimated using Monte Carlo simulations. We present here series of prices of five representative tranches (out of 100 tranches in total)—the tranches at 10% level from the bottom of the portfolio, at 30% level, at 50% level, at 70% level, and at 90% level.

We then let ρ_v change across vintages and examine how the dynamics of ρ_v affect the distribution of tranche prices across vintages. In Fig. 4.11, we compare the histograms of tranche prices when the default correlation parameter ρ_v is fixed at 0.5 and when ρ_v switches between 0.3 and 0.7 according to Equation 4.7 or 4.10. The corresponding QQ plots are shown in Fig. 4.12. We can see from this figure that the distributions of tranche prices are obviously different for a constant ρ_v and for a varying ρ_v. Furthermore, the differences in distribution vary across tranches. For example, for a thin slice of MBS tranche created at the 50% level from the bottom of a mortgage pool, the distribution of its tranche prices across vintages have thinner left tail when ρ_v is time varying compared with when ρ_v is a constant. On the other hand, for a thin MBS tranche at

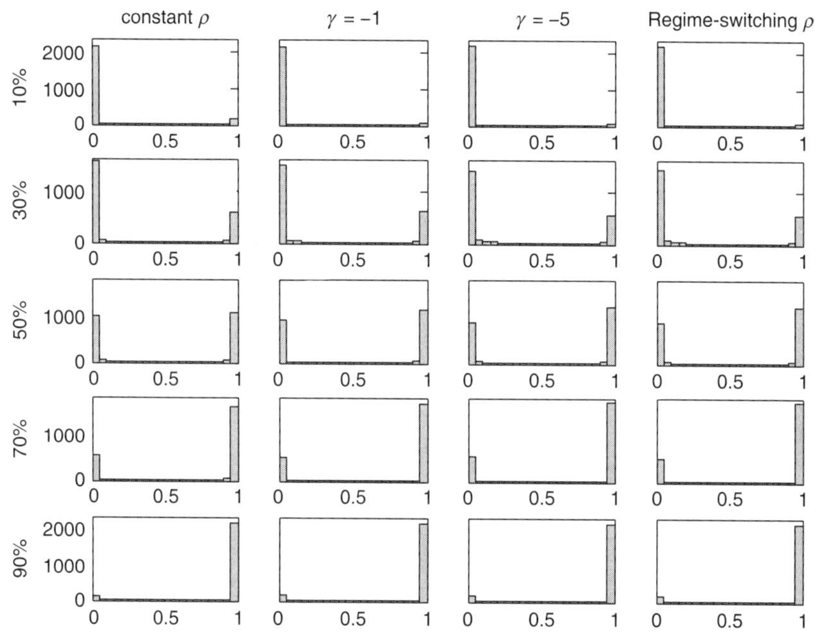

FIGURE 4.11 The histograms of high-frequency tranche prices over vintages. In the first column, the value of ρ_v is fixed at 0.5. In the second and third column, the value of ρ_v changes between 0.3 and 0.7 according to Equation 4.10, with $\gamma = -1$ in the second column and $\gamma = -5$ in the third column. In the fourth column, the value of ρ_v switches between 0.3 and 0.7 according to Equation 4.7. The state variable Z_v is assumed to follow an $AR(1)$ process where the first order coefficient $\phi = 0.5$. The unconditional default probability is assumed to be 50% .

90% level of a mortgage pool, the distribution of its tranche prices has fatter tails when ρ_v is dynamic relative to when ρ_v is constant. Also notice that when ρ_v has a logistic transition structure, the resulting tranche prices converge in distribution to constant-ρ_v tranche prices as γ approaches 0. They converge in distribution to regime-switching-ρ_v tranche prices as γ decreases to negative infinity.

A noteworthy observation is that for certain tranches, such as the 90% tranche in Fig. 4.11, the distortion of the price distribution caused by the dynamics of ρ_v is relatively small. This fact suggests that for certain tranches, the simple Gaussian copula model is good enough to model tranche prices as long as it correctly specifies the mean value of default correlation. On the other hand, for certain tranches such as the 50% tranche, the distortion of price distribution from the baseline model is relatively big, suggesting that a simple Gaussian Copula model is inappropriate to capture the distribution of tranche prices when default correlation is indeed varying across vintages.

This observation also holds when Z_v does not exhibit serial correlation. This can be seen in Figs. 4.13 and 4.14, where we set Z_v to be a series of i.i.d. standard Gaussian variables.

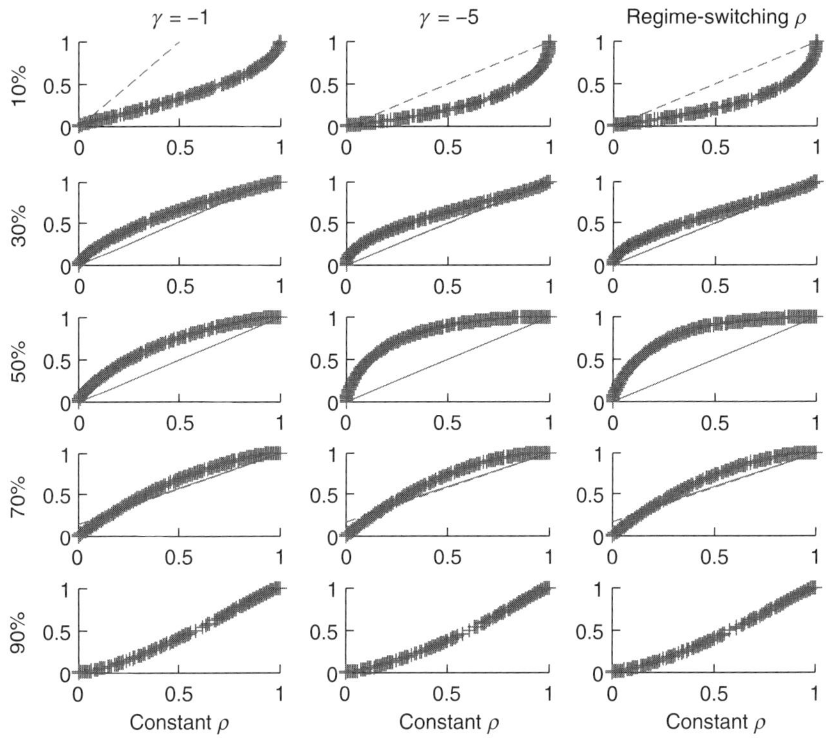

FIGURE 4.12 QQ plot of constant ρ_v versus varying ρ_v. In these figures, we display the quantile–quantile plot of high-frequency tranche prices when default correlation is constant versus tranche prices when default correlation is stochastic. In all figures, the horizontal axis denotes the case where ρ_v is constant. The vertical axis denotes the cases where ρ_v varies across vintage. In the first column, the value of ρ_v has a logistic transition model according to Equation 4.10, where $\gamma = -1$. In the second column, the value of ρ_v has a logistic transition model according to Equation 4.10, where $\gamma = -5$. In the third column, the value of ρ_v has a regime-switching model and varies between 0.3 and 0.7 according to Equation 4.7. The number in percentage in front of each row indicates the position of that tranche. For example, the number 10% on the first row means that the tranche of that row is located at the 10% position from the bottom of the MBS portfolio. The state variable Z_v is assumed to follow an $AR(1)$ process where the first order coefficient $\phi = 0.5$. The unconditional default probability is assumed to be 50%.

4.5 Conclusion

We find that introducing dynamics into the state variable does not affect the distribution of tranche prices across vintages. On the other hand, the dynamics of default correlation do influence the distribution of tranche prices. The smoothness of the change of default correlation also matters. If the default correlation changes smoothly according to the value of Z_v, the distortion tends to be small, and vice versa.

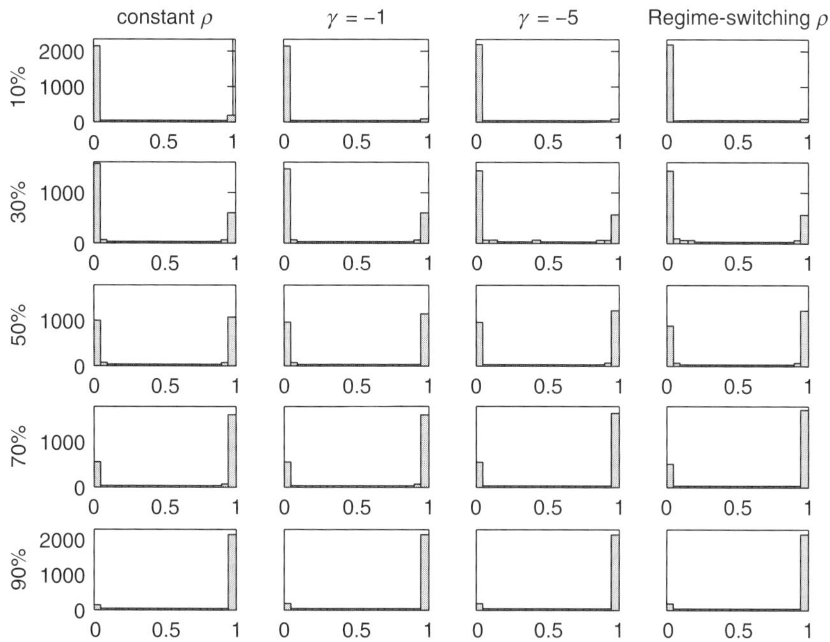

FIGURE 4.13 The histograms of high-frequency tranche prices over vintages. In the first column, the value of ρ_v is fixed at 0.5. In the second and third column, the value of ρ_v changes between 0.3 and 0.7 according to Equation 4.10, with $\gamma = -1$ in the second column and $\gamma = -5$ in the third column. In the fourth column, the value of ρ_v switches between 0.3 and 0.7 according to Equation 4.7. The state variable Z_v is assumed to have no serial correlation. The unconditional default probability is assumed to be 50%.

The distortions of distributions caused by the dynamics of default correlation parameter ρ_v is determined by seniority of the tranche. In general, if the tranche price is positively correlated with default correlation, the distribution of the price of the tranche tends to have fatter tails when ρ_v is negatively correlated with the conditional default probability. The exact opposite is true for a tranche whose price is negatively correlated with default correlation.

The findings above prompt us to study the sensitivity of high-frequency tranching prices to change in default correlation. We find that the tranche price as a function of the seniority is a transition with locus at a threshold whose distance from the bottom of the MBS portfolio is positively correlated with the unconditional default probability.

The results in this chapter have important implications for risk management. If the default correlation changes across vintages either in a regime-switching model or in a logistic transition, our findings suggest that a Gaussian copula model that assumes a constant default correlation ρ_v underestimates the default risk of a senior tranche while overestimating the default risk for an equity tranche, even if it correctly characterizes the mean value of ρ_v and the true unconditional default probability.

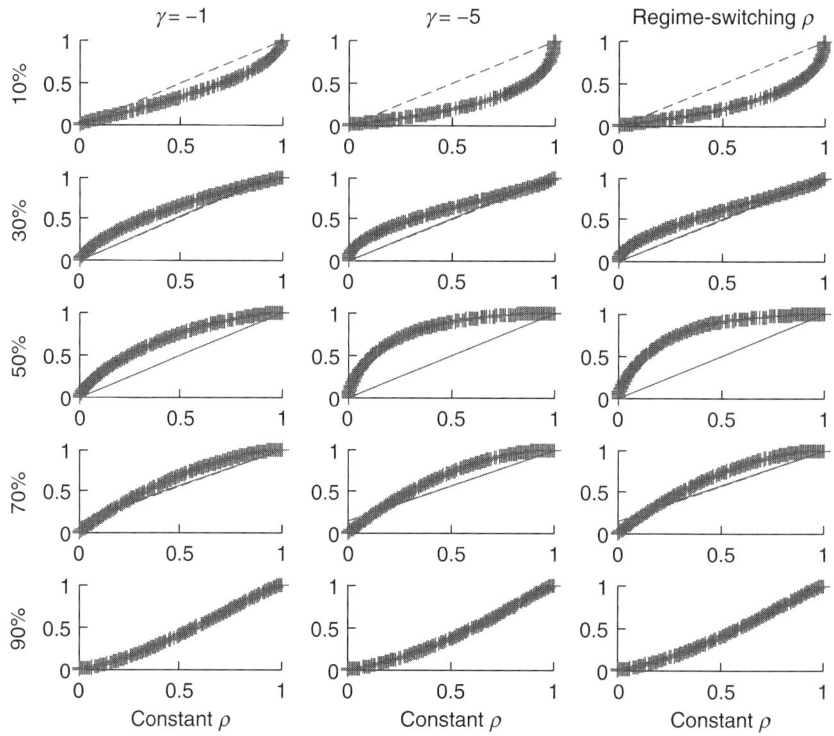

FIGURE 4.14 QQ plot of constant ρ_v versus varying ρ_v. In these figures, we display the quantile–quantile plot of high-frequency tranche prices when default correlation is constant versus tranche prices when default correlation is stochastic. In all figures, the horizontal axis denotes the case where ρ_v is constant. The vertical axis denotes the cases where ρ_v varies across vintage. In the first column, the value of ρ_v has a logistic transition model according to Equation 4.10, where $\gamma = -1$. In the second column, the value of ρ_v has a logistic transition model according to Equation 4.10, where $\gamma = -5$. In the third column, the value of ρ_v has a regime-switching model and varies between 0.3 and 0.7 according to Equation 4.7. The number in percentage in front of each row indicates the position of that tranche. For example, the number 10% in the first row means that the tranche of that row is located at the 10% position from the bottom of the MBS portfolio. The state variable Z_v is assumed to have no serial correlation. The unconditional default probability is assumed to be 50%.

REFERENCES

Andersen L, Sidenius J. Extensions to the Gaussian copula: random recovery and random factor loadings. J Credit Risk 2005;1(1):29–70.

Berd A, Engle R, Voronov A. The underlying dynamics of credit correlations. J Credit Risk 2007;3(2):27–62.

Das SR, Freed L, Geng G, Kapadia N. Correlated default risk. J Fixed Income 2006;16(2):7–32.

Gorton G. The panic of 2007. Working Paper 14358, NBER; 2008.

Hillebrand E, Sengupta A, Xu J. Temporal correlation of defaults in subprime securitization. Working paper; 2010.

Hull J, Predescu M, White A. The valuation of correlation-dependent credit derivatives using a structural model. Working paper; 2009.

Li D. On default correlation: a copula function approach. J Fixed Income 2000;9(4):43–54.

Meng C, Sengupta A. CDO tranche sensitivities in the Gaussian copula model. Int J Theor Appl Finance 2011, Upcoming.

Servigny A, Renault O. Default correlation: empirical evidence. Working paper, Standard and Poor's; 2002.

CHAPTER FIVE

Construction of Volatility Indices Using A Multinomial Tree Approximation Method

DRAGOS BOZDOG, IONUŢ FLORESCU, KHALDOUN KHASHANAH, and HONGWEI QIU

Department of Mathematical Sciences, Stevens Institute of Technology, Hoboken, NJ

5.1 Introduction

The Chicago Board Options Exchange (CBOE) Market Volatility Index (VIX) was introduced by Professor Robert Whaley in 1993. It is a forward-looking index that provides the expected stock market volatility over the next 30 calendar days. There were two purposes for creating this index. First, it was intended to provide a benchmark of the expected short-term market volatility. And second, it was created to provide an index on which options and futures contracts can be written. In 2003 the methodology was revised and VIX started trading future contracts in 2004.

The VIX index is computed directly from options written on the Standards and Poor 500 equity index (SPX) or the ETF that tracks it (the SPY), thus its movement is determined by the market demand of calls and puts written on

Handbook of Modeling High-Frequency Data in Finance, First Edition.
Edited by Frederi G. Viens, Maria C. Mariani, and Ionuţ Florescu.

the S&P500. Indeed, Bollen and Whaley (2004) show that the demand to buy out-of-the-money and at-the-money SPX puts is a key driver in the movement in SPX implied volatility measures such as VIX. The reason given is that the option market became dominated by portfolio insurers or hedgers, who routinely buy out-of-the-money and at-the-money SPX index put options for insurance purposes to protect their portfolio from a potential market crash. Very often, the VIX index was termed as an *investor fear gauge*. This is due to the fact that the VIX spikes during periods of market turmoil.

5.1.1 CALCULATION OF VIX BY CBOE

The current calculation of VIX by CBOE is based on the concept of fair value of future variance developed by Demeterfi *et al.* (1999). The fair value of future variance is determined from market observables such as option prices and interest rates independent of any option pricing model. The fair value of future variance is defined as following (Eq. (26) in Demeterfi *et al.* (1999)):

$$K_{\text{var}} = \frac{2}{T}\left\{rT - \left[\frac{S_0}{S_*}e^{rT} - 1\right] - \log\left(\frac{S_*}{S_0}\right) + e^{rT}\int_0^{S_*}\frac{P(T,K)}{K^2}dK \right.$$
$$\left. + e^{rT}\int_{S_*}^{\infty}\frac{C(T,K)}{K^2}dK\right\}, \tag{5.1}$$

where S_0 is the current asset price, C and P are call and put prices, respectively, r is the risk-free rate, T and K are option maturity and strike price, respectively, and S_* is an arbitrary stock price which is typically chosen to be close to the forward price.

The calculation of VIX by CBOE follows Equation 5.1, as explained in the CBOE white paper see CBOE (2003). CBOE calculates the VIX index using the following formula:

$$\sigma_{\text{VIX}}^2 = \frac{2}{T}\sum_i \frac{\Delta K_i}{K_i^2}e^{rT}Q(T,K_i) - \frac{1}{T}\left(\frac{F_0}{K_0} - 1\right)^2, \tag{5.2}$$

where

- σ_{vix} is the $\frac{\text{VIX}}{100}$.
- T is the time to expiration.
- F_0 is the forward index level derived from index option prices;
- K_i is the ith out-of-money option; a call if $K_i > F_0$ and a put if $K_i < F_0$.
- ΔK_i is the interval between strike prices-half the distance between the strike on either side of K_i

$$\Delta K_i = \frac{K_{i+1} - K_{i-1}}{2}. \tag{5.3}$$

Please note that ΔK for the lowest or highest strike is simply the difference between the lowest or highest strike and the next strike price.

- K_0 is the first strike below the forward index level.
- r is the risk-free interest rate to expiration.
- And $Q(T, K_i)$ is the midpoint of the bid-ask spread of each option with strike K_i.

A step-by-step calculation and an example that replicates the value of the VIX for a particular day is provided in Appendix A.

5.1.2 ISSUES WITH CBOE PROCEDURE FOR VIX CALCULATION

As shown by Jiang and Tian (2007), there are differences between the fair value of future variance and the practical implementation of VIX provided by CBOE. The main differences come from the following:

1. The calculation of fair value of future variance uses continuous strike prices. However, strike price vectors on CBOE or any other exchange are generally discrete.
2. The calculation of fair value of future variance uses strike prices between 0 and ∞. But in reality, the strike prices have a small range.
3. The fair value of future variance produce the expected variance (volatility) corresponding to the maturity date of the options used. In reality, options with exact 30-day maturity are not available. VIX is obtained by linearly interpolating the variances of options with near term and next term maturity.

Owing to the truncation of the data and the discreteness of the data, the CBOE procedure can generate errors (Jiang and Tian, 2007).

5.2 New Methodology

5.2.1 THEORETICAL FRAME OF STOCHASTIC VOLATILITY QUADRINOMIAL TREE METHOD

Stochastic volatility models have been proposed to better model the complexity of the market. The quadrinomial tree approximation developed by Florescu and Viens (2008) has demonstrated that it can be used to estimate option values and that it produces option chain values which are within bid-ask spread. The quadrinomial tree method outperforms other approximating techniques (with the exception of analytical solutions) in terms of both error and time. In this work, we use this methodology to approximate an underlying asset price process following:

$$\mathrm{d}X_t = \left(r - \frac{\varphi_t^2}{2}\right)\mathrm{d}t + \varphi_t S_t \mathrm{d}W_t, \tag{5.4}$$

where $X_t = \log S_t$ and S_t is the asset price, r is the short-term risk-free rate of interest, and W_t a standard Brownian motions. φ_t models the stochastic volatility process. It has been proved that for any proxy of the current stochastic volatility distribution at t the option prices calculated at time t converge to the true option prices (Theorem 4.6 in Florescu and Viens (2008)).

When using Stochastic volatility models, we are faced with a real problem when trying to come up with ONE number describing the volatility. The model intrinsically has an entire distribution describing the volatility and therefore providing a number is nonsensical. However, since a number we need to provide the idea of this approach is to produce the price of a synthetic one-month option with strike exactly the spot price and calculate the implied volatility value corresponding to the price we produce. The real challenge is to come up with a stochastic volatility distribution characteristic of the current market conditions.

In the current work, we take the simplest approach possible. We use a proxy for this φ_t calculated directly from the implied volatility values characterizing the option chains. This is used in conjunction with a highly recombining quadrinomial tree method to compute the price of options. The quadrinomial tree method is described in details in Florescu and Viens (2008). In Appendix B, we describe a one-step quadrinomial tree construction.

5.2.2 DIFFERENCE BETWEEN CBOE PROCEDURE AND QUADRINOMIAL TREE METHOD

1. CBOE procedure calculates two variances from near term and next term out-of-money options chains and then it obtains the expected variance in 30 days by linearly interpolating the variance from near term and next term options chain. This arbitrary linear interpolation lacks a theoretical base. Using the quadrinomial tree method, we can compute the expected market volatility in exactly 30 days.
2. Criteria for selection of the options used for the calculation are different. In CBOE procedure, the out-of-money options are first arranged according to the increase in strike price. All the individual options in the near term and next term out-of-money options are selected as long as two options next to each other do not have zero price at the same time. However, in our analysis, we observe that some of the options selected are not actively traded and therefore their price may not reflect the expectation of the current market conditions. In the quadrinomial tree method, we select all the options (regardless of being out-of-money or not) as long as they reflect the market volatility. This is ensured by selecting all options with volume higher than 0.
3. In the CBOE procedure, eight days before the maturity of the near term options chain, CBOE will roll over to the next/third options chains. The argument is that when the options are close to maturity, their price is more volatile and thus cannot represent the market volatility. However, it is also well known that options with larger maturities tends to have volatility close to the long term market mean volatility and this can lead to underestimating

the market volatility. In the quadrinomial tree method, we use all the data of near term and next term options chains.

4. In this work, we use all relevant options weighted accordingly. In theory all options with different maturities may be incorporated as they reflect the market volatility. Only the near term and next term options chains are used in this work, as from empirical studies including options with longer maturities have associated little weight and they do not generally influence the final result.

5.3 Results and Discussions

5.3.1 CONSTRUCTING A VOLATILITY INDEX USING DIFFERENT INPUTS

Options written on S&P500 have three near term expiration months followed by three additional expiration months from the March quarterly cycle. We note that for the VIX calculation by CBOE, the closest near term options chain and the next term options chain are used. Also, when the maturity of the near term options is less than eight days, next term options and the ones after will be used in the calculation. For the quadrinomial tree model, we explore the effects of using different option types and maturity on the resulting VIX. In the next figures, we compare constructed indices using five different ways.

1. First, we consider only call options with the near term maturity and we obtain an index we denote cVIX-1. Figure 5.1a presents this index versus the CBOE VIX. It is evident that when only the near term options are used, the cVIX-1 is very unstable. When options are very close to maturity, they become more volatile and overestimate the true market volatility. This is the reason why CBOE avoids using options with maturity less than eight days.
2. Next we calculate cVIX-2, which uses only the next term call options chain (the maturity is larger than one month but less than two months). cVIX-2 is represented by the dotted line in Fig. 5.1b. It appears that cVIX-2 has a similar pattern as that of the CBOE VIX. However, the value of cVIX-2 is generally smaller than that of VIX index. As we shall see this is due to the fact that we only use data from call options in this calculation.
3. In the third method, we use data from both call options chains (call options with the near term and next term maturities). However, the importance of data from these two options chains is different. The significance of each options chain is evaluated by a linear relationship depending on which maturity is closer to day 30. This is ensured by setting the probability of using the near term option data as:

$$p_{\text{near term}} = (30 - T_1)/(T_2 - T_1), \tag{5.5}$$

where T_1 is the maturity of the near term options in days, and T_2 is the maturity of next term options in days. The probability of the next term values is $p_{\text{next term}} = 1 - p_{\text{near term}}$.

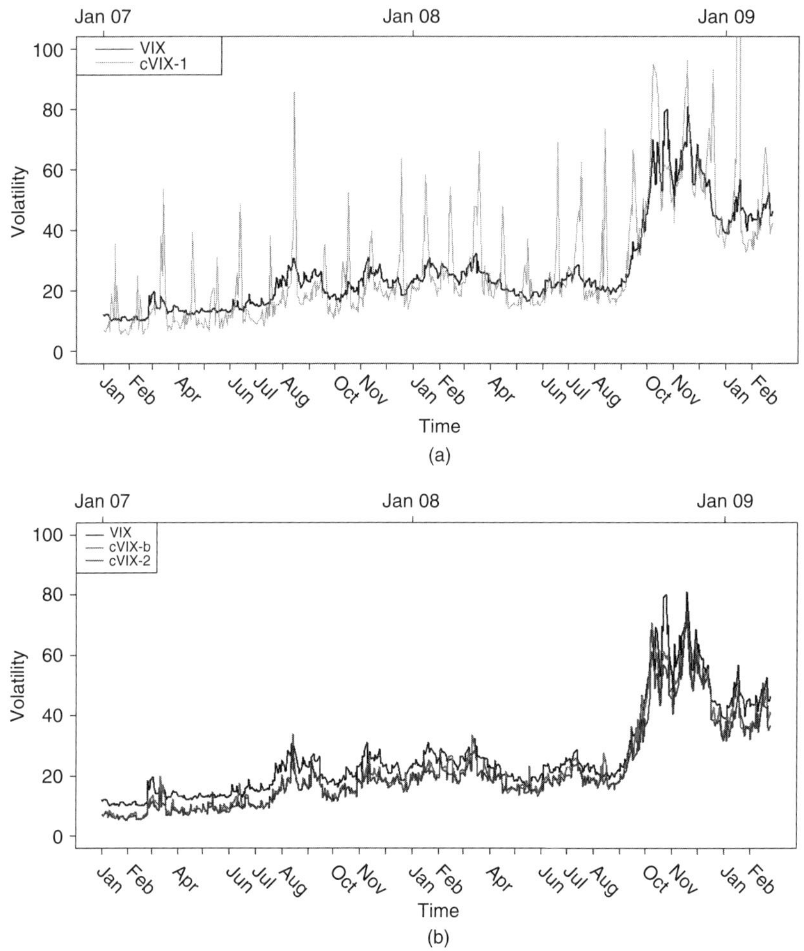

FIGURE 5.1 **Comparison of VIX constructed using different methods: (a) cVIX-1 which is computed from actively traded call options with the nearest maturity; (b) cVIX-2 (computed from actively traded call options with more than one month but less than two-month maturity) and cVIX-b (constructed using call options with less than two-month maturity).**

The index obtained by this method is denoted with cVIX-b and is shown in Fig. 5.1b by the gray line. We note that the cVIX-b has a similar pattern as the CBOE VIX. Similarly with the cVIX-2, the values are generally lower than the VIX. When comparing cVIX-b to cVIX-2, due to the effect of incorporation more volatile data, occasionally cVIX-b has higher value than cVIX-2, especially when there is a spike in the VIX value.

4. As previously observed using only call options (cVIX-b or cVIX-2) tends to produce smaller values than the VIX. Thus, we next use only data coming from the put options. The computed pVIX-b uses both near term and next option with linear weight ratio, and is plotted in Fig. 5.2. The figure clearly

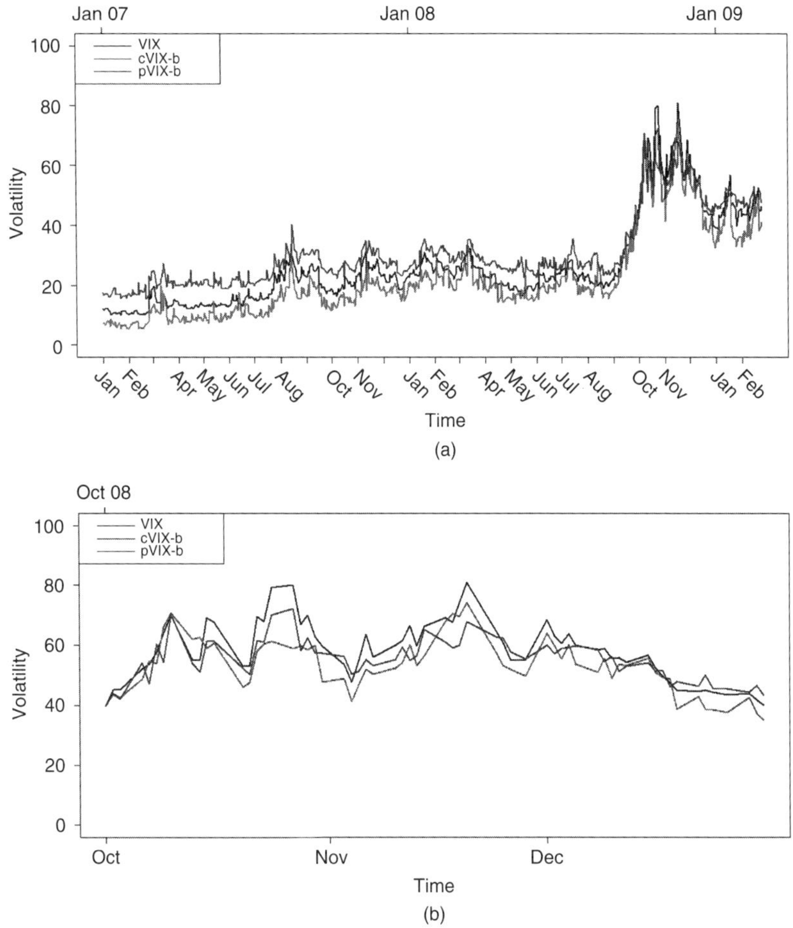

FIGURE 5.2 **Comparison between constructed VIX using call options and put options for period: (a) January 2007 to February 2009; and (b) October 2008 to December 2008.**

shows that the CBOE VIX values tend to be between the cVIX-b and the pVIX-b.

5. Since the third and fourth methods produce indices that are bounding the CBOE VIX, we next are using both call options and put options. During the construction, since the number of call and put options are different, we set the probability of using the call data or put data proportional to their numbers. The probability of using near term options is determined by the same Equation 5.5. The result, which is named as VIX′, is shown in Fig. 5.3a along with VIX. We also plot the arithmetic average of cVIX-b and pVIX-b (cpVIX). For clarity in Fig. 5.3b we plot the differences between these indices. With the exception of the crash period the differences are consistent.

In Table 5.1, we summarize all the indices constructed.

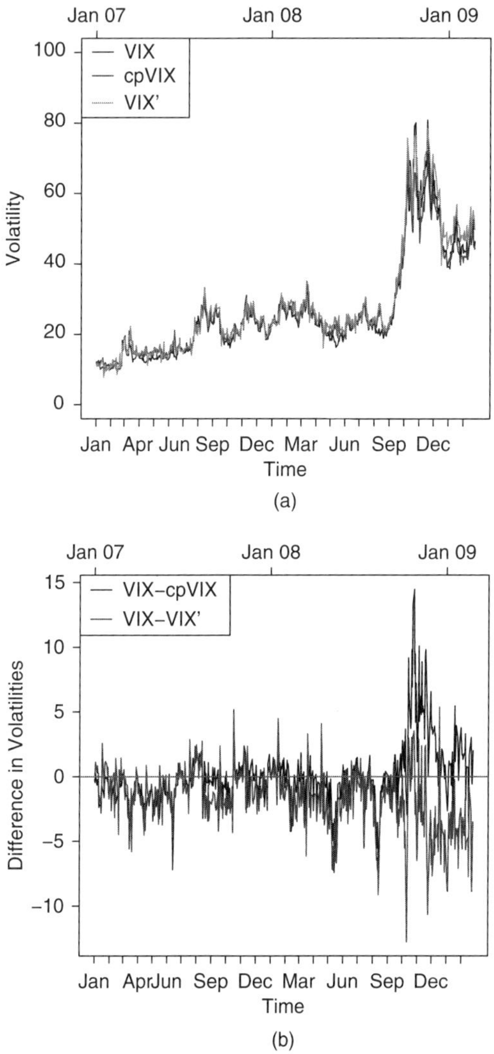

FIGURE 5.3 Comparison among VIX, cpVIX, and VIX′. (a) Plot of the actual indices and (b) differences. End of 2009 shows higher VIX′ than VIX value.

TABLE 5.1 **The Names of Constructed VIX and Data Used**

Type of Constructed VIX	Data Used
cVIX-1	Near term call options
cVIX-2	Next term call options
cVIX-b	Both near and next term call options
pVIX-b	Both near and next term put options
cpVIX	Average of cVIX-b and pVIX-b
VIX′	Both near and next term call and put options

5.3.2 CONVERGENCE OF THE METHOD USED IN THE CONSTRUCTION OF INDICES

We study the convergence of the results obtained using the quadrinomial tree method when computing various indices. We use different number of steps in the tree (10, 50, and 100 steps) as well as different number of trees (10, 50, and 200 times). This is exemplified using the cVIX-b calculation. To avoid image clutter, we only show a reduced number of results in Fig. 5.4. The index converges as the trees becomes larger. This is in agreement with the theoretical results from Florescu abd Viens (2008).

5.3.3 COMPARISON BETWEEN CONSTRUCTED VIX USING CALL AND PUT OPTIONS CHAINS

In the calculation of VIX, CBOE uses the out-of-money call and out-of-money put options. As detailed in the description, we may use any type of options and produce various types of indices. In this section, we analyze the resulting indices separately using call options and put options. Figure 5.2a, presents the cVIX-b (using calls) and pVIX-b using puts in comparison to the VIX. Generally, the cVIX-b has lower values than the VIX, while the pVIX-b has higher values than the CBOE index. This is perhaps best explained by Bollen and Whaley (2004), who remark that the index option market such as S&P500 became dominated by portfolio insurers or hedgers, who routinely buy out-of-the-money and at-the-money SPX put options for insurance purposes. This drives up the price of put options and therefore the implied volatilities from put options tends to be higher. This leads to the differences between the constructed VIX using call options and put options.

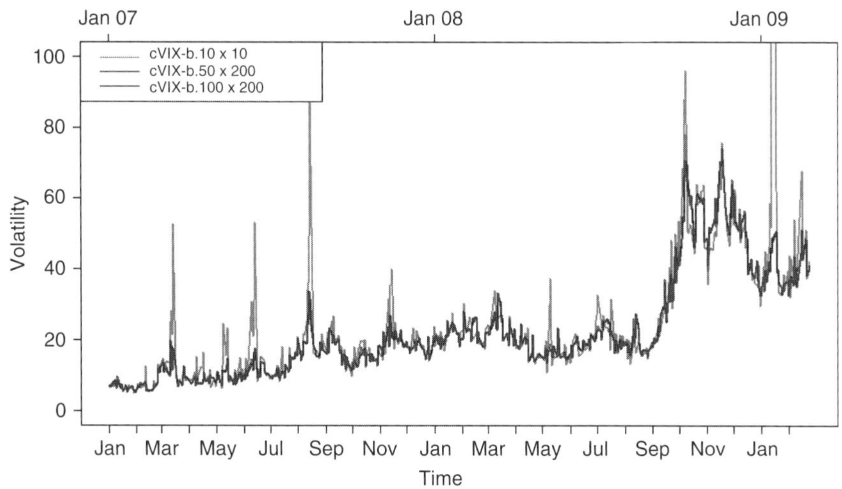

FIGURE 5.4 Convergence of constructed volatility index using quadrinomial tree method.

In Fig. 5.2b, we zoom into turbulent financial time between October and December 2008. It is clear that during this period, the VIX is generally the higher than either cVIX or pVIX. This seem to indicate us that during this period the demand for put options seems to be extraordinary. We should also note that during this period of time, the market was very volatile and the observed VIX index went as high as 80. Furthermore, when looking at the difference between the call based index (cVIX-b) and the put based index (pVIX-b) the spread between these volatilities was the smallest for this particular period. In Fig. 5.5, we showcase this feature and we observe that the spread becomes negative before the market crash and stays negative for an extended period during the crash.

5.3.4 A COMPARISON OF THE CORRELATION BETWEEN THE CONSTRUCTED INDICES/S&P500 AND VIX/S&P500

It is well documented that a negative relationship exists between the index S&P500 and the CBOE VIX; when the S&P500 index goes up/down, VIX tends to go down/up. In Table 5.2, we present the R^2 of the linear relationship between S&P500 and various indices. The data does not show major differences between these correlations.

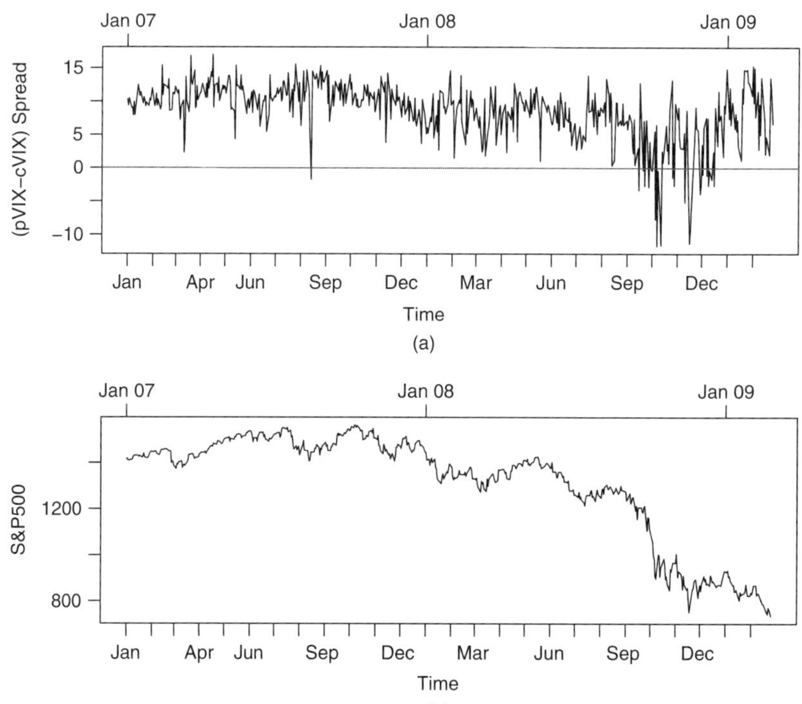

FIGURE 5.5 The difference (spread) pVIX′cVIX. A decrease in spread seems to indicate a decrease in the market index.

TABLE 5.2 The Correlation Between Constructed VIX and VIX to S&P500

S&P500	VIX	cVIX-2	cVIX-b	pVIX-2	pVIX-b	cpVIX-b	cpVIX-2
R^2	0.7818	0.7944	0.7805	0.7875	0.7912	0.8004	0.8030

5.3.5 AN ANALYSIS OF THE PREDICTIVE POWER OF THE DIFFERENT INDICES

In this section, we analyze the relationship between the volatility and the return of the S&P500. Specifically, we are interested in determining whether a significant increase in the volatility is followed by a significant drop in the S&P500 prices and to determine which VIX variant proves to be a better predictor of this relationship. We analyze the same day observations as well as one day forecast. Furthermore, we investigate the relationship for a selection of observations centered around major financial events as presented in Table 5.3. We consider the VIX from CBOE and the following index variants: cpVIX, VIX′, cVIX-b, and pVIX-b.

TABLE 5.3 Important Events That Happened During January 2007 to February 2009 Period

Central banks increase money supply	August 10, 2007
Countywide job slashes	September 7, 2007
Bush calls for economic stimulus package	January 18, 2008
Central European banks plan emergency cash infusion	March 11, 2008
Bear Stearns gets emergency funds	March 14, 2008
J.P. Morgan to acquire Bear Stearns	March 16, 2008
Federal Reserve cuts rates by 0.75	March 18, 2008
IMF may sell 400 tons of gold	April 8, 2008
Citigroup anticipates a giant loss, Fed cuts rate again	April 30, 2008
US backs lending firms	July 13, 2008
US inflation at 26-year high	July 16, 2008
Mortgage firms bail out	September 7, 2008
Lehman Brothers files for bankruptcy	September 14, 2008
Bush hails the financial rescue plan	September 19, 2008
$700 billion package failed	September 29, 2008
House backs the bail-out plan	October 3, 2008
Plans to buy 125 billion stakes in banks	October 14–29, 2008
Citigroup cuts 75,000 jobs	November 17, 2008
Citigroup gets US Treasury lifeline	November 23, 2008
800 billion stimulus package announced	November 25, 2008
Bank of America cuts 30,000 jobs	December 11, 2008
Madoff 50 billion scandal	December 13, 2008
Auto industry bail-out	December 19, 2009
US financial sector stocks decline sharply	January 20, 2009
New bank bail-out	February 10, 2009

For each of these variants, we calculate the rate of change and we estimate the conditional probability that S&P500 is moving in the opposite direction.

$$Prob(\text{Return}_{\text{S\&P500}} < 0 \mid (\text{Return}_{\text{Vol Index}} > L, \text{lag} = d)), \text{ and} \qquad (5.6)$$
$$Prob(\text{Return}_{\text{S\&P500}} > 0 \mid (\text{Return}_{\text{Vol Index}} < L, \text{lag} = d)),$$

where $\text{Return}_{\text{S\&P500}}$ is the return of S&P500, $\text{Return}_{\text{Vol Index}}$ is the return of the particular VIX, L is a threshold for the index return, and d represents the same day for $d = 0$, and the previous day for $d = 1$.

The graphs presented are grouped in two sections corresponding to the same day $d = 0$ or the forecast for the next day $d = 1$. On all of these graphs the x-axis plots the respective threshold that conditions the probabilities in Equation 5.6, while the y-axis plots the percent of days where the S&P500 moved in the predicted direction. The left image in a figure presents all the dataset, while the right image is restricted to the important financial events detailed in Table 5.3.

We analyze separately the positive and negative movement in Figs. 5.6 and 5.7. It is pretty clear from these images that the CBOE VIX is the best indicator for the return/volatility evolution within the same day ($d = 0$). The profile of the probability curves for the major events selection follows a similar profile to the probability curves for all data analyzed. However, the fact that an increase in the VIX calculated from the calls indicates a drop in the S&P500 index was a surprise to us.

For prediction purposes, we analyze the relationship between the previous day VIX and the return on the S&P500 the following day. The corresponding graphs once again split by the positive and negative thresholds are presented in Figs. 5.8 and 5.9, respectively.

This time we observe that the CBOE VIX is one of the worst indicators for future day evolution of the S&P500. In some cases the probability of predicting a positive return correctly is well below 50%.

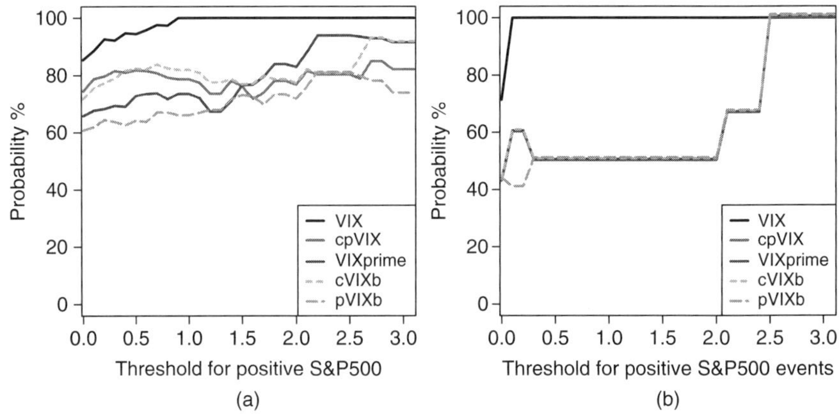

FIGURE 5.6 Probability of a positive return on S&P500 when $d = 0$.

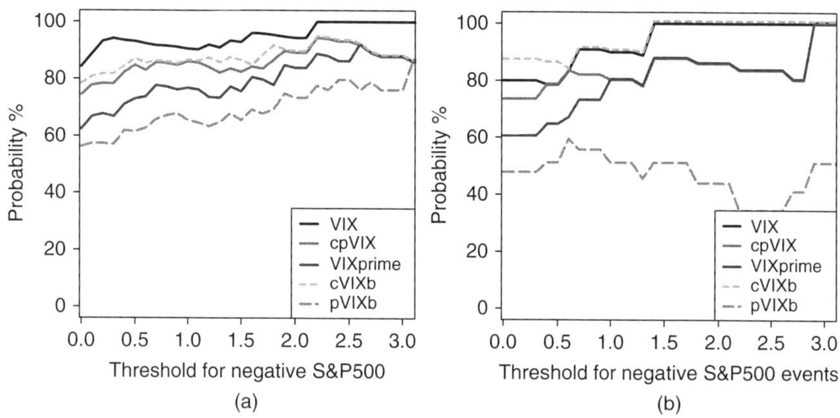

FIGURE 5.7 Probability of a negative return on S&P500 when $d = 0$.

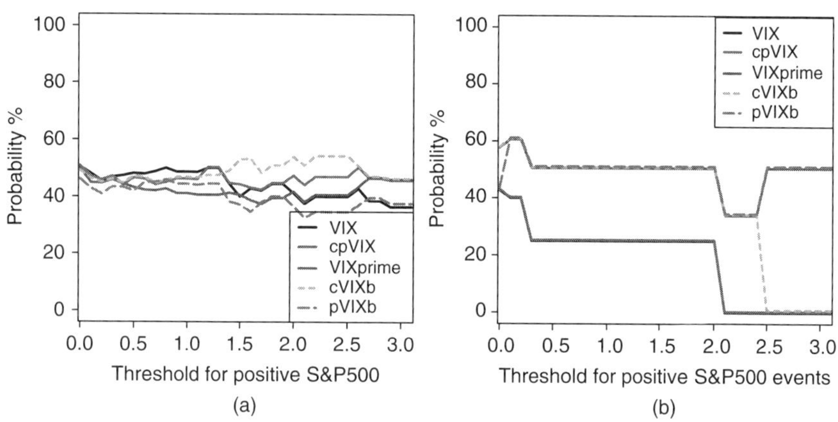

FIGURE 5.8 Probability of a positive return on S&P500 when $d = 1$.

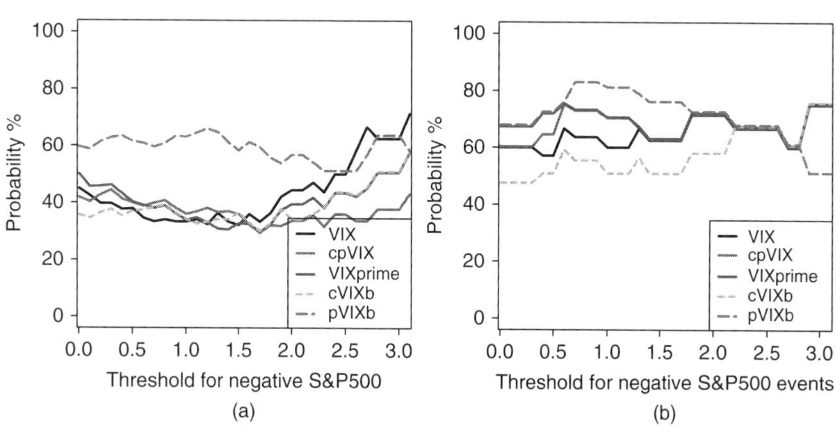

FIGURE 5.9 Probability of a negative return on S&P500 when $d = 1$.

In contrast, two of the indices that we calculated stand out. We note that a drop in the cVIX-b (calculated from call options) forecasts with the highest probability a positive return of the S&P500. Furthermore, an increase in the pVIX-b (calculated from the put options) has a clear advantage in forecasting second day negative S&P500 returns. The probabilities for the pVIX-b are in fact very high for all data sample and also for the major events in the market considered in this analysis.

We hope that we convinced the reader that using different types of options in the VIX calculation has the potential to reveal more information about the market than the VIX.

5.4 Summary and Conclusion

We propose a new methodology of calculating a value that represents the market volatility at a given moment in time by implementing a stochastic volatility technique. We believe this technique is a viable way to produce a market index. We propose several variants of such indices and we believe each of them is valuable as an indicator of a market movement. The index constructed from calls (cVIX-b) may be considered as an indicator of market's positive movement while the index constructed from put options (pVIX-b) as an indicator of future negative movement in the market. The difference (spread) between the two indices may be indicative of future market movement. The average of these two indices (cpVIX) and the index constructed with all options (VIX′) both have value in determining when the VIX undervalues or overvalues the market volatility.

Finally, we analyze the relations between all these types of indices. We believe all of them bring more information about the market and the methodology has the potential to produce market indicators each indicative of a certain aspect of the financial market.

Appendix A.1: Step-by-Step Explanation of the CBOE Procedure for Calculating VIX Index

Using data obtained at the market close on September 8, 2009, we replicate the VIX value following the CBOE procedure. First, we need to do some calculation and rearrangement of the data. The procedure is described below.

1. *Selection of Options Chains.* VIX generally uses put and call options in the two nearest-term expiration months while there are more options chains trading in the market. Also, it should be pointed out that, with eight days left to expiration, the VIX "rolls" to the second and third contract months in order to minimize the pricing anomalies that might occur close to the maturity.

2. T, the time to expiration, is measured in minutes rather than in days. Specifically, the calculation of T is given by the following expression:

$$T = \{M_{\text{currentday}} + M_{\text{settlementday}} + M_{\text{otherdays}}\}/M_{\text{year}}, \tag{5.7}$$

where $M_{\text{currentday}}$ is the number of minutes remaining until midnight of the current day, $M_{\text{settlementday}}$ is the number of minutes from midnight until 8:30 a.m. on SPX settlement day, and $M_{\text{otherdays}}$ is the number of minutes in all the days between current day and the settlement day, and M_{year} is the number of minutes in a year.

3. Calculating the at-the-money strike. This is done by finding the strike price at which the difference between the call and put prices is the smallest.
4. Calculation of F, the forward index level. This is based on the previously determined at-the-money option prices and the corresponding strike price:

$$F = \text{Strikeprice} + e^{rT}(\text{Call price} - \text{Put price}) \tag{5.8}$$

Note that since two options chains are used in the calculation, two forward index level should be obtained, for the near term and next term options chains.

5. Selection of K_0, the strike price immediately below the forward index level, F.

In the following, we demonstrate how to obtain the VIX value using CBOE procedure using data obtained when the S&500 options stopped trading at 3:15 p.m. (Middle time) on September 8, 2009.

Step 1. Calculate the time to expiration T, forward index level F, K_0, the strike price immediately below F, and data arrangement:

$$\begin{aligned}
T_1 &= \{M_{\text{currentday}} + M_{\text{settlementday}} + M_{\text{otherdays}}\}/M_{\text{year}} \\
&= (525 + 510 + 12{,}960)/525{,}600 \\
&= 0.026626712 \\
T_2 &= \{M_{\text{currentday}} + M_{\text{settlementday}} + M_{\text{otherdays}}\}/M_{\text{year}} \\
&= (525 + 510 + 53{,}280)/525{,}600 \\
&= 0.103339041
\end{aligned}$$

We should note that the total days in a year is 365 days. Since the smallest difference between call and put price is at strike \$1025, the at-the-money strike is determined to be at \$1025 for both near term options and next term options. Therefore, using federal funds effective rate at 0.15%, the forward index level F_1 for the near term options and forward index level F_2 for the next term options are

$$F_1 = \text{Strike price} + e^{rT_1}(\text{Call price} - \text{Put price})$$
$$= 1025 + e^{0.0015\times 0.026626712}(13.25 - 13.9) = 1024.35$$
$$F_2 = \text{Strike price} + e^{rT_2}(\text{Call price} - \text{Put price})$$
$$= 1025 + e^{0.0015\times 0.103339041}(29.15 - 30.35) = 1023.80$$

We also obtain K_0, the strike price immediately below F, which is \$1020 for both expirations. Then we select call and put options that have strike prices greater and smaller, respectively, than K_0 (it is 1020 here) and nonzero bid price. After encountering two consecutive options with a bid price of zero, do not select any other option. Note that the prices of the options are calculated using the mid-point of the bid-ask spread. At K_0, the average of call and put price is used. The data selected is summarized below:

- Calculation of time to maturity:
  $T_1 = 0.026626712$
  $T_2 = 0.103339041$
- At-the-money strike: \$1025 for both near term options and next term options.
- Federal funds effective rate: 0.15%.
- The forward index level F_1 for the near term options and forward index level F_2 for the next term options are
  $F_1 = 1024.35$
  $F_2 = 1023.80$
- K_0, the strike price immediately below F, is \$1020 for both expirations.

Step 2. Calculate the volatility for near term and next term options. We apply the following equations to calculate the VIX to the near term and next term options:

$$\sigma_1^2 = \frac{2}{T_1}\sum_i \frac{\Delta K_i}{K_i^2} e^{rT_1} Q(T_1, K_i) - \frac{1}{T_1}\left(\frac{F_1}{K_0} - 1\right)^2, \tag{5.9}$$

$$\sigma_2^2 = \frac{2}{T_2}\sum_i \frac{\Delta K_i}{K_i^2} e^{rT_2} Q(T_2, K_i) - \frac{1}{T_2}\left(\frac{F_2}{K_0} - 1\right)^2. \tag{5.10}$$

We need to pay attention to value of ΔK_i. Generally, ΔK_i is half the distance between the strike on either side of K_i, but at the upper and lower ends of any options chain, ΔK_i is simply the distance between K_i and the adjacent strike price.
We obtain: $\sigma_1^2 = 0.055576664$ and $\sigma_2^2 = 0.066630428$.

Step 3. Interpolate σ_1^2 and σ_2^2 to get a single value with a constant maturity of 30 days. VIX is 100 times of the square root of this value.

$$\sigma^2 = \left\{ T_1\sigma_1^2 \frac{N_{T_2} - N_{30}}{N_{T_2} - N_{T_1}} + T_2\sigma_2^2 \frac{N_{30} - N_{T_1}}{N_{T_2} - N_{T_1}} \right\} \frac{N_{365}}{N_{30}}, \tag{5.11}$$

where

N_{T_1} is the maturity of the near term options in minutes (13,995),
N_{T_2} is the maturity of the next term options in minutes (54,315),
N_{T_2} is the maturity of a 30-day options in minutes (43,200),
N_{365} is the number of minutes in a year (525,600).

Therefore, the $VIX = 100 \times \sigma = 25.62$, which is exactly the same value as the one provided by CBOE.

Appendix B.1: Explanation of the New Volatility Index Calculation

The following gives details about the quadrinomial tree approximation and the new volatility estimation. In Fig. 5.10, we present a one-step construction. Assume that we are given an (empirical or theoretical) distribution for the stochastic volatility process at the time t when pricing is done. Sample from this volatility distribution to obtain the value φ. Given this value, we construct a grid of points of the form $l\varphi\sqrt{\Delta t}$ with l taking integer values. No matter where the parent x is, it will fall at one such point or between two grid points. In this grid, let j be the integer that corresponds to the point right above x. Mathematically, j is the integer equal to the integer part of $\frac{x}{\varphi\sqrt{\Delta t}} + 1$, as $x_3 < x < x_2$. We will have

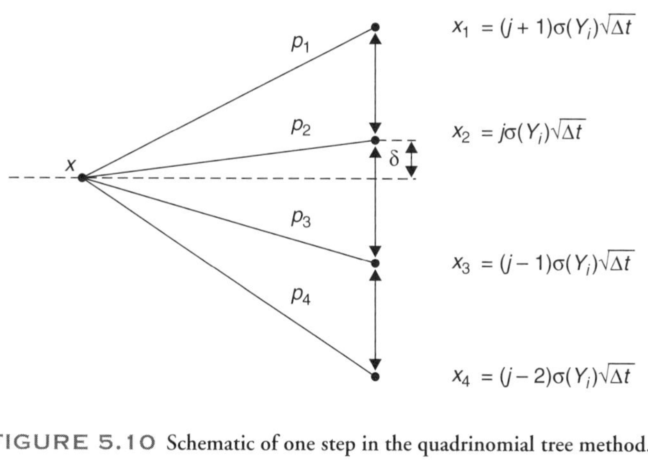

FIGURE 5.10 Schematic of one step in the quadrinomial tree method.

two possible cases: either the point $j\varphi\sqrt{\Delta t}$ on the grid corresponding to j (above) is closer to x, or the point $(j-1)\varphi\sqrt{\Delta t}$ corresponding to $j-1$ (below) is closer. We use δ to denote the distance from the parent x and the closest successor on the grid. We use q to denote the standardized value, that is,

$$q := \frac{\delta}{\varphi\sqrt{\Delta t}}. \tag{5.12}$$

There are two cases: first when x_2 is closer to x and the second when x_3 is closer to x. In the first case by considering the mean of the increment converging to the drift of the process X_t, the probabilities corresponding to each of the points on the grid can be calculated as

$$\begin{aligned} p_1 &= \frac{1}{2}(1+q+q^2) - p \\ p_2 &= 3p - q^2 \\ p_3 &= \frac{1}{2}(1-q+q^2) - 3p \\ p_4 &= p \end{aligned} \tag{5.13}$$

In the second case, when x_3 is closer to x the probabilities are

$$\begin{aligned} p_1 &= p \\ p_2 &= \frac{1}{2}(1+q+q^2) - 3p \\ p_3 &= 3p - q^2 \\ p_4 &= \frac{1}{2}(1-q+q^2) - p \end{aligned} \tag{5.14}$$

where $p \in [\frac{1}{12}, \frac{1}{6}]$. It is observed that when p is close to $\frac{1}{6}$, the option values obtained are stable even with few replications (Fig. 5.4 in Florescu and Viens (2008)). In this chapter, we set $p = 0.135$ throughout the algorithm.

APPENDIX B.2: STEP-BY-STEP EXPLANATION OF THE CONSTRUCTION OF VIX USING STOCHASTIC VOLATILITY QUADRINOMIAL TREE METHOD

Here we use quadrinomial tree model to compute the price of a synthetic options with exact 30 days maturity using distribution of implied volatility obtained from S&P500 as input. Then by Black and Scholes (1973) formula, we obtain the implied volatility of this synthetic option. We want to study whether or not this implied volatility multiplied with 100 can better reflect the market volatility.

There are four steps in the construction of this VIX as follows:

- Compute the implied volatilities of entire option chain on SP500 and construct an estimate for the distribution of current market volatility. The implied volatility is calculated by applying Black–Scholes formula.
- Use this estimated distribution as input to the quadrinomial tree method. Obtain the price of an at-the-money synthetic option with exactly 30-day maturity.
- Compute the implied volatility of the synthetic option based on Black–Scholes formula once the 30-day synthetic option is priced.
- Obtain the estimated VIX by multiplying the implied volatility of the synthetic option by 100.

Please note that the most important step in the estimation is the choice of proxy for the current stochastic volatility distribution.

REFERENCES

Black F, Scholes M. The valuation of options and corporate liability. J Polit Econ 1973;81:637–654.

Bollen N, Whaley R. Does net buying pressure affect the shape of implied volatility functions? J Finance 2004;59(2):711–753.

CBOE. The new CBOE volatility index-vix. White papers, CBOE; 2003, http://www.cboe.com/micro/vix/vixwhite.pdf.

Demeterfi K, Derman E, Kamal M, Zou J. More than you ever wanted to know about volatility swaps. Technical report, Goldman Sachs Quantitative Strategies Research Notes; 1999, http://www.ederman.com/new/docs/gs-volatility_swaps.pdf.

Florescu I, Viens F. Stochastic volatility: option pricing using a multinomial recombining tree. Appl Math Finance J 2008;15:151–181.

Jiang GJ, Tian YS. Extracting model-free volatility from option prices: an examination of the VIX index. J Deriv 2007;14(3):35–60.

PART TWO

Long Range Dependence Models

CHAPTER SIX

Long Correlations Applied to the Study of Memory Effects in High Frequency (Tick) Data, the Dow Jones Index, and International Indices

ERNEST BARANY
Department of Mathematical Sciences, New Mexico State University, Las Cruces, NM

MARIA PIA BECCAR VARELA
Department of Mathematical Sciences, University of Texas at El Paso, El Paso, TX

6.1 Introduction

In recent years, a growing concern is the presence of long-term memory effects in financial time series. The empirical characterization of stochastic processes usually requires the study of temporal correlations and the determination of asymptotic probability density function (pdfs). Major stock indices in developed countries have been previously analyzed in literature, see [1–11] and the references therein.

Handbook of Modeling High-Frequency Data in Finance, First Edition.
Edited by Frederi G. Viens, Maria C. Mariani, and Ionuţ Florescu.

The estimated statistical properties of the temporal time series have been of a great importance comparing the financial markets.

The first model that described the evolution of option prices was the Brownian motion. This model assumes that the increment of the logarithm of prices follows a diffusive process with Gaussian distribution [12]. However, the empirical study of temporal series of some of the most important indices shows that in short time intervals, the associated pdfs have greater kurtosis than a Gaussian distribution [5]. The first step to explain this behavior was done in 1963 by Mandelbrot [13]. He developed a model for the evolution of cotton prices by a stable stochastic non-Gaussian Levy process; these types of non-Gaussian processes were first introduced and studied by Levy [14]. The other major problem encountered in the analysis of the behavior of different time-series data is the existence of long-term or short-term correlations in the behavior of financial markets (established versus emerging markets [15], developed countries' market indices [1–5], Bombay stock exchange index [16], Latin American indices [17], and the references therein). Studies that focus on particular country indices [16–18] generally show that a long-term memory effect exists.

These problems may also be avoided considering a temporal evolution of financial markets described by a truncated Levy flight (TLF) [19] or by a standardized TLF, and this is the model used in this work. On the basis of our results we conclude that using the TLF model is an important and useful tool in the analysis of long-memory effects in time series. In many cases, TLF model fits the data very well. However, for a further clarification of the results the analysis should be complemented with the R/S and DFA (detrended fluctuation analysis) methods since in many cases these approaches bring new facts into the picture. Previous literature has concluded that the time series of financial indices are explained by the *TLF* model [17–19]. The Rescaled Range Analysis (R/S) and DFA methods are used to investigate long-range correlations. Previous work has shown that both methods are very powerful for characterizing fractional behavior [16–18, 20,21]. Since the exponents calculated can serve as verification and comparison of the results, both methods are used in this work.

To display the versatility of these models, we apply them to distinct sets of data. We analyze stock indices in developed and developing countries using daily data, and we also present an analysis of high frequency data.

One of the main interests in this work is to compare the international stock market indices with US market indices such as the S&P500. Specifically, this paper seeks to determine whether long-memory effects are present in well-diversified international market indices.

Long correlation behavior for a financial index along with the rate of return of all companies within the index is analyzed as well. We detect long-range correlations in the rate of return of the companies and briefly discuss some features specific to the equity in comparison to the conclusions obtained for the financial indices.

We also apply our methodology to high frequency data. Most of the previous studies that detected long-range correlations in financial indices concentrated on daily data. We wish to verify if the same conclusion applies to high frequency data. Following this line, we analyze a sample of 26 stocks of trade-by-trade (tick) data for a very typical day (April 10, 2007) devoid of any major events.

We found that all unit-root tests performed rejected the existence of a unit-root type nonstationarity. The p-values of the tests were all under 0.01. We use Rescaled Range Analysis (R/S) and DFA methods to determine long-range correlations. Both methods characterize fractional behavior, but R/S analysis can yield more accurate results for small and stationary data sets and DFA analysis yields more accurate result for nonstationary data sets. The exponents calculated are complementary and could serve as verification and comparison of the results; therefore, both methods are used.

We found evidence that even in an ordinary day without any notable information for about 75% of the market, the use of short-term memory models is inappropriate.

Specifically, in only 23% of the studied cases one of the tests performed did not reject the Gaussian hypothesis (no memory or very short-term memory). There were no stocks for which both tests performed agreed that the data may be Gaussian.

Finally, we study high frequency data corresponding to the Bear Stearns crash. On Friday, March 14, 2008, at about 9:14 a.m., JP Morgan Chase together with the Federal Reserve Bank of New York announced an emergency loan to Bear Stearns (about 29 billion, terms undisclosed) to prevent the firm from becoming insolvent. This bailout was declared to prevent the very likely crash of the market as a result of the fall of one of the biggest investment banks at the time. This measure proved to be insufficient for keeping the firm alive, and two days later, on Sunday March 16, 2008, Bear Stearns signed a merger agreement with JP Morgan Chase essentially selling the company for \$2 a share (price revised on March 24 to \$10/share). The same stock traded at \$172 in January 2007 and \$93 a share in February 2007. Today, this collapse is viewed as the first sign of the risk management meltdown of investment bank industry in September 2008 and the subsequent global financial crisis and recession.

In this chapter we are not concerned with the details and causes that lead to the demise of Bear Stearns. Instead, we have two major objectives in mind. First, we would like to know how soon an investor who was lacking insider information but had at his/her disposal all the information contained in the equity prices could have discovered that a crash is imminent and take the necessary precautions. Second, although the crisis was restricted to the financial companies, we wish to find out if it was a market-wide phenomenon and if its effects may be observed in the evolution of price of technology companies or food producers for example (which technically should not be affected by the crisis in the financial sector).

The premise we make in this study is a simple one. In the normal market conditions, all the participating agents have diverse views and accordingly the price process should not exhibit large long-term memory effects. Of course, even in normal market conditions, when working with high frequency data, the price process is far from the log-normal specification. On the other hand, when a crisis situation is anticipated all the agents start to behave in a similar way and accordingly the resulting price process starts to exhibit large memory effects. There is ample recent evidence for this fact, we only mention [8 and 9] and the references therein.

We estimate the Hurst parameter (H) as well as the Detrended Fluctuation parameter (α) and we compare with 0.5. The further these parameters are from

0.5 the stronger the evidence of a crash event waiting to happen. The reason why we estimate both parameters is that the alpha parameter works better with nonstationary data than H. On the other hand, when working with stationary data H is much more relevant. The estimation methodology is described below.

We conclude that stochastic volatility models, jump diffusion models, and general Levy processes seem to be needed for the modeling of high frequency data in any situation.

6.2 Methods Used for Data Analysis

In this section we give details about the methodology used in data analysis.

6.2.1 THE TRUNCATED LEVY FLIGHT

Levy [22] and Khintchine [23] solved the problem of the determination of the functional form that all the stable distributions must follow. They found that the most general representation is through the characteristic function $\varphi(q)$, by the following equation:

$$\ln(\varphi(q)) = \begin{cases} i\mu q - \gamma|q|^{\alpha}\left[1 - i\beta\dfrac{q}{|q|}\tan\left(\dfrac{\pi}{2}\alpha\right)\right] & (\alpha \neq 1) \\ i\mu q - \gamma|q|\left[1 + i\beta\dfrac{q}{|q|}\dfrac{2}{\pi}\ln|q|\right] & (\alpha = 1) \end{cases} \tag{6.1}$$

where $0 < \alpha \leq 2$, γ is a positive scale factor, μ is a real number, and β is an asymmetry parameter that takes values in the interval $[-1, 1]$.

The analytic form for a stable Levy distribution is known only in these cases:

$\alpha = 1/2, \beta = 1$, (Levy–Smirnov distribution),
$\alpha = 1, \beta = 0$ (Lorentz distribution),
$\alpha = 2$ (Gaussian distribution).

In this work, symmetric distributions ($\beta = 0$) with zero mean value ($\mu = 0$) are considered. In this case, the characteristic function takes the form:

$$\varphi(q) = \mathrm{e}^{-\gamma|q|^{\alpha}} \tag{6.2}$$

As the characteristic function of a distribution is its Fourier transform, the stable distribution of index α and scale factor γ is

$$P_{\mathrm{L}}(x) \equiv \frac{1}{\pi}\int_{0}^{\infty} \mathrm{e}^{-\gamma|q|^{\alpha}} \cos(qx)\,\mathrm{d}q \tag{6.3}$$

The asymptotic behavior of the distribution for large values of the absolute value of x is given by

$$P_L(|x|) \approx \frac{\gamma\Gamma(1+\alpha)\sin(\pi\alpha/2)}{\pi|x|^{1+\alpha}} \approx |x|^{-(1+\alpha)} \tag{6.4}$$

and the value in zero $P_L(x=0)$ by

$$P_L(x=0) = \frac{\Gamma(1/\alpha)}{\pi\alpha\gamma^{1/\alpha}} \tag{6.5}$$

The fact that the asymptotic behavior for huge values of x is a power law has as a consequence that the stable Levy processes have infinite variance. To avoid the problems arising in the infinite second moment, Mantegna and Stanley [19] considered a stochastic process with finite variance that follows scale relations called *TLF*. The *TLF* distribution is defined by

$$P(x) = \begin{cases} 0 & x > l \\ cP_L(\mathrm{x}) & -l < x < l \\ 0 & x < -l \end{cases} \tag{6.6}$$

where $P_L(x)$ is a symmetric Levy distribution and c is a normalization constant. The only stable distributions are the Levy distributions. The TLF distribution is not stable, but it has finite variance, thus independent variables from this distribution satisfy a regular central limit theorem. However, depending on the size of the parameter l (the cutoff length) the convergence may be very slow [15]. If the parameter l is small (so that the convergence is fast), the cut that it presents in its tails is very abrupt. In order to have continuous tails, Koponen [24] considered a TLF in which the cut function is a decreasing exponential characterized by a parameter l. The characteristic function of this distribution is defined as

$$\varphi(q) = \exp\left\{c_0 - c_1\frac{(q^2+1/l^2)^{\alpha/2}}{\cos(\pi\alpha/2)}\cos[\alpha\ \arctan(l|q|)]\right\} \tag{6.7}$$

with c_1 a scale factor and

$$c_0 \equiv \frac{l^{-\alpha}}{\cos(\pi\alpha/2)} \tag{6.8}$$

If one discretizes the time interval with steps Δt, it is found that $T = N\Delta t$. At the end of each interval one must calculate the sum of N stochastic variables that are independent and identically distributed. The new characteristic function will be

$$\varphi(q,N) = \exp\left\{c_0N - c_1\frac{N(q^2+1/l^2)^{\alpha/2}}{\cos(\pi\alpha/2)}\cos[\alpha\ \arctan(l|q|)]\right\} \tag{6.9}$$

For small values of N the return probability will be very similar to the stable Levy distribution:

$$P_L(x=0) = \frac{\Gamma(1/\alpha)}{\pi\alpha(\gamma N)^{1/\alpha}} \tag{6.10}$$

We note that an alternative way to deal with the convergence of the distribution to a Gaussian in the sense of central limit theorem is to use a scale-invariant truncated Lévy process (STL) as in [25]. This process uses correlated increments and exhibits Lévy type stability for the increments. We do not use this process in estimation.

Instead, we use in this work a standardized truncated Lévy flight model. There are two major advantages to standardize the TLF model. First, since it is accepted that the volatility of the return of a financial index is largely proportional to the time scale, normalization over variance allows us to directly compare the statistical properties under different time frames. Second, different markets usually have different risks. This is particularly true when one compares a well-developed market with an emerging market. Standardization essentially implements risk-adjustment, which allows us to compare the behaviors across both developed and emergent markets.

In Koponen's model the variance can be calculated from the characteristic function:

$$\sigma^2(t) = -\left.\frac{\partial^2\varphi(q)}{\partial q^2}\right|_{q=0} = t\left[\frac{2A\pi(1-\alpha)}{\Gamma(\alpha)\sin(\pi\alpha)}\right]l^{2-\alpha} \tag{6.11}$$

In order to standardize Koponen's model to describe the returns of the indices, given that

$$\sigma^2 = -\left.\frac{\partial^2\varphi(q)}{\partial q^2}\right|_{q=0} \tag{6.12}$$

It follows that

$$-\left.\frac{\partial^2\varphi(q/\sigma)}{\partial q^2}\right|_{q=0} = -\frac{1}{\sigma^2}\left.\frac{\partial^2\varphi(q)}{\partial q^2}\right|_{q=0} = 1 \tag{6.13}$$

Therefore, by performing a change of variable, a standardized model with characteristic function $\varphi_{SL}(q)$ and volatility 1 can be obtained as

$$\begin{aligned}\ln\varphi_{SL}(q) &= \ln\varphi\left(\frac{q}{\sigma}\right)\\ &= c_0 - c_1\frac{\left((q/\sigma)^2+1/l^2\right)^{\alpha/2}}{\cos(\pi\alpha/2)}\cos\left[\alpha\arctan\left(l\frac{|q|}{\sigma}\right)\right]\\ &= \frac{2\pi A l^{-\alpha}t}{\alpha\Gamma(\alpha)\sin(\pi\alpha)}\left(1-\left(\left(\frac{ql}{\sigma}\right)^2+1\right)^{\alpha/2}\cos\left(\alpha\arctan\left(\frac{ql}{\sigma}\right)\right)\right)\end{aligned} \tag{6.14}$$

This is the standardized Levy model that will be used for the numerical analysis.

To simulate the normalized truncated Levy model, a Matlab module was developed. The parameter l is fixed at 1, and then the parameter A and the characteristic exponent α are adjusted simultaneously in order to fit the cumulative function of the observed returns. On the same grid, the cumulative distribution of the observed and simulated returns are plotted for different time lags T in order to visualize how good the fitting is. Time lag $T = 1$ means the returns are calculated by using two consecutive observations; for a general T, the returns are calculated by using: $r_t = \log(X_t/X_{t-T})$.

The reader unfamiliar with the α-stable Levy processes (also called *Levy flight*) may wonder how they can have independent increments and yet be designated as long-memory processes. Indeed, this is the case for these processes because of the fact that the increments are heavy tailed. For a detailed discussion, please consult Chapter III in [27]. In fact, the parameter α of the Levy distribution is inversely proportional to the Hurst parameter. The Hurst parameter is an indicator of the memory effects coming from the fractional Brownian motion, which has correlated increments. Furthermore, the TLF maintains statistical properties that are indistinguishable from the Levy flights [15].

6.2.2 RESCALED RANGE ANALYSIS

Hurst [27] initially developed the Rescaled range analysis (R/S analysis). He observed many natural phenomena that followed a biased random walk, that is, every phenomenon showed a pattern. He measured the trend using an exponent now called the *Hurst exponent*. Mandelbrot [28,29] later introduced a generalized form of the Brownian motion model, the fractional Brownian motion to model the Hurst effect.

The numerical procedure to estimate the Hurst exponent H by using the R/S analysis is presented next (for more details, please see [27] and references therein).

1. Let N be the length of time series $(y_1, y_2, y_3, \ldots, y_N)$. The logarithmic ratio of the time series is obtained. The length of the new time series $M(t)$ will be $N - 1$.

$$M(t) = \log\left(\frac{y_{t+1}}{y_t}\right), t = 1, 2, \ldots, (N-1)$$

2. The time series is then divided into m subseries of length $n.n$ represents the number of elements in the series, and m represents the number of subseries. Thus $m \times n = N - 1$. Each subseries can be labeled as Q_a where $a = 1, 2, \ldots, m$ and each element in Q_a can be labeled as $L_{k,a}$ for $k = 1, 2, \ldots, n$.
3. For each Q_a, the average value is calculated:

$$Z_a = \frac{1}{n}\sum_{k=1}^{n} L_{k,a}$$

4. The cumulative deviation in each Q_a is calculated:

$$C_{k,a} = \sum_{j=1}^{k} (L_{j,a} - Z_a) k = 1, 2, \ldots, n$$

5. Thus the range of each subseries Q_a is given as

$$R(Q_a) = \max(C_{k,a}) - \min(C_{k,a})$$

6. The standard deviation of each subseries Q_a is calculated:

$$S(Q_a) = \sqrt{\left(\frac{1}{n}\right) \sum_{j=1}^{n} (L_{j,a} - Z_a)^2}$$

7. Each subseries is normalized by dividing the range, $R(Q_a)$ by the standard deviation, $S(Q_a)$. The average value of R/S for subseries of length n is obtained by

$$\left(\frac{R}{S}\right)_n = \frac{1}{m} \sum_{a=1}^{m} \frac{R(Q_a)}{S(Q_a)}$$

8. Steps 2 through 7 are repeated for all possible values of n, thus obtaining the corresponding R/S values for each n.
   The relationship between length of the subseries, n and the rescaled range R/S is

$$\frac{R}{S} = (c * n)^H$$

   where R/S is the rescaled range, n is the length of the subseries of the time series, and H is the Hurst exponent. Taking logarithms yields

$$\log\left(\frac{R}{S}\right) = H \log n + H \log c$$

9. An ordinary least squares regression is performed using $\log(R/S)$ as a dependent variable and $\log(n)$ as an independent variable. The slope of the equation is the estimate of the Hurst exponent, H.

If the Hurst exponent H for the investigated time series is 0.5, then it implies that the time series follows a random walk, which is a process with independent increments. For data series with long-memory effects, H would lie between 0.5 and 1. It suggests all the elements of the observation are dependent. This means that what happens now would have an impact on the future. Time series that exhibit this property are called *persistent time series*, and this character enables prediction of any time series as it shows a trend. If H lies between 0 and 0.5, it implies that the time-series possess antipersistent behavior (negative autocorrelation).

6.2.3 DETRENDED FLUCTUATION ANALYSIS

The DFA method is an important technique in revealing long-range correlations in nonstationary time series. This method was developed by Peng [20,21] and has been successfully applied to the study of cloud breaking [30], Latin–American market indices [17], DNA [21,31,32], cardiac dynamics [20,33], climatic studies [34,35], solid state physics [36,37], and economic time series [38–40]. The advantages of DFA over conventional methods are that it permits the detection of intrinsic self-similarity embedded in a seemingly nonstationary time series, and also avoids the spurious detection of apparent self-similarity, which may be an artifact of extrinsic trends.

First, the absolute value of $M(t)$, that is, the logarithmic returns of the indices calculated in the R/S analysis, is integrated:

$$y(t) = \sum_{i}^{t} |M(i)|$$

Then the integrated time series of length N is divided into m boxes of equal length n with no intersection between them. As the data is divided into equal-length intervals, there may be some left over at the end. In order to take account of these leftover values, the same procedure is repeated but beginning from the end, obtaining $2N/n$ boxes. Then, a least squares line is fitted to each box, representing the trend in each box, thus obtaining $(y_n(t))$. Finally the root mean square fluctuation is calculated using the formula:

$$F(n) = \sqrt{\frac{1}{2N} \sum_{t=1}^{2N} \left[y(t) - y_n(t)\right]^2}$$

This computation is repeated over all box sizes to characterize a relationship between the box size n and $F(n)$. A linear relationship between the $F(n)$ and n (i.e., box size) in a log–log plot reveals that the fluctuations can be characterized by a scaling exponent (α), the slope of the line relating log $F(n)$ to log n.

For data series with no correlations or short-range correlation, α is expected to be 0.5. For data series with long-range power law correlations, α would lie between 0.5 and 1 and for power law anticorrelations; α would lie between 0 and 0.5. This method was used to measure correlations in financial series of high frequencies and in the daily evolution of some of the most relevant indices.

6.2.4 STATIONARITY AND UNIT-ROOT TEST

In order to study the fractional behavior of a times series using the R/S or the DFA analysis, it is important to investigate whether the underlying time series is stationary or not. The first method is more adequate when analyzing stationary data sets, whereas the second one is more adequate for nonstationary data sets. Assume that $\{y_t\}$ is an univariate stochastic autoregressive process of order p (AR(p)); that is, $\{y_t\}$ obeys the equation

$$y_t = a_0 + a_1 y_{t-1} + a_2 y_{t-2} + \cdots + a_p y_{t-p} + \varepsilon_t$$

where $\varepsilon_t \sim$ iid mean 0, constant variance σ^2).

We define the roots of the AR(p) process as the solutions to the characteristic polynomial

$$z^p - a_1 z^{p-1} - a_2 z^{p-2} - \cdots - a_p$$

The AR(p) process is said to be stationary if all its roots are greater than one in modulus. In this case shocks into the system will dissipate over time. However, if the AR(p) process has a unit-root, it is said to be unit-root nonstationary; then the effect of shocks dies out at a much slower rate.

6.3 Data

We first studied the behavior of international market indices: iShares MSCI EAFE Index and the iShares MSCI Emerging Markets Index. We mention a previous study of long-memory behavior in some Eastern European economies transitioning to EU [41].

6.3.1 MSCI EAFE

The MSCI EAFE is a stock index of foreign stocks maintained by Morgan Stanley Capital International. The index includes stocks from 21 developed countries excluding United States and Canada; it is considered as one of the most prominent foreign stock funds benchmark.

6.3.2 MSCI EMERGING MARKETS INDEX

The MSCI Emerging Markets Index is a market capitalization index that measures the equity market performance in global emerging markets. It is maintained by Morgan Stanley Capital International.

Daily closing values of these indices are considered for this study: iShares MSCI EAFE Index (EFA), from August 27, 2001 to May 1, 2009 (1930 data points), and the iShares MSCI Emerging Markets Index (EEM), from April 15, 2003 to May 1, 2009 (1523 data points). We also used the data of the S&P500, the New York Stock Exchange index from August 27, 2001 to May 1, 2007 (1930 data points).

6.3.3 DOW JONES INDEX

We studied the behavior of stock prices comprising the Dow Jones industrial average (DJIA) with the index itself. Dow Jones Index is selected for this analysis because of its importance and also because of the fact that it is widely quoted index over other financial stock market indices. We studied the behavior of all the 30 stocks of the DJIA index from January 2, 1985 to June 30, 2010. In order to check the time-series stationarity, we performed two of the most well known unit-root tests: the augmented Dickey–Fuller (ADF) and the Phillips–Peron (PP) tests. For both tests, the null hypothesis is the presence of a unit-root and failing to reject the null hypothesis is equivalent to failing to reject the nonstationarity of the time series. The test is done using the tseries package in R.

We chose to apply the DFA and R/S analysis to individual companies to compare them with the behavior of the indices.

6.3.4 HIGH FREQUENCY DATA FROM A TYPICAL DAY

We study high frequency data for 26 stocks traded on NYSE during April 10, 2007. We chose this particular day since we want to study the typical behavior of the equity data, during a day when there are no major events influencing the returns. We pick a sample of 26 highly traded stocks and for obvious reasons we call them Stock 1, Stock 2, ..., Stock 26. Since we use every trade, it is very common to find many consecutive trades at the same price. We cumulate all such consecutive trades into one data point since they do not indicate price movement. Throughout this work, the stochastic variable analyzed is the continuously compounded return (r_t), defined as the difference of the logarithm of two consecutive equity prices: $r_t = \log(S_t) - \log(S_{t-1})$.

Owing to the nature of the stock movement (only moves in \$0.01 increments) the resulting values for the return are in fact discretized. There are many more data points where the stock changes just by one cent from transaction to transaction than points where the change in the stock price is higher. We can see this aspect of the data exemplified in Fig. 6.1.

The next images show the result obtained when comparing this empirical distribution function with the normal log-normal and logistic family of distributions. Additionally, we have compared with many other properly scaled families of distribution including Exponential, Gamma, and Weibull types. Of course, all these are constructed assuming little or no memory in the dataset.

The Table 6.1 in the following page shows the results of the unit-root test as well as the Hurst and DFA exponents.

It is worth mentioning that while the stationarity tests reject the presence of the unit root in the characteristic polynomial that does not necessarily mean that the data is stationary, only that the particular type of nonstationarity indicated

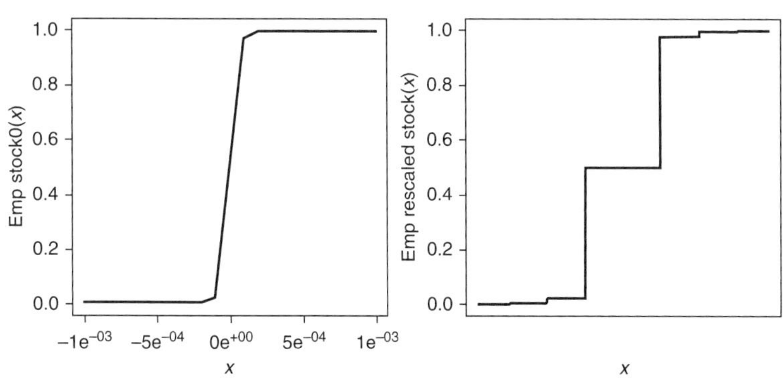

FIGURE 6.1 Plot of the empirical CDF of the returns for Stock 1. (a) The image contains the original CDF. (b) The image is the same empirical CDF but rescaled so that the discontinuities are clearly seen.

TABLE 6.1 DFA and Hurst Analysis

Data	ADF (*p*-value)	PP (*p*-value)	KPSS (*p*-value)	DFA	HURST
Stock 1	<0.01	<0.01	>0.1	0.525178	0.561643
				0.007037	0.005423
Stock 2	<0.01	<0.01	>0.1	0.64812	0.490789
				0.01512	0.006462
Stock 3	<0.01	<0.01	>0.1	0.66368	0.628440
				0.01465	0.006138
Stock 4	<0.01	<0.01	>0.1	0.66969	0.644534
				0.01506	0.005527
Stock 5	<0.01	<0.01	>0.1	0.65525	0.65044
				0.02916	0.02908
Stock 6	<0.01	<0.01	>0.1	0.74206	0.722893
				0.01032	0.008662
Stock 7	<0.01	<0.01	>0.1	0.50432	0.644820
				0.01212	0.008521
Stock 8	<0.01	<0.01	>0.1	0.66184	0.38046
				0.01681	0.01673
Stock 9	<0.01	<0.01	>0.1	0.72729	0.635075
				0.01383	0.006374
Stock 10	<0.01	<0.01	0.07686	0.79322	0.654970
				0.01158	0.006413
Stock 11	<0.01	<0.01	>0.1	0.322432	0.52485
				0.007075	0.01265
Stock 12	<0.01	<0.01	>0.1	0.70352	0.596178
				0.01429	0.007172
Stock 13	<0.01	<0.01	>0.1	0.74889	0.58279
				0.02081	0.00825
Stock 14	<0.01	<0.01	>0.1	0.70976	0.578053
				0.01062	0.007177
Stock 15	<0.01	<0.01	>0.1	0.76746	0.588555
				0.01029	0.004527
Stock 16	<0.01	<0.01	>0.1	0.62549	0.61023
				0.01554	0.01083
Stock 17	<0.01	<0.01	>0.1	0.80534	0.591336
				0.02432	0.006912
Stock 18	<0.01	<0.01	0.076	0.69134	0.596003
				0.01336	0.001927
Stock 19	<0.01	<0.01	>0.1	0.678050	0.596190
				0.009018	0.005278
Stock 20	<0.01	<0.01	>0.1	0.48603	0.59426
				0.01462	0.01829
Stock 21	<0.01	<0.01	>0.1	0.65553	0.50115
				0.02517	0.01086
Stock 22	<0.01	<0.01	>0.1	0.70807	0.552367
				0.01081	0.009506
Stock 23	<0.01	<0.01	>0.1	0.717223	0.594051
				0.009553	0.006709
Stock 24	<0.01	<0.01	>0.1	0.45403	0.37129
				0.01370	0.02267

TABLE 6.1 *(Continued)*

Data	ADF (p-value)	PP (p-value)	KPSS (p-value)	DFA	HURST
Stock 25	<0.01	<0.01	0.02718	0.63043	0.646725
				0.01200	0.005784
Stock 26	<0.01	<0.01	>0.1	0.59568	0.51591
				0.01464	0.01586

Abbreviations: ADF, augmented Dickey–Fuller test for unit-root stationarity; PP, Phillips–Perron unit-root test; KPSS, Kwiatkowski–Phillips–Schmidt–ShinKwiatkowski–Phillips–Schmidt–Shin test for unit-root Stationarity; DFA, detrended fluctuation analysis; Hurst, rescale range analysis.
For the ADF and the PP the null hypothesis is the nonstationarity, and for the KPSS the null hypothesis is stationarity.
With two small exceptions the tests reject the unit-root type nonstationarity.

by the unit root is absent. For this reason we proceed with both tests even though conventional wisdom would recommend the use of the Hurst analysis at this point.

The Fig. 6.3 below show the plot of

$$\log\left(\frac{R}{S}\right) = H * (\log n + \log c) \text{ for Hurst}$$

and the plot of

$$\log F(n) = \alpha * (\log n + \log c) \text{ for DFA}$$

for four stocks. The plots for the entire sample of 26 stocks can be obtained at www.math.stevens.edu/~ifloresc/fractional.html.

Points close to a straight line indicate good parameter estimators.

6.3.5 HIGH FREQUENCY DATA CORRESPONDING TO THE BEAR STEARNS CRASH

The data used is comprised of the five trading days March 10–14, 2008 predating the merging announcement over the weekend as well as the two trading days March 17 and 18 following the event. We shall use the first five days to answer the first question (how soon an investor could have detected the crisis). If what the federals declared is true, that is—the financial crisis has been averted; we should see evidence of the market returning to normality on the last two days and especially on March 18. Furthermore, we shall use selected equity from the universe of over 7000 equity traded on the US market to answer both questions. The data used consists of the closing value within each minute of the trading day (8.5 h). We analyze 18 very large companies grouped by sector. Specifically, we consider the following sectors:

- Entertainment sector: Disney Co. (DIS),
- Technology sector: Google (GOOG), International Business Machines (IBM), Intel Co. (INTC), and Microsoft (MSFT),

- Retail sector: Costco (COST), Target (TGT), and Walmart (WMT),
- Oil sector: Chevron Co. (CVX), PetroChina Co. (PTR), Royal Dutch Shell (RDS.A), and Exxon Mobile (XOM),
- Financial Sector: Bank of America (BAC), City Bank (C), Goldman Sachs (GS), JPMorgan (JPM), Lehman Brothers (LBC), and Wells Fargo (WFC).

There is no particular reason for our specific choices other than these are the largest companies in each sector judging by the market capitalization numbers at the time.

We first estimate the Hurst parameter H using an R/S analysis. Results are presented in Table 6.2. Quite surprisingly these results do not tell us much. We may see that the estimates for the entire week are similar for all the equity under consideration. Furthermore when divided by day the new numbers do not bring anything new and judging by these numbers it would appear that all the week and the two days after stocks behave very similarly. It is not surprising that the Hurst parameter estimates are all close to 0.6—we expected this since our previous analysis told us that even during a normal day when analyzing data sampled with high frequency the prices exhibit long-memory effects the surprise is the small differences in the parameter behavior across equity. Indeed, judging by these numbers it seems there is no difference in the parameter behavior for a foreign oil stock (PTR) versus a financial company (GS). Surely, the financial crisis during that week should have affected differently the behavior of these stocks.

To investigate further we perform a DFA (the results are presented in Table 6.3).

6.4 Results and Discussions

6.4.1 ANALYSIS OF DAILY SAMPLED INDICES

Hurst as well as DFA analysis is performed to find the persistence of long correlations. Table 6.4 presents the results of unit-root stationarity tests. Table 6.5 presents the estimated Hurst and the DFA parameters for the entire respective period. The Hurst exponent and the alpha values obtained are significantly >0.5, thus implying the existence of long-term correlations in the financial time-series of all the indices analyzed. The values obtained for the Hurst parameters for the three indices are not significantly different. The vales obtained for the DFA alphas are not significantly different between the EEM and S&P500 or between EFA and S&P500. The difference is significant between the EFA and EEM indices.

We note from Table 6.5 that the value range of the exponents of the EFA and the EEM index are similar with the values obtained for S&P500. This does not necessarily mean that the extent of the memory effects is the same for all these indices. Indeed, the EFA and EEM indices include stocks from different countries and cannot be expected to move in the same direction as the US Stocks that influence the S&P500. Furthermore, as we can see in Figs. 6.1–6.3,

TABLE 6.2 Comparison of the Estimated Hurst Parameter for the High Frequency Data Corresponding to the Crash Week (March 10–March 14) and the Following Two Days in 2008

	Monday 3/10/08	Tuesday 3/11/08	Wednesday 3/12/08	Thursday 3/13/08	Friday 3/14/08	Monday 3/10/08	Tuesday 3/11/08	7 d
DIS	0.65	0.64	0.62	0.62	0.65	0.60	0.58	0.63
GOOG	0.66	0.65	0.59	0.59	0.62	0.61	0.65	0.62
IBM	0.62	0.67	0.59	0.59	0.62	0.67	0.56	0.62
INTC	0.62	0.69	0.62	0.60	0.62	0.64	0.64	0.63
MSFT	0.66	0.72	0.70	0.60	0.65	0.68	0.62	0.66
COST	0.60	0.61	0.63	0.64	0.62	0.61	0.62	0.62
TGT	0.61	0.64	0.63	0.63	0.61	0.63	0.66	0.63
WMT	0.68	0.60	0.60	0.60	0.62	0.64	0.59	0.62
CVX (Chevron)	0.65	0.64	0.67	0.62	0.58	0.69	0.58	0.63
PTR (PetroChina)	0.60	0.64	0.66	0.62	0.60	0.63	0.67	0.63
RDS.A (Shell)	0.64	0.61	0.58	0.58	0.62	0.61	0.61	0.61
XOM	0.62	0.63	0.61	0.61	0.59	0.67	0.65	0.63
BAC	0.62	0.68	0.67	0.59	0.57	0.61	0.63	0.62
C (City)	0.63	0.67	0.65	0.64	0.64	0.65	0.71	0.65
GS (Goldman Sachs)	0.61	0.64	0.63	0.64	0.59	0.61	0.68	0.62
JPM	0.59	0.66	0.65	0.58	0.57	0.63	0.63	0.62
LBC (Lehman Br)	0.50	NA	0.48	0.65	NA	NA	NA	NA
WFC (Wells Fargo)	0.62	0.62	0.69	0.59	0.55	0.60	0.68	0.61

Abbreviation: NA, not available.

TABLE 6.3 Comparison of the Estimated DFA Parameter for the High Frequency Data Corresponding to the Crash Week (March 10–14) and the Following Two Days in 2008

	Monday 3/10/08	Tuesday 3/11/08	Wednesday 3/12/08	Thursday 3/13/08	Friday 3/14/08	Monday 3/10/08	Tuesday 3/11/08	7 d
DIS	0.70	0.69	0.60	0.58	0.57	0.61	0.71	0.63
GOOG	0.65	0.53	0.64	0.58	0.64	0.65	0.85	0.64
IBM	0.57	0.83	0.60	0.57	0.47	0.60	0.70	0.68
INTC	0.54	0.60	0.51	0.67	0.69	0.60	0.74	0.68
MSFT	0.56	0.56	0.53	0.64	0.73	0.67	0.80	0.75
COST	0.60	0.69	0.50	0.76	0.59	0.58	0.81	0.71
TGT (Target)	0.66	0.64	0.66	0.66	0.62	0.59	0.74	0.72
WMT	0.73	0.63	0.56	0.64	0.51	0.49	0.63	0.66
CVX (Chevron)	0.58	0.58	0.60	0.67	0.46	0.69	0.68	0.67
PTR (PetroChina)	0.64	0.68	0.55	0.60	0.43	0.67	0.57	0.60
RDS.A (Shell)	0.66	0.62	0.65	0.60	0.59	0.53	0.52	0.60
XOM	0.58	0.57	0.63	0.67	0.44	0.66	0.58	0.64
BAC	0.62	0.67	0.53	0.78	0.57	0.78	0.65	0.72
C (City)	0.61	0.65	0.57	0.72	0.57	0.59	0.66	0.61
GS (Goldman Sachs)	0.65	0.53	0.67	0.63	0.45	0.73	0.69	0.60
JPM	0.66	0.61	0.55	0.69	0.63	0.63	0.73	0.69
LBC (Lehman Br)	0.67	0.59	0.57	0.72	0.79	0.82	0.78	0.79
WFC (Wells Fargo)	0.71	0.61	0.62	0.75	0.48	0.64	0.81	0.66

TABLE 6.4 ***p*-Values for the Unit-Root Stationarity Test, EAFE Index**[a]

Index	PP	ADF	KPSS
EAFE index (EFA)	<0.01	<0.01	>0.1
Emerging markets index (EEM)	<0.01	<0.01	>0.1
S&P500 (SP500)	<0.01	<0.01	>0.1

Abbreviations: DFA, detrended fluctuation analysis; Hurst, rescale range analysis; ADF, augmented Dickey–Fuller test for unit-root stationarity; PP, Phillips–Perron unit-root test; KPSS, Kwiatkowski–Phillips–Schmidt–Shin test for unit-root Stationarity.

[a]For the ADF and the PP the null hypothesis is the unit-root nonstationarity, and for the KPSS the null hypothesis is stationarity. The tests reject the unit-root type nonstationarity. So it is reasonable to assume that the data does not possess evidence of unit-root nonstationarity.

TABLE 6.5 **Values of Exponent α and H for All Indices Calculated Using DFA Method and R/S Analysis, respectively**[a]

Index	DFA Exponent		Hurst Exponent	
	A	error	H	error
EAFE index (EFA)	0.6067	0.0220	0.5761	0.0053
Emerging markets index (EEM)	0.743	0.0390	0.5779	0.0047
S&P500	0.6707	0.0202	0.5665	0.0041

[a]The entire period available was used for each index.

the pattern of the correlations in EFA and EEM is less stable compared to the pattern characterizing the S&P500. This may be attributed to the fact that the international indices encompass a widely diversified set of stocks from various countries over the world. This raises a question relevant to an investor who looks for the best portfolio profitability: is it better to invest in US market only, or should an investor look for opportunities in external markets?

When considering long-term investments, investors can focus in analyzing the long-memory effects to construct a well-diversified, low volatility portfolio. In general it is thought that by diversifying a portfolio in general its variance is reduced. That is only true for investments that behave relatively independently from the current assets already existing in the portfolio. This is why it is crucial to establish the asset's behavior before adding it to a portfolio. From Fig. 6.1 through Fig. 6.3, it seems that the memory effects are entirely different between the S&P500 and the international indices. Specifically, we see that the DFA analysis for the two international indices is much weaker than the analysis for the S&P500. Thus, by diversification into these markets a portfolio manager could potentially lower the variability of the portfolio.

To shed light onto this issue we divide the available data by years and perform the analysis separately within each year. Tables 6.5–6.7 present the results obtained for each index and for each year available to study. We also present the results of estimating the Levy flight parameter. We recall that a value close to 2.0 indicates Gaussian behavior of the daily return. We do not present in detail the plots similar to Figs. 6.1–6.3 because of the lack of

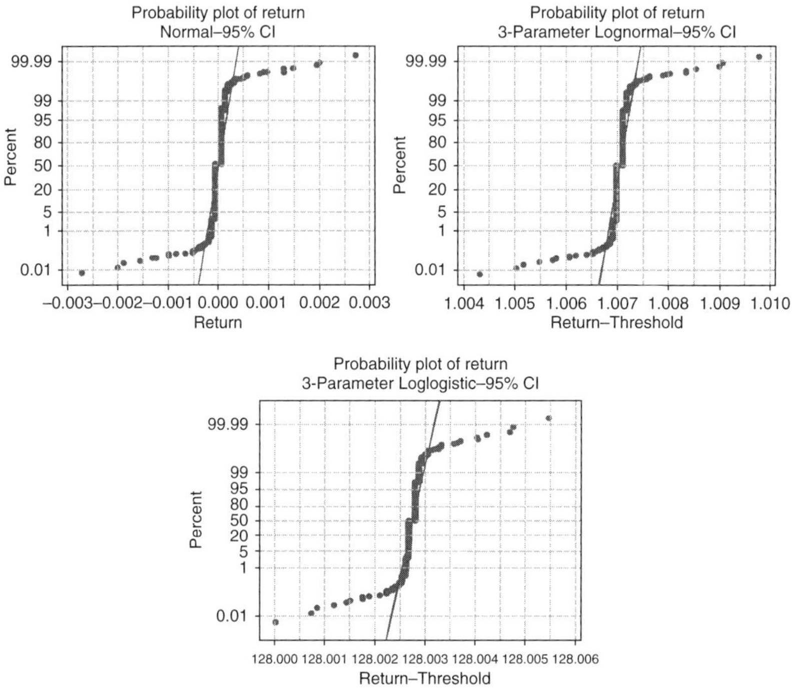

FIGURE 6.2 **Quantile–Quantile plots of the empirical CDF of the returns for Stock 1 versus several candidate distributions. The plots and the numerical results reject all these traditional distributions.**

space in this article, they are available on the article's accompanying webpage: http://www.math.stevens.edu/~ifloresc/indicesAnalysis.html.

There are several things that jump into view once we study these tables. First and the most important, Hurst parameter analysis gives different results from either DFA analysis or Levy Flight analysis. Specifically, during the years where both DFA and TLF methods detect strong departures from normality (2002 and 2008) R/S estimation does not seem to behave any differently than the previous years (Tables 6.5–6.7). This may be explained by the fact that the Hurst parameter estimation works best when the data is stationary. While we have tested for unit root nonstationarity in Table 6.5 and that hypothesis was rejected we cannot guarantee that the data does not possess other types of nonstationarity. There is currently no other type of nonstationarity that may be tested.

Second, looking at several years for which we have an idea of what the results should look like we notice that our hypotheses were confirmed. Specifically, in 2001 and partially in 2002, we expect to see high parameter values due to the end of the dot-com bubble. Again in 2008, we expect to see high values due to the housing crisis and the subsequent market crash in September 2008. Surprisingly, the most reliable confirmation is in the Levy Flight parameter values, they are all much smaller than 2.0 "the normal behavior" parameter value.

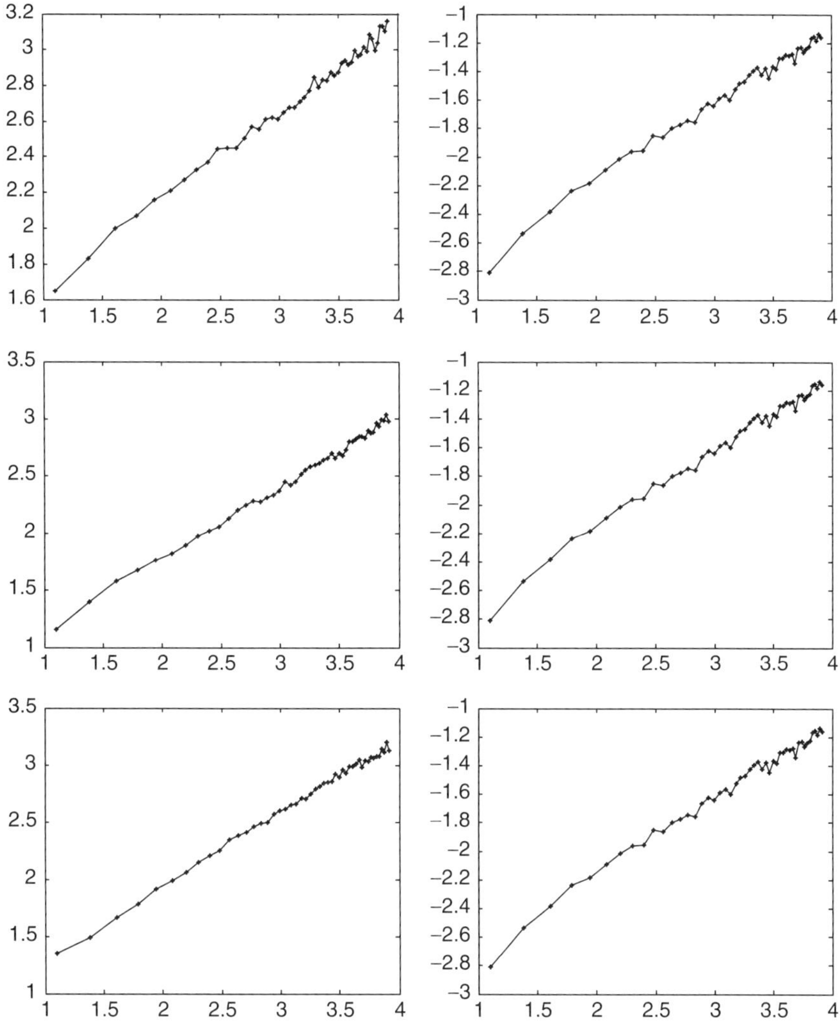

FIGURE 6.3 Hurst and DFA regression plots for a sample of three stocks. Plots on the left depict the Hurst method while the plots on the right show the results obtained using the DFA method.

Third, one of the purposes of the study was to see if we could indicate to the potential investors the markets that possess the greatest opportunities for diversification. Analyzing the values obtained for the three indices we can see that the behavior of EFA and S&P500 indices are somewhat similar. We are concentrating the analysis toward the crisis years that are the times when potential investors are faced with the critical investment issue. On the other hand it seems that EEM is representative of markets where investments opportunities are presenting themselves during those times of crisis. We point the reader to the crisis years (2008) and especially to the years after the crisis (2003 and 2009) in

TABLE 6.6 Values of DFA exponent α, Hurst exponent H, and Levy Flight Parameter α for the EAFE Index (EFA) Year by Year

EAFE Index	DFA		Hurst		Levy Flight Parameter (α)			
(EFA)	A	Error	H	Error	$\alpha@T=1$	$\alpha@T=4$	$\alpha@T=8$	$\alpha@T=16$
2001	0.8173	0.0282	0.8098	0.0218	1.70	1.40	1.40	1.60
2002	0.6844	0.0156	0.5929	0.0088	1.80	1.70	1.60	2.00
2003	0.5066	0.0111	0.5526	0.0134	1.80	1.90	1.70	1.60
2004	0.6186	0.0130	0.5534	0.0095	1.85	1.70	1.70	2.00
2005	0.6098	0.0204	0.5593	0.0114	2.00	1.80	1.99	2.00
2006	0.6016	0.0111	0.5750	0.0128	1.60	1.40	1.40	1.40
2007	0.6300	0.0119	0.5504	0.0092	1.80	1.80	1.90	1.90
2008	0.7870	0.0290	0.5484	0.0084	1.30	1.30	130	1.30
2009	0.4877	0.0157	0.5742	0.0134	1.70	1.90	1.90	1.90

TABLE 6.7 Values of DFA Exponent α, Hurst Exponent H, and Levy Flight Parameter α for the Emerging Markets Index (EEM) Year by Year

Emerging Markets	DFA		Hurst		Levy Flight Parameter (α)			
Index (EEM)	A	Error	H	Error	$\alpha@T=1$	$\alpha@T=4$	$\alpha@T=8$	$\alpha@T=16$
2003	0.4474	0.0123	0.5835	0.0113	2.00	2.00	2.00	2.00
2004	0.6970	0.0229	0.6264	0.0074	1.70	1.60	1.60	1.60
2005	0.6064	0.0202	0.6203	0.0079	1.80	1.75	1.70	1.70
2006	0.6373	0.0196	0.5300	0.0126	1.50	1.60	1.50	1.40
2007	0.6657	0.0138	0.5318	0.0109	1.70	1.80	1.70	1.80
2008	0.5546	0.0448	0.5236	0.0102	1.40	1.40	1.40	1.40
2009	0.3866	0.0120	0.5605	0.0190	1.85	1.99	2.00	2.00

Table 6.4. All the indicators show a more pronounced closeness to the normal distribution than the indicators for the other two indices. Table 6.6 displaying results for normality tests confirm this observation as well. This is surprising since EEM is an emerging market index and those markets are traditionally regarded as hit the most during crisis periods. Additionally, recall that the analysis is done only using only partial data for the year 2009 so even though these conclusions may be evident at the time of publication they were not so when the analysis was performed. In any case the conclusion we draw is that the investment opportunities in these emerging markets are *different*, not necessarily better during crisis periods.

Fourth, the Hurst and DFA estimation for the years 2003 and 2009 and in 2006 for the S&P500 alone give contradictory results. Case in point, the DFA analysis for these years reports antipersistent behavior while the R/S analysis reports persistent behavior. For further clarification we fit Gaussian distributions for these years to see if the hypothesis of normality can be rejected. The results

TABLE 6.8 Values of the DFA Exponent α, Hurst Exponent H, and Levy Flight Parameter α for the S&P500 Index Year by Year

S&P 500	DFA		Hurst		Levy Flight Parameter (α)			
Index	A	Error	H	Error	$\alpha@T=1$	$\alpha@T=4$	$\alpha@T=8$	$\alpha@T=16$
2001	0.6888	0.0188	0.7836	0.0152	1.40	1.30	1.30	1.30
2002	0.7434	0.0189	0.5865	0.0098	1.50	1.40	1.50	1.60
2003	0.4979	0.0114	0.5702	0.0082	1.50	1.60	1.50	1.50
2004	0.5199	0.0124	0.6080	0.0070	1.90	1.80	1.90	2.00
2005	0.6674	0.0132	0.5589	0.0086	1.90	1.80	1.90	2.00
2006	0.4745	0.0131	0.5170	0.0135	1.60	1.99	1.60	1.70
2007	0.6574	0.0185	0.5220	0.0104	1.60	1.80	1.70	2.00
2008	0.7677	0.0287	0.5168	0.0097	1.40	1.40	1.40	1.40
2009	0.4449	0.0159	0.5639	0.0150	1.50	1.80	1.90	1.50

are presented in Table 6.8 and the relevant numbers are in bold. The p-values should be read while keeping in mind that they are obtained under the hypothesis that the observations are iid (which is not the case with the rest of the tests) and they are presented only for information purposes. We see that for 2003 the return behavior was that of a Gaussian process. However, for S&P500 in 2006 the normality hypothesis is rejected. In fact it seems that the results parallel the conclusions drawn following the Levy flight parameter estimation. For a wealth of analysis and complete results we again direct the interested reader to the above mentioned webpage.

Finally, we want to point out the analysis for the year 2009, the year after the great crisis of 2008. The analysis only contains the first seven months of this year (we are in August at the date of writing this article). Normality hypothesis is rejected for S&P500 and the EFA index but cannot be rejected for the EEM index (Table 6.9). We see the same dichotomy pointed out earlier in the behavior of the three indices. The analysis seems to indicate that while the S&P500 and

TABLE 6.9 Goodness of fit p-Values for Fitting the Gaussian Distribution to the Return Data of the Three Indices

	EFA Index	EEM Index	S&P500 Index
2001	0.023		0.303
2002	0.074		0.086
2003	**0.283**	**0.668**	**0.327**
2004	0.138	0.060	0.026
2005	<0.005	0.031	0.133
2006	<0.005	0.013	<0.005
2007	<0.005	<0.005	<0.005
2008	<0.005	<0.005	<0.005
2009	**0.035**	**0.100**	**0.033**

the EFA indices may still possess long-memory behavior, the EEM index already returned to the normal precrisis behavior (Figs. 6.4–6.7).

Thus, fitting the three different methods to the data under study we found the behavior we expected to see reflected best in the TLF analysis. However, we also discovered that DFA and R/S methods provided complementary answers and ideas to the ones already provided by the TLF analysis.

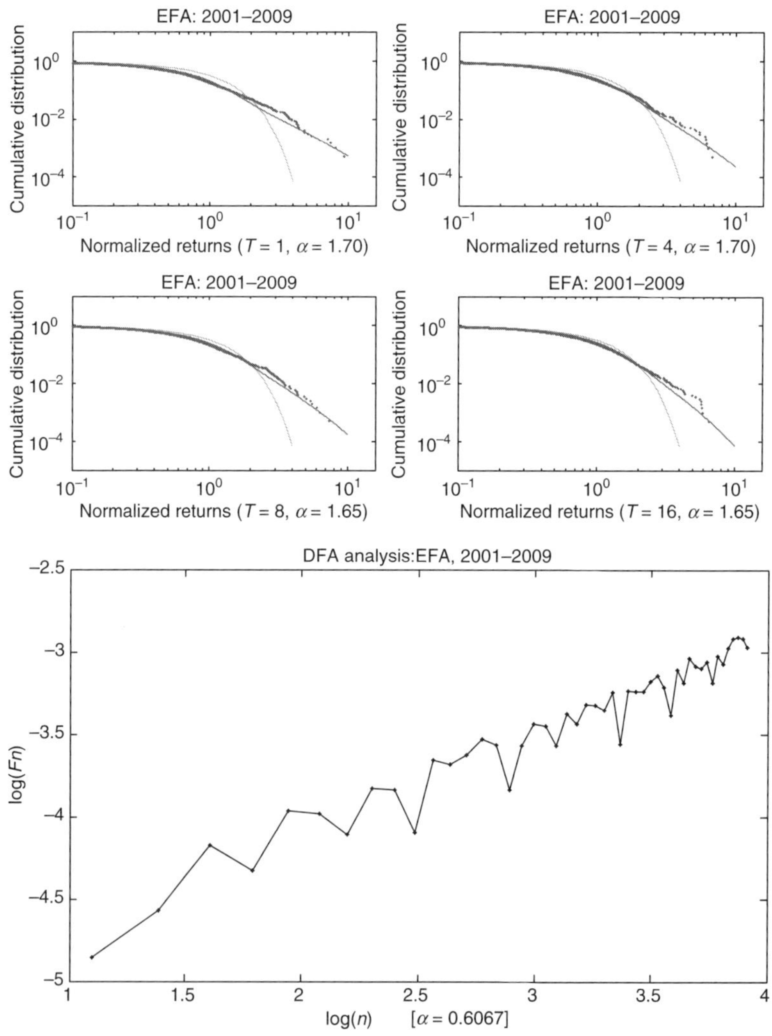

FIGURE 6.4 Analysis results for EFA index using the entire period available. (a): Fitting using TLF. Black points represent the empirical distribution; gray curve the best fitted TLF distribution; light gray curve best Gaussian curve fit. There are four fitted distribution one for each return lag T considered. (b): results for the DFA analysis. Points should be close to a line, the slope of the line is the DFA parameter (α). (c): results for the R/S analysis. Points should be close to a line, the slope is the Hurst parameter (H).

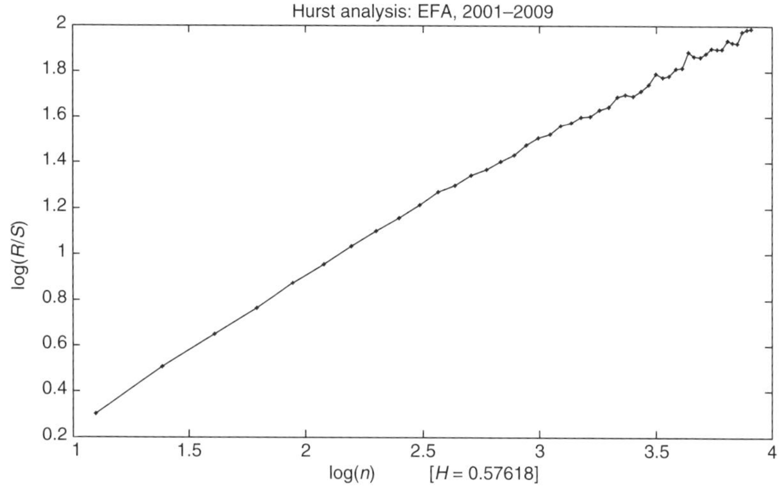

FIGURE 6.4 (*Continued*)

Additionally, we find that the behavior of the three indices under study is different during the crisis period, but mostly after a crisis period. An investor would be served well by searching for investment opportunities and switching his/her investments when the crisis is coming. Diversifying into emerging markets during and especially after a crisis periods seems to be the right way to proceed.

6.4.2 ANALYSIS OF DOW JONES DATA

A unit-root test is conducted first in order to investigate if the underlying time series is stationary, and to figure it out which analysis is better. Hurst as well as DFA analysis is performed to find the persistence of long correlations. The unit-root test results are used to figure out which analysis is better. The results obtained for all the DJIA components are presented in Table 6.10. Figs. 6.8–6.11 show results from selected examples of the 30 DJIA components. Even if the DJIA index is nonstationary, most of the components show a stationary behavior (based on the 5% level of significance). All figures corresponding to the components that are not showed exhibited a similar pattern as shown from the selected samples. The values obtained from the Hurst and DFA analysis confirm the existence of long correlations (long-memory effects). The financial index along with the specific companies possesses long-memory effects in their time series.

The Hurst analysis shows that the least long correlation effect among the components is on Exxon stock (0.5294) and the maximum long correlation effect is on JP Morgan Chase (0.6009). The correlation on the index is 0.5797 and is believed to capture all the varying correlation effects of its components. The pattern of memory effects could not be observed clearly from the figures obtained using R/S analysis in Fig. 6.12. However, we could clearly see them in the figures obtained using the DFA method.

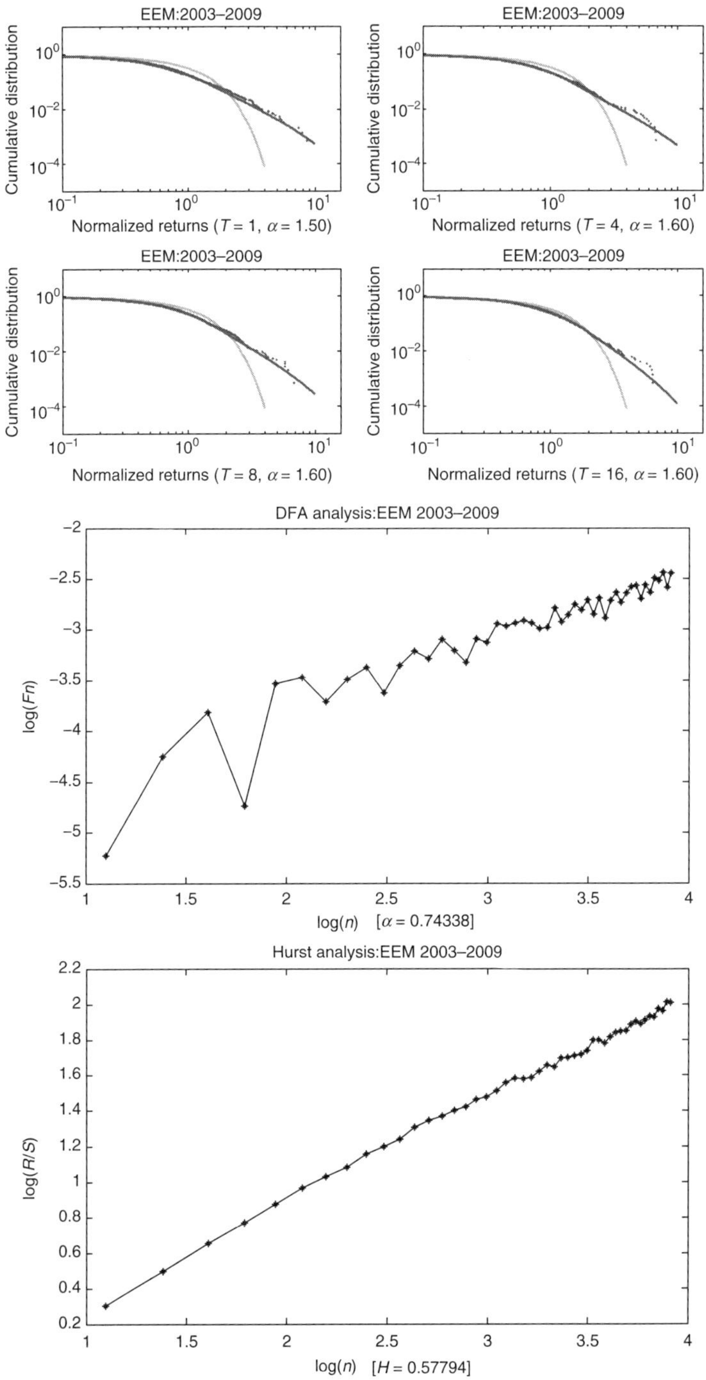

FIGURE 6.5 Analysis results for EEM index using the entire period available.

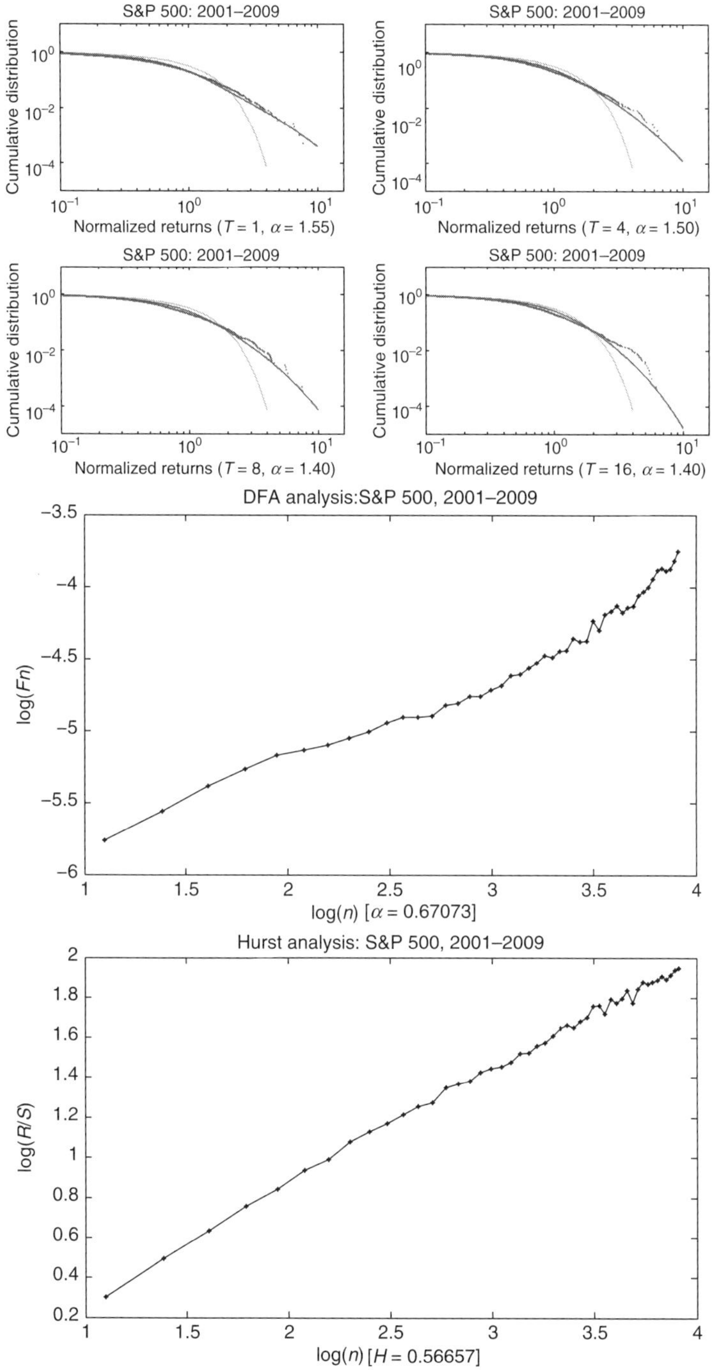

FIGURE 6.6 Analysis results for S&P500 index using the entire period available.

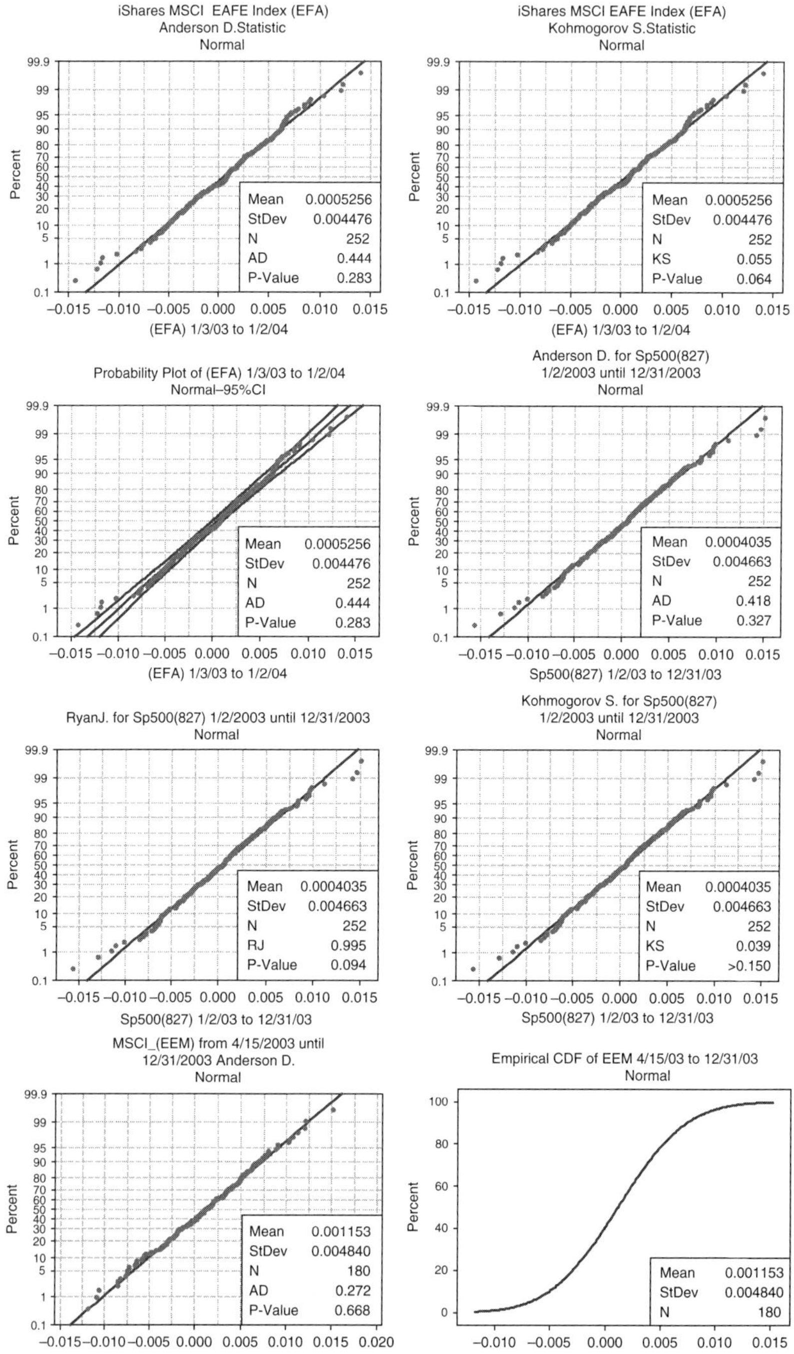

FIGURE 6.7 Several normality tests for 2003 using the three indices.

TABLE 6.10 Dow Jones Index and its Components: p-Value of the ADF and PP Tests of Unit Root, H Exponent and α Exponent Calculated Using R/S and DFA Analysis for All Components and Index

Symbol	Company	ADF	PP	H (Hurst Exponent)	Error	α (DFA Method)	Error
DJI	Dow Jones Industrial Ave	0.48	0.53	0.5797	0.01	0.6879	0.06
AA	ALCOA	0.08	0.06	0.5974	0.01	0.5692	0.05
AIG	AMER INTL GROUP	0.01	0.01	0.5804	0.02	0.6107	0.04
AXP	AMER EXPRESS	0.50	0.41	0.5614	0.02	0.6275	0.07
BA	BOEING	0.56	0.44	0.5694	0.01	0.5844	0.03
C	CITIGROUP	0.02	0.04	0.5750	0.02	0.6074	0.03
CAT	CATERPILLAR	0.01	0.01	0.5948	0.02	0.5852	0.05
DD	DU PONT E I DE NEM	0.05	0.03	0.5816	0.01	0.6038	0.10
DIS	WALT DISNEY-DISNEY	0.02	0.01	0.5850	0.02	0.5781	0.06
GE	GEN ELECTRIC	0.09	0.06	0.5680	0.02	0.5752	0.06
GM	GEN MOTORS	0.04	0.09	0.5860	0.01	0.6096	0.03
HD	HOME DEPOT	0.04	0.02	0.5712	0.02	0.5865	0.03
HON	HONEYWELL INTL	0.07	0.06	0.5660	0.02	0.6502	0.05
HPQ	HEWLETT PACKARD	0.23	0.35	0.5640	0.02	0.5796	0.04
IBM	INTL BUSINESS MACH	0.02	0.01	0.6033	0.01	0.5796	0.04
INTC	INTEL CP	0.24	0.25	0.5744	0.02	0.5800	0.03
JNJ	JOHNSON AND JOHNS DC	0.02	0.01	0.5737	0.02	0.5779	0.05
JPM	JP MORGAN CHASE	0.47	0.52	0.6009	0.02	0.6078	0.03
KO	COCA COLA	0.01	0.01	0.5902	0.01	0.5985	0.06
MCD	MCDONALDS CP	0.37	0.28	0.5694	0.02	0.5713	0.05
MMM	3M	0.06	0.03	0.5707	0.02	0.5846	0.07
MO	ALTRIA GROUP	0.08	0.08	0.5710	0.01	0.6833	0.11
MRK	MERCK	0.11	0.07	0.5776	0.01	0.5991	0.07
MSFT	MICROSOFT CP	0.15	0.04	0.5869	0.01	0.5793	0.04
PFE	PFIZER	0.05	0.04	0.5713	0.01	0.5618	0.04
PG	PROCTER GAMBLE	0.01	0.01	0.5574	0.02	0.5659	0.04
T	AT&T.	0.18	0.06	0.5938	0.02	0.5913	0.09
UTX	UNITED TECH	0.02	0.01	0.5536	0.02	0.5644	0.04
VZ	VERIZON COMMUN	0.01	0.01	0.5809	0.02	0.5630	0.04
WMT	WAL MART STORES	0.09	0.07	0.5724	0.02	0.6041	0.06
XOM	EXXON MOBIL CP	0.36	0.29	0.5294	0.02	0.5963	0.08

From Fig. 6.9 (DFA method) we conclude that the pattern of long-memory effects is stable in Boeing, HPQ, Intel, and JP Morgan. We also noted that some have a fluctuating memory effect for 3M, Alcoa, Altria, American Express, and Merck. We recall that the unit-root tests rejected the null hypothesis of nonstationarity for all the mentioned companies. By looking at Figs. 6.8 and 6.13, we can observe the composition of all memory effects transformed into the index. The pattern of memory effects in DJIA index does not fluctuate greatly, but it does have some leaps and bounds. This is due to the adverse behaving of some companies discussed earlier. The value obtained using the DFA method

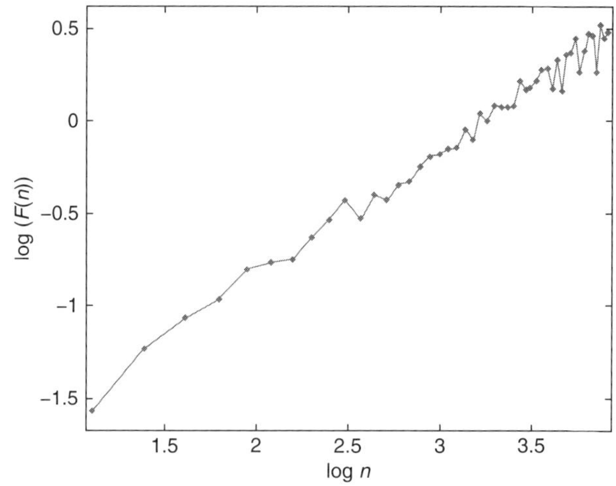

FIGURE 6.8 DFA method applied to the data series of DJIA index.

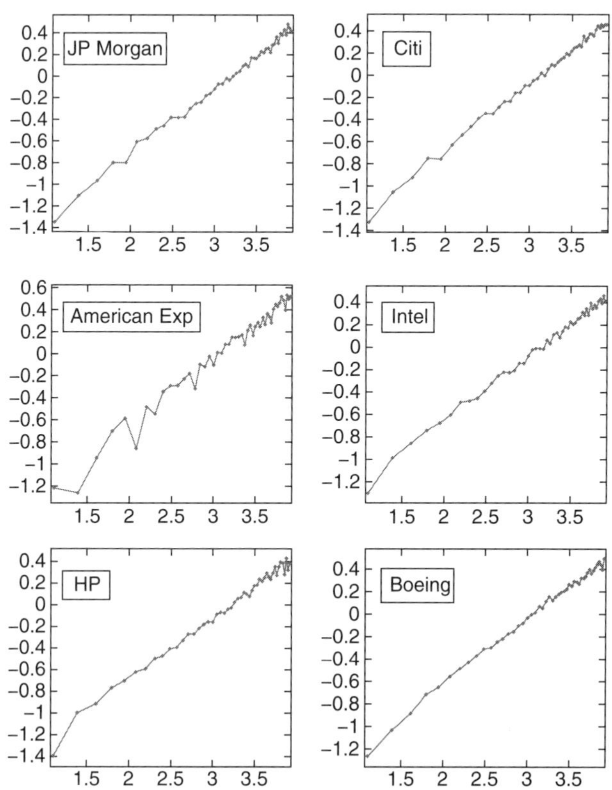

FIGURE 6.9 DFA method applied to the data series of the components of DJIA Index index.

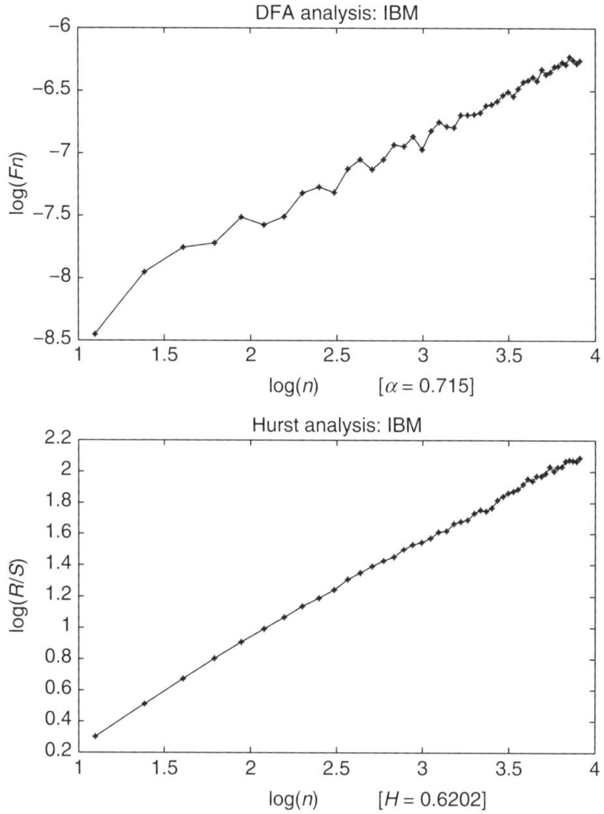

FIGURE 6.10 DFA and Hurst methods applied to the data series of IBM.

for the index is greater than all the values of other components of the index. The companies' exponents' values are very fluctuating greatly as compared to the results of R/S analysis. This might be a reason for the higher value for the index. However, the value obtained is expected to represent the long memory in various stocks from Fig. 6.3.

Based on the results, we conclude that the large, strong firms of the DJIA index exhibit long-term memory effects in a moment similar to the index.

6.4.3 ANALYSIS OF HIGH FREQUENCY TICK DATA FOR THE 26 EQUITY (FOR A TYPICAL DAY)

The estimated values for the slopes are presented in the last two columns of Table 6.1. With one exception the results obtained using the two methods agree. Nineteen out of the 26 equity data analyzed (or about 73% of the data) exhibited long-memory effects that were recognized by both DFA and R/S methods. For 6 out of the 26 (about 23%), one of the two tests did not indicate correlations in the data. In one case (Stock 7) the results were contradictory; both tests indicated the

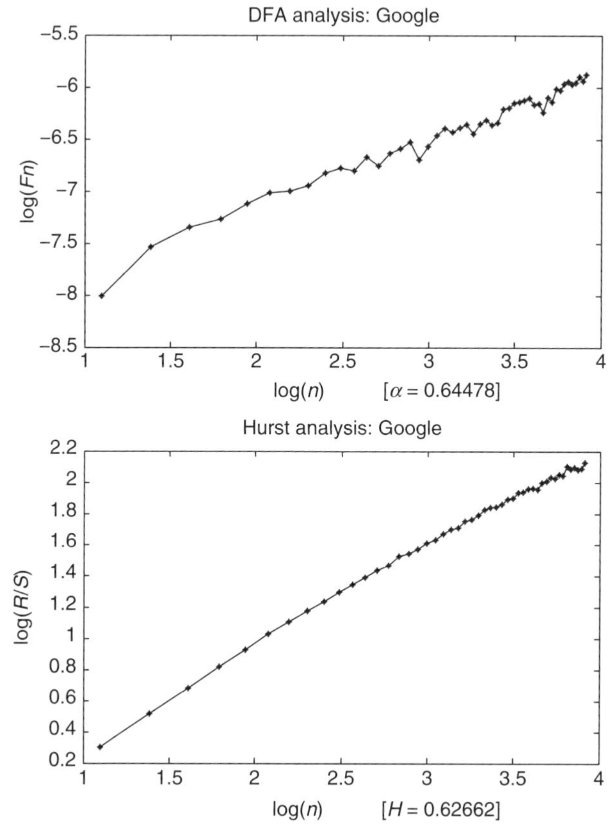

FIGURE 6.11 DFA and Hurst methods applied to the data series of Google.

presence of the long-memory effects, however, while R/S indicated a persistent behavior, the DFA shows an antipersistent activity (negative correlation). Of the 19 stocks that show definite evidence of long-memory effects 18 show a persistent and only 1 an antipersistent activity.

We found evidence that even in an ordinary day without any notable information for about 75% of the market, the use of short-term memory models is inappropriate. We conclude that stochastic volatility models, jump diffusion models, and general Levy processes seem to be needed for the modeling of high frequency data in any situation.

6.4.4 ANALYSIS OF HIGH FREQUENCY (1 MIN) DATA FROM THE WEEK CORRESPONDING TO THE BEAR STEARNS CRASH

We first stress that the data used for this analysis is not the tick data used in the previous study. Here we use the 1-min sampled data since this was the highest

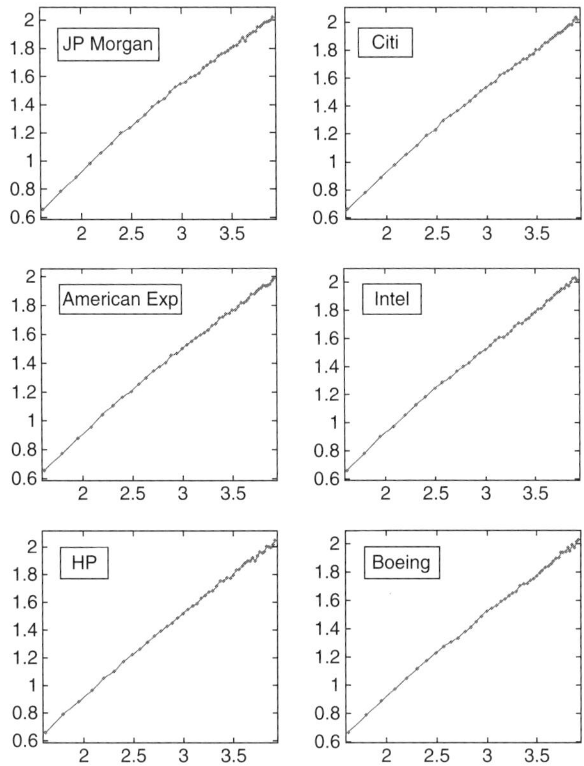

FIGURE 6.12 R/S analysis applied to the data series of the components of DJIA index.

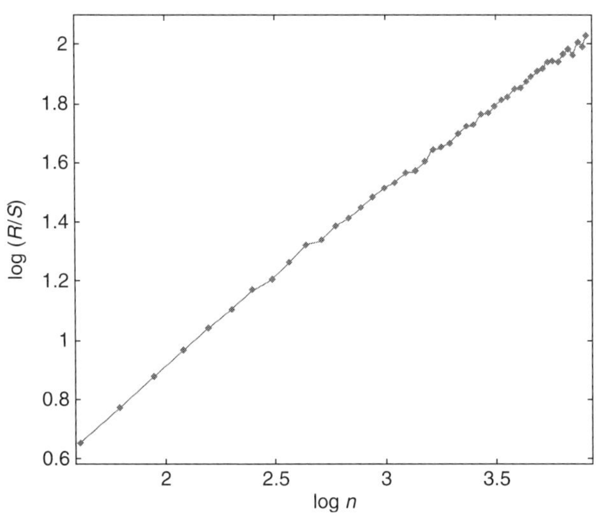

FIGURE 6.13 R/S analysis applied to the data series of DJIA index.

frequency we were able to obtain data about the crash. The estimates we obtain should not be dependent on the frequency of the data and the results should remain comparable. Table 6.2 presents the results obtained when estimating the Hurst parameter and Table 6.3 presents the results from the DFA.

When analyzing the results in Table 6.2 (H estimates) we see that the estimates for the entertainment, technology, and retail sector are unaffected by the events. For the oil companies Chevron and Exxon show drops in estimates during the day of the crash and much increases estimates the following Monday. However, the financial sector estimates are quite different. With the exception of City (no change) and Lehman Br. (suspended trading that made the estimation impossible) all the other equity show a decrease of the estimates preceding and following the crisis on Friday. This is in line with the study of the indices behavior using daily data. We have seen that immediately *before* a crisis the estimates of the long memory increase while *during* the time of crisis the stocks start behaving randomly and therefore their H estimates are closer to the estimates for a Brownian motion (0.5).

Looking at the DFA estimates (Table 6.3), we recognize this behavior in other equity as well. What we also see here is that *after* the crisis (on Monday and especially Tuesday) the estimates increase to much higher levels than before the crisis.

The stocks unaffected by this behavior are Shell (drop in estimates is on Monday and Tuesday) and Lehman. It is worth mentioning that for the later the DFA analysis was performed despite the periods of suspended trading, which may explain the increase in parameter estimates during the time of the crisis. The Lehman strange behavior is interesting and we wanted to include this study in the view of the Lehman bankruptcy in September of the same year (2008). We may see from the data we have available that maintaining normal behavior for LBC was a struggle for regulators even in March six months before the bankruptcy. Figs. 6.10, 6.11, 6.14–6.27 illustrate the DFA and Hurst analysis applied to several companies.

6.5 Conclusion

In this work we have presented several methods of estimating the long-term behavior in time series. These methods are not new but their application is. We have exemplified the methods with different type of data. The time frequency of the data used varied from data sampled daily to data sampled every minute of the trading day to tick data containing every trade.

There are several observations we may gather when we look at all these results. First, the long-term memory behavior was found to be present in the majority of data studied. The long-term memory effects are present during the normal trading day that is devoid of major events. This conclusion is based on studying the tick data. Second, in the presence of a crash the equity behavior is quite different. Preceding the crash the parameter estimating the long-term memory effects seems to increase. During the crash the parameter gets closer to 0.5

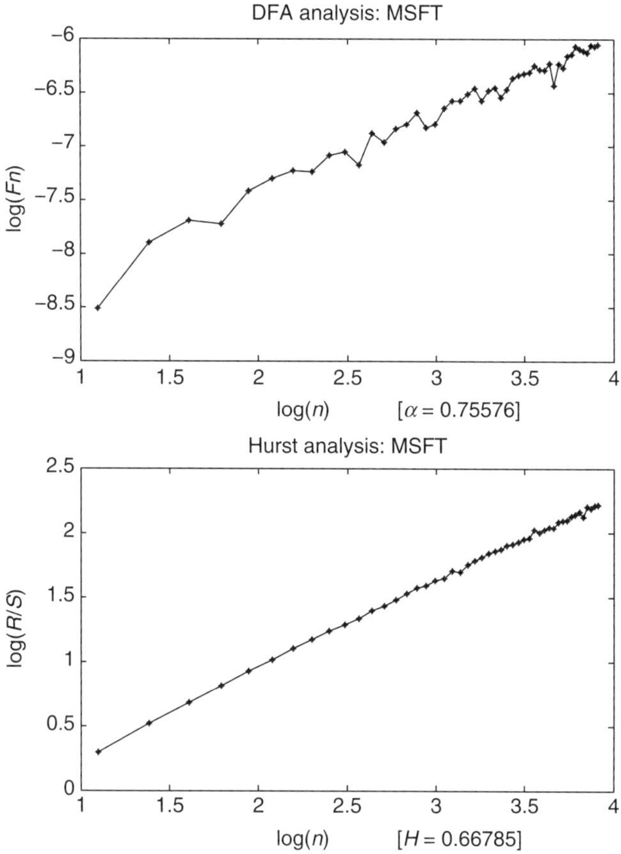

FIGURE 6.14 DFA and Hurst methods applied to the data series of MSFT.

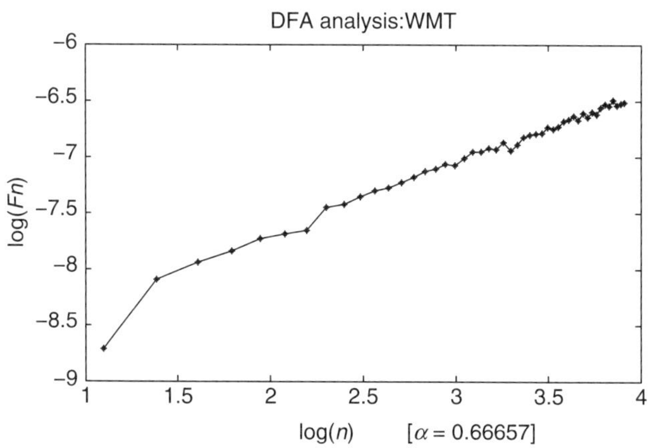

FIGURE 6.15 DFA and Hurst methods applied to the data series of WMT.

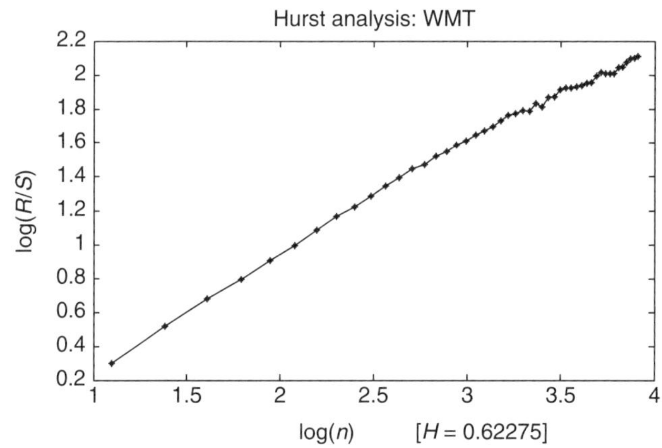

FIGURE 6.15 (*Continued*)

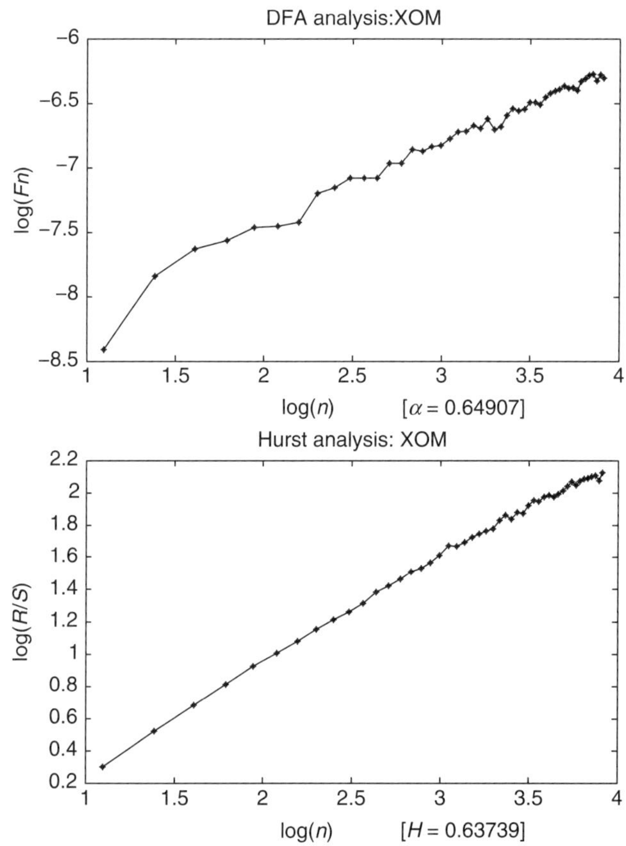

FIGURE 6.16 DFA and Hurst methods applied to the data series of XOM.

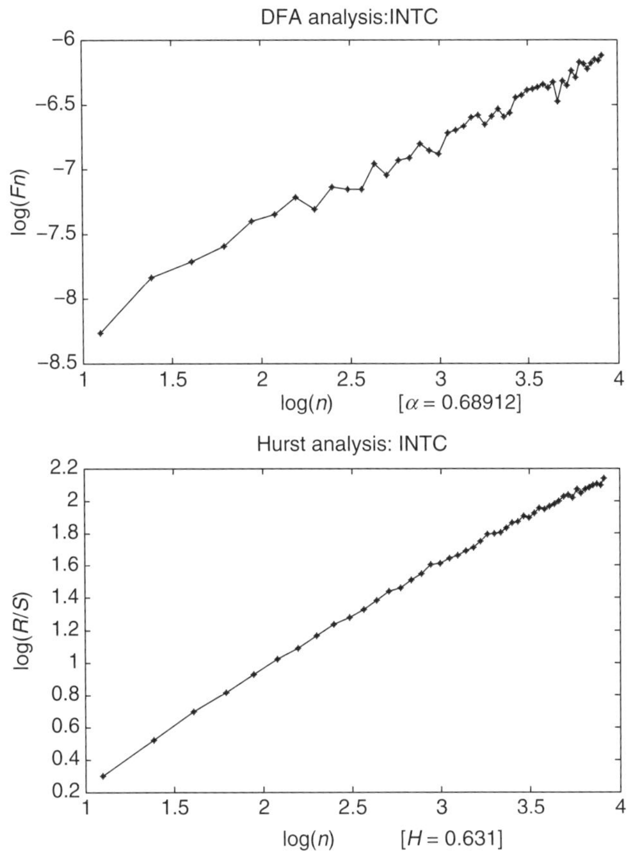

FIGURE 6.17 DFA and Hurst methods applied to the data series of INTC.

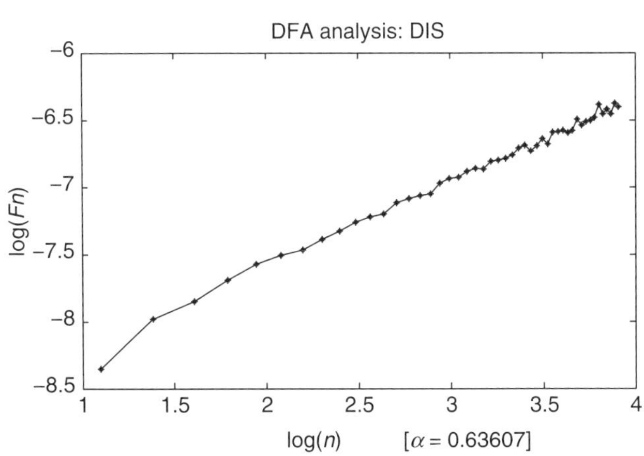

FIGURE 6.18 DFA and Hurst methods applied to the data series of DIS.

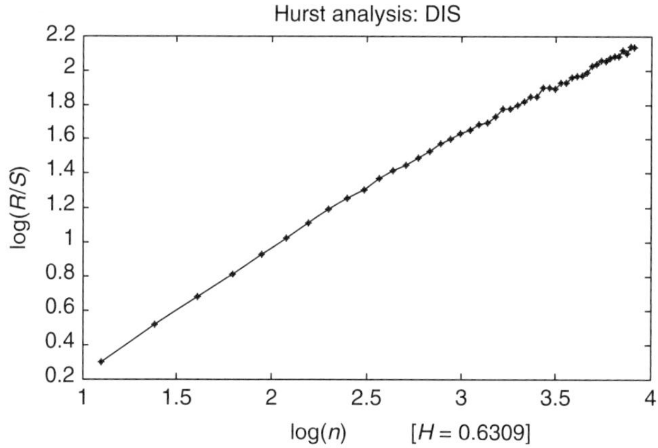

FIGURE 6.18 *(Continued)*

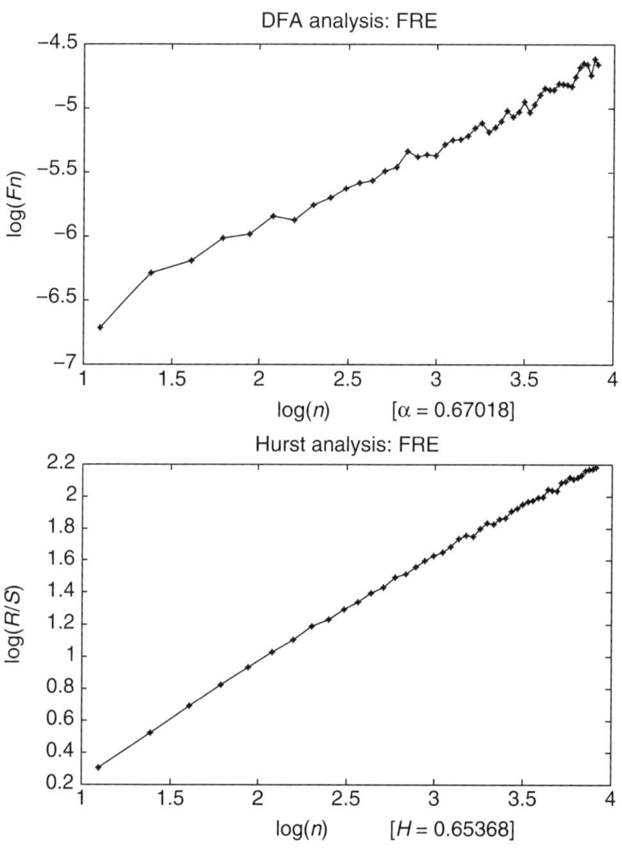

FIGURE 6.19 DFA and Hurst methods applied to the data series of FRE.

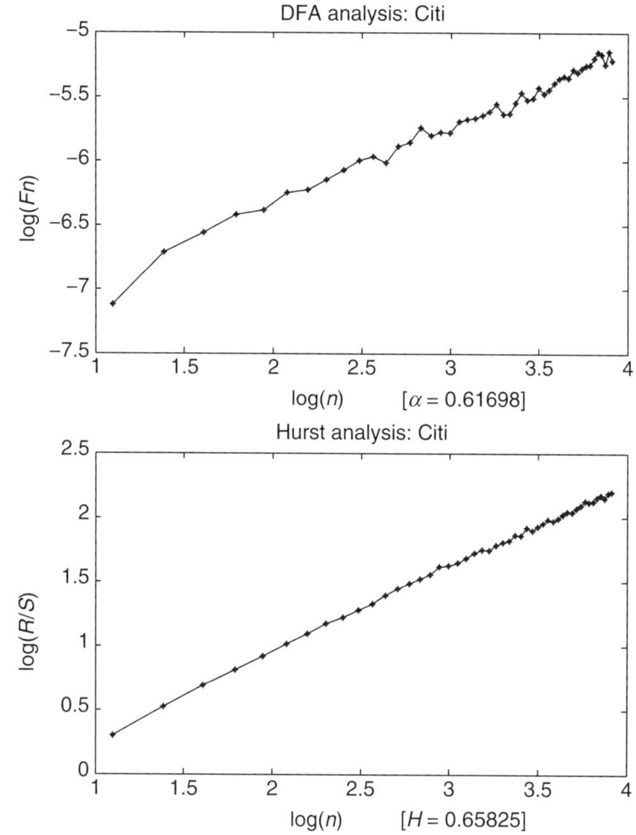

FIGURE 6.20 DFA and Hurst methods applied to the data series of Citi.

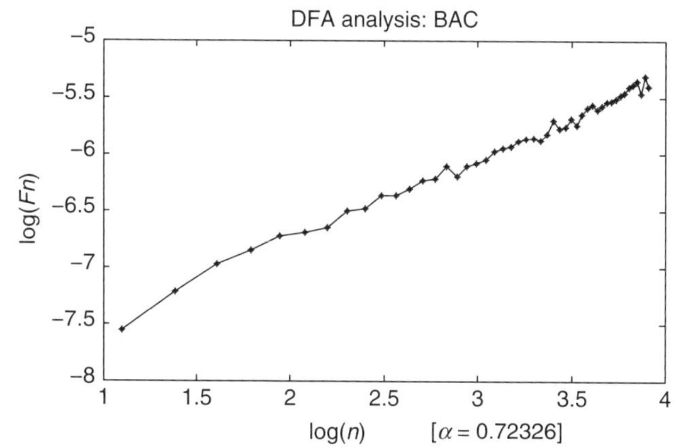

FIGURE 6.21 DFA and Hurst methods applied to the data series of BAC.

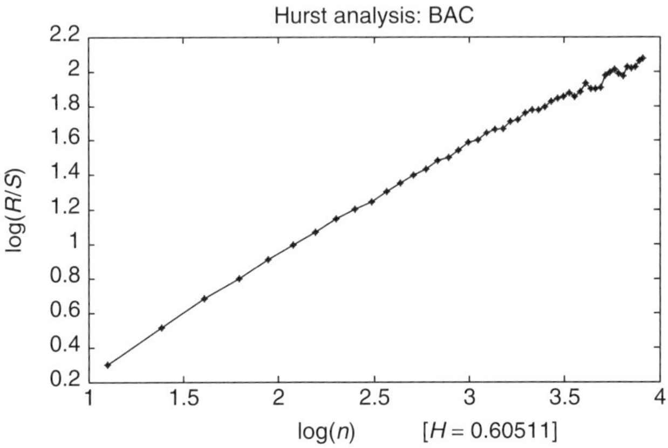

FIGURE 6.21 (*Continued*)

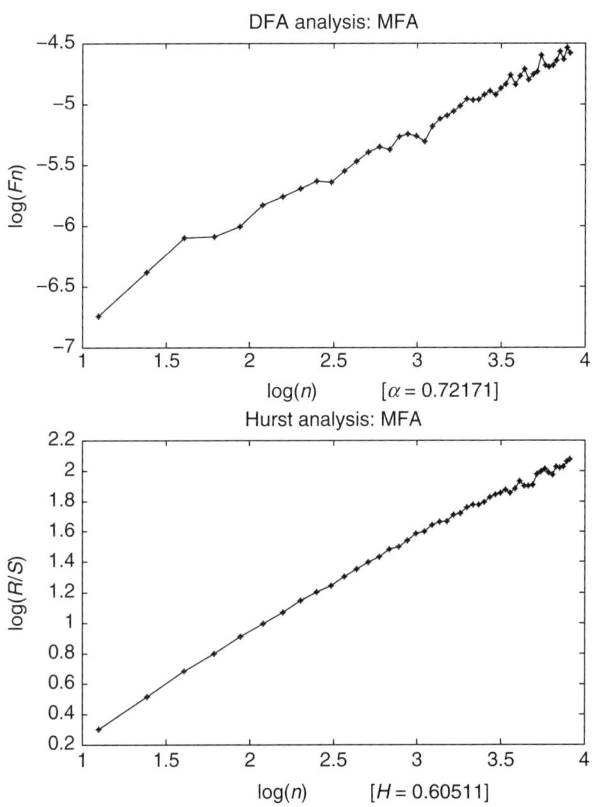

FIGURE 6.22 DFA and Hurst methods applied to the data series of MFA.

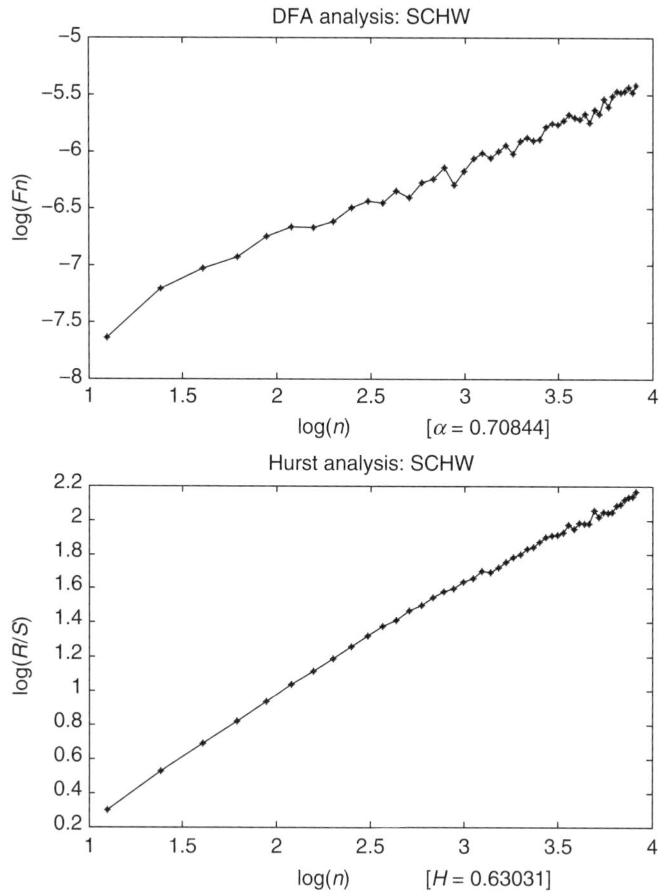

FIGURE 6.23 DFA and Hurst methods applied to the data series of SCHW.

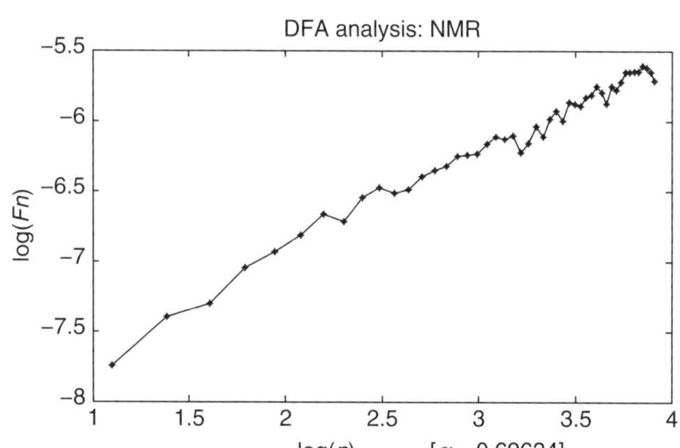

FIGURE 6.24 DFA and Hurst methods applied to the data series of NMR.

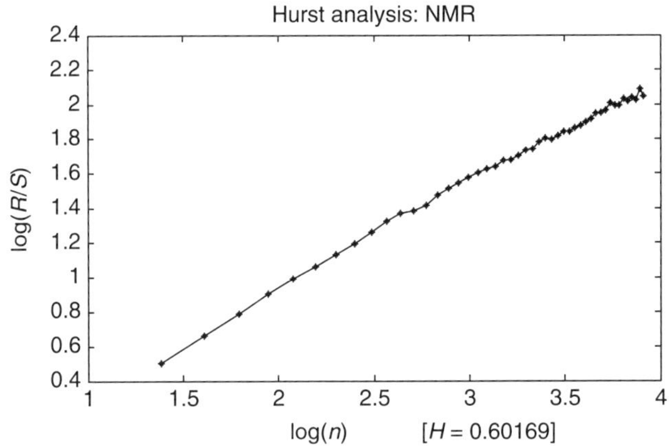

FIGURE 6.24 *(Continued)*

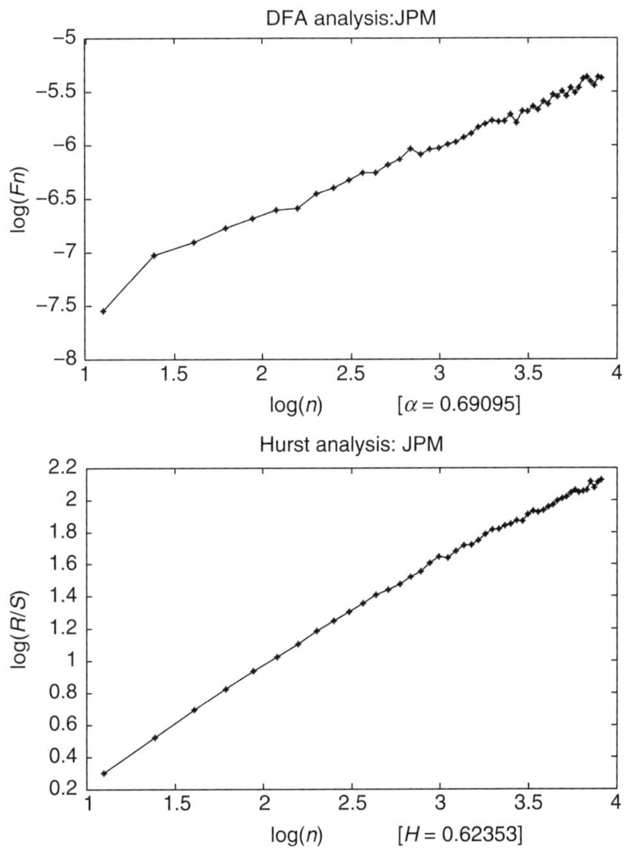

FIGURE 6.25 DFA and Hurst methods applied to the data series of JPM.

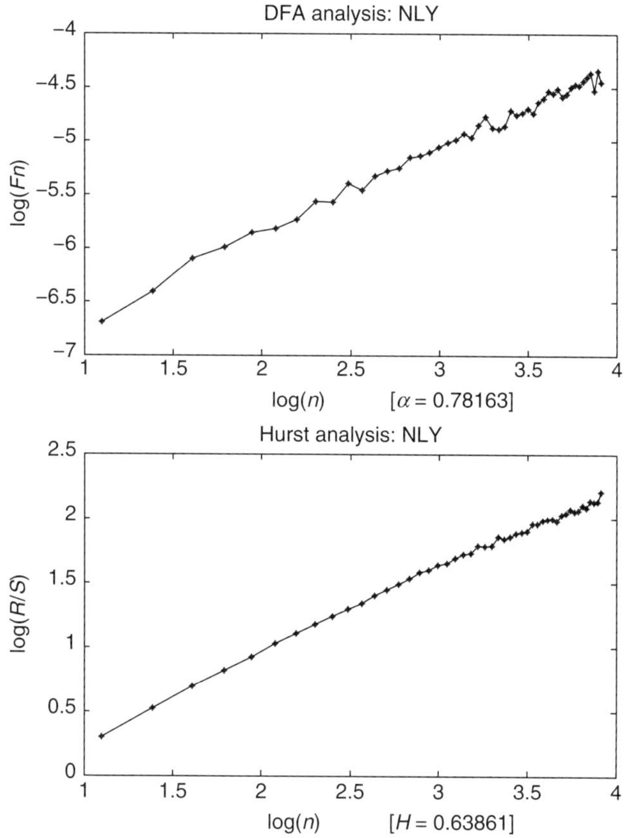

FIGURE 6.26 DFA and Hurst methods applied to the data series of NLY.

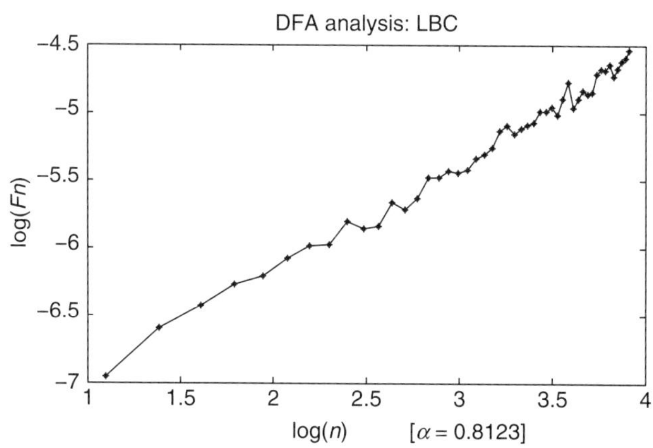

FIGURE 6.27 DFA and Hurst methods applied to the data series of LBC.

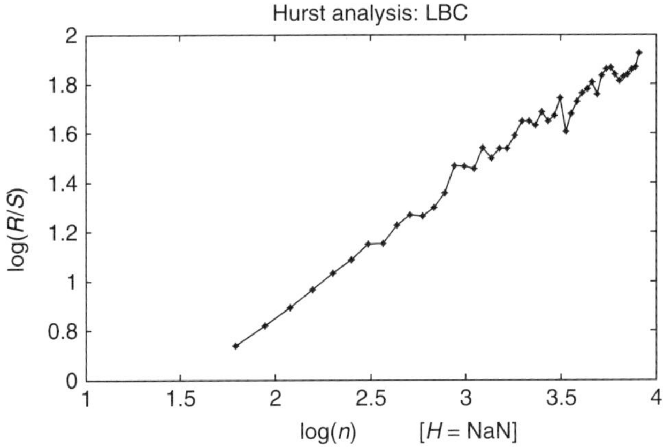

FIGURE 6.27 (*Continued*)

(a level specific to no memory behavior). Immediately after the crash the process returns to exhibiting long-term memory parameter levels and in some cases parameter estimates are at levels higher than those before the event.

This type of behavior was exhibited by the majority of data affected by the crisis, the daily index data, and most evidently, the financial data sampled every minute.

REFERENCES

1. Mantegna RN, Stanley HE. An introduction to econophysics: correlations and complexity in finance. Cambridge: Cambridge University Press; 1999.
2. Stanley HE, Amaral LAN, Canning D, Gopikrishnan P, Lee Y, Liu Y. Econophysics: can physicists contribute to the science of economics? Physica A 1999;269:156–169 [Proceedings of 1998 Econophysics Workshop].
3. Ausloos M, Vandewalle N, Boveroux Ph, Minguet A, Ivanova K. Applications of statistical physics to economic and financial topics. Physica A 1999;274:229–240.
4. Bouchaud JPh, Potters M. Théorie des riques financiers. Paris: Alea-Saclay/Eyrolles; 1997.
5. Mantegna RN, Stanley HE. Scaling behaviour in the dynamics of an economic index. Nature 1995;376:46–49.
6. Figueroa MG, Mariani MC, Ferraro M. The effects of the Asian Crisis of 1997 on emergent markets through a critical phenomena model. Int J Theor Appl Finance 2003;6:605–612.
7. Matia K, Pal M, Salunkay H, Stanley HE. Scale-dependent price fluctuations for the Indian stock market. Europhys Lett 2004;66(6):909–914.
8. Mariani MC, Liu Y. A new analysis of intermittence, scale invariance and characteristic scales applied to the behavior of financial indices near a crash. Physica A 2006;367:345–352.

9. Mariani MC, Liu Y. A new analysis of the effects of the Asian crisis of 1997 on emergent markets. Physica A 2007;380:307–316.
10. Amster P, Averbuj C, Mariani MC, Rial D. A Black-Scholes option pricing model with transaction costs. J Math Anal Appl 2005;303:688–695.
11. Podobnik B, Horvatic D, Pammolli F, Wang F, Stanley HE, Grosse I. Size-dependent standard deviation for growth rates: empirical results and theoretical modeling. Phys Rev E 2008;77:056102.
12. Willmott P, Dewynne JN, Howison SD, Option pricing: mathematical models and computation. Oxford: Oxford Financial Press; 1993.
13. Mandelbrot BB. The variation of certain speculative prices. J Bus 1963;36:394–419.
14. Levy P. Théorie de l'Addition des Variables Aléatoires. Paris: Gauthier-Villars; 1937.
15. Beben M, Orlowski A. Correlations in financial time series: established versus emerging markets. Eur Phys J 2001;B20:527–530.
16. Razdan A. Scaling in the Bombay stock exchange index. PRAMANA 2002;58(3):537–544.
17. Jaroszewicz S, Mariani MC, Ferraro M. Long correlations and truncated Levy walks applied to the study of Latin-American market indices. Physica A 2005;355:461–474.
18. Stanley HE. Statistical physics and economic fluctuations: do outliers exist? Physica A 2003;318:279–292 [Proceedings of International Statistical Physics Conference, Kolkata].
19. Mantegna RN, Stanley HE. Stochastic process with ultra-slow convergence to a Gaussian: the truncated Levy flight. Phys Rev Lett 1994;73:2946–2949.
20. Peng CK, Mietus J, Hausdorff JM, Havlin S, Stanley HE, Goldberger AL. Long-range anticorrelations and non-Gaussian behavior of the heartbeat. Phys Rev Lett 1993;70:1343–1346.
21. Peng CK, Buldyrev SV, Havlin S, Simons M, Stanley HE, Goldberger AL. Mosaic organization of DNA nucleotides. Phys Rev E 1994;49:1685–1689.
22. Levy P. Calcul des probabilités. Paris: Gauthier-Villars; 1925.
23. Khintchine AYa, Levy P. Sur les lois stables. C R Acad Sci Paris 1936;202:374–376.
24. Koponen I. Analytic approach to the problem of convergence of truncated Levy flights towards the Gaussian stochastic process. Phys Rev E 1995;52:1197–1199.
25. Podobnik B, Ivanov PCh, Lee Y, Stanley HE. Scale-invariant truncated Levy process. Europhys Lett 2000;52:491–497.
26. Shiryaev AN. Essentials of the stochastic finance. World Scientific, Hackensack, New Jersey; 2008.
27. Hurst HE. Long term storage of reservoirs. Trans Am Soc Civ Eng 1950;116:770–808.
28. Mandelbrot BB, Van Ness JW. Fractional Brownian motions, fractional noises and applications. SIAM Rev 1968;10(4): 422–437.
29. Mandelbrot BB. The fractal geometry of nature. New York: Freeman and Co.; 1982.
30. Ivanova K, Ausloos M. Application of the Detrended Fluctuation Analysis (DFA) method for describing cloud breaking. Physica A 1999;274:349–354.

31. Buldyrev SV, Buldyrev SV, Goldberger AL, Havlin S, Mantegna RN, Matsa ME, Peng CK, Simons M, Stanley HE. Long-range correlation properties of coding and noncoding DNA sequences: GenBank analysis. Phys Rev E 1995;51:5084–5091.
32. Peng CK, Buldyrev SV, Goldberger AL, Mantegna RN, Simons M, Stanley HE. Statistical properties of DNA sequences. Physica A 1995;221:180–192 [Proceeding of International IUPAP Conf. on Statistical Physics, Taipei].
33. Peng CK, Havlin S, Stanley HE, Goldberger AL. In: Glass L, editor. Quantification of scaling exponents and crossover phenomena in nonstationary heartbeat time series, Chaos, Vol. 5; 1995. p 82–87 [Proceedings of NATO Dynamical Disease Conference].
34. Koscienly-Bunde E, Roman HE, Bunde A, Havlin S, Schellnhuber HJ. Long-range power-law correlations in local daily temperature fluctuations. Philos Mag B 1998;77:1331–1339.
35. Koscienly-Bunde E, Bunde A, Havlin S, Roman HE, Goldreich Y, Schellnhuber HJ. Indication of universal persistence law governing atmospheric variability. Phys Rev Lett 1998;81:729–732.
36. Kantelhardt JW, Berkovits R, Havlin S, Bunde A. Are the phases in the Anderson model long-range correlated?. Physica A 1999;266:461–464.
37. Vandewalle N, Ausloos M, Houssa M, Mertens PW, Heyns MM. Non-Gaussian behavior and anticorrelations in ultrathin gate oxides after soft breakdown. Appl Phys Lett 1999;74:1579–1581.
38. Liu YH, Cizeau P, Meyer M, Peng CK, Stanley HE. Quantification of correlations in economic time series. Physica A 1997;245:437–440.
39. Cizeau P, Liu YH, Meyer M, Peng CK, Stanley HE. Volatility distribution in the S&P500 stock index. Physica A 1997;245:441–445.
40. Ausloos M, Ivanova K. Introducing false EUR and false EUR exchange rates. Physica A 2000;286:353–366.
41. Podobnik B, Fu D, Jagric T, Grosse I, Stanley HE. Fractionally integrated process for transition economics. Physica A 2006;362(2):465–470.

CHAPTER SEVEN

Risk Forecasting with GARCH, Skewed t Distributions, and Multiple Timescales

ALEC N. KERCHEVAL and YANG LIU
Department of Mathematics, Florida State University, Tallahassee, FL

7.1 Introduction

This chapter is about forecasting risk. The vague word "risk" refers to the degree of future variability of a quantity of interest, such as price return. A risk model is a quantitative approach to making a numerical risk forecast based on observed data, and such models are central to the practice of investing.

The classical risk forecast, as developed by Markowitz (1952) and Sharpe (1964), is a forecast of the standard deviation (StD) of portfolio return at a fixed time horizon, but there are several other measures of risk in common use, such as value at risk (VaR), expected shortfall (ES), and others (see Artzner *et al.*, 1999; Rockafellar and Uryasev, 2002). Each of these is a kind of measure of the width of a probability density function (pdf) describing the future return. Ultimately, the real underlying risk forecast is a forecast of the full probability distribution of returns, from which any numerical risk measure is determined.

The historical emphasis on a single number to measure risk has tended to hide the fact that most risk models, in fact, implicitly generate the forecast of

Handbook of Modeling High-Frequency Data in Finance, First Edition.
Edited by Frederi G. Viens, Maria C. Mariani, and Ionuţ Florescu.

a full distribution and, therefore, represent an implicit choice of a family of distributions from which the forecast is to be made. This choice is difficult to avoid, even if it is not explicit.

For example, given a historical time series of monthly returns for a stock index, one could compute the sample StD over the history and use that as a forecast for the coming month. However, this is approximately equivalent to a maximum likelihood fitting of the data to the normal distribution and, therefore, implicitly uses the normal model for the returns distribution forecast.

It is now well acknowledged that financial returns are poorly described by normal distributions, even in one dimension, because of the prevalence of extreme outcomes (fat tails of the probability density function). What other choices do we have? The empirical distribution defined by the data is usually a poor choice because it has inadequate tail behavior. However, there are heavy-tailed parametric families in common use now, such as variance gamma, hyperbolic, Student t, skewed t, and normal inverse Gaussian. (These will be defined later.) See Hu and Kercheval (2007, 2008, 2010), Hu (2005), McNeil *et al.* (2005), Aas and Hobaek Haff (2006), Keel and Geering (2006).

Two questions immediately arise for these more complicated distributions. Does it matter for practical risk management? And, is it computationally practical to use these families?

The answer to both questions is yes. For example, the composition of portfolios on the efficient frontier, whether risk is measured via StD, VaR, or ES, depends on the choice of distribution family. Moreover, the use of these heavier-tailed distributions leads to much better fit of the returns data and has become practical with the application of the expectation-maximization (EM) algorithm (described below) to the maximum likelihood problem.

The method of Hu and Kercheval (2007), in brief, is to use a GARCH filter to remove serial dependence in a financial returns series, fit the filtered returns to a heavy-tailed distribution family using the EM algorithm, and then defilter the resulting pdf to get a risk forecast conditional on current information.

This works well, but a drawback of this method is that a relatively large amount of data is required for numerical stability of the estimate—in our experiments, around 750 to 1000 observations are required for reliable results. This is fine for daily returns, but impractical for a monthly risk forecast. Here, we address this difficulty by introducing a way to use higher frequency data, which is in more plentiful supply, to estimate risk on a lower frequency horizon. In this way, weekly or monthly risk forecasts can be made with daily or weekly data. The method we describe applies to any frequency, so we also illustrate it briefly with intraday data at high frequency.

The article is organized as follows. In Section 7.2, we define a useful general class of probability distributions called the generalized hyperbolic (GH) distributions. These include as special cases the variance gamma, hyperbolic, normal inverse Gaussian, Student t, and skewed t distributions; we focus primarily on the last of these in the remainder of the article. We discuss in detail how the distribution parameters can be estimated from data using the EM algorithm.

Section 7.3 describes the GARCH filter and how it can be used to forecast risk on a fixed timescale, with specific emphasis on VaR (although the methods apply equally well to StD, ES, or any other common risk measure). In Section 7.4, we introduce a method for using high frequency data to forecast risk on a lower frequency horizon, using the generalized autoregressive conditionally heteroskedastic (GARCH) methodology. The method proves viable through backtesting in Section 7.5, which includes multiple-day and monthly VaR forecasts, as well as some experiments with high frequency intraday data. Section 7.6 provides some further discussion of the long-term behavior of the GARCH process, along with additional analysis of the comparison between the multiscale approach and the fixed scale approach.

7.2 The Skewed *t* Distributions

The generalized hyperbolic (GH) distributions are becoming well used to describe financial data. This family of probability distributions was introduced in Barndorff-Nielsen (1977, 1978) and further explored in Barndorff-Nielson and Blæsild (1981) (see also McNeil *et al.* 2005). It includes as subfamilies or limiting subfamilies many of the popular distributions in current modeling use, including Gaussian, Student *t*, skewed *t*, variance gamma, normal inverse Gaussian, and hyperbolic distributions. Our primary interest is in the skewed *t* distribution because of its efficient fitting of equity returns data (see Hu and Kercheval, 2007, 2010). We first describe the GH distributions and some of their properties and then focus on the skewed *t* distributions. A detailed description of parameter estimation using the EM algorithm follows.

7.2.1 NORMAL MEAN–VARIANCE MIXTURE DISTRIBUTIONS

DEFINITION 7.1

The random vector $\boldsymbol{X}$ is said to have a (multivariate) normal mean–variance mixture distribution if

$$\boldsymbol{X} \stackrel{d}{=} \boldsymbol{\mu} + W\boldsymbol{\gamma} + \sqrt{W}A\boldsymbol{Z}, \tag{7.1}$$

where

1. $\boldsymbol{Z} \sim N_k(\mathbf{0}, I_k)$ is the standard k-dimensional normal distribution;
2. $W \geq 0$ is a nonnegative, scalar-valued random variable (r.v.) independent of $\boldsymbol{Z}$;
3. $A \in \mathbb{R}^{d\times k}$ is a matrix of constants;
4. $\boldsymbol{\mu} \in \mathbb{R}^d$ and $\boldsymbol{\gamma} \in \mathbb{R}^d$ are vectors of constants.

From the definition, we can see that

$$\boldsymbol{X}|W \sim N_d(\boldsymbol{\mu} + W\boldsymbol{\gamma}, W\Sigma), \tag{7.2}$$

where $\Sigma = AA'$, the covariance of $N(0, A\boldsymbol{Z})$. This is also why the distribution is called a normal mean–variance mixture. Simple calculation yields the following moment formulas

$$E(\boldsymbol{X}) = E(E(\boldsymbol{X}|W)) = \boldsymbol{\mu} + E(W)\boldsymbol{\gamma}, \tag{7.3}$$

$$\text{cov}(\boldsymbol{X}) = E(\text{cov}(\boldsymbol{X}|W)) + \text{cov}(E(\boldsymbol{X}|W)) = E(W)\Sigma + \text{var}(W)\boldsymbol{\gamma}\boldsymbol{\gamma}'. \tag{7.4}$$

In the context of modeling risk-factor returns, the mixing variable W can be interpreted as a shock that arises from new information and impacts the mean and volatility of stocks.

7.2.2 SKEWED t: A SPECIAL CASE OF GH DISTRIBUTIONS

DEFINITION 7.2 Modified Bessel Function of the Third Kind.

The modified Bessel function of the third kind with index λ is defined by the integral

$$K_\lambda(x) = \frac{1}{2}\int_0^\infty y^{\lambda-1} e^{-\frac{x}{2}(y+y^{-1})} dy, \quad x > 0. \tag{7.5}$$

When $\lambda < 0$, the following asymptotic property of the Bessel function is useful for computing the limiting density of generalized inverse Gaussian (GIG) and GH,

$$K_\lambda(x) \sim \Gamma(-\lambda)2^{-\lambda-1}x^\lambda \quad \text{as } x \to 0^+. \tag{7.6}$$

The following formulas for a GIG distributed r.v. X will be used later,

$$E(X^\alpha) = \left(\frac{\chi}{\psi}\right)^{\alpha/2} \frac{K_{\lambda+\alpha}(\sqrt{\chi\psi})}{K_\lambda(\sqrt{\chi\psi})} \tag{7.7}$$

and

$$E(\log X) = \frac{dE(X^\alpha)}{d\alpha}\Big|_{\alpha=0}, \tag{7.8}$$

where Equation 7.8 needs to be evaluated numerically. More details on the properties of GIG can be found in Jørgensen (1982).

DEFINITION 7.3 The Generalized Inverse Gaussian (GIG) Distribution.

The random variable X has a GIG distribution, written $X \sim N^{-}(\lambda, \chi, \psi)$, if its density is

$$h(x; \lambda, \chi, \psi) = \frac{\chi^{-\lambda}(\sqrt{\chi\psi})^{\lambda}}{2K_{\lambda}(\sqrt{\chi\psi})} x^{\lambda-1} \exp\left(-\frac{1}{2}(\chi x^{-1} + \psi x)\right), \quad x > 0, \tag{7.9}$$

where K_{λ} is a modified Bessel function of the third kind with index λ and the parameters satisfy

$$\begin{cases} \chi > 0, \psi \geq 0 & \text{if} \quad \lambda < 0; \\ \chi > 0, \psi > 0 & \text{if} \quad \lambda = 0; \\ \chi \geq 0, \psi > 0 & \text{if} \quad \lambda > 0. \end{cases}$$

THEOREM 7.4 The Generalized Hyperbolic (GH) Distribution.

If a random vector $\boldsymbol{X}$ has a normal mean–variance mixture distribution $\boldsymbol{X} \stackrel{d}{=} \boldsymbol{\mu} + W\boldsymbol{\gamma} + \sqrt{W}A\boldsymbol{Z}$ and the mixing variable $W \sim N^{-}(\lambda, \chi, \psi)$, then $\boldsymbol{X}$ is said to have a GH distribution, denoted by $\boldsymbol{X} \sim GH_d(\lambda, \chi, \psi, \boldsymbol{\mu}, \Sigma, \boldsymbol{\gamma})$. Its density is given by

$$f(\boldsymbol{x}) = c \frac{\left(K_{\lambda - \frac{d}{2}}\left(\sqrt{[\chi + (\boldsymbol{x} - \boldsymbol{\mu})'\Sigma^{-1}(\boldsymbol{x} - \boldsymbol{\mu})](\psi + \boldsymbol{\gamma}'\Sigma^{-1}\boldsymbol{\gamma})}\right) \times e^{(\boldsymbol{x} - \boldsymbol{\mu})'\Sigma^{-1}\boldsymbol{\gamma}} \right)}{\left(\sqrt{[\chi + (\boldsymbol{x} - \boldsymbol{\mu})'\Sigma^{-1}(\boldsymbol{x} - \boldsymbol{\mu})](\psi + \boldsymbol{\gamma}'\Sigma^{-1}\boldsymbol{\gamma})}\right)^{\frac{d}{2} - \lambda}}, \tag{7.10}$$

where the normalizing constant c is

$$c = \frac{(\sqrt{\chi\psi})^{-\lambda}\psi^{\lambda}(\psi + \boldsymbol{\gamma}'\Sigma^{-1}\boldsymbol{\gamma})^{\frac{d}{2} - \lambda}}{(2\pi)^{\frac{d}{2}}|\Sigma|^{\frac{1}{2}}K_{\lambda}(\sqrt{\chi\psi})}$$

and $|\cdot|$ denotes the determinant.

Proof. From the definition of the normal mean–variance mixture distribution, the density of $\boldsymbol{X}$ is given by

$$
\begin{aligned}
f(\boldsymbol{x}) &= \int_0^\infty f_{\boldsymbol{X}|W}(\boldsymbol{x}|w)h(w)\mathrm{d}w \\
&= \int_0^\infty \frac{1}{(2\pi)^{\frac{d}{2}}|\Sigma|^{\frac{1}{2}}w^{\frac{d}{2}}} \\
&\qquad \exp\left\{-\frac{(\boldsymbol{x}-\boldsymbol{\mu}-w\boldsymbol{\gamma})'(w\Sigma)^{-1}(\boldsymbol{x}-\boldsymbol{\mu}-w\boldsymbol{\gamma})}{2}\right\}h(w)\mathrm{d}w,
\end{aligned}
$$

where $h(w)$ is the density of W.

$f(\boldsymbol{x})$ can be rewritten as

$$
\begin{aligned}
f(\boldsymbol{x}) &= \int_0^\infty \frac{\mathrm{e}^{(\boldsymbol{x}-\boldsymbol{\mu})'\Sigma^{-1}\gamma}}{(2\pi)^{\frac{d}{2}}|\Sigma|^{\frac{1}{2}}w^{\frac{d}{2}}} \\
&\qquad \exp\left\{-\frac{(\boldsymbol{x}-\boldsymbol{\mu})'\Sigma^{-1}(\boldsymbol{x}-\boldsymbol{\mu})}{2w} - \frac{\boldsymbol{\gamma}'\Sigma^{-1}\boldsymbol{\gamma}}{2/w}\right\}h(w)\mathrm{d}w.
\end{aligned} \tag{7.11}
$$

Using (7.7) and some rearrangements, we get

$$
\begin{aligned}
f(\boldsymbol{x}) &= \frac{(\sqrt{\chi\psi})^{-\lambda}\psi^{\lambda}\mathrm{e}^{(\boldsymbol{x}-\boldsymbol{\mu})'\Sigma^{-1}\gamma}}{(2\pi)^{\frac{d}{2}}|\Sigma|^{\frac{1}{2}}K_\lambda(\sqrt{\chi\psi})} \\
&\quad \times \frac{1}{2}\int_0^\infty w^{\lambda-\frac{d}{2}-1}\exp\left\{-\frac{(\boldsymbol{x}-\boldsymbol{\mu})'\Sigma^{-1}(\boldsymbol{x}-\boldsymbol{\mu})+\chi}{2w} - \frac{\boldsymbol{\gamma}'\Sigma^{-1}\boldsymbol{\gamma}+\psi}{2/w}\right\}\mathrm{d}w.
\end{aligned}
$$

By setting

$$
y = w\frac{\sqrt{\psi+\boldsymbol{\gamma}'\Sigma^{-1}\boldsymbol{\gamma}}}{\sqrt{\chi+(\boldsymbol{x}-\boldsymbol{\mu})'\Sigma^{-1}(\boldsymbol{x}-\boldsymbol{\mu})}} \tag{7.12}
$$

and after further rearrangements, we obtain

$$
\begin{aligned}
f(\boldsymbol{x}) &= c\frac{\mathrm{e}^{(\boldsymbol{x}-\boldsymbol{\mu})'\Sigma^{-1}\gamma}}{\left(\sqrt{(\chi+(\boldsymbol{x}-\boldsymbol{\mu})'\Sigma^{-1}(\boldsymbol{x}-\boldsymbol{\mu}))(\psi+\boldsymbol{\gamma}'\Sigma^{-1}\boldsymbol{\gamma})}\right)^{\frac{d}{2}}} \\
&\quad \times \frac{1}{2}\int_0^\infty y^{\lambda-\frac{d}{2}-1} \\
&\quad \exp\left\{-\frac{1}{2}\sqrt{(\chi+(\boldsymbol{x}-\boldsymbol{\mu})'\Sigma^{-1}(\boldsymbol{x}-\boldsymbol{\mu}))(\psi+\boldsymbol{\gamma}'\Sigma^{-1}\boldsymbol{\gamma})}\left[\frac{1}{y}+y\right]\right\}\mathrm{d}y.
\end{aligned}
$$

■

By Equation 7.5, we can get the density of GH distributions.

For a d-dimensional normal r.v. $\boldsymbol{X} \sim N_d(\boldsymbol{\mu}, \Sigma)$, it is well known that its characteristic function is

$$\phi_{\boldsymbol{X}}(\boldsymbol{t}) = E(e^{i\boldsymbol{t}'\boldsymbol{X}}) = \exp\left(i\boldsymbol{t}'\boldsymbol{\mu} - \frac{\boldsymbol{t}'\Sigma\boldsymbol{t}}{2}\right). \tag{7.13}$$

From the mean–variance mixture definition, we obtain the characteristic function of the GH r.v. $\boldsymbol{X} \sim GH_d(\lambda, \chi, \psi, \boldsymbol{\mu}, \Sigma, \boldsymbol{\gamma})$:

$$\begin{aligned}\phi_{\boldsymbol{X}}(\boldsymbol{t}) = E(E(\exp(i\boldsymbol{t}'\boldsymbol{X})|W)) &= E\left(\exp\left(i\boldsymbol{t}'\boldsymbol{\mu} + W\boldsymbol{t}'\boldsymbol{\gamma} - \frac{1}{2}W\boldsymbol{t}'\Sigma\boldsymbol{t}\right)\right)\\ &= \exp(i\boldsymbol{t}'\boldsymbol{\mu})\widehat{H}\left(\frac{\boldsymbol{t}'\Sigma\boldsymbol{t}}{2} - i\boldsymbol{t}'\boldsymbol{\gamma}\right),\end{aligned}$$

where $\widehat{H}(\theta) = E(e^{-\theta W})$ is the Laplace transform of the density function h of W.

With the help of the characteristic function, we can show that GH distributions are closed under linear transformations.

PROPOSITION 7.5

If $\boldsymbol{X} \sim GH_d(\lambda, \chi, \psi, \boldsymbol{\mu}, \Sigma, \boldsymbol{\gamma})$ and $\boldsymbol{Y} = B\boldsymbol{X} + \boldsymbol{b}$, where $B \in \mathbb{R}^{k\times d}$ and $\boldsymbol{b} \in \mathbb{R}^k$, then $\boldsymbol{Y} \sim GH_k(\lambda, \chi, \psi, B\boldsymbol{\mu} + \boldsymbol{b}, B\Sigma B', B\boldsymbol{\gamma})$.

Proof.

$$\phi_{\boldsymbol{Y}}(\boldsymbol{t}) = E(e^{i\boldsymbol{t}'(B\boldsymbol{X}+\boldsymbol{b})}) = e^{i\boldsymbol{t}'\boldsymbol{b}}\phi_{\boldsymbol{X}}(B'\boldsymbol{t}) = e^{i\boldsymbol{t}'(B\boldsymbol{\mu}+\boldsymbol{b})}\widehat{H}\left(\frac{\boldsymbol{t}'B\Sigma B'\boldsymbol{t}}{2} - i\boldsymbol{t}'B\boldsymbol{\gamma}\right). \blacksquare$$

This proposition shows that linear transformations of GH distributions remain in the class of GH distributions generated by the same GIG distribution $N^-(\lambda, \chi, \psi)$, which is a useful property in portfolio management.

COROLLARY 7.6

If $B = \boldsymbol{\omega}' = (\omega_1, \ldots, \omega_d)'$ and $\boldsymbol{b} = \boldsymbol{0}$, then $y = \boldsymbol{\omega}'\boldsymbol{X}$ is a one-dimensional GH distribution, and

$$y \sim GH_1(\lambda, \chi, \psi, \boldsymbol{\omega}'\boldsymbol{\mu}, \boldsymbol{\omega}'\Sigma\boldsymbol{\omega}, \boldsymbol{\omega}'\boldsymbol{\gamma}).$$

More specifically, the margins of $\boldsymbol{X}$ is

$$\mathbf{X}_i \sim GH_1(\lambda, \chi, \psi, \mu_i, \Sigma_{ii}, \gamma_i).$$

This corollary shows that the method used in portfolio risk management based on multivariate normal distribution is also applicable to GH distribution.

When $\psi = 0$ and $\lambda < 0$, a GIG distribution becomes the so-called inverse gamma distribution and the corresponding limiting case of the GH distribution is known as the skewed t distribution. Using the GH density and the asymptotic formula in Equation 7.6, we can get the density of the skewed t distribution.

DEFINITION 7.7 Skewed *t* Distribution

If $\boldsymbol{X} \sim GH_d(\lambda, \chi, \psi, \boldsymbol{\mu}, \Sigma, \boldsymbol{\gamma})$, $\lambda = -\frac{1}{2}\nu$, $\chi = \nu$ and $\psi = 0$, $\boldsymbol{X}$ is of skewed t distribution, denoted as SkewT(ν, μ, γ, σ). Its density is given by

$$f(\boldsymbol{x}) = c \frac{K_{\frac{\nu+d}{2}}\left(\sqrt{(\nu + \rho_x)(\boldsymbol{\gamma}'\Sigma^{-1}\boldsymbol{\gamma})}\right) e^{(\boldsymbol{x}-\boldsymbol{\mu})'\Sigma^{-1}\gamma}}{\left(\sqrt{(\nu + \rho_x)(\boldsymbol{\gamma}'\Sigma^{-1}\boldsymbol{\gamma})}\right)^{\frac{\nu+d}{2}} (1 + \frac{\rho_x}{\nu})^{\frac{\nu+d}{2}}}, \tag{7.14}$$

where the normalizing constant c is

$$c = \frac{2^{1-\frac{\nu+d}{2}}}{\Gamma(\frac{\nu}{2})(\pi\nu)^{\frac{d}{2}}|\Sigma|^{\frac{1}{2}}} \tag{7.15}$$

and

$$\rho_x = (\boldsymbol{x} - \boldsymbol{\mu})'\Sigma^{-1}(\boldsymbol{x} - \boldsymbol{\mu}). \tag{7.16}$$

The mean and covariance of a skewed t distributed r.v. $\boldsymbol{X}$ are

$$E(\boldsymbol{X}) = \boldsymbol{\mu} + \boldsymbol{\gamma}\frac{\nu}{\nu - 2}, \tag{7.17}$$

$$\text{cov}(\boldsymbol{X}) = \frac{\nu}{\nu - 2}\Sigma + \boldsymbol{\gamma}\boldsymbol{\gamma}'\frac{2\nu^2}{(\nu - 2)^2(\nu - 4)}, \tag{7.18}$$

where the covariance matrix is only defined when $\nu > 4$.

Moreover, when $\boldsymbol{\gamma} = 0$, the skewed t distribution degenerates into the Student t distribution.

As implied by its name, an inverse gamma r.v. is the inverse of a gamma r.v. Together with the mean–variance mixture definition, we can generate a skewed t r.v. accordingly.

ALGORITHM 7.8 Simulation of the Skewed t Distribution.

1. Generate Y from a $Gamma(\frac{\nu}{2}, \frac{\nu}{2})$ distribution.
2. Set $W = Y^{-1}$. By definition, $W \sim InverseGamma(\frac{\nu}{2}, \frac{\nu}{2})$.
3. Generate a d-dimensional normal random vector $\boldsymbol{Z} \sim N_d(\mathbf{0}, I_d)$.
4. Let

$$\boldsymbol{X} = \boldsymbol{\mu} + W\boldsymbol{\gamma} + \sqrt{W}AZ.$$

Then $X \sim SkewT(\nu, \boldsymbol{\mu}, \Sigma, \boldsymbol{\gamma})$.

Other subfamilies of the GH distribution include

Hyperbolic Distributions

If $\lambda = (d+1)/2$, we refer to the distribution as a d-dimensional hyperbolic distribution.

If $\lambda = 1$, we get the multivariate distribution whose univariate margins are one-dimensional hyperbolic distributions.

Normal Inverse Gaussian (NIG) Distributions

If $\lambda = -1/2$, GIG becomes the inverse Gaussian distribution. The corresponding GH distribution is known as the NIG distribution.

Variance Gamma (VG) Distributions

If $\lambda > 0$ and $\chi = 0$, GIG becomes the gamma distribution. The corresponding GH limiting distribution is known as the VG distribution.

7.2.3 THE EM ALGORITHM

GH distributions can be fitted with an iterative procedure known as the EM algorithm. To illustrate the idea behind it, we will present a compact derivation of the formulas used in the EM algorithm for the skewed t distribution. Further details and an array of formulas for other subfamilies of the GH distributions can be found in Hu (2005).

DEFINITION 7.9 Likelihood Function.

Let $f(x|\theta_1, \ldots, \theta_k)$ denote the probability density function (pdf) or the probability mass function (pmf, the discrete version of a pdf) of an independent and identically distributed (i.i.d.) sample $X_1, \ldots, X_n$, with parameters $\theta = (\theta_1, \ldots, \theta_k)$. Given an observation $x = \{x_1, \ldots, x_n\}$, the function of θ defined by

$$L(\theta|\mathbf{x}) = \prod_{i=1}^{n} f(x_i|\theta_1, \ldots, \theta_k)$$

is called the likelihood function.

DEFINITION 7.10 Maximum Likelihood Estimator (MLE).

> For each sample point x, let $\hat{\theta}(x)$ be a parameter value at which $L(\theta|x)$ attains its maximum as a function of θ, with x held fixed. Then $\hat{\theta}(x)$ is called a maximum likelihood estimator of the parameter θ based on the sample X.

Assume we have i.i.d. data $\boldsymbol{x}_1, \ldots, \boldsymbol{x}_n \in \mathbb{R}^d$ and want to fit a skewed t distribution. Summarize the parameters by $\boldsymbol{\theta} = (\nu, \boldsymbol{\mu}, \Sigma, \boldsymbol{\gamma})$, and the problem is to maximize the log likelihood

$$\log L(\boldsymbol{\theta}; \boldsymbol{x}_1, \ldots, \boldsymbol{x}_n) = \sum_{i=1}^{n} \log f_X(\boldsymbol{x}_i; \boldsymbol{\theta}), \tag{7.19}$$

where $f_X(\cdot; \boldsymbol{\theta})$ denotes the skewed t density function.

The problem looks formidable at first glance because of the number of parameters and the necessity of maximizing over covariance matrices Σ. However, if the latent mixing variables $W_1, \ldots, W_n$ were observable, the optimization would be much easier. The joint density of any pair $\boldsymbol{X}_i$ and W_i is given by

$$f_{\boldsymbol{X},W}(\boldsymbol{x}, w; \boldsymbol{\theta}) = f_{\boldsymbol{X}|W}(\boldsymbol{x}|w; \boldsymbol{\mu}, \Sigma, \boldsymbol{\gamma}) h_W(w; \nu), \tag{7.20}$$

where $h_W(\cdot; \nu)$ is the density of *InverseGamma*$(\nu/2, \nu/2)$. We could then construct the augmented log likelihood

$$\begin{aligned} \log \tilde{L}(\boldsymbol{\theta}; \boldsymbol{x}_1, \ldots, \boldsymbol{x}_n, w_1, \ldots, w_n) &= \sum_{i=1}^{n} \log f_X(\boldsymbol{x}_i, w_i; \boldsymbol{\theta}) \\ &= \sum_{i=1}^{n} \log f_{\boldsymbol{X}|W}(\boldsymbol{x}_i|w_i; \boldsymbol{\mu}, \Sigma, \boldsymbol{\gamma}) + \sum_{i=1}^{n} h_W(w_i; \nu) \qquad (7.21) \\ &= L_1(\boldsymbol{\mu}, \Sigma, \boldsymbol{\gamma}; \boldsymbol{x}_1, \ldots, \boldsymbol{x}_n | w_1, \ldots, w_n) + L_2(\nu; w_1, \ldots, w_n), \end{aligned}$$

where $f_{\boldsymbol{X}|W}(\cdot|w_i; \boldsymbol{\mu}, \Sigma, \boldsymbol{\gamma})$ is the density of the condition normal $N(\boldsymbol{\mu} + w\boldsymbol{\gamma}, w\Sigma)$. L_1 and L_2 could be maximized separately if the latent mixing variables were observable.

To overcome such latency, we maximize the *expected value* of the augmented-likelihood $\log \tilde{L}$ conditional on the observed data and a guess for the parameters $\boldsymbol{\theta}$. Such conditioning is necessary because the distribution of W depends on the parameters. Maximizing the expectation of $\log \tilde{L}$ produces an updated guess for $\boldsymbol{\theta}$, which we then use to repeat the procedure until convergence.

This can be summarized as an iterated two-step process consisting of an E-step and an M-step.

E-step: Compute an objective function

$$Q(\boldsymbol{\theta}; \boldsymbol{\theta}^{[k]}) = E\Big(\log \tilde{L}(\boldsymbol{\theta}; \boldsymbol{x}_1, \ldots, \boldsymbol{x}_n, W_1, \ldots, W_n) \Big| \boldsymbol{x}_1, \ldots, \boldsymbol{x}_n; \boldsymbol{\theta}^{[k]} \Big), \quad (7.22)$$

where $\boldsymbol{\theta}^{[k]}$ denotes the parameter estimate after the kth step.

M-step: Maximize Q with respect to $\boldsymbol{\theta}$ to get the updated estimate $\boldsymbol{\theta}^{[k+1]}$. Repeat.

Now we will derive the formulas necessary for the implementation of the EM algorithm.

Similar to Equation 7.11, the density of the conditional normal distribution can be written as

$$f_{\boldsymbol{X}|W}(x|w) = \frac{1}{(2\pi)^{\frac{d}{2}} |\Sigma|^{\frac{1}{2}} w^{\frac{d}{2}}} e^{(\boldsymbol{x}-\boldsymbol{\mu})'\Sigma^{-1}\boldsymbol{\gamma} - \frac{\rho}{2w} - \frac{w}{2}\boldsymbol{\gamma}'\Sigma^{-1}\boldsymbol{\gamma}}, \quad (7.23)$$

where ρ is the quadratic form defined in Equation 7.16.

Therefore,

$$\begin{aligned} &L_1(\boldsymbol{\mu}, \Sigma, \boldsymbol{\gamma}; \boldsymbol{x}_1, \ldots, \boldsymbol{x}_n | w_1, \ldots, w_n) = \\ &-\frac{n}{2}\log|\Sigma| - \frac{d}{2}\sum_{i=1}^{n}\log w_i + \sum_{i=1}^{n}(\boldsymbol{x}_i - \boldsymbol{\mu})'\Sigma^{-1}\boldsymbol{\gamma} \quad (7.24) \\ &-\frac{1}{2}\sum_{i=1}^{n}\frac{\rho_i}{w_i} - \frac{1}{2}\boldsymbol{\gamma}'\Sigma^{-1}\boldsymbol{\gamma}\sum_{i=1}^{n} w_i. \end{aligned}$$

From Equations 7.6 and 7.9,

$$\begin{aligned} &L_2(\nu; w_1, \ldots, w_n) = \\ &-\left(\frac{\nu}{2} - 1\right)\sum_{i=1}^{n}\log w_i - \frac{\nu}{2}\sum_{i=1}^{n} w_i^{-1} - n\log\Gamma\left(\frac{\nu}{2}\right) + \frac{n\nu}{2}\log\frac{\nu}{2} \quad (7.25) \end{aligned}$$

From Equations 7.24 and 7.25, it can be seen that computing the objective function $Q(\boldsymbol{\theta}; \boldsymbol{\theta}^{[k]})$ requires formulas for three types of quantities:

$$E(W_i|\boldsymbol{x}_i; \boldsymbol{\theta}^{[k]}), E(W_i^{-1}|\boldsymbol{x}_i; \boldsymbol{\theta}^{[k]}), \text{ and } E(\log W_i|\boldsymbol{x}_i; \boldsymbol{\theta}^{[k]}).$$

To calculate these conditional expectations, we compute the following conditional density function of W

$$f_{W|\boldsymbol{X}}(w|\boldsymbol{x}; \boldsymbol{\theta}) = \frac{f_{\boldsymbol{X}|W}(\boldsymbol{x}|w; \boldsymbol{\theta}) h_W(w)}{f_{\boldsymbol{X}}(\boldsymbol{x}; \boldsymbol{\theta})}. \quad (7.26)$$

By some algebra and Equation 7.9, we can get

$$W_i|\boldsymbol{X}_i \sim N^-\left(-\frac{d+\nu}{2}, \rho_i+\nu, \boldsymbol{\gamma}'\Sigma^{-1}\boldsymbol{\gamma}\right). \tag{7.27}$$

For convenience, we will use a standard notation of Liu and Rubin (1994), Protassov (2004) and McNeil *et al.* (2005).

$$\delta_i^{[\cdot]} = E(W_i^{-1}|\boldsymbol{x}_i;\boldsymbol{\theta}^{[\cdot]}), \quad \eta_i^{[\cdot]} = E(W_i|\boldsymbol{x}_i;\boldsymbol{\theta}^{[\cdot]}), \quad \xi_i^{[\cdot]} = E(\log W_i|\boldsymbol{x}_i;\boldsymbol{\theta}^{[\cdot]}), \tag{7.28}$$

and

$$\bar{\delta} = \frac{1}{n}\sum_{i=1}^{n}\delta_i, \quad \bar{\eta} = \frac{1}{n}\sum_{i=1}^{n}\eta_i, \quad \bar{\xi} = \frac{1}{n}\sum_{i=1}^{n}\xi_i \tag{7.29}$$

Using Equations 7.8 and 7.9, we get

$$\delta_i^{[k]} = \left(\frac{A^{[k]}}{B^{[k]}}\right)^{-\frac{1}{2}} \frac{K_{\frac{\nu+d+2}{2}}\left(\sqrt{A^{[k]}B^{[k]}}\right)}{K_{\frac{\nu+d}{2}}\left(\sqrt{A^{[k]}B^{[k]}}\right)}, \tag{7.30}$$

$$\eta_i^{[k]} = \left(\frac{A^{[k]}}{B^{[k]}}\right)^{\frac{1}{2}} \frac{K_{\frac{\nu+d-2}{2}}\left(\sqrt{A^{[k]}B^{[k]}}\right)}{K_{\frac{\nu+d}{2}}\left(\sqrt{A^{[k]}B^{[k]}}\right)}, \tag{7.31}$$

$$\xi_i^{[k]} = \frac{1}{2}\log\left(\frac{A^{[k]}}{B^{[k]}}\right) \frac{\frac{\partial K_{-\frac{\nu+d}{2}+\alpha}\left(\sqrt{A^{[k]}B^{[k]}}\right)}{\partial\alpha}|_{\alpha=0}}{K_{\frac{\nu+d}{2}}\left(\sqrt{A^{[k]}B^{[k]}}\right)}, \tag{7.32}$$

where

$$A^{[k]} = \rho_i^{[k]} + \nu^{[k]} \quad \text{and} \quad B^{[k]} = \boldsymbol{\gamma}^{[k]'}\Sigma^{[k]^{-1}}\boldsymbol{\gamma}^{[k]}.$$

In the M-step, L_1 can be maximized by taking its partial derivative with respect to $\boldsymbol{\mu}$, Σ, and $\boldsymbol{\gamma}$, and set

$$\frac{\partial L}{\partial\boldsymbol{\mu}} = \mathbf{0}, \quad \frac{\partial L}{\partial\Sigma} = \mathbf{0}, \quad \text{and} \quad \frac{\partial L}{\partial\boldsymbol{\gamma}} = \mathbf{0}. \tag{7.33}$$

Solving the above equation array, we get the following estimates:

$$\boldsymbol{\gamma} = \frac{n^{-1}\sum_{i=1}^{n} w_i^{-1}(\bar{\boldsymbol{x}} - \boldsymbol{x}_i)}{n^{-2}(\sum_{i=1}^{n} w_i)(\sum_{i=1}^{n} w_i^{-1}) - 1}, \tag{7.34}$$

$$\boldsymbol{\mu} = \frac{n^{-1}\sum_{i=1}^{n} w_i^{-1}\boldsymbol{x}_i - \boldsymbol{\gamma}}{n^{-1}\sum_{i=1}^{n} w_i^{-1}}, \tag{7.35}$$

$$\Sigma = \frac{1}{n}\sum_{i=1}^{n} w_i^{-1}(\boldsymbol{x}_i - \boldsymbol{\mu})(\boldsymbol{x}_i - \boldsymbol{\mu})' - \frac{1}{n}\sum_{i=1}^{n} w_i \boldsymbol{\gamma}\boldsymbol{\gamma}'. \tag{7.36}$$

Setting $\partial L_2/\partial \nu = 0$, we get the following equation:

$$-\frac{\Gamma'\left(\frac{\nu}{2}\right)}{\Gamma\left(\frac{\nu}{2}\right)} + \log\left(\frac{\nu}{2}\right) + 1 - \frac{1}{n}\sum_{i=1}^{n} w_i^{-1} - \frac{1}{n}\sum_{i=1}^{n} \log w_i = 0, \tag{7.37}$$

which can be solved numerically to get the estimate of ν.

Applying the δ, η, ξ notation to Equations 7.34–7.37, we get the detailed algorithm.

ALGORITHM 7.11 EM Algorithm for Skewed *t* Distributions.

1. Set the iteration counter $k = 1$, and select starting values for $\boldsymbol{\theta}^{[1]}$. Reasonable starting values for $\boldsymbol{\mu}$, Σ, and $\boldsymbol{\gamma}$ are the sample mean, the sample covariance matrix, and the zero vector, respectively.
2. Compute $\delta_i^{[k]}$, $\eta_i^{[k]}$, and $\xi_i^{[k]}$ and their averages $\bar{\delta}^{[k]}$, $\bar{\eta}^{[k]}$, and $\bar{\xi}^{[k]}$ using Equations 7.30–7.32.
3. Update $\boldsymbol{\gamma}$, $\boldsymbol{\mu}$, and Σ according to

$$\boldsymbol{\gamma}^{[k+1]} = \frac{n^{-1}\sum_{i=1}^{n} \delta_i^{[k]}(\bar{\boldsymbol{x}} - \boldsymbol{x}_i)}{\bar{\delta}^{[k]}\bar{\eta}^{[k]} - 1}, \tag{7.38}$$

$$\boldsymbol{\mu}^{[k+1]} = \frac{n^{-1}\sum_{i=1}^{n} \delta_i^{[k]}\boldsymbol{x}_i - \boldsymbol{\gamma}^{[k+1]}}{\bar{\delta}^{[k]}}, \tag{7.39}$$

$$\Sigma^{[k+1]} = \frac{1}{n}\sum_{i=1}^{n} \delta_i^{[k]}(\boldsymbol{x}_i - \boldsymbol{\mu}^{[k+1]})(\boldsymbol{x}_i - \boldsymbol{\mu}^{[k+1]})' - \bar{\eta}^{[k]}\boldsymbol{\gamma}^{[k+1]}\boldsymbol{\gamma}^{[k+1]'}. \tag{7.40}$$

4. Compute $\nu^{[k+1]}$ by numerically solving the equation

$$-\frac{\Gamma'\left(\frac{\nu}{2}\right)}{\Gamma\left(\frac{\nu}{2}\right)} + \log\left(\frac{\nu}{2}\right) + 1 - \bar{\xi}^{[k]} - \bar{\delta}^{[k]} = 0. \tag{7.41}$$

5. Set counter $k = k+1$ and go back to step 2 unless the relative increment of log likelihood is below a given tolerance.

7.3 Risk Forecasts on a Fixed Timescale

In this section, we describe the GARCH method for filtering time series data and for forecasting risk in the simplest case of a fixed timescale, as discussed in Hu and Kercheval (2010, 2007). The method allows us to forecast the full pdf of the returns distribution, but for simplicity and concreteness, we focus here on forecasting VaR; other kinds of risk forecasts will be similar.

7.3.1 VALUE AT RISK

DEFINITION 7.12 Value at Risk (VaR).

Given $\alpha \in (0, 1)$, the value at risk at confidence level α for loss L of a security or a portfolio is defined as

$$\mathrm{VaR}_\alpha(L) = \inf\{l \in \mathbb{R} : F_L(l) \geq \alpha\},$$

where F_L is the cumulative distribution function of L.

In probabilistic terms, VaR is a quantile of the loss distribution. Typical values for α are between 0.95 and 0.995. VaR can also be based on returns instead of losses, in which case α takes a small value such as 0.05 or 0.01.

For example, intuitively, a 95% value at risk, $\mathrm{VaR}_{0.95}$, is a level L such that a loss exceeding L has only a 5% chance of occurring.

7.3.2 DATA AND STYLIZED FACTS

Given a set of daily closing prices for some index, we first convert them into negative log returns and then would like to calibrate a skewed t distribution with the EM algorithm. However, there is another complication: financial data are not i.i.d. and the maximum likelihood method is not yet applicable.

Financial time series, such as log returns on equities, indexes, exchange rates, and commodity prices, are studied extensively and a collection of deeply entrenched empirical observations, and inferences has been established. Some of these so-called "stylized facts" include

1. Returns series are not i.i.d., although they show little serial correlation.
2. Series of absolute or squared returns show profound serial correlation.
3. Conditional expected returns are close to zero.
4. Volatility appears to vary over time and is clustered.
5. Returns series are leptokurtic and skewed.

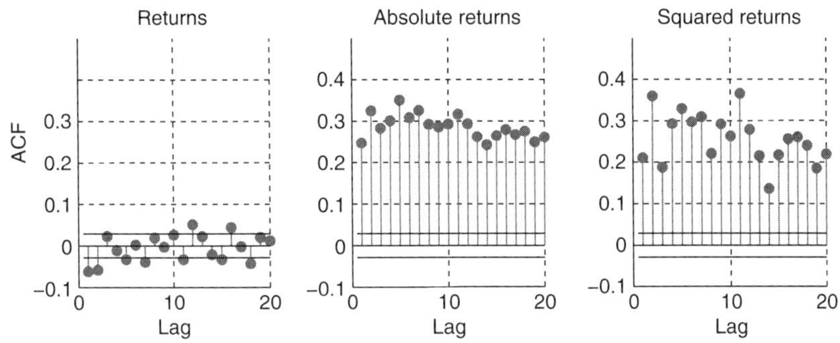

FIGURE 7.1 Autocorrelation function (ACF) for unfiltered S&P500 daily returns data, 1991–2009.

These facts persist on all time intervals ranging from intraday returns to weekly or monthly returns.

In this chapter, our primary data set consists of daily returns of the S&P500 index (based on adjusted daily closing prices) from January 1, 1991, to December 31, 2009, about 4750 observations.

Facts (1) and (2) can be illustrated through Fig. 7.1.

7.3.3 GARCH FILTER

A GARCH model can be used to filter the negative log returns into an approximately i.i.d. series. We provide some of the essentials of the classical time series analysis, which are most relevant to the GARCH model. A more comprehensive summary based on standard texts such as Brockwell and Davis (2002) can be found in McNeil *et al.* (2005). In the following, $\mathbb{Z}$ denotes either the positive integers or the nonnegative integers.

DEFINITION 7.13 Covariance Stationarity

A sequence of r.v.s $(X_t)_{t\in\mathbb{Z}}$ is *covariance stationary* if the first two moments exist and satisfy

$$E(X_t) = \mu, \quad t \in \mathbb{Z},$$
$$E(X_t X_s) = E(X_{t+k} X_{s+k}), \quad t, s, k \in \mathbb{Z}.$$

DEFINITION 7.14 Strict White Noise

$(X_t)_{t\in\mathbb{Z}}$ is a *strict white noise process* if it is a sequence of i.i.d. r.v.s with finite variance. A strict white noise process with mean 0 and variance σ^2 is denoted as SWN$(0, \sigma^2)$.

DEFINITION 7.15 Martingale Difference

$(X_t)_{t\in\mathbb{Z}}$ is a martingale-difference sequence with respect to the filtration $\{\mathcal{F}_t\}_{t\in\mathbb{Z}}$ if $E|X_t| < \infty$, X_t is $\mathcal{F}_t$ measurable and

$$E(X_t|\mathcal{F}_{t-1}) = 0, \forall t \in \mathbb{Z}.$$

The unconditional mean of such a process is also zero:

$$E(X_t) = E(E(X_t|\mathcal{F}_{t-1})) = 0.$$

Moreover, if $E(X_t^2) < \infty$, then autocovariances satisfy

$$E(X_tX_s) = \begin{cases} E(E(X_tX_s|\mathcal{F}_{s-1})) = E(X_tE(X_s|\mathcal{F}_{s-1})) = 0, & t < s, \\ E(E(X_tX_s|\mathcal{F}_{t-1})) = E(X_sE(X_t|\mathcal{F}_{t-1})) = 0, & t > s. \end{cases} \tag{7.42}$$

Thus a finite-variance martingale-difference process has zero mean and zero covariance. If the variance is constant for all t, the process is covariance stationary.

DEFINITION 7.16 GARCH(p,q) Process

Let $(Z_t)_{t\in\mathbb{Z}}$ be SWN(0, 1). The process $(X_t)_{t\in\mathbb{Z}}$ is a GARCH(p,q) process if it satisfies the following equations:

$$X_t = \sigma_t Z_t, \tag{7.43}$$

$$\sigma_t^2 = \alpha_0 + \sum_{i=1}^{p} \alpha_i X_{t-i}^2 + \sum_{j=1}^{q} \beta_j \sigma_{t-j}^2, \tag{7.44}$$

where $\alpha_0 > 0, \alpha_i \geq 0, i = 1, \ldots, p$ and $\beta_j \geq 0, j = 1, \ldots, q$ are constants, and Z_t is independent of $(X_s)_{s<t}$ for each t. The r.v.s Z_t are called the innovations.

Let $\mathcal{F}_t = \sigma\{X_s : s \leq t\}$ denote the sigma algebra representing the history of the process up to time t so that $\{\mathcal{F}_t\}_{t\in\mathbb{Z}}$ is the natural filtration. It can be easily verified that the GARCH process has the martingale-difference property with respect to $\{\mathcal{F}_t\}_{t\in\mathbb{Z}}$. Zero covariance implies zero autocorrelation, which suits stylized fact 1. We will further show that it has constant variance and is therefore covariance stationary.

In practice, low order GARCH models are most widely used and their mathematical analysis is relatively straightforward. We will concentrate on the GARCH(1,1) process.

It follows from Equations 7.43 and 7.44 that for a GARCH(1,1) process we have

$$\sigma_t^2 = \alpha_0 + \alpha_1 X_{t-1}^2 + \beta\sigma_{t-1}^2 = \alpha_0 + (\alpha_1 Z_{t-1}^2 + \beta)\sigma_{t-1}^2. \tag{7.45}$$

This is a stochastic recurrence equation (SRE) of the form $Y_t = A_t Y_{t-1} + B_t$, where $(A_t)_{t\in\mathbb{Z}}$ and $(B_t)_{t\in\mathbb{Z}}$ are i.i.d. r.v.s. As shown by Brandt (1986), sufficient conditions for a solution are that

$$E(\max\{0, \log|B_t|\}) < \infty \text{ and } E(\log|A_t|) < 0. \tag{7.46}$$

The unique solution is given by

$$Y_t = B_t + \sum_{i=1}^{\infty} B_{t-i} \prod_{j=0}^{i-1} A_{t-j}, \tag{7.47}$$

where the sum converges absolutely, almost surely.

We will use these facts about SREs to derive the sufficient and necessary condition for the covariance stationarity of the GARCH(1,1) process.

PROPOSITION 7.17

> The GARCH(1,1) process is a covariance-stationary process if and only if $\alpha_1 + \beta < 1$. The variance of the covariance-stationary process is given by $\alpha_0/(1 - \alpha_1 - \beta)$.

Proof. Assuming covariance stationarity, it follows from Equation 7.45 and $E(Z_t^2) = 1$ that

$$\sigma^2 = E(\sigma_t^2) = \alpha_0 + (\alpha_1 E(Z_t^2) + \beta)E(\sigma_{t-1}^2) = \alpha_0 + (\alpha_1 + \beta)\sigma^2.$$

As a result, $\sigma^2 = \alpha_0/(1 - \alpha_1 - \beta)$, and we must have $\alpha_1 + \beta < 1$ since $\alpha_0 > 0$.

Since Z_t is independent of $(X_s)_{s<t}$, σ_t and Z_t are independent immediately from Equation 7.45. By Equation 7.43 and such independence,

$$\operatorname{var}(X_t) = E(X_t^2) = E(\sigma_t^2)E(Z_t^2) = \sigma^2 \cdot 1 = \alpha_0/(1 - \alpha_1 - \beta).$$

Conversely, if $\alpha_1 + \beta < 1$, by Jensen's inequality,

$$E(\log((\alpha_1 Z_{t-1}^2 + \beta)\sigma_{t-1}^2)) < \log(E((\alpha_1 Z_{t-1}^2 + \beta)\sigma_{t-1}^2)) = \log(\alpha_1 + \beta) < 0.$$

On the other hand, since α_0 is a constant,

$$E(\max\{0, \log|\alpha_0|\}) < \infty.$$

Now that both two sufficient conditions in Equation 7.46 are satisfied, by Equation 7.47, the solution to Equation 7.45 is

$$\sigma_t^2 = \alpha_0 + \alpha_0 \sum_{i=1}^{\infty} \prod_{j=0}^{i-1} (\alpha_1 Z_{t-j}^2 + \beta). \tag{7.48}$$

Take expectation, then by $E(Z_t^2) = 1$,

$$\begin{aligned} E(\sigma_t^2) &= \alpha_0 + \alpha_0 \sum_{i=1}^{\infty} \prod_{j=0}^{i-1} (\alpha_1 E(Z_{t-j}^2) + \beta) \\ &= \alpha_0 + \alpha_0 \sum_{i=1}^{\infty} \prod_{j=0}^{i-1} (\alpha_1 + \beta) \\ &= \alpha_0 \sum_{i=0}^{\infty} (\alpha_1 + \beta)^i = \frac{\alpha_0}{(1 - \alpha_1 - \beta)}. \end{aligned}$$

■

While the GARCH(1,1) process has constant variance, its conditional variance is given by

$$\text{var}(X_t|\mathcal{F}_{t-1}) = E(\sigma_t^2 Z_t^2|\mathcal{F}_{t-1}) = \sigma_t^2 E(Z_t^2) = \sigma_t^2 = \alpha_0 + \alpha_1 X_{t-1}^2 + \beta \sigma_{t-1}^2.$$

In other words, its conditional StD σ_t, or volatility, is a continually changing function of both $|X_{t-1}|$ and σ_{t-1}. If one or both are particularly large, then X_t is effectively drawn from a distribution with large variance and more likely to be large itself. In this way, the model generates volatility clusters as described by stylized fact 4.

Assuming a GARCH(1,1) process has a fourth moment, we can calculate the kurtosis of X_t. Square both sides of Equation 7.48, take expectations and by stationarity,

$$E(\sigma_t^4) = \alpha_0^2 + (\alpha_1^2 \kappa_Z + \beta^2 + 2\alpha_1 \beta) E(\sigma_t^4) + 2\alpha_0(\alpha_1 + \beta) E(\sigma_t^2),$$

where $\kappa_Z = E(Z_t^4)/(E(Z_t^2))^2 = E(Z_t^4)$ denotes the kurtosis of the innovations. Solve for $E(\sigma_t^4)$ and using $E(\sigma_t^2) = E(X_t^2) = \alpha_0/(1 - \alpha_1 - \beta)$, we will get

$$E(X_t^4) = \kappa_Z E(\sigma_t^4) = \frac{\alpha_0^2 \kappa_Z (1 - (\alpha_1 + \beta)^2)}{(1 - \alpha_1 - \beta)^2 (1 - \alpha_1^2 \kappa_Z - \beta^2 - 2\alpha_1 \beta)},$$

from which it follows that

$$\kappa_X = \frac{\kappa_Z(1 - (\alpha_1 + \beta)^2)}{1 - \alpha_1^2 \kappa_Z - \beta^2 - 2\alpha_1\beta}.$$

It can be seen that whenever $\kappa_Z > 1$, the kurtosis of X_t is inflated in comparison with that of Z_t. Therefore, the stationary distribution of the GARCH process is leptokurtic (i.e., $\kappa_X > 3$) for Gaussian or Student t innovations, capturing stylized fact (5).

Higher order GARCH models have the same general behavior as GARCH(1,1). The necessary and sufficient condition for covariance stationarity is $\sum_{i=1}^{p} \alpha_i + \sum_{j=1}^{q} \beta_j < 1$, and the constant variance is $\alpha_0/(1 - \sum_{i=1}^{p} \alpha_i - \sum_{j=1}^{q} \beta_j)$. For more details, see Bougerol and Picard (1992).

There are many variants on and extensions of the basic GARCH model, such as the following:

DEFINITION 7.18 ARMA Process with GARCH Errors

Let $(Z_t)_{t\in\mathbb{Z}}$ be SWN(0, 1). The process $(X_t)_{t\in\mathbb{Z}}$ is an ARMA(p_1, q_1) process with GARCH(p_2, q_2) errors if it is covariance stationary and satisfies the equations:

$$X_t = \mu_t + \sigma_t Z_t, \tag{7.49}$$

$$\mu_t = \mu_0 + \sum_{i=1}^{p_1} \phi_i (X_i - \mu) + \sum_{j=1}^{q_1} \theta_j (X_{t-j} - \mu_{t-j}), \tag{7.50}$$

$$\sigma_t^2 = \alpha_0 + \sum_{i=1}^{p_2} \alpha_i (X_{t-i} - \mu_{t-i})^2 + \sum_{j=1}^{q_2} \beta_j \sigma_{t-j}^2, \tag{7.51}$$

where $\sum_{i=1}^{p_2} \alpha_i + \sum_{j=1}^{q_2} \beta_j < 1, \alpha_0 > 0, \alpha_i \geq 0, i = 1, \ldots, p_2$ and $\beta_j \geq 0$, $j = 1, \ldots, q_2$, and the innovation Z_t is independent of $(X_s)_{s<t}$ for all t.

Since return series show little serial correlation, the ARMA component is unnecessary, that is, we choose $p_1 = q_1 = 0$. On the other hand, stylized fact 3 states that conditional expected returns are close but not equal to zero. Therefore, we retain the constant μ_0 in Equation 7.50. We will use such a standard GARCH(1,1) model with a constant nonzero mean to filter the negative log return process and get an approximately i.i.d. series. Hu and Kercheval (2007) demonstrated in this context that the traditional normal distribution is a poor candidate for the distribution of the filtered returns due to its thin tails. We adopt the more heavy-tailed skewed t distribution, which has shown good results in

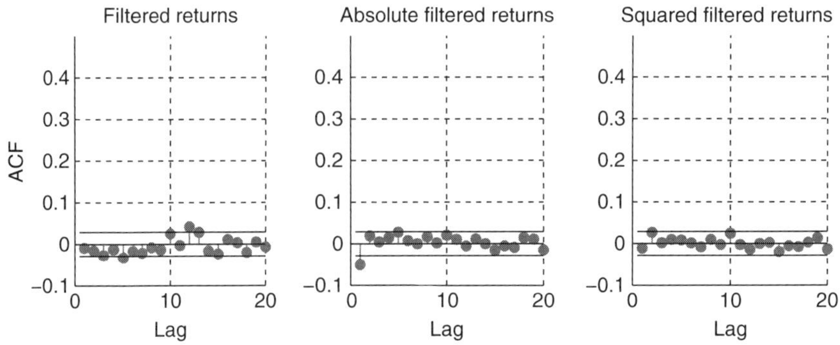

FIGURE 7.2 ACF for filtered S&P500 daily returns data, 1991–2009.

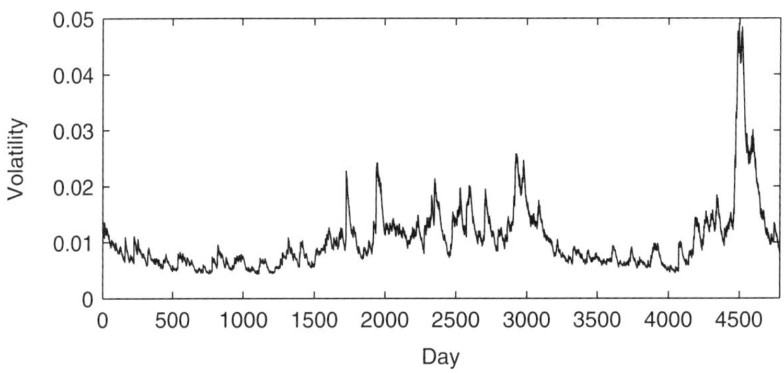

FIGURE 7.3 GARCH volatility for S&P500 daily returns data, 1991–2009.

comparison to common heavy-tailed alternatives. For the same reason, we choose Student t innovations when calibrating GARCH. Correlograms of the filtered series (Fig. 7.2) are included to show the performance of the GARCH filter.

In Fig. 7.3, we plot $\{\sigma_t\}$ of the fitted GARCH process to illustrate stylized fact 4.

7.3.4 VaR FORECASTING

Once the distribution of the filtered data is calibrated with the EM algorithm, VaR forecasts can be immediately derived via defiltering. At time T, since σ_{T+1} is $\mathcal{F}_T$ measurable and Z_{T+1} is independent of $\{X_t\}_{t\leq T+1}$, $\mathcal{F}_T$, the conditional VaR for time $T+1$, will be

$$\begin{aligned}\mathrm{VaR}_\alpha(X_{T+1}|\mathcal{F}_T) &= \mathrm{VaR}_\alpha(\sigma_{T+1}Z_{T+1} + \mu_0|\mathcal{F}_T)\\ &= \sigma_{T+1}\mathrm{VaR}_\alpha(Z_{T+1}) + \mu_0 = \sigma_{T+1}q_\alpha + \mu_0,\end{aligned}$$

where q_α is the α-quantile of the calibrated skewed t distribution.

7.3.5 DRAWBACKS OF THE FIXED-FREQUENCY APPROACH

The EM algorithm uses a maximum likelihood method, which requires a sufficient amount of input data for accuracy. Therefore, as the time horizon grows, data availability can become an issue of major concern.

To investigate the extent to which the EM algorithm depends on the sample size, we generate skewed t r.v.s with $\nu = 6.4$, $\mu = -0.14$, $\gamma = 0.12$, and $\sigma = 0.65$[1] and apply the EM algorithm to samples of different sizes. The calibration of each sample size is repeated 20 times, and the performance is recorded in Tables 7.1 and 7.2.

When the sample size is small, the means of calibrated parameters differ greatly from the exact values and StDs are huge. In other words, calibration results are highly unstable between different groups of simulated r.v.s. An overly small sample size implies a high probability of encountering intractable samples whose empirical distribution is far from representative of the underlying skewed t density (Fig. 7.4**a**–c are included to illustrate such situations). The algorithm struggles to handle such samples, as reflected by high ratios of blowup[2] and a large StD of the number of iterations. As the sample size increases, notably after reaching 750 or 1000, all these anomalies disappear and calibration results are much improved.

TABLE 7.1 **Dependance of EM Algorithm on Sample Size Part I**

	ν		μ		γ		σ	
Sample Size	Mean	StD	Mean	StD	Mean	StD	Mean	StD
100	25.80	23.58	−0.536	0.977	0.491	0.947	0.650	0.118
250	10.45	7.64	−0.210	0.218	0.191	0.198	0.662	0.108
500	7.07	2.08	−0.134	0.147	0.116	0.111	0.641	0.064
750	7.14	2.01	−0.161	0.137	0.132	0.104	0.668	0.050
1000	7.15	1.44	−0.171	0.085	0.148	0.077	0.656	0.040
5000	6.55	0.50	−0.161	0.046	0.136	0.034	0.650	0.018

TABLE 7.2 **Dependance of EM Algorithm on Sample Size Part II**

	Performance		Number of Iterations	
Sample Size	Blowup	Success	Mean	StD
100	10	10	65	157.85
250	4	16	82	120.41
500	1	19	76	44.76
750	1	19	73	45.65
1000	0	20	73	37.76
5000	0	20	62	16.42

[1]These values are the long-term averages obtained from calibrating historical data.

[2]When the maximum iteration number (usually between 250 and 300) is reached, the relative increment is still above the tolerance (usually set as 10^{-5} or 10^{-6}).

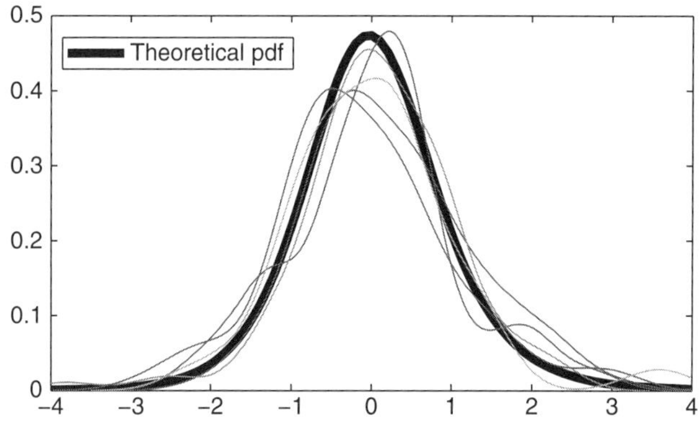

FIGURE 7.4a Theoretical pdf versus sample pdfs, sample size = 100.

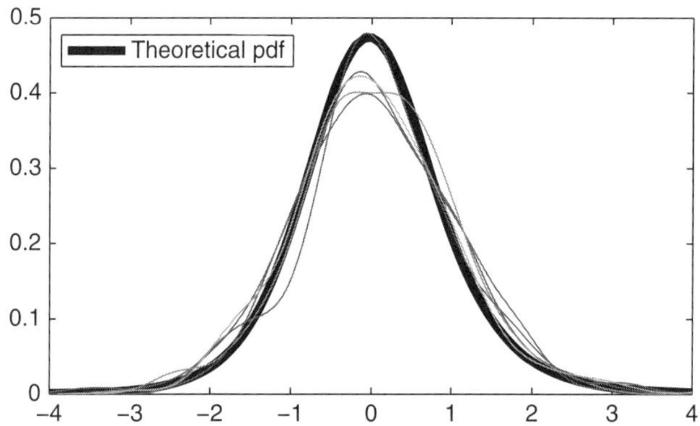

FIGURE 7.4b Theoretical pdf versus sample pdfs, sample size = 250.

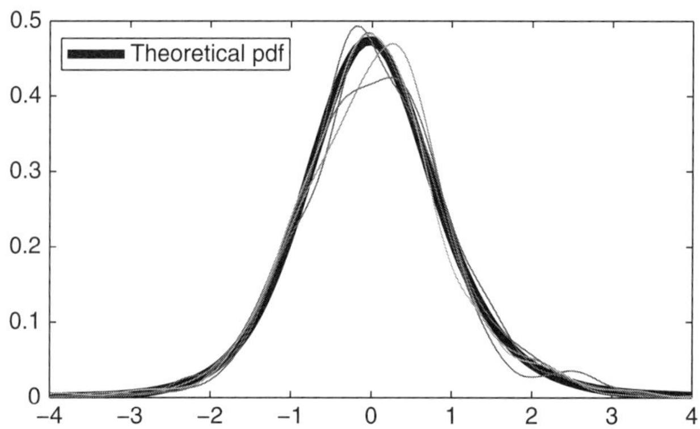

FIGURE 7.4c Theoretical pdf versus sample pdfs, sample size = 500.

TABLE 7.3 **Dependence of GARCH Calibration on Sample Size**

	μ_0		α_0		α_1		β_1	
Sample Size	Mean	StD	Mean	StD	Mean	StD	Mean	StD
100	8.05e-04	9.31e-04	7.31e-05	3.03e-04	0.095	0.134	0.539	0.383
250	8.61e-04	5.49e-04	1.79e-05	2.25e-05	0.066	0.068	0.747	0.297
500	8.78e-04	3.83e-04	1.03e-05	1.48e-05	0.054	0.033	0.853	0.155
750	8.65e-04	2.95e-04	9.09e-06	1.63e-05	0.054	0.026	0.863	0.186
1000	8.81e-04	2.79e-04	7.07e-06	9.74e-06	0.051	0.021	0.881	0.139
5000	8.66e-04	1.21e-04	4.26e-06	9.63e-07	0.048	0.007	0.917	0.013

Calibrating GARCH parameters[3] to non-i.i.d. data uses the same idea of maximum likelihood estimation. To ensure effective filtering, we also need a reasonably large sample.

We simulate a GARCH(1,1) process with $\mu_0 = 8.71 \times 10^{-4}$, $\alpha_0 = 4.26 \times 10^{-6}$, $\alpha_1 = 0.0486$, and $\beta_1 = 0.9161$,[4] then filter the simulated processes of different lengths with GARCH repeatedly (100 times each). Similar to our earlier experiment, Table 7.3 indicates that we need at least 750–1000 samples to approximately retrieve exact parameters.

A minimum of 750 observations is equivalent to about $750/52 \approx 14$ years of weekly data. This may already exceed the entire history for certain stocks (e.g., emerging markets). When it comes to monthly forecasts, a commonly used time horizon for portfolio management, the figure will further grow to $750/12 \approx 62$ years, making it all but impossible to implement the entire framework.[5]

Even if enough data are documented, changes at all market levels (e.g., the integration of global markets, the increasing use of financial derivatives, an industry changed fundamentally by new technology, and a firm after merger and acquisition) can still render historical data outdated or irrelevant. As a result, the validity of forecasts will be dubious.

7.4 Multiple Timescale Forecasts

To overcome the aforementioned drawbacks, we will introduce a high–low frequency approach. Given an *n*-day time horizon, instead of basing calibration and forecasts on the low frequency *n*-day return data, we will use high frequency data (e.g., daily returns) to calibrate the return distribution, then switch back to the lower frequency and make forecasts on the *n*-day timescale. If this approach can be implemented successfully, the restrictions imposed by the scarcity of weekly and monthly historical data will be substantially reduced.

Now we will describe the procedure for this high–low frequency approach.

[3]We use the GARCH Toolbox in Matlab.

[4]Again, to make results more relevant to the application we have in mind, these parameters come from historical data.

[5]Daily data of major indexes such as DOW and SP500 date back only to the 1950s.

ALGORITHM 7.19 High–Low Frequency VaR Forecast

1. Choose a conversion factor K based on the amount of available historical data and/or the time range considered most relevant. When the time horizon is n days, K can be any factor of n except 1. For the sake of simplicity, we will assume $K = n$, that is, n-day is the low frequency, daily is the high frequency.
2. Filter daily data with GARCH(1,1) to get an approximately i.i.d. sequence.
3. Calibrate the skewed t distribution to the filtered data. Denote the corresponding parameter set as $(\nu, \mu, \gamma, \sigma)$.
4. At time T, forecast n days into the future using the GARCH(1,1) mechanism[6]:
For $t = T + 1, \ldots, T + n$

$$X_t = \mu_0 + \sigma_t Z_t,$$
$$\sigma_t^2 = \alpha_0 + \alpha_1 (X_{t-1} - \mu_0)^2 + \beta_1 \sigma_{t-1}^2,$$

where innovations $Z_t \sim \text{SkewT}(\nu, \mu, \gamma, \sigma)$ and $\mu_0, \alpha_0, \alpha_1, \beta_1$ are GARCH parameters from step 2.[7]
5. Make n-day *VaR* forecasts based on the distributions of $X_{T+1}, \ldots, X_{T+n}$.

7.4.1 SIMULATION OF THE GARCH SUM

When this high–low frequency approach is used, VaR estimates must be based on a sequence of n forecasts $X_{T+1}, \ldots, X_{T+n}$. Further, since VaR is not even subadditive, we must consider their sum. Expanding this sum according to Equation 7.49, we get

$$\sum_{i=1}^{n} X_{T+i} = n\mu_0 + \sigma_{T+1} Z_{T+1} + \cdots + \sigma_{T+n} Z_{T+n}. \tag{7.52}$$

Except for σ_{T+1},[8] all volatility coefficients are themselves r.v.s. And by the very nature of GARCH, they are serially correlated.

Since it is extremely difficult to analytically determine the distribution of this GARCH sum, we will compute VaR estimates by Monte Carlo simulation of the GARCH sum distribution:

[6]We will justify using multiple steps of GARCH later in Section 7.5.

[7]Since $Z_t \sim \mathit{SkewT}(\nu, \mu, \gamma, \sigma)$ instead of SWN(0,1), strictly speaking, these forecasts are no longer a GARCH process.

[8]σ_{T+1} is solely determined by observed data, thus constant.

- For each of M independent simulations, generate n i.i.d. $SkewT(\nu, \mu, \gamma, \sigma)$ variates by Algorithm 7.8. Compute $X_{T+1}, \ldots, X_{T+n}$ one by one according to GARCH, then add them up to get the n-day negative log returns $L_1, \ldots, L_M$ (i.e., losses).
- Let$\hat{F}_{L,M}(x)$ denote the empirical distribution of losses based on M simulations,

$$\hat{F}_{L,M}(x) = \frac{1}{M}\sum_{i=1}^{M} 1_{\{L_i \leq x\}}.$$

Estimate VaR_α by the empirical quantile $\hat{x}_\alpha$

$$\widehat{\text{VaR}}_\alpha\left(\sum_{i=1}^{n} X_{T+i}|\mathcal{F}_T\right) = \hat{x}_\alpha = \hat{F}^{-1}_{L,M}(\alpha),$$

where the inverse of the piecewise constant function$\hat{F}_{L,M}$ is defined as

$$\hat{F}^{-1}_{L,M}(u) = \inf\{u : \hat{F}_{L,M}(x) \geq u\}.$$

7.4.2 CONFIDENCE INTERVALS FOR THE FORECASTS

The empirical quantile $\hat{x}_\alpha$ converges to the true quantile x_α with probability 1 as $M \to \infty$. Assuming that L has a strictly positive density f in the neighborhood of x_α, a central limit theorem, as shown in Serfling (1980), states that

$$\sqrt{M}(\hat{x}_\alpha - x_\alpha) \sim \frac{\sqrt{\alpha(1-\alpha)}}{f(x_\alpha)} N(0, 1).$$

This provides the basis for a large-sample $1 - p$ confidence interval[9] for x_α of the form

$$\hat{x}_\alpha \pm z_{p/2}\frac{\sqrt{\alpha(1-\alpha)}}{f(x_\alpha)\sqrt{M}},$$

where $z_{p/2}$ is the $p/2$-quantile of standard normal distribution. Since the density f is unknown, we can divide the sample of M simulations into batches, compute an estimate $\hat{x}_\alpha$ for each batch, and form a confidence interval based on the sample StD of the estimates across batches.

Glasserman (2003) proposed an alternative way without computing the sample StD. Using the fact that the number of samples exceeding x_α has

[9]Later we will use confidence intervals to see if the difference between high–low frequency and fixed-frequency forecasts is statistically significant.

binomial distribution with parameters M and α, we can form the confidence interval without relying on a central limit theorem. Let

$$L_{(1)} \leq L_{(2)} \leq \cdots \leq L_{(M)}$$

denote the order statistics of the losses. An interval of the form $(L_{(r)}, L_{(s)})$, $r < s$, covers x_α with probability

$$P(L_{(r)} \leq x_\alpha < L_{(s)}) = \sum_{i=r}^{s-1} \binom{M}{i} (1-\alpha)^i \alpha^{M-i}.$$

Choose r, s so that this probability is close to the desired confidence level.

7.5 Backtesting

GARCH plays dual roles in the high–low frequency approach. First, it removes serial dependence in historical data so that the maximum likelihood method is applicable for distribution fitting. Later, it is used to mimic the return process n days into the future to enable the switch from the high frequency back to the low frequency. Being an effective filter[10] does not necessarily ensure being a good simulation mechanism. We must justify its validity through backtests.

7.5.1 INDEPENDENCE OF VIOLATION INDICATORS

Define indicator variables

$$I_{t+1}^{\alpha} = 1_{\{\sum_{i=1}^{n} X_{t+i} > \mathrm{VaR}_\alpha(\sum_{i=1}^{n} X_{t+i}|\mathcal{F}_t)\}},$$

which indicates whether the actual losses over the next n days exceeds the conditional VaR forecasted at time t.

Recall that

$$\sum_{i=1}^{n} X_{t+i} = n\mu_0 + \sigma_{t+1} Z_{t+1} + \cdots + \sigma_{t+n} Z_{t+n}.$$

Since $\sigma_{t+2}, \ldots, \sigma_{t+n}$ are actually determined by $\sigma_{t+1}, Z_{t+1}, \ldots, Z_{t+n-1}$, we can summarize this sum as

$$\sum_{i=1}^{n} X_{t+i} = f(\mu_0, \sigma_{t+1}, Z_{t+1}, \ldots, Z_{t+n}).$$

[10]As illustrated in Figs. 7.1 and 7.2. Hu and Kercheval (2007) also provided favorable evidence.

Similarly, the conditional VaR can be expressed as

$$\mathrm{VaR}_\alpha\left(\sum_{i=1}^{n} X_{t+i}|\mathcal{F}_t\right) = g(\mu_0, \sigma_{t+1}, Z^{(1)}, \ldots, Z^{(n)}).^{11}$$

Noticing that μ_0 and the distribution of $Z^{(1)}, \ldots, Z^{(n)}$ hold constant throughout the GARCH process, we can further reduce the above notation to

$$\mathrm{VaR}_\alpha\left(\sum_{i=1}^{n} X_{t+i}|\mathcal{F}_t\right) = g(\sigma_{t+1}).$$

Now consider two indicator variables

$$I_{t+1}^{\alpha} = 1_{\{f(\mu_0, \sigma_{t+1}, Z_{t+1}, \ldots, Z_{t+n}) > g(\sigma_{t+1})\}}$$

and

$$I_{t+j+1}^{\alpha} = 1_{\{f(\mu_0, \sigma_{t+j+1}, Z_{t+j+1}, \ldots, Z_{t+j+n}) > g(\sigma_{t+j+1})\}}.$$

Among the variables, μ_0 is a constant. Both σ_{t+1} and σ_{t+j+1} are $\mathcal{F}_{t+j}$ measurable, so they are deterministic at time $t + j$. Therefore, as long as $Z_{t+1}, \ldots, Z_{t+n}$ and $Z_{t+j+1}, \ldots, Z_{t+j+n}$ do not overlap, that is, $j \geq n$, these i.i.d. innovations will ensure that I_{t+1}^{α} and I_{t+j+1}^{α} are independent.

7.5.2 BACKTEST ALGORITHM

Given a data set of N daily negative log returns $\{X_1, \ldots, X_N\}$, suppose our target time horizon is n days and the sample size for skewed t calibration is C. Use the following algorithm for backtest.

ALGORITHM 7.20 Backtest

For $t = C, C + n, C + 2n, \ldots, C + kn, \ldots$

1. Apply GARCH filter to $\{X_{t-C+1}, \ldots, X_t\}$ and calibrate the skewed t distribution.
2. Compute $\widehat{\mathrm{VaR}}_\alpha(\sum_{i=1}^{n} X_{t+i}|\mathcal{F}_t)$, the estimate for conditional VaR_α, for $\alpha = 0.95, 0.975, 0.99$, and 0.995 with Monte Carlo simulation.
3. Compare the sum of next n observations with $\widehat{\mathrm{VaR}}_\alpha$. Violation is counted by $I_{t+1}^{\alpha} = 1_{\{\sum_{i=1}^{n} X_{t+i} > \widehat{\mathrm{VaR}}_\alpha(\sum_{i=1}^{n} X_{t+i}|\mathcal{F}_t)\}}$.

[11] VaR is based on the distribution of $\sum_{i=1}^{n} X_{t+i}$, not the actual values of $Z_{t+1}, \ldots, Z_{t+n}$. Distinguishing Zs with a time index is no longer necessary. It suffices to use $Z^{(1)}, \ldots, Z^{(n)}$, that is, n i.i.d. skewed t r.v.s.

7.5.3 STATISTICAL TESTS

DEFINITION 7.21 Bernoulli(p) Distribution.

A random variable X has a Bernoulli(p) distribution if

$$X = \begin{cases} 1 & \text{with probability } p \\ 0 & \text{with probability } 1-p, \end{cases} \qquad 0 \le p \le 1.$$

If the estimates of conditional VaR are successful, the violation indicators should behave like i.i.d. Bernoulli($1-\alpha$) trials.

PROPOSITION 7.22 Bernoulli MLE

Let $X_1, \dots, X_n$ be i.i.d. Bernoulli(p). The likelihood function is

$$L(p|\mathbf{x}) = \prod_{i=1}^{n} p^{x_i}(1-p)^{1-x_i} = p^y(1-p)^{n-y},$$

where $y = \sum_{i=1}^{n} x_i$. The maximum likelihood estimator (MLE) of p is $\sum_{i=1}^{n} X_i/n$.

Proof. $L(p|\mathbf{x}) = p^y(1-p)^{n-y}$ follows immediately from the definition of likelihood functions and the pmf of Bernoulli(p). $L(p|\mathbf{x}) = p^y(1-p)^{n-y}$ is not too hard to differentiate, but it is easier to differentiate the log likelihood

$$\log L(p|\mathbf{x}) = y \log p + (n-y)\log(1-p).$$

If $0 < y < n$, differentiating $\log L(p|\mathbf{x})$ and setting the result equal to 0 yields the solution $\hat{p} = y/n$. It can be easily verified that y/n is the global maximum. If $y = 0$ or $y = 1$, it is again straightforward to verify that $\hat{p} = y/n$. Thus, $\sum_{i=1}^{n} X_i/n$ is the MLE of p. ■

DEFINITION 7.23 Likelihood Ratio Test Statistic

Let Θ denote the entire parameter space, and Θ_0 some parameter subset. The likelihood ratio test (LRT) statistic for testing $H_0 : \theta \in \Theta_0$ versus $H_1 : \theta \in \Theta_0^c$ is

$$\lambda(\mathbf{x}) = \frac{\sup_{\Theta_0} L(\theta|\mathbf{x})}{\sup_{\Theta} L(\theta|\mathbf{x})}.$$

To understand the rationale behind the LRT, consider a sample of discrete r.v.s, in which case the likelihood function is the product of pmfs (i.e., discrete probabilities). The numerator of $\lambda(\boldsymbol{x})$ is the maximum probability, computed over parameters in the null hypothesis, of the observed sample. The denominator is the maximum probability over all possible parameters. The ratio of these two maxima is small if there are parameter points in the alternative hypothesis for which the observed sample is much more likely than for any parameter point in the null hypothesis. In that case, the LRT criterion concludes that H_0 should be rejected.

PROPOSITION 7.24 Bernoulli LRT

Let $X_1, \ldots, X_n$ be a random sample from a Bernoulli(p) population. Consider testing $H_0 : p = p_0$ versus $H_1 : p \neq p_0$. The LRT statistic is

$$\lambda(\mathbf{x}) = \frac{p_0^y (1 - p_0)^{n-y}}{\left(\frac{y}{n}\right)^y \left(1 - \frac{y}{n}\right)^{n-y}}.$$

Proof. Since there is only one value specified by H_0, the numerator of $\lambda(\mathbf{x})$ is $L(p_0|\mathbf{x})$. The MLE of p is y/n by Proposition 7.21, so the denominator is $L(\frac{y}{n}|\mathbf{x})$. Together, the LRT statistic is

$$\lambda(\mathbf{x}) = \frac{L(p_0|\mathbf{x})}{L(\frac{y}{n}|\mathbf{x})} = \frac{p_0^y (1 - p_0)^{n-y}}{\left(\frac{y}{n}\right)^y \left(1 - \frac{y}{n}\right)^{n-y}}.$$

■

DEFINITION 7.25 Asymptotic Distribution of the LRT

For testing $H_0 : \theta = \theta_0$ versus $H_1 : \theta \neq \theta_0$, suppose $X_1, \ldots, X_n$ are i.i.d. with pdf or pmf $f(x|\theta)$, $\hat{\theta}$ is the MLE of θ, and $f(x|\theta)$ satisfies certain regularity conditions. Then under H_0, as $n \to \infty$,

$$-2 \log \lambda(\mathbf{x}) \to \chi^2(1) \text{ in distribution.}$$

Proof. See Casella and Berger (2002). ■

Recall that we did a sequence of backtests by counting VaR violations. Suppose there are altogether Y tests, and let y denote the number of total violations. The actual violation frequency is y/Y, which is the MLE of a Bernoulli distribution, while the expected violation probability, q, should be 0.05, 0.025, 0.01, and 0.005.

We then evaluate the backtest results with the likelihood ratio test[12] based on Theorem 7.24:

$$\begin{cases} H_0: & \text{The expected violation ratio} = q, \\ H_1: & \text{The expected violation ratio} \neq q. \end{cases}$$

Under the null hypothesis, the test statistic is

$$-2[(Y-y)\log(1-q)+y\log(q)]+2[(Y-y)\log(1-y/Y)+y\log(y/Y)],$$

which is asymptotically $\chi^2(1)$ distributed.

The stepsize of the backtest algorithm is set as n to ensure the independence of violation indicators. As a result, the number of tests that can be done on a fixed amount of daily data will shrink substantially when the time horizon increases. To extract more information on the violations, we can implement the backtest algorithm n times, each with a different starting point in the time index (i.e., $t = C, C+1, \ldots, C+n-1$). Each of the n backtests will contain the same total number of tests Y, but a different number of violations $y_1, \ldots, y_n$.

7.5.4 *n*-DAY HORIZON

We list the actual violation ratios and the corresponding p-values of the likelihood ratio test (LRT) in Tables 7.4–7.13. All VaR backtesting is based on S&P500 daily close prices from January 1, 1991, to December 31, 2009. A thousand samples are used to calibrate each skewed t distribution. Depending on the length of the time horizon, the total number of backtests ranges between 500 and 1900. For an n-day horizon, we have n groups of results representing different starting points in the time index.

From a 2-day to a 10-day horizon, altogether $(2+10)\times 9\times 4/2 = 216$ LRTs are done, among which the five p-values <0.05[13] are sparsely distributed. Setting the confidence level of the LRT to be 95% implies that even if the model is perfect, we will still have a 5% chance of observing LRT failures (i.e., type I errors). Since the failure ratio of the backtests 5/216≈2.3% is much lower than 5%, we consider our model performance is satisfactory.

TABLE 7.4 Backtest Results: Two Days

	Violation Ratio				p-Value			
q	0.05	0.025	0.01	0.005	0.05	0.025	0.01	0.005
Group 1	0.059	0.026	0.010	0.005	0.076	0.809	0.827	0.864
Group 2	0.050	0.027	0.010	0.007	0.975	0.596	0.827	0.277

[12]Since the sum of i.i.d. Bernoulli r.v. is a binomial r.v., another alternative is a standard two-sided binomial test, as described by Casella and Berger (2002).

[13]We reject the null hypothesis when the p-value is <0.05.

TABLE 7.5 Backtest Results: Three Days

	Violation Ratio				p-Value			
q	0.05	0.025	0.01	0.005	0.05	0.025	0.01	0.005
Group 1	0.057	0.027	0.012	0.008	0.260	0.663	0.513	0.175
Group 2	0.054	0.032	0.013	0.009	0.532	0.143	0.239	0.091
Group 3	0.052	0.025	0.012	0.007	0.807	0.921	0.513	0.313

TABLE 7.6 Backtest Results: Four Days

	Violation Ratio				p-Value			
q	0.05	0.025	0.01	0.005	0.05	0.025	0.01	0.005
Group 1	0.055	0.025	0.012	0.004	0.490	0.942	0.624	0.730
Group 2	0.041	0.030	0.013	0.006	0.202	0.378	0.426	0.574
Group 3	0.052	0.023	0.013	0.005	0.801	0.728	0.426	0.902
Group 4	0.053	0.030	0.020	0.008	0.690	0.378	**0.006**	0.170

TABLE 7.7 Backtest Results: Five Days

	Violation Ratio				p-Value			
q	0.05	0.025	0.01	0.005	0.05	0.025	0.01	0.005
Group 1	0.045	0.024	0.007	0.005	0.514	0.828	0.317	0.913
Group 2	0.053	0.026	0.012	0.008	0.722	0.804	0.612	0.293
Group 3	0.046	0.029	0.011	0.008	0.630	0.485	0.876	0.293
Group 4	0.052	0.026	0.016	0.011	0.849	0.804	0.136	0.059
Group 5	0.057	0.037	0.012	0.005	0.400	**0.048**	0.612	0.913

TABLE 7.8 Backtest Results: Six Days

	Violation Ratio				p-Value			
q	0.05	0.025	0.01	0.005	0.05	0.025	0.01	0.005
Group 1	0.052	0.019	0.011	0.006	0.785	0.318	0.783	0.645
Group 2	0.049	0.022	0.013	0.008	0.927	0.649	0.514	0.336
Group 3	0.056	0.025	0.011	0.008	0.529	0.949	0.783	0.336
Group 4	0.048	0.021	0.014	0.011	0.782	0.470	0.310	0.061
Group 5	0.057	0.030	0.011	0.006	0.421	0.422	0.783	0.645
Group 6	0.051	0.032	0.011	0.006	0.927	0.298	0.783	0.645

TABLE 7.9 Backtest Results: Seven Days

	Violation Ratio				*p*-Value			
q	0.05	0.025	0.01	0.005	0.05	0.025	0.01	0.005
Group 1	0.043	0.024	0.011	0.007	0.418	0.890	0.799	0.459
Group 2	0.044	0.017	0.013	0.006	0.546	0.187	0.508	0.857
Group 3	0.041	0.033	0.013	0.004	0.308	0.238	0.508	0.654
Group 4	0.044	0.024	0.013	0.006	0.546	0.890	0.508	0.857
Group 5	0.039	0.024	0.019	0.013	0.218	0.890	0.075	**0.029**
Group 6	0.054	0.020	0.011	0.007	0.696	0.477	0.799	0.459
Group 7	0.059	0.030	0.006	0.006	0.337	0.503	0.257	0.857

TABLE 7.10 Backtest Results: Eight Days

	Violation Ratio				*p*-Value			
q	0.05	0.025	0.01	0.005	0.05	0.025	0.01	0.005
Group 1	0.034	0.021	0.013	0.006	0.089	0.586	0.570	0.689
Group 2	0.055	0.023	0.015	0.006	0.618	0.811	0.325	0.689
Group 3	0.047	0.028	0.008	0.004	0.733	0.728	0.732	0.809
Group 4	0.038	0.017	0.015	0.006	0.218	0.235	0.325	0.689
Group 5	0.051	0.030	0.008	0.004	0.933	0.528	0.732	0.809
Group 6	0.053	0.017	0.008	0.006	0.770	0.235	0.732	0.689
Group 7	0.044	0.023	0.015	0.008	0.576	0.811	0.325	0.331
Group 8	0.049	0.023	0.006	0.004	0.899	0.811	0.394	0.809

TABLE 7.11 Backtest Results: Nine Days

	Violation Ratio				*p*-Value			
q	0.05	0.025	0.01	0.005	0.05	0.025	0.01	0.005
Group 1	0.036	0.014	0.007	0.005	0.158	0.127	0.535	0.944
Group 2	0.045	0.024	0.012	0.005	0.649	0.875	0.703	0.944
Group 3	0.043	0.029	0.010	0.005	0.492	0.647	0.921	0.944
Group 4	0.033	0.021	0.010	0.002	0.096	0.631	0.921	0.396
Group 5	0.048	0.024	0.007	0.005	0.822	0.875	0.535	0.944
Group 6	0.057	0.026	0.014	0.010	0.511	0.877	0.407	0.243
Group 7	0.052	0.031	0.017	0.014	0.824	0.451	0.210	**0.028**
Group 8	0.052	0.024	0.014	0.010	0.824	0.875	0.407	0.243
Group 9	0.040	0.017	0.010	0.002	0.355	0.245	0.921	0.396

TABLE 7.12 **Backtest Results: 10 Days**

	Violation Ratio				*p*-Value			
q	0.05	0.025	0.01	0.005	0.05	0.025	0.01	0.005
Group 1	0.040	0.016	0.011	0.008	0.340	0.224	0.910	0.456
Group 2	0.048	0.026	0.016	0.008	0.831	0.858	0.290	0.456
Group 3	0.048	0.024	0.021	0.016	0.831	0.881	0.058	**0.017**
Group 4	0.040	0.019	0.013	0.008	0.340	0.398	0.548	0.456
Group 5	0.034	0.016	0.005	0.005	0.141	0.224	0.312	0.937
Group 6	0.032	0.016	0.013	0.008	0.082	0.224	0.548	0.456
Group 7	0.040	0.016	0.008	0.008	0.340	0.224	0.676	0.456
Group 8	0.048	0.026	0.011	0.005	0.831	0.858	0.910	0.937
Group 9	0.042	0.026	0.016	0.008	0.483	0.858	0.290	0.456
Group 10	0.053	0.032	0.011	0.005	0.797	0.420	0.910	0.937

TABLE 7.13 **Backtest Results: 15 Days**

	Violation Ratio				*p*-Value			
q	0.05	0.025	0.01	0.005	0.05	0.025	0.01	0.005
Group 1	0.046	0.036	0.015	0.010	0.645	0.118	0.230	0.117
Group 2	0.049	0.034	0.014	0.010	0.940	0.184	0.405	0.117
Group 3	0.044	0.029	0.020	0.010	0.512	0.553	**0.026**	0.117
Group 4	0.058	0.031	0.012	0.007	0.395	0.399	0.652	0.557
Group 5	0.054	0.027	0.015	0.012	0.627	0.735	0.230	**0.044**
Group 6	0.054	0.031	0.017	0.012	0.627	0.399	0.121	**0.044**
Group 7	0.054	0.041	0.020	0.007	0.627	**0.024**	**0.026**	0.557
Group 8	0.060	0.034	0.019	0.007	0.303	0.184	0.058	0.557
Group 9	0.056	0.037	0.017	0.012	0.504	0.072	0.121	**0.044**
Group 10	0.056	0.029	0.015	0.012	0.504	0.553	0.230	**0.044**
Group 11	0.061	0.041	0.014	0.009	0.227	**0.024**	0.405	0.274
Group 12	0.065	0.032	0.014	0.007	0.119	0.277	0.405	0.557
Group 13	0.056	0.032	0.014	0.009	0.504	0.277	0.405	0.274
Group 14	0.058	0.031	0.014	0.012	0.395	0.399	0.405	**0.044**
Group 15	0.058	0.029	0.015	0.010	0.395	0.553	0.230	0.117

Still, the high–low frequency method does have its limits. As shown in Table 7.13, when the time horizon is extended to 15 days, nine failures are observed in 60 LRTs. This is not surprising. As the time horizon stretches, we are ignoring more and more new information, leading to deteriorating GARCH performance.

7.5.5 A VARIANT BACKTEST: FORECASTING A ONE-DAY RETURN, *n* DAYS AHEAD

The backtest above evaluates the accuracy of the simulated sum $\sum_{i=1}^{n} X_{t+i}$ as a whole. To further examine each term inside that sum, we can slightly modify the previous backtest algorithm.

ALGORITHM 7.26 Alternative Backtest

For $t = C, C+n, C+2n, \ldots, C+kn, \ldots$

1. Apply GARCH filter to $\{X_{t-C+1}, \ldots, X_t\}$, and calibrate the skewed t distribution.
2. Compute $\widehat{\text{VaR}}_\alpha(X_{t+n}|\mathcal{F}_t)$, that is, VaR for day $t+n$, for $\alpha = 0.95, 0.975, 0.99$, and 0.995 with Monte Carlo simulation.
3. Compare the observation on day $t+n$ with $\widehat{\text{VaR}}_\alpha(X_{t+n}|\mathcal{F}_t)$. Violation is counted if $X_{t+n} > \widehat{\text{VaR}}_\alpha(X_{t+n}|\mathcal{F}_t)$.

Repeat this alternative version with stepsize from 2 to n days, and a day-by-day picture of the performance of GARCH simulation will be obtained. We list the results in Tables 7.14–7.22.

Not a single LRT failure is observed up to the seven-day horizon. Successfully forecasting day-by-day VaR lends further confidence to the high–low frequency method.

7.5.6 A NOTE ON THE MONTHLY FORECAST HORIZON

As shown above, when the target horizon is monthly, a daily frequency is no longer appropriate for the high frequency level. In the high–low frequency approach, timescales on both levels are evenly spaced. However, physical months are of varying lengths (in terms of trading days). We must first find some substitute for the monthly horizon.

Not considering occasional national holidays, each year typically has 260 trading days and thereby $260/12 = 21.7$ days each month on average. We will

TABLE 7.14 Alternative Backtest Results: Two Days

	Violation Ratio				p-Value			
q	0.05	0.025	0.01	0.005	0.05	0.025	0.01	0.005
Group 1	0.058	0.030	0.011	0.006	0.165	0.229	0.611	0.595
Group 2	0.048	0.027	0.007	0.004	0.721	0.682	0.276	0.569

TABLE 7.15 Alternative Backtest Results: Three Days

	Violation Ratio				p-Value			
q	0.05	0.025	0.01	0.005	0.05	0.025	0.01	0.005
Group 1	0.055	0.030	0.010	0.003	0.475	0.326	1.000	0.333
Group 2	0.052	0.027	0.007	0.005	0.773	0.689	0.314	1.000
Group 3	0.054	0.027	0.011	0.006	0.566	0.689	0.754	0.664

TABLE 7.16 Alternative Backtest Results: Four Days

	Violation Ratio				p-Value			
q	0.05	0.025	0.01	0.005	0.05	0.025	0.01	0.005
Group 1	0.063	0.033	0.011	0.004	0.125	0.164	0.856	0.687
Group 2	0.043	0.020	0.011	0.003	0.345	0.364	0.856	0.320
Group 3	0.055	0.021	0.008	0.007	0.563	0.510	0.568	0.538
Group 4	0.061	0.033	0.009	0.005	0.168	0.164	0.853	0.898

TABLE 7.17 Alternative Backtest Results: Five Days

	Violation Ratio				p-Value			
q	0.05	0.025	0.01	0.005	0.05	0.025	0.01	0.005
Group 1	0.050	0.022	0.005	0.003	1.000	0.593	0.173	0.538
Group 2	0.063	0.028	0.010	0.007	0.149	0.608	1.000	0.582
Group 3	0.057	0.030	0.010	0.007	0.463	0.447	1.000	0.582
Group 4	0.043	0.030	0.012	0.005	0.444	0.447	0.689	1.000
Group 5	0.053	0.028	0.010	0.005	0.711	0.608	1.000	1.000

TABLE 7.18 Alternative Backtest Results: Six Days

	Violation Ratio				p-Value			
q	0.05	0.025	0.01	0.005	0.05	0.025	0.01	0.005
Group 1	0.056	0.034	0.010	0.006	0.546	0.221	1.000	0.759
Group 2	0.050	0.018	0.004	0.004	1.000	0.292	0.125	0.743
Group 3	0.056	0.022	0.008	0.006	0.546	0.661	0.641	0.759
Group 4	0.048	0.030	0.010	0.006	0.836	0.487	1.000	0.759
Group 5	0.060	0.032	0.008	0.006	0.319	0.336	0.641	0.759
Group 6	0.054	0.032	0.012	0.002	0.685	0.336	0.663	0.279

TABLE 7.19 Alternative Backtest Results: Seven Days

	Violation Ratio				p-Value			
q	0.05	0.025	0.01	0.005	0.05	0.025	0.01	0.005
Group 1	0.056	0.028	0.014	0.009	0.571	0.693	0.431	0.256
Group 2	0.070	0.037	0.007	0.005	0.071	0.126	0.511	0.923
Group 3	0.061	0.023	0.009	0.005	0.323	0.827	0.891	0.923
Group 4	0.051	0.023	0.007	0.005	0.895	0.827	0.511	0.923
Group 5	0.042	0.023	0.009	0.005	0.439	0.827	0.891	0.923
Group 6	0.056	0.026	0.009	0.005	0.571	0.926	0.891	0.923
Group 7	0.051	0.030	0.012	0.009	0.895	0.491	0.733	0.256

TABLE 7.20 **Alternative Backtest Results: Eight Days**

	Violation Ratio				*p*-Value			
q	0.05	0.025	0.01	0.005	0.05	0.025	0.01	0.005
Group 1	0.051	0.035	0.008	0.005	0.953	0.257	0.687	0.928
Group 2	0.040	0.024	0.008	0.008	0.358	0.901	0.687	0.449
Group 3	0.059	0.029	0.008	0.005	0.453	0.601	0.687	0.928
Group 4	0.069	0.040	0.011	0.008	0.104	0.087	0.898	0.449
Group 5	0.061	0.035	0.011	0.008	0.330	0.257	0.898	0.449
Group 6	0.051	0.021	0.005	0.000	0.953	0.641	0.319	NaN[a]
Group 7	0.053	0.021	0.008	0.008	0.769	0.641	0.687	0.449
Group 8	0.056	0.027	0.008	0.005	0.601	0.838	0.687	0.928

[a]NaN (not a number) arises from log 0 in the likelihood ratio statistic when violation count is 0.

TABLE 7.21 **Alternative Backtest Results: Nine Days**

	Violation Ratio				*p*-Value			
q	0.05	0.025	0.01	0.005	0.05	0.025	0.01	0.005
Group 1	0.051	0.024	0.009	0.003	0.930	0.909	0.853	0.577
Group 2	0.054	0.021	0.006	0.000	0.737	0.633	0.429	NaN[a]
Group 3	0.075	0.030	0.015	0.006	0.050	0.569	0.392	0.801
Group 4	0.060	0.030	0.009	0.006	0.414	0.569	0.853	0.801
Group 5	0.069	0.036	0.009	0.006	0.130	0.226	0.853	0.801
Group 6	0.045	0.018	0.009	0.009	0.673	0.391	0.853	0.351
Group 7	0.066	0.042	0.018	0.012	0.199	0.069	0.186	0.125
Group 8	0.042	0.024	0.012	0.006	0.494	0.909	0.721	0.801
Group 9	0.039	0.024	0.009	0.003	0.341	0.909	0.853	0.577

[a]NaN (not a number) arises from log 0 in the likelihood ratio statistic when violation count is 0.

TABLE 7.22 **Alternative Backtest Results: 10 Days**

	Violation Ratio				*p*-Value			
q	0.05	0.025	0.01	0.005	0.05	0.025	0.01	0.005
Group 1	0.047	0.017	0.003	0.000	0.789	0.326	0.178	NaN[a]
Group 2	0.050	0.027	0.003	0.000	1.000	0.855	0.178	NaN[a]
Group 3	0.070	0.030	0.013	0.010	0.133	0.591	0.581	0.280
Group 4	0.043	0.030	0.007	0.007	0.588	0.591	0.537	0.697
Group 5	0.067	0.030	0.007	0.000	0.207	0.591	0.537	NaN[a]
Group 6	0.053	0.030	0.013	0.010	0.793	0.591	0.581	0.280
Group 7	0.070	0.027	0.017	0.010	0.133	0.855	0.290	0.280
Group 8	0.053	0.027	0.010	0.007	0.793	0.855	1.000	0.697
Group 9	0.043	0.030	0.010	0.007	0.588	0.591	1.000	0.697
Group 10	0.070	0.023	0.010	0.007	0.133	0.852	1.000	0.697

[a]NaN (not a number) arises from log 0 in the likelihood ratio statistic when violation count is 0.

use 20 or 21 days as the monthly horizon, as they are divisible by reasonable conversion factors.[14] LRT results are presented in Tables 7.23–7.26[15]. Again, the high–low frequency model passes the backtests.

7.5.7 STABILITY OF THE LIKELIHOOD RATIO TEST AND ALGORITHM SPEED

VaR estimates based on Monte Carlo simulation are inherently random. If we run a specific backtest more than once, the number of VaR violations will not be a fixed number. Will such uncertainty affect the conclusion of LRTs?

TABLE 7.23 Backtest Results: 7–21 Days

	Violation Ratio				*p*-Value			
q	0.05	0.025	0.01	0.005	0.05	0.025	0.01	0.005
Group 1	0.054	0.021	0.012	0.012	0.747	0.627	0.725	0.126
Group 2	0.051	0.030	0.018	0.006	0.940	0.575	0.188	0.804
Group 3	0.045	0.018	0.012	0.012	0.664	0.386	0.725	0.126

TABLE 7.24 Backtest Results: 5–20 Days

	Violation Ratio				*p*-Value			
q	0.05	0.025	0.01	0.005	0.05	0.025	0.01	0.005
Group 1	0.060	0.032	0.018	0.008	0.340	0.351	0.110	0.389
Group 2	0.052	0.028	0.012	0.008	0.871	0.695	0.677	0.389
Group 3	0.044	0.026	0.012	0.006	0.504	0.910	0.677	0.769
Group 4	0.054	0.028	0.012	0.008	0.716	0.695	0.677	0.389

TABLE 7.25 Backtest Results: 4–20 Days

	Violation Ratio				*p*-Value			
q	0.05	0.025	0.01	0.005	0.05	0.025	0.01	0.005
Group 1	0.045	0.030	0.018	0.008	0.570	0.460	0.100	0.371
Group 2	0.045	0.026	0.012	0.010	0.570	0.853	0.643	0.157
Group 3	0.051	0.028	0.008	0.006	0.951	0.641	0.660	0.744
Group 4	0.053	0.026	0.016	0.010	0.790	0.853	0.204	0.157
Group 5	0.061	0.030	0.014	0.006	0.289	0.460	0.381	0.744

[14] Reasonable conversion factors are those that can effectively reduce reliance on data availability without going beyond the limits of GARCH forecasting. For example, the conversion factors for the 22-day horizon can be 2, 11, or 22. Using 11 and 22 risks extrapolating much too far into the future while choosing 2 means you still need 30 years of data.

[15] To get enough backtests, the data set is expanded to 1971–2009.

TABLE 7.26 **Backtest Results: 3–21 Days**

	Violation Ratio				*p*-Value			
q	0.05	0.025	0.01	0.005	0.05	0.025	0.01	0.005
Group 1	0.041	0.021	0.017	0.013	0.335	0.606	0.161	**0.045**
Group 2	0.043	0.017	0.011	0.011	0.460	0.246	0.883	0.130
Group 3	0.058	0.021	0.013	0.009	0.456	0.606	0.557	0.323
Group 4	0.058	0.032	0.013	0.006	0.456	0.349	0.557	0.679
Group 5	0.064	0.036	0.017	0.017	0.179	0.141	0.161	**0.004**
Group 6	0.049	0.032	0.011	0.006	0.932	0.349	0.883	0.679
Group 7	0.038	0.024	0.011	0.009	0.233	0.834	0.883	0.323

To investigate this problem, we first backtest a daily VaR forecast using the fixed-frequency method. Since VaR is computed using numerical integration and root finding, the resulting violation numbers are constant and can be used as a benchmark. We then replace the VaR forecast step with Monte Carlo simulation as used in the high–low frequency method, repeat the same backtest again and again, and examine the discrepancy between violation numbers and the benchmark.

As shown in Tables 7.27–7.30, all 20 trials, with either 10K or 25K simulations, lead to the same conclusion for the LRTs. As a matter of fact, over the entire course, the error in violation count never exceeds six, which is a tiny fraction of the 8843 tests[16] and also minimal when compared with the acceptable band[17] of LRTs. Therefore, we can conclude that when 25K simulations[18] are used, the randomness of the violation counts is already immaterial, and the LRT results are stable.

In our experience, filtering a sample of 1000 data with GARCH can be finished within a second or two.[19] It then takes the EM algorithm about 2 min[20] to calibrate the skewed *t* distribution. In the forecast step, depending on the conversion factor, every 10K simulation costs about 1.5–3 s. Since the target horizon for the high–low frequency approach is at least two days, the model is quick enough to produce a single VaR forecast to any desired accuracy level

[16]Using 1971–2009 daily returns.

[17]Kupiec (1995) provided an extensive survey of the performance of the LRT in the context of risk management.

[18]Although using 25K simulations reduces both relative error and absolute error in VaR by about one-third as compared to 10K, in terms of average discrepancy and maximum discrepancy, there is not much difference. Still, to be cautious, we performed all backtests listed in tables prior to Table 7.6. A using 30K simulations.

[19]We use a laptop with 2.8 GHz CPU and 2 GB memory. The software used is MATLAB R2007b.

[20]In backtest, the time spent on calibration can be significantly reduced. Since most data are overlapping, we can use the parameters from calibration results of the previous period as the initial values and start from scratch only infrequently, say every 200 days, to avoid overestimation.

TABLE 7.27 Stability of Violation Counts Monte Carlo simulations (MC) = 10K

α	95%	97.50%	99%	99.50%
Benchmark	451	238	91	46
Trial 1	455	244	90	50
Trial 2	445	242	89	47
Trial 3	452	243	92	48
Trial 4	447	244	93	50
Trial 5	450	240	93	49
Trial 6	455	244	90	50
Trial 7	445	242	89	47
Trial 8	452	243	92	48
Trial 9	447	244	93	50
Trial 10	450	240	93	49
Average Error	3.2	4.6	1.6	2.8
Maximum Error	6	6	2	4

TABLE 7.28 Stability of Violation Counts MC = 25K

α	95%	97.50%	99%	99.50%
Benchmark	451	238	91	46
Trial 1	451	239	89	48
Trial 2	445	239	88	47
Trial 3	446	244	88	48
Trial 4	449	238	90	45
Trial 5	446	241	88	51
Trial 6	453	243	94	48
Trial 7	451	242	90	49
Trial 8	451	235	91	50
Trial 9	451	237	92	49
Trial 10	446	241	91	47
Average Error	2.5	2.7	1.7	2.4
Maximum Error	6	6	3	5

TABLE 7.29 VaR Error

	Mean Absolute Error[a]				Mean Relative Error			
α	95%	97.50%	99%	99.50%	95%	97.50%	99%	99.50%
10K	0.00020	0.00029	0.00049	0.00074	1.30%	1.49%	1.95%	2.51%
25K	0.00013	0.00019	0.00031	0.00047	0.83%	0.95%	1.25%	1.62%

[a]As compared with the forecast made by the fixed frequency method, with absolute value taken.

TABLE 7.30 Acceptable[a] Band of LRT

α	95%	97.50%	99%	99.50%
Expected Violation	442	221	89	42
Min Acceptable	403	193	71	32
Max Acceptable	482	250	107	57

[a]So that p-value >0.05.

(by increasing the number of simulations). When 25K simulations are used, the mean absolute error and relative error for $\text{VaR}_{95\%}$ are 0.00013 and 0.83%, respectively.

7.5.8 A QUICK LOOK AT INTRADAY DATA

As mentioned earlier, financial data behave similarly on all time intervals. The entire approach can be readily applied to intraday data. However, as the time interval is shortened to minutes or even seconds, data typically get more noisy and the order of the GARCH filter must be increased to get satisfactory results. To illustrate this, we examined a time series of 1-min returns of a US long-term bond index futures contract over the week of March 16, 2009. Autocorrelation of GARCH filtering at different orders is shown in Fig. 7.5**a**–c.

VaR is not traditionally used for time horizons less than one day, but to illuminate the possibilities for high frequency applications, we show multiscale VaR forecast backtest results for 2- through 5-min horizons, based on the same intraday data, in Tables 7.31–7.33 .

We see some rejections of the backtest null hypothesis for GARCH(1,1), but GARCH(2,2) and GARCH(3,3) behave quite reasonably. Therefore, at least for this high frequency returns series, intraday VaR forecasts are a viable option with the multiscale GARCH method. Practitioners should test their own data for suitability of this approach for their own use.

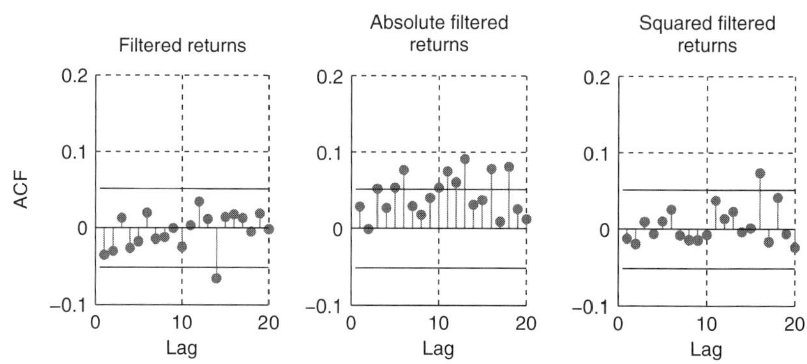

FIGURE 7.5a ACF for minute data using GARCH(1,1).

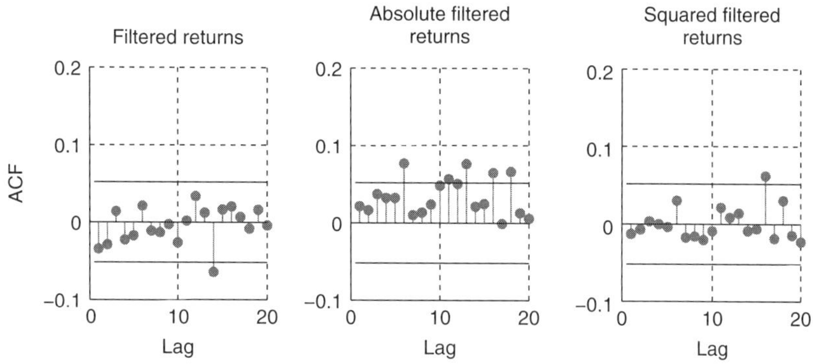

FIGURE 7.5b ACF for minute data using GARCH(2,2).

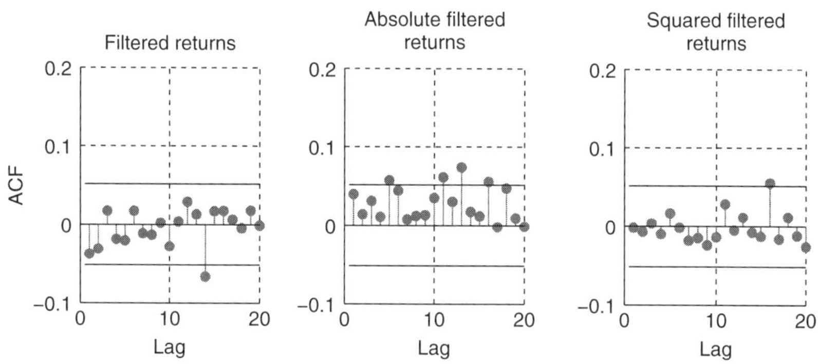

FIGURE 7.5c ACF for minute data using GARCH(3,3).

7.6 Further Analysis: Long-Term GARCH and Comparisons using Simulated Data

7.6.1 LONG-TERM BEHAVIOR OF GARCH

The results in Section 7.5.4 suggest that the conversion factor of the high–low frequency approach cannot be set too high. In this section, we discuss the long-horizon behavior of GARCH forecasts, in particular, the conditional variances $\mathrm{var}(X_{t+n}|\mathcal{F}_t)$ and $\mathrm{var}(\sum_{i=1}^{n} X_{t+i}|\mathcal{F}_t)$ as n grows, to find some explanation for such restrictions. We see below that GARCH forecasts begin to degenerate at long horizons, so that they are bound to lose their usefulness once n grows too large.

When $n > 1$ and since $E(Z_t^2) = 1$, we have, by measurability of σ_t with respect to $\mathcal{F}_{t-1}$ and independence of Z_t from $\{\mathcal{F}_s\}_{s<t}$,

$$\begin{aligned}\mathrm{var}(X_{t+n}|\mathcal{F}_t) &= E(\sigma_{t+n}^2 Z_{t+n}^2|\mathcal{F}_t) = E\left[E(\sigma_{t+n}^2 Z_{t+n}^2|\mathcal{F}_{t+n-1})|\mathcal{F}_t\right]\\ &= E\left[\sigma_{t+n}^2 E(Z_{t+n}^2|\mathcal{F}_{t+n-1})|\mathcal{F}_t\right] = E(\sigma_{t+n}^2|\mathcal{F}_t).\end{aligned}$$

TABLE 7.31 Backtest Results (p-Values) Using GARCH(1,1)

2-min Horizon				
α	95%	97.5%	99%	99.5%
Group 1	0.349	0.344	0.438	0.050
Group 2	0.059	0.510	**0.047**	0.114
3-min Horizon				
α	95%	97.5%	99%	99.5%
Group 1	0.317	0.513	0.526	0.392
Group 2	0.264	0.406	0.225	0.196
Group 3	0.177	0.631	0.129	**0.022**
4-min Horizon				
α	95%	97.5%	99%	99.5%
Group 1	0.552	0.571	0.113	0.094
Group 2	0.096	0.867	**0.049**	**0.020**
Group 3	0.465	0.441	0.704	0.263
Group 4	0.317	0.441	0.379	0.871
5-min Horizon				
α	95%	97.5%	99%	99.5%
Group 1	0.354	**0.024**	**0.027**	NaN[a]
Group 2	**0.036**	0.453	0.182	0.055
Group 3	**0.036**	0.453	0.838	0.508
Group 4	0.881	0.081	0.573	0.885
Group 5	0.530	0.744	0.838	0.508

[a]NaN (not a number) arises from log 0 in the likelihood ratio statistic when violation count is 0.

TABLE 7.32 Backtest Results (p-Values) Using GARCH(2,2)

2-min Horizon				
α	95%	97.5%	99%	99.5%
Group 1	0.157	0.652	0.583	0.380
Group 2	0.089	0.967	0.917	0.050
3-min Horizon				
α	95%	97.5%	99%	99.5%
Group 1	0.317	0.631	0.526	0.655
Group 2	0.444	0.840	0.526	0.196
Group 3	0.217	0.593	0.225	0.078
4-min Horizon				
α	95%	97.5%	99%	99.5%
Group 1	0.851	0.871	0.113	0.095
Group 2	0.053	0.542	0.113	0.095
Group 3	0.961	0.675	0.585	0.536
Group 4	0.460	0.542	0.222	0.095
5-min Horizon				
α	95%	97.5%	99%	99.5%
Group 1	0.744	0.584	0.079	NaN[a]
Group 2	0.888	0.921	0.349	0.509
Group 3	0.744	0.438	0.349	0.509
Group 4	0.864	0.212	0.183	0.055
Group 5	0.631	0.738	0.840	0.216

[a]NaN (not a number) arises from log 0 in the likelihood ratio statistic when violation count is 0.

TABLE 7.33 Backtest Results (*p*-Values) Using GARCH(3,3)

2-min Horizon				
α	95%	97.5%	99%	99.5%
Group 1	0.259	0.752	0.583	0.584
Group 2	0.108	0.323	0.438	0.050
3-min Horizon				
α	95%	97.5%	99%	99.5%
Group 1	0.518	0.513	0.932	0.655
Group 2	0.114	0.593	0.661	0.196
Group 3	0.377	0.712	0.526	0.196
4-min Horizon				
α	95%	97.5%	99%	99.5%
Group 1	0.202	0.871	0.380	0.264
Group 2	0.053	0.973	0.222	**0.020**
Group 3	0.744	0.675	0.821	0.536
Group 4	0.053	0.542	0.113	0.095
5-min Horizon				
α	95%	97.5%	99%	99.5%
Group 1	0.350	0.584	0.183	NaN
Group 2	0.764	0.584	0.840	0.055
Group 3	0.864	0.585	0.575	0.738
Group 4	0.631	0.212	0.575	0.216
Group 5	0.094	0.921	0.575	0.216

Using similar arguments and Equation 7.45,

$$\begin{aligned}
E(\sigma^2_{t+n}|\mathcal{F}_t) &= E\left[E(\sigma^2_{t+n}|\mathcal{F}_{t+n-2})|\mathcal{F}_t\right] \\
&= E\left[E(\alpha_0 + \alpha_1\sigma^2_{t+n-1}Z^2_{t+n-1} + \beta\sigma^2_{t+n-1}|\mathcal{F}_{t+n-2})|\mathcal{F}_t\right] \\
&= E\left[\alpha_0 + \alpha_1\sigma^2_{t+n-1}E(Z^2_{t+n-1}|\mathcal{F}_{t+n-2}) + \beta\sigma^2_{t+n-1}|\mathcal{F}_t\right] \\
&= E\left[\alpha_0 + (\alpha_1+\beta)\sigma^2_{t+n-1}|\mathcal{F}_t\right] = \alpha_0 + (\alpha_1+\beta)E(\sigma^2_{t+n-1}|\mathcal{F}_t).
\end{aligned}$$

$E(\sigma^2_{t+n}|\mathcal{F}_t) = \alpha_0 + (\alpha_1+\beta)E(\sigma^2_{t+n-1}|\mathcal{F}_t)$ can be transformed into

$$E(\sigma^2_{t+n}|\mathcal{F}_t) - \frac{\alpha_0}{1-\alpha_1-\beta} = (\alpha_1+\beta)\left[E(\sigma^2_{t+n-1}|\mathcal{F}_t) - \frac{\alpha_0}{1-\alpha_1-\beta}\right]. \tag{7.53}$$

Since $\mathrm{var}(X_{t+n}|\mathcal{F}_t) = E(\sigma^2_{t+n}|\mathcal{F}_t)$, repeating Equation 7.53 and rearranging terms produces

$$\mathrm{var}(X_{t+n}|\mathcal{F}_t) = \frac{\alpha_0}{1-\alpha_1-\beta} + (\alpha_1+\beta)^{n-1}\left[E(\sigma^2_{t+1}|\mathcal{F}_t) - \frac{\alpha_0}{1-\alpha_1-\beta}\right], \tag{7.54}$$

where

$$E(\sigma_{t+1}^2|\mathcal{F}_t) = \sigma_{t+1}^2 = \alpha_0 + \alpha_1\sigma_t^2 Z_t^2 + \beta\sigma_t^2$$

as σ_t and Z_t are already observed at time t.

This shows that the conditional variance will converge to the unconditional variance $\alpha_0/(1-\alpha_1-\beta)$ as the second term in Equation 7.54 decays geometrically (we have previously assumed $\alpha_1+\beta<1$ for the sake of covariance stationarity). That is, the variance forecast is eventually completely insensitive to the current information at time t.

We next compute the conditional variance $\text{var}(\sum_{i=1}^{n} X_{t+i}|\mathcal{F}_t)$. By similar arguments as in Equation 7.42, it can be shown that $\text{cov}(X_{t+i}X_{t+j}|\mathcal{F}_t) = 0$ when $i \neq j$. Therefore,

$$\text{var}\left(\sum_{i=1}^{n} X_{t+i}|\mathcal{F}_t\right) = \sum_{i=1}^{n} \text{var}(X_{t+i}|\mathcal{F}_t). \tag{7.55}$$

Further algebra based on Equation 7.54 yields

$$\text{var}\left(\sum_{i=1}^{n} X_{t+i}|\mathcal{F}_t\right) = \frac{n\alpha_0}{1-\alpha_1-\beta} + \frac{1-(\alpha_1+\beta)^n}{1-\alpha_1-\beta}\left[E(\sigma_{t+1}^2|\mathcal{F}_t) - \frac{\alpha_0}{1-\alpha_1-\beta}\right], \tag{7.56}$$

which implies that when n is large so that $(\alpha_1+\beta)^n$ is close to 0, the conditional variance will grow linearly in n.

Consider $\text{var}(\sum_{i=1}^{n} X_{t+i}|\mathcal{F}_t^{[1]})$ and $\text{var}(\sum_{i=1}^{n} X_{t+i}|\mathcal{F}_t^{[2]})$, a pair of conditional variances with the same GARCH parameter α_0, α_1, and β, but different initial volatility $E(\sigma_{t+1}^2|\mathcal{F}_t^{[1]}) = \sigma_{t+1}^{[1]}$ and $E(\sigma_{t+1}^2|\mathcal{F}_t^{[2]}) = \sigma_{t+1}^{[2]}$. Their difference is given by

$$\frac{1-(\alpha_1+\beta)^n}{1-\alpha_1-\beta}\left[\sigma_{t+1}^{[1]} - \sigma_{t+1}^{[2]}\right], \tag{7.57}$$

which grows/decays nonlinearly at first but ultimately becomes almost a constant. A constant gap between $\text{var}(\sum_{i=1}^{n} X_{t+i}|\mathcal{F}_t^{[1]})$ and $\text{var}(\sum_{i=1}^{n} X_{t+i}|\mathcal{F}_t^{[2]})$ means the power of the difference in the conditioning information $\sigma_{t+1}^{[1]}$ and $\sigma_{t+1}^{[2]}$ to influence the variance of the sum $\sum_{i=1}^{n} X_{t+n}$ has reached its limit.

We expect these results about the variance of sums of high frequency returns to carry over to similar results about VaR. Since the analysis for VaR is more difficult, we instead illustrate the results for VaR via simulation. That is, we fix initial values of σ_t and X_t, set $n = 250$, and compute via MC simulation two sequences of length 250: the conditional variances analyzed above

$$\left\{\text{var}\left(\sum_{i=1}^{n} X_{t+i}|\mathcal{F}_t\right)\right\}_{n=1}^{250},$$

and the conditional VaRs

$$\left\{ \mathrm{VaR}_{95\%} \left(\sum_{i=1}^{n} X_{t+i} | \mathcal{F}_t \right) \right\}_{n=1}^{250}.$$

Not surprisingly, we found that they are closely correlated with correlation $\rho \approx 0.98$ for a variety of choices of initial conditions. This supports our expectation that the conditional VaR will behave similarly to the conditional variance.

The analog of Equation 7.57 for VaR is illustrated by the initially widening and then the almost constant gap between the curves in Fig. 7.6, which plots simulated conditional VaR as a function of n for two different initial values of σ_t and Z_t.[21] The resulting conditional VaR of n-day returns as an asymptotically linear function of the time horizon n is obviously unrealistic and therefore should fail backtests with real data for large enough n.

Results for the general GARCH(p,q) are similar. By similar arguments, the iterative equation for the conditional variance of the GARCH(p,q) process is

$$\begin{aligned} E(\sigma_{t+n}^2 | \mathcal{F}_t) &- \frac{\alpha_0}{1 - \sum_{i=1}^{p} \alpha_i - \sum_{j=1}^{q} \beta_j} \\ &= \sum_{k=1}^{\max(p,q)} (\alpha_k + \beta_k) \left[E(\sigma_{t+n-k}^2 | \mathcal{F}_t) - \frac{\alpha_0}{1 - \sum_{i=1}^{p} \alpha_i - \sum_{j=1}^{q} \beta_j} \right], \end{aligned} \quad (7.58)$$

where $\alpha_k = 0$ if $k > p$ and $\beta_k = 0$ if $k > q$.

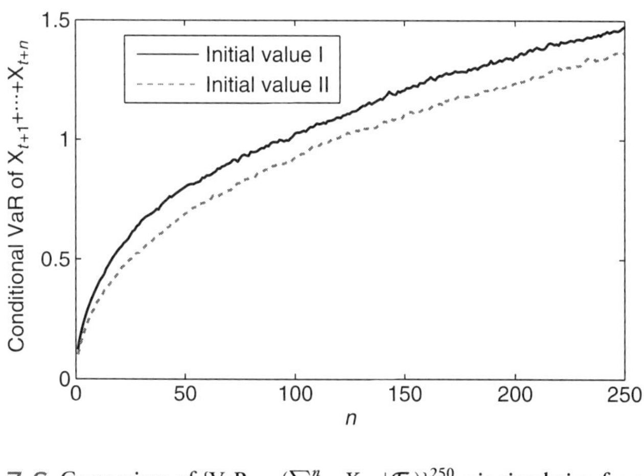

FIGURE 7.6 **Comparison of $\{\mathrm{VaR}_{95\%}(\sum_{i=1}^{n} X_{t+i} | \mathcal{F}_t)\}_{n=1}^{250}$ via simulation for two different initial GARCH volatilities.**

[21] $\mu_0 = 0$, $\alpha_0 = 0.00005$, $\alpha_1 = 0.04$, $\beta = 0.95$; $\sigma_t^{[1]} = 0.08$, $Z_t^{[1]} = 0.375$; and $\sigma_t^{[2]} = 0.05$, $Z_t^{[2]} = 0.25$.

Denote $Y_k = E(\sigma_{t+k}^2|\mathcal{F}_t) - \sum_{i=1}^{p}\alpha_i - \sum_{j=1}^{q}\beta_j$ and $d = \max(p, q)$, then an array of iterative equations in the form of Equation 7.58 can be rewritten in matrices:

$$\begin{pmatrix} Y_n \\ \vdots \\ Y_{n-d+1} \end{pmatrix} = A\begin{pmatrix} Y_{n-1} \\ \vdots \\ Y_{n-d} \end{pmatrix} = \cdots = A^{n-d}\begin{pmatrix} Y_d \\ \vdots \\ Y_1 \end{pmatrix}, \tag{7.59}$$

where

$$A_{ij} = \begin{cases} \alpha_i + \beta_i & \text{if} \quad i = j, \\ 1 & \text{if} \quad i = j+1, \\ 0 & \text{otherwise.} \end{cases}$$

The lower diagonal matrix A can be diagonalized, and then A^{n-d} will be straightforward to compute. Each term in the initial vector can be calculated through the known observations $\{\sigma_{t-i}, Z_{t-i}\}_{i=0}^{d-1}$. Again, thanks to the covariance stationarity condition $\sum_{i=1}^{p}\alpha_i + \sum_{j=1}^{q}\beta_j < 1$, the conditional variance will converge to $\alpha_0/(1 - \sum_{i=1}^{p}\alpha_i - \sum_{j=1}^{q}\beta_j)$, the unconditional variance.

7.6.2 HIGH–LOW VERSUS FIXED FREQUENCY WITH ABUNDANT DATA

So far, the high–low frequency approach has been used to reduce reliance on data availability. What if data is in plentiful supply? Will it still be a worthy alternative?

Within a fixed time range, the high–low frequency approach utilizes at least twice as much data as the fixed-frequency approach. Intuitively, this may reveal information not previously captured.

Suppose we have a sequence of n-day negative log returns $X_1^{(L)}, \ldots, X_T^{(L)}$[22] and the calibrated distribution of the filtered data (i.e., innovations $Z_t^{(L)}$) is skewed t with parameters $(\nu, \mu, \gamma, \sigma)$.

Since $X_{T+1}^{(L)} = \mu_0 + \sigma_{T+1}Z_{T+1}^{(L)}$ and σ_{T+1} is a constant at time T, by Proposition 7.5:

$$X_{T+1}^{(L)} \sim \text{Skew}T(\nu, \mu_0 + \sigma_{T+1}\mu, \sigma_{T+1}\sigma, \sigma_{T+1}\gamma).$$

On the other hand, if we use the high–low frequency approach based on daily data on the same period $X_1^{(H)}, \ldots, X_{nT}^{(H)}$, the distribution of the next n-day return can be determined by simulating the sum $X_{nT+1}^{(H)} + \cdots + X_{nT+n}^{(H)}$. Since both $X_{T+1}^{(L)}$ and $X_{nT+1}^{(H)} + \cdots + X_{nT+n}^{(H)}$ denote the negative log return in the same period, we can compare the fixed- and high–low frequency approach by plotting the skewed t density of $X_{T+1}^{(L)}$ and the density function[23] of the simulated $X_{nT+1}^{(H)} + \cdots + X_{nT+n}^{(H)}$ for various values of T in our standard S&P500 data time series. See Figs. 7.7**a**–d.

[22] L stands for low frequency and H stands for high frequency.

[23] Using a kernel smoothing method.

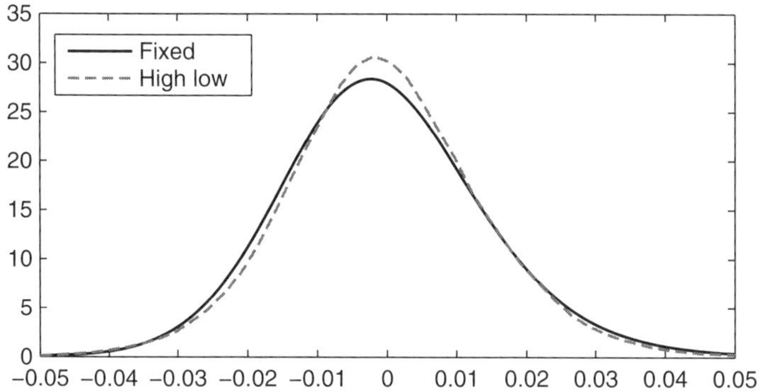

FIGURE 7.7a Forecast pdf for a two-day negative log return on day 4740 (S&P500 daily data).

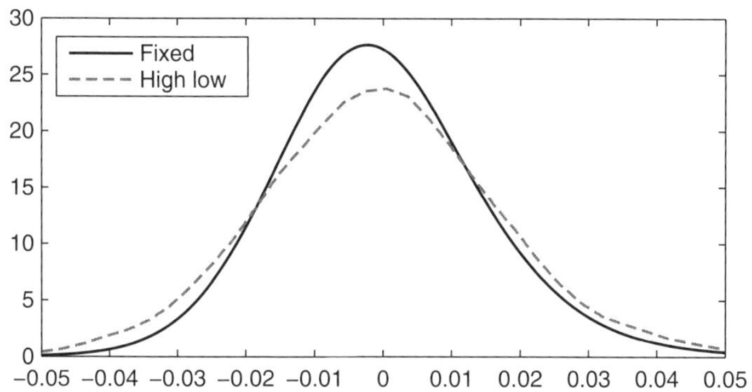

FIGURE 7.7b Forecast pdf for a two-day negative log return on day 4750 (S&P500 daily data).

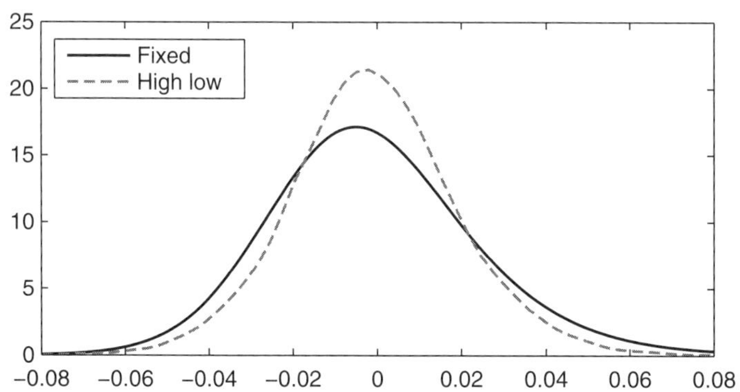

FIGURE 7.7c Forecast pdf for a four-day negative log return on day 4740 (S&P500 daily data).

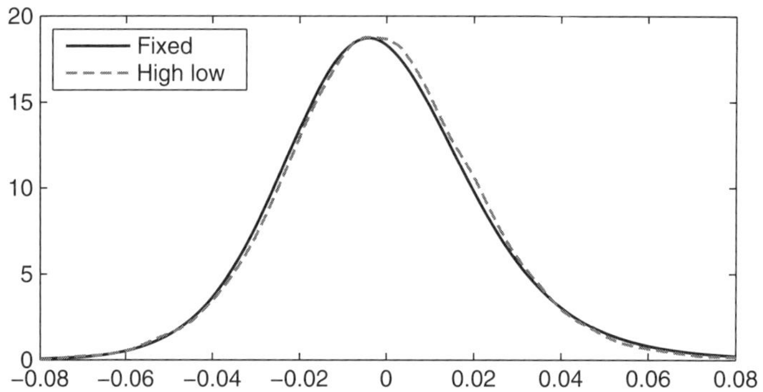

FIGURE 7.7d Forecast pdf for a five-day negative log return on day 4740 (S&P500 daily data).

The difference between fixed-frequency density and high–low frequency density does not shown any predictable pattern. The high–low frequency density can have higher peaks and thinner tails (Fig. 7.7**a**), but the reverse can also be true (Fig. 7.7**b**). Further, such reversal can be quite volatile. The results in (Fig. 7.7**b**) was obtained only 10 days (2 weeks) after those in (Fig. 7.7**a**) tiny lag given the 3750 daily (750 weekly) returns used for calibration.

As time horizon increases, the difference in densities does not widen steadily. For example, there can be greater deviation under the 4-day horizon (Fig. 7.7**c**) than the 2-day horizon (Fig. 7.7**a**). However, 5-day densities (Fig. 7.7**d**) can be hardly distinguishable. To further explore their relationship in the long run, we reexamined our S&P500 daily returns series for the years 1971–2009.[24] After a lead-in period of 750 weeks for fitting the parameters, we made weekly VaR forecasts for the next 1200 weeks, using both the fixed-frequency method with a weekly horizon and the high–low frequency method based on daily data.

We have the following observations from Table 7.34 and Fig. 7.8.

- Daily and week-based forecasts are closely correlated, with $\rho \approx 0.92$. As a result, their long-term trends are roughly the same.
- Less than 10% of the week-based forecasts fall within the 95% confidence interval of daily-based forecast. So the difference between the two methods is statistically significant.
- Both models have passed the backtest, so unsurprisingly they record approximately the same number of VaR violations. However, the timings of these violations are different. More than 85% of $\text{VaR}_{95\%}$ violations arrived simultaneously, while the rate declines to 60% at the 99.5% level.
- Daily-based forecasts are more volatile, magnifying the fluctuations in week-based forecasts.

[24]VaR forecasts in this study have to be for nonoverlapping weeks to make violation indicators independent. Therefore, we again expand our data set.

TABLE 7.34 VaR_{Fixed} vs VaR_{HL}: Weekly Forecasts, 1971–2009

α	95%	97.5%	99%	99.5%
Violations of VaR_{Fixed}	62	34	15	8
Violations of VaR_{HL}	60	32	17	10
Simultaneous Violations	50	25	12	5
VaR_{Fixed} outside 95% confidence interval[a]	1108	1103	1112	1099
VaR_{Fixed} inside 95% confidence interval	92	97	88	101
Correlation of VaR_{Fixed} and VaR_{HL}	0.918	0.917	0.916	0.913
Variance of VaR_{Fixed}	0.0003	0.0004	0.0007	0.001
Variance of VaR_{HL}	0.0005	0.0008	0.0012	0.0016

[a]Of VaR_{HL}.

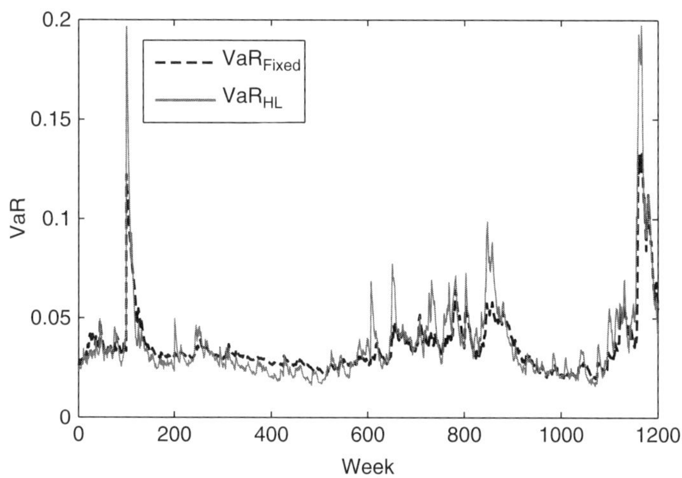

FIGURE 7.8 VaR_{Fixed} **vs** VaR_{HL}**: Weekly forecasts for S&P500 returns, 1971–2009. Week 0 in the figure corresponds to the 750th week after January 1, 1971.**

When we take the fixed-frequency approach, GARCH is applied on the weekly scale. Correspondingly, what is most directly responsible for the VaR forecasts is the return and volatility of the previous week.[25] Similarly, when GARCH is applied on the daily scale, as in the high–low frequency method, VaR forecasts are most susceptible to the previous day, not week.

Daily return/volatility and weekly return/volatility are bound to be correlated, and they exhibit similar patterns when viewed globally. However, having

[25]Since the innovation terms in a GARCH process are SWN(0,1), the filtered returns will approximately have mean 0 and variance 1. Even though the calibration of skewed t distributions produces different parameters as time evolves, the scale of these distributions will not differ greatly. As a result, σ_{t+1} in the defiltering/forecasting equation $X_{t+1} = \mu_0 + \sigma_{t+1} Z_{t+1}$ is the most decisive factor for the scale (i.e., variance) of X_{t+1} and consequently the size of VaR.

less time to smooth out or recover from extreme events, daily data are more volatile and will give rise to steeper ups and downs, as well as forecasts different from the week-based ones.

The last feature makes high–low frequency method a quicker responder to volatility changes. For example, if volatility starts to rise only in the last week of a particular month, its severity may be dampened by the first three good or uneventful weeks. By paying more attention to the most recent week, the high–low frequency model will have a better chance to detect this signal, which is otherwise masked in a fixed monthly horizon.

Admittedly, the opposite situation can also happen, especially when the conversion factor between high and low frequencies is too large. For example, a daily return/volatility may hardly reflect what is actually happening in an entire month. Despite the possibility of false alarms, high–low frequency approach can at least offer an alternative view of risk. If a risk manager intends to be more cautious, he may implement both models and pick the VaR forecast that is higher.

7.6.3 A SIMULATED WEEKLY RETURNS SCENARIO

To illustrate the potential advantage of the high–low frequency approach, we will compare the two methods using simulated data.[26] A weekly returns time series is simulated using GARCH, the parameters of which are derived from historical S&P500 weekly returns. The total length of the simulated series is 1950 months. The first 750 months are used as history to make the first monthly VaR forecast starting at month 751. We then make a series of 1200 monthly VaR forecasts using both the fixed-frequency (monthly horizon) and high–low frequency (weekly–monthly) methods.[27] Additionally, now that the weekly return process is strictly GARCH, we can nail down the true values of each monthly VaR, again using MC simulation.

As pointed out earlier, the size of VaR is closely related to return volatilities in previous periods, which we will measure in four ways:

- StD of weekly returns in the previous month. (*MonthlyStD*)
- Sum of absolute values of weekly returns in the previous month. (*AbsMonthly*)
- Average of weekly volatilities in the previous month. (*VolAvg*)
- StD of weekly volatilities in the previous month. (*VolStD*)

Table 7.35 presents correlations between VaR_{True}, the true monthly VaR; VaR_{HL}, the VaR computed using the high–low frequency method; VaR_{Fixed}, the VaR computed using the fixed-frequency method; and the four volatility measures. It shows

[26] Direct comparison of model performance in terms of error size is impossible when historical data is used, as we do not the know the "true" VaR.

[27] We will only examine $VaR_{95\%}$ in this section.

TABLE 7.35 Comparison Using Simulated *Weekly* Data: Correlations Part I

	VaR_{True}	VaR_{HL}	VaR_{Fixed}	VolAvg	VolStD	AbsMonthly	MonthlyStD
VaR_{True}	1	0.9937	0.7887	0.9886	0.4626	0.6098	0.5960
VaR_{HL}		1	0.7867	0.9860	0.4506	0.5968	0.5807
VaR_{Fixed}			1	0.7791	0.3683	0.4568	0.4443
VolAvg				1	0.5195	0.6565	0.6386
VolStd					1	0.6424	0.6577
AbsMonthly						1	0.9262
MonthlyStd							1

- Among the proposed volatility measures, VolAvg is most closely related to VaR_{True}.
- VaR_{HL} is almost perfectly correlated to both VaR_{True} and VolAvg.
- The correlations between VaR_{Fixed} and all four volatility measures are weaker than those between VaR_{HL} and all four volatility measures.

Tables 7.36 and 7.37 and Fig. 7.9**a** study errors and show

- Relative errors of VaR_{Fixed} are negatively correlated to all four volatility measures. Graphically (Fig. 7.9**a**), errors tend to be negative when VolStD rises and vice versa. In other words, the fixed-frequency approach underestimates VaR when volatility surges and overestimates VaR when volatility subsides.
- The correlation between relative errors of VaR_{HL} and VolStD, *AbsMonthly* is minimal, which shows that the accuracy of the high–low frequency approach is relatively immune to volatility changes.
- Absolute errors of VaR_{HL} have significantly lower mean and StD compared to absolute errors of VaR_{Fixed}.

TABLE 7.36 Comparison Using Simulated *Weekly* Data: Correlations Part II

	VolAvg	VolStD	AbsMonthly	MonthlyStD
Error[a] of VaR_{HL}	0.1804	0.0358	0.0364	0.0187
Error of VaR_{Fixed}	−0.4452	−0.1996	−0.3127	−0.3042

[a]Error = (estimate − true) /true.

TABLE 7.37 Comparison Using Simulated *Weekly* Data: Error

	Mean of Absolute Error[a]	StD
Error of VaR_{HL}	0.0022	0.0025
Error of VaR_{Fixed}	0.0091	0.0128

[a]With absolute value taken.

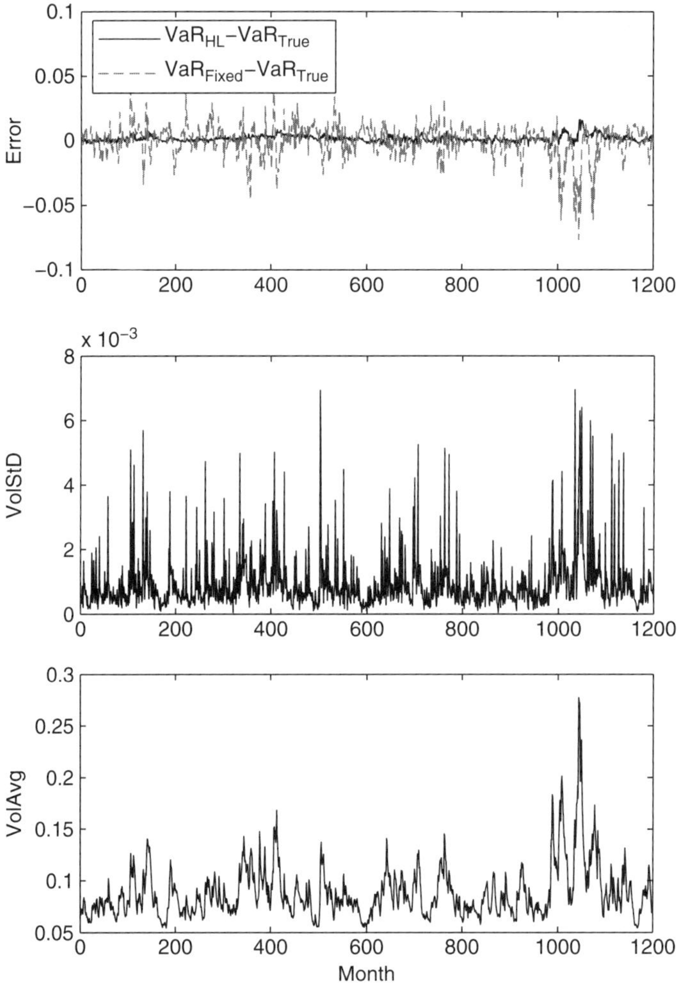

FIGURE 7.9a Error comparison of VaR_{Fixed} and VaR_{HL}.

At the 1044th month (Fig. 7.9**b**), VaR_{True} for the next month is 22.43%, almost the global maximum in our entire 1200 simulated months (the global maximum VaR_{True} is 22.65%). If we zoom in on the time leading to that month (Fig. 7.9**b**), we can see that both VolAvg and VolStD have been increasing since the 1035th month and approaching their respective global maximum as well. During this "chaotic" period, the gap between $VaR_{fixed} - VaR_{True}$ and $VaR_{HL} - VaR_{True}$ is widening steadily. As a result, VaR_{fixed} is merely 14.78%, seriously underestimated. In contrast, VaR_{HL}, at 23.22%, is much closer to VaR_{True}.

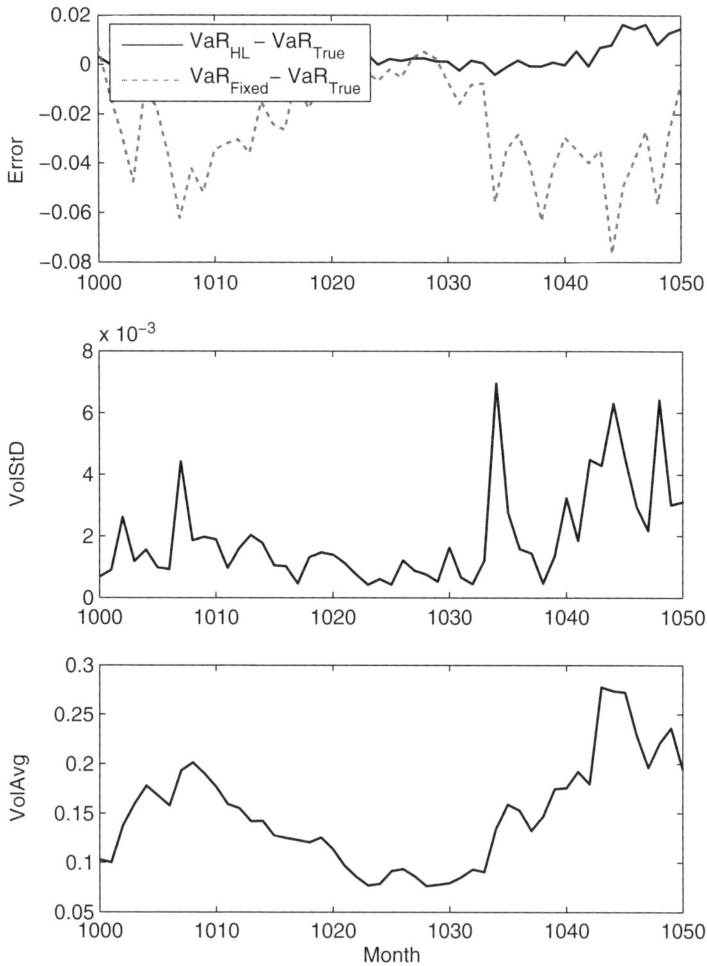

FIGURE 7.9b Error comparison of VaR_{Fixed} and VaR_{HL} (Detail, centered at month 1025).

7.6.4 A SIMULATED DAILY RETURNS SCENARIO

It can be argued that the simulated weekly GARCH process has an unfair advantage in the above comparison, since the weekly simulation frequency matches the weekly high frequency horizon in our high–low frequency approach. To address[28] such bias, we will simulate a daily GARCH process, aggregate daily returns into weekly returns, and then repeat our earlier experiment using the same weekly/monthly horizons.

As shown in Tables 7.38–7.40, the high–low frequency method still beats the fixed-frequency method by displaying stronger correlation between volatility

[28]Completely eliminating this bias is impossible since one cannot simulate a monthly GARCH process and then split it into weekly returns for the high–low frequency method to work on.

TABLE 7.38 Comparison Using Simulated *Daily* Data: Correlations Part I

	VaR_{True}	VaR_{HL}	VaR_{Fixed}	VolAvg	VolStD	AbsMonthly	MonthlyStD
VaR_{True}	1	0.8647	0.6339	0.9475	0.5810	0.7308	0.6848
VaR_{HL}		1	0.7659	0.8746	0.4639	0.8233	0.7752
VaR_{Fixed}			1	0.6697	0.3470	0.5419	0.3892
VolAvg				1	0.5318	0.6881	0.6378
VolStD					1	0.3739	0.3590
AbsMonthly						1	0.8938
MonthlyStD							1

TABLE 7.39 Comparison Using Simulated *Daily* Data: Correlations Part II

	VolAvg	VolStD	AbsMonthly	MonthlyStD
Error of VaR_{HL}	−0.4029	−0.3368	−0.0750	−0.0659
Error of VaR_{Fixed}	−0.6181	−0.4151	−0.4516	−0.5116

TABLE 7.40 Comparison Using Simulated *Daily* Data: Error

	Mean of Absolute Error	StD
Error of VaR_{HL}	0.0074	0.01
Error of VaR_{Fixed}	0.0114	0.0155

measures and lower errors. However, now that the GARCH mechanism operates on a daily level, filtering the weekly returns with GARCH will not perfectly capture the varying volatilities. As a result, correlations between errors of VaR_{HL} and volatility measures turn negative. Still, the magnitude of those negative correlation coefficients is smaller than what the fixed frequency method can offer.

Since the stylized facts pervade all scales of financial data, the high–low frequency approach will always uncover volatility changes ignored by the coarser fixed-frequency method and thus be a quicker responder. These simulated data studies refer to "weeks" and "months," but the timescales are in fact arbitrary so long as they are adequately modeled by a GARCH process. The practitioner need only take care that the conversion factor between the two timescales are not too large.

7.7 Conclusion

Financial returns are fat tailed, heteroskedastic, and exhibit serial dependence. To make a risk forecast based on historical returns, we need to remove the serial dependence and calibrate a fat-tailed distribution to the filtered series. This is accomplished using GARCH as a filter, and GH distributions, notably the skewed t distribution, for calibration. This approach is successful, provided we have sufficient data for the calibration.

The focus of this chapter has been to examine a way to use higher frequency data to form a lower frequency risk forecast by using the calibrated GARCH process to forecast the intermediate time steps. When the ratio between the long horizon and the short horizon is no more than about 10, this works well in our studies based on S&P500 daily returns, as well as for simulated data.

Risk managers making fixed-horizon risk forecasts should consider this multiscale method because

- by reducing the required lead-in period by at least a factor of 2, it makes forecasts possible for a security with a history otherwise too short to train the GARCH filter and the skewed t distribution;
- it enables the removal of outdated and thus irrelevant data in earlier periods;
- the greater abundance of higher frequency data makes statistical estimation more robust and more stable numerically;
- risk forecasts will be quicker to react to changing conditions, for example, by better reflecting a change in the volatility regime that might occur late in the previous period.

All the results reported here pertain to the one-dimensional case of returns of a single index; naturally, it will be important to carry out a similar investigation in the multidimensional case of portfolios of N assets. In that case, the forecast will be a forecast of the N-dimensional distribution of the N vector of all the asset returns, from which the portfolio return is obtained, as usual, as an inner product with the vector of portfolio holdings. The full N-dimensional fitted distribution of returns will be required for typical portfolio optimization applications. This is the subject of subsequent research.

REFERENCES

Aas K, Hobaek Haff I. The generalized hyperbolic skew student's t-distribution. J Financ Econometrics 2006;4(2):275–309.

Artzner P, Delbaen F, Eber J, Heath D. Coherent measures of risk. Math Finance 1999;9:203–228.

Barndorff-Nielson OE. Exponentially decreasing distributions for the logarithm of the particle size. Proc R Soc Lond Math Phys Sci 1977;350:401–419.

Barndorff-Nielson OE. Hyperbolic distribution and distribution on hyperbolae. Scand J Stat 1978;5:151–157.

Barndorff-Nielson OE, Blæsild P. Hyperbolic distributions and ramifications: contribution to theory and applications. In: Taillie C, Patil G, Baldessari B, editors. Statistical Distributions in Scientific Work. Volume 4, Dordrecht: Reidel; 1981. p 19–44.

Bougerol P, Picard N. Stationarity of GARCH processes and of some non-negative time series. J Econometrics 1992;52:115–127.

Brandt A. The stochastic equation $y_{n+1} = a_n y_n + b_n$ with stationary coefficients. Adv Appl Probab 1986;18:211–220.

Brockwell PJ, Davis RA. Introduction to time series and forecasting. 2nd ed. Springer, New York; 2002.

Casella G, Berger RL. Statistical inference. Pacific Grove, CA: Duxbury; 2002.

Glasserman P. Monte Carlo methods in financial engineering. Springer, New York; 2003.

Hu W. Calibration of multivariate generalized hyperbolic distributions using the EM ALgorithm, with applications in risk management, portfolio optimization and portfolio credit risk [Phd dissertation]. Tallahasse (FL): Florida State University; 2005.

Hu W, Kercheval AN. Risk management with generalized hyperbolic distributions. Proceedings of the fourth IASTED International conference on financial engineering and applications. Calgary: ACTA Press; 2007. p 19–24.

Hu W, Kercheval AN. The skewed t distribution for portfolio credit risk. Adv Econometrics 2008;22:55–83.

Hu W, Kercheval AN. Portfolio optimization for *t* and skewed *t* returns. Quant Finance 2010;10(1):91–105.

Jørgensen B. Satistical properties of the generalized inverse Gaussian distribution. Lecture notes in statistics. Heidelberg: Springer; 1982.

Keel S, Herzog F, Geering H. Optimal portfolios with skewed and heavy-tailed distributions. Proceedings of the Third IASTED International conference on financial engineering and applications, Cambridge, MA; 2006 p. 42–48.

Kupiec P. Techniques for verifying the accuracy of risk measurement models. J Deriv 1995;Winter 3(2):73–84.

Liu C, Rubin DB. The ECME algorithm: a simple extension of EM and ECM with faster monotone convergence. Biometrika 1994;81:633–648.

Markowitz H. Portfolio selection. J Finance 1952;7(1):77–91.

McNeil A, Frey R, Embrechts P. Quantitative risk management: concepts, techniques and tools. Princeton University Press, Princeton, NJ; 2005.

Protassov RS. EM-based maximum likelihood parameter estimation of multivariate generalized hyperbolic distributions with fixed λ. Stat Comput 2004;14:67–77.

Rockafellar R, Uryasev S. Conditional value-at-risk for general loss distributions. J Bank Finance 2002;26:1443–1471.

Serfling RJ. Approximation theorems of mathematical statistics. New York: Wiley; 1980.

Sharpe WF. Capital asset prices-a theory of market equilibrium under conditions of risk. J Finance 1964;19(3):425–42.

CHAPTER EIGHT

Parameter Estimation and Calibration for Long-Memory Stochastic Volatility Models

ALEXANDRA CHRONOPOULOU
INRIA, Nancy, France

8.1 Introduction

It has been observed that there exists a discrepancy between European option prices calculated under the Black and Scholes (1973) model with constant volatility and the market-traded option prices. In general, the volatility exhibits an intermittent behavior with periods of high values and periods of low values. As a result, implied volatilities at market prices are not constant across a range of options, but vary with respect to strike prices and create the so-called volatility smile (or smirk). Stochastic volatility models were introduced in order to model this observed random behavior of the market volatility. Under such a model, the volatility is described by a stochastic process. Among the first models in the literature were these by Taylor (1986) and Hull and White (1987), under which the volatility dynamics are described by an Ornstein–Uhlenbeck process. Classical references for specific stochastic volatility models are Ball and Roma

Handbook of Modeling High-Frequency Data in Finance, First Edition.
Edited by Frederi G. Viens, Maria C. Mariani, and Ionuţ Florescu.

(1994), Heston (1993), and Scott (1987) whereas a presentation of properties, option pricing techniques, and statistical inference methods can be found in the book by Fouque et al. (2000a).

It is widely believed that volatility smiles can be explained to a great extent by stochastic volatility models. However, it has been well documented that volatility is highly persistent, which means that even for options with long maturity, there exist pronounced smile effects. Furthermore, a unit root behavior of the conditional variance process is observed, particularly when we work with high frequency data. To better describe this behavior, Comte and Renault (1998) introduced a stochastic volatility model with long memory.

Long-memory in financial datasets has been observed in practice in the past, long before the use of long-range dependent stochastic volatility models. For example, Ding et al. (1993), De Lima and Crato (1994), and Breidt et al. (1998), among others, observed that the squared returns of market indexes have the long-memory property, which intuitively means that observations that are far apart are highly correlated. Harvey (1998) and Breidt et al. (1998) independently introduced a discrete time model under which the log-volatility is modeled as a fractional ARIMA(p,d,q) process, while at the same time Comte and Renault (1998) introduced a continuous-time long-range dependent volatility model.

In this chapter, we consider the *continuous-time* long-memory stochastic volatility (LMSV) model by Comte and Renault (1998): If X_t are the log-returns of the price process S_t and Y_t is the volatility process, then

$$\begin{cases} dX_t &= \left(\mu - \dfrac{\sigma^2(Y_t)}{2}\right) dt + \sigma(Y_t)\, dW_t, \\ dY_t &= \alpha\ Y_t\ dt + \beta\ dB_t^H, \end{cases} \tag{8.1}$$

where W_t is a standard Brownian motion and B_t^H is a fractional Brownian motion with Hurst index $H \in (0, 1]$.

The *fractional Brownian motion* (fBm) with Hurst parameter $H \in (0, 1]$ is a Gaussian process with almost surely continuous paths and covariance structure given by

$$\mathrm{Cov}(B_t^H, B_s^H) = \frac{1}{2}\left(|t|^{2H} + |s|^{2H} - |t-s|^{2H}\right).$$

For $H = 1/2$ the process is the well-known standard Brownian motion.

Formally, we say that a process exhibits *long-range dependence* when the series of the autocorrelation function is nonsummable, that is

$$\sum_{n=1}^{+\infty} \rho(n) = +\infty.$$

From the covariance function of the fractional Brownian motion, we can easily deduce that the autocorrelation function of the increments of fBm is of order n^{2H-2}. This implies that when $H > 1/2$ the process exhibits long-range dependence, while for $H < 1/2$ the process has what we describe by "short" memory. The parameter H is the long-memory parameter and is also known as Hurst index. More details regarding the properties of the fractional Brownian motion can be found in the book by Beran (1994).

As in the case of a classical stochastic volatility models, the volatility process is not directly observed. As a consequence, estimation of the parameters of the model is not straightforward. In the LMSV model (Eq. 8.1), apart from the drift μ, the rate of mean reversion α and the volatility of the volatility β, we also need to estimate the long-memory parameter H.

Our goal in this chapter is to study the most popular methods in the literature for parameter estimation under the LMSV model (Eq. 8.1). We focus on the estimation of the Hurst parameter, but we also discuss techniques for the remaining parameters of the model. First, we consider the log-periodogram regression, initially introduced by Robinson (1995a) and the GPH estimator due to Geweke and Porter-Hudak (1983) for estimating the parameter H. Moreover, we study a Whittle-type criterion, which was introduced by Fox and Taqqu (1986) in order to estimate the long-memory parameter of functionals of Gaussian processes and adapted to the LMSV case by Gao et al. (2001) and Casas and Gao (2008). This approach not only estimates the Hurst parameter, but also provides estimators for the remaining parameters of the model. Finally, we compute the implied Hurst index proposed by Chronopoulou and Viens (2010), which is obtained by calibrating the model with realized option prices.

In this chapter, we compare the two parameter estimation procedures using high frequency simulated data and we conclude that the Whittle-type estimator for H is better than the GPH estimator. In order to study the implied H method, we treat a real-data example and we price options on the S&P 500 index. Since the implied H approach is inherently linked with option pricing, we also describe a multinomial recombining tree algorithm adapted in the LMSV case by Chronopoulou and Viens (2010), which we then apply to option pricing, using estimated parameters from all three different approaches. We conclude that the computed option prices using the implied Hurst parameter are closer to market-realized prices.

The structure of the chapter is as follows: In Section 8.2, we discuss the three parameter estimation techniques for the LMSV model. In Section 8.3, we use simulated data to test the preformance of the described methodologies, while in Section 8.4, we apply them in real data. In the last section, we summarize our results.

8.2 Statistical Inference Under the LMSV Model

The main goal of this section is to present the most popular methods for statistical inference under the LMSV model (Eq. 8.1). The model is in continuous-time and the volatility process is not observed, but we only have access to discrete time observations of historical stock prices. However, we assume that we are able to obtain high frequency (intraday) data, for example, tick-by-tick observations.

8.2.1 LOG-PERIODOGRAM REGRESSION HURST PARAMETER ESTIMATOR

A common practice in the literature is the use of the absolute or log squared returns in order to estimate the long-memory parameter semiparametrically. For example, the reader can refer to Breidt et al. (1998) and Andersen and Bollerslev (1997). The estimator used in these cases is the well-known GPH estimator that was initially introduced by Geweke and Porter-Hudak (1983) and is based on the log-periodogram regression.

The asymptotic behavior of the GPH estimator in the case of Gaussian observations has been studied by Robinson (1995a,b) and Hurvich, Deo and Brodsky (1998). However, the log squared returns in the discrete time LMSV model are not Gaussian and asymptotic properties of the estimator in this case have been established by Deo and Hurvich (2001).

Our model is in continuous time, thus, we are going to discretize it first before applying the log-periodogram method. This is a common approach when we deal with continuous-time models and is also suggested by Comte and Renault (1998).

REMARK 8.1

For convenience in the illustration of the method, we drop the drift term.

Thus, we discretize the process of the log-returns in (Eq. 8.1) with step Δ and we obtain

$$X_{t\Delta} - X_{(t-1)\Delta} = \sigma(Y_{(t-1)\Delta})\,(W_{t\Delta} - W_{(t-1)\Delta}),\ t = 1, 2, \ldots, T. \tag{8.2}$$

Equivalently we can write

$$\frac{X_{t\Delta} - Y_{(t-1)\Delta}}{\Delta} = \sigma(Y_{(t-1)\Delta})\,\varepsilon_t\sqrt{\frac{1}{\Delta}},\ t = 1, 2, \ldots, T, \tag{8.3}$$

where ε_t is a sequence of i.i.d. normal errors with mean 0 and variance 1. In the following step, we exploit the fact that we can linearize model (Eq. 8.1) by taking the logarithm, thus

$$Z_t = \mu + 2\log\sigma(Y_{(t-1)\Delta}) + e_t,\ t = 1, 2, \ldots, T, \tag{8.4}$$

where we set $Z_t = \log\left(\frac{X_{t\Delta}-X_{(t-1)\Delta}}{\Delta}\right)^2$, $e_t = \log\varepsilon_t^2 - \mathbf{E}[\log\varepsilon_t^2]$, and $\mu = \mathbf{E}[\log\varepsilon_t^2] - \log\Delta$.

In order to describe the procedure for computing the GPH estimator, we are going to work on the spectral domain. Recall that the spectral density function is defined as the inverse Fourier transform of the autocovariance function $\gamma(h)$ of the stationary process Y_t into consideration, that is,

$$\phi_Y(\omega) := \frac{1}{2\pi}\int_{-\infty}^{\infty} \mathrm{e}^{-i\omega h}\gamma(h)\mathrm{d}h,\quad \omega \in (-\infty, +\infty).$$

It can be proved that the spectral density of the discrete process Y_t for $-\frac{\pi}{\Delta} \le \omega \le \frac{\pi}{\Delta}$ is the superposition of the continuous process ϕ_Y for frequencies $\omega, \omega \pm \frac{2k\pi}{\Delta}, \ldots$ and can be written as

$$f_Y(\omega) = \sum_{k=-\infty}^{\infty} \phi_Y\left(\omega + \frac{2k\pi}{\Delta}\right).$$

Moreover, the spectral density of the linearized process Z_t satisfies the following property:

$$f_Z(\omega) = 4f_Y(\omega) + \frac{\pi}{4}. \tag{8.5}$$

Therefore, we observe that the spectral density of Z behaves in a similar way as the spectral density of Y at low frequencies. The GPH estimator will be based on the linearized process Z. In order to construct the estimator, we are going to use an estimate of the spectral density, the so-called periodogram. We define the periodogram of the observations $Z_0, Z_1, \ldots, Z_{n-1}$ of the jth Fourier frequency $\omega_j = 2\pi j/n$ by

$$I_j^Z = \frac{1}{2\pi n}\left|\sum_{t=0}^{n-1} Z_t \mathrm{e}^{it\omega_j}\right|^2. \tag{8.6}$$

The Geweke and Porter-Hudak estimator of H is computed using the first m Fourier frequencies as follows:

$$\hat{H}_{\mathrm{GPH}} = \frac{1}{2} - \frac{1}{2\sum_{j=1}^{m}(X_j - \bar{X})^2}\sum_{j=1}^{m}(X_j - \bar{X})\log I_j^Z, \tag{8.7}$$

where $X_j = \log\left|2\sin\left(\frac{\omega_j}{2}\right)\right|$. Expressions for the asymptotic variance and asymptotic bias of this estimator can be found in Deo and Hurvich (2001). The same authors also proved that the estimator is asymptotically normal under some strong conditions on m.

Up to now we have described a procedure for estimating only the long-memory parameter. Following the steps of Comte and Renault (1998), we estimate H through the GPH estimators and then we approximate the volatility process Y_t using the quadratic variation of the stock price returns X_t.

Indeed, observe that $\langle X\rangle_t = \int_0^t Y_s^2 ds$ and if we have a partition $\{t_1, \ldots, t_m\}$ of $[0, t]$ with step $\Delta = \max_{1\leq i\leq m}\{|t_i - t_{i-1}|\}$ and $t_0 = 0$, then

$$\lim_{\Delta\to 0}\sum_{k=1}^{m}(X_{t_k} - X_{t_{k-1}})^2 = \langle X\rangle_t,$$

in probability. Then

$$\frac{\langle X\rangle_t - \langle X\rangle_{t-h}}{h} \to Y_s^2, \text{ as } h \to 0, \text{ a.s.}$$

If we have high frequency data available, then we can obtain an estimate of the quadratic variation, by considering a partition of the partition and by taking the two limits as follows: Let $[0, T]$ be the interval of observation with partition that we denote here by $t_k = kT/N$, where $N = np$ are the dates of observations. Let X_{t_k}, $k = 0, \ldots, N$, denote the sample of observations of the log-prices. Then, we have n blocks of length p and we estimate the quadratic variation of $\langle X\rangle_t$ by

$$\langle \hat{X}\rangle_t^N = \sum_{k=0}^{[tN/T]}(X_{t_k} - X_{t_{k-1}})^2.$$

Then, we observe that if $\frac{\langle \hat{X}\rangle_t^N - \langle \hat{X}\rangle_{t-h}^N}{h}$ is computed for $h = T/N$, then

$$\hat{Y}^2_{(n,p)}(t) = \frac{n}{T}\sum_{k=[tN/T]-p+1}^{[tN/T]}(X_{t_k} - X_{t_{k-1}})^2. \tag{8.8}$$

REMARK 8.2

In general, p must be as large as possible in order to obtain the optimal rate of convergence of $\hat{Y}^2_{(n,p)}$. However, as one would expect there is a trade-off between n and p. For more details regarding the optimal choice of these parameters can be found in Comte and Renault (1998).

Finally, the remaining parameter to estimate is the drift μ, which is obtained using a classical approach by Renault and Touzi (1993) through the estimator

$$\hat{\mu} = \frac{1}{T} \sum_{k=1}^{np} \frac{S_{t_k} - S_{t_{k-1}}}{S_{t_{k-1}}},$$

where n and p are as above.

8.2.2 WHITTLE-BASED APPROACH FOR HURST INDEX ESTIMATION

Another classical approach for estimating the Hurst index is the Whittle maximum likelihood estimator (mle), which is an estimator based on the discrete approximation of the likelihood of the underlying model on the spectral domain. In the LMSV context, we use the Gauss–Whittle contrast function to jointly estimate all the parameters of the model, suggested Gao et al. (2001) and revisited by Casas and Gao (2008).

As in the previous section, in order to make use of the discrete stock price observations that we have available, we work with the discrete linear version of the model (Eq. 8.4). Recall also that the spectral density of Z is given by (Equation 8.5) and the corresponding periodogram by (Equation 8.6) .

The reason why we do not use an exact likelihood approach is the computational complexity of this method in practice (for more details the reader can refer to Beran, (1993). Thus, we use the celebrated Whittle approximation of the likelihood and consequently of the mle.

For the LMSV model and its discretization, we write the Whittle contrast function

$$W_n(\theta) = \frac{1}{4\pi} \int_{-\pi}^{\pi} \left\{ \log f(\omega) + \frac{I_n(\omega)}{f(\omega)} \right\} d\omega \tag{8.9}$$

from which the Whittle maximum likelihood estimate of the unknown parameters $\theta = (\alpha, \beta, H)$ is given by

$$\tilde{\theta}_n = \arg \min_{\theta \in \Theta_0} W_n(\theta),$$

where $\Theta_0 = \{0 < \alpha < \infty, 0 < H < 1, 0 < \beta < \infty\}$. In order to reduce the computational needs to compute the Whittle mle, we consider a discretized version of W_n as follows:

$$\bar{W}_n(\theta) = \frac{1}{2n} \sum_{s=1}^{n-1} \left\{ \log f(\omega_s) + \frac{I_n(\omega_s)}{f(\omega_s)} \right\},$$

where $\omega_s = \frac{2\pi s}{n}$.

Under certain assumptions it can be proved that both mles obtained either through the continuous or the discrete Whittle function are strongly consistent as well as asymptotically normal with the same asymptotic variance. More details on the proof of these results can be found in Heyde and Gay (1993), Gao (2004), and Casas and Gao (2008).

8.2.3 IMPLIED HURST INDEX

The implied Hurst parameter was initially introduced by Chronopoulou and Viens (2010) and is directly linked with an option pricing procedure. Therefore, first we are going to discuss the option pricing algorithm and then the methodology that we follow in order to determine the implied value of H.

As we also mentioned in the introduction, although the model is in continuous time, we only have available discrete time observations, the historical stock prices. The option pricing algorithm consists of two main parts. In the first part, our goal is to compute the empirical distribution of the unobserved volatility process. This is handled by adapting a genetic-type particle filtering algorithm by Del Moral et al. (2001) introduced into finance by Florescu and Viens (2008). The main idea of this algorithm is to simulate the model, that is, pairs of simulated stock returns and volatility values (mutation step), and then weigh the pairs appropriately so that we assign higher weights to those pairs with simulated values closer to the observed stock returns (selection step). We repeat this procedure and in the end we obtain the discrete empirical distribution of the unobserved volatility, which is known as the *volatility particle filter*.

The second part of the algorithm is a multinomial recombining tree algorithm. The level of recombination of the tree is high, since at each step the volatility is sampled from the volatility particle filter. As a result the branches of the tree recombine fast and unevenly. Moreover, the gain we have by using a tree-based pricing scheme is that we can price not only European options, but also American as well as other path-dependent options. For more details on this approach the reader can refer to Chronopoulou and Viens (2010).

Now, that we have selected our pricing scheme we can determine the implied long-memory parameter, H, by calibrating the model with realized option prices. More specifically the approach is the following: For each value of H varying from 0.5 to 0.95 with a relatively fine step:

1. we compute the corresponding empirical distribution of Y.
2. we use the tree algorithm to compute option prices for a certain range of strike prices.
3. we consider the center of the bid-ask spread and we compute the mean square error (MSE) of the computed option prices from the center of the bid-ask spread.

The implied Hurst index is the value of H with the smallest MSE.

REMARK 8.3

> Depending on the options that we want to price (put or call) and our needs, that is, if we wish to buy or sell an option, we can compare our computed option prices with the bid or the ask, instead of the center of the bid-ask spread.

In order to compute the remaining parameters of the model, we adapt classical techniques, for example, the variogram as discussed in the book by Fouque et al. (2000b).

8.3 Simulation Results

In this section we are going to compare the GPH and Whittle estimator for H using simulated data. We simulate model (Eq. 8.1) using an Euler discretization scheme with $\sigma(y) = \exp(y)$. We consider an equidistant Euler scheme with step Δ:

$$\begin{cases} X_{n\Delta} &= X_{(n-1)\Delta} + \left(\mu - \frac{\sigma(Y_{(n-1)\Delta})^2}{2}\right)\Delta + \sigma(Y_{(n-1)\Delta})\sqrt{\Delta}\varepsilon_n, \\ Y_{n\Delta} &= Y_{(n-1)\Delta} + \alpha Y_{(n-1)\Delta}\Delta + \beta(B^H_{n\Delta} - B^H_{(n-1)\Delta}). \end{cases}$$

Since we want high frequency data, we use n samples with length 500, where we have generated 5000 points for the continuous-time model with step 0.01, which means that we keep one point out of ten for estimation. We consider parameters $\mu = 0.1$, $\alpha = 0.2$, $\beta = 1$, and three different values of $H = 0.5, 0.6,$ and 0.85. The simulated model for $H = 0.6$ is illustrated in Fig. 8.1. We consider sample sizes of paths with $n = 512$, 1024, 2048. The estimated values of H are computed as the average of the estimators for 500 samples and thus we also obtain the corresponding standard errors. The results are summarized in Table 8.1.

We observe that both estimators work quite well in this simulated data example, but not in a satisfying way, thus the question how well they perform in real data remains open. From Table 8.1, we observe that the Whittle estimator is better than the GPH estimator in the three different values of H we considered. We also computed the CPU time required for each of the two procedures and we conclude that the GPH estimator is significantly faster than the Whittle. On the other hand, it is important to mention that the Whittle method provides estimates for all the parameters of the model (thus, it is reasonable to be slower), while the GPH method is only an estimation procedure for the long-memory parameter and we still need to use another technique for estimating the remaining parameters of the model.

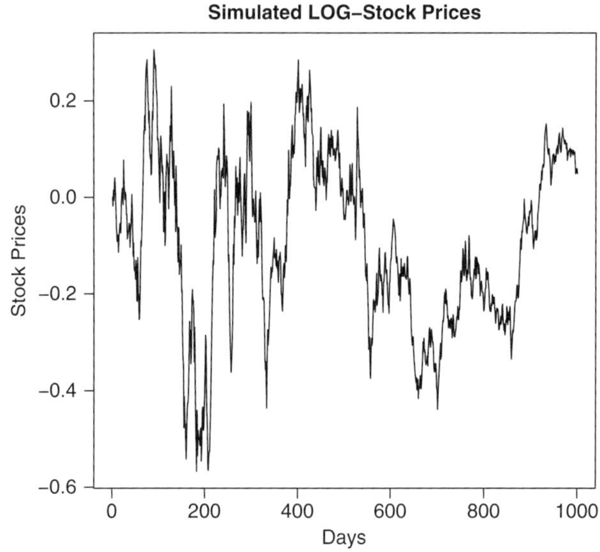

FIGURE 8.1 Sample path of the stock price with parameters: $\mu = 0.1$, $\alpha = 0.2$, $\beta = 1$, and $H = 0.6$.

8.4 Application to the S&P Index

Empirical evidence shows that the S&P 500 exhibits long memory, for example, the reader can refer to Chronopoulou and Viens (2010). In this section, we apply the implied H approach for pricing a European call option on the S&P 500.

In order to find the implied Hurst parameter, we construct the empirical distribution of the volatility for values of H from 0.5 to 0.95 with step 0.01. Before constructing each volatility filter, we estimate the other parameters of the model using the variogram method and high frequency stock prices (intraday tick-by-tick data). For the construction of the filter we do not use high frequency data, since empirical evidence shows that the implied value of H is the same, irrespectively of the frequency of the historical stock prices. For each filter, we generate 1000 particles and the model in the mutation step is constructed using 600 Euler steps.

We price a European call option written on the S&P 500 on March 30th, 2009 that expires in 35 business days. The interest rate during this period is $r = 0.21\%$ and the stock price "today" is $S_0 = \$787.53$. We choose the implied H by comparing our calculated option prices with the center of the bid-ask spread. The strike prices we consider vary from $K = \$670$ to $K = \$850$. The implied value of H is $\hat{H}_{\text{implied}} = 0.53$, while the GPH estimator we obtain is $\hat{H}_{\text{GPH}} = 0.67$. Using high frequency data the estimated parameters of the model for $\hat{H}_{\text{implied}} = 0.53$ are provided in Table 8.2.

Now, using the implied value of H and the GPH estimator as well as the corresponding estimated parameters for each model, we price the above European call option. At the tree algorithm we use $N = 100$ tree steps. In addition, we

TABLE 8.1 Hurst Parameter Estimators Using the Whittle and GPH Methods

	$n = 512$	$n = 1024$	$n = 2048$
$H = 0.50$			
Whittle procedure	0.4960	0.4968	0.4965
	(0.0150)	(0.0157)	(0.0129)
GPH estimator	0.5122	0.5099	0.5088
	(0.0431)	(0.0343)	(0.0291)
$H = 0.60$			
Whittle procedure	0.6103	0.6073	0.6099
	(0.0115)	(0.0148)	(0.0152)
GPH estimator	0.6233	0.6205	0.6189
	(0.0523)	(0.0488)	(0.0399)
$H = 0.85$			
Whittle procedure	0.8424	0.8499	0.8592
	(0.0234)	(0.0198)	(0.0125)
GPH estimator	0.8724	0.8697	0.8679
	(0.0735)	(0.0536)	(0.0487)

generate 1000 trees and we average the calculated values in order to obtain the option price "today". The results are presented in Table 8.3.

From Table 8.3 we observe that the option prices computed using the implied value of H are much closer to the center of the bid-ask spread than the prices computed using the GPH estimator. Thus, we conclude that following the suggested multinomial recombining tree approach for option pricing (using the volatility particle filter) we compute option prices that are closer to realized option prices using the implied value of H and not the GPH estimator.

8.5 Conclusion

In this chapter we reviewed the most popular techniques for parameter estimation under a continuous-time stochastic volatility model with long memory. We discussed two semiparametric methods, the log-periodogram regression estimator,

TABLE 8.2 Estimated Parameters of the Model (Eq. 8.1) Using High-Frequency S&P 500 Index Data

Parameter	Value
$\hat{H}_{\text{implied}}$	0.53
$\hat{\alpha}$	−0.0357
$\hat{\beta}$	0.231
$\hat{\mu}$	0.00015

TABLE 8.3 Computed European Call Option Prices on the S&P 500 Using Two Different Values of H; the Implied and the GPH

Strike Price	Bid	Ask	Implied $\hat{H} = 0.53$	GPH $\hat{H} = 0.67$
670	126.9	130.3	123.96	128.548998
680	118.5	121.9	115.819	120.8243045
690	110.4	113.8	107.935	113.8934418
700	102.6	105.9	100.324	106.9046677
710	94.6	98	92.9996	99.93005803
720	87.1	90.5	85.9752	92.98605016
730	79.8	83.2	79.2616	86.02413154
740	73	76.2	72.8693	79.05452604
750	66	69.5	66.805	72.61403562
760	59.7	63	61.0704	67.94887532
770	53.5	57	55.6668	63.3240498
780	47.8	51.3	50.5955	58.6024026
790	42.6	45.7	45.8526	53.96178084
800	37.4	40.8	41.4336	49.29507786
810	32.8	36.2	37.3349	44.66005889
820	28.3	31	33.5426	40.02346866
830	24.6	27.9	30.0468	35.47853205
840	20.8	24.3	26.8366	33.070406
850	18.9	20.8	23.9021	30.58178489

and the Whittle maximum likelihood estimator. We compared these two approaches using simulated data, concluding that the second one performs better. Moreover, we presented a real-data example and compared option prices calculated using the implied Hurst index and the GPH estimator of H. We observe that the option prices computed using the implied Hurst index are significantly closer to the realized option prices.

REFERENCES

Andersen A, Bollerslev T. Heterogenous information arrivals and return volatility dynamics: uncovering the long-run in high frequency returns. J Finance 1997;52:975–1005.

Ball C, Roma A. Stochastic volatility option pricing. J Financ Quant Anal 1994;29(4):589–607.

Beran J. Statistics for long-memory processes. Chapman and Hall, USA; 1994.

Black F, Scholes M. The valuation of options and corporate liability. J Polit Econ 1973;81:637–654.

Breidt FJ, Crato N, De Lima P. The detection and estimation of long-memory in stochastic volatility. J Econometrics 1998;83:325–348.

Casas I, Gao J. Econometric estimation in long-range dependent volatility models: theory and practice. J Econometrics 2008;147:72–83.

Chronopoulou A, Viens F. Estimation and pricing under long-memory stochastic volatility. Ann Finance 2010.

Comte F, Renault E. Long memory in continuous-time stochastic volatility models. Math Finance 1998;8(4):291–323.

De Lima P, Crato N. Long-range dependence in the conditional variance of stock returns. Econ Lett 1994;45(3):281–285.

Del Moral P, Jacod J, Protter P. The Monte-Carlo method for filtering with discrete time observations. Probab Theor Relat Field 2001;120:346–368.

Deo RS, Hurvich CM. On the log periodogram regression estimator of the memory parameter in long memory stochastic volatility models. Economet Theor 2001;17:686–710.

Ding ZC, Granger WJ, Engle RF. A long memory property of stock market returns and a new model. J Empir Finance 1993;1:1.

Florescu I, Viens FG. Stochastic volatility: option pricing using a multinomial recombining tree. Appl Math Finance 2008;15(2):151–181.

Fouque JP, Papanicolaou G, Sircar KR. Derivatives in financial markets with stochastic volatility. Cambridge University Press; 2000a.

Fouque JP, Papanicolaou G, Sircar KR. Mean-reverting stochastic volatility. Int J Theor Appl Finance 2000b;3(1):101–142.

Fox R, Taqqu MS. Large-sample properties of parameter estimates for strongly dependent stationary Gaussian time series. Ann Stat 1986;14:512–532.

Gao J. Modeling long-range dependent Gaussian processes with application in continuous-time financial models. J Appl Probab 2004;41:467–482.

Gao J, Anh V, Heyde C, Tieng Q. Parameter estimation of stochastic processes with long-range dependence and intermittency. J Time Anal 2001;22:527–535.

Geweke J, Porter-Hudak S. The estimation and application of long-memory time-series models. J Time Anal 1983;4:221–237.

Harvey AC. Long memory in stochastic volatility. In: Knight J, Satchell S, editors. Forecasting volatility in financial markets. Oxford: Butterworth-Haineman; 1998, p 307–320.

Heston S. A closed-form solution for options with stochastic volatility with applications to bond and currency options. Rev Financ Stud 1993;6(2):327–343.

Heyde C, Gay R. Smoothed periodogram asymptotics and estimation for processes and fields with possible long-range dependence. Stoch Proc Appl 1993;45:169–182.

Hull J, White A. The pricing of options on assets with stochastic volatility. J Finance 1987;42:281–300.

Hurvich CM, Deo RS, Brodsky J. The mean squared error of Geweke and Porter-Hudak's estimator of the memory parameter of a long-memory time series. J Time Ser Anal 1998;19:19–46.

Renault E, Touzi N. Option hedging and implicit volatilities in a stochastic volatility model. Math Finance 1993;6:215–236.

Robinson P. Log periodogram regression of time series with long range dependence. Ann Stat 1995a;23:1048–1072.

Robinson P. Gaussian semiparametric estimation of long-range dependence. Ann Stat 1995b;23:1630–1661.

Scott L. Option pricing when the variance changes randomly: theory, estimation, and an application. J Financ Quant Anal 1987;22(4):419–438.

Taylor S. Modeling financial timeseries. John Wiley and Sons, New York; 1986.

PART THREE

Analytical Results

CHAPTER NINE

A Market Microstructure Model of Ultra High Frequency Trading

CARLOS A. ULIBARRI and PETER C. ANSELMO
Department of Management, New Mexico Institute of Mining and Technology, Socorro, NM

9.1 Introduction

In the United States ultra high frequency traders (UHFTs) compete across a network market involving some 50 exchange institutions by submitting buy/sell orders algorithmically to a given exchange for execution. Automated trading platforms at these exchanges instantaneously route orders among one another in finding the best pricing. A striking feature of this network market is the high volume of UHFT activity. As of 2009 UHFTs represented only 2% of the nearly 20,000 trading firms operating in US markets. Nonetheless, the relatively few firms accounted for over 70% of US stock trading (Iati, 2009). Most UHFT volume reflects situations where broker-dealers shift orders among exchanges to find better prices and shorter trade execution times; or market conditions where stock indexes may lag momentarily in reflecting the falling or rising prices of their component stocks. In either case, the high UHFT volume is an economic consequence of trader-agents attempting to exploit arbitrage opportunities in

Handbook of Modeling High-Frequency Data in Finance, First Edition.
Edited by Frederi G. Viens, Maria C. Mariani, and Ionuţ Florescu.

milliseconds—akin to gathering pennies at the rate of some 1000 times per second (1000 ms) or more.

UHFT market activities have received critical attention in the analysis of the "flash-crash" of May 6th, 2010, when the Dow Jones fell 573 points in several minutes only to recover 543 points in an even shorter time interval. Market regulators confirmed the event initiated from the automated execution of a single large sell order at the Chicago Mercantile Exchange (CME): the sale of 75,000 E-mini S&P 500 futures contracts.[1] The price drop gained momentum as a result of a colossal imbalance in buy/sell orders. Studies by Easley *et al.* (2011) and Kirilenko *et al.* (2011) provide evidence that UHFT orders did not cause of the crash, yet the algorithmic response to selling pressure wound up talking liquidity from the network market. Specifically, UHFTs either submitted large numbers of small-sized sell orders (Kirilenko *et al.*), or stopped trading in order to avoid adverse selection risk (Easley *et al.*), i.e. potential losses from trading with better-informed agents. These actions resulted in a "liquidity bottleneck" and raise concerns that UHFT may interfere with the self-correcting tendencies of financial markets.

The microstructure model developed in this chapter offers insights on UHFT behavior, market liquidity and securities pricing in network markets. Increased liquidity benefits trader-agents by allowing for the immediate exchange of a security at more favorable prices, as reflected by narrower bid-ask spreads (Demsetz, 1968). Conversely, agents pay a higher price for liquidity as it becomes scarce, reflected in wider spreads.[2] In these situations sellers have a lesser chance of finding buyers resulting in higher liquidity costs (Ulibarri and Schatzberg, 2003). Various authors have opened the way for examining liquidity costs in high frequency trade domains. In particular, Mandelbrot (2004) and Engle (2000) describe time-scaling problems in modeling high frequency trade; Engle (2000) and Campbell *et al.* (1997) provide econometric guidance in applying trading time-intervals; and Ait-Shalia and Yu (2009) provide a state-of-the-art econometric approach for obtaining liquidity measures from 'noisy' high frequency data.

In keeping with these intellectual directions and the theme of this handbook, our study focuses on the affects of UHFT on bid-ask price behavior and market liquidity. We do so by simulating Poisson order arrival rates for UHFT and non-UHFT agents over time-intervals of 1000 and 1 ms. The comparative analysis offers some insights on the impacts of UHFT on liquidity provision, and some of the challenging theoretical and empirical issues in modeling split-second arbitrage opportunities and intraday trading behavior.

---

[1]CFTC-SEC (2010), esp. p. 3.

[2]Bloomberg News reported spreads widening during the May 6th crash "beyond belief"—from as low as one penny a share to as high as $100,000 a share. See Bloomberg Business Week Nov. 15–21, esp. p. 12.

9.2 Microstructural Model

We consider UHFT and non-UHFT trading of a security in the context of a double-auction market, where buyers enter competitive bid prices and sellers enter competitive ask prices simultaneously (Garman, 1976). Our model assumes N dealer-agents operate under monopolistic competition by submitting limit or market orders to buy or sell the security over a sequence of short time intervals.[3] The population of traders includes UHFT and non-UHFT dealer-agents, and we assume both subpopulations trade based on perceived arbitrage opportunities by maximizing their expected profits. A transaction occurs at the exact point of time where a limit order is executed at the first best price. Consequently, the first-best bid-ask prices in a given time interval are conditioned by the size and composition of the trading population.

Our microstructural model considers a trading horizon spanning a base time interval $[0, t = 1]$, which could represent 1 day, 1 h, 1 s, or 1 ms. This interpretation of the trading horizon allows for the occurrence of k transactions in any of the possible subintervals, that is, $0 = t_0 < t_1 < t_2 < \cdots < t_N = 1$. We assume UHFT and non-UHFT orders arrive randomly over time according to Poisson processes, where buy and sell orders (in theory) can take on any values from zero to infinity. We also assume the stochastic order flow process is noninformative in regard to future price movements and other market parameters.

Of course, no abstract model of market microstructure can capture the full complexity of market phenomenon, and the present framework is no exception. Here, we take a pragmatic approach in studying the UHFT market by imposing additional restrictions: (i) in any given subinterval $[0, t]$, there exist a large number of potential traders; (ii) each trader acts independently in submitting orders; (iii) no one trader can generate an infinite number of orders in a finite time interval; and (iv) no subset of traders can dominate order generation (subsequently relaxed). These restrictions have important theoretical and empirical implications.

First, our focus on independent agents is a cornerstone of monopolistic competition models, where agents make independent pricing decisions without conspiring to influence trade (Vives, 1998). And applying the Poisson process in this setting rules out the possibility that some traders know more about the next price ticks than other traders (see O'Hara (2008), pp. 16 and 45).[4] Second, our focus on extremely short trading horizons motivates us to represent the fundamental asset value as a fixed parameter. This approach seems realistic in the present situation but could be relaxed in a more general analysis. Finally, the caveat that no subset of agents can dominate order generation is central to the present study, and accordingly, we examine this restriction more closely in the context of a UHFT/non-UHFT trading platform.

[3]See Stigler (1968) for an interesting discussion of the historical underpinnings of monopolistic competition theory set forth by Chamberlin (1937).

[4]This is a simplifying restriction having important order flow implications, and it could be treated directly in a more general information-based framework. See O'Hara (2008) for a review of information-based models.

The following lemma describes the limiting probability of k orders arriving in the base time interval $[0, t = 1]$, and thus the essence of the order flow process.

LEMMA 9.1

Let $B_T = B_1 + B_2$ and $S_T = S_1 + S_2$ be the Poisson random variables defining the aggregate volumes of buy and sell orders submitted by UHFT (subscript 1) and non-UHFT (subscript 2) traders in the base time interval $[0, t = 1]$. Also, let the average arrival rates for the buy and sell orders be defined by $\bar{\mu}_N = \bar{\mu}_1^B + \bar{\mu}_2^B$ and $\bar{\gamma}_N = \bar{\gamma}_1^S + \bar{\gamma}_2^S$. It follows that the corresponding probabilities of k-order arrivals in the time interval $[0, t = 1]$ are given by $\Pr B_T(k) = (\mu_1^B + \mu_2^B)^k \frac{e^{-(\mu_1^B + \mu_2^B)}}{k!}$ and $\Pr S_T(k) = (\gamma_1^S + \gamma_2^S)^k \frac{e^{-(\gamma_1^S + \gamma_2^S)}}{k!}$ (proof given in Johnson pp. 162–163).

The following theorem defines the probability of buy and sell orders arriving in a fraction of the base time interval $[0, t]$, representing 1 s or ms.

THEOREM 9.2

The probability of k buy or sell orders arriving in the subintervals $[0, t]$ are given by $\Pr B_T(k) = [(\mu_1^B + \mu_2^B)t]^k \frac{e^{-[(\mu_1^B + \mu_2^B)t]}}{k!}$ and $\Pr S_T(k) = [(\gamma_1^S + \gamma_2^S)t]^k \frac{e^{-[(\gamma_1^S + \gamma_2^S)t]}}{k!}$ (see Johnson for proof).

Our analysis of market pricing and liquidity assumes dealers are well diversified and choose bid and ask prices so as to maximize their expected arbitrage profits for a single stock. Under "common knowledge," any one dealer is aware that the other N-1 dealers may use UHFT technology and quotes double-auction prices that are "regret free," that is, the dealer does not regret transacting at the bid or ask price after the fact. Under this pricing rule, the electronic limit book contains a regret-free price schedule for any quantity of buy and sell orders. Thus, dealer A may have posted a limit order to buy 10 shares at the price of 8. Another dealer may have posted a limit order to sell 5 shares at the price of 9. Assuming these are the first best prices received on each side of the market, the best regret-free two-way price is 8–9.

More generally, we view the double-auction prices as the outcome of orders crossing between the population of dealer-agents: buy orders are crossed at the ask price and sell orders are crossed at the bid price. Here, we focus on the resulting bid-ask spread obtained under conditions of monopolistic competition, which assumes agents maximize expected profits per unit time. The buy and sell order rate functions for a representative trader are $B_i = [(\mu_i^B, P_a | P_a = \phi(\mu_N)]$

and $S_i = [(\gamma_i^S, P_b | P_b = \varphi(\gamma_N))]$, where P_a and P_b denote the regret-free ask and bid prices and μ_N and γ_N denote aggregate volumes of buy and sell orders in a given time interval, that is, $\mu_N = \sum \mu_i^B$ and $\gamma_N = \sum \gamma_i^S$. Correspondingly, the ith trader's cost and revenue functions are given by $C_i^S = \gamma_i^S \varphi(\gamma_N)$ and $R_i^B = \mu_i^B \phi(\mu_N)$, with derivative marginal cost and revenue functions $MC_i^S = \varphi(\gamma_N) + \gamma_i^S \varphi'(\gamma_N)$ and $MR_i^B = \phi(\mu_N) + \mu_i^B \phi'(\mu_N)$.

To represent the "inside spread"—the difference between the regret-free bid and ask prices—we multiply each marginal condition by the population of traders (N). We then substitute and rearrange terms to express each marginal condition in elasticity form: $MC_i^S = P_b(1 + (N\varepsilon)^{-1})$ and $MR_i^B = P_a(1 + (N\theta)^{-1})$, where θ and ε denote the market elasticities of buy and sell orders, that is, $\theta = \frac{d\mu}{dP_a}\frac{P_a}{\mu} < 0$ and $\varepsilon = \frac{d\gamma}{dP_b}\frac{P_b}{\gamma} > 0$. Equating the resulting marginal conditions establishes the "inside spread," $S^* = P_a^* - P_b^* = \frac{1}{N}\left(\frac{P_b^*}{\varepsilon} - \frac{P_a^*}{\theta}\right)$, where P_a^* and P_b^* are the regret-free bid and ask prices.

Below, we make static comparisons of the inside-spread over a fractured time interval, with dealer-agents exploiting minute arbitrage opportunities. The comparisons rely on the above lemma and theorem in examining how the inside spread varies with the mix of arbitrage traders and the corresponding price elasticities for buy and sell orders.

9.3 Static Comparisons

Here we use comparative analysis to sample critical parameter values underlying the inside spread. Key inputs in this analysis include the random arrival of buy and sell orders with aggregate mean arrival rates $(\bar{\mu}_N, \bar{\gamma}_N)$. Key outputs of the analysis include (i) simulated order flows for the UHFT/non-UHFT trading platform, (ii) the price elasticities for aggregate order flows, and (iii) the inside spread. For convenience and tractability, our market comparisons use linear order rate functions $P_a = \delta^{-1}(c^B - \bar{\mu}_N)$ and $P_b = \beta^{-1}(\bar{\gamma}_N - c^S)$, reflecting Poisson distributed order-arrival rates in a given time interval, that is, $[0, t = 0.001]$ or $[0, t = 1]$. Buyers enter competitive bid prices, and sellers (simultaneously) enter competitive ask prices. Accordingly, their embedded transaction costs influence the order decisions and trading prices of the stock.

As noted earlier, applying the Poisson order-arrival process requires dealer-agents to act independently, with no subset of agents dominating order generation (see O'Hara, pp. 16 and 45). We examine this restriction by simulating the market dropping toward UHFT as dealer-agents exploit perceived arbitrage opportunities, thus affecting the inside spread. Let $\bar{\pi}_t^B$ and $\bar{\pi}_t^S$ denote expected profits to be had by submitting buy and sell orders in the time interval $[t, t + \Delta t]$. We assume random order arrivals govern the dynamic adjustment of arbitrage profits, as specified by $\frac{\Delta\bar{\pi}_t^B}{\bar{\pi}_t^B} = -(\bar{\mu}_N - \bar{\gamma}_N)\Delta t < 0$ and $\frac{\Delta\bar{\pi}_t^S}{\bar{\pi}_t^S} = -(\bar{\gamma}_N - \bar{\mu}_N)\Delta t < 0$. The necessary conditions for arbitrage profits to dissipate in the time interval Δt require $\bar{\mu}_N - \bar{\gamma}_N > 0$ or $\bar{\gamma}_N - \bar{\mu}_N > 0$.

To model order generation tipping toward UHFT, let $N_1 = \alpha N$denote UHFT dealer-agents and $N_2 = (1-\alpha)N$all other agents where $0 < \alpha < 1$. Correspondingly, the weighted arrival rates for buy and sell orders are $\bar{\mu}_N = \alpha\mu_1^B + (1-\alpha)\mu_2^B$ and $\bar{\gamma}_N = \alpha\gamma_1^S + (1-\alpha)\gamma_2^S$. In the event UHFT agents dominate order generation ($\alpha \to 1$), the arrival rates governing arbitrage become $\bar{\mu}_N \to \mu_1^B$ and $\bar{\gamma}_N \to \gamma_1^S$. We examine how the arbitrage process impacts the inside spread S^* by simulating order-arrival counts for the two subpopulations. Our experiments compare trading time intervals of 1 ms $[0, t = 0.001]$ and 1000 ms $[0, t = 1]$ using the following parameter values for the order rate functions: $\delta = \beta = 40, c^B = 50$, and $c^S = -18$.

Experiment 1. Our first experiment models the 1-ms time interval $[0, t = 0.001]$ assuming UHFT dominates order generation $N_1 = 50, N_2 = 0$. The order arrivals are simulated using a random number generator and Poisson probabilities reflecting average arrival rates of $\mu_1^B = \gamma_1^S = 1$, that is, one trade per millisecond. Given these order rate characteristics, the regret-free bid and ask prices were computed for 20 simulation trials by minimizing the sum of the bid-ask spreads subject to the price-parameter constraint $c^S = -18$.

Experiment 2. Our second experiment models the 1000-ms time interval $[0, t = 1]$ assuming UHFT and non-UHFT agents participate in order generation $N_1 = 50, N_2 = 40$. In this case, buy and sell orders are simulated using the random number generator with Poisson probabilities reflecting weighted arrival rates of $\bar{\mu}_N = \bar{\gamma}_N = 555$ trades per second. Using these order rates, we recomputed the regret-free bid and ask prices over 20 simulation trials, with the bid-ask spreads minimized subject to the same price-parameter constraint $c^S = -18$. Table 9.1 describes summary statistics for the outcomes of the two experiments in terms of the means, ranges, and standard deviations of the order flow elasticities (θ, ε) and the inside spread (S^*).

Our results show the mean value of the simulated inside spread is relatively narrow in the fractured time interval compared to the longer time interval, that is, $S^* = 0.0026$ versus 0.0056. The tighter spread in the fractured time interval is explained by more elastic buy and sell order flows: $\theta = -35.86$ versus -4.13

TABLE 9.1 Simulation Results for Experiments 1 and 2

	Experiment 1 $[0, t = 0.001]$			Experiment 2 $[0, t = 1.0]$		
	S^*	ϑ	ε	S^*	ϑ	ε
Mean	0.0026	−35.86	10.52	0.0056	−4.13	2.89
Minimum	0.0010	−49.0	3.0	0.0042	−6.56	2.29
Maximum	0.006	−6.14	19.0	0.0070	−2.76	3.81
Standard Deviation	0.0015	18.52	6.49	0.0009	1.03	0.39

Notes: Experiment 1 uses parameter settings $N_1 = 50, N_2 = 0$, and $\mu = \gamma = 1$ trade per millisecond. Experiment 2 uses parameter settings $N_1 = 50, N_2 = 40$, and $\mu = \gamma = 555$ trade per second. In both cases, buy (and sell) orders correspond to the perception that the underlying asset is undervalued (overvalued) relative to the perceived "fair-value" price, yielding expected arbitrage profits. The inside spread is computed using excel solver to minimize the sum of- differences in regret-free prices across 20 simulation trials subject to the price constraint $c^s = -18$.

for buy orders and $\varepsilon = 10.52$ versus 2.89 for sell orders. These results are consistent with the belief UHFT dealer-agents have relatively lower transaction costs allowing them to exploit flash arbitrage opportunities. Correspondingly, UHFT orders exhibit a higher degree of price responsiveness. Interestingly, both the ranges and standard deviations of the inside spread are lower in the longer time interval, where non-UHFT agents participate in the arbitrage process, that is, $\sigma = 0.0009$ versus 0.0015. These observations underscore the potential for UHFT orders to destabilize market prices and liquidity provision.

9.4 Questions for Future Research

The microstructure model considered in the present study is motivated by the May 6, 2010, crash in stock index prices, when the Dow Jones industrials lost nearly 1000 points in less than half hour (biggest drop ever). Following this event the U.S. Securities and Exchange Commission (SEC) took swift steps to regulate UHFT. On one hand, the SEC began coordinating the use and scope of "circuit breakers" on single stocks. For example, trade in any S&P stock that rises or falls 10% or more in a 5-min interval is now halted for 5 min to give the primary listing market sufficient time to generate liquidity and reopen the stock at a more rational price. Also, the SEC has added "erroneous trade-break rules," which give traders greater confidence in foul prices that would result in broken trades (reference given in ff. 2 citation).

Our conceptual model offers insights on the potential for UHFT to affect market liquidity and price continuity. The simulation analysis of the model shows that UHFT orders *tend to* exhibit greater price responsiveness and contribute to lower bid-ask spreads. At the same time, we observe the potential for UHFT to contribute to price volatility, as reflected by the ranges and standard deviations of the inside spread. Clearly, the potential dominance of UHFT in generating buy and sell orders in a given time interval has important implications for market liquidity and deserves closer scrutiny relative to the price responsiveness of order flows.

In future work, it would be interesting to examine the means by which UHFT poses potential trade execution problems for non-UHFT broker-dealers, as well as its impact on market volatility. We believe further work along these lines may help guide policy discussions concerning the regulation of UHFT. Toward this end we thank the authors of this handbook for the opportunity to share our conceptual insights.

ACKNOWLEDGMENTS

The authors are most grateful for the comments and suggestions received from the anonymous reviewers of this chapter and to other participants at the Conference on Modeling High Frequency Data II at the Stevens Institute of Technology. Support funding for this research is also acknowledged to ICASA (Institute of Complex Additive Systems Analysis), New Mexico Institute of Mining and Technology.

REFERENCES

Ait-Shalia Y, Yu J. High frequency market microstructure noise estimates and liquidity measures. Ann Appl Stat 2009;1:422–457.

Campbell JY, Lo AW, MacKinlay C. The econometrics of financial markets. Princeton, NJ: Princeton University Press; 1997.

CFTC-SEC. Findings regarding the market events of May 6, 2010; September 30, 2010.

Chamberlin EH. The theory of monopolistic competition. London: Oxford University Press; 1937.

Condon B. Recipe for disaster? Albuquerque J 2010.

Demsetz H. The cost of transacting. Q J Econ 1968;82:33–53.

Easley D, Lopez de Prado MM, O'Hara M. The microstructure of the 'flash crash:' flow toxicity, liquidity crashes and the probability of informed trading. J Portfolio Management 2011;37:118–128.

Engle RE. The econometrics of ultra-high frequency data. Econometrica 2000;1:1–22.

Garman M. Market microstructure. J Financ Econ 1976;3:257–275.

Iati R. High frequency trading technology. TABB Group; 2009.

Johnson J. Probability and statistics for computer science. John Wiley & Sons Inc.; Hoboken, NJ; 2003.

Kirilenko A, Kyle A, Samadi M, Tuzun T. The flash crash: the impact of high frequency trading on an electronic market. Working Paper 2011. Available at http://ssrn.com/abstract=1686004.

Mandelbrot B, Hudson RL. The (mis) behavior of markets. New York: Basic Books; 2004.

O'Hara M. Market microstructure theory. Malden, MA: Blackwell Publishing; 2008.

Podobnik B *et al.* ARCH-GARCH approaches to modeling high-frequency financial data. Physica 2004;344:216–220.

Stigler GJ. The organization of industry. Chicago: University of Chicago Press; 1968.

Ulibarri CA, Schatzberg J. Liquidity costs: screen-based trading versus open outcry. Rev Financ Econ 2003;12:381–396.

Ulibarri CA, Anselmo PC, Trabatti MX. Cournot model of brokered FX trading. J Int Financ Market Inst Money 2005;15:425–436.

CHAPTER TEN

Multivariate Volatility Estimation with High Frequency Data Using Fourier Method

MARIA ELVIRA MANCINO
Department of Mathematics for Decisions, University of Firenze, Italy
SIMONA SANFELICI
Department of Economics, University of Parma, Italy

10.1 Introduction

Volatility and covolatility measurement/forecasting is a key issue in finance. Volatility can be computed through parametric or nonparametric methods, see for instance the review by Andersen *et al.* (2010a). In the first case, the expected volatility is modeled through a functional form of market or latent variables. On the contrary, nonparametric methods address the computation of the historical volatility without assuming any functional form of the volatility. As volatility changes over time, its computation through nonparametric methods concentrates on a small time window (a day, a week), and high frequency data should be employed.

Availability of high frequency data has improved the capability of computing volatility in an efficient way. Nevertheless measuring the diffusion coefficient

Handbook of Modeling High-Frequency Data in Finance, First Edition.
Edited by Frederi G. Viens, Maria C. Mariani, and Ionuţ Florescu.

of a continuous time semimartingale (i.e., the instantaneous volatility) from the observed asset prices is challenging for two main reasons: data are not available in continuous time and observed asset prices are not generated by the theoretical model (frictionless price), but they are affected by noise microstructure effects. Further, when computing covariances between returns recorded at the highest available observation frequency, returns are obviously asynchronous across different assets, thus the estimation of covariances suffers from a downward bias when the sampling interval is reduced (known as *Epps effect*, by Epps (1979)).

Motivated by the consequences of the combined effect of asynchronous trading and microstructure noise, a number of alternative covariance estimators have been proposed in the literature; nevertheless, most of them rely on the *quadratic covariation* formula, a classical result essentially due to Wiener. Following the study by Martens (2004), the different approaches to the estimation of covariances can be split in two groups. The first group uses interpolation of data in order to obtain synchronous returns, which are necessary to construct the *realized covariance–quadratic variation* estimator; for instance, Scholes and Williams (1977) modified the standard realized covariance estimator by adding the first lead and lag of the sample autocovariance, Dimson (1979) and Cohen *et al.* (1983) generalize this estimator to include k leads and lags, and Zhang (2009) provides a consistent two scales realized covariance estimator using the previous tick method. A different approach to data synchronization is given by the *refresh time* procedure proposed by Barndorff-Nielsen *et al.* (2008b) in order to construct the multivariate realized kernels estimators; this synchronization procedure is employed also by Jacod *et al.* (2009) and Christensen *et al.* (2010) who construct an estimator based on a preaveraging method. The second group utilizes all transaction data (Harris *et al.*, 1995; De Jong and Nijman, 1997; Brandt and Diebold, 2006). In particular, De Jong and Nijman (1997) and Hayashi and Yoshida (2005) propose an alternative to the realized covariance estimator that uses tick-by-tick data and does not rely on any synchronization methods. Sheppard (2006) introduces the concept of scrambling to describe the link between the price generating process and the sampling process.

The impact of microstructure noise has been studied extensively in the context of univariate volatility measurement, (Ait-Sahalia *et al.*, 2005a; Barndorff-Nielsen *et al.*, 2005; Zhang *et al.*, 2005; Hansen and Lunde, 2006; Bandi and Russel, 2006a). For the multivariate case, Bandi and Russel (2005) provide an analytical study of the realized covariance in the presence of noise, but they do not address the nonsynchronicity issue. Griffin and Oomen (2011) find that the ordering of covariance estimators in terms of efficiency depends crucially on the level of microstructure noise. The multivariate realized kernel by Barndorff-Nielsen *et al.* (2008b) and the modulated realized covariation by Kinnebrock and Podolskij (2008) are consistent estimators in the presence of certain types of microstructure noise.

In Malliavin and Mancino (2002), an alternative nonparametric method to compute multivariate volatility based on Fourier series has been proposed. We refer to this estimator as the *Fourier* estimator. The method allows to compute both the instantaneous volatility and the volatility in a time interval (integrated volatility). The Fourier estimator uses all the available observations and avoids any "synchronization" of the original data, being based on the integration of the time series of returns rather than on its differentiation. Therefore, it is particularly suitable for employing high frequency data and for computing volatility/covariance of financial time series. Since the method was proposed, it has been extended/applied in several directions.

In this chapter, we aim at reviewing some results which explicitly focus on the properties of the Fourier estimator and its performance when applied to high frequency data. This chapter is organized as follows. In Section 10.2, we present the Fourier method for computing multivariate volatilities developed in Malliavin and Mancino (2009) and the asymptotic properties of the Fourier estimator under general asynchronous observations. Moreover, we show that starting from the observation of a price trajectory it is possible to recover the latent variable trajectory (volatility) as a *stochastic function of time* in the univariate and multivariate settings, and then, by iterating the procedure, the volatility of the volatility process and the leverage component (asset price–volatility covariance) can be obtained by the Fourier method. In Section 10.3, the finite sample properties of the Fourier estimator of integrated volatility under market microstructure noise are studied. Analytic expressions for the bias and the mean squared error (MSE) of the contaminated estimator are derived, and an empirical analysis based on a simulation study is conducted, showing the efficiency of the Fourier estimator. In particular, a feasible procedure to design an optimal MSE-based estimator is derived. Section 10.4 analyzes the effects of market microstructure on the Fourier estimator of multivariate integrated volatilities. We prove that with high frequency data, the estimator has a competitive performance even in comparison to bias-adjusted estimators in all the different scenarios considered, without requiring any ad hoc adjustment. Our theoretical results are confirmed by the Monte Carlo experiments. In Section 10.5, we analyze the forecasting performance of the Fourier estimator, both in the univariate and multivariate cases. We show that the Fourier estimator outperforms the realized volatility/covariance estimator to a significant extent, in particular for high frequency observations and when the noise component is relevant; in general, it has a better performance even in comparison to the methods specifically designed to handle market microstructure contaminations. Finally, in Section 10.6, we consider the gains offered by the Fourier estimator over other covariance measures from the perspective of an asset-allocation decision problem, following the approach of Fleming *et al.* (2001), who study the impact of volatility timing versus unconditional mean–variance efficient static asset-allocation strategies and of selecting the appropriate sampling frequency or choosing between different bias and variance reduction techniques for the realized covariance matrices. In particular, we show that the Fourier estimator carefully extracts information from noisy high frequency asset price data for the purpose of realized variance/covariance estimation and allows for nonnegligible utility gains in portfolio management.

10.2 Fourier Estimator of Multivariate Spot Volatility

Suppose that the prices of n assets $p(t) = (p^1(t), \dots, p^n(t))$ are observed at a continuous time, whose evolutions are continuous semimartingales satisfying the following Itô stochastic differential equations

$$dp^j(t) = \sum_{i=1}^{d} \sigma_i^j(t) dW^i + b^j(t)\, dt, j = 1, \dots, n, \tag{10.1}$$

where $W = (W^1, \dots, W^d)$ are independent Brownian motions on a filtered probability space satisfying the *usual conditions* and σ_*^* and b^* are adapted random processes satisfying

$$(\mathbf{H})\, E\left[\int_0^T (b^i(t))^2 dt\right] < \infty, \quad E\left[\int_0^T (\sigma_i^j(t))^4 dt\right] < \infty$$
$$i = 1, \dots, d, \quad j = 1, \dots, n.$$

From the representation (Eq. 10.1) the *(time dependent) volatility matrix* is defined by

$$\Sigma^{j,k}(t) = \sum_{i=1}^{d} \sigma_i^j(t) \sigma_i^k(t). \tag{10.2}$$

For notational simplicity, we will refer to the case of two assets whose prices are $(p^1(t), p^2(t))$. By a change of the origin and rescaling the unit of time, we can always reduce ourselves to the case where the time window $[0, T]$ becomes $[0, 2\pi]$.

The main result of this section is formula (Eq. 10.4), on which the construction of the volatility estimator relies. We recall some definitions from harmonic analysis theory (see for instance Malliavin (1995)): given a function ϕ on the circle S^1, we consider its *Fourier transform*

$$\mathcal{F}(\phi)(k) := \frac{1}{2\pi} \int_0^{2\pi} \phi(\vartheta) \exp(-ik\vartheta)\, d\vartheta, \quad \text{for } k \in \mathbf{Z}. \tag{10.3}$$

Further, we define

$$\mathcal{F}(d\phi)(k) := \frac{1}{2\pi} \int_0^{2\pi} \exp(-ik\vartheta)\, d\phi(\vartheta).$$

The following result contains the identity relating the Fourier transform of the price process $p(t)$ to the Fourier transform of the volatility matrix $\Sigma(t)$ (Malliavin and Mancino, 2009).

THEOREM 10.1

Consider a process p satisfying the assumption (**H**). Then we have for $i, j = 1, 2$ and for all integers k

$$\frac{1}{2\pi}\mathcal{F}(\Sigma^{ij})(k) = \lim_{N\to\infty}\frac{1}{2N+1}\sum_{s=-N}^{N}\mathcal{F}(dp^i)(s)\mathcal{F}(dp^j)(k-s), \quad (10.4)$$

where the convergence (Eq. 10.4) is attained in probability.

By Theorem 10.1, we gather all the Fourier coefficients of the volatility matrix by means of the Fourier transform of the log-returns. Then the reconstruction of the cross-volatility function $\Sigma^{ij}(t)$ from its Fourier coefficients can be obtained as follows: define for $i = 1, 2$

$$\Phi^i_N(k) := \mathcal{F}(dp^i)(k) \quad \text{for } |k| \leq 2N \text{ and 0 otherwise}$$

and for any $|k| \leq N$,

$$\Psi^{ij}_N(k) := \frac{1}{2N+1}\sum_{s\in\mathbf{Z}}\Phi^i_N(s)\Phi^j_N(k-s).$$

If $\Sigma^{ij}(t)$ is continuous, then the Fourier–Fejer summation gives almost everywhere

$$\Sigma^{ij}(t) = \lim_{N\to\infty}\sum_{|k|<N}(1-\frac{|k|}{N})\Psi^{ij}_N(k)\exp(ikt) \quad \text{for all } t \in (0, 2\pi). \quad (10.5)$$

In the case of a single asset, the computation of the volatility can be derived from Theorem 10.1 and is specified by the following.

COROLLARY 10.2

Suppose that the log-price process $p(t)$ follows the Itô process

$$dp(t) = b(t)dt + \sigma(t)dW(t),$$

and assumption (H) holds. Then the Fourier coefficients of volatility $\sigma^2(t)$ are obtained by

$$\frac{1}{2\pi}\mathcal{F}(\sigma^2)(k) = \lim_{N\to\infty}\frac{1}{2N+1}\sum_{|s|\leq N}\mathcal{F}(dp)(s)\,\mathcal{F}(dp)(k-s), \quad (10.6)$$

where the limit is attained in probability.

The financial econometric's literature mainly focuses on the *integrated* (co)volatility, that is, $\int_0^T \sigma^2(t)dt$, where $[0, T]$ is a fixed time horizon, e.g. a day, exploiting the quadratic (co)variation formula. In fact, a classical result, essentially due to Wiener, states the following formula holds almost surely

$$QV|_0^T(p) = \int_0^T \sigma^2(s)\,ds,$$

where

$$QV|_0^T(p) := \lim_{n\to\infty} \sum_{0\le k<T2^n} \left(p((k+1)2^{-n}) - p(k2^{-n})\right)^2.$$

The spot volatility is then obtained by numerical differentiation, and therefore, it is quite instable. In the context of Fourier estimation methodology, the integrated volatility and covolatilities are computed by considering the $k = 0$ coefficient, respectively, in the formulae 10.4 and 10.6. Moreover, the Fourier estimation theory presented in this section is more powerful, as it allows to recover the entire volatility curve pathwise from the observation of an asset price trajectory by Equation 10.5. The knowledge of the volatility function, in contrast to the integrated volatility alone, is essential when a stochastic derivation of volatility along the time evolution is performed as in contingent claim pricing-hedging, (Barucci *et al.*, 2003, Malliavin and Thalmaier, 2006), or when we study the geometry of the Heath–Jarrow–Morton interest rates dynamics, given the observation of a single market trajectory (Malliavin *et al.*, 2007).

10.2.1 ASYMPTOTIC PROPERTIES OF THE FOURIER ESTIMATOR

Starting from the analysis above, the Fourier estimator of covariances based on discrete observations of prices can be derived by considering a piecewise-constant approximation of the price process $p(t)$. The peculiarity of the Fourier estimator is that it uses all the available observations because it is based on the integration of the time series of returns rather than on its differentiation. Further, from the practitioner's point of view, it is easy to implement, as it does not rely on any choice of synchronization methods or sampling schemes. The definition of the Fourier estimator does not induce any synchronization bias as it happens for all realized covariance-type estimators. Thus, the Fourier estimator of instantaneous (and integrated) covolatility is consistent under asynchronous trading.

Let $\mathcal{T}_{n_l} := \{t^l_{i,n_l}, i = 0, \ldots, n_l\}$, $l = 1, 2$, be the trading times for the two assets. For the ease of notation, we often omit the second index n_l. For simplicity, suppose that both assets trade at $t_0 = 0$ and $t^1_{n_1} = t^2_{n_2} = 2\pi$. It is not restrictive to suppose that $n_1 = n_2 := n$. Denote for $l = 1, 2$, $\theta^l(n) := \max_{0\le h\le n-1} |t^l_{h+1} - t^l_h|$, and suppose that $\theta(n) := \theta^1(n) \vee \theta^2(n) \to 0$ as $n \to \infty$. Consider the following interpolation formula

$$p_n^*(t) := \sum_{i=0}^{n-1} p^*(t_i^*) I_{[t_i^*,\, t_{i+1}^*]}(t).$$

Set $I_i^* := [t_i^*, t_{i+1}^*]$ and $\delta_{I_i^*}(p^*) := p^*(t_{i+1}^*) - p^*(t_i^*)$. For any integer k, $|k| \leq 2N$, define

$$c_k(\mathrm{d}p_n^*) = \frac{1}{2\pi} \sum_{i=0}^{n-1} \exp(-\mathrm{i}kt_i^*)\delta_{I_i^*}(p^*). \tag{10.7}$$

THEOREM 10.3

Let $c_k(\mathrm{d}p_n^*)$ and $\mathcal{F}(\Sigma^{12})(k)$ be as defined in Equations (10.7) and (10.4), respectively. Define

$$c_k(\Sigma_{n,N}^{12}) := \frac{2\pi}{2N+1} \sum_{|s| \leq N} c_s(\mathrm{d}p_n^1) c_{k-s}(\mathrm{d}p_n^2) \quad \forall |k| \leq N, \tag{10.8}$$

and

$$\widehat{\Sigma}_{n,N}^{12}(t) := \sum_{|k|<N} \left(1 - \frac{|k|}{N}\right) c_k(\Sigma_{n,N}^{12}) \mathrm{e}^{\mathrm{i}kt}. \tag{10.9}$$

Suppose that $N\theta(n) \to 0$ as $N, n \to \infty$. Then the following results hold in probability:

$$\text{(i)} \quad \lim_{n,N\to\infty} c_k(\Sigma_{n,N}^{12}) = \mathcal{F}(\Sigma^{12})(k), \tag{10.10}$$

$$\text{(ii)} \quad \lim_{n,N\to\infty} \sup_{0 \leq t \leq 2\pi} |\widehat{\Sigma}_{n,N}^{12}(t) - \Sigma^{12}(t)| = 0.$$

The random function $\widehat{\Sigma}_{n,N}^{12}(t)$ in Equation 10.9 will be called the *Fourier estimator* of the instantaneous covolatility $\Sigma^{12}(t)$. Theorem 10.3 proves the convergence in probability of the random function (Eq. 10.9) to the covolatility function $\Sigma^{12}(t)$ uniformly in t, as N and n go to infinity (see Malliavin and Mancino (2009) for the proof).

Finally, we state the weak convergence of the instantaneous covolatility estimator defined in Equation 10.9 to the volatility process $\Sigma^{12}(t)$ (see Malliavin and Mancino (2009) for the proof). As a corollary, the asymptotic normality for the error of the integrated covolatility estimators is derived.

The asymptotic result below is obtained as the width of the partition $\theta(n)$, goes to zero, and the interval $[0, 2\pi]$ remains fixed. Nevertheless, as we suppose to have irregularly spaced grids, some conditions are needed. Following Mykland and Zhang (2006) we consider

(A) (i) $\theta(n) \to 0$ and $n\theta(n) = 0(1)$

(ii) $H_n(t) := \frac{n}{2\pi} \sum_{t^1_{i+1} \wedge t^2_{j+1} \leq t} (t^1_{i+1} \wedge t^2_{j+1} - t^1_i \vee t^2_j)^2 I_{\{t^1_i \vee t^2_j < t^1_{i+1} \wedge t^2_{j+1}\}} \to$ $H(t)$ as $n \to \infty$

iii) $H(t)$ is continuously differentiable.

We note that if the partitions are evenly spaced, then $H(t) = t$ and $H'(t) = 1$.

THEOREM 10.4

Let $\widehat{\Sigma}^{12}_{n,N}(t)$ be defined in Equation 10.9. Suppose $\theta(n) \to 0$, $N \to \infty$, and assumption **(A)** holds. Then, for any function $h \in Lip(\alpha)$, $\alpha > 2/3$, with compact support in $(0, 2\pi)$,

$$(\theta(n))^{-\frac{1}{2}} \int_0^{2\pi} h(t)(\overline{\widehat{\Sigma}^{12}_{n,N}(t)} - \Sigma^{12}(t))\mathrm{d}t \tag{10.11}$$

converges in law to a mixture of Gaussian distribution with variance $\int_0^{2\pi} H'(t)h^2(t)(\Sigma^{11}(t)\Sigma^{22}(t) + (\Sigma^{12}(t))^2)\mathrm{d}t$, provided that $\theta(n)N^{2\alpha} \to \infty$ and $\theta(n)N^{4/3} \to 0$.

10.2.2 FOURIER ESTIMATOR OF THE VOLATILITY OF THE VARIANCE AND OF THE LEVERAGE

The Fourier estimation method is particularly suitable to build an estimator of the volatility of the variance and of the "leverage," that is, the covariance between the stochastic variance process and the asset price process. In fact, once we have reconstructed the variance path as a function of t, the Fourier methodology allows us to iterate the procedure to compute the diffusion coefficient of the variance process and the covariance between the variance and the asset price, handling the variance as a second observable process.

We consider a fairly general class of stochastic volatility models in continuous time. Suppose that the log price–variance processes (p, v) satisfy

$$\begin{cases} \mathrm{d}p(t) = \sigma(t)\mathrm{d}W(t) + a(t)\mathrm{d}t \\ \mathrm{d}v(t) = \gamma(t)\mathrm{d}Z(t) + b(t)\mathrm{d}t \end{cases} \tag{10.12}$$

where $v(t) := \sigma^2(t)$ is the variance process, W and Z are correlated Brownian motions, and $\sigma(t)$, $\gamma(t)$ and $a(t)$, $b(t)$ are adapted random processes satisfying

$$(\mathbf{H}') \quad E[\int_0^{2\pi} (a^2(t) + b^2(t))\,\mathrm{d}t] < \infty, E[\int_0^{2\pi} (\sigma^4(t) + \gamma^4(t))\,\mathrm{d}t] < \infty.$$

Barucci and Mancino (2010) apply Fourier estimation method to compute pathwise the diffusion coefficients in Equation 10.12, that is $\sigma(t), \gamma(t)$ and the covariance between the price and the instantaneous variance, which we denote by $\rho(t)$, starting from the observation of the asset price trajectory $p(t), t \in [0, 2\pi]$. The Fourier coefficients of the unobservable instantaneous variance process $v(t)$ are expressed in terms of the Fourier coefficients of the log-returns; then the variance function $v(t)$ is reconstructed from its Fourier coefficients by the Fourier–Fejer summation method. Thanks to this step, the instantaneous variance can be handled as an observable variable and we can iterate the procedure in order to compute the volatility of the variance process identifying the two components: volatility of variance ($\gamma(t)$) and asset price–variance covariance ($\rho(t)$).

In order to obtain the Fourier estimator of the stochastic function $\gamma^2(t)$, we have to derive an estimator for the Fourier coefficients $\mathcal{F}(\gamma^2)(k)$ of $\gamma^2(t)$, given the discrete observations of the variance process. The following result extends Theorem 10.3: given the Fourier estimator $c_k(v_{n,M})$ of the kth coefficient of the variance process, it is shown that $c_k(\gamma^2_{n,N,M})$ defined in Equation 10.14 is a consistent estimator of the kth Fourier coefficient of $\gamma^2(t)$. More precisely, the following result holds (see Barucci and Mancino (2010) for the proof).

THEOREM 10.5

Suppose that $N^4/M \to 0$ and $M^{5/4}\theta(n) \to 0$ for $n, N, M \to \infty$. Then, in probability,

$$\lim_{n,N,M\to\infty} c_k(\gamma^2_{n,N,M}) = \mathcal{F}(\gamma^2)(k) \tag{10.13}$$

where $\gamma^2(t)$ is the spot variance of the variance process,

$$c_k(\gamma^2_{n,N,M}) := \frac{2\pi}{2N+1} \sum_{|j|\le N} c_j(\mathrm{d}v_{n,M}) c_{k-j}(\mathrm{d}v_{n,M}) \tag{10.14}$$

and

$$c_j(\mathrm{d}v_{n,M}) := \mathrm{i}j\, c_j(v_{n,M}) + \frac{1}{2\pi}(v_{n,M}(2\pi) - v_{n,M}(0)). \tag{10.15}$$

We remark that the effective reconstruction of the Fourier coefficient of the variance of variance process is realized as superposition of three limits, that we can handle in this way: first, we compute the kth coefficient of the variance process by means of M frequencies and n observations of the price process; second, we perform a convolution over N Fourier coefficients of the derivative of the variance process. The convergence in probability is achieved under the specified growth conditions on N, M, and n. Choosing these parameters according to the above conditions allows for strong reduction of both bias and MSE in finite samples as well.

Given the Fourier coefficients of $\gamma^2(t)$, the variance of the variance process can be reconstructed by the Fourier–Fejer summation as follows:

$$\gamma^2(t) = \lim_{Q\to\infty} \sum_{|q|\le Q} \left(1 - \frac{|q|}{Q}\right) e^{iqt}\mathcal{F}(\gamma^2)(q) \quad t \in (0, 2\pi),$$

where the limit is in probability uniformly in time, by Theorem 10.3.

To compute the instantaneous covariance $\rho(t)$, we exploit the multivariate version of Fourier estimator presented in Section 10.2.1. The estimator proposed in Barucci and Mancino (2010) is obtained by means of the convolution product of the Fourier transform of the asset price function and the Fourier transform of the variance function, as follows.

THEOREM 10.6

Suppose that $N^2/M \to 0$ and $M\theta(n) \to 0$ for $n, N, M \to \infty$. The following convergence in probability holds

$$\lim_{n,N,M\to\infty} c_k(\rho_{n,N,M}) = \mathcal{F}(\rho)(k), \tag{10.16}$$

where $\rho(t)$ is the covariance between asset price and variance,

$$c_k(\rho_{n,N,M}) := \frac{2\pi}{2N+1} \sum_{|j|\le N} c_j(\mathrm{d}p_n)c_{k-j}(\mathrm{d}v_{n,M}),$$

$c_k(dv_{n,M})$ is defined in Equation 10.15.

Finally, the covariance function $\rho(t)$ can be obtained by the Fourier–Fejer summation given its Fourier coefficients from Equation 10.16.

10.3 Fourier Estimator of Integrated Volatility in the Presence of Microstructure Noise

The aim of this section is to analyze the *robustness* of the Fourier estimator of integrated volatility toward microstructure effects, such as price discreteness, different trading prices for buyers and sellers, and other contaminations. These results have been obtained in Mancino and Sanfelici (2008).

We suppose that the logarithm of the observed price process is given by

$$\widetilde{p}(t) = p(t) + \eta(t), \tag{10.17}$$

where $p(t)$ is the efficient log-price process and $\eta(t)$ is the microstructure noise. We can think of $p(t)$ as the log-price in equilibrium, that is, the price that would prevail in the absence of market microstructure frictions. The econometrician does not observe the true return series but the returns contaminated by market microstructure effects. Therefore, an estimator of the integrated volatility should be constructed using the contaminated returns.

Suppose that the process is observed at a discrete unevenly spaced grid $\{0 \leq t_{0,n} \leq t_{1,n} \leq \cdots \leq t_{k_n,n} \leq 2\pi\}$ for any fixed $n \geq 1$. In this section, we make the following assumptions:

A.I $p(t)$ is a continuous semimartingale satisfying assumption $(\boldsymbol{H})$.

A.II The random shocks $\eta(t_{j,n})$, for $0 \leq j \leq k_n$ and for all n, are independent and identically distributed (i.i.d.) with mean zero and bounded fourth moment.

A.III The true return process $\delta_{j,n}(p) := p(t_{j+1,n}) - p(t_{j,n})$ is independent of $\eta(t_{j,n})$ for any j, n.

To simplify the notation, in the sequel we will write $\delta_j(p)$ and η_j instead of $\delta_{j,n}(p)$ and $\eta(t_{j,n})$, respectively.

We note that the instantaneous volatility process is allowed to display jumps, diurnal effects, high persistence, nonstationarities, and leverage effects. The hypothesis that the η_js are independent of the increments $\delta_j(p)$ is discussed in Hansen and Lunde (2006). Their empirical work suggests that the independence assumption is not too damaging statistically, when we analyze data in tickly traded stocks recorded every minute. Therefore, our analysis is mainly developed in this setting, although in Mancino and Sanfelici (2008) the robustness of the Fourier estimator is studied under more general microstructure noise dependence assumptions.

10.3.1 BIAS AND MSE COMPUTATION

Denote $\delta_j(\tilde{p}) := \tilde{p}(t_{j+1}) - \tilde{p}(t_j)$ where $\tilde{p}$ is defined in Equation 10.17 and $\varepsilon_j := \eta_{j+1} - \eta_j$. Put

$$\hat{V}_n = \sum_{j=0}^{n-1} (\delta_j(\tilde{p}))^2, \tag{10.18}$$

where n is the number of observations in the trading interval $[0, 2\pi]$. Then $\hat{V}_n$ is the *realized volatility* estimator of the integrated volatility $\int_0^{2\pi} \sigma^2(t)\mathrm{d}t$, henceforth denoted by IV. The realized volatility is a consistent estimator of integrated volatility in the hypothesis that the prices are observed without measurement errors. However, in practice, because of market microstructure noise, sampling at the highest frequency leads to a bias problem (Zhou, 1996). Under the hypothesis that $2\pi/n$ is the time distance between adjacent logarithmic prices, the realized volatility estimator $\hat{V}_n$ diverges as the number n of observations increases, and the bias is the following

$$E[\hat{V}_n - \mathrm{IV}] = 2nE[\eta^2]. \tag{10.19}$$

The Fourier estimator of integrated volatility is obtained by the univariate version of Equation 10.8, taking $k = 0$

$$\hat{\sigma}^2_{n,N} := \frac{(2\pi)^2}{2N+1} \sum_{s=-N}^{N} c_s(\mathrm{d}\tilde{p}_n)c_{-s}(\mathrm{d}\tilde{p}_n). \tag{10.20}$$

The definition of the Fourier estimator does not require evenly spaced data. Anyway, for simplicity of computation, we will suppose that the observations are equidistant in time and that $2\pi/n$ is the distance between two observations, where $[0, 2\pi]$ is the trading period. Then the bias is computed as follows (Mancino and Sanfelici, 2008).

THEOREM 10.7

For any fixed integers n, N the following identity holds

$$E[\hat{\sigma}^2_{n,N} - \mathrm{IV}] = 2nE[\eta^2]\left(1 - D_N\left(\frac{2\pi}{n}\right)\right), \tag{10.21}$$

where

$$D_N(t) := \frac{1}{2N+1} \frac{\sin[(2N+1)\frac{\pi}{n}]}{\sin(\frac{\pi}{n})}. \tag{10.22}$$

Then, under the condition $N^2/n \to 0$, it holds

$$\lim_{n,N\to\infty} E[\hat{\sigma}^2_{n,N} - \mathrm{IV}] = 0.$$

We can derive the following conclusion: the Fourier estimator is asymptotically unbiased under the condition $N^2/n \to 0$. Moreover, the result (Eq. 10.21) shows that for fixed n, that is, for a finite sample, a suitable choice of N allows for lower bias with respect to the realized volatility estimator (cfr. Equation 10.19).

Second, we compute the mean squared error (MSE) of the Fourier estimator conditional on the volatility path. For simplicity, we will suppose that the volatility process is independent of W, namely, we assume that the no-leverage hypothesis holds (see Andersen *et al.* (2010a) and Meddahi, (2002) for a justification of the no-leverage assumption in the literature).

In Bandi and Russel (2008) and Hansen and Lunde (2006), under the hypothesis that $2\pi/n$ is the time distance between adjacent logarithmic prices, it is proved that the MSE of the realized volatility estimator (Eq. 10.20) is the following

$$E[(\hat{V}_n - \mathrm{IV})^2] = 2\frac{2\pi}{n}(\mathrm{IQ} + o(1)) + \Lambda_n, \qquad (10.23)$$

where IQ is the so-called *integrated quarticity* $\int_0^{2\pi} \sigma^4(s)ds$, $o(1)$ is a term which goes to zero as n goes to infinity, and

$$\Lambda_n := n^2\alpha + n\beta + \gamma,$$

with

$$\alpha := 4E[\eta^2]^2, \beta := 4E[\eta^4], \ \gamma := 8E[\eta^2]\mathrm{IV} + 2E[\eta^2]^2 - 2E[\eta^4]. \qquad (10.24)$$

The following result contains the computation of the MSE of the Fourier volatility estimator (Mancino and Sanfelici, 2008).

THEOREM 10.8

For any fixed n, N the following relation holds

$$E[(\hat{\sigma}^2_{n,N} - \mathrm{IV})^2] = 2\frac{2\pi}{n}(IQ + o(1)) + n^2\hat{\alpha}(n,N) + n\hat{\beta}(n,N) + \hat{\gamma}(n,N), \qquad (10.25)$$

where

$$\hat{\alpha}(n,N) := \alpha(1 + D_N^2(\frac{2\pi}{n}) - 2D_N(\frac{2\pi}{n})), \qquad (10.26)$$

$$\hat{\beta}(n,N) := \beta(1 + D_N^2(\frac{2\pi}{n}) - 2D_N(\frac{2\pi}{n})), \qquad (10.27)$$

$$\hat{\gamma}(n,N) := \gamma + 4\,IQ\frac{2\pi}{2N+1} + 4(E[\eta^2]^2 + E[\eta^4])(2D_N(\frac{2\pi}{n}) - D_N^2(\frac{2\pi}{n})), \qquad (10.28)$$

with α, β, and γ as in Equation 10.24, and $D_N(t)$ is the rescaled Dirichlet (DIR) kernel defined in (Equation 10.22).

The above result needs some comments. In the absence of microstructure effects, the MSE of the realized volatility estimator goes to zero as $n \to \infty$, while in the presence of microstructure effects the MSE of the realized volatility estimator diverges as $n \to \infty$ because of the presence of the terms of order n^2 and n in (10.23).

Analogously, we now make the comparison of the MSE of the Fourier estimator without microstructure noise, denoted by $\mathrm{MSE_F}$, and with microstructure noise, denoted by $\mathrm{MSE_{Fm}}$. We have that $\mathrm{MSE_F}$ goes to zero as N, n go to infinity. Moreover,

$$\mathrm{MSE_{Fm}} = \mathrm{MSE_F} + n^2\hat{\alpha}(n, N) + n\hat{\beta}(n, N) + \widetilde{\gamma}(n, N),$$

where $\hat{\alpha}(n, N)$ and $\hat{\beta}(n, N)$ are defined in Equations (10.26) and (10.27), while

$$\widetilde{\gamma}(n, N) := \gamma + 4(E[\eta^2]^2 + E[\eta^4])(2D_N(\frac{2\pi}{n}) - D_N^2(\frac{2\pi}{n})).$$

We note that if $N^2/n \to 0$, then

$$\lim_{n,N\to\infty} n^2\hat{\alpha}(n, N) + n\hat{\beta}(n, N) = 0$$

and

$$\lim_{n,N\to\infty} \widetilde{\gamma}(n, N) = 8E[\eta^2]\mathrm{IV} + 2E[\eta^4] + 6E[\eta^2]^2. \tag{10.29}$$

It follows that the MSE of the Fourier estimator does not diverge, and it is not significantly affected by microstructure noise; in fact, by conveniently choosing N, we obtain that $\mathrm{MSE_F}$ and $\mathrm{MSE_{Fm}}$ differ by the positive constant term (Eq. 10.29).

We conclude that the Fourier estimator needs no correction in order to be asymptotically unbiased and robust to market frictions of MA(1)-type, that is, the microstructure noise is represented by independent identically distributed random variables. The result is generalized to noise correlated with the efficient returns in Mancino and Sanfelici (2008).

10.3.2 MONTE CARLO ANALYSIS

The theoretical results above can be reproduced by simulating discrete data from a continuous time stochastic volatility model with microstructure noise as in Mancino and Sanfelici (2008). The authors show that when $N = n/2$, the Fourier estimator behaves like the realized volatility estimator and it does explode as the sampling interval goes to zero; nevertheless, both bias and MSE can be strongly reduced by choosing N conveniently.

Assume that the infinitesimal variation of the true log-price process, and spot volatility is given by the Cox, Ingersoll, Ross (CIR) square-root model (Cox *et al.*, 1985)

$$\begin{aligned} \mathrm{d}p(t) &= \sigma(t)\mathrm{d}W_1(t) \\ \mathrm{d}\sigma^2(t) &= \alpha(\beta - \sigma^2(t))\mathrm{d}t + \nu\sigma(t)\mathrm{d}W_2(t), \end{aligned} \tag{10.30}$$

where W_1 and W_2 are independent Brownian motions. Moreover, we assume that the logarithmic noises η are i.i.d. Gaussian and independent from p; this is typical of the bid-ask bounce effects in the case of exchange rates and, to a lesser extent, in the case of equities. The contaminated process becomes

$$\tilde{p}(t_j) = p(t_j) + \eta(t_j), \eta(t_j) \sim N(0, \xi^2),$$

so that

$$\delta_j(\tilde{p}) = \delta_j(p) + \varepsilon_j,$$

where the ε_j follows an MA(1) process with negative first-order autocorrelation. Since $\delta_j(p)$ and ε_j are independent, the variance and covariance of contaminated returns can be easily computed

$$\mathrm{var}(\delta_j(\tilde{p})) = \int_{t_{j+1}}^{t_{j+1}} \sigma^2(s)\mathrm{d}s + 2\xi^2, \ \mathrm{cov}(\delta_j(\tilde{p}), \delta_{j+1}(\tilde{p})) = -\xi^2.$$

Hence, we notice that $\delta_j(\tilde{p})$ exhibits spurious volatility and negative serial correlation as a consequence of noise contamination.

The parameter values used in the simulations are taken from the unpublished Appendix in Bandi and Russel (2008) and reflect the features of IBM time series: $\alpha = 0.01$, $\beta = 1.0$, $\nu = 0.05$, and $\xi = 0.000142$. The initial value of σ^2 is set to one, while $p(0) = \log 100$. The simulations are run for 500 daily replications using the computer language Matlab.

In order to avoid other data manipulations such as interpolation and imputation, which might affect the numerical results, we generate (through simple Euler Monte Carlo discretization, see Kloeden and Platen (1999)) high frequency, evenly sampled, efficient and observed returns by simulating second-by-second return and variance paths over a daily trading period of $T = 6$ h for a total of 21,600 observations per day. Then we sample the observations uniformly for different choices of the sampling interval $\theta(n) = T/n$ so that we obtain different data sets $(t_j, \tilde{p}(t_j), j = 0, 1 \ldots n)$, with σ recorded at every t. While implementing the Fourier estimator $\hat{\sigma}^2_{n,N}$, the smallest wavelength that can be evaluated in order to avoid aliasing effects is twice the smallest distance between two consecutive prices, which yields $N \leq n/2$ (*Nyquist frequency*). For 1-min returns, it corresponds to $N \leq 180$.

As a matter of fact, when analyzing high frequency time series the diffusion model (Eq. 10.30) does not hold for small time steps and microstructure effects can affect the computation of the Fourier coefficients. This is shown in Fig. 10.1, where the average $\hat{\sigma}^2_{n,N}$ is plotted as a function of the highest frequency N employed in the Fourier expansion, when all the observations are used (n =21,600). As remarked in Barucci and Renò (2002), if the observed process $d\tilde{p}(t)$ was normally distributed, then, as N increases, the plot should tend to the fixed (and known) average integrated variance value (i.e., 0.2499). This is not the case: for a frequency larger than a certain value (denoted by N_{cut}), the Fourier coefficients tend to increase inconsistently as a consequence of the negative serial correlation of the contaminated returns. In our setting, this happens approximately for $N_{\text{cut}} = 90$, which corresponds roughly to a time step of $6 \cdot 60/(2N_{\text{cut}}) = 2$ min.

This suggests to cut out the highest frequencies in the computation of the integrated volatility, that is, we compute the Fourier expansion for $N = \min(n/2, N_{\text{cut}})$ when n grows too high, that is, for high frequency data. Moreover, from the theoretical results of Section 10.3.1, this cutting procedure should result in a smaller bias and MSE of the Fourier estimator, and ultimately, it should provide "near" consistency of $\hat{\sigma}^2_{n,N}$ as $N^2/n \to 0$.

When computing the true bias and MSE, the value IV is obtained from σ by numerical integration. On the other hand, the estimated bias and MSE are computed by Equations (10.21) and (10.25), respectively. The practical calculation hinges on the estimation of the relevant noise moments and on the preliminary identification of IV and IQ. Since the noise moments do not vary across frequencies under the MA(1) model, in computing the MSE estimates we use sample moments constructed using quote-to-quote return data in order to estimate the relevant population moments of the noise components according to Bandi and Russel (2008). Preliminary estimates of IV and IQ are obtained by computing $\hat{\sigma}^2_{n,N}$ and the estimator $\widehat{\text{IQ}} = n/(6\pi) \sum_{j=1}^{n} (\delta_j(\tilde{p}))^4$ for the integrated quarticity, using 2-min returns.

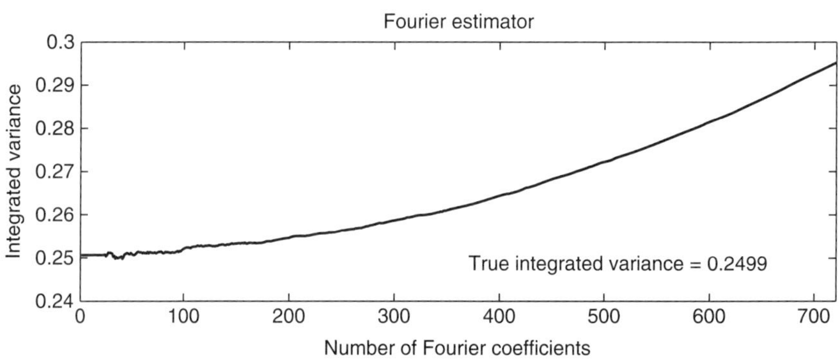

FIGURE 10.1 Average $\hat{\sigma}^2_{n,N}$ as a function of the highest frequency N employed in the Fourier expansion and n =21,600 (quote-to-quote returns).

Figure 10.2a shows the true (dotted line) and estimated bias, given by Equation 10.21, as a function of the sampling interval for different values of $N_{\mathrm{cut}} = 360, 180, 90, 10$. All the plots coincide for large sampling interval and start to separate from each other at the time step corresponding to the chosen cutting frequency, that is, at $\Delta t = 6 \cdot 60/(2N_{\mathrm{cut}})$. Moreover, as the cutting frequency N_{cut} is reduced, the Fourier estimator is characterized by smaller bias for every choice of the sampling interval, with the minimum attained for quote-to-quote returns where the estimator is almost unbiased. On the contrary, the MSE (Fig. 10.2b) shows a more complicated behavior: as the cutting frequency N_{cut} is reduced from 360 to 90, the MSE is reduced as well for every choice of the sampling interval; however, further reduction of N_{cut} (e.g., $N_{\mathrm{cut}} = 10$) results in a larger MSE, especially for very high frequency data. This is due to the $O((2N+1)^{-1})$ term in the addendum (Eq. 10.28) of the MSE estimate. As noticed in Nielsen and Frederiksen (2006), this behavior of the Fourier estimator can be attributed to the decomposition of the integrated variance into components of varying frequencies. That is, cutting out the highest frequencies in the Fourier expansion implies that high frequency noise or short-run noise is

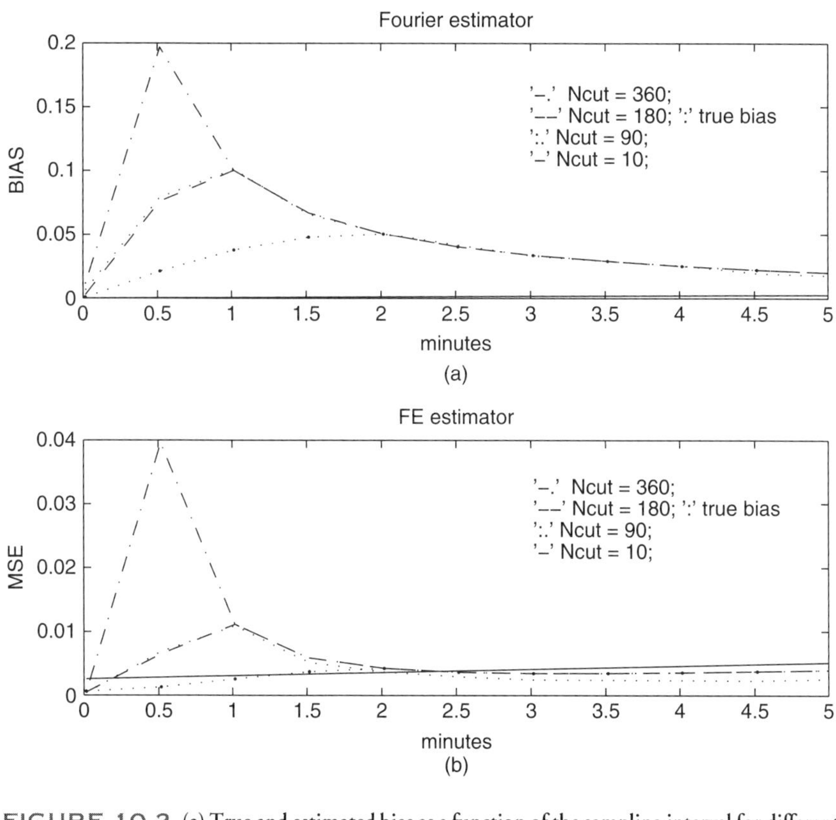

FIGURE 10.2 (a) True and estimated bias as a function of the sampling interval for different values of N_{cut}. (b) Same format for the MSE.

ignored by the estimator. Hence, by choosing a smaller number of low frequency ordinates to be used for estimation, that is, by choosing N_{cut} small, it is in principle possible to render the Fourier estimator invariant to short-run noise introduced by market microstructure effects.

The analysis above suggests to use quote-to-quote returns and try to minimize the MSE as a function of the cutting frequency N_{cut}. This minimization over the integer variable N_{cut} can be performed easily by comparison of the computed MSE values. This is done in Fig. 10.3, where the true and estimated bias and MSE of the Fourier estimator are plotted as a function of the number of the Fourier coefficients. The minimum of the true MSE is 2.88e−4 and is attained for $N_{cut} = 264$, which, at least theoretically, corresponds to a sampling frequency of $6 \cdot 60/(2 \cdot 264) = 0.68$ min. On the other hand, the minimum of the estimated MSE is attained for $N_{cut} = 240$, which, at least theoretically, corresponds to a sampling frequency of $6 \cdot 60/(2 \cdot 240) = 0.75$ min. At this frequency, the true MSE is $2.92e - 4$. Hence, a feasible and easily implementable procedure to select an optimal MSE-based cutting frequency N_{cut} from noisy observed returns is defined by minimizing the MSE estimate (Eq. 10.25).

Finally, we try to understand more deeply from an empirical point of view how the Fourier estimator relates to other estimators that have been specifically proposed to handle the microstructure noise. In our analysis, besides the realized

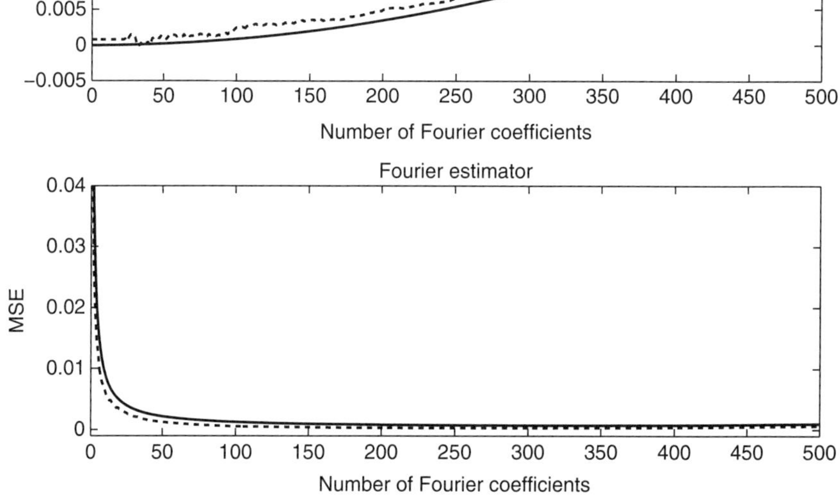

FIGURE 10.3 True (---) and estimated (-) bias and MSE of the Fourier estimator as a function of the number of the Fourier coefficients. Quote-to-quote returns.

volatility $\hat{V}_n$, we consider the following estimators: the bias corrected estimator by Hansen and Lunde (2006)

$$\hat{V}_n^{\mathrm{HL}} := \hat{V}_n + 2\frac{n}{n-1}\sum_{j=1}^{n-1} \delta_j(\tilde{p})\delta_{j+1}(\tilde{p});$$

the *flat-top realized kernels* by Barndorff-Nielsen *et al.* (2008a) and Barndorff-Nielsen *et al.* (2010)

$$\sum_{h=1}^{H} k\left(\frac{h-1}{H}\right)\{\sum_{j=1}^{n} \delta_j(\tilde{p})\delta_{j-h}(\tilde{p}) + \sum_{j=1}^{n} \delta_j(\tilde{p})\delta_{j+h}(\tilde{p})\}.$$

with kernels of *Bartlett* type $k(x) = 1 - x$, of *Cubic* type $k(x) = 1 - 3x^2 + 2x^3$, and of TH_2 type $k(x) = \sin^2\left(\frac{\pi}{2}(1-x)^2\right)$. The realized kernels may be considered as unbiased corrections of the realized volatility by means of the first H autocovariances of the returns. In particular, when H is selected to be zero, the realized kernels become the realized volatility. The last estimator is the *two-scale estimator* by Zhang *et al.* (2005) (henceforth ZMA)

$$\hat{V}_n^S := \frac{1}{S}\sum_{s=1}^{S} \hat{V}_{n_S}^{\mathcal{G}^{(s)}} - \frac{n-S+1}{nS}\hat{V}_n.$$

The two-scale (subsampling) estimator is a bias-adjusted average of lower frequency realized volatilities computed on S nonoverlapping observation subgrids $\mathcal{G}^{(s)}$ containing n_S observations.

Finite sample MSE optimal rules for these estimators are considered in Bandi and Russel (2006b). In our analysis, we differentiate from their study in that the optimal MSE-based estimators are designed relying on the true MSE. The comparative analysis of these methods is shown in Tables 10.1 and 10.2. The Fourier estimator is implemented both in its original form (10.20) with DIR kernel and with Fejer (FEJ) kernel (Mancino and Sanfelici, 2011a)

$$\tilde{\sigma}_{n,N}^2 := \frac{(2\pi)^2}{N+1}\sum_{|s|<N}\left(1 - \frac{|s|}{N}\right) c_s(d\tilde{p}_n)c_{-s}(d\tilde{p}_n).$$

Both Fourier estimators are optimally designed in order to minimize the true MSE with respect to the number of Fourier coefficients N for a given sampling interval $\theta = 1$ s, 30 s, 1 min, and 5 min. The realized kernels are optimized according to the same criterion with respect to the number of autocovariances H and the two-scale ZMA estimator with respect to the number of subgrids S.

We notice that at a sampling frequency of 5 min, the effects of microstructure noise are not evident. Therefore, the optimal MSE-based value of the parameter H is automatically selected to be zero, and the realized kernels become the

TABLE 10.1 Comparison of Optimized Integrated Volatility Estimators

	MSE				BIAS			
	1 s	30 s	1 min	5 min	1 s	30 s	1 min	5 min
Fourier DIR	2.88e−4	1.11e−3	1.51e−3	2.31e−3	7.04e−3	1.67e−2	1.49e−2	1.52e−2
Fourier FEJ	2.53e−4	9.64e−4	1.28e−3	2.05e−3	6.79e−3	1.29e−2	1.44e−2	7.41e−3
Bartlett Kernel	9.18e−5	7.50e−4	1.34e−3	2.32e−3	5.96e−4	−2.76e−4	1.56e−4	1.52e−2
Cubic Kernel	9.93e−5	7.50e−4	1.34e−3	2.32e−3	7.47e−4	−2.76e−4	1.56e−4	1.52e−2
TH_2 Kernel	8.99e−5	7.27e−4	1.26e−3	2.32e−3	6.26e−4	−2.56e−4	6.39e−5	1.52e−2
Two-scale ZMA	1.82e−4	2.00e−3	3.24e−3	9.31e−3	−6.45e−3	−2.75e−2	−3.64e−2	−6.47e−2
Realized Volatility HL	3.43e−3	9.24e−4	1.34e−3	5.51e−3	−3.55e−4	−4.49e−4	1.56e−4	−3.70e−3
Realized Volatility	3.76e+1	4.12e−2	1.13e−2	2.32e−3	6.13e+0	2.01e−1	1.03e−1	1.52e−2

TABLE 10.2 Optimal MSE-Based Parameter Values for N, H, S. When H Is Selected to be Zero, the Realized Kernels Become the Realized Volatility

Optimal MSE-based parameter values for N, H, S									
	1 s	30 s	1 min	5 min		1 s	30 s	1 min	5 min
Fourier DIR	264	79	53	35	Bartlett Kernel	13	2	1	0
Fourier FEJ	386	107	84	50	Cubic Kernel	14	2	1	0
Two-scale ZMA	37	10	8	5	TH_2 Kernel	19	3	2	0

realized volatility. The optimal MSE-based two-scale ZMA estimator exhibits a larger MSE and negative bias, while the HL estimator shows a slightly larger MSE and a very small bias. Both the Fourier estimators perform comparably and, in particular, the FEJ kernel allows for smaller MSE and bias. At 1-min frequency, the noise induced autocorrelation of returns becomes effective and the realized volatility starts to strongly overestimate the underlying integrated volatility. In this setting, the optimal MSE-based values for H are 1 for the Bartlett and Cubic kernels and 2 for the TH_2 kernel. This correction results in a smaller MSE and negligible bias. Identical performance is obtained with the HL estimator, while the two-scale ZMA shows a larger MSE and negative bias. Both the optimal MSE-based Fourier estimators perform very well in terms of MSE, while having only a slightly higher bias. At higher sampling frequencies, the impact from market microstructure effects becomes more evident and the realized volatility becomes progressively unstable. At the highest frequency, the realized kernels provide the best estimate both in terms of MSE and bias. Moreover, as already observed in the literature, the finite sample performance of the cubic and Bartlett kernels is virtually identical, and the Bartlett kernel is slightly preferable at 1-s frequency. The smooth TH_2 kernel provides the best volatility estimate and tends to select more lags than the others. Very strikingly, for all the sampling frequencies, the optimally designed Fourier estimators provide very good results and are practically unaffected by noise, having only a slightly higher MSE for quote-to-quote returns. Notice that the use of the FEJ kernel allows to slightly improve the behavior of the Fourier estimator for very high frequencies. Hence, the Fourier method remains a very attractive estimator even in comparison with methods specifically designed to handle market microstructure contaminations. More specifically, the Fourier estimator is competitive in terms of MSE for sampling frequencies up to 30 s, while having only a slightly higher bias.

10.4 Fourier Estimator of Integrated Covariance in the Presence of Microstructure Noise

When sampling high frequency returns, two difficulties arise in the computation of the covariance of financial asset returns: the distortion from efficient prices due to the market microstructure contamination and the so-called Epps effect (Epps, 1979). By means of the Fourier–Fejer summation, as suggested in Malliavin and Mancino (2009), the *Fourier estimator* of the integrated covariance $\int_0^{2\pi} \Sigma^{12}(t)dt$ is obtained as

$$\widehat{\Sigma}^{12}_{N,n_1,n_2} := \frac{(2\pi)^2}{N+1} \sum_{|s|<N} (1 - \frac{|s|}{N}) c_s(dp^1_{n_1}) c_{-s}(dp^2_{n_2}), \tag{10.31}$$

where $c_s(dp^*_*)$ are defined in Equation 10.7. The positive semidefiniteness of this estimator is proved in Mancino and Sanfelici (2011b).

The finite sample properties of the Fourier covariance estimator in the presence of asynchronous data and microstructure effects are studied in Mancino and Sanfelici (2011a): the authors derive the analytical expression of the bias and MSE of the Fourier estimator for two given finite sample sizes and a given number of Fourier coefficients included in the estimation and prove that the bias of the Fourier estimator converges to zero, under a suitable growth condition for these parameters. Further, they provide a practical way to optimize the finite sample performance of the Fourier estimator as a function of the number of frequencies by the minimization of the MSE for a given number of intradaily observations.

Without loss of generality, we consider the following model for the observed log-returns

$$\widetilde{p}^i(t) := p^i(t) + \eta^i(t) \quad \text{for } i = 1, 2, \tag{10.32}$$

where

$$dp^i(t) = \sum_{k=1}^{2} \sigma^i_k(t) dW^k(t) \tag{10.33}$$

and hypothesis **(H)** holds. Moreover, the following assumptions hold:

(M1) $p := (p^1, p^2)$ and $\eta := (\eta^1, \eta^2)$ are independent processes; moreover, $\eta(t)$ and $\eta(s)$ are independent for $s \neq t$ and $E[\eta(t)] = 0$ for any t.

(M2) $E[\eta^i(t)\eta^j(t)] = \omega_{ij} < \infty$ for any t, $i, j = 1, 2$.

10.4.1 BIAS AND MSE COMPUTATION

Consider the case of *regular asynchronous trading* analyzed in Voev and Lunde (2007): the asset 1 trades at regular points $\Pi^1 = \{t^1_i : i = 1, \ldots, n_1$ and $t^1_{i+1} - t^1_i = \frac{2\pi}{n_1 - 1}\}$, and asset 2 also trades at regular points $\Pi^2 = \{t^2_j : j = 1, \ldots, n_2$ and $t^2_{j+1} - t^2_j = \frac{4\pi}{n_1 - 1}\}$, where $n_2 = n_1/2$, but no trade of asset 1 occurs at the same time of a trade of asset 2. Specifically, the link between the trading times of the two assets is the following: $t^2_j = t^1_{2(j-1)+1} + \frac{\pi}{n_1 - 1}$ for $j = 1, \ldots, n_2$. Moreover, suppose $t^1_1 = 0$ and $t^1_{n_1} = 2\pi$. For simplicity, denote $n := n_1$ and assume n is even.

The following theorem provides the bias of the Fourier covariance estimator under microstructure noise, neglecting minor end effects (for the proof, see Mancino and Sanfelici (2011a)).

THEOREM 10.9

Under the asynchronous trading model specified above and if the microstructure noise satisfies **(M1)** and **(M2)**, the bias of the Fourier covariance estimator is

$$E\left[\widehat{\Sigma}^{12}_{N,n} - \int_0^{2\pi} \Sigma^{12}(t)\mathrm{d}t\right]$$

$$= \sum_{j=1}^{\frac{n}{2}-1} \sum_{i=2(j-1)+1}^{2(j-1)+3} (V_N(t_i^1 - t_j^2) - 1)E\left[\int_{t_i^1}^{t_{i+1}^1} \Sigma^{12}(t)\mathrm{d}t\right], \qquad (10.34)$$

where $V_N(t) = (\sin Nt/Nt)^2$. Therefore, the Fourier covariance estimator is asymptotically unbiased in the presence of microstructure noise satisfying **(M1)** and **(M2)**, under the condition $\theta(n)N \to 0$ as $n, N \to \infty$.

THEOREM 10.10

Under the above specified asynchronous trading setting and noise satisfying assumptions (**M1**) and (**M2**), it holds

$$E\left[(\widehat{\Sigma}^{12}_{N,n} - \int_0^{2\pi} \Sigma^{12}(t)\mathrm{d}t)^2\right]$$

$$= o(1) + 2\omega_{22} \sum_{i=1}^{n-1} V_N^2(t_i^1 - t_{\frac{n}{2}-1}^2)E[\int_{t_i^1}^{t_{i+1}^1} \Sigma^{11}(t)\mathrm{d}t] \qquad (10.35)$$

$$+ 2\omega_{11} \sum_{j=1}^{\frac{n}{2}-1} V_N^2(t_{n-1}^1 - t_j^2)E[\int_{t_j^2}^{t_{j+1}^2} \Sigma^{22}(t)\mathrm{d}t]$$

$$+ 4\,\omega_{22}\omega_{11}\, V_N^2(t_{n-1}^1 - t_{\frac{n}{2}-1}^2),$$

where $o(1)$ is a term which goes to zero, for $\theta(n)N \to 0$ as $n, N \to \infty$.

REMARK 10.11

The $o(1)$ term in Equation 10.35 is explicitly computed in Mancino and Sanfelici (2011a). The other terms arise from the corrections due to microstructure effects.

The sampling scheme considered above does not allow to consider the totally synchronous case. Nevertheless, in Mancino and Sanfelici (2011a), the bivariate case with synchronous trading is also considered.

Theorem 10.9 shows that under asynchronous observations, when the noise satisfies the assumptions **(M1)** and **(M2)**, the bias of the Fourier estimator is not affected by the presence of microstructure noise, and the Fourier estimator remains asymptotically unbiased. The next step is the computation of the Fourier estimator's MSE in the presence of microstructure noise.

We remark that in the expression (Eq. 10.35), there are four terms: the first one tends to zero as the number of observations increases, the other terms are bounded and particularly the term $4\omega_{11}\omega_{22} V_N^2(t^1_{n-1} - t^2_{\frac{n}{2}-1})$ converges to the constant $4\omega_{11}\omega_{22}$ as n, N increase at the proper rate $\theta(n)N \to 0$. In summary, the Fourier estimator of multivariate volatility is consistent under asynchronous observations; moreover, in the presence of microstructure noise satisfying (**M1**) and (**M2**), the MSE does not diverge at the highest frequencies.

10.4.2 MONTE CARLO ANALYSIS

We recall the definition of some covariance estimators proposed in the recent literature, which will constitute a benchmark for our simulation study.

The quadratic covariation-*realized covariance* estimator is defined by

$$\mathrm{RC}^{12} := \sum_{i=1}^{n-1} \delta_i(p^1)\delta_i(p^2),$$

where $\delta_i(p^*) = p^*(\tau_{i+1}) - p^*(\tau_i)$ and the observations times $\{0 \le \tau_1 \le \tau_2 \le \cdots \le \tau_n \le 2\pi\}$ for both assets are obtained through a synchronization procedure, such as interpolation or imputation (i.e., last-tick interpolation). The realized covariance estimator is not consistent under asynchronous trading. The *realized covariance plus leads and lags*

$$\mathrm{RCLL}^{12} := \sum_i \sum_{h=-l}^{L} \delta_{i+h}(p^1)\delta_i(p^2), \tag{10.36}$$

has good properties under microstructure noise contaminations of the prices, but it is still not consistent for asynchronous observations.

Hayashi and Yoshida (2005) have proposed an estimator that is consistent under asynchronous observations of the prices:

$$\mathrm{AO}^{12}_{n_1,n_2} := \sum_{i,j} \delta_{I^1_i}(p^1)\delta_{I^2_j}(p^2) I_{(I^1_i \cap I^2_j \neq \emptyset)}, \tag{10.37}$$

where $I_P = 1$ if proposition P is true and $I_P = 0$ if proposition P is false. We will refer to estimator (Eq. 10.39) as the *all-overlapping* (AO) estimator. The AO estimator is unbiased in the absence of noise, but it does not guarantee positivity. Moreover, the studies by Griffin and Oomen (2011) and Voev and Lunde (2007) show that the AO estimator is not efficient in the presence of microstructure noise.

Barndorff-Nielsen *et al.* (2008b) introduce the *multivariate realized kernel* estimator, which is defined by

$$\mathrm{K}^{12} := \sum_{h=-n}^{n} k\left(\frac{h}{H+1}\right)\Gamma^{12}_h, \tag{10.38}$$

where Γ^{12}_h is the hth realized autocovariance of the two assets and $k(\cdot)$ belongs to a suitable class of kernel functions. Here, we will consider the Parzen weight function defined as $1 - 6x^2 + 6x^3$ for $0 \le x \le 0.5$, $2(1-x)^3$ for $0.5 < x \le 1$ and 0 otherwise. The synchronization procedure uses the *refresh time*, that is, the first time when both posted prices are updated, setting the price of the quicker asset to its most recent value (last-tick interpolation). In order to reduce end effects, the asymptotic theory dictates we need to average ν prices at the very beginning and end of each day. Barndorff-Nielsen *et al.* (2008b) prove that the estimator is positive semidefinite and robust to various type of noise.

Kinnebrock and Podolskij (2008) propose a preaveraging technique in order to reduce the microstructure effects. The idea is again that if one averages a number of observed log-prices, one is closer to the latent process $p(t)$. They obtain a consistent estimator of the integrated covariance called *modulated realized covariation*

$$\mathrm{MRC}^{12} = \frac{\sqrt{\Delta}}{\theta\psi_2}\sum_{s=0}^{n-k_n+1}\bar{\delta}_s(p^1)\bar{\delta}_s(p^2) - \frac{\psi_1\Delta}{2\theta^2\psi_2}\sum_{s=1}^{n}\delta_s(p^1)\delta_s(p^2),$$

where the preaveraged return process is given by

$$\bar{\delta}_s(p^i) = \sum_{r=1}^{k_n} g\left(\frac{r}{k_n}\right)\delta_{s+r}(p^i)$$

and g is a suitable continuous, piecewise differentiable function. Although this estimator retains the optimal rate of convergence, its positive definitiveness is not guaranteed. The refresh time synchronization method is employed to apply the estimator to nonsynchronous data observation.

In the following, we show some numerical results from Mancino and Sanfelici (2011a) in order to compare the performance of the Fourier estimator of the integrated covariance to the behavior of the realized covariance RC^{12}, the realized covariance plus leads and lags $RCLL^{12}$, the AO estimator AO^{12}, the multivariate realized kernel K^{12}, and the modulated realized covariation MRC^{12}.

We simulate discrete data from the continuous time bivariate generalized autoregressive conditionally heteroskedastic (GARCH) model (Hoshikawa *et al.*, 2008)

$$\begin{bmatrix} dp^1(t) \\ dp^2(t) \end{bmatrix} = \begin{bmatrix} \beta_1\sigma_1^2(t) \\ \beta_2\sigma_4^2(t) \end{bmatrix} dt + \begin{bmatrix} \sigma_1(t) & \sigma_2(t) \\ \sigma_3(t) & \sigma_4(t) \end{bmatrix} \begin{bmatrix} dW_5(t) \\ dW_6(t) \end{bmatrix}$$
$$d\sigma_i^2(t) = (\omega_i - \phi_i\sigma_i^2(t))dt + \alpha_i\sigma_i^2(t)dW_i(t), \quad i = 1, \ldots, 4,$$

where $\{W_i(t)\}_{i=1}^6$ are independent Wiener processes. Moreover, we assume that the logarithmic noises $\eta^1(t), \eta^2(t)$ are i.i.d. Gaussian, possibly contemporaneously correlated and independent from p. We also consider the case of dependent noise, assuming for simplicity $\eta_i^j = \alpha(p^j(t_i^j) - p^j(t_{i-1}^j)) + \bar{\eta}_i^j$, for $j = 1, 2$ and $\bar{\eta}_i^j$ i.i.d. Gaussian. Voev and Lunde (2007) define the noise variance to be 90% of the total variance for 1-s returns, which is in fact quite moderate. For instance, Ait-Sahalia *et al.* (2005a) report a study of 274 NYSE stocks in which the noise is 12 times this amount. Therefore, in our simulations, we consider both the case of 90% noise variance and 10 times such an amount, which we call *increased noise term*. When the noise correlation matrix is not diagonal, the correlation is set to 0.5. From the simulated data, integrated covariance estimates can be compared to the value of the true variance quantities.

We generate (through simple Euler Monte Carlo discretization) high frequency, evenly sampled, true, and observed returns by simulating second-by-second return and variance paths over a daily trading period of $h = 6$ h, for a total of 21,600 observations per day. Then we sample the observations according to different trading scenarios: *regular synchronous trading* with duration $\theta_1 = \theta(n_1)$ between trades for the first asset and $\theta_2 = 2\theta_1$ for the second, that is, the second asset trades each second time the first asset trades; *regular nonsynchronous trading* with duration θ_1 between trades for the first asset and $\theta_2 = 2\theta_1$ for the second and displacement $\delta \cdot \theta_1$ between the two, that is, the second asset starts trading $\delta \cdot \theta_1$ seconds later; *Poisson trading* with durations between observations drawn from an exponential distribution with means λ_1 and λ_2 for the two assets, respectively. The other parameters of the model are $\alpha_1 = 0.1$, $\alpha_2 = 0.1$, $\alpha_3 = 0.2$, $\alpha_4 = 0.2$, $\beta_1 = 0.02$, $\beta_2 = 0.01$, $\omega_1 = 0.1$, $\omega_2 = 0.1$, $\omega_3 = 0.2$, $\omega_4 = 0.2$, $\phi_1 = 0.1$, $\phi_2 = 0.1$, $\phi_3 = 0.1$, $\phi_4 = 0.1$, and $\alpha = 0.1$. The simulations are run for 500 daily replications, using the computer language Matlab.

In implementing the Fourier estimator $\hat{\Sigma}_{N,n_1,n_2}^{12}$ on finite samples, the smallest wavelength that can be evaluated in order to avoid aliasing effects is twice the smallest distance between two consecutive prices (*Nyquist frequency*). Nevertheless, as pointed out in Mancino and Sanfelici (2011a), smaller values of N may provide better variance/covariance measures. The optimal MSE-based Fourier estimator is obtained by minimizing the true MSE with respect to N on each day. However, we notice that this procedure is unfeasible when dealing with empirical data since the true MSE is not available; in Mancino and Sanfelici (2010a), a feasible approach is proposed.

The optimal MSE-based covariance estimator is compared to the realized covariance $RC^{12}_{0.5\,\text{min}}$ based on half-a-minute returns, the realized covariance $RC^{12}_{1\text{min}}$ based on 1-min returns, the realized covariance $RC^{12}_{5\text{min}}$ based on 5-min returns, and the corresponding realized covariance plus leads and lags $RCLL^{12}_{0.5\text{min}}$, $RCLL^{12}_{1\text{min}}$, and $RCLL^{12}_{5\text{min}}$, with $l = L = 1$; the AO estimator AO^{12}; the Parzen kernel K^{12}; and the modulated realized covariation MRC^{12}. The low frequency returns necessary for the realized covariance-type estimators are obtained by imputation on a uniform grid. As any estimator based on interpolated prices, these methods suffer from the Epps effect when trading is nonsynchronous, but the lead–lag correction reduces such an effect. The kernel estimator and the modulated realized covariation use synchronized data obtained by the refresh time procedure. The Fourier and AO estimators use all tick-by-tick data.

When implementing the multivariate realized kernel, a single bandwidth parameter H should be considered for both variances and covariances on each day to guarantee the positive definiteness property of the estimator. Possible choices are the minimum, the maximum, or the average bandwidth. Therefore, we apply the univariate optimal MSE bandwidth selection to each asset price individually as suggested by Barndorff-Nielsen *et al.* (2008b) and get $H_i = c^* \xi_i^{4/5} n^{3/5}$, where $c^* = (144/0.269)^{1/5}$, $\xi_i^2 = \omega_{ii}/\sqrt{Q_{ii}}$, and Q_{ii} is the integrated quarticity of asset i estimated by means of low frequency returns. These two bandwidths are then averaged to obtain the global H value. The jittering parameter is set to $\nu = 2$. In the case of the modulated realized covariation, we choose $g(x) = \min(x, 1 - x)$; hence, $\psi_1 = 1$ and $\psi_2 = 1/12$. Inspired by Barndorff-Nielsen *et al.* (2008b), we choose $k_n = (k_n^{(1)} + k_n^{(2)}2)/2$, where $k_n^{(i)} = \theta_i n^{3/5}$ and $\theta_i = c^* \xi_i^{4/5}$.

The results are reported in Tables 10.3 and 10.4. Within each table, entries are the values of the MSE and bias, using 500 Monte Carlo replications. In the first day, the initial values for p_is and σ_is are extracted from independent standard half normal distributions and are the same for all the trading setting; then, in the upcoming days, they are set equal to the closing value of the previous day. Columns correspond to the trading scenarios and rows to different estimators. The trading settings are denoted by the terms Reg-S, Reg-NS, Poisson, while the second term (Unc, Cor, Dep) refers to the type of noise, namely, contemporaneously uncorrelated (i.e., $\omega_{ij} = 0$ for $i \neq j$), contemporaneously correlated, and dependent on the price process, respectively.

When we consider covariance estimates, an important effect to deal with is the Epps effect. In fact, from Table 10.3, we see that in the Reg-NS setting without noise, the effects imputable to nonsynchronicity are evident and spoil all the realized covariance-type estimates based on synchronization. The best performance is given by the AO and Fourier estimator, followed by the kernel

TABLE 10.3 Comparison of Integrated Volatility Estimators. The Noise Variance is 90% of the Total Variance for 1-s Returns. $\theta_1 = 5$ s, $\theta_2 = 10$ s with a Displacement of 0 s for Reg-S and 2 s for Reg-NS Trading and $\lambda_1 = 5$ s and $\lambda_2 = 10$ s for Poisson Trading

	Reg-NS		Reg-S + Unc		Reg-NS + Unc		Reg-NS + Cor	
	MSE	Bias	MSE	Bias	MSE	Bias	MSE	Bias
$\hat{\Sigma}^{12}_{N,n_1,n_2}$	5.72e−4	−9.88e−3	3.35e−4	−6.09e−3	7.29e−4	−1.12e−2	4.73e−4	−8.82e−3
$RC^{12}_{0.5\,min}$	2.96e−2	−1.68e−1	1.06e−3	8.80e−4	3.45e−2	−1.80e−1	3.20e−2	−1.74e−1
$RC^{12}_{1\,min}$	9.14e−3	−8.44e−2	2.08e−3	2.70e−3	1.12e−2	−9.16e−2	9.74e−3	−8.65e−2
$RC^{12}_{5\,min}$	1.16e−2	−1.80e−2	1.14e−2	5.00e−3	1.44e−2	−2.33e−2	1.13e−2	−1.68e−2
$RCLL^{12}_{0.5\,min}$	2.88e−3	−1.68e−3	3.34e−3	2.94e−3	3.71e−3	−2.43e−3	3.15e−3	−1.55e−3
$RCLL^{12}_{1\,min}$	6.40e−3	−3.13e−3	6.42e−3	5.04e−3	8.00e−3	−3.37e−4	6.13e−3	3.09e−3
$RCLL^{12}_{5\,min}$	3.35e−2	1.11e−2	3.12e−2	3.15e−4	4.23e−2	−7.22e−3	3.61e−2	6.79e−3
AO^{12}	4.72e−4	−1.20e−3	4.47e−4	−1.08e−3	6.88e−4	9.45e−4	5.98e−4	−5.91e−4
K^{12}	9.33e−4	−8.13e−3	9.13e−4	−5.22e−4	1.28e−3	−6.32e−3	1.09e−3	−7.18e−3
MRC^{12}	2.80e−3	−3.27e−2	2.57e−3	−2.55e−2	3.38e−3	−3.01e−2	2.91e−3	−2.87e−2
	Reg-NS + Dep		Poisson + Unc		Poisson + Cor		Poisson + Dep	
	MSE	Bias	MSE	Bias	MSE	Bias	MSE	Bias
$\hat{\Sigma}^{12}_{N,n_1,n_2}$	3.96e−4	−6.32e−3	1.07e−3	−1.38e−2	1.18e−3	−1.53e−2	1.00e−3	−1.43e−2
$RC^{12}_{0.5\,min}$	3.02e−2	−1.66e−1	3.33e−2	−1.76e−1	3.11e−2	−1.70e−1	2.91e−2	−1.64e−1
$RC^{12}_{1\,min}$	9.97e−3	−8.17e−2	1.08e−2	−8.95e−2	1.05e−2	−8.85e−2	1.03e−2	−8.62e−2
$RC^{12}_{5\,min}$	1.47e−2	−1.70e−2	1.28e−2	−2.50e−2	1.36e−2	−2.06e−2	1.23e−2	−2.64e−2
$RCLL^{12}_{0.5\,min}$	4.42e−3	3.20e−3	3.81e−3	−7.98e−3	3.40e−3	−6.84e−3	3.73e−3	−9.08e−3
$RCLL^{12}_{1\,min}$	8.06e−3	−9.21e−4	6.81e−3	−3.41e−3	7.23e−3	1.26e−3	7.80e−3	3.78e−3
$RCLL^{12}_{5\,min}$	3.59e−2	−1.60e−2	3.31e−2	−3.59e−3	3.74e−2	6.35e−3	3.67e−2	−1.47e−2
AO^{12}	7.42e−3	7.46e−2	1.29e−3	−8.75e−4	1.24e−3	9.32e−3	8.10e−3	7.49e−2
K^{12}	5.25e−3	5.43e−2	5.88e−3	−6.35e−2	4.57e−3	−5.46e−2	2.85e−3	−1.95e−2
MRC^{12}	3.93e−3	−1.59e−2	4.19e−3	−3.00e−2	3.71e−3	−2.71e−2	4.72e−3	−2.24e−2

TABLE 10.4 Comparison of Integrated Volatility Estimators. The Noise is 10 Times than that in Table 10.1. $\theta_1 = 5$ s, $\theta_2 = 10$ s with a Displacement of 0 s for Reg-S and 2 s for Reg-NS Trading and $\lambda_1 = 5$ s and $\lambda_2 = 10$ s for Poisson Trading

	Reg-S + Unc		Reg-NS + Unc		Reg-NS + Cor		Reg-NS + Dep	
	MSE	Bias	MSE	Bias	MSE	Bias	MSE	Bias
$\hat{\Sigma}^{12}_{N,n_1,n_2}$	3.41e−4	−6.07e−3	6.14e−4	−9.26e−3	4.84e−4	−8.06e−3	3.50e−4	−4.88e−3
$RC^{12}_{0.5\,min}$	2.00e−3	4.20e−4	3.65e−2	−1.81e−1	3.41e−2	−1.78e−1	5.71e−2	−1.68e−1
$RC^{12}_{1\,min}$	2.69e−3	−2.10e−3	1.22e−2	−9.36e−2	1.09e−2	−8.71e−2	2.34e−2	−8.50e−2
$RC^{12}_{5\,min}$	1.10e−2	−2.29e−3	1.61e−2	−1.84e−2	1.38e−2	−1.92e−2	1.87e−2	−1.59e−2
$RCLL^{12}_{0.5\,min}$	3.95e−3	−3.33e−3	5.03e−3	−1.63e−4	4.24e−3	7.19e−4	1.83e−2	−1.31e−3
$RCLL^{12}_{1\,min}$	6.94e−3	1.29e−3	9.24e−3	−3.85e−3	8.14e−3	4.15e−3	1.88e−2	3.26e−3
$RCLL^{12}_{5\,min}$	2.98e−2	6.90e−3	4.56e−2	−7.88e−4	3.93e−2	7.38e−4	4.14e−2	1.37e−2
AO^{12}	1.95e−3	7.56e−4	2.18e−3	1.54e−3	2.23e−3	4.78e−3	4.42e−2	7.40e−2
K^{12}	1.71e−3	−1.01e−3	2.18e−3	−1.90e−3	2.18e−3	2.87e−6	2.39e−2	5.62e−2
MRC^{12}	3.19e−3	−1.54e−2	4.33e−3	−1.71e−2	3.82e−3	−1.45e−2	6.56e−3	−1.17e−2
	Poisson + Unc		Poisson + Cor		Poisson + Dep			
	MSE	Bias	MSE	Bias	MSE	Bias		
$\hat{\Sigma}^{12}_{N,n_1,n_2}$	1.26e−3	−1.68e−2	1.10e−3	−1.40e−2	5.36e−4	−8.04e−3		
$RC^{12}_{0.5\,min}$	3.50e−2	−1.80e−1	3.00e−2	−1.63e−1	4.95e−2	−1.57e−1		
$RC^{12}_{1\,min}$	1.24e−2	−9.53e−2	1.09e−2	−8.32e−2	2.58e−2	−8.45e−2		
$RC^{12}_{5\,min}$	1.27e−2	−2.36e−2	1.48e−2	−5.81e−3	1.98e−2	−7.07e−3		
$RCLL^{12}_{0.5\,min}$	4.62e−3	−1.01e−2	5.61e−3	−6.71e−3	2.16e−2	−4.23e−3		
$RCLL^{12}_{1\,min}$	7.61e−3	−1.24e−3	9.35e−3	7.58e−3	1.90e−2	3.88e−3		
$RCLL^{12}_{5\,min}$	3.83e−2	−1.34e−2	4.21e−2	1.83e−2	4.43e−2	1.59e−3		
AO^{12}	2.58e−3	−3.12e−3	1.38e−2	1.06e−1	4.42e−2	8.25e−2		
K^{12}	6.95e−3	−6.62e−2	2.88e−3	−5.89e−3	2.13e−2	−9.48e−3		
MRC^{12}	5.03e−3	−2.23e−2	5.26e−3	−1.55e−2	7.78e−3	−1.13e−2		

estimator. The 0.5-min return lead–lag realized covariance $\mathrm{RCLL}^{12}_{0.5\,\mathrm{min}}$ offers a good alternative, as it mitigates the bias induced by nonsynchronicity by adding one lead and one lag of the empirical autocovariance function of returns to the realized covariance measure. The addition of a moderate amount of independent and uncorrelated noise does not have great effect on the estimates. On the contrary, it may, in some sense, even compensate the effects due to nonsynchronicity, see for instance the realized covariance measures $\mathrm{RCLL}^{12}_{1\,\mathrm{min}}$ and $\mathrm{RCLL}^{12}_{5\,\mathrm{min}}$ having smaller biases. In the Reg-S setting (i.e., no displacement), the best performances are provided by Fourier and the AO, followed by the kernel estimator, which has a slightly lower bias. On the contrary, the modulated realized covariation estimator is not competitive at this low noise level. In the Reg-NS setting with noise, the AO estimator provides the best results together with the Fourier estimator, which shows a slightly larger bias. An exception to this ranking is provided by the case Reg-NS with dependent noise, where the Fourier estimator is indisputably the most efficient. In the case of Poisson trading setting, the best performance is provided by the Fourier and AO estimator, which shows a slightly smaller bias. However, when we allow the noise to be dependent on the price process, the AO estimator looses efficiency and again the Fourier estimator is indisputably the most efficient.

In Table 10.4, the noise term is increased to 10 times the one in Table 10.3. We can see that in all the trading scenarios, the Fourier estimator outperforms the other estimators. The AO estimator can sometimes become less effective, as can be seen in the Poisson trading scheme with correlated noise and in the trading settings with dependent noise. In fact, the AO remains unbiased under independent noise whenever the probability of trades occurring at the same time is zero, which is not the case for Poisson arrivals. In particular, in the trading scenarios with noise dependent on the price process, the Fourier estimator remains a robust alternative that outperforms all the other methods.

Therefore, we can conclude that in agreement with our theoretical analysis, the Fourier covariance estimator is not much affected by the presence of noise and asynchronicity so that it becomes a very interesting alternative especially when microstructure effects are particularly relevant in the available data.

10.5 Forecasting Properties of Fourier Estimator

Risk and asset management practices, as well as derivative pricing, rely on a precise measure/forecast of volatility and covariances. Availability of high frequency data has improved the capability of computing volatility in an efficient way. Empirical analysis has shown that the forecasting performance of the realized volatility is superior to that of classical autoregressive conditionally heteroskedastic (ARCH) models (Andersen *et al.*, 2003). By treating volatility as observed rather than latent, nonparametric estimation methods improve forecasting performance using simple methods directly based on observable variables.

10.5.1 FORECASTING VOLATILITY

The forecasting performance of the Fourier estimator of integrated volatility is analyzed in Barucci *et al.* (2010). The authors prove that the Fourier estimator outperforms the realized volatility in a significant measure, in particular, for high frequency observations and when the noise component is relevant. Compared to other realized volatility measures, the Fourier estimator generally has a better performance, even in comparison with methods specifically designed to handle market microstructure contaminations, for example, the Zhou (1996) estimator, the two-scale estimator by Zhang *et al.* (2005), or the realized kernel estimators by Barndorff-Nielsen *et al.* (2010).

In this section, we review the results by Barucci *et al.* (2010). Given a measure of the integrated volatility in the period $[t-1, t]$ obtained through the realized volatility or the Fourier methodology, we intend to evaluate its capability of forecasting the integrated volatility on day $[t, t+1]$: to this end the linear regression of the one-day-ahead integrated volatility over the today volatility is considered. In this setting, the forecasting performance can be evaluated through the R^2 of the linear regression.

We suppose that the logarithm of the observed asset price $\widetilde{p}(s)$ follows the model (Eq. 10.17) where we assume that the logarithm of the efficient price $p(s)$ evolves as

$$dp(s) = \sigma(s)dW^1(s). \tag{10.39}$$

W^1 is a Brownian motion on a filtered probability space $(\Omega, (\mathcal{F}_s)_{s\in[0,T]}, P)$ and σ is a continuous adapted stochastic process such that $E[\int_0^T \sigma^4(s)ds] < \infty$. We will assume that σ and W^1 are independent processes. The one period, say $[t-1, t]$, integrated volatility is defined

$$\text{IV}(t) := \int_{t-1}^{t} \sigma^2(s)ds \tag{10.40}$$

and the corresponding multiperiod measure

$$\text{IV}(t+1 : t+m) := \sum_{j=1}^{m} \text{IV}(t+j) = \int_{t}^{t+m} \sigma^2(s)ds, \tag{10.41}$$

where m is an integer (e.g., days).

Assume that the spot volatility model belongs to the class of eigenfunction stochastic volatility (ESV) models introduced by Meddahi (2001). The ESV class of models includes most continuous time stochastic volatility models analyzed in the literature. Suppose that the volatility process is driven by a single (latent) state variable: then the corresponding one-factor ESV representation takes the form

$$\sigma^2(s) = \sum_{l=0}^{p} a_l P_l(f(s)), \tag{10.42}$$

where the integer p may be infinite and the latent state variable $f(s)$ evolves according to the process

$$df(s) = m(f(s))dt + \sqrt{v(f(s))}dW^2(s), \tag{10.43}$$

where W^2 is a Brownian motion independent of W^1. The coefficients a_l are real numbers, $P_l(f(s))$ are the eigenfunctions of the infinitesimal generator associated with $f(s)$, and by $-\lambda_l$, we denote the eigenvalue corresponding to $P_l(f(s))$. The properties of the ESV class of models allow to derive the moments of discretely sampled returns, see Andersen *et al.* (2010b) where such explicit computations are obtained.

Given n equally spaced observations in the time period $[t-1, t]$, in the following, we denote by $\mathrm{RV}_n(t)$ and by $\mathrm{FM}_{n,N}(t)$ the realized volatility and the Fourier estimator of volatility in the absence of microstructure noise, and by $\widetilde{\mathrm{RV}}_n(t)$ and $\widetilde{\mathrm{FM}}_{n,N}(t)$, the realized volatility and the Fourier estimator in the presence of microstructure noise, whose definitions are in Equations 10.20 and 10.22.

In Andersen *et al.* (2010b), under the no-leverage hypothesis, it is proved that

$$R^2_{\widetilde{\mathrm{RV}}} := \frac{\mathrm{Cov}(\mathrm{IV}(t+1), \widetilde{\mathrm{RV}}_n(t))^2}{\mathrm{Var}[\mathrm{IV}(t)]\mathrm{Var}[\widetilde{\mathrm{RV}}_n(t)]} = \frac{\mathrm{Cov}(\mathrm{IV}(t+1), \mathrm{IV}(t))^2}{\mathrm{Var}[\mathrm{IV}(t)]\mathrm{Var}[\widetilde{\mathrm{RV}}_n(t)]}. \tag{10.44}$$

As far as the Fourier estimator is concerned, in Barucci *et al.* (2010), it is proved that under the no-leverage hypothesis, the following result holds:

$$R^2_{\widetilde{\mathrm{FM}}} := \frac{\mathrm{Cov}(\mathrm{IV}(t+1), \widetilde{\mathrm{FM}}_{n,N}(t))^2}{\mathrm{Var}[\mathrm{IV}(t)]\mathrm{Var}[\widetilde{\mathrm{FM}}_{n,N}(t)]} = \frac{\mathrm{Cov}(\mathrm{IV}(t+1), \mathrm{IV}(t))^2}{\mathrm{Var}[\mathrm{IV}(t)]\mathrm{Var}[\widetilde{\mathrm{FM}}_{n,N}(t)]}. \tag{10.45}$$

Formulas 10.44 and 10.45 show that maximizing the R^2 of the linear regression is equivalent to minimizing the variance of the considered estimator. Hence, minimum variance estimators should have better forecasting performances. A direct comparison of the forecasting performance of the two methodologies is possible by comparing the variance formulae varying the microstructure noise parameters.

It is possible to compute analytically the variances of the two estimators and to study their behavior as n goes to infinity, with similar arguments as in Section 10.3.1, see Barucci *et al.* (2010) for details. In particular, given a sampling frequency n, using the explicit formulae obtained in Theorem 10.8, it is possible to determine the optimal (in the sense of minimizing the variance) Fourier cutting frequency N_{cut}, having good effects on the forecasting performance.

In the analysis below, we will also consider several other realized volatility measures explicitly designed to account for high frequency microstructure noise and we will compute the R^2 of the linear regression of a realized-volatility-type estimate over the past Fourier volatility estimate and vice versa, namely,

$$R^2 = \frac{\text{Cov}(\text{FM}_{n,N}(t+1:t+m), \text{RM}_n(t))^2}{\text{Var}[\text{FM}_{n,N}(t+1:t+m)]\text{Var}[\text{RM}_n(t)]}, \quad (10.46)$$

where $\text{RM}_n(t)$ denotes any realized volatility measure. For an analytic expression of Equation 10.46 in the class of ESV models, see Barucci *et al.* (2010).

10.5.2 MONTE CARLO ANALYSIS

In this section, we evaluate the capability of realized-volatility-type measures and of the Fourier estimator to forecast the integrated volatility one step (day) ahead. We consider three different data generating processes, as in Andersen *et al.* (2010b):

(M1) - GARCH Model

$$\text{d}\sigma^2(t) = \kappa(\theta - \sigma^2(t))\text{d}t + \overline{\sigma}\sigma^2(t)\text{d}W^2(t)$$

with $\kappa = 0.035$, $\theta = 0.636$, and $\overline{\sigma} = 0.1439$; note that $E[\text{IV}(t)] = \theta = 0.636$,

(M2) - Two-Factor Affine

$$\sigma^2(t) = \sigma_1^2(t) + \sigma_2^2(t),$$
$$\text{d}\sigma_i(t) = \kappa_i(\theta_i - \sigma_i^2(t))\text{d}t + \overline{\sigma}_i\sigma_i^2(t)\text{d}W^2(t) \quad i = 1, 2$$

with $\kappa_1 = 0.5708, \theta_1 = 0.3257, \overline{\sigma}_1 = 0.2286, \kappa_2 = 0.0757, \theta_2 = 0.1786$, and $\overline{\sigma}_2 = 0.1096$; note that $E[\text{IV}(t)] = \theta_1 + \theta_2 = 0.5043$,

(M3) - Log-Normal Diffusion

$$\text{d}\log\sigma^2(t) = \kappa(\theta - \log\sigma^2(t))\text{d}t + \overline{\sigma}\text{d}W^2(t)$$

with $\kappa = 0.0136$, $\theta = -0.8382$, and $\overline{\sigma} = 0.1148$; note that $E[\text{IV}(t)] = e^{\theta + \frac{\sigma^2}{4\kappa}} = 0.5510$.

Through a simple Euler Monte Carlo discretization procedure, we generate high frequency, evenly sampled, theoretical prices $p(t)$ and observed returns by simulating second-by-second return and variance paths over $K = 240$ trading days (one trading year). A trading day is made up of $T = 6$ h for a total of 21,600 observations (a tick corresponds to a second). Then, we sample the observations varying the uniform sampling interval $\theta(n) = T/n$, obtaining data sets with different frequencies. The initial point of the simulation of the volatility process is set at $E[\text{IV}(t)]$. Observed prices differ from theoretical prices for the microstructure noise component. For each observation t_j, the observed asset price is obtained by adding the microstructure noise component to the theoretical price: realizations $\{\eta(t_j)\}(j = 0, 1, \ldots, n)$ come from a sequence of identically and independent random variables with zero mean and constant variance.

Microstructure noise variance is set equal to a given percentage of the integrated volatility. In particular, we consider a model without microstructure noise and two different noise levels:

$$\text{Var}[\eta(t)] = \lambda E[\text{IV}(t)] \quad \text{with} \quad \lambda = 0,\ 0.1,\ \text{and}\ 0.5\%.$$

In our analysis, we consider the following sampling periods:

n	2160	1440	720	360	288	96	48	24	12	6
$\theta(n)$	10″	15″	30″	1′	1′ 15″	3′45″	7′30″	15′	30′	1 h

Let us consider the problem of forecasting future integrated volatility through the realized volatility observed today. Given the volatility process of the theoretical asset price, we calculate the exact integrated volatility. The comparison between the realized and the Fourier volatility methodology is accomplished through the R^2 associated with the Mincer–Zarnowitz style regression of the integrated volatility at date $t + 1$ ($\text{IV}(t + 1)$) onto a constant, and the integrated volatility of the previous day is computed according to the realized volatility method and the Fourier method, see formulae 10.44 and 10.45.

In Table 10.5, we provide the value of the R^2 for the realized volatility and for the Fourier estimator (with the optimal N), varying the sampling frequency and the microstructure noise. The column N reports the frequency employed for the Fourier estimator that yields the highest R^2.

Concerning the realized volatility estimator, we observe a result that has been already obtained in Andersen *et al.* (2010b): the R^2 goes up monotonically as the sampling horizon decreases only in a model without noise; if noise is added, then the R^2 reaches the highest value for a sampling horizon between 1 and 5 min. The phenomenon is not observed for the Fourier estimator: the R^2 increases with the sampling frequency also in a model with microstructure noise. The forecasting performance of the two estimators is quite similar in a model without noise. When noise is added, the Fourier estimator outperforms the realized volatility estimator to a significant extent, in particular, for high frequency observations and when the noise component is relevant. Note that when the noise increases, even maintaining the same size of the grid, the cutting frequency of the Fourier estimator becomes smaller and smaller: cutting the highest frequencies in the Fourier expansion, we ignore high frequency noise, as remarked in Mancino and Sanfelici (2008). Hence, by choosing a small number of low frequency ordinates, it is in principle possible to render the Fourier estimator invariant to market microstructure effects.

We now compare the quality of the forecasts obtained through the Fourier method with that obtained by variants of the realized volatility estimator that turn out to be robust to microstructure noise (Andersen *et al.*, 2010b). The

TABLE 10.5 R^2 **for Integrated Variance Forecasts: Linear Regression of the Integrated Volatility at Time $t+1$ onto a Constant and the Volatility at Time t Computed as the Realized Volatility or as the Fourier Volatility. λ Indicates the Noise Fraction; n, the Number of Observations; and N, the Cutting Frequency of the Fourier Estimator. M1, M2, and M3 Refer to the Three Stochastic Volatility Models**

		M1			M3			M3		
λ	n	$R^2(\mathrm{RV}(n,\lambda))$	$R^2(\mathrm{FM}_N(n,\lambda))$	N	$R^2(\mathrm{RV}(n,\lambda))$	$R^2(\mathrm{FM}_N(n,\lambda))$	N	$R^2(\mathrm{RV}(n,\lambda))$	$R^2(\mathrm{FM}_N(n,\lambda))$	N
0%	2160	0.9035	0.9053	581	0.5707	0.5701	806	0.9010	0.9013	788
	1440	0.9028	0.9036	536	0.5575	0.5612	458	0.8914	0.8918	533
	720	0.8998	0.9033	326	0.5551	0.5579	335	0.8771	0.8806	345
	360	0.8919	0.8926	178	0.5097	0.5112	178	0.8592	0.8592	180
	288	0.8837	0.8862	124	0.5036	0.5049	144	0.8326	0.8349	143
	96	0.8025	0.8044	42	0.3846	0.3908	46	0.7270	0.7273	48
	48	0.7336	0.7344	24	0.3197	0.3170	24	0.6148	0.6170	24
	24	0.5750	0.5792	12	0.2176	0.2134	12	0.4571	0.4652	11
	12	0.4476	0.4538	5	0.1619	0.1709	5	0.3466	0.3315	6
	6	0.3037	0.3207	3	0.1039	0.1035	3	0.2268	0.2298	2
0.1%	2160	0.6931	0.8861	170	0.3995	0.5377	251	0.8380	0.8771	386
	1440	0.7533	0.8763	143	0.4060	0.5232	218	0.8397	0.8639	267
	720	0.8103	0.8616	182	0.5040	0.5154	176	0.8413	0.8464	182
	360	0.8238	0.8435	121	0.4387	0.4601	155	0.8311	0.8336	180
	288	0.8085	0.8296	82	0.4238	0.4410	99	0.8216	0.8217	139
	96	0.7476	0.7506	42	0.3369	0.3536	37	0.7020	0.7007	47

(continued)

TABLE 10.5 (*Continued*)

		M1			M3			M3		
λ	n	$R^2(\mathrm{RV}(n,\lambda))$	$R^2(\mathrm{FM}_N(n,\lambda))$	N	$R^2(\mathrm{RV}(n,\lambda))$	$R^2(\mathrm{FM}_N(n,\lambda))$	N	$R^2(\mathrm{RV}(n,\lambda))$	$R^2(\mathrm{FM}_N(n,\lambda))$	N
	48	0.6633	0.6595	23	0.2876	0.2929	23	0.6027	0.6016	23
	24	0.5456	0.5459	12	0.2020	0.1975	12	0.4495	0.4603	11
	12	0.4244	0.4301	5	0.1605	0.1672	5	0.3433	0.3306	5
	6	0.2897	0.2963	3	0.1009	0.0994	3	0.2270	0.2295	2
0.5%	2160	0.2224	0.8422	86	0.0878	0.4402	80	0.4317	0.8099	140
	1440	0.2249	0.8211	62	0.1086	0.3972	61	0.4415	0.7888	125
	720	0.3439	0.8019	50	0.1850	0.3790	51	0.6434	0.7486	98
	360	0.3776	0.7419	50	0.1973	0.3500	35	0.6667	0.7222	75
	288	0.4837	0.7099	31	0.2042	0.2749	32	0.6128	0.6683	60
	96	0.5254	0.6100	17	0.2429	0.2669	30	0.6021	0.6185	24
	48	0.4857	0.5757	18	0.2341	0.2395	24	0.5679	0.5719	23
	24	0.4650	0.4675	10	0.1550	0.1536	5	0.4139	0.4202	11
	12	0.3696	0.3907	4	0.1399	0.1450	5	0.3244	0.3088	6
	6	0.2589	0.2746	3	0.0829	0.0723	3	0.2154	0.2302	2

methods basically combine a fast time grid with some other slow time grids. As in Andersen *et al*. (2010b) for all the estimators, the step of the principal grid is set at 15 s while we change the level of the noise as we did in Table 10.5. The considered estimators are the *sparse estimator*, which is the equally spaced 75-s grid subsampled from the principal one; the *average estimator* by Zhang *et al*. (2005); the *two-scaled estimator*, which consists essentially the combination of the previously described average estimator with the classic realized volatility over the principal grid; the *two-scaled adjusted estimators* (Zhang, 2006); the estimator proposed by Zhou (1996), which extends the classical realized volatility by considering also the first-order serial correlation of high frequency returns; and the *Kernel estimator* in Barndorff-Nielsen *et al*. (2008a), for which we consider only the modified Tukey–Hanning one.

Zhang *et al*. (2005) rank the performance of realized volatility's estimators as follows: $\mathrm{RV}_n(t)$ as the fifth best realized variance estimator, choosing a lower sampling frequency ($\mathrm{RV}^{\mathrm{sparse}}(t)$) as the fourth best, and sampling at an optimal sampling frequency as the third best. Then they put the $\mathrm{RV}^{\mathrm{average}}$ as the second best realized volatility estimator and finally the two scaled (adjusted or not) as the best one. Numerical results in Table 10.6 confirm essentially this ranking. In fact, surely, a wider step of the grid allows us to avoid a greater amount of noise. On the other hand, this feature also leads us to loose important information about the variance process. The average and the two-scale estimator bypass this problem considering many short-step grids shifted in time (the first method) or combining slow and fast time grids (the second one). As it is described by Andersen *et al*. (2010b) and by our results, the first strategy allows to get better results in terms of prediction of the future volatility. Even the Kernel estimator gets remarkable results. Excluding two cases (M1 with 0.1% , M3 with 0.5% and $\mathrm{RV}^{\mathrm{average}}$), the Fourier method performs better than realized volatility estimators that are designed to cope with microstructure noise. This can be easily explained by recalling what we said about analyzing the results in Table 10.5: the Fourier method always uses all the information of the price signal (the fastest grid possible) and cuts out the noise in the frequency domain.

Finally Barucci *et al*. (2010), analyze how the estimators behave when the integrated volatility process is unknown, that is, when using real data, by means of the analytical formulae (Eq. 10.46). To this end, the authors perform a cross-correlation analysis in order to find the best dependent-independent variable--estimator combination for different levels of noise. With regard to the combination that gives rise to the best results in terms of prediction, the competition is between the average realized volatility estimator and the Fourier estimator: in three settings, the first method prevails, but the R^2 difference is rather small, and in the other ones, the Fourier methodology prevails in a significant extent. Barucci *et al*. (2010) conclude that the Fourier methodology tends to prevail when the noise level is high.

TABLE 10.6 R^2 for Integrated Variance Forecasts: Linear Regression of the Integrated Volatility at Time $t+1$ onto a Constant and the Volatility at Time t Computed as a Realized-Type Volatility Estimator or as the Fourier Volatility. λ Indicates the Noise F and N the Cutting Frequency of the Fourier Estimator. M1, M2, and M3 Refer to the Three Stochastic Volatility Models

		M1		M2		M3	
λ	Model	R^2	N	R^2	N	R^2	N
0.1%	RV_t^{all}	0.7533		0.3995		0.8397	
	RV_t^{sparse}	0.8085		0.4238		0.8311	
	$RV_t^{average}$	0.8796		0.5084		0.8581	
	RV_t^{TS}	0.8703		0.4853		0.8417	
	$RV_t^{TS_{Adj}}$	0.8703		0.4853		0.8417	
	RV_t^{Zhou}	0.7830		0.4512		0.8254	
	RV_t^{Ker}	0.8610		0.4977		0.8464	
	FM_t^N	0.8763	143	0.5232	218	0.8639	182
0.5%	RV_t^{all}	0.2249		0.0878		0.4415	
	RV_t^{sparse}	0.3837		0.2042		0.6128	
	$RV_t^{average}$	0.7608		0.3928		0.8022	
	RV_t^{TS}	0.7391		0.3598		0.7886	
	$RV_t^{TS_{Adj}}$	0.7391		0.3598		0.7886	
	RV_t^{Zhou}	0.2251		0.1005		0.5059	
	RV_t^{Ker}	0.6043		0.2516		0.7498	
	FM_t^N	0.8211	62	0.3972	61	0.7888	98

10.5.3 FORECASTING COVARIANCE: A MONTE CARLO ANALYSIS

In this section, we evaluate the forecasting power of different estimators of the integrated covariance, illustrating the results in Mancino and Sanfelici (2011b). In our analysis, besides the Fourier estimator, we will consider the following ones: the realized covariance (RC) estimator, the realized covariance plus leads and lags estimator (RCLL), the estimator proposed by Hayashi and Yoshida (2005) (AO), the subsampled version of the AO estimator proposed by Voev and Lunde (2007) (AO_{sub}), and finally, the multivariate realized kernel of Barndorff-Nielsen *et al.* (2008b) (K).

Following a large literature, we simulate discrete data from the continuous time bivariate Heston model

$$
\begin{aligned}
dp^1(t) &= \left(\mu_1 - \sigma_1^2(t)/2\right) dt + \sigma_1(t) dW_1 \\
dp^2(t) &= \left(\mu_2 - \sigma_2^2(t)/2\right) dt + \sigma_2(t) dW_2 \\
d\sigma_1^2(t) &= k_1(\alpha_1 - \sigma_1^2(t))dt + \gamma_1\sigma_1(t)dW_3, \\
d\sigma_2^2(t) &= k_2(\alpha_2 - \sigma_2^2(t))dt + \gamma_2\sigma_2(t)dW_4,
\end{aligned}
$$

where $\text{corr}(W_1, W_2) = 0.35$, $\text{corr}(W_1, W_3) = -0.5$, and $\text{corr}(W_2, W_4) = -0.55$. The other parameters of the model are as in Zhang *et al.* (2005): $\mu_1 = 0.05$, $\mu_2 = 0.055$, $k_1 = 5$, $k_2 = 5.5$, $\alpha_1 = 0.05$, $\alpha_2 = 0.045$, $\gamma_1 = 0.5$, and $\gamma_2 = 0.5$. The volatility parameters satisfy Feller's condition $2k\alpha \geq \gamma^2$, which makes the zero boundary unattainable by the volatility process. Moreover, we assume that the additive logarithmic noises $\eta_l^1 = \eta^1(t_l^1)$ and $\eta_l^2 = \eta^2(t_l^2)$ are i.i.d. Gaussian, contemporaneously correlated, and independent from p. The correlation is set to 0.5, and we assume $\omega_{ii}^{1/2} = (E[(\eta^i)^2])^{1/2}$ equal to 0 or 0.004. We also consider the case of dependent noise, assuming for simplicity $\eta_l^i = \alpha(p^i(t_l^i) - p^i(t_{l-1}^i)) + \bar{\eta}_l^i$, for $i = 1, 2$ and $\bar{\eta}_l^i$ i.i.d. Gaussian. We set $\alpha = 0.1$. From the simulated data, integrated covariance estimates can be compared to the value of the true covariance quantities.

We generate (through simple Euler Monte Carlo discretization) high frequency, evenly sampled, efficient, and observed returns by simulating second-by-second return and variance paths over a daily trading period of $h = 6$ h, for a total of 21,600 observations per day. In order to simulate high frequency unevenly sampled data, we extract the observation times in such a way that the duration between the observations is drawn from an exponential distribution with means $\lambda_1 = 6$ s and $\lambda_2 = 8$ s for the two assets. Therefore, on each trading day, the processes are observed at a different discrete unevenly spaced grid $\{0 = t_1^i \leq t_2^i \leq \cdots \leq t_{n_i}^i \leq 2\pi\}$ for any $i = 1, 2$.

In the tradition of Mincer and Zarnowitz (1969), we regress the real daily integrated covariance over the forecasting period on one-step-ahead forecasts obtained by means of each covariance measure. More precisely, following Andersen and Bollerslev (1998), we split our samples into two parts: the first one containing 30% of total estimates is used as a "burn-in" period to fit a univariate AR(1) model for the estimated covariance time series and then the fitted model is used to forecast integrated covariance on the next day. The choice of the AR(1) model comes from Ait-Sahalia and Mancini (2008), who consider the univariate Heston data generating process. The total number of out-of-sample forecasts m is equal to 525. Each time a new forecast is performed, the corresponding actual covariance measure is moved from the forecasting horizon to the first sample, and the AR(1) parameters are reestimated in real time. For each time series of covariance forecasts, we project the real daily integrated covariance on day $[t, t+1]$ on a constant and the corresponding one-step-ahead forecasts $\hat{C}_t^{\text{Fourier}}$ obtained from the series of Fourier estimates and from each of the other covariance measures $\hat{C}_t$. The regression takes the form

$$\int_t^{t+1} \Sigma^{12}(s)ds = \phi_0 + \phi_1 \hat{C}_t^{\text{Fourier}} + \phi_2 \hat{C}_t + \text{error}_t,$$

where $t = 1, 2, \ldots, m$. The R^2 from these regressions provides a direct assessment of the variability in the integrated covariance that is explained by the particular estimates in the regressions. The R^2 can therefore be interpreted as a simple gauge of the degree of predictability in the volatility process and hence of the potential economic significance of the volatility forecasts.

The results are reported in Tables 10.7–10.9 for different shapes and extents of the noise, using a Newey–West covariance matrix. Let us start with Table 10.7, the case with no noise. In this case, the optimally sampled realized covariance and the subsampled AO estimator reduce to the 1-min realized covariance and to the AO estimator, respectively, (i.e., no subsampling is needed), and hence, they are omitted. When we consider a single regressor, the R^2 is the highest for the AO estimator, immediately followed by Fourier and the kernel estimator while $RCLL^{10min}$ explains less than 5% of the time series variability. For none of the estimators we can reject the hypothesis that $\phi_0 = 0$ and $\phi_1 = 1$ (or $\phi_0 = 0$ and $\phi_2 = 1$) using the corresponding t tests. When we include alternative forecasts besides Fourier estimator in the regression, the R^2 improves very little relative to the R^2 based solely on Fourier. Moreover, the coefficient estimates for ϕ_1 are generally close to unity, while for the other estimators, the coefficients are not significantly different from zero at the 5% level. The only exceptions are given by the multiple regression on Fourier and AO forecasts, as a consequence of the higher accuracy and lower variability of AO covariance estimates, and by the multiple regression on Fourier and kernel forecasts, which has no statistically significant coefficients at the 5% level, although the F-statistic is 64.57. In the latter case, the explanatory powers of the explanatory variables overlap, and the marginal contribution of each explanatory variable is quite small.

In the upper panel of Table 10.8, simultaneous correlated noise is considered, and the highest R^2 is now achieved by the subsampled AO estimator, immediately followed by the Fourier estimator. For none of the estimators we can reject the hypothesis that $\phi_0 = 0$ and $\phi_1 = 1$ (or $\phi_0 = 0$ and $\phi_2 = 1$), except for RC^{5min}, AO, and K. When we include alternative forecasts besides Fourier estimator in the regression, the R^2 are generally slightly increased relative to the R^2 based solely on Fourier, but, in general, the coefficient ϕ_2 does not significantly differ from zero. Exceptions are given by RC^{opt}, AO, and AO_{sub}. In particular, in both the regressions involving the AO estimator, the intercept ϕ_0 differs significantly from zero, and, in particular, in the multiple regression, it represents a large part of the true integrated volatility.

Finally, let us consider the case with noise dependent on the efficient price. In the upper panel of Table 10.9, the highest R^2 is achieved by the subsampled AO estimator and the Fourier estimator. When we include alternative forecasts besides Fourier estimator in the regression, the R^2 slightly increases, but the coefficients ϕ_2 remain not significantly different from zero, while the coefficient estimates for ϕ_1 are generally close to unity and significant at the 5% level. The last two regressions in the table provide coefficients all of which significantly differ from zero and the highest R^2.

Therefore, we can conclude that the above results confirm the ranking between different covariance estimators obtained in Section 10.4.2 because the higher accuracy and lower variability of Fourier and subsampled AO covariance estimates translate into superior forecasts of future covariances.

TABLE 10.7 OLS Estimates from Regressions of Real Integrated Covariance on a Constant and Each Covariance Forecast Over the Forecasting Horizon for $\omega_{ii} = 0$. Heteroskedasticity Robust Standard Errors are Listed in Parentheses

Method	ϕ_0	ϕ_1	ϕ_2	R^2
Fourier	−0.000357 (0.000344)	1.189359 (0.102915)	—	0.193886
$RC^{1\,min}$	−0.000160 (0.000326)	—	1.175931 (0.101524)	0.189368
$RC^{5\,min}$	−0.000875 (0.000559)	—	1.253498 (0.155701)	0.131912
$RC^{10\,min}$	−0.000633 (0.000718)	—	1.180675 (0.199363)	0.095597
$RCLL^{1\,min}$	−0.000431 (0.000429)	—	1.101692 (0.115191)	0.156135
$RCLL^{5\,min}$	0.000481 (0.000467)	—	0.872040 (0.129550)	0.095959
$RCLL^{10\,min}$	0.000494 (0.000693)	—	0.878594 (0.193523)	0.042197
AO	−0.000432 (0.000326)	—	1.115636 (0.090716)	0.208508
K	−0.000345 (0.000351)	—	1.189693 (0.106857)	0.193926
$F + RC^{1\,min}$	−0.000367 (0.000342)	0.763583 (0.388643)	0.445468 (0.380325)	0.196213
$F + RC^{5\,min}$	−0.000523 (0.000547)	1.120893 (0.205312)	0.109524 (0.282750)	0.194250
$F + RC^{10\,min}$	−0.000494 (0.000655)	1.156734 (0.141495)	0.067775 (0.247474)	0.194055
$F + RCLL^{1\,min}$	−0.000411 (0.000422)	1.132873 (0.273765)	0.065820 (0.294081)	0.194006
$F + RCLL^{5\,min}$	−0.000536 (0.000436)	1.117881 (0.142965)	0.114582 (0.168453)	0.194842
$F + RCLL^{10\,min}$	−0.000274 (0.000674)	1.199005 (0.125196)	−0.031849 (0.224384)	0.193928
F+ AO	−0.000407 (0.000337)	−0.156772 (0.499995)	1.253392 (0.449527)	0.208696
F+ K	−0.000443 (0.000345)	0.606863 (0.411885)	0.609752 (0.409939)	0.198321

TABLE 10.8 OLS Estimates from Regressions of Real Integrated Covariance on a Constant and Each Covariance Forecast Over the Forecasting Horizon for $\omega_{ii}^{1/2} = 0.004$. Heteroskedasticity Robust Standard Errors are Listed in parentheses

Method	ϕ_0	ϕ_1	ϕ_2	R^2
Fourier	0.000289 (0.000447)	0.934596 (0.127683)	—	0.159878
$RC^{1\,min}$	0.000238 (0.000594)	—	0.958151 (0.171193)	0.097955
$RC^{5\,min}$	0.001138 (0.000365)	—	0.708021 (0.106029)	0.106261
$RC^{10\,min}$	0.000822 (0.000476)	—	0.821870 (0.138801)	0.089039
$RCLL^{1\,min}$	0.000152 (0.000493)	—	0.981620 (0.141241)	0.124185
$RCLL^{5\,min}$	0.000602 (0.000617)	—	0.871933 (0.174710)	0.068160
$RCLL^{10\,min}$	0.000421 (0.000808)	—	0.899933 (0.223244)	0.047621
RC^{opt}	0.000094 (0.000511)	—	1.032842 (0.142621)	0.153681
AO	−0.006479 (0.001467)	—	0.960790 (0.141400)	0.120925
K	0.000697 (0.000472)	—	0.744498 (0.120660)	0.078797
AO_{sub}	0.000027 (0.000472)	—	0.900493 (0.119631)	0.163476
$F + RC^{1\,min}$	−0.000290 (0.000584)	0.934879 (0.160315)	−0.000472 (0.209145)	0.159878
$F + RC^{5\,min}$	0.000156 (0.000456)	0.804672 (0.162177)	0.166798 (0.125648)	0.162685
$F + RC^{10\,min}$	−0.000005 (0.000529)	0.829524 (0.143006)	0.192210 (0.148598)	0.162727
$F + RCLL^{1\,min}$	−0.000147 (0.000507)	0.725966 (0.180395)	0.330217 (0.201237)	0.165964
$F + RCLL^{5\,min}$	−0.000122 (0.000632)	0.860920 (0.143192)	0.189859 (0.188459)	0.162116
$F + RCLL^{10\,min}$	−0.000534 (0.000770)	0.869414 (0.134253)	0.288530 (0.216120)	0.163995
$F + RC^{opt}$	−0.000302 (0.000530)	0.560295 (0.154433)	0.531720 (0.201200)	0.174964
F+ AO	−0.002963 (0.001259)	0.712225 (0.142840)	0.383016 (0.136055)	0.170044
F+ K	0.000325 (0.000486)	0.947413 (0.166833)	−0.020439 (0.142337)	0.159907
$F + AO_{sub}$	−0.000017 (0.000482)	0.430555 (0.231898)	0.525662 (0.234024)	0.169082

TABLE 10.9 OLS Estimates from Regressions of Real Integrated Covariance on a Constant and Each Covariance Forecast Over the Forecasting Horizon for $\omega_{ii}^{1/2} = 0.004$ and Dependent Noise. Heteroskedasticity Robust Standard Errors are Listed in Parentheses

Method	ϕ_0	ϕ_1	ϕ_2	R^2
Fourier	−0.000553 (0.000360)	1.206333 (0.101268)	—	0.228107
$RC^{1\,min}$	−0.000092 (0.000433)	—	1.156458 (0.130600)	0.133428
$RC^{5\,min}$	−0.000428 (0.000619)	—	1.175871 (0.168303)	0.077988
$RC^{10\,min}$	−0.001231 (0.001051)	—	1.337231 (0.274826)	0.057487
$RCLL^{1\,min}$	0.000376 (0.000429)	—	0.916729 (0.112831)	0.108334
$RCLL^{5\,min}$	−0.000642 (0.000861)	—	1.144396 (0.219782)	0.065329
$RCLL^{10\,min}$	0.000993 (0.000656)	—	0.700703 (0.158462)	0.055697
RC^{opt}	−0.000223 (0.000438)	—	1.133138 (0.125219)	0.155574
AO	−0.000139 (0.000423)	—	0.950547 (0.103165)	0.132463
K	−0.000353 (0.000460)	—	1.088604 (0.122791)	0.162078
AO_{sub}	−0.000498 (0.000325)	—	1.128151 (0.084872)	0.229336
$F + RC^{1\,min}$	−0.000565 (0.000421)	1.200380 (0.152692)	0.009791 (0.184195)	0.228111
$F + RC^{5\,min}$	0.000013 (0.000556)	1.307011 (0.138977)	−0.255483 (0.208519)	0.230200
$F + RC^{10\,min}$	0.000415 (0.000998)	1.296528 (0.121808)	−0.339960 (0.312605)	0.230547
$F + RCLL^{1\,min}$	−0.000405 (0.000405)	1.275637 (0.160140)	−0.105193 (0.169297)	0.228781
$F + RCLL^{5\,min}$	−0.000477 (0.000769)	1.214562 (0.119038)	−0.026815 (0.231508)	0.228132
$F + RCLL^{10\,min}$	−0.000942 (0.000627)	1.157871 (0.123250)	0.137724 (0.187821)	0.229891
$F + RC^{opt}$	−0.000611 (0.000411)	1.164916 (0.173187)	0.058059 (0.198324)	0.228247
$F + AO$	−0.000712 (0.000412)	1.138820 (0.151219)	0.096222 (0.145790)	0.228750
$F + K$	−0.001014 (0.000446)	0.985978 (0.126263)	0.326911 (0.143702)	0.235112
$F + AO_{sub}$	−0.000689 (0.000349)	0.603879 (0.265580)	0.605376 (0.230310)	0.237252

10.6 Application: Asset Allocation

In this section, we consider a different approach to the comparison of covariance estimators with high frequency data, in the context of a relevant economic criterion, developed in Mancino and Sanfelici (2011b). We consider the gains offered by the Fourier estimator over other covariance measures from the perspective of an asset-allocation decision problem, following the approach of Fleming *et al.* (2001, 2003), Engle and Colacito (2006), Bandi *et al.* (2008), and De Pooter *et al.* (2008), who study the impact of volatility timing versus unconditional mean–variance efficient static asset-allocation strategies and of selecting the appropriate sampling frequency or choosing between different bias and variance reduction techniques for the realized covariance matrices. We compare the portfolio utility obtained by virtue of covariance forecasts based on the Fourier estimator to the utility obtained through covariance forecasts constructed using the more familiar realized covariance and other recently proposed estimators. The choice of a quadratic utility function is consistent with the mean–variance Markowitz-type optimization used to build the optimal portfolio and with the MSE-based procedure used to optimize the different covariance measures. A different approach is the one of De Pooter *et al.* (2008), who optimize the variance estimators directly by maximizing the utility that a risk-averse investor receives from alternative volatility-timing trading strategies. In the following, we adopt a notation that is common in the literature about portfolio management.

Let R^f and R_{t+1} be the risk-free return and the return vector on k risky assets over a day $[t, t+1]$, respectively. Define $\mu_t = E_t[R_{t+1}]$ and $\Phi_t = E_t[(R_{t+1} - \mu_t)(R_{t+1} - \mu_t)']$ the conditional expected value and the conditional covariance matrix of R_{t+1}, respectively. We consider a mean–variance investor who solves the problem

$$\min_{w_t} w_t'\Phi_t w_t, \text{ subject to } w_t'\mu_t + (1 - w_t'\mathbf{1}_k)R^f = \mu_p,$$

where w_t is a k-vector of portfolio weights, μ_p is a target expected return on the portfolio, and $\mathbf{1}_k$ is a $k \times 1$ vector of ones. The solution to this program is

$$w_t = \frac{(\mu_p - R^f)\Phi_t^{-1}(\mu_t - R^f\mathbf{1}_k)}{(\mu_t - R^f\mathbf{1}_k)'\Phi_t^{-1}(\mu_t - R^f\mathbf{1}_k)}. \tag{10.47}$$

We estimate Φ_t using one-day-ahead forecasts $\hat{C}_t$ given a time series of daily covariance estimates, obtained using the Fourier estimator, the realized covariance estimator, the realized covariance plus leads and lags estimator, the AO estimator and its subsampled version and the kernel estimator. The out-of-sample forecast is based on a univariate ARMA model.

Given the sensible choices of R^f, μ_p, and μ_t, each one-day-ahead forecast leads to the determination of a daily portfolio weight w_t. The time series of daily portfolio weights then leads to daily portfolio returns. In order to concentrate ourselves on volatility approximation and to abstract from the issues that would be posed by expected stock return predictability, for all times t, we set the components of the vector $\mu_t = E_t[R_{t+1}]$ equal to the sample means of the returns on the risky assets over the forecasting horizon. Finally, we employ the investor's long-run mean–variance utility as a metric to evaluate the economic benefit of alternative covariance forecasts $\hat{C}_t$, that is,

$$U^* = \bar{R}^p - \frac{\lambda}{2}\frac{1}{m}\sum_{t=1}^{m}(R^p_{t+1} - \bar{R}^p)^2,$$

where $R^p_{t+1} = R^f + w'_t(R_{t+1} - R^f\mathbf{1}_k)$ is the return on the portfolio with estimated weights w_t, $\bar{R}^p = \frac{1}{m}\sum_{t=1}^{m} R^p_{t+1}$ is the sample mean of the portfolio returns across $m \leq n$ days, and λ is the coefficient of risk aversion.

Following Bandi *et al.* (2008), in order to avoid contaminations induced by noisy first moment estimation, we simply look at the variance component of U^*, namely,

$$U = \frac{\lambda}{2}\frac{1}{m}\sum_{t=1}^{m}(R^p_{t+1} - \bar{R}^p)^2, \tag{10.48}$$

see Engle and Colacito (2006) for further justifications of this approach. The difference between two utility estimations, say $U^A - U^B$, can be interpreted as the fee that the investor would be willing to pay to switch from covariance forecasts based on estimator A to covariance forecasts based on estimator B. In other words, $U^A - U^B$ is the utility gain that can be obtained by investing in portfolio B, with the lowest variance for a given target return μ_p.

We consider again the model of Section 10.5.3. Given any time series of daily variance/covariance estimates, we split our samples of 750 days into two parts: the first one containing 30% of total estimates is used as a "burn-in" period, while the second one is saved for out-of-sample purposes. The out-of-sample forecast is based on univariate ARMA models for each variance/covariance estimates separately, as in Section 10.5.3. We implement the criterion in Equation 10.50 by setting R_f equal to 0.03 and considering three targets μ_p, namely, 0.09, 0.12, and 0.15. For all times t, the conditional covariance matrix is computed as an out-of-sample forecast based on the different variance/covariance estimates.

We interpret the difference $U^{\hat{C}} - U^{\text{Fourier}}$ between the average utility computed on the basis of the Fourier estimator and that based on alternative estimators $\hat{C}$ as the fee that the investor would be willing to pay to switch from covariance forecasts based on estimator $\hat{C}$ to covariance forecasts based on the Fourier estimator. Tables 10.10 and 10.11 contain the results for three levels of risk aversion and three target expected returns in two different noise scenarios. We remark that the optimal sampling frequencies for the realized variances and covariances are generally different because of the different effects of microstructure noise and nonsynchronicity on the volatility

TABLE 10.10 Annualized Fees $U^{\hat{C}} - U^{\text{Fourier}}$ (in Basis Points) that a Mean–Variance Investor would be Willing to Pay to Switch from $\hat{C}$ to Fourier Estimates. Contemporaneously Correlated Noise, with $\omega_{ii}^{1/2} = 0.002$

Method	$\mu_p = 0.09$			$\mu_p = 0.12$			$\mu_p = 0.15$		
λ	2	7	10	2	7	10	2	7	10
$RC^{1\,\text{min}}$	1.907	6.675	9.536	4.291	15.019	21.456	7.629	26.701	38.144
$RC^{5\,\text{min}}$	0.361	1.262	1.803	0.811	2.839	4.056	1.442	5.048	7.211
$RC^{10\,\text{min}}$	1.801	6.303	9.004	4.052	14.181	20.258	7.203	25.210	36.014
$RCLL^{1\,\text{min}}$	−1.817	−6.359	−9.084	−4.088	−14.308	−20.439	− 7.267	−25.436	−36.337
$RCLL^{5\,\text{min}}$	3.245	11.359	16.227	7.302	25.557	36.510	12.981	45.435	64.906
$RCLL^{10\,\text{min}}$	8.587	30.056	42.937	19.321	67.625	96.607	34.349	120.222	171.746
RC^{opt}	0.110	0.385	0.551	0.248	0.867	1.239	0.441	1.542	2.203
AO	5.236	18.326	26.180	11.781	41.133	58.905	20.944	73.304	104.720
K	−1.169	−4.090	−5.844	−2.630	−9.204	−13.148	−4.675	− 16.362	−23.374
AO_{sub}	−0.980	−3.429	−4.898	−2.204	−7.714	−11.020	−3.918	−13.714	−19.592

TABLE 10.11 **Annualized Fees $U^{\hat{C}} - U^{\text{Fourier}}$ (in Basis Points) that a Mean–Variance Investor would be Willing to Pay to Switch from $\hat{C}$ to Fourier Estimates. Dependent Noise, with $\omega_{ii}^{1/2} = 0.004$**

Method	$\mu_p = 0.09$			$\mu_p = 0.12$			$\mu_p = 0.15$		
λ	2	7	10	2	7	10	2	7	10
$RC^{1\,\text{min}}$	4.944	17.305	24.722	11.125	38.937	55.624	19.778	69.221	98.887
$RC^{5\,\text{min}}$	1.805	6.316	9.023	4.060	14.211	20.301	7.218	25.264	36.091
$RC^{10\,\text{min}}$	2.311	8.090	11.557	5.201	18.202	26.002	9.245	32.359	46.227
$RCLL^{1\,\text{min}}$	−0.066	−0.232	−0.332	−0.149	−0.522	−0.746	−0.265	−0.929	−1.327
$RCLL^{5\,\text{min}}$	2.823	9.880	14.115	6.352	22.231	31.758	11.292	39.521	56.458
$RCLL^{10\,\text{min}}$	4.689	16.412	23.446	10.551	36.927	52.753	18.757	65.649	93.784
RC^{opt}	1.555	5.442	7.774	3.498	12.243	17.491	6.219	21.766	31.094
AO	8.509	29.782	42.546	19.146	67.010	95.728	34.037	119.128	170.183
K	0.918	3.213	4.590	2.066	7.229	10.328	3.672	12.852	18.360
AO_{sub}	−0.417	−1.461	−2.087	−0.939	−3.287	−4.695	−1.669	-5.843	−8.347

measures. Therefore, in the asset-allocation, application we choose to use a unique sampling frequency for realized variances and covariances, given by the maximum among the optimal sampling intervals corresponding to variances and covariances.

Consider Table 10.10, corresponding to $\omega_{ii}^{1/2} = 0.002$. The entries represent the difference $U^{\hat{C}} - U^{\text{Fourier}}$ for three levels of risk aversion and three target expected returns; therefore, a positive number is evidence in favor of better performance of the Fourier estimator over $\hat{C}$. For instance, when $\hat{C} = \text{RC}^{1\,\text{min}}$ and the target is 0.09, the investor would pay between 1.9 (when $\lambda = 2$) and 9.5 basis points (when $\lambda = 10$) per year to use the Fourier estimator versus the $\text{RC}^{1\,\text{min}}$ estimator. When the target is 0.12, the investor would pay between 4.3 (when $\lambda = 2$) and 21.5 basis points (when $\lambda = 10$). Finally, when the target is 0.15, the investor would pay between 7.6 (when $\lambda = 2$) and 38.1 basis points (when $\lambda = 10$). The same investor would pay marginally less to abandon $\text{RC}^{5\,\text{min}}$. The remaining part of the table can be read similarly[1]. In the last two lines, the negative values imply a better performance of the kernel and subsampled AO estimators. Unexpectedly, a minor but statistically significant utility loss is encountered when considering the $\text{RCLL}^{1\,\text{min}}$ estimator. Notice that the optimally sampled realized covariance estimator cannot achieve the same performance. In particular, this evidence partially contradicts the conclusions of De Pooter *et al.* (2008) about the greater effects obtainable by a careful choice of the sampling interval rather than by bias correction procedures. When we allow for dependency between noise and price (Table 10.11), we get a modest utility loss moving from the subsampled AO estimator to Fourier estimator, according to the good in-sample properties of the former estimator for the whole covariance matrix, which translate into precise forecasts. Unexpectedly, a modest utility loss is encountered when considering the $\text{RCLL}^{1\,\text{min}}$ estimator as well. In all the other cases, there are nonnegligible utility gains to the investor associated to the Fourier method.

In conclusion, we can say that the Fourier estimator carefully extracts information from noisy high frequency asset price data and allows for nonnegligible utility gains in portfolio management. Specifically, our simulations show that the gains yielded by the Fourier methodology are statistically significant and can be economically large, while only the subsampled AO estimator and, for low levels of market microstructure noise, the realized covariance with one lead–lag bias correction and suitable sampling frequency can be competitive.

REFERENCES

Ait-Sahalia Y, Mancini L. Out of sample forecasts of quadratic variations. J Econometrics 2008;147:17–33.

[1]As already noted by Bandi et al. (2008) , the risk-aversion coefficient simply rescales the portfolio variances but does not affect the portfolio holding directly. Hence, the gains/losses are monotonic in the value of this coefficient.

Ait-Sahalia Y, Mykland P, Zhang L. How often to sample a continuous-time process in the presence of market microstructure noise. Rev Financ Stud 2005;18:351–416.

Andersen T, Bollerslev T. Answering the skeptics: yes, standard volatility models do provide accurate forecasts. Int Econ Rev 1998;39/4:885–905.

Andersen T, Bollerslev T, Diebold F. Parametric and nonparametric volatility measurement. In: Hansen L. P., Ait-Sahalia Y, editors. Handbook of Financial Econometrics. Amsterdam: North Holland; 2010.67–138.

Andersen T, Bollerslev T, Diebold F, Labys P. Modeling and forecasting realized volatility. Econometrica 2003;71:579–625.

Andersen TG, Bollerslev T, Frederiksen PH, Nielsen MØ. Comment on P. R. Hansen and A. Lunde: realized variance and market microstructure noise. J Bus Econ Stat 2006;24:173–179.

Andersen T, Bollerslev T, Meddahi N. Realized volatility forecasting and market microstructure noise. J Econometrics 2010;160:220–234.

Bandi FM, Russel JR. Realized covariation, realized beta and microstructure noise. Working Paper, Graduate School of Business, University of Chicago, 2005.

Bandi FM, Russel JR. Separating market microstructure noise from volatility. J Financ Econ 2006;79:655–692.

Bandi FM, Russell JR. Market microstructure noise, integrated variance estimators, and the accuracy of asymptotic approximations. J Econometrics 2011;160(1):145–159.

Bandi FM, Russell JR. Microstructure noise, realized variance and optimal sampling. Rev Econ Stud 2008;75(2):339–369.

Bandi FM, Russel JR, Zhu Y. Using high-frequency data in dynamic portfolio choice. Economet Rev 2008;27/1-3:163–198.

Barndorff-Nielsen OE, Graversen SE, Jacod J, Shephard N. Limit theorems for bipower variation in financial econometrics. Economet Theor 2006;22(4):677–719.

Barndorff-Nielsen OE, Hansen PR, Lunde A, Shephard N. Realized kernels can consistently estimate integrated variance: correcting realized variance for the effect of market frictions. Working paper, 2005.

Barndorff-Nielsen OE, Hansen PR, Lunde A, Shephard N. Designing realized kernels to measure the ex-post variation of equity prices in the presence of noise. Econometrica 2008;76/6:1481–1536.

Barndorff-Nielsen OE, Hansen PR, Lunde A, Shephard N. Multivariate realized kernels: consistent positive semi-definite estimators of the covariation of equity prices with noise and non-synchronous trading. Working paper, 2008.

Barndorff-Nielsen OE, Hansen PR, Lunde A, Shephard N. Subsampling realized kernels. J Econometrics 2010;160:204–219.

Barndorff-Nielsen OE, Shephard N. Econometric analysis of realized volatility and its use in estimating stochastic volatility models. J Roy Stat Soc B 2002;64:253–280.

Barndorff-Nielsen OE, Shephard N. Econometric analysis of realized covariation: high frequency based covariance, regression and correlation in financial economics. Econometrica 2004;72/3:885–925.

Barndorff-Nielsen OE, Shephard N. Econometrics of testing for jumps in financial economics using bipower variation. J Financ Econometrics 2006;4:1–30.

Barucci E, Mancino ME. Computation of volatility in stochastic volatility models with high frequency data. Int J Theor Appl Finance 2010;13(5):1–21.

Barucci E, Malliavin P, Mancino ME, Renò R, Thalmaier A. The price-volatility feedback rate: an implementable mathematical indicator of market stability. Math Finance 2003;13:17–35.

Barucci E, Magno D, Mancino ME. Fourier volatility forecasting with high frequency data and microstructure noise. Quant Finance 2010, Available online: 20 April 2010.

Barucci E, Renò R. On measuring volatility and the GARCH forecasting performance. J Int Financ Market Inst Money 2002;12:183–200.

Brandt MW, Diebold FX. A no-arbitrage approach to range-based estimation of return covariances and correlations. J Bus 2006;79:61–73.

Christensen K, Kinnebrock S, Podolskij M. Pre-averaging estimators of the ex-post covariance matrix in noisy diffusion models with non-synchronous data. J Econometrics 2010;159(1):116–133.

Cohen KJ, Hawawini GA, Maier SF, Schwartz RA, Whitcomb DK. Friction in the trading process and the estimation of systematic risk. J Financ Econ 1983;12:263–278.

Cox JC, Ingersoll JE, Ross SA. A theory of the term structure of interest rates. Econometrica 1985;53:385–408.

De Jong F, Nijman T. High frequency analysis of lead-lag relationships between financial markets. J Empir Finance 1997;4:259–277.

De Pooter M, Martens M, van Dijk Dick. Predicting the daily covariance matrix for S&P100 stocks using intraday data: but which frequency to use? Economet Rev 2008;27:199–229.

Dimson E. Risk measurement when shares are subject to infrequent trading. J Financ Econ 1979;7:197–226.

Engle R, Colacito R. Testing and valuing dynamic correlations for asset allocation. J Bus Econ Stat 2006;24(2):238–253.

Epps T. Comovements in stock prices in the very short run. J Am Stat Assoc 1979;74:291–298.

Fleming J, Kirby C, Ostdiek B. The economic value of volatility timing. J Finance 2001;LVI(1):329–352.

Fleming J, Kirby C, Ostdiek B. The economic value of volatility timing using "realized" volatility. J Financ Econ 2001;67:473–509.

Griffin JE, Oomen RCA. Covariance measurement in the presence of non-synchronous trading and market microstructure noise. J Econometrics 2011;160(1):58–68.

Hayashi T, Yoshida N. On covariance estimation of nonsynchronously observed diffusion processes. Bernoulli 2005;11(2):359–379.

Hansen PR, Lunde A. Realized variance and market microstructure noise (with discussions). J Bus Econ Stat 2006;24:127–218.

Harris FH, de B, McInish TH, Shoesmith GL, Wood RA. Cointegration, error correction, and price discovery on informationally linked security markets. J Financ Quant Anal 1995;30:563–579.

Hoshikawa T, Kanatani T, Nagai K, Nishiyama Y. Nonparametric estimation methods of integrated multivariate volatilities. Economet Rev 2008;27(1):112–138.

Jacod J, Li Y, Mykland PA, Podolskij M, Vetter M. Microstructure noise in the continuous case: the pre-averaging approach. Stoch Proc Appl 2009;119:2249–2276.

Kinnebrock S, Podolskij M. An econometric analysis of modulated realized covariance, regression and correlation in noisy diffusion models. CREATES Research Paper; 2008, 2008-23. p 1–48.

Kloeden PE, Platen EM. Numerical solution of stochastic differential equations. Springer Verlag, Berlin-Heidelberg; 1999.

Malliavin P. Integration and probability. Springer Verlag, New York; 1995.

Malliavin P, Mancino ME. Fourier series method for measurement of multivariate volatilities. Finance Stochast 2002;4:49–61.

Malliavin P, Mancino ME. A Fourier transform method for nonparametric estimation of multivariate volatility. Ann Stat 2005;37(4):1983–2010.

Malliavin P, Mancino ME, Recchioni MC. A non-parametric calibration of the HJM geometry: an application of Itô calculus to financial statistics. Jpn J Math 2007;2:55–77.

Malliavin P, Thalmaier A. Stochastic calculus of variations in mathematical finance. Springer Finance, Berlin-Heidelberg; 2006.

Mancino ME, Sanfelici S. Robustness of Fourier estimator of integrated volatility in the presence of microstructure noise. Comput Stat Data Anal 2008;52(6):2966–2989.

Mancino ME, Sanfelici S. Estimating covariance via Fourier method in the presence of asynchronous trading and microstructure noise. J Financ Econometrics 2011a;9(2):367–408.

Mancino ME, Sanfelici S. Covariance estimation and dynamic asset allocation under microstructure effects via Fourier methodology. In: Gregoriou GN, Pascalau R, editors. Financial Econometrics Modeling: Market Microstructure, Factor Models and Financial Risk Measures. London, UK: Palgrave-MacMillan; 2011b:3–32.

Martens M. Estimating unbiased and precise realized covariances. EFA 2004 Maastricht Meetings Paper No. 4299, 2004, Maastricht, The Netherlands.

Meddahi N. An eigenfunction approach for volatility modeling. Working paper, 2001.

Meddahi N. A theoretical comparison between integrated and realized volatility. J Appl Econometrics 2002;17:475–508.

Mincer J, Zarnowitz V. The evaluation of economic forecasts. In: Mincer J, editor. Economic forecasts and expectations. New York: National Bureau of Economic Research; 1969.

Mykland PA. A Gaussian calculus for inference from high frequency data. Ann Finance 2010. Published online: 30 April 2010.

Mykland P, Zhang L. Anova for diffusions. Ann Stat 2006;34(4):1931–1963.

Nielsen MO, Frederiksen PH. Finite sample accuracy and choice of sampling frequency in integrated volatility estimation. J Empir Finance 2006;15:265–286.

Podolskij M, Vetter M. Estimation of volatility functionals in the simultaneous presence of microstructure noise and jumps. Bernoulli 2009;15(3):634–658.

Scholes M, Williams J. Estimating betas from nonsynchronous data. J Financ Econ 1977;5:309–327.

Sheppard K. Realized covariance and scrambling. 2006 preprint.

Voev V, Lunde A. Integrated covariance estimation using high-frequency data in the presence of noise. J Financ Econometrics 2007;5(1):68–104.

Zhang L. Efficient estimation of stochastic volatility using noisy observations: a multi-scale approach. Bernoulli 2006;12(6):1019–1043.

Zhang L. Estimating covariation: Epps effect, microstructure noise. J Econometrics 2009, forthcoming.

Zhang L, Mykland P, Ait-Sahalia Y. A tale of two time scales: determining integrated volatility with noisy high frequency data. J Am Stat Assoc 2005;100:1394–1411.

Zhou B. High frequency data and volatility in foreign-exchange rates. J Bus Econ Stat 1996;14(1):45–52.

CHAPTER ELEVEN

The "Retirement" Problem

CRISTIAN PASARICA
Stevens Institute of Technology, Hoboken, NJ

11.1 Introduction

Problems of expected utility go back at least to the articles of Samuelson and Merton (1969) and Merton (1971), and have been studied extensively in recent years, for instance, by Pliska (1986), Karatzas *et al.* (1987), Cox and Huang (1989), Karatzas and Wang (2000), Jeanblanc and Lakner (2001), Koike and Morimoto (2003). Most of the literature shares the common setting of an agent who receives a deterministic initial capital, which he must invest in a market (complete or incomplete) so as to maximize the expected utility of his wealth and/or consumption, up to a *prespecified* terminal time. Karatzas and Wang (2000) allowed the agent freely to stop *before or at* prespecified final time, in order to maximize the expected utility of his wealth and/or consumption up to the stopping time.

In this chapter, we consider a problem proposed in Karatzas and Wang (2000), namely, of an investor who remains in the stock market up until a "retirement" time τ of his choice. At this point he consumes a lump-sum amount $\xi \geq 0$ of his choice (say, to buy a new house, or to finance some other "retirement-related" activity); and from then on he keeps his holdings in the money market, making withdrawals for consumption at some rate, up until $t = T$. For the infinite horizon, constant coefficients and only one stock in the market, some specific versions of this problem have been solved by Jeanblanc *et al.* (2004) by partial differential equations (PDE) methods and Koike and Morimoto

Handbook of Modeling High-Frequency Data in Finance, First Edition.
Edited by Frederi G. Viens, Maria C. Mariani, and Ionuţ Florescu.

(2003) by means of viscosity solutions. By extending the convex duality method of Karatzas and Wang (2000) to the case of infinite horizon, we prove that there is no duality gap in the case of constant coefficients and a modification of the results in Dayanik and Karatzas (2003) allow us to give sufficient conditions for the existence of an optimal stopping/consumption strategy, in a market with m stocks available. We consider different types of utility functions, give conditions for the existence of an optimal solution, and present cases in which an explicit solution can be computed. We also consider an extension of this problem, in which we allow to stop at randomized stopping times and use randomized strategies and prove that this extension will always have a solution. The main restriction of our approach is that we require that the interest rate to be "locked-in" after retirement.

11.2 The Market Model

We adopt a model consisting in a money market, with price $P_0(\cdot)$ given by

$$dP_0(t) = P_0(t)r(t)dt, \; P_0(0) = 1, \tag{11.1}$$

and of m stocks with prices-per-share $P_i(\cdot)$ satisfying the equations

$$dP_i(t) = P_i[b_i(t)dt + \sum_{i=1}^{m} \sigma_{ij}(t)dW_j(t)], \; i = 1, \ldots, m. \tag{11.2}$$

Here $W(\cdot) = (W_1(\cdot), \ldots, W_m(\cdot))^*$ is an m-dimensional Brownian motion on a complete probability space $(\Omega, \mathbf{F}, \mathbf{P})$. We shall denote by $\mathbf{F} = \{\mathcal{F}_t\}_{\{0 \le t \le T\}}$ the $\mathbf{P}$-augmentation of the filtration generated by $W(\cdot)$. Here and in what follows, we denote by $\mathcal{S}_{[s,t]}$ the class of $\mathbf{F}$-stopping times $\tau : \Omega \to [s, t]$ for $0 \le s \le t \le T$, and let $\mathcal{S} \equiv \mathcal{S}_{[0,T]}$. The coefficients $r(\cdot)$, $\sigma(\cdot)$, and $b(\cdot)$ follow the usual setting (see Karatzas and Wang 2000) with the only difference that we require the following:

STANDING ASSUMPTION 11.1

We shall assume that the interest rate process is "locked-in" after retirement, namely, $r(t) = r(\tau)$ for any $t \in [\tau, T]$, and any $\tau \in \mathcal{S}_{[0,T]}$.

STANDING ASSUMPTION 11.2

We shall assume that the $m \times m$ matrix $\sigma(s)$ is invertible, we can define the "relative risk" process

$$\theta(s) \triangleq \sigma^{-1}(s)[b(s) - r(s)\mathbf{1}_m], \tag{11.3}$$

with $\mathbf{1}_m = (1, .., 1)^*$, the discount process.

$$\gamma(t) \triangleq \frac{1}{P_0(t)} = \exp\left\{-\int_0^t r(s)\mathrm{d}s\right\}, \tag{11.4}$$

the exponential martingale (or *likelihood ratio* process).

$$Z_0(t) \triangleq \exp\left\{-\int_0^t \theta(s)^*\mathrm{d}W(s) - \frac{1}{2}\int_0^t \| \theta(s) \|^2 \,\mathrm{d}s\right\} \tag{11.5}$$

and the state-price-density process

$$H(t) \triangleq \gamma(t)Z_0(t),\ 0 \le t \le T. \tag{11.6}$$

We shall also introduce the process $\{Y^{(t,y)}(s)\}_{\{s\ge t\}}$ defined as

$$Y^{(t,y)}(s) \triangleq \exp\left\{-\int_t^s (r(u)-\beta)\mathrm{d}u - \int_t^s \theta(u)'\mathrm{d}W_u \right.$$
$$\left. -\frac{1}{2}\int_t^s \| \theta(u) \|^2 \,\mathrm{d}u\right\},\ s \ge t,$$

which is an Itö process with linear dynamics

$$\mathrm{d}Y^{(t,y)}(s) = Y^{(t,y)}(s)\left[(\beta - r(s))\mathrm{d}s - \theta(s)'\mathrm{d}W(s)\right],\ Y^{(t,y)}(t) = y. \tag{11.7}$$

For simplicity, we shall denote

$$Y^y(t) \triangleq Y^{(0,y)}(t),\ 0 \le t \le T. \tag{11.8}$$

11.3 Portfolio and Wealth Processes

A *portfolio* $\pi(\cdot) = (\pi_1(\cdot), \ldots, \pi_m(\cdot))^*$ is an $\mathbf{R}^m$-valued process, and the *cumulative consumption* is a process takes $C : [0, T] \times \Omega \to [0, \infty)$ with increasing paths and $C(0) = 0$; these are both progressively measurable and satisfy

$$C(T) + \int_0^T \| \pi(t) \|^2 \,\mathrm{d}t < \infty, \ \text{a.s.}$$

Furthermore, we shall assume that the *cumulative consumption* process has a continuous and a singular part with respect to the Lebesgue measure, namely,

$$C(t) \triangleq \int_0^t c(u)\mathrm{d}u + \xi \cdot \mathbf{1}_{[\tau,T]}(t),\ 0 \le t \le T \tag{11.9}$$

is "the cumulative consumption up to time t." This process consists of a stopping time $\tau \in \mathcal{S}$, a consumption process $c(\cdot)$ positive and $\mathcal{F}$−progressively measurable, and an $\mathcal{F}_\tau$ measurable random variable $\xi : \Omega \to [0, \infty)$ representing the lump-sum consumption at time τ. We regard $\pi_i(t)$ as the proportion of an agent's wealth invested in stock i at time t; the remaining proportion $1 - \pi^*(t)\mathbf{1}_m = 1 - \sum_{i=1}^m \pi_i(t)$ is invested in the money market. These proportions are *not* constrained to take values in the interval $[0, 1]$; in other words, we allow both short selling of stocks and borrowing at the interest rate of the bond. For a given, nonrandom, initial capital $x > 0$, let $X(\cdot) = X^{x,\pi,C}(\cdot)$ denote the *wealth process* corresponding to a portfolio/consumption pair $(\pi(\cdot), C(\cdot))$ as above. This wealth process is defined by the initial condition $X^{x,\pi,C}(0) = x$ and the equation

$$\begin{aligned} dX(t) &= \sum_{i=1}^m \pi_i(t)X(t)\{b_i(t)dt + \sum_{i=1}^m \sigma_{ij}(t)dW_j(t)\} \\ &\quad + \{1 - \sum_{i=1}^m \pi_i(t)\}X(t)r(t)dt - dC(t) \\ &= r(t)X(t)dt + X(t)\pi^*(t)\sigma(t)dW_0(t) - dC(t), \qquad X(0) = x > 0, \end{aligned} \tag{11.10}$$

where we have set

$$W_0(t) \triangleq W(t) + \int_0^t \theta(s)ds, \qquad 0 \le t \le T. \tag{11.11}$$

In other words,

$$\begin{aligned} d(\gamma(t)X^{x,\pi,C}(t)) &= \gamma(t)X^{x,\pi,C}(t)\pi^*(t)\sigma(t)dW_0(t) \\ &\quad - \gamma(t)dC(t),\ 0 \le t \le T. \end{aligned} \tag{11.12}$$

The process $W_0(t)$ of Equation 11.11 is Brownian motion under the *equivalent martingale measure*

$$\mathbf{P}_0(A) \triangleq \mathbf{E}[Z_0(T)\mathbf{1}_A], \qquad A \in \mathcal{F}_T, \tag{11.13}$$

by the Girsanov theorem (Section 3.5 in Karatzas and Shreve (1991)). We shall say that a portfolio/consumption process pair is available at initial capital $x > 0$ if the corresponding wealth process $X^{x,\pi,C}(\cdot)$ is strictly positive on $[0, T]$ a.s. An application of Itö's rule to the product of the processes $Z_0(\cdot)$ and $\gamma(\cdot)X^{x,\pi,C}(\cdot)$ leads to

$$\begin{aligned} H(t)X^{x,\pi,C}(t) &+ \int_{(0,t]} H(s)dC(s) \\ &= x + \int_0^t H(s)X^{x,\pi,C}(s)(\sigma^*(s)\pi(s) - \theta(s))^*dW(s). \end{aligned} \tag{11.14}$$

This shows, in particular, that for any pair (π, C) available at initial capital $x > 0$, the process $H(\cdot)X^{x,\pi,C}(\cdot) + \int_{(0,\cdot]} H(s)\mathrm{d}C(s)$ is a continuous, positive local martingale, hence a supermartingale, under $\mathbf{P}$. Consequently, the optional sampling theorem gives

$$\mathbf{E}\left[H(\tau)X^{x,\pi,C}(\tau) + \int_{(0,\tau]} H(s)\mathrm{d}C(s)\right] \leq x, \qquad \tau \in \mathcal{S}_{[0,T]}. \quad (11.15)$$

11.4 Utility Function

A function $U : (0, \infty) \to \mathbf{R}$ will be called *utility function* if it is strictly increasing, strictly concave, continuously differentiable, and satisfies

$$U'(0+) \triangleq \lim_{x\to 0} U'(x) = \infty, \qquad U'(\infty) \triangleq \lim_{x\to\infty} U'(x) = 0. \quad (11.16)$$

We shall denote by $I(\cdot)$ the (continuous, strictly decreasing) inverse of the marginal utility function $U'(\cdot)$; this function maps $(0, \infty)$ onto itself and satisfies $I(0+) = \infty, I(\infty) = 0$. We also introduce the Legendre–Fenchel transform

$$\tilde{U}(y) \triangleq \max_{x>0}[U(x) - xy] = U(I(y)) - yI(y), \qquad 0 < y < \infty, \quad (11.17)$$

of $-U(-x)$; this function $\tilde{U}(\cdot)$ is strictly decreasing, strictly convex, and satisfies

$$\tilde{U}'(y) = -I(y), \qquad 0 < y < \infty, \quad (11.18)$$

$$U(x) = \min_{y>0}[\tilde{U}(y) + xy] = \tilde{U}(U'(x)) + xU'(x), \qquad 0 < x < \infty. \quad (11.19)$$

The inequality

$$U(I(y)) \geq U(x) + y[I(y) - x] \qquad x > 0, y > 0 \quad (11.20)$$

is a direct consequence of Equation 11.17.

11.5 The Optimization Problem in the Case $\pi_{(\tau,T]} \equiv 0$

The expression to be maximized has the form $\int_0^\tau \mathrm{e}^{-\beta t} U_1(c(t))\mathrm{d}t + \mathrm{e}^{-\beta\tau} U_2(\xi) + \int_\tau^T \mathrm{e}^{-\beta t} U_3(c(t))\mathrm{d}t$, where ξ represents a lump sum that the agent consumes at time τ. The utility functions $U_1(\cdot)$, $U_2(\cdot)$, $U_3(\cdot)$ measure his utility before and after retirement, respectively, whereas $\beta \geq 0$ stands for a discount factor. If the agent uses the portfolio/consumption strategy (π, C) available at initial capital $x > 0$, and the stopping rule $\tau \in \mathcal{S}$, his *expected discounted utility* is

$$J(x; \pi, C, \tau) \triangleq \mathbf{E}\left[\int_0^\tau e^{-\beta t} U_1(c(t))dt + e^{-\beta\tau} U_2(\xi) + \int_\tau^T e^{-\beta t} U_3(c(t))dt\right]. \tag{11.21}$$

The optimization problem considered in this chapter is the following: to maximize *the expected discounted utility* above over the class $\mathcal{A}(x)$ of (ξ, C, τ) of Equation 5.1, for which the expectation is well defined, that is,

$$\mathbf{E}\left[\int_0^\tau e^{-\beta t} U_1^-(c(t))dt + e^{-\beta\tau} U_2^-(\xi) + \int_\tau^T e^{-\beta t} U_3^-(c(t))dt\right] < \infty. \tag{11.22}$$

The value function of this problem will be denoted by

$$V(x) \triangleq \sup_{(\pi,C,\tau)\in\mathcal{A}(x)} \mathbf{E}\left[\int_0^\tau e^{-\beta t} U_1(c(t))dt + e^{-\beta\tau} U_2(\xi) + \int_\tau^T e^{-\beta t} U_3(c(t))dt\right]. \tag{11.23}$$

STANDING ASSUMPTION 11.3

$V(x) < \infty, \forall x \in (0, \infty)$.

REMARK 11.4

A sufficient condition for Standing Assumption 11.3 to hold, is that

$$\max\{U_1(x), U_2(x), U_3(x)\} \leq k_1 + k_2 x^\gamma, \ \forall x \in (0, \infty) \tag{11.24}$$

holds for some $k_1 > 0$, $k_2 > 0$, $\gamma \in (0, 1)$; cf. Remark 3.6.8 in Karatzas and Shreve (1998).

11.6 Duality Approach

For any stopping time $\tau \in \mathcal{S}_{[0,T]}$, we denote by $\Pi_\tau(x)$ the set of portfolio/consumption-rate processes triplets (π, C) for which $(\pi, C, \tau) \in \mathcal{A}(x)$. For fixed $\tau \in \mathcal{S}$, we consider the utility maximization problem

$$V_\tau(x) \triangleq \sup_{(\pi,C)\in\Pi_\tau(x)} J(x; \pi, C, \tau). \tag{11.25}$$

Not allowing our agent to invest in the stock market ($\pi_{(\tau,T]} \equiv 0$) after retirement, creates an incomplete market in which the problem is difficult to solve explicitly. However, under the additional Assumption (11.1) that the interest rate is locked after retirement, we can solve the optimization problem after retirement explicitly by pathwise optimization given the information available at retirement time $\mathcal{F}_\tau$. Equation 11.12 with $\pi_{(\tau,T]} \equiv 0$ implies that we have the following constraint

$$\int_\tau^\infty \gamma(t)c(t)\mathrm{d}t \leq \gamma(\tau)(X^{x,\pi,C} - \xi), \text{ a.s.} \tag{11.26}$$

In conjunction with Equation 11.15 this constraint leads to

$$\begin{aligned}
&\mathbf{E}\left[\frac{H(\tau)}{\gamma(\tau)}\int_\tau^T \gamma(t)c(t)\mathrm{d}t + H(\tau)\xi + \int_0^\tau H(s)c(s)\mathrm{d}s\right] \\
&\quad \leq \mathbf{E}\left[H(\tau)(X^{x,\pi,C}(\tau) - \xi) + H(\tau)\xi + \int_0^\tau H(s)c(s)\mathrm{d}s\right] \leq x.
\end{aligned}$$

The problem can be solved as usual, with the introduction of a Lagrange multiplier $\lambda > 0$:

$$\begin{aligned}
J(x;\pi,C,\tau) &= \mathbf{E}\left[\int_0^\tau \mathrm{e}^{-\beta t}U_1(c(t))\mathrm{d}t + \mathrm{e}^{-\beta\tau}U_2(\xi) + \int_\tau^T \mathrm{e}^{-\beta t}U_3(c(t))\mathrm{d}t\right] \\
&\leq \mathbf{E}\left[\int_0^\tau \mathrm{e}^{-\beta t}\tilde{U}_1(\lambda \mathrm{e}^{\beta t}H(t))\mathrm{d}t + \mathrm{e}^{-\beta\tau}\tilde{U}_2(\lambda \mathrm{e}^{\beta\tau}H(\tau))\right. \\
&\quad \left. + \int_\tau^T \mathrm{e}^{-\beta t}\tilde{U}_3\left(\lambda \mathrm{e}^{\beta t}\frac{H(\tau)}{\gamma(\tau)}\gamma(t)\right)\mathrm{d}t\right] \\
&\quad + \lambda \cdot \mathbf{E}\left[\int_0^\tau H(t)c(t)\mathrm{d}s + H(\tau)\xi + \frac{H(\tau)}{\gamma(\tau)}\int_\tau^T \gamma(t)c(t)\mathrm{d}t\right] \\
&\leq \mathbf{E}\left[\int_0^\tau \mathrm{e}^{-\beta t}\tilde{U}_1(\lambda \mathrm{e}^{\beta t}H(t))\mathrm{d}t + \mathrm{e}^{-\beta\tau}\tilde{U}_2(\lambda \mathrm{e}^{\beta\tau}H(\tau))\right. \\
&\quad \left. + \int_\tau^T \mathrm{e}^{-\beta t}\tilde{U}_3\left(\lambda \mathrm{e}^{\beta t}\frac{H(\tau)}{\gamma(\tau)}\gamma(t)\right)\mathrm{d}t\right] \\
&\quad + \lambda x
\end{aligned}$$

with equality if and only if

$$c(t) = \begin{cases} I_1(\lambda \mathrm{e}^{\beta t}H(t)) & 0 < t < \tau, \\ I_3\left(\lambda \mathrm{e}^{\beta t}\dfrac{H(\tau)}{\gamma(\tau)}\gamma(t)\right) & \tau < t \leq T. \end{cases} \tag{11.27}$$

$$\xi = I_2(\lambda \mathrm{e}^{\beta\tau}H(\tau)) \text{ and } X^{x,\pi,C} - \xi = \int_\tau^T \frac{\gamma(s)}{\gamma(\tau)} I_3\left(\lambda \mathrm{e}^{\beta s}\frac{H(\tau)}{\gamma(\tau)}\gamma(s)\right)\mathrm{d}s, \tag{11.28}$$

$$\mathbf{E}\left[\int_0^\tau H(t)c(t)\mathrm{d}t + H(\tau)\xi + \frac{H(\tau)}{\gamma(\tau)}\int_\tau^T \gamma(t)c(t)\mathrm{d}t\right] = x. \tag{11.29}$$

Note that Equation 11.26 is verified a.s. with the choice of $c(\cdot)$, $X - \xi$ defined above. In order to proceed we shall need the following assumption:

STANDING ASSUMPTION 11.5

$$\mathbf{E}\left[\sup_{0\le t\le T}\int_0^t H(s)I_3(\lambda e^{\beta t}H(t))\mathrm{d}s + H(t)\cdot\left(I_2(\lambda e^{\beta t}H(t)) + \int_t^T \frac{\gamma(s)}{\gamma(\tau)}I_3(\lambda e^{\beta s}\frac{H(\tau)}{\gamma(\tau)}\gamma(s))\mathrm{d}s\right)\right] < \infty$$

Under this assumption, for any given $\tau \in S$, the function $\mathcal{X}_\tau : (0,\infty) \to (0,\infty)$ defined by

$$\mathcal{X}_\tau(\lambda) \triangleq \mathbf{E}\left[\int_0^\tau H(s)I_1(\lambda e^{\beta s}H(s))\mathrm{d}s + H(\tau)\left(I_2\left(\lambda e^{\beta\tau}H(\tau)\right) + \int_\tau^T \frac{\gamma(s)}{\gamma(\tau)}I_3(\lambda e^{\beta s}\frac{H(\tau)}{\gamma(\tau)}\gamma(s))\mathrm{d}s\right)\right]$$

is a continuous, strictly decreasing mapping of $(0,\infty)$ onto itself with $\mathcal{X}_\tau(0+) = \infty$, $\mathcal{X}_\tau(\infty) = 0$; thus, $\lambda \to \mathcal{X}_\tau(\cdot)$ has a continuous, strictly decreasing inverse denoted by $\mathcal{Y}_\tau(\cdot)$ from $(0,\infty)$ to itself. Taking into account that we can rewrite $e^{\beta s}\frac{H(\tau)}{\gamma(\tau)}\gamma(s)$ as $e^{\beta\tau}H(\tau)e^{(\beta-r(\tau))(t-\tau)}$, we define

$$\xi^x = I_2(\mathcal{Y}_\tau(x)e^{\beta\tau}H(\tau)), \text{ and} \tag{11.30}$$

$$c_\tau(t) = \begin{cases} I_1(\mathcal{Y}_\tau(x)e^{\beta t}H(t)) & 0 < t < \tau, \\ I_3(\mathcal{Y}_\tau(x)e^{\beta\tau}H(\tau)e^{(\beta-r(\tau))(t-\tau)}) & \tau < t \le T, \end{cases} \tag{11.31}$$

so that, in particular, Equations (11.26) and (11.29) hold. The existence of the a portfolio is based on the market completeness assumption and is stated in the following lemma.

LEMMA 11.6

For any $\tau \in \mathcal{S}$, any positive measurable $\mathcal{F}_\tau$ random variable B with $P[B > 0] = 1$, and any progressively measurable consumption process

$c(\cdot) \geq 0$, such that $\mathbf{E}[\int_0^\tau H(s)c(s)ds + H(\tau)B] = x$, there exist a portfolio process $\pi(\cdot)$ that satisfies $\pi_{(\tau,T]} \equiv 0$ a.s. such that

$$X^{(x,\pi,C)} > 0,\ 0 \leq t < T \text{ and } X^{(x,\pi,C)}(\tau) = B. \tag{11.32}$$

Let us introduce some notations related to the dual problem, namely,

$$\tilde{J}(\lambda;\tau) \triangleq \mathbf{E}\left[\int_0^\tau e^{-\beta t}\tilde{U}_1(\lambda e^{\beta t}H(t))dt + e^{-\beta\tau}\tilde{U}_2(\lambda e^{\beta\tau}H(\tau)) + \int_\tau^T e^{-\beta t}\tilde{U}_3\left(\lambda e^{\beta t}\frac{H(\tau)}{\gamma(\tau)}\gamma(t)\right)dt\right]$$

and the dual value function

$$\begin{aligned}\tilde{V}(\lambda) &\triangleq \sup_{\tau\in\mathcal{S}}\tilde{J}(\lambda;\tau)\\ &= \sup_{\tau\in\mathcal{S}}\mathbf{E}\left[\int_0^\tau e^{-\beta t}\tilde{U}_1(\lambda e^{\beta t}H(t))dt + e^{-\beta\tau}\tilde{U}_2(\lambda e^{\beta\tau}H(\tau))\right.\\ &\quad\left. + \int_\tau^T e^{-\beta t}\tilde{U}_3\left(\lambda e^{\beta t}\frac{H(\tau)}{\gamma(\tau)}\gamma(t)\right)dt\right].\end{aligned} \tag{11.33}$$

To ensure that the problem is meaningful, we have to impose the following assumption throughout.

STANDING ASSUMPTION 11.7

For all $\lambda > 0$, we have $\tilde{V}(\lambda) < \infty$ and there exist a stopping time τ_λ, which is optimal in the previous expression such that $\tilde{V}(\lambda) = \tilde{J}(\lambda;\tau_\lambda)$.

The following lemma is a consequence of Equations 11.30–11.31 and Lemma 11.6.

PROPOSITION 11.8

Under Assumption 11.5, for any $\tau \in \mathcal{S}$ we have

$$V_\tau(x) = \inf_{\lambda>0}\left[\tilde{J}(\lambda;\tau) + \lambda x\right] = \tilde{J}(\mathcal{Y}_\tau(x);\tau) + \mathcal{Y}_\tau(x)x \tag{11.34}$$

and the supremum in Equation 11.25 is attained by the consumption strategy:

$$\xi^x = I_2(\mathcal{Y}_\tau(x)e^{\beta\tau}H(\tau)) \quad \text{and}$$

$$c_\tau(t) = \begin{cases} I_1(\mathcal{Y}_\tau(x)e^{\beta t}H(t)) & 0 < t < \tau, \\ I_3(\mathcal{Y}_\tau(x)e^{\beta\tau}H(\tau)e^{(\beta - r(\tau))(t-\tau)}) & \tau < t \le T, \end{cases} \tag{11.35}$$

and some portfolio $\hat{\pi}(\cdot)$ as guaranteed by Lemma 11.6. Moreover,

$$\begin{aligned} V(x) &= \sup_{\tau\in\mathcal{S}} V_\tau(x) = \sup_{\tau\in\mathcal{S}_0} \inf_{\lambda>0} \left[\tilde{J}(\lambda;\tau) + x\lambda\right] \\ &= \sup_{\tau\in\mathcal{S}_0} \inf_{\lambda>0} \left[\tilde{J}(\mathcal{Y}_\tau(x);\tau) + x\mathcal{Y}_\tau(x)\right]. \end{aligned}$$

We also have the following straightforward property

$$V(x) \le \sup_{\tau\in\mathcal{S}_0} \inf_{\lambda>0} \left[\tilde{J}(\lambda;\tau) + \lambda x\right] \le \inf_{\lambda>0} \left[\sup_{\tau\in\mathcal{S}_0} \tilde{J}(\lambda;\tau) + \lambda x\right] = \inf_{\lambda>0} \left[\tilde{V}(\lambda) + \lambda x\right].$$

In the following, we list some results

THEOREM 11.9

1. For any $x \in \mathcal{G} \triangleq \cup_{\lambda>0}\{\mathcal{X}_{\tau_\lambda}(\lambda)/\tau_\lambda$ is optimal for Equation 11.33$\}$,

$$V(x) = \inf_{\lambda>0} \left[\tilde{V}(\lambda) + \lambda x\right] \tag{11.36}$$

and the value function $V(x)$ is attainable.
2. If $x \in (0, \infty)$ such that the previous equality is satisfied, we have $x \in \mathcal{G}$.
3. If $\tilde{V}(\cdot)$ is differentiable everywhere then Equation 11.36 holds.

REMARK 11.10

A more general situation of why Equation 11.36 holds even though there is no optimal portfolio/consumption process will be provided at the end of the chapter by using randomized stopping times.

EXAMPLE 11.11

Utility Functions of Power Type. $U_j(x) = x^\alpha/\alpha$, where $0 < \alpha < 1$, $j = 1 : 3$. In this case we have that $I_j(y) = y^{-1/(1-\alpha)}$ and $\tilde{U}_j(y) = y^{-\gamma}/\gamma$ with $\gamma = -\alpha/(1-\alpha)$. We obtain easily

$$\tilde{V}(\lambda) = \sup_{\tau \in \mathcal{S}} \mathbf{E}\left[\int_0^\tau \mathrm{e}^{-\beta t}\tilde{U}_1(\lambda \mathrm{e}^{\beta t}H(t))\mathrm{d}t + \mathrm{e}^{-\beta\tau}\tilde{U}_2(\lambda \mathrm{e}^{\beta\tau}H(\tau)) + \mathrm{e}^{-\beta\tau}\int_0^{T-\tau} \mathrm{e}^{-\beta s}\tilde{U}_3(\lambda \mathrm{e}^{\beta\tau}H(\tau)\mathrm{e}^{(\beta - r(\tau))t})\mathrm{d}t\right] = \frac{K}{\gamma}\lambda^{-\gamma}$$

with

$$K \triangleq \sup_{\tau \in \mathcal{S}} \mathbf{E}\left[\int_0^\tau \mathrm{e}^{-(1+\gamma)\beta t}(H(t))^{-\gamma}\mathrm{d}t + \mathrm{e}^{-(1+\gamma)\beta\tau}H(\tau)^{-\gamma}\cdot \left(1 + \int_0^{T-\tau} \mathrm{e}^{-(\beta + (\beta - r(\tau))\gamma)s}\mathrm{d}s/\gamma\right)\right].$$

It is almost straightforward to check that $\hat{\tau} \equiv 0$, $K = 1$ if

$$\beta \geq \gamma\left[\frac{r(t)}{1+\gamma} + \frac{1}{2} \parallel \theta(t) \parallel^2\right], \ \forall\, 0 \leq t \leq T$$

holds a.s., and that $\hat{\tau} \equiv T$ if

$$\beta \leq \gamma\left[\frac{r(t)}{1+\gamma} + \frac{1}{2} \parallel \theta(t) \parallel^2\right], \ \forall\, 0 \leq t \leq T$$

holds a.s. Derivation of the optimal portfolio/consumption processes can be obtained from Lemma 11.6.

11.7 Infinite Horizon Case

We will extend now the convex duality method to the case of infinite horizon and discuss the constant coefficients case in detail. We assume that the market model remains the same for this case with the only exception that $T = \infty$. For the simplicity of the results, we make the additional assumption that the interest rate is fixed.

11.7.1 PORTFOLIO AND WEALTH PROCESSES

A *portfolio* $\pi(\cdot) = (\pi_1(\cdot), \ldots, \pi_m(\cdot))^*$ is an $\mathbf{R}^m$-valued process, and the *cumulative consumption* is a process takes $C : [0, \infty) \times \Omega \to [0, \infty)$ with increasing paths and $C(0) = 0$; these are both progressively measurable and satisfy

$$C(T) + \int_0^T \parallel \pi(t) \parallel^2 \mathrm{d}t < \infty, \ \forall \ T > 0 \ \text{a.s.}$$

Furthermore, we shall assume that the *cumulative consumption* process can be decomposed in a continuous and singular part with respect to the Lebesgue measure, namely,

$$C(t) \triangleq \int_0^t c(u)\mathrm{d}u + \xi \cdot \mathbf{1}_{([\tau,\infty))}(t) \cdot \mathbf{1}_{\{\tau<\infty\}}, \ 0 \le t < \infty \tag{11.37}$$

is "the cumulative consumption up to time t." This process consists of a stopping time $\tau \in \mathcal{S}_0$, a consumption process $c(\cdot)$ positive and $\mathcal{F}-$progressively measurable, and an $\mathcal{F}_\tau$ measurable random variable $\xi : \Omega \rightarrow [0, \infty)$ representing the lump-sum consumption at time τ. We regard $\pi_i(t)$ as the proportion of an agent's wealth invested in stock i at time t; the remaining proportion $1 - \pi^*(t)\mathbf{1}_m = 1 - \sum_{i=1}^m \pi_i(t)$ is invested in the money market. These proportions are *not* constrained to take values in the interval $[0, 1]$; in other words, we allow both short selling of stocks and borrowing at the interest rate of the bond. For a given, nonrandom, initial capital $x > 0$, let $X(\cdot) = X^{x,\pi,C}(\cdot)$ denote the *wealth process* corresponding to a portfolio/consumption pair $(\pi(\cdot), C(\cdot))$ as above. This wealth process is defined by the initial condition $X^{x,\pi,C}(0) = x$ and the equation

$$\begin{aligned} \mathrm{d}X(t) &= \sum_{i=1}^m \pi_i(t)X(t)\{b_i(t)\mathrm{d}t + \sum_{i=1}^m \sigma_{ij}(t)\mathrm{d}W_j(t)\} \\ &\quad + \{1 - \sum_{i=1}^m \pi_i(t)\}X(t)r\mathrm{d}t - \mathrm{d}C(t) \\ &= rX(t)\mathrm{d}t + X(t)\pi^*(t)\sigma(t)\mathrm{d}W_0(t) - \mathrm{d}C(t), \qquad X(0) = x > 0, \end{aligned} \tag{11.38}$$

where we have set

$$W_0(t) \triangleq W(t) + \int_0^t \theta(s)\mathrm{d}s, \qquad 0 \le t < \infty. \tag{11.39}$$

In other words

$$\mathrm{d}(\gamma(t)X^{x,\pi,C}(t)) = \gamma(t)X^{x,\pi,C}(t)\pi^*(t)\sigma(t)\mathrm{d}W_0(t) - \gamma(t)\mathrm{d}C(t), 0 \le t < \infty. \tag{11.40}$$

The process $W_0(t)$ of Equation 11.39 is Brownian motion under the *equivalent martingale measure*

$$\mathbf{P}_0(A) \triangleq \mathbf{E}[Z_0(T)\mathbf{1}_A], \qquad A \in \mathcal{F}_T \tag{11.41}$$

by the Girsanov theorem (Section 3.5 in Karatzas and Shreve (1991)). We shall say that a portfolio/consumption process pair is available at initial capital $x > 0$ if the corresponding wealth process $X^{x,\pi,C}(\cdot)$ is strictly positive on $[0, \infty)$ a.s. An application of Itö's rule to the product of the processes $Z_0(\cdot)$ and $\gamma(\cdot)X^{x,\pi,C}(\cdot)$ leads to

$$H(t)X^{x,\pi,C}(t) + \int_{(0,t]} H(s)\mathrm{d}C(s)$$
$$= x + \int_0^t H(s)X^{x,\pi,C}(s)(\sigma^*(s)\pi(s) - \theta(s))^*\mathrm{d}W(s), \qquad 0 < t < \infty. \quad (11.42)$$

This shows, in particular, that for any pair (π, C) available at initial capital $x > 0$, the process $H(\cdot)X^{x,\pi,C}(\cdot) + \int_{(0,\cdot]} H(s)\mathrm{d}C(s)$ is a continuous, positive local martingale, hence a supermartingale, under $\mathbf{P}$. Thus the limit $\lim_{t\to\infty} H(t)X^{x,\pi,C}(t) + \int_{(0,t]} H(s)\mathrm{d}C(s)$ exists *a.e.* and the optional sampling theorem gives

$$\mathbf{E}\left[H(\tau)X^{x,\pi,C}(\tau) + \int_{(0,\tau]} H(s)\mathrm{d}C(s)\right] \le x, \qquad \tau \in \mathcal{S}_0. \quad (11.43)$$

11.7.2 THE OPTIMIZATION PROBLEM

The infinite horizon problem has not been treated by Karatzas and Wang (2000) with the convex duality methods as it presents the challenge that wealth can be accumulated at $\tau = \infty$. For *fixed* stopping time $\tau \in \mathcal{S}_0$ define

$$J_\infty(x; \pi, C, \tau) \triangleq \mathbf{E}\left[\int_0^\tau e^{-\beta t}U_1(c(t)) + \left(e^{-\beta\tau}U_2(\xi) + \int_\tau^\infty e^{-\beta t}U_3(c(t))\mathrm{d}t\right)\cdot \mathbf{1}_{\{\tau<\infty\}}\right].$$

The optimization problem considered in this chapter is the following: to maximize *the expected discounted utility* above over the class $\mathcal{A}_\infty(x)$ of (π, C, τ), for which the expectation is well defined, that is,

$$\mathbf{E}\left[\int_0^\tau e^{-\beta t}U_1^-(c(t))\mathrm{d}t + \left(e^{-\beta\tau}U_2^-(\xi) + \int_\tau^\infty e^{-\beta t}U_3^-(c(t))\mathrm{d}t\right)\cdot \mathbf{1}_{\{\tau<\infty\}}\right] < \infty.$$

The value function of this problem will be denoted by

$$V_\infty(x) \triangleq \sup_{(\pi,C,\tau)\in\mathcal{A}_\infty(x)} \mathbf{E}\left[\int_0^\tau e^{-\beta t}U_1(c(t)) + \left(e^{-\beta\tau}U_2(\xi) + \int_\tau^\infty e^{-\beta t}U_3(c(t))\mathrm{d}t\right)\cdot \mathbf{1}_{\{\tau<\infty\}}\right]. \quad (11.44)$$

11.7.3 DUALITY APPROACH

Equation 11.42 with $\pi_{(\tau,\infty)} \equiv 0$ implies that we have the following constraint

$$\int_{\tau}^{\infty} \gamma(t)c(t)\mathrm{d}t \leq \gamma(\tau)(X^{x,\pi,C} - \xi), \text{ a.s., } \{\tau < \infty\}. \tag{11.45}$$

In conjunction with Equation 11.43 this constraint leads to

$$\mathbf{E}\left[\left(\frac{H(\tau)}{\gamma(\tau)}\int_{\tau}^{\infty} \gamma(t)c(t)\mathrm{d}t + H(\tau)\xi\right) \cdot \mathbf{1}_{\{\tau<\infty\}} + \int_0^{\tau} H(s)c(s)\mathrm{d}s\right]$$
$$\leq \mathbf{E}\left[\left(H(\tau)(X^{x,\pi,C}(\tau) - \xi) + H(\tau)\xi\right) \cdot \mathbf{1}_{\{\tau<\infty\}} + \int_0^{\tau} H(s)c(s)\mathrm{d}s\right] \leq x. \tag{11.46}$$

For *fixed* stopping time $\tau \in \mathcal{S}_0$, we denote by $\Pi_\tau(x)$ the fixed portfolio/consumption processes pairs (π, C) for which $(\pi, C, \tau) \in \mathcal{A}_\infty(x)$. The solution to the optimization problem

$$V_\tau(x) = \sup_{(\pi,C)\in\Pi_\tau(x)} J_\infty(x; \pi, C, \tau) \tag{11.47}$$

can be derived with some modifications in the same manner as in KLS (1987). To simplify notations, we will introduce the functions $\tilde{U}, I : (0,\infty) \to \mathbf{R}$.

DEFINITION 11.12

$$\tilde{U}(y) \triangleq \tilde{U}_2(y) + \int_0^{\infty} \mathrm{e}^{-\beta s}\tilde{U}_3(y\mathrm{e}^{(\beta-r)s})\mathrm{d}s,$$
$$I(y) \triangleq I_2(y) + \int_0^{\infty} \mathrm{e}^{-\beta s}I_3(y\mathrm{e}^{(\beta-r)s})\mathrm{d}s,$$

such that the Legendre–Fenchel transform of the convex function $\tilde{U}$ is an utility function that sums up the utility from consumption at and after retirement.

In terms of $\tilde{U}$, for any triple $(\pi, C, \tau) \in \mathcal{A}_\infty(x)$ and any real number $\lambda > 0$ using Equation 11.46

$$J_\infty(x; \pi, C, \tau) = \mathbf{E}\left[\int_0^{\tau} \mathrm{e}^{-\beta t}U_1(c(t))\mathrm{d}t + \left(\mathrm{e}^{-\beta\tau}U_2(\xi) + \int_{\tau}^{\infty} \mathrm{e}^{-\beta t}U_3(c(t))\mathrm{d}t\right)\right.$$
$$\left.\cdot\mathbf{1}_{\{\tau<\infty\}}\right]$$

$$\leq \mathbf{E}\Bigg[\int_0^\tau e^{-\beta t}\tilde{U}_1(\lambda e^{\beta t}H(t))dt + \Big(e^{-\beta\tau}\tilde{U}_2(\lambda e^{\beta\tau}H(\tau))$$

$$+ \int_\tau^\infty e^{-\beta t}\tilde{U}_3\left(\lambda e^{\beta t}\frac{H(\tau)}{\gamma(\tau)}\gamma(t)\right)dt\Big)\cdot \mathbf{1}_{\{\tau<\infty\}}\Bigg]$$

$$+\lambda\cdot\mathbf{E}\left[\int_0^\tau H(t)c(t)ds + \left(H(\tau)\xi + \frac{H(\tau)}{\gamma(\tau)}\int_\tau^\infty \gamma(t)c(t)dt\right)\cdot\mathbf{1}_{\{\tau<\infty\}}\right]$$

$$\leq \mathbf{E}\Bigg[\int_0^\tau e^{-\beta t}\tilde{U}_1(\lambda e^{\beta t}H(t))dt$$

$$+e^{-\beta\tau}\left(\tilde{U}_2(\lambda e^{\beta\tau}H(\tau)) + \int_0^\infty e^{-\beta s}\tilde{U}_3\left(\lambda e^{(\beta-r)s}e^{\beta\tau}H(\tau)\right)ds\right)\cdot\mathbf{1}_{\{\tau<\infty\}}\Bigg] + \lambda x$$

$$= \mathbf{E}\left[\int_0^\tau e^{-\beta t}\tilde{U}_1(\lambda e^{\beta t}H(t))dt + e^{-\beta\tau}\tilde{U}(\lambda e^{\beta\tau}H(\tau))\cdot\mathbf{1}_{\{\tau<\infty\}}\right] + \lambda x$$

with equality only if and only if

$$c(t) = \begin{cases} I_1(\lambda e^{\beta t}H(t)) & 0 < t < \tau, \\ I_3\left(\lambda e^{\beta t}\dfrac{H(\tau)}{\gamma(\tau)}\gamma(t)\right) & \tau < t < \infty, \end{cases} \tag{11.48}$$

$$\text{on } \{\tau < \infty\},\ \xi = I_2(\lambda e^{\beta\tau}H(\tau)),\ \text{and } X^{x,\pi,C}(\tau) - \xi$$
$$= \int_\tau^\infty \frac{\gamma(s)}{\gamma(\tau)}I_3\left(\lambda e^{\beta s}\frac{H(\tau)}{\gamma(\tau)}\gamma(s)\right)ds$$

$$\mathbf{E}\left[\int_0^\tau H(t)c(t)dt + \left(H(\tau)\xi + \frac{H(\tau)}{\gamma(\tau)}\int_\tau^\infty \gamma(t)c(t)dt\right)\cdot\mathbf{1}_{\{\tau<\infty\}}\right] = x. \tag{11.50}$$

In order for both Equations 11.47 and 11.43 to hold, it is necessary

$$\limsup_{t\to\infty} H(t)X^{x,\pi,C}(t) \equiv 0,\ \text{on } \{\tau = \infty\}. \tag{11.51}$$

Let us recall the quantities associated with the dual value function from the finite horizon case (e.g., $\mathcal{X}_\tau(\cdot)$ and $\tilde{V}(\cdot)$ of Equation 11.33)

$$\tilde{J}_\infty(\lambda;\tau) \triangleq \mathbf{E}\left[\int_0^\tau e^{-\beta t}\tilde{U}_1(\lambda e^{\beta t}H(t))dt + e^{-\beta\tau}\tilde{U}(\lambda e^{\beta\tau}H(\tau))\cdot\mathbf{1}_{\{\tau<\infty\}}\right], \tag{11.52}$$

$$\tilde{V}_\infty(\lambda) \triangleq \sup_{\tau\in\mathcal{S}_0}\tilde{J}_\infty(\lambda;\tau)$$
$$= \sup_{\tau\in\mathcal{S}_0}\mathbf{E}\left[\int_0^\tau e^{-\beta t}\tilde{U}_1(\lambda e^{\beta t}H(t))dt + e^{-\beta\tau}\tilde{U}(\lambda e^{\beta\tau}H(\tau))\cdot\mathbf{1}_{\{\tau<\infty\}}\right], \tag{11.53}$$

$$\mathcal{X}_\tau^\infty(\lambda) \triangleq \mathbf{E}\left[\int_0^\tau H(s)I_1(\lambda e^{\beta s}H(s))ds + H(\tau)I(\lambda e^{\beta\tau}H(\tau))\cdot\mathbf{1}_{\{\tau<\infty\}}\right]. \tag{11.54}$$

In order to ensure that the above quantities are well defined we shall need the following assumption.

ASSUMPTION 11.13

$$\mathbf{E}\left[\sup_{0\le t<\infty}\int_0^t H(s)I_3(\lambda e^{\beta t}H(t))ds + H(t)I(\lambda e^{\beta t}H(t))\right] < \infty,\ \forall\lambda > 0.$$

All the arguments from the finite horizon case stand except for Lemma 11.6 because of the additional requirement (Eq. 11.51). We state now the infinite horizon version of this lemma.

LEMMA 11.14

For any $\tau \in \mathcal{S}_0$, any positive progressively measurable process $B(t)$ with $B(\tau) > 0$, on $\{\tau < \infty\}$ and any progressively measurable consumption process $c(\cdot) \ge 0$ that satisfies $c(\cdot) \equiv 0$ *a.e.* on (τ, ∞) on $\{\tau < \infty\}$ as well as $\mathbf{E}\left[\int_0^\tau c(s)H(s)ds + H(\tau)B(\tau)\cdot \mathbf{1}_{\{\tau<\infty\}}\right] = x$, there exist a portfolio process $\pi(\cdot)$ that satisfies $\pi_{(\tau,\infty)} \equiv 0$ on $\{\tau < \infty\}$ a.e. such that

$$X^{(x,\pi,C)} > 0,\ 0 \le t < \infty \text{ and } X^{(x,\pi,C)}(\tau) = B(\tau) \text{ on } \{\tau < \infty\},$$
$$\limsup_{t\to\infty} H(t)X^{(x,\pi,C)}(t) \equiv 0, \text{ on } \{\tau = \infty\}.$$

Proof. Consider the positive process

$$X(t) = \frac{1}{\gamma(t)}\mathbf{E}_0\left[\gamma(\tau)B(\tau)\cdot\mathbf{1}_{\{\tau<\infty\}} + \int_{t\wedge\tau}^{\tau} c(s)ds\middle|\mathcal{F}_t\right],\ 0 \le t < \infty,$$

which is strictly positive on $\{\tau < \infty\}$. This process satisfies

$$\begin{aligned} X(0) &= \mathbf{E}_0\left[\int_0^\tau \gamma(s)c(s)ds + \gamma(\tau)B(\tau)\cdot\mathbf{1}_{\{\tau<\infty\}}\middle|\mathcal{F}_0\right] \\ &= \mathbf{E}\left[\int_0^\tau H(s)c(s)ds + H(\tau)B(\tau)\cdot\mathbf{1}_{\{\tau<\infty\}}\right] = x, \end{aligned}$$

and $X(\tau) = B(\tau)\cdot\mathbf{1}_{\{\tau<\infty\}}$. On the other hand, the $\mathbb{P}_0$-martingale

$$\begin{aligned} M(\cdot) &\triangleq \gamma(\cdot)X(\cdot) + \int_0^{\cdot\wedge\tau}\gamma(s)c(s)ds \\ &= \mathbf{E}_0\left[\gamma(\tau)B(\tau)\cdot\mathbf{1}_{\{\tau<\infty\}} + \int_{t\wedge\tau}^{\tau} c(s)ds\middle|\mathcal{F}_t\right] \end{aligned}$$

admits the stochastic integral representation

$$M(t) = x + \int_0^t \psi^*(s)\mathrm{d}W_0(s),\ 0 \leq t < \infty,$$

for some $\mathbb{F}-$ adapted process $\psi(\cdot)$ that satisfies $\int_0^T \parallel \psi(s) \parallel^2 \mathrm{d}s < \infty$, for all $T > 0$ (e.g., Karatzas and Shreve (1998), Theorem 4.15). By the continuity of the Brownian filtration and integrability of $H(\tau)B(\tau) \cdot \mathbf{1}_{\{\tau<\infty\}} + \int_0^\tau c(s)H(s)\mathrm{d}s$, we have

$$\begin{aligned}\lim_{t\to\infty} H(t)X^{(x,\pi,C)}(t) &= \lim_{t\to\infty} \mathbf{E}\left[H(\tau)B(\tau) \cdot \mathbf{1}_{\{\tau<\infty\}} + \int_{t\wedge\tau}^{\tau} c(s)H(s)\mathrm{d}s \middle| \mathcal{F}_t\right] \\ &= H(\tau)B(\tau) \cdot \mathbf{1}_{\{\tau<\infty\}},\end{aligned}$$

which concludes the proof. ■

11.7.4 THE CASE OF CONSTANT COEFFICIENTS

In what follows we shall try to convert the original optimization problem into a family of *pure optimal stopping* problems for which we have a better understanding. We provide an explicit solution for the optimization problem in a Markovian setting for some general utility functions $U_1(\cdot)$, $U_2(\cdot)$, and $U_3(\cdot)$. In order to obtain an explicit solution, we place ourselves on an infinite time-horizon so that all stopping times $\tau \in \mathcal{S}_0$ are admissible. Furthermore, we assume that the coefficients of the model $r(\cdot) \equiv r$, $b(\cdot) \equiv b$, $\sigma(\cdot) \equiv \sigma > 0$, are constant and we impose the assumption $b \neq r\mathbf{1}_m$, or equivalently, $\theta(\cdot) \equiv \theta \neq 0_m$.

Before we proceed, we need to introduce some notations and prove some results.

11.7.5 SOME RESULTS ON OPTIMAL STOPPING FOR ONE-DIMENSIONAL DIFFUSIONS

Consider the one-dimensional diffusion process driven by an m-dimensional Brownian motion $\{W_t\}$

$$\mathrm{d}Y(t) = (\beta - r)Y(t)\mathrm{d}t - Y(t)\theta\mathrm{d}W_t,\ Y(0) \in (0,\infty) \qquad (11.55)$$

and the optimal stopping problem

$$W(y) = \sup_{\tau\in\mathcal{S}_0} \mathbf{E}_y\left[\mathrm{e}^{-\beta\tau}h(Y(\tau)) \cdot \mathbf{1}_{\{\tau<\infty\}}\right]. \qquad (11.56)$$

Here $\mathbf{E}_y$ denotes expectation given $Y(0) = y$, $h : (0,\infty) \to \mathbf{R}^+$ is assumed to be $C^2((0,\infty))$. Consider the differential operator $\mathcal{L}$ acting on functions $\phi : (0,\infty) \to \mathbf{R}$ which are twice continuously differentiable is defined as follows:

$$\mathcal{L}\phi \triangleq \frac{1}{2} \parallel \theta \parallel^2 y^2\phi_{yy} + (\beta - r)y\phi_y - \beta\phi.$$

There are two linearly independent *fundamental solutions*, $\psi(x) = x^{\rho_+}$ monotonically increasing and $\varphi(x) = x^{\rho_-}$ monotonically decreasing spanning the set of solutions of the ordinary differential equation $\mathcal{L}u = 0$. Here ρ_+, ρ_- are the solutions to the following quadratic equation

$$\parallel \theta \parallel^2 /2\rho^2 + (\beta - r - \theta^2/2)\rho - \beta = 0. \tag{11.57}$$

and we can verify that due to $r > 0$, $\beta > 0$ we have $\rho_+ > 1$ and $\rho_- < 0$. In terms of the these fundamental solutions, we have this useful representation (e.g., Dayanik and Karatzas (2003), equality (11.7))

$$\mathbf{E}_x\left[e^{-\beta\tau_y}\right] = \begin{cases} \dfrac{\psi(x)}{\psi(y)}, & x \le y, \\ \dfrac{\varphi(x)}{\varphi(y)}, & x > y. \end{cases} \tag{11.58}$$

In order for $W(y) < \infty$, $\forall y \in (0, \infty)$, we need to impose the following assumption cf. Dayanik and Karatzas (2003), Proposition 5.7

STANDING ASSUMPTION 11.15

$$l_0 = x \downarrow 0 \frac{h^+(x)}{x^{\rho_-}} < \infty, \text{ and } l_\infty = x \uparrow \infty \frac{h^+(x)}{x^{\rho_+}}.$$

Let us denote by

$$\tau_x \triangleq \inf\{t \ge 0 \ / \ Y(t) = x\}, \ x > 0,$$

the first hitting time of level x. The reduction of the optimal stopping problem to the Brownian motion case has been studied by Dayanik and Karatzas in the case when the diffusion was driven by one-dimensional Brownian motion. Their results hold also for the case in which we have a m-dimensional Brownian motion with the only modification in the equation solved by the Green functions ψ and φ. Still, the problem is solved explicitly for the Brownian motion case by using a graphical method. By taking advantage of the theory developed in Dayanik and Karatzas (2003), in terms of the existence of an optimal stopping time and provided that we can either solve or determine the shape of intervals that form

$$C_0 \triangleq \{y > 0/\mathcal{L}g(y) > 0\}, \tag{11.59}$$

then the value function is the supremum over stopping times which are exit times from open intervals that contain C_0. This observation appears everywhere in literature (see Karatzas and Wang (2000), Oksendal (1998), etc.) but it is either solved on a specific case or under some uniform integrability conditions for the reward and boundness of the optimal stopping time. We clearly formulate this for the case in which C_0 is an open interval which contains the left or right boundary of the diffusion $Y(t)$ in the next proposition.

PROPOSITION 11.16

Provided that there exist an optimal stopping time, the value function $W(\cdot)$ of Equation 11.56 has the following form

1. If $C_0 = (0, a)$ then $C_* \triangleq \sup_{y>0} \frac{h(y)}{y^{\rho+}} = \max_{y>0} \frac{h(y)}{y^{\rho+}} < \infty$. By denoting with a_*, the largest value such that $\frac{h(a_*)}{a_*^{\rho+}} = C_*$, we have $a < a_* < \infty$. With this notations, the value function $W(\cdot)$ is $C^1((0,\infty))$ and given by

$$W(y) = \begin{cases} C_* y^{\rho+} & y \in (0, a_*), \\ h(y) & y \in [a_*, \infty), \end{cases} \tag{11.60}$$

and the optimal stopping time is $\tau_{(0,a^*)} = \inf\{t \geq 0 / Y(t) \notin (0, a_*)\}$.

2. If $C_0 = (0, a)$ then $C_* \triangleq \sup_{y>0} \frac{h(y)}{y^{\rho-}} = \max_{y>0} \frac{h(y)}{y^{\rho-}} < \infty$. By denoting with a_*, the lowest value such that $\frac{h(a_*)}{a_*^{\rho-}} = C_*$, we have $0 < a_* < a$. With this notations, the value function $W(\cdot)$ is $C^1((0,\infty))$ and given by

$$W(y) = \begin{cases} h(y) & y \in (0, a_*), \\ C_* y^{\rho+} & y \in [a_*, \infty), \end{cases} \tag{11.61}$$

and the optimal stopping time is $\tau_{(a^*,\infty)} = \inf\{t \geq 0 Y(t) \notin (a_*, \infty)\}$.

Proof. We proceed in two steps. First, we prove that there exist an open interval $(0, a_*)$ that contains C_0, such that the stopping time $\tau_{(0,a_*)}$ is optimal for all $y \leq a_*$ and maximal. Second, we prove that for $y \in (a_*, \infty)$, it is sufficient to restrict ourself to stopping times bounded by $\tau_{(0,a_*)}$ and the maximum over this stopping times is attained for $\tau \equiv 0$.

Step 1. First we need to prove that if suffices to restrict ourself to stopping times that are exit times from open intervals of $(0, \infty)$, namely,

$$W(y) = \sup_{0 \leq l \leq y \leq r \leq \infty} \mathbf{E}_y \left[e^{-\beta \tau_l \wedge \tau_r} h(Y(\tau_l \wedge \tau_r)) \cdot \mathbf{1}_{\{\tau_l \wedge \tau_r < \infty\}} \right]. \tag{11.62}$$

To prove this, let us consider the value function of Equation 11.56. By the continuity of the value function as proved in Dayanik and Karatzas (2003), the continuation region defined

$$\mathcal{C} = \{x > 0 / W(x) > h(x)\}$$

is an open set of $(0, \infty)$. By the countability of the topological base of the ordinary topology on $\mathbf{R}$, C can be written as a disjoint union of open intervals of $(0, \infty)$. Moreover, provided that there exist a stopping time, τ_* defined as

$$\tau_* \triangleq \inf\{t \geq 0 / Y(t) \notin \mathcal{C}\}$$

is an optimal stopping time and we have

$$W(y) = \mathbf{E}_y \left[e^{-\beta \tau_*} h(Y(\tau_*)) \cdot \mathbf{1}_{\{\tau_* < \infty\}} \right].$$

It is straightforward that

$$\sup_{0 \leq l \leq y \leq r \leq \infty} \mathbf{E}_y \left[e^{-\beta \tau_l \wedge \tau_r} h(Y(\tau_l \wedge \tau_r)) \cdot \mathbf{1}_{\{\tau_l \wedge \tau_r < \infty\}} \right]$$
$$\leq \mathbf{E}_y \left[e^{-\beta \tau_*} h(Y(\tau_*)) \cdot \mathbf{1}_{\{\tau_* < \infty\}} \right] = W(y)$$

and taking into account that τ_* is an exit time from open disjoint intervals, implies that

$$\sup_{0 \leq l \leq y \leq r \leq \infty} \mathbf{E}_y \left[e^{-\beta \tau_l \wedge \tau_r} h(Y(\tau_l \wedge \tau_r)) \cdot \mathbf{1}_{\{\tau_l \wedge \tau_r < \infty\}} \right] \geq W(y).$$

This proves the other direction of the inequality and concludes Equation 11.62. Next, we need to prove that C_0 is included in the continuation region $\mathcal{C}$. Fix $y \in C_0$ then there exist $\varepsilon > 0$ such that $(y - \varepsilon, y + \varepsilon)$ is included in C_0. By Dynkin's formula taking into account that h is $C^2((0, \infty))$, $\mathbf{E}_y \left[\tau_{y-\varepsilon} \wedge \tau_{y+\varepsilon} \right] < \infty$, we have

$$\mathbf{E}_y[e^{-\beta \tau_{y-\varepsilon} \wedge \tau_{y+\varepsilon}} h(Y(\tau_{y-\varepsilon} \wedge \tau_{y+\varepsilon}))] = h(y) + \mathbf{E}_y \left[\int_0^{\tau_{y-\varepsilon} \wedge \tau_{y+\varepsilon}} \mathcal{L}h(Y(t)) \mathrm{d}t \right] > h(y).$$

This implies that $y \in \mathcal{C}$ and therefore the region $(0, a) \subset \mathcal{C}$.
Fix $y \in C_0$ and taking into account that C_0 is included into the continuation region $\mathcal{C}$, it suffices to maximize Equation 11.62 over intervals of form $(0, x)$ with $x \geq a$.

$$\begin{aligned} W(y) &= \sup_{\{x > 0 / y \leq x\}} \mathbf{E}_y \left[e^{-\beta \tau_x} h(Y(\tau_x)) \right] = \sup_{\{x \geq a\}} \mathbf{E}_y \left[e^{-\beta \tau_x} h(Y(\tau_x)) \cdot \mathbf{1}_{\{\tau_x < \infty\}} \right], \\ &= \sup_{\{x \geq a\}} h(x) \cdot \mathbf{E}_y \left[e^{-\beta \tau_x} \cdot \mathbf{1}_{\{\tau_x < \infty\}} \right] = \sup_{\{x \geq a\}} \left(\frac{y}{x} \right)^{\rho_+} h(x), \\ &= \sup_{\{x \geq a\}} \frac{h(x)}{x^{\rho_+}} \cdot y_+^{\rho}. \end{aligned} \tag{11.63}$$

Here we used the fact that by Equation 11.58 and monotone convergence theorem, we have $\mathbf{E}_y[\mathrm{e}^{-\beta\tau_x}] = \mathbf{E}_y\left[\mathrm{e}^{-\beta\tau_x}\cdot\mathbf{1}_{\{\tau_x<\infty\}}\right] = \left(\frac{y}{x}\right)^{\rho+}$, for $y \le x$. If $C_* = \sup_{\{x|0<x\}}\frac{h(x)}{x^{\rho+}} = \infty$, then we will prove that this contradicts the fact that the value function is finite. By Equation 11.40, we have for all $\varepsilon > 0$, there exist $x_0 > 0$ such $\frac{h(x)}{x^{\rho-}} < (l_0+\varepsilon)$ for all $x < x_0$. This implies

$$\frac{h(x)}{x^{\rho+}} \le (l_0+\varepsilon)\frac{x^{\rho-}}{x^{\rho+}} \le (l_0+\varepsilon)\frac{x_0^{\rho-}}{x_0^{\rho+}},\ \forall x < x_0$$

so the function $\frac{h(x)}{x^{\rho+}}$ is bounded in a neighborhood of 0. If $C_* = \infty$ then there exist a sequence x_n convergent to $x_0 > 0$ such that $\lim\frac{h(x_n)}{x_n^{\rho+}} \to \infty$. Then by choosing $y < x_0$ we have

$$W(y) \ge \lim_n \mathbf{E}_y[\mathrm{e}^{-\beta\tau_{x_n}}h(Y(\tau_{x_n}))] = \lim_n \frac{h(x_n)}{x_n^{\rho+}}y_+^{\rho} = \infty$$

contradicting that the value function is finite. Thus the supremum in Equation 11.63 is attained for some $a_* \in (a,\infty)$. To conclude the proof that for $y \in C_0$, τ_{a_*} is an optimal stopping time let us notice that

$$\mathbf{E}_y[\mathrm{e}^{-\beta\tau}h(Y(\tau))\cdot\mathbf{1}_{\{\tau<\infty\}}] = \mathbf{E}_y\left[\frac{h(Y(\tau))}{Y(\tau)^{\rho+}}\mathrm{e}^{-\beta\tau}Y(\tau)^{\rho+}\cdot\mathbf{1}_{\{\tau<\infty\}}\right]$$
$$\le C_*\mathbf{E}_y\left[\mathrm{e}^{-\beta\tau}Y(\tau)^{\rho+}\cdot\mathbf{1}_{\{\tau<\infty\}}\right] \le C_*y^{\rho+},\ \forall y\in C_0,$$

and choosing stopping time $\tau = \tau_{a_*}$ proves the other direction of the inequality. The maximum in Equation 11.63, it is not unique and for $y \in C_0$, any a_* that attains the maximum in Equation 11.63 will be optimal. By choosing a_* to be the largest value implies that $(0, a_*)$ the maximal element that contains C_0. This implies that for any $y \in (a_*,\infty)$, we have by Equation 11.62 that

$$\begin{aligned} W(y) &= \sup_{a_*<l\le y\le r\le\infty}\mathbf{E}_y\left[\mathrm{e}^{-\beta\tau_l\wedge\tau_r}h(Y(\tau_l\wedge\tau_r))\right], \\ &= \sup_\tau \mathbf{E}_y\left[\mathrm{e}^{-\beta\tau\wedge\tau_{a*}}h(Y(\tau\wedge\tau_{a*}))\cdot\mathbf{1}_{\{\tau\wedge\tau_{a*}<\infty\}}\right]. \quad (11.64)\end{aligned}$$

Step 2. We will prove that for any $y \in (a_*,\infty)$ we have $W(y) = h(y)$. Note that it suffices to prove that $W(y) \le h(y)$ for any $y \in (a_*,\infty)$. By applying Ito's rule to the stopped diffusion, $\mathrm{e}^{-\beta t\wedge\tau_{a*}}h(Y(t\wedge\tau_{a*}))$, we have that

$$\mathrm{e}^{-\beta t}h(Y^y(t\wedge\tau_{a_*}) = h(y) + \int_0^{t\wedge\tau_{a*}}\mathcal{L}h(Y^y(t))\mathrm{d}t - \int_0^{t\wedge\tau_{a*}}h'(Y_t)\theta\,\mathrm{d}W_t, t\ge 0.$$

Taking into account that $h(\cdot)$ is positive, the positive, local supermartingale $\{\mathrm{e}^{-\beta t\wedge\tau_{a*}}h(Y(t\wedge\tau_{a_*}))\}$ is a true supermartingale and, in particular,

$\lim_{t\to\infty} \mathrm{e}^{-\beta t\wedge\tau_{(a*,\infty)}} h(Y^y(t \wedge \tau_{(a_*,\infty)}))$ exists a.s. By the Optional sampling theorem, we now have that

$$\mathbf{E}_y[\mathrm{e}^{\beta\tau\wedge\tau_{a*}} h(Y(\tau \wedge \tau_{a_*}))\mathbf{1}_{\{\tau<\infty\}}] \le \mathbf{E}[\mathrm{e}^{\beta\tau\wedge\tau_{a*}} h(Y(\tau \wedge \tau_{a_*}))] \le h(y)$$

holds for any stopping time $\tau \in \mathcal{S}_0$.
This implies that for any $y \in (a_*, \infty)$ we have that

$$W(y) = \sup_{\tau\in\mathcal{S}} \mathbf{E}[\mathrm{e}^{-\beta\tau\wedge\tau_{(a*,\infty)}} h(Y^y(\tau \wedge \tau_{(a_*,\infty)}))] \le h(y)$$

and that the supremum is attained for $\tau \equiv 0$.
Differentiability of $W(\cdot)$ in a_* comes from observing that due to the differentiability of $h(\cdot)$, and the fact that a_* is a maximum point of $\frac{h(y)}{y^{\rho+}}$ implies $\frac{\mathrm{d}}{\mathrm{d}y}\frac{h(y)}{y^{\rho+}}|_{y=a_*} = 0$ and as a consequence

$$\frac{\mathrm{d}}{\mathrm{d}y}\frac{h(y)}{y^{\rho+}}|_{y=a_*} = \frac{\mathrm{d}}{\mathrm{d}y} C_* y^{\rho+}|_{y=a_*},$$

gives the "smooth-fit." This completes the proof of Case 1 of this proposition. Case 2 follows by same type of reasoning.

■

REMARK 11.17

Sufficient and necessary conditions for the existence of optimal stopping times for infinite horizon one-dimensional diffusions have been established by Karatzas and Dayanik. Note that although their theory requires that the diffusion is driven by a one-dimensional Brownian motion, their results hold for our case and a sufficient assumption for the existence of an optimal stopping time is (Proposition 5.14 Dayanik and Karatzas (2003))

ASSUMPTION 11.18

$$l_0 = \limsup_{x\downarrow 0} \frac{h(x)}{\varphi(x)} = 0, \text{ and } \limsup_{x\uparrow\infty} \frac{h(x)}{\psi(x)} = 0.$$

We can also solve using the same method problems of the type

$$W(y) = \sup_{\tau\in\mathcal{S}_0} \mathbf{E}\left[\int_0^\tau \mathrm{e}^{-\beta t} f(Y^y(t))\mathrm{d}t + \mathrm{e}^{-\beta\tau} h(Y^y(\tau)) \cdot \mathbf{1}_{\{\tau<\infty\}}\right], \qquad (11.65)$$

where $f(\cdot), h(\cdot) : (0,\infty) \to \mathbf{R}$ are assumed to be $C^2((0,\infty))$. As a consequence of the strong Markov Property, we can furthermore simplify the expression (Eq. 11.65)

$$
\begin{aligned}
W(y) &= \mathbf{E}\left[\int_0^{\infty} \mathrm{e}^{-\beta t} f(Y^y(t))\mathrm{d}t - \int_{\tau}^{\infty} \mathrm{e}^{-\beta t} f(Y^y(t))\mathrm{d}t + \mathrm{e}^{-\beta\tau} h(Y^y(\tau)) \cdot \mathbf{1}_{\{\tau<\infty\}}\right] \\
&= (R_\beta f)(y) + \mathbf{E}\left[\left(\mathrm{e}^{-\beta\tau}(h(Y^y(\tau)) - (R_\beta f)(Y^y(\tau))\right) \cdot \mathbf{1}_{\{\tau<\infty\}}\right], \qquad (11.66)
\end{aligned}
$$

where the $(R_\beta f)(\lambda)$ can be calculated by probabilistic methods using the Green function and speed measure, see Alvarez (2001) p. 319., Karatzas and Shreve (1998) p. 148

$$
\begin{aligned}
(R_\beta f)(y) &\triangleq \mathbf{E}\left[\int_0^{\infty} \mathrm{e}^{-\beta t} f(Y^y(t))\mathrm{d}t\right] \\
&= \frac{1}{(\rho_+ - \rho_-)\theta^2/2}\left[y^{\rho_-}\int_0^y \eta^{-\rho_- -1} f(\eta)\mathrm{d}\eta + y^{\rho_+}\int_y^{\infty} \eta^{-\rho_+ -1} f(\eta)\mathrm{d}\eta\right].
\end{aligned}
\qquad (11.67)
$$

The following proposition is an extension of general results (e.g., Theorem 9.3.3 in Oksendal (1998)) for the specific case of one-dimensional diffusions, to accommodate the case in which the stopping time is ∞ with strictly positive probability.

STANDING ASSUMPTION 11.19

[Proposition 11.19 Solution of the Combined Stochastic and Dirichlet Problem] Let τ_D be the first exit time of the diffusion $Y(t)$ from the open domain $D \subset (0,\infty)$ and ϕ be $C((0,\infty))$. Then

$$
w(x) \triangleq \mathbf{E}_x\left[\mathrm{e}^{-\beta\tau_D}\phi(Y(\tau_D))\mathbf{1}_{\{\tau_D<\infty\}}\right] \qquad (11.68)
$$

verifies

$$
\mathcal{L}w = 0, \text{ in } D, \qquad (11.69)
$$

$$
\lim_{t\to\tau_D} w(Y^y(t)) = \phi(Y^y(\tau_D)) \text{ on}\{\tau_D < \infty\}. \qquad (11.70)
$$

Proof. D open can be represented as a disjoint union of open intervals. There are two types of these intervals one that contain the left or the right bound of the diffusion (e.g., $(0,a)$ or (a,∞)) and intervals of type (a,b) with $0 < a < b < \infty$. For the second type of intervals the problem verifies the conditions from the classical theory (e.g., Theorem 9.3.3 in Oksendal (1998)). The problem with intervals that contain either the right or left limit of the diffusion process (i.e., 0 or ∞) is that the first exit time can be ∞ with strictly positive probability and thus the classical conditions are not verified. Let us study now this case, namely, $D = (0, a)$ with $a > 0$. Direct computation gives

$$w_a(x) \triangleq \mathbf{E}_x\left[\phi(Y(\tau_a))\mathbf{1}_{\{\tau_a<\infty\}}\right] = \phi(a)\frac{\psi(x)}{\psi(a)}.$$

Thus, $w(x)$ is $C^2((0, a))$ satisfies Equation 11.69 and is continuous on $(0, a]$. Equation 11.70 is a consequence of the continuity of $Y(t)$. The proof when $D = (a, \infty)$ is similar. ■

11.7.6 EXPLICIT FORMULAS FOR THE RETIREMENT PROBLEM

Let us write now the value function for the constant coefficients case. For fixed stopping time τ, in terms of $\tilde{U}(\cdot)$, $I(\cdot)$ and the diffusion $Y(t)$, $\mathcal{X}_\tau^\infty(\cdot)$ and the dual value function $\tilde{V}_\infty(\cdot)$ of Equations 7.18 and 7.17, respectively, become

$$\begin{aligned}
\mathcal{X}_\tau^\infty(\lambda) &= \mathbf{E}\left[\int_0^\tau H(s)I_1(\lambda e^{\beta s}H(s))\mathrm{d}s + H(\tau)I(\lambda e^{\beta\tau}H(\tau))) \cdot \mathbf{1}_{\{\tau<\infty\}}\right], \\
&= \frac{1}{\lambda} \cdot \mathbf{E}_\lambda\left[\int_0^\tau e^{-\beta s}Y(s)I_1(Y(s))\mathrm{d}s + e^{-\beta\tau}Y(\tau)I(Y(\tau)) \cdot \mathbf{1}_{\{\tau<\infty\}}\right], \qquad (11.71)
\end{aligned}$$

$$\begin{aligned}
\tilde{V}_\infty(\lambda) &= \sup_{\tau\in\mathcal{S}_0} \mathbf{E}\left[\int_0^\tau e^{-\beta t}\tilde{U}_1(\lambda e^{\beta t}H(t))\mathrm{d}t + e^{-\beta\tau}\tilde{U}(\lambda e^{\beta\tau}H(\tau)) \cdot \mathbf{1}_{\{\tau<\infty\}}\right], \\
&= \sup_{\tau\in\mathcal{S}_0} \mathbf{E}_\lambda\left[\int_0^\tau e^{-\beta t}\tilde{U}_1(Y(t))\mathrm{d}t + e^{-\beta\tau}\tilde{U}(Y(\tau)) \cdot \mathbf{1}_{\{\tau<\infty\}}\right]. \qquad (11.72)
\end{aligned}$$

Recall that the inverse of the continuous, strictly increasing function $\mathcal{X}_\tau^\infty(\cdot)$ is denoted $\mathcal{Y}_\tau^\infty(\cdot)$. Under Assumption 11.38 (e.g., if Assumption 11.42 holds) an optimal stopping time exists, the continuation region

$$\mathcal{C} \triangleq \{y > 0/\tilde{V}_\infty(y) > \tilde{U}(y)\},$$

and the stopping time defined $\tau_\lambda \triangleq \inf\{t \geq /Y^\lambda(t) \notin \mathcal{C}\}$ is optimal in Equation 11.72.

PROPOSITION 11.20

With the notations defined above provided that Assumption 11.13 holds, we do not have a duality gap

$$V_\infty(x) = \inf_{\lambda>0}\left[\tilde{V}_\infty(\lambda) + \lambda x\right] \qquad (11.73)$$

and $V_\infty(x)$ is attainable for any $x > 0$. Given initial wealth $x > 0$, there exist a unique $y = \mathcal{Y}_{\tau_*}^{\infty}(x)$ that attains the minimum in the RHS of Equation 11.73; the stopping time $\tau^* = \tau_y$, which is the first exit time of the process $Y^y(t)$ from the open set $\mathcal{C}$ is optimal.

Proof. The value function $\tilde{V}_\infty(\cdot)$ of Equation 11.72, satisfies the "smooth-fit" principle, namely, is $C^1((0,\infty))$ by Dayanik and Karatzas (2003), Corollary 7.1. Thus, $\tilde{V}_\infty(\cdot)$ is $C^1((0,\infty))$ and by Theorem 6.5 2. implies that we do not have a duality gap, namely, the equality (Eq. 11.73) holds and the value function $V_\infty(\cdot)$ is attainable for any initial wealth $x > 0$. ■

PROPOSITION 11.21

For fixed initial wealth $x > 0$, $\tau^* \triangleq \tau_{\mathcal{Y}_{\tau^*}^{\infty}(x)}$ is the optimal stopping time and the optimal wealth process is given by

$$X^x(s) = \mathcal{X}_{\tau^*}^{\infty}(Y^{\mathcal{Y}_{\tau^*}^{\infty}(x)}(s)) \cdot \mathbf{1}_{\{\tau^* < \infty\}},\ 0 \le s \le \tau_*, \tag{11.74}$$

where $\mathcal{X}_{\tau^*}^{\infty}(\cdot)$ is $C^2(\mathcal{C}) \cap C(\bar{\mathcal{C}})$ is the solution of the boundary value problem

$$\frac{1}{2} \parallel \theta \parallel^2 y^2 \mathcal{X}_{\tau_*}^{\infty\prime\prime}(y) + (\parallel \theta \parallel^2 - r + \beta) y \mathcal{X}_{\tau_*}^{\infty\prime}(y) - r\mathcal{X}_{\tau_*}(y)$$

$$= -I(y), y \in \mathcal{C}, \tag{11.75}$$

$$\lim_{t \to \tau_*} \mathcal{X}_{\tau_*}^{\infty}(Y^y(t)) = I(Y^y(\tau_*)), a.s.;\ \forall y \in \mathcal{C}. \tag{11.76}$$

In terms of $X^x(\cdot)$, the optimal portfolio and the consumption/rate processes $\Pi_\infty^x(\cdot)$ and $c^x(\cdot)$ are given, in the feedback form

$$\Pi_\infty^x(t) = \begin{cases} -(\sigma\sigma')^{-1}[b - r\mathbf{1}_m] \dfrac{\mathcal{Y}_{\tau_*}^{\infty}(X^x(t))}{\mathcal{Y}_{\tau_*}^{\infty\prime}(X^x(t))} & 0 \le t \le \tau, \\ 0 & \tau_* < t, \end{cases} \tag{11.77}$$

$$c^x(t) = \begin{cases} I_1(\mathcal{Y}_{\tau_*}^{\infty}(X^x(t))) & 0 \le t < \tau_*, \\ I_3(\mathcal{Y}_{\tau}^{\infty}(X^x(\tau_*))e^{(\beta-r)(t-\tau_*)}) & \tau_* < t, \end{cases} \tag{11.78}$$

$$\xi = I_2(\mathcal{Y}_{\tau_*}^{\infty}(X^x(\tau_*))), \tag{11.79}$$

$$\tau_* = \inf\{t \ge 0 / X^x(t) \notin \mathcal{X}_{\tau_*}^{\infty}(\mathcal{C})\}. \tag{11.80}$$

Proof. The proof follows the reasoning of Karatzas and Shreve (1998) p.144 Corrolary 9.15. Let $x \in \mathcal{X}_{\tau_*}^{\infty}(\mathcal{C})$ be given and denote with $y = \mathcal{Y}_{\tau^*}^{\infty}(x)$. The optimal wealth at $t = \tau^*$ is given by Equation 11.49,

$$X^x(\tau_*) = \int_0^{\tau_*} H(s) I_1\left(ye^{\beta s} H(s)\right) \mathrm{d}s + H(\tau_*) \cdot I\left(ye^{\beta\tau_*} H(\tau_*)\right) \cdot \mathbf{1}_{\{\tau_* < \infty\}},$$

and the optimal wealth process with initial condition x is given by the proof of Lemma 11.14

$$\begin{aligned} X^x(t) &= \frac{1}{\gamma(t)} \mathbf{E}_0 \left[\gamma(\tau_*) I(Y^y(\tau)) + \int_{t\wedge\tau_*}^{\tau_*} \gamma(s) I_1(Y^y(s)) \mathrm{d}s \middle| \mathcal{F}_t \right], \\ &= \frac{1}{\gamma(t)} \mathbf{E}_0 \left[\gamma(\tau_*) I\left(Y^y(t) \frac{Y^y(\tau_*)}{Y^y(t)} \right) + \int_{t\wedge\tau_*}^{\tau_*} \gamma(s) I_1\left(Y^y(t) \frac{Y^y(s)}{Y^y(t)} \right) \mathrm{d}s \middle| Y^y(t) \right], \\ &= \frac{1}{\gamma(t)} \mathbf{E}_{Y^y(t)} \left[\gamma(t)\gamma(\tau) I(Y(\tau)) + \gamma(t) \int_0^{\tau} \gamma(s) I_1(Y(s)) \mathrm{d}s \right], \\ &= \mathbf{E}_{Y^y(t)} \left[\gamma(\tau) I(Y(\tau)) + \int_0^{\tau} \gamma(s) I_1(Y(s)) \mathrm{d}s \right], \\ &= \mathcal{X}_{\tau_*}^{\infty}(Y^y(t)), \end{aligned}$$

using the strong Markov property of $Y(t)$. Define $S_{\tau*}^{\infty}(x)$ by

$$S_{\tau^*}^{\infty}(x) \triangleq \mathbf{E}_x \left[\int_0^{\tau^*} e^{-\beta s} Y(s) I_1(Y(s)) \mathrm{d}s + e^{-\beta\tau^*} Y(\tau^*) I(Y(\tau^*)) \cdot \mathbf{1}_{\{\tau^* < \infty\}} \right],$$

then function $S_{\tau_*}^{\infty}(x)$ by Proposition 11.19 is $C^2(\mathcal{C}) \cap C(\bar{\mathcal{C}})$ and verifies

$$\begin{aligned} &\mathcal{L} S_{\tau_*}^{\infty}(x) + y I_1(x) = 0;\ x \in \mathcal{C}, \\ &\lim_{t\to\tau_*} S_{\tau_*}^{\infty}(Y^x(t)) = Y(\tau^*) I(Y^x(\tau^*)),\ a.s.;\ \{\tau^* < \infty\}\ \forall x \in \mathcal{C}. \end{aligned}$$

Since $S_{\tau_*}^{\infty}(x) = x\mathcal{X}_{\tau_*}^{\infty}(x)$, it follows that $\mathcal{X}_{\tau_*}^{\infty}(\cdot)$ is $C^2(\mathcal{C}) \cap C(\bar{\mathcal{C}})$ and solves the boundary value problem

$$\begin{aligned} &\frac{1}{2} \parallel \theta \parallel^2 y^2 \mathcal{X}_{\tau_*}^{\infty\prime\prime}(y) + (\parallel \theta \parallel^2 - r + \beta) y \mathcal{X}_{\tau_*}^{\infty\prime}(y) - r\mathcal{X}_{\tau_*}(y) \\ &\quad = -I(y), y \in \mathcal{C}, && (11.81) \\ &\lim_{t\to\tau_*} \mathcal{X}_{\tau_*}^{\infty}(Y^y(t)) = I(Y^y(\tau_*)), a.s.;\ \forall y \in \mathcal{C}. && (11.82) \end{aligned}$$

The function $x \to \mathcal{X}_{\tau_*}^{\infty}(x)$ is $C^2(\mathcal{C}) \cap C(\bar{\mathcal{C}})$, and by applying Ito's rule the process $t \to \mathcal{X}_{\tau_*}^{\infty}(Y(t \wedge \tau_*))$ in conjunction with Equation 11.81, we have

$$\mathrm{d}(e^{-rt}\mathcal{X}_{\tau_*}^{\infty}(Y(t))) = -e^{(\beta-r)t} Y(t) \mathcal{X}_{\tau_*}^{\infty\prime}(Y(t)) \theta \mathrm{d}W_0(t) - e^{-\beta t} Y(t) I_1(Y(t)) \mathrm{d}t,$$

and a comparison with Equation 11.40 shows that the optimal portfolio process is

$$\pi(x) = -(\sigma)^{-1}\theta e^{\beta t} Y^y(t) \mathcal{X}_{\tau^*}^{\infty\prime}(e^{\beta t} Y^y(t)).$$

But $e^{\beta t} Y^y(t) = \mathcal{Y}_{\tau^*}^{\infty}(X^x(t))$, and by the implicit functions theorem $\mathcal{Y}_{\tau^*}^{\infty}(\cdot) \in C^2(\mathcal{X}_{\tau^*}^{\infty}(\mathcal{C}))$, we have

$$\mathcal{X}_{\tau^*}^{\infty\prime}(\mathcal{Y}_{\tau^*}^{\infty}(x))\mathcal{Y}_{\tau^*}^{\infty\prime}(x) = 1, \ \forall x \in \mathcal{X}_{\tau^*}^{\infty}(\mathcal{C}).$$

Taking into account that $\mathcal{X}_{\tau^*}^{\infty\prime}(e^{\beta t} Y^y(t)) = 1/\mathcal{Y}_{\tau^*}^{\infty\prime}(X(t))$, which proves Equation 11.77. ■

EXAMPLE 11.22

Logarithmic Utility Functions. $U_1(x) = \alpha \log(x)$, $U_2(x) = \log x$, and $U_3(x) = \log x$.

In this case, we have $I_2(y) = 1/y$, $\tilde{U}_2(y) = -\log y - 1$. Let us note that the linear transformation of an utility $U_1 \triangleq aU(\cdot) + b$, then its Legendre–Fenchel transform can be expressed in terms of the dual

$$\begin{aligned}\tilde{U}_1(\lambda) &= \sup_{x>0}(aU(x) + b - \lambda x) = b + a \sup_{x>0}\left(U(x) - \frac{\lambda}{a}x\right)\\ &= b + a\tilde{U}(\lambda/a).\end{aligned}$$

The optimization problem and the dual value function (Eq. 11.72) are

$$V_\infty(x) = \sup_{(\pi,C,\tau)\in\mathcal{A}_\infty(x)} \mathbf{E}\left[\alpha \int_0^\tau \log c(t)dt + \left(e^{-\beta\tau}\log\xi + \int_\tau^\infty \log c(t)dt\right)\cdot \mathbf{1}_{\{\tau<\infty\}}\right],$$

$$\begin{aligned}\tilde{V}_\infty(\lambda) &= \sup_{\tau\in\mathcal{S}_0} \mathbf{E}\left[\int_0^\tau e^{-\beta t}\tilde{U}_1(\lambda e^{\beta t}H(t))dt + \left(e^{-\beta\tau}(\tilde{U}(Y^\lambda(\tau)))\right)\cdot \mathbf{1}_{\{\tau<\infty\}}\right],\\ &= \alpha(R_\beta U_1)(\lambda/\alpha) + \sup_{\tau\in\mathcal{S}_0} \mathbf{E}_\lambda\left[e^{-\beta\tau}\left(\tilde{U}(Y(\tau)) - \alpha(R_\beta U_1)(Y(\tau)/\alpha)\right)\cdot \mathbf{1}_{\{\tau<\infty\}}\right].\end{aligned}$$

We can use formulas (Eq. 11.67) and compute the resolvent $(R_\beta \tilde{U}_1)(y) \triangleq \frac{-\log y - 1}{\beta} - \frac{\beta - r - \theta^2/2}{\beta^2}$ and $\alpha(R_\beta\tilde{U}_1)(y/\alpha) = (\alpha/\beta)(-\log y - 1) - \frac{\alpha}{\beta^2}(\beta - r - \theta^2/2 + \log\alpha)$. Straightforward computations yield the utility after retirement Definition (11.48)

$$\tilde{U}(y) = \frac{-\log y - 1}{\beta} + \frac{r-\beta}{\beta^2} + (-\log y - 1),$$

$$\tilde{U}(y) - \alpha(R_\beta\tilde{U}_1)(y/\alpha) = \tilde{U}_2(y) + \int_0^\infty e^{-\beta s}(-\log(ye^{(\beta-r)s}) - 1)ds - \alpha(R_\beta\tilde{U}_1)(y/\alpha),$$

$$= \frac{\beta + 1 - \alpha}{\beta}(-\log y - 1) + \frac{r - \beta + \alpha(r - \beta + \theta^2/2 - \log\alpha)}{\beta^2}.$$

In order to ensure that an optimal stopping time exists and the value function is finite, we compute

$$l_0 = \limsup_{y\to 0} \frac{\tilde{U}(y) - \alpha(R_\beta \tilde{U}_1)(y/\alpha)}{x^{\rho_-}} = 0, l_\infty = \limsup_{y\to\infty} \frac{\tilde{U}(y) - \alpha(R_\beta \tilde{U}_1)(y/\alpha)}{x^{\rho_+}} = 0,$$

thus, an optimal stopping time exists by Assumption 11.18.

The hypothesis of Proposition 11.16 are verified, the optimal stopping time will be an exit time of the process $Y(t)$ from an open interval that contains

$$C_0 \triangleq \{y > 0/\mathcal{L}\tilde{U}(y) > 0\} = \begin{cases} (0, a) & \beta + 1 - \alpha < 0, \\ (a, \infty) & \beta + 1 - \alpha > 0, \end{cases}$$

with $a = \mathrm{e}^{\frac{\|\theta\|^2/2 + r - (\alpha - 1)}{(\alpha-1)-\beta}}$. This enables us to determine the shape of the continuation region, namely, either a hitting time of a lower level or a hitting time of a upper level and divide the problem in two parts according to this.

Case 1. We have $\beta + 1 < \alpha$. We can now proceed and compute the optimal stopping boundary using Proposition 11.16

$$a_* \triangleq argmax_{y>0} \frac{\tilde{U}(y) - \alpha(R_\beta \tilde{U}_1)(y/\alpha)}{y^{\rho_+}} = \mathrm{e}^{1/\rho_+ - 1 + \frac{r - \beta + \alpha(r - \beta + \theta^2/2 - \log\alpha)}{\beta(\beta + 1 - \alpha)}}$$

and denote with $C^* \triangleq \tilde{U}(a_*) - \alpha(R_\beta \tilde{U}_1)(a_*/\alpha)$. This gives us the optimal stopping time in the state price form

$$\tau_\lambda = \inf\{t \geq 0/Y^\lambda(t) \geq a_*\}.$$

The solution of the optimal stopping time gives us the value of the dual problem by Proposition 11.16

$$\tilde{V}_\infty(y) = \begin{cases} (y/a_*)^{\rho_+} C^* + \alpha(R_\beta \tilde{U}_1)(y/\alpha) & y \in \mathcal{C} = \{0 \leq y \leq a_*\}, \\ \tilde{U}(y) & y \in \mathcal{S} = \{y > a_*\}. \end{cases}$$

We can now compute the optimal portfolio/consumption process using the Proposition 11.21

$$\mathcal{X}^\infty_{\tau_*}(y) = -\tilde{V}'_\infty(y) = \begin{cases} -\rho_+(y/a_*)^{\rho_+ - 1}\dfrac{C^*}{a_*} - (R_\beta \tilde{U}_1)'(y/\alpha) & y \in \mathcal{C} = \{0 \leq y \leq a_*\}, \\ -\tilde{U}'(y) & y \in \mathcal{S} = \{y > a_*\}, \end{cases}$$

and as usual we denote with $\mathcal{Y}^\infty_{\tau_*}(\cdot) \triangleq \mathcal{X}^{\infty\,-1}_{\tau_*}(\cdot)$, which does not have a closed form. The optimal wealth process $X^x(\cdot)$ is given by Equation 11.74

$$X^x(t) = \mathcal{X}_{\tau_*}^{\infty}(Y^{\mathcal{Y}_{\tau_*}^{\infty}(x)}(t)),\ 0 \le t \le \tau_*.$$

In terms of $X^x(\cdot)$, the optimal portfolio and consumption/rate processes $\Pi_\infty^x(\cdot)$, $c^{(t,x)}$ are given, in the feedback form by formulas 11.77–11.80,

$$\Pi^x(t) = \begin{cases} -(\sigma\sigma')^{-1}[b - r\mathbf{1}_d]\dfrac{\mathcal{Y}_{\tau_*}^{\infty}(X^x(t))}{\mathcal{Y}_{\tau_*}^{\infty}(X^x(t))} & 0 \le t \le \tau_*, \\ 0 & \tau_* \le t, \end{cases}$$

$$= \begin{cases} (\sigma\sigma')^{-1}[b - r\mathbf{1}_d]\left(\rho_+(\rho_+ - 1)\mathcal{Y}_{\tau_*}^{\infty}(X^x(t))^{\rho_+ - 1}\dfrac{C_*}{a_*^{\rho_+}} + \dfrac{\alpha}{\beta\mathcal{Y}_{\tau_*}^{\infty}(X^x(t))}\right) & 0 \le t \le \tau_*, \\ 0 & \tau_* \le t, \end{cases}$$

$$c^x(t) = \begin{cases} I_1(\mathcal{Y}_{\tau_*}^{\infty}(X^x(t))) & 0 \le t \le \tau_*, \\ X^{(x)}(\tau)\dfrac{\beta}{1+\beta}e^{(r-\beta)(t-\tau_*)} & \tau_* \le t, \end{cases}$$

$$\tau_* = \inf\{t \ge 0/X^x(t) \le \mathcal{X}_{\tau_*}(a_*)\},$$

$$\xi = \frac{\beta}{1+\beta}X^x(\tau),$$

respectively.

REMARK 11.23

Note that the case in which $\alpha > \beta + 1$ corresponds to the situation of an agent that has a bigger utility before stopping and after stopping, and that is why he just keeps a small portion of his wealth for retirement. The situation $\beta + 1 > \alpha$ follows a similar manner, only that we are stopping when the wealth attains a level high enough to ensure "happy" consumption through the retirement. Note that it is possible that agent never retires, namely, $P(\tau_* < \infty) < 1$ iff $\beta - r - \parallel \theta \parallel^2 /2 < 0$.

Case 2. ($\beta + 1 > 0$). Let us consider now the situation in which we do not have utility from consumption before the retirement ($\alpha = 0$). This implies that $\beta + 1 > 0$ where the shape of the continuation region is different and everything can be solved explicitly.

$$a_* = e^{1/\rho_- 1 + \dfrac{r-\beta}{\beta(\beta+1)}},$$

$$\tau_* = \inf\{t \ge 0 | Y(t) \le a_*\},$$

$$\tilde{V}_\infty(y) = \begin{cases} -\dfrac{\beta+1}{\beta\rho_-}(y/a_*)^{\rho_-} & y \ge a_*, \\ \dfrac{\beta+1}{\beta}(-\log y - 1) + \dfrac{r-\beta}{\beta^2} & 0 < y \le a_*, \end{cases}$$

$$\mathcal{X}_{\tau_*}^{\infty}(y) = \begin{cases} \dfrac{\beta+1}{\beta a_*}(y/a_*)^{\rho_-1} & y \geq a_*, \\ \dfrac{\beta+1}{\beta}\dfrac{1}{y} & 0 < y \leq a_*, \end{cases}$$

$$\mathcal{Y}_{\tau_*}^{\infty}(y) = \begin{cases} \dfrac{\beta}{\beta+1}^{1/(\rho_-1)} a_*^{\rho_-/(\rho_-1)} y^{1/(\rho_-1)} & 0 < y \leq \dfrac{\beta+1}{\beta a_*}, \\ \dfrac{\beta+1}{\beta}\dfrac{1}{y} & \dfrac{\beta+1}{\beta a_*} < y. \end{cases}$$

The optimal wealth can be expressed now in terms of the state price process and $\mathcal{Y}_{\tau_*}^{\infty}(\cdot)$. In terms of $X^x(\cdot)$, the optimal portfolio and consumption/rate processes $\Pi_{\infty}^{x}(\cdot)$, (c, ξ) are given, in the feedback form by

$$\Pi_{\infty}^{x}(t) = \begin{cases} -(\sigma\sigma')^{-1}[b - r\mathbf{1}_d](\rho_-1)X^x(t) & 0 \leq t \leq \tau_*, \\ 0 & \tau_* \leq t, \end{cases}$$

$$c^x(t) = \begin{cases} 0 & 0 \leq t \leq \tau_*, \\ X^x(\tau)\dfrac{\beta}{1+\beta}e^{(r-\beta)(t-\tau_*)} & \tau_* \leq t, \end{cases}$$

$$\tau_* = \inf\{t \geq 0/X^x(t) \geq \mathcal{X}_{\tau_*}(a_*) = \frac{\beta+1}{\beta}e^{-1/\rho_-+1-\frac{r-\beta}{\beta(\beta+1)}}\},$$

$$\xi = \frac{\beta}{1+\beta}X^x(\tau),$$

respectively.

REMARK 11.24

Note that $P(\tau_* < \infty) = 1$ if $\beta - r - \theta^2/2 < 0$ and $P(\tau_* < \infty) < 1$, if $\beta - r - \theta^2/2 > 0$.

REFERENCES

Alvarez L. Reward functionals, salvage values, and optimal stopping. Math Meth Oper Res 2001;54:315–337.

Cox J, Huang CF. Optimal consumption and portfolio policies when asset prices follow a diffusion process. J Econ Theor 1989;49:33–83.

Dayanik S, Karatzas I. On the optimal stopping problem for one-dimensional diffusions. Stoch Proc Appl 2003;107:173–212.

Jeanblanc M, Lakner P. Optimal bankruptcy time and consumption/investment policies on an infinite horizon with a continuous debt repayment until bankruptcy, preprint. New York: New York University; 2001.

Jeanblanc M, Lakner P, Kadam A. Optimal bankruptcy time and consumption/investment policies on an infinite horizon with a continuous debt repayment until bankruptcy. Math Oper Res 2004;29:649–671.

Karatzas I, Lehoczky JP, Shreve SE. Optimal portfolio and consumption decisions for a small investor on a finite time-horizon. SIAM J Control Optim 1987;25:1557–1586.

Karatzas I, Shreve SE. Brownian motion and stochastic calculus. 2nd ed. New York: Springer; 1991.

Karatzas I, Shreve SE. Methods of mathematical finance. New York: Springer; 1998.

Karatzas I, Wang H. Utility maximization with discretionary stopping. SIAM J Control Optim 2000;39:306–329.

Koike S, Morimoto H. Optimal consumption with choice with stopping. Funkcialaj Ekvacioj 2005;48:183–202.

Merton RC. Optimum consumption and portfolio rules in continuous-time model. J Econ Theor 1971;3:373–413; Erratum, 6 (1973), 213–214.

Oksendal B. Stochastic differential equations. 5th ed. New York: Springer; 1998.

Pliska SR. A stochastic calculus model of continuous trading: optimal portfolios. Math Oper Res 1986;11:371–382.

Samuelson PA, Merton RC. A complete model of warrant-pricing that maximizes utility. Ind Manag Rev 1969;10:17–46.

CHAPTER TWELVE

Stochastic Differential Equations and Levy Models with Applications to High Frequency Data

ERNEST BARANY
Department of Mathematical Sciences, New Mexico State University, Las Cruces, NM
MARIA PIA BECCAR VARELA
Department of Mathematical Sciences, University of Texas at El Paso, El Paso, TX

12.1 Solutions to Stochastic Differential Equations

We first present some necessary steps in order to find an analytical solution for a class of stochastic differential equations (SDEs) that arises in population models. Consider the following nonlinear SDE for the stochastic process $X = \{X_t : t \in T\}$:

$$\mathrm{d}X_t = rX_t(k - X_t^m)\mathrm{d}t + \beta X_t \mathrm{d}B_t \tag{12.1}$$

Handbook of Modeling High-Frequency Data in Finance, First Edition.
Edited by Frederi G. Viens, Maria C. Mariani, and Ionuţ Florescu.

where B_t indicates the Brownian motion [1–3].

If $m = 2$ this equation arises in modeling the growth of a population of size X_t in a stochastic, crowded environment. The constant $k > 0$ is called the *carrying capacity* of the environment, the constant $r \in R$ is the growth rate and is a measure of the quality of the environment, and the constant $\beta \in R$ is a measure of the strength of the noise in the system.

Step 1. It is possible to find an integrating factor F_t for Equation 12.1 In this case, F_t is given by

$$F_t = \exp\left(-\beta B_t + \frac{1}{2}\beta^2 t\right)$$

More generally, if we consider the following SDE

$$dX_t = f(t, X_t)dt + c(t)X_t dB_t$$

then

$$F_t = \exp\left(-\int_0^t c(s)dB_s + \frac{1}{2}\int_0^t c(s)^2 ds\right).$$

In this case, $c(s) = \beta$ constant, so

$$F_t = \exp\left(-\int_0^t \beta dB_s + \frac{1}{2}\int_0^t \beta^2 ds\right) = \exp\left(-\beta B_t + \frac{1}{2}\beta^2 t\right)$$

Step 2. We know that for X_t, Y_t Ito's processes:

$$d(X_t Y_t) = X_t dY_t + Y_t dX_t + dX_t dY_t.$$

This formula is also called *integration by parts*, or *derivative of a product* for two stochastic processes.

The proof of this identity is done by using the two dimensional Ito's formula below, and $(dX_t)^2$, $(dY_t)^2$, $dX_t dY_t$ are computed by using that $dtdt = dtdB_t = dB_t dt = 0$, and $dB_t dB_t = dt$.

THEOREM 12.1

Two dimensional Ito's formula:

If X_t and Y_t are Ito's processes given by

$$dX_t = \mu_1 dt + v_1 dB_t$$

$$\mathrm{d}Y_t = \mu_2 \mathrm{d}t + v_2 \mathrm{d}B_t$$

and $Z_t = g(t, X_t, Y_t)$, where g is a C^2 function, then Z_t is also an Ito's process and

$$\begin{aligned} \mathrm{d}(Z_t) = \mathrm{d}(g(t, X_t, Y_t)) &= \frac{\partial g}{\partial t}(t, X_t, Y_t)\mathrm{d}t + \frac{\partial g}{\partial x}(t, X_t, Y_t)\mathrm{d}X_t \\ &+ \frac{\partial g}{\partial y}(t, X_t, Y_t)\mathrm{d}Y_t + \frac{1}{2}\frac{\partial^2 g}{\partial x^2}(t, X_t, Y_t)(\mathrm{d}X_t)^2 \\ &+ \frac{1}{2}\frac{\partial^2 g}{\partial y^2}(t, X_t, Y_t)(\mathrm{d}Y_t)^2 + \frac{\partial^2 g}{\partial x \partial y}(t, X_t, Y_t)\mathrm{d}X_t \mathrm{d}Y_t. \end{aligned}$$

Step 3. Compute dF_t.

In order to compute $\mathrm{d}F_t$, we will use the one-dimensional Ito's formula below:

THEOREM 12.2

One-dimensional Ito's formula. If Z_t is an Ito's process given by

$$\mathrm{d}Z_t = \mu \mathrm{d}t + v \mathrm{d}B_t$$

and $Y_t = g(t, Z_t)$ where g is a C^2 function, then Y_t is also an Ito's process and

$$\mathrm{d}Y_t = \frac{\partial g}{\partial t}(t, Z_t)\mathrm{d}t + \frac{\partial g}{\partial x}(t, Z_t)\mathrm{d}B_t + \frac{1}{2}\frac{\partial^2 g}{\partial x^2}(t, Z_t)(\mathrm{d}Z_t)^2.$$

In this case, as F_t is given by

$$F_t = \exp\left(-\beta B_t + \frac{1}{2}\beta^2 t\right),$$

then we can take $Z_t = B_t$ in the one-dimensional Ito's formula above, that is, $\mu = 0$, $v = 1$, and $Y_t = F_t = g(t, B_t)$, with

$$g(t, x) = \exp\left(-\beta x + \frac{1}{2}\beta^2 t\right)$$

therefore,

$$\frac{\partial g}{\partial t} = g\frac{1}{2}\beta^2$$
$$\frac{\partial g}{\partial x} = g(-\beta)$$

and

$$\frac{1}{2}\frac{\partial^2 g}{\partial x^2} = \frac{1}{2}\frac{\partial g(-\beta)}{\partial x} = \frac{1}{2}(-\beta)\frac{\partial g}{\partial x} = \frac{1}{2}(-\beta)g(-\beta) = \frac{1}{2}\beta^2 g$$

As $g = F_t$, we have that

$$\mathrm{d}F_t = \frac{1}{2}F_t\beta^2\mathrm{d}t + F_t(-\beta)\mathrm{d}B_t + \frac{1}{2}F_t\beta^2(\mathrm{d}B_t)^2 = -\beta F_t\mathrm{d}B_t + F_t\beta^2\mathrm{d}t$$

Step 4. Now, we will compute

$$\mathrm{d}(X_tF_t) = X_t\mathrm{d}F_t + F_t\mathrm{d}X_t + \mathrm{d}F_t\mathrm{d}X_t$$

where

$$\mathrm{d}X_t = rX_t(k - X_t^m)\mathrm{d}t + \beta X_t\mathrm{d}B_t$$
$$\mathrm{d}F_t = -\beta F_t\mathrm{d}B_t + \beta^2 F_t\mathrm{d}t.$$

We have that

$$F_t\mathrm{d}X_t = F_t rX_t(k - X_t^m)\mathrm{d}t + F_t\beta X_t\mathrm{d}B_t$$
$$X_t\mathrm{d}F_t = -\beta X_tF_t\mathrm{d}B_t + \beta^2 X_tF_t\mathrm{d}t$$

and

$$\begin{aligned}\mathrm{d}X_t\mathrm{d}F_t &= (rX_t(k - X_t^m)\mathrm{d}t + \beta X_t\mathrm{d}B_t)(-\beta F_t\mathrm{d}B_t + \beta^2 F_t\mathrm{d}t)\\ &= -\beta^2 F_tX_t(\mathrm{d}B_t)^2 = -\beta^2 F_tX_t\mathrm{d}t.\end{aligned}$$

Then finally,

$$\begin{aligned}\mathrm{d}(X_tF_t) &= F_trX_t(k - X_t^m)\mathrm{d}t + F_t\beta X_t\mathrm{d}B_t - \beta X_tF_t\mathrm{d}B_t\\ &\quad + \beta^2 X_tF_t\mathrm{d}t - \beta^2 F_tX_t\mathrm{d}t = rF_tX_t(k - X_t^m)\mathrm{d}t.\end{aligned}$$

REMARK 12.3

We observe that in this last equation, we do not have anymore dB_t, so the integrating factor transformed the original equation in an equation that is not only exact, but also a deterministic equation.

Now, setting $Y_t = F_t X_t$, we have that

$$dY_t = d(F_t X_t) = rF_t X_t (k - X_t^m)dt = rY_t \left(k - \frac{Y_t^m}{F_t^m}\right) dt$$

or

$$\frac{dY}{dt} = rY\left(k - \frac{Y^m}{F_t^m}\right) = rkY - r\frac{Y^{m+1}}{F_t^m}$$

where we call $Y = Y_t$.

REMARK 12.4

We observe that the last equation is not anymore a SDE, it is a deterministic one. That is why we call $Y = Y_t$, in order to use the classical notation for ordinary differential equations.

Step 5. By change of variables, the last equation can be transformed in a linear equation: Setting

$$z = -\frac{Y^{1-(m+1)}}{1-(m+1)} = \frac{Y^{-m}}{m}$$

then

$$mz = Y^{-m}$$

and

$$mdz = -mY^{-(m+1)}dY$$

so

$$dz = -Y^{-(m+1)}dY$$

or

$$dY = -Y^{m+1}dz.$$

Therefore, the equation

$$dY = \left(rkY - r\frac{Y^{m+1}}{F_t^m}\right)dt$$

becomes

$$-Y^{m+1}dz = \left(rkY - r\frac{Y^{m+1}}{F_t^m}\right)dt$$

or, equivalently,

$$dz = \left(-rkY^{1-m-1} + r\frac{Y^{m+1-m-1}}{F_t^m}\right)dt.$$

Hence,

$$dz = \left(-rkY^{-m} + \frac{r}{F_t^m}\right)dt = \left(-rkmz + \frac{r}{F_t^m}\right)dt.$$

that can be written as

$$\frac{dz}{dt} = -rkmz + \frac{r}{F_t^m}$$

or

$$\frac{dz}{dt} + rkmz = \frac{r}{F_t^m}.$$

Step 6. Solutions for the differential equation.
The solution to the equation

$$\frac{dz}{dt} + P(t)z = Q(t)$$

is given by

$$z(t) = \frac{1}{\mu(t)}\left[\int_0^t \mu(s)Q(s)ds + C\right]$$

with $\mu(t) = \exp(\int_0^t P(s)ds)$, because if we want an integrating factor $\mu(t)$ for the equation

$$dz + P(t)zdt - Q(t)dt = 0$$

then

$$\mu(t)\mathrm{d}z + \mu(t)(P(t)z - Q(t))\mathrm{d}t$$

needs to be exact, that is, there exists F so that

$$\mathrm{d}F = \mu(t)\mathrm{d}z + \mu(t)(P(t)z - Q(t))\mathrm{d}t,$$

hence,

$$\frac{\partial \mu}{\partial t} = \frac{\partial[\mu(t)(P(t)z - Q(t))]}{\partial z}$$

and therefore,

$$\frac{\mathrm{d}\mu}{\mathrm{d}t} = \mu(t)P(t)$$

or equivalently, $\frac{1}{\mu(t)}\frac{\mathrm{d}\mu}{\mathrm{d}t} = P(t)$. So, integrating we have that

$$\mu(t) = \exp\left(\int_0^t P(s)\mathrm{d}s\right)$$

see Ref. 4 for details.

In this case, $P(t) = rkm$, so $\mu(t) = \exp(rkmt)$, and

$$z(t) = \exp(-rkmt)\left[\int_0^t \exp(rkms)\frac{r}{F_s^m}\mathrm{d}s + C\right].$$

As $Z = \frac{Y^{-m}}{m}$, where $Y = Y_t$ and $Y_t = X_t F_t$, we obtain that $Y = (mz)^{-\frac{1}{m}}$ and finally,

$$X_t = \frac{Y_t}{F_t} = \frac{(mz)^{-\frac{1}{m}}}{F_t}$$

Now, as

$$F_t = \exp\left(-\beta B_t + \frac{1}{2}\beta^2 t\right)$$

If $m = 1$, we obtain that

$$X_t = \frac{z^{-1}}{F_t}$$

and hence

$$X_t = \frac{1}{\exp\left(-\beta B_t + \frac{1}{2}\beta^2 t\right)}\frac{1}{\exp(-rkt)}$$

$$\frac{1}{\int_0^t \exp(rks)\frac{r}{\exp\left(-\beta B_s + \frac{1}{2}\beta^2 s\right)} ds + C\exp(-rkt)}$$

where C is a constant that will be fixed with the initial condition, or equivalently,

$$X_t = \frac{\exp\left(\beta B_t - \left(\frac{1}{2}\beta^2 - rk\right)t\right)}{r\int_0^t \exp\left(\left(-\frac{1}{2}\beta^2 + rk\right)s + \beta B_s\right) ds + C}$$

Similarly, if $m = 2$ we obtain that

$$X_t = \frac{(2z)^{-1/2}}{F_t}$$

and hence

$$X_t = \frac{2^{-1/2}\exp\left(\beta B_t - \left(\frac{1}{2}\beta^2 - 2rk\right)t\right)}{\left[r\int_0^t \exp\left(\left(-\frac{1}{2}\beta^2 + 2rk\right)s + \beta B_s\right) ds + C\right]^{1/2}}$$

12.2 Stable Distributions

It is known that the Black–Scholes is not appropriated for the study of high frequency data, or for the study of financial indices or asset prices when a market crash takes place. For these financial data are more appropriated other models, like the Levy—like stochastic processes. In order to introduce these models, we first present a brief introduction of Stable distributions.

Consider the sum of n independent identically distributed (i.i.d.) random variables x_i,

$$S_n = x_1 + x_2 + x_3 + \cdots + x_n = x(n\Delta t)$$

Observe that S_n can be regarded as the sum of n random variables or as the position of a single walker at time $t = n\Delta t$, where n is the number of steps performed, and Δt the time required to perform one step.

As the variables are independent, the sum can be obtained as the convolution, namely,

$$P[x(2\Delta t)] = P(x_1) \otimes P(x_2)$$

or more generally,

$$P[x(n\Delta t)] = P(x_1) \otimes P(x_2) \cdots \otimes P(x_n).$$

We say that the distribution is stable if the functional form of $P[x(n\Delta t)]$ is the same as the functional form of $P[x(\Delta t)]$. Specifically, given a random variable X, if we denote with $Law(X)$ its probability density function (for example, for a Gaussian random variable, we write $Law(X) = N(\mu, \sigma^2)$) then we say that the random variable X is stable, or that it has a stable distribution if for any $n \geq 2$ there exists a positive number C_n and a number D_n so that

$$Law(X_1 + X_2 + \cdots + X_n) = Law(C_n X + D_n)$$

where $X_1, X_2, \ldots, X_n$ are independent random copies of X, this means that $Law(X_i) = Law(X)$ for $i = 1, 2, \ldots, n$.

If $D_n = 0$, X is said to be a strictly stable variable.

It can be shown (see Ref. 5) that

$$C_n = n^{\frac{1}{\alpha}}$$

for some parameter α, $0 < \alpha \leq 2$.

For example, if X is a Lorentzian random variable,

$$P(x) = \frac{\gamma}{\pi} \frac{1}{\gamma^2 + x^2}$$

and its characteristic function (that is, its Fourier transform) is given by

$$\varphi(q) = \int_{\mathbb{R}} \exp(iqx) f(x) \mathrm{d}x = E(\exp(iqx))$$

where $f(x)$ is the probability density function associated to the distribution $P(x)$. In this case, we obtain that

$$\varphi(q) = \exp(-\gamma |q|)x$$

Now, if X_1, X_2 are two i.i.d. Lorentzian random variables, we have that

$$P[X(2\Delta t)] = P(X_1) \otimes P(X_2) = \frac{2\gamma}{\pi} \frac{1}{4\gamma^2 + x^2}.$$

Also, as the Fourier transform of a convolution is the product of the Fourier transforms, we obtain

$$\varphi_2(q) = \exp(-2\gamma |q|) = (\varphi(q))^2$$

and in general,

$$\varphi_n(q) = (\varphi(q))^n.$$

As a second example, if X is a Gaussian random variable,

$$P(X) = \frac{1}{\sqrt{2\pi}\sigma} \exp\left(\frac{-x^2}{2\sigma^2}\right),$$

its characteristic function is

$$\varphi(q) = \exp\left(-\frac{\sigma^2}{2}|q|^2) = \exp(-\gamma|q|^2\right).$$

where $\gamma = \frac{\sigma^2}{2}$, and again, we have that

$$\varphi_2(q) = (\varphi(q))^2.$$

By performing the inverse Fourier transform, we obtain

$$P_2[X(2\Delta t)] = \frac{1}{\sqrt{8\pi\gamma}} \exp\left(\frac{-x^2}{8\gamma}\right) = \frac{1}{\sqrt{2\pi}(\sqrt{2}\sigma)} \exp\left(\frac{-x^2}{2(\sqrt{2}\sigma)^2}\right).$$

That is, the variance is now $\sigma_2^2 = 2\sigma^2$.

So, two stable stochastic processes exist: Lorentzian and Gaussian, and in both cases, their Fourier transform has the form

$$\varphi(q) = \exp(-\gamma|q|^\alpha)$$

with $\alpha = 1$ for the Lorentzian, and $\alpha = 2$ for the Gaussian.

It could be guessed that distributions with characteristic function

$$\varphi(q) = \exp(-\gamma|q|^\alpha)$$

for $1 \leq \alpha \leq 2$ will be stable.

In the next section, we see the form of all stable distributions also called *Levy distributions*.

12.3 The Levy Flight Models

Levy [6] and *Khintchine* [7] solved the problem of determining the functional form that all the stable distributions must follow. They found that the most general representation is through the characteristic functions $\varphi(q)$, that are defined by the following equation

$$\ln(\varphi(q)) = i\mu q - \gamma |q|^{\alpha} \left[1 - i\beta \frac{q}{|q|} \tan\left(\frac{\pi\alpha}{2}\right)\right]$$

if $\alpha \neq 1$, and

$$\ln(\varphi(q)) = \mu q - \gamma |q| \left[1 + i\beta \frac{q}{|q|} \frac{2}{\pi} \log(q)\right]$$

if $\alpha = 1$, where $0 < \alpha \leq 2$ (that is, the same parameter mentioned before) is called the *stability exponent* or the *characteristic parameter*; γ is a positive scale factor, μ is a real number, called the *location parameter* and β is an asymmetry parameter ranging from -1 to 1, which is called the *skewness parameter*.

The analytical form of the Levy-stable distribution is known only for a few values of α and β

1. $\cdot\ \alpha = \frac{1}{2}$, $\beta = 1$ (Levy–Smirnov).
This distribution is also called the *one sided stable distribution* on (μ, ∞) with density

$$\left(\frac{\gamma}{2\pi}\right)^{\frac{1}{2}} \frac{1}{(x-\mu)^{\frac{3}{2}}} \exp\left(-\frac{\gamma}{2(x-\mu)}\right).$$

2. $\cdot\ \alpha = 1$, $\beta = 0$ (Lorentzian).
This distribution is also called the *Cauchy stable distribution* with density

$$\frac{\gamma}{\pi} \frac{1}{\gamma^2 + (x-\mu)^2}.$$

3. $\cdot\ \alpha = 2$, $\beta = 0$ (Gaussian).
This distribution is also called the *normal distribution* with density

$$\frac{1}{\sqrt{2\pi}\gamma} \exp\left(\frac{-(x-\mu)^2}{2\gamma^2}\right).$$

From the previous discussion, it is clear that μ will be (in same cases) the mean, and that γ^2 will coincide in same cases with the variance σ^2.

We consider the symmetric distribution ($\beta = 0$) with a zero mean ($\mu = 0$). In this case the characteristic function takes the form

$$\varphi(q) = \exp(-\gamma |q|^{\alpha}).$$

As the characteristic function of a distribution is its Fourier transform, the stable distribution of index α and scale factor γ is

$$P_L(x) = \frac{1}{\pi} \int_0^{\infty} \exp(-\gamma |q|^{\alpha}) \cos(qx) dq.$$

The asymptotic behavior of the distribution for big values of the absolute value of x is given by

$$P_L(x) \simeq \frac{\gamma\Gamma(1+\alpha)\sin\dfrac{\pi\alpha}{2}}{\pi|x|^{1+\alpha}} \simeq |x|^{-(1+\alpha)}$$

and the value at zero $P_L(x=0)$ by

$$P_L(x=0) = \frac{\Gamma(1/\alpha)}{\pi\alpha\gamma^{1/\alpha}}.$$

The fact that the asymptotic behavior for big values of x is a power law has as a consequence that $E[|x|^n]$ diverges for $n \geq \alpha$ when $\alpha < 2$. In particular, all the stable Levy processes with $\alpha < 2$ have infinite variance. In order to avoid the problems arising in the infinite second moment *Mantegna and Stanley* considered a stochastic process with finite variance that follows scale relations called *Truncated Levy flight* (TLF) [8].

The *TLF* distribution is defined by

$$T(x) = cP(x)\chi_{(-l,l)}(x)$$

with $P(x)$ a symmetric Levy distribution.

The *TLF* distribution is not stable, but it has finite variance, thus independent variables from this distribution satisfy a regular central limit theorem. However, depending on the size of the parameter l (the cutoff length) the convergence may be very slow [8]. If the parameter l is small (so that the convergence is fast) the cut that it presents in its tails is very abrupt. In order to have continuous tails, *Koponen* [9] considered a *TLF* in which the cut function is a decreasing exponential characterized by a parameter l.

The characteristic function of this distribution is defined as

$$\varphi(q) = \exp\left\{c_0 - c_1\frac{(q^2+1/l^2)^{\frac{\alpha}{2}}}{\cos(\pi\alpha/2)}\cos(\alpha\arctan(l|q|))\right\}$$

with c_1 a scale factor:

$$c_1 = \frac{2\pi\cos(\pi\alpha/2)}{\alpha\Gamma(\alpha)\sin(\pi\alpha)}At$$

and

$$c_0 = \frac{l^{-\alpha}}{\cos(\pi\alpha/2)}c_1 = \frac{2\pi}{\alpha\Gamma(\alpha)\sin(\pi\alpha)}Al^{-\alpha}t.$$

The variance can be calculated from the characteristic function

$$\sigma^2(t) = \frac{\partial^2\varphi(q)}{\partial q^2}\Big|_{q=0} = t\frac{2A\pi(1-\alpha)}{\Gamma(\alpha)\sin(\pi\alpha)}l^{2-\alpha}$$

If we discretize in time with steps Δt, we obtain that $T = N\Delta t$.

Following the discussion in the previous session, we can think that at the end of each interval we must calculate the sum of N stochastic variables that are independent and identically distributed. Therefore, the new characteristic function will be

$$\varphi(q, N) = \varphi(q)^N = \exp\left\{c_0 N - c_1 \frac{N(q^2 + 1/l^2)^{\alpha/2}}{\cos(\pi\alpha/2)} \cos(\alpha \arctan(l|q|))\right\}.$$

For small values of N the probability will be very similar to the stable Levy distribution:

$$P_L(x = 0) = \frac{\Gamma(1/\alpha)}{\pi\alpha(\gamma N)^{1/\alpha}}.$$

Observe that here γ has been changed by $N\gamma$.

The model can be improved by standardizing it. If the variance is given by

$$\sigma^2 = -\frac{\partial^2\varphi(q)}{\partial q^2}|_{q=0}.$$

we have that

$$-\frac{\partial^2\varphi(q/\sigma)}{\partial q^2}|_{q=0} = -\frac{1}{\sigma^2}\frac{\partial^2\varphi(q)}{\partial q^2}|_{q=0} = 1.$$

Therefore, a standardized model is

$$\ln\varphi_N(q) = \ln\varphi\left(\frac{q}{\sigma}\right) = c_0 - c_1 \frac{\left((q/\sigma)^2 + 1/l^2\right)^{\alpha/2}}{\cos(\pi\alpha/2)} \cos\left(\alpha \arctan\left(l\frac{|q|}{\sigma}\right)\right),$$

$$= \frac{2\pi A l^{-\alpha} t}{\alpha\Gamma(\alpha)\sin(\pi\alpha)}\left[1 - \left(\left(\frac{ql}{\sigma}\right)^2 + 1\right)^{\alpha/2} \cos\left(\alpha \arctan\left(\frac{ql}{\sigma}\right)\right)\right].$$

To simulate the standardized truncated Levy model, a Matlab module was developed. The parameter l is fixed at 1 and then the parameter A and the characteristic exponent α are adjusted simultaneously in order to fit the cumulative function. On the same grid the cumulative distribution of the simulated data are plotted for different time lags T in order to visualize how good the fitting is. Time lag $T = 1$ means the fit is done by using two consecutive data; and for a general T, by using: $\log\frac{X_t}{X_{t-T}}$.

REMARK 12.5

It is very remarkable the fact that the stable Levy processes (also called *Levy flight*) have independent increments but are designated as long memory processes. Indeed, this is the case for these processes due to the fact that the increments are heavy tailed.

12.4 Numerical Simulations and Levy Models: Applications to Models Arising in Financial Indices and High Frequency Data

We implemented a numerical simulation of the solution to the SDE by using *R* and Matlab.

The standardized Levy models are applied to the analysis of three different sets of data: the simulated data from the SDE (Fig. 12.1), the stock prices comprising the Dow Jones Industrial Average Index (DJIA), along with the index itself (Figs. 12.2–12.5), and to the study of high frequency data from several influential companies (Figs. 12.6–12.10).

The analyzed stochastic variable is the return r_t, defined as the difference of the logarithm of two consecutive stock (or index) prices. In this case, we plot on the same grid the cumulative distribution of the observed returns for different time lags T in order to visualize how good the fitting is. Time lag $T = 1$ means

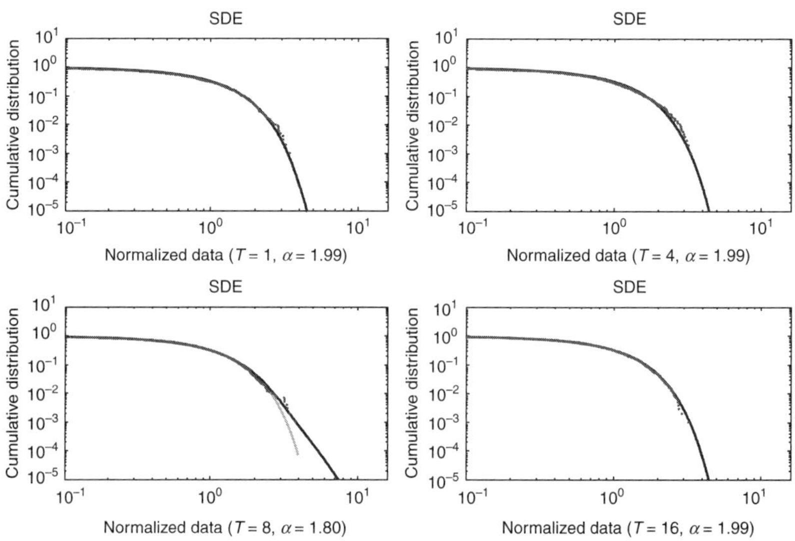

FIGURE 12.1 The figure shows the estimating of the Levy flight parameter for the solution of the SDE.

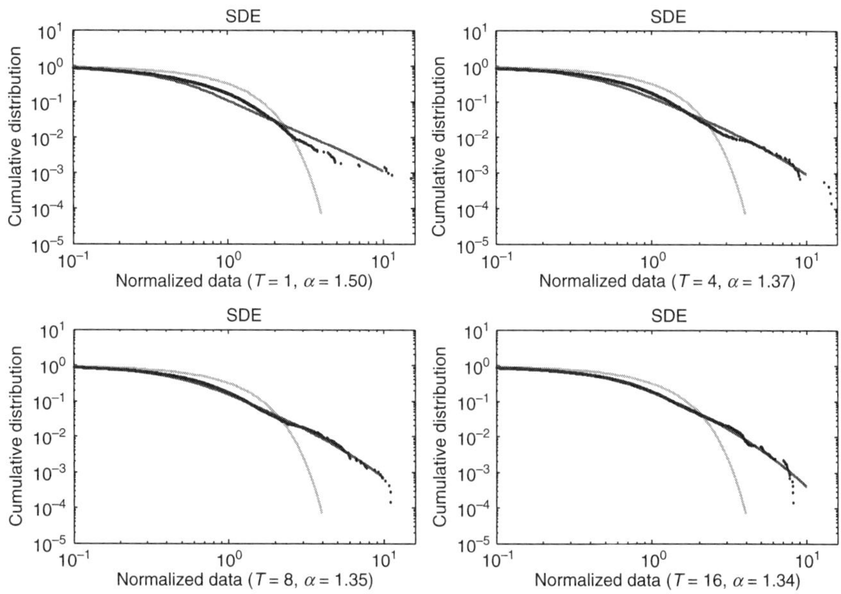

FIGURE 12.2 The figure shows the estimating of the Levy flight parameter for City Group.

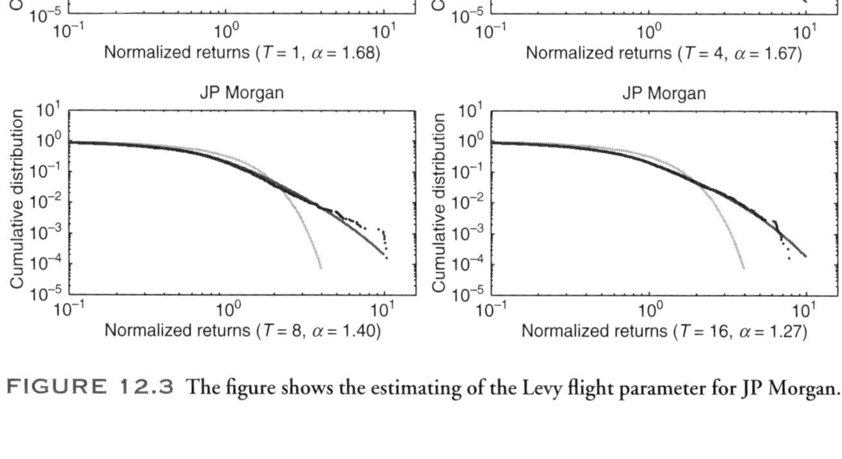

FIGURE 12.3 The figure shows the estimating of the Levy flight parameter for JP Morgan.

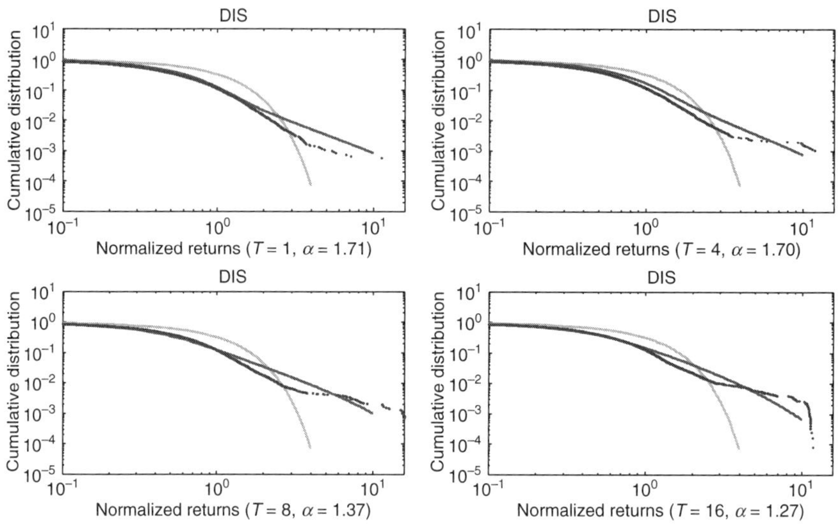

FIGURE 12.4 The figure shows the estimating of The Levy flight parameter for the Walt Disney Company.

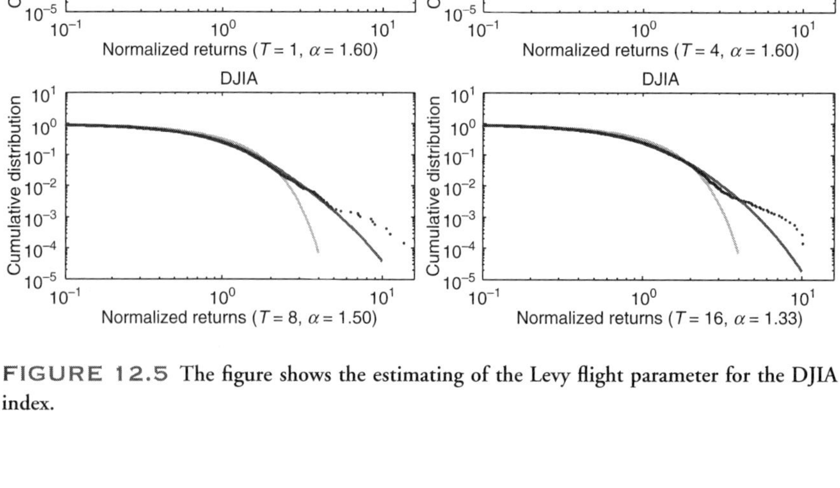

FIGURE 12.5 The figure shows the estimating of the Levy flight parameter for the DJIA index.

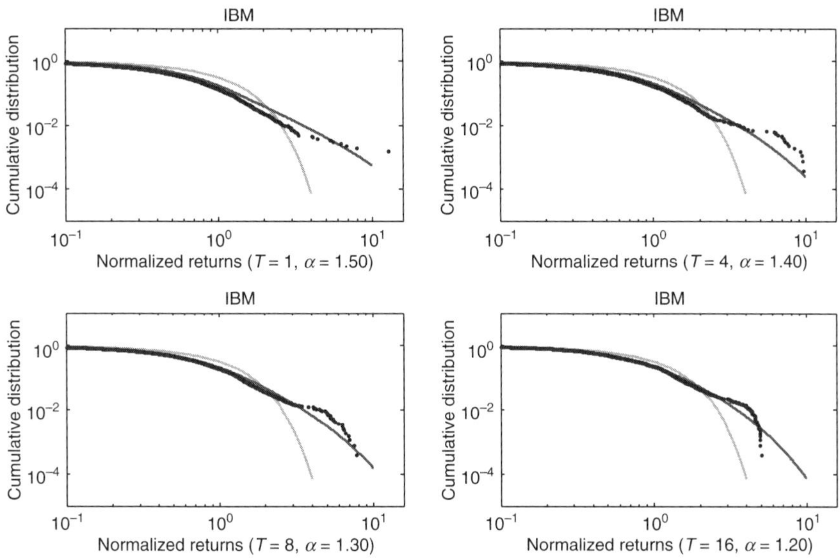

FIGURE 12.6 The figure shows the estimating of the Levy flight parameter for IBM. These are high frequency (tick) data.

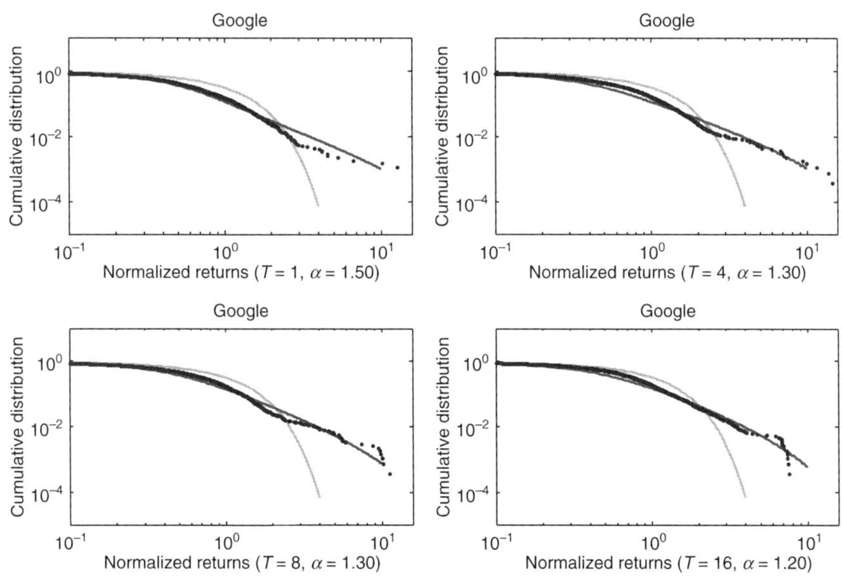

FIGURE 12.7 The figure shows the estimating of the Levy flight parameter for Google. These are high frequency (tick) data.

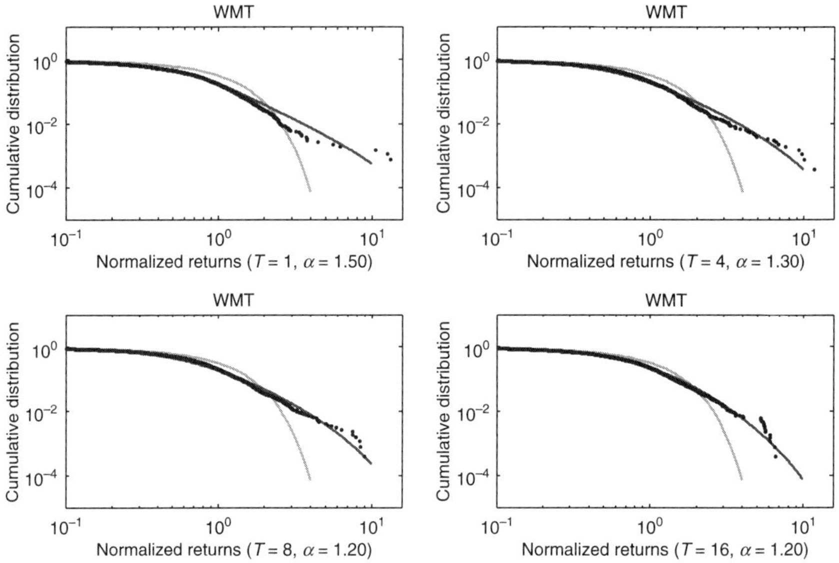

FIGURE 12.8 The figure shows the estimating of the Levy flight parameter for Walmart. These are high frequency (tick) data.

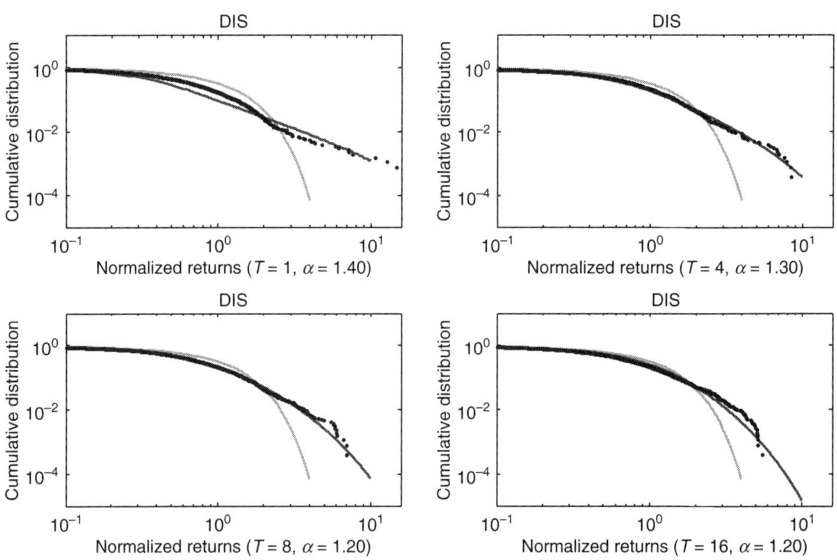

FIGURE 12.9 The figure shows the estimating of the Levy flight parameter for The Walt Disney Company. These are high frequency (tick) data.

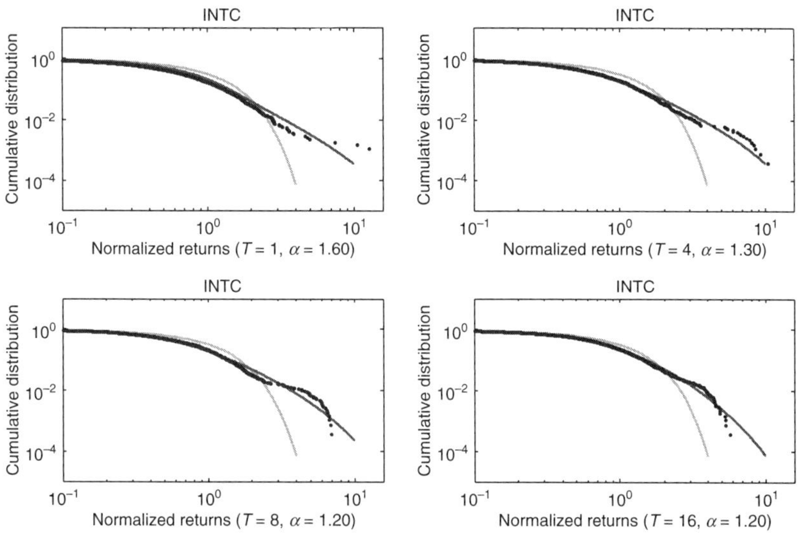

FIGURE 12.10 The figure shows the estimating of the Levy flight parameter for Intel Corporation. These are high frequency (tick) data.

the returns are calculated by using two consecutive observations; for a general T, the returns are calculated by using $r_t = \log(Xt/Xt - T)$. Now, $X_t = I_t$, where I_t denotes the stock (or index) price at time t, and T is the difference (in labor days) between two values of the stock, or index.

We study the behavior of stock prices comprising the DJIA, along with the index itself. The values are from 1985 to 2010.

We finally analyzed high frequency (minute) data from 2008. In this case T is the difference in minutes between two values of the stock.

We conclude that the Levy flights are appropriate for modeling the three different set of data. We recall that a value close to 2.0 indicates Gaussian behavior of the stochastic variable.

12.5 Discussion and Conclusions

We did a study of the statistical behavior of data arising in population models, of a financial index along with the rate of return of specific companies within the index, and of high frequency data by using a standardized TLF model. In all the cases we obtained that the evolution of data can be described by the model. We can see that all the values obtained for the exponent α are lower than 2.

In previous works (see Ref. 10 and the references therein) it was found that the exponents calculated for market indices were strictly greater than 2. Weron [10] concluded that these values could be a consequence of working with finite samples. This behavior was compatible with a slow convergence to a Gaussian distribution but it was not possible to conclude that the Levy distribution was the appropriated stochastic process for explaining the financial indices evolution. The authors believe that the standardized Levy model that was used in this work, together with computation of the constants involved in the model, allowed them to more accurately complete a numerical analysis. This standardized Levy model is suitable for better working with finite samples, and it offers a new way for analyzing financial indices, as well as other phenomena with similar behavior.

The figures show the log–log plot of the cumulative distribution of the normalized return for four different values of time scale. The dark gray line is the best fit of the Levy distribution. The light gray line indicates the Gaussian distribution. In the cumulative distribution curve of each fund there are some outlying points. Those outlying points correspond to the significant drops in a very short period (1 or 2 days, or 1 or 2 min, depending on the data) that happened to the data. This is exactly the way in which a market crash is defined: A market crash is an outlying point in the cumulative probability distribution of the stochastic process described by the Levy model. It should be noted that outlying points exactly reflect the crash of the corresponding financial indices/stocks.

12.5.1 ACKNOWLEDGMENT

We are especially grateful to Dr. Ionuţ Florescu for having shared high frequency data with us.

REFERENCES

1. Casella G, Berger R. Statistical inference. 2nd ed. Duxbury, Pacific Grove, California; 2002.
2. Oksendal B. Stochastic differential equations. 6th ed. Springer, New York; 2007.
3. Ross SM. Introduction to probability models. 9th ed. Elsevier, San Diego, California; 2007.
4. Nagle KB, Saff EB, Snider AD. Fundaments of differential equations. 6th ed. Addison Wesley, Boston, Massachusetts; 2003.
5. Samorodnitsky G, Taqqu MS. Stable non-Gaussian random processes: stochastic models with infinite variance. New York: Chapman and Hall; 1994.
6. Levy P. Calcul des probabilités. Paris: Gauthier-Villars; 1925.
7. Khintchine AYa, Levy P. Sur les lois stables. C R Acad Sci Paris;1936;202:374.
8. Mantegna RN, Stanley HE. Stochastic process with ultra-slow convergence to a Gaussian: the truncated Levy flight. Phys Rev Lett;1994;73:2946–2949.
9. Koponen I. Analytic approach to the problem of convergence of truncated Levy flights towards the Gaussian stochastic process. Phys Rev E;1995;52:1197–1199.
10. Weron R. Levy-stable distributions revisited: tail index> 2 does not exclude the Levy-stable regime. Int J Mod Phys C; 2001;12:209–223.

CHAPTER THIRTEEN

Solutions to Integro-Differential Parabolic Problem Arising on Financial Mathematics

MARIA C. MARIANI
Department of Mathematical Sciences, University of Texas at El Paso, El Paso, TX

MARC SALAS
New Mexico State University, Las Cruces, NM

INDRANIL SENGUPTA
Department of Mathematical Sciences, University of Texas at El Paso, El Paso, TX

13.1 Introduction

Jumps were introduced in the asset-price dynamics since the classical work of Nobel laureate Robert Merton in his 1976 paper *Option Pricing When Underlying Returns are Discontinuous* [1]. From the perspective of the mathematical and financial theory, it has been more convenient to work with models in which asset prices are described by pure diffusion processes evolving continuously in time. Researchers and practitioners have generally favored these models more for their

Handbook of Modeling High-Frequency Data in Finance, First Edition.
Edited by Frederi G. Viens, Maria C. Mariani, and Ionuţ Florescu.

simplicity than their realism. In particular, the pricing of derivative securities in this framework can be reduced to the solution of partial differential equations, allowing the application of an extensive body of mathematical knowledge from that field.

Recently, there has been a resurgence of interest in asset-price models that capture jumps and diffusions. In this setting, the price of derivative securities is described not by partial differential equations but rather by *partial integro-differential equations* (PIDE), the integral terms arising from jumps. This presents new research challenges. We should mention that much of the material in the first three sections of this chapter has been covered in Ref. 2. A few corrections and additions have been made.

We recall that an option is a contract that gives the holder the right to buy or sell a particular asset in the future at a previously agreed price. In each financial mathematics model, we will look at the value of a European option, $F = F(S, t)$ of a particular asset will be modeled by a nonlinear parabolic PDE known as a *Black–Scholes* PDE. Here, S is the asset price and t is time. We should note that the acronym PDE is typically used to denote partial differential equation, whereas PDEs is used for the plural form. In addition to depending on the asset price and time, the option price could also depend on the stochastic volatility of the asset price. In this case, the option value is given by $F = F(S, \sigma, t)$, where σ is a measure of the asset-price volatility.

Through a change of variables, one can transform a parabolic problem in F, S, t, and (possibly) σ into a problem involving some new variables $u = u(x, \tau)$, x, τ, and σ. If the volatility is stochastic, then x will be related to S and σ, if not, x will just be related to S. This change of variables will give us a nonlinear parabolic PDE for u. Since the value of an option will be studied over some finite time interval, this parabolic PDE will be defined in $Q_T = \Omega \times (0, T) \subset \mathbb{R}^{d+1}$, where $\Omega \subset \mathbb{R}^d$ is an unbounded, open set and $d = 1, 2$. The value of d will depend on whether or not we assume constant or stochastic volatility. Typically, a terminal condition is specified for the value of an option at expiration. Through the change of variables, this terminal condition is translated into an initial condition for u.

After introducing our models from financial mathematics, we will try to generalize these models to more general parabolic domains of the form $Q_T = \Omega \times (0, T) \in \mathbb{R}^{d+1}$. Here, $\Omega \subset \mathbb{R}^d$ will be a bounded or an unbounded open set with a smooth boundary $\partial\Omega$, and $T > 0$ will be a terminal time. Finally, we will prove the existence of solutions to these particular classes of generalized models. We will do this by using iterative methods. We will also prove the uniqueness of our solutions.

Before we continue any further, we should introduce some notation that we will be using. Also, we will define a few function spaces that are commonly used when studying the theory of partial differential equations.

13.1.1 DEFINITIONS

For $d \geq 1$, $\Omega \subset \mathbb{R}^d$ will be an open set, and $Q_T = \Omega \times (0, T)$ will be a parabolic domain for some $T > 0$. If Ω has a boundary, $\partial\Omega$, then $\partial\Omega$ will be smooth.

A multiindex of nonnegative integers will be denoted by $\alpha = (\alpha_1, \ldots, \alpha_d)$ with $|\alpha| = \alpha_1 + \ldots + \alpha_d$. We will let k be a nonnegative integer and δ be a positive constant with $0 < \delta < 1$. Unless otherwise indicated, we will always use the standard Lebesgue integral.

DEFINITION 13.1

Let $u, v \in L^1_{\text{loc}}(Q_T)$. For a nonnegative integer ρ, we say v is the $\alpha\rho$th weak partial derivative of u of order $|\alpha| + \rho$, $D^\alpha \partial_t^\rho u = v$, provided

$$\iint_{Q_T} u D^\alpha \partial_t^\rho \phi \ \mathrm{d}x\,\mathrm{d}t = (-1)^{|\alpha|+\rho} \iint_{Q_T} v\phi \ \mathrm{d}x\,\mathrm{d}t,$$

for any test function $\phi \in C_0^\infty(Q_T)$. The space $C_0^\infty(Q_T)$ is the set of all functions in $C^\infty(Q_T)$ with compact support.

It can be shown that weak derivatives are unique up to a set of zero measure. The definition of a weak derivative of a function in $u \in L^1_{\text{loc}}(\Omega)$, should be clear.

DEFINITION 13.2

Let $1 \le p \le \infty$ and $k \in \mathbb{N} = \{1, 2, 3, \ldots\}$. We define the following Sobolev spaces

$$W_p^k(\Omega) := \{u \in L^p(\Omega) \mid D^\alpha u \in L^p(\Omega),\ 1 \le |\alpha| \le k\}, \tag{13.1}$$

$$W_p^{2k,k}(Q_T) := \{u \in L^p(Q_T) \mid D^\alpha \partial_t^\rho u \in L^p(Q_T),\ 1 \le |\alpha| + 2\rho \le 2k\}. \tag{13.2}$$

The spaces above become Banach spaces if we endow them with the respective norms

$$\|u\|_{W_p^k(\Omega)} = \sum_{0 \le |\alpha| \le k} \|D^\alpha u\|_{L^p(\Omega)}, \tag{13.3}$$

$$\|u\|_{W_p^{2k,k}(Q_T)} = \sum_{0 \le |\alpha| + 2\rho \le 2k} \|D^\alpha \partial_t^\rho u\|_{L^p(Q_T)}. \tag{13.4}$$

For the theory of Sobolev spaces, we refer the reader to Ref. 3.

Next, we discuss spaces with classical derivatives, known as *Hölder spaces*. We will follow the notation and definitions given in the books [4, 5]. We define $C^k_{\text{loc}}(\Omega)$ to be the set of all real-valued functions $u = u(x)$ with continuous classical derivatives $D^\alpha u$ in Ω, where $0 \le |\alpha| \le k$. Next, we set

$$|u|_{0;\Omega} = [u]_{0;\Omega} = \sup_{\Omega} |u|,$$
$$[u]_{k;\Omega} = \max_{|\alpha|=k} |D^\alpha u|_{0;\Omega}.$$

DEFINITION 13.3

The space $C^k(\Omega)$ is the set of all functions $u \in C^k_{\text{loc}}(\Omega)$ such that the norm

$$|u|_{k;\Omega} = \sum_{j=0}^{k} [u]_{j;\Omega}$$

is finite. With this norm, it can be shown that $C^k(\Omega)$ is a Banach space.

If the seminorm

$$[u]_{\delta;\Omega} = \sup_{\substack{x,y\in\Omega \\ x\neq y}} \frac{|u(x) - u(y)|}{|x-y|^\delta}$$

is finite, then we say the real-valued function u is *Hölder continuous in* Ω with exponent δ. For a k-times differentiable function, we will set

$$[u]_{k+\delta;\Omega} = \max_{|\alpha|=k} \left[D^\alpha u\right]_{\delta;\Omega}.$$

DEFINITION 13.4

The Hölder space $C^{k+\delta}(\overline{\Omega})$ is the set of all functions $u \in C^k(\Omega)$ such that the norm

$$|u|_{k+\delta;\Omega} = |u|_{k;\Omega} + [u]_{k+\delta;\Omega}$$

is finite. With this norm, it can be shown that $C^{k+\delta}(\overline{\Omega})$ is a Banach space.

For any two points $P_1 = (x_1, t_1), P_2 = (x_2, y_2) \in Q_T$, we define the parabolic distance between them as

$$\mathrm{d}(P_1, P_2) = \left(|x_1 - x_2|^2 + |t_1 - t_2|\right)^{1/2}.$$

For a real-valued function $u = u(x, t)$ on Q_T, let us define the seminorm

$$[u]_{\delta,\delta/2;Q_T} = \sup_{\substack{P_1,P_2 \in Q_T \\ P_1 \neq P_2}} \frac{|u(x_1, t_1) - u(x_2, t_2)|}{d^\delta(P_1, P_2)}.$$

If this seminorm is finite for some u, then we say u is *Hölder continuous with exponent* δ. The maximum norm of u is given by

$$|u|_{0;Q_T} = \sup_{(x,t)\in Q_T} |u(x, t)|.$$

DEFINITION 13.5

The space $C^{\delta,\delta/2}\left(\overline{Q}_T\right)$ is the set of all functions $u \in Q_T$ such that the norm

$$|u|_{\delta,\delta/2;Q_T} = |u|_{0;Q_T} + [u]_{\delta,\delta/2;Q_T}$$

is finite. Furthermore, we define

$$C^{2k+\delta,k+\delta/2}\left(\overline{Q}_T\right) = \{u : D^\alpha \partial_t^\rho u \in C^{\delta,\delta/2}\left(\overline{Q}_T\right),\ 0 \leq |\alpha| + 2\rho \leq 2k\}.$$

We define a seminorm on $C^{2k+\delta,k+\delta/2}\left(\overline{Q}_T\right)$ by

$$[u]_{2k+\delta,k+\delta/2;Q_T} = \sum_{|\alpha|+2\rho=2k} [D^\alpha \partial_t^\rho u]_{\delta,\delta/2;Q_T},$$

and a norm by

$$|u|_{2k+\delta,k+\delta/2;Q_T} = \sum_{0\leq|\alpha|+2\rho\leq 2k} |D^\alpha \partial_t^\rho u|_{\delta,\delta/2;Q_T}.$$

Using this norm, it can be shown that $C^{2k+\delta,k+\delta/2}\left(\overline{Q}_T\right)$ is a Banach space.

13.2 Method of Upper and Lower Solutions

The authors of Refs 6 and 7 used the method of upper and lower solutions to study generalizations of two different Black–Scholes models for option pricing. In their work, they proved the existence of so-called *strong solutions* to these problems in parabolic Sobolev spaces $W_p^{2,1}(Q_T)$ for some $p \geq 1$. A strong solution to the first initial-boundary value problem is a function in $W_p^{2,1}(Q_T)$, which satisfies the PDE almost everywhere and the initial/boundary conditions.

In this section, we improve on the earlier work of these authors and obtain a stronger existence result in a bounded domain. In particular, we prove the existence of classical solutions to these two generalized problems in a bounded parabolic domain. Furthermore, under a suitable assumption, we show that the solution to each problem is unique. We then expand on the diagonal argument given in Refs 6 and 7 to show how one can obtain the existence of a strong solution in an unbounded parabolic domain.

13.2.1 INTRODUCTION AND STATEMENT OF PROBLEM

In recent years, there has been an increasing interest in solving PDE problems arising in financial mathematics and, in particular, on option pricing. The standard approach to this problem leads to the study of equations of parabolic type.

In financial mathematics, the Black–Scholes model [1,8–12] is usually used for pricing options, by means of a backward parabolic differential equation. In this model, an important quantity is the volatility, which is a measure of the fluctuation (risk) in the asset prices, and corresponds to the diffusion coefficient in the Black–Scholes equation.

In the standard Black–Scholes model, a basic assumption is that the volatility is constant. However, several models proposed in recent years, such as the model found in Ref. 13, have allowed the volatility to be nonconstant or a stochastic variable. In this model, the underlying security S follows, as in the Black–Scholes model, a stochastic process

$$dS_t = \mu S_t dt + \sigma_t S_t dZ_t,$$

where Z is a standard Brownian motion. Unlike the classical model, the variance $v(t) = \sigma^2(t)$ also follows a stochastic process given by

$$dv_t = \kappa(\theta - v(t))dt + \gamma\sqrt{v_t} dW_t,$$

where W is another standard Brownian motion. The correlation coefficient between W and Z is denoted by ρ:

$$\text{Cov}(dZ_t, dW_t) = \rho\, dt.$$

This leads to a generalized Black–Scholes equation

$$\frac{1}{2}vS^2\frac{\partial^2 F}{\partial S^2} + \rho\gamma vS\frac{\partial^2 F}{\partial v \partial S} + \frac{1}{2}v\gamma^2\frac{\partial^2 F}{\partial v^2} + rS\frac{\partial F}{\partial S} + [\kappa(\theta - v) - \lambda v]\frac{\partial F}{\partial v} - rF + \frac{\partial F}{\partial t} = 0. \tag{13.5}$$

If $F(S, v, t)$ is the value of a European option with expiration time $t = T$ and strike price $K > 0$, then F satisfies Equation 13.5 with the terminal condition

$$F(S_T, v_T, T) = \max(S_T - K, 0).$$

A similar model has been considered in Ref. 14.

Through a change of variables, the following more general model with stochastic volatility has been proposed [15] using the Feynman–Kac lemma:

$$\begin{aligned} u_t &= \frac{1}{2} Tr\left(M(x,\tau)D^2 u\right) + q(x,\tau)\cdot Du, \qquad (13.6)\\ u(x,0) &= u_0(x). \end{aligned}$$

Here, M is some diffusion matrix, and u_0 is some payoff function.

The Black–Scholes models with jumps arise from the fact that the driving Brownian motion is a continuous process, and so there are difficulties fitting the financial data presenting large fluctuations. The necessity of taking into account large market movements and a great amount of information arriving suddenly (i.e., a jump) has led to the study of PIDE in which the integral term is modeling the jump.

In Refs 1 and 16, the following PIDE in the variables t and S is obtained:

$$\frac{1}{2}\sigma^2 S^2 F_{SS} + (r - \lambda k)SF_S + F_t - rF + \lambda\varepsilon\{F(SY,t) - F(S,t)\} = 0, \qquad (13.7)$$

where the volatility is assumed to be constant. Here, r denotes the riskless rate, λ the jump intensity, and $k = \varepsilon(Y - 1)$, where ε is the expectation operator. The random variable $Y - 1$ measures the percentage change in the stock price if the jump, modeled by a Poisson process, occurs. See Refs 1 and 16 for details.

The following PIDE is a generalization of Equation 13.7 for N assets with prices $S_1, \ldots, S_N$ and constant volatility:

$$\begin{aligned} &\sum_{i=1}^{N} \frac{1}{2}\sigma_i^2 S_i^2 \frac{\partial^2 F}{\partial S_i^2} + \sum_{i \neq j} \frac{1}{2}\rho_{ij}\sigma_i\sigma_j S_i S_j \frac{\partial^2 F}{\partial S_i \partial S_j}\\ &\quad + \sum_{i=1}^{N} (r - \lambda k_i) S_i \frac{\partial F}{\partial S_i} + \frac{\partial F}{\partial t} - rF\\ &\quad + \lambda \int [F(S_1Y_1, \ldots, S_dY_d, t) - F(S_1, \ldots, S_d, t)]\\ &g(Y_1, \ldots, Y_d)\mathrm{d}Y_1, \ldots, \mathrm{d}Y_d = 0 \qquad (13.8) \end{aligned}$$

with the correlation coefficients

$$\rho_{ij}\mathrm{d}t = \varepsilon\{\mathrm{d}z_i, \mathrm{d}z_j\}.$$

We recall that the case in which F is decreasing and all jumps are negative corresponds to the evolution of a call option near a crash (see Ref. 17 and the references therein).

When the volatility is stochastic, we may consider the processes

$$\begin{aligned} \mathrm{d}S &= S\sigma \mathrm{d}Z + S\mu \mathrm{d}t, \\ \mathrm{d}\sigma &= \beta\sigma \mathrm{d}W + \alpha\sigma \mathrm{d}t, \end{aligned}$$

where Z and W are two standard Brownian motions with correlation coefficient ρ. If $F(S, \sigma, t)$ is the price of an option depending on the price of the asset S, then by Ito's lemma [11] we have

$$\mathrm{d}F(S, \sigma, t) = F_S \mathrm{d}S + F_\sigma \mathrm{d}\sigma + \mathcal{L}F \mathrm{d}t,$$

where $\mathcal{L}$ is a second-order differential operator given by

$$\mathcal{L} = \partial_t + \frac{1}{2}\sigma^2 S^2 \frac{\partial^2}{\partial S^2} + \frac{1}{2}\beta^2\sigma^2 \frac{\partial^2}{\partial \sigma^2} + \rho\sigma^2 S\beta \frac{\partial^2}{\partial S \partial \sigma}.$$

Under an appropriate choice of the portfolio, the stochastic term of the equation vanishes (for details, see Ref. 14).

A generalized tree process has been developed in Refs 18 and 19 that approximates any stochastic volatility model. Unlike the nonrandom volatility case, the tree construction is stochastic every time it is created because that is the only way we are able to deal with the huge complexity involved.

If, in this model, we add a jump component modeled by a compound Poisson process to the process S, and we follow Merton [1], we obtain the following PIDE:

$$\begin{aligned} &\frac{\partial F}{\partial t} + \frac{1}{2}\sigma^2 S^2 \frac{\partial^2 F}{\partial S^2} + \frac{1}{2}\sigma^2\beta^2 \frac{\partial^2 F}{\partial \sigma^2} + \rho\sigma^2\beta S \frac{\partial^2 F}{\partial S \partial \sigma} \\ &\quad + (r - \lambda k) S \frac{\partial F}{\partial S} - \frac{1}{2}\rho\sigma^2\beta \frac{\partial F}{\partial \sigma} \\ &\quad + \lambda \int_{\mathbb{R}} [F(SY, \sigma, t) - F(S, \sigma, t)]\, g(Y)\, \mathrm{d}Y - rF = 0. \end{aligned} \tag{13.9}$$

Once again, r is the riskless rate, λ is the jump intensity, and $k = \varepsilon(Y - 1)$. Here, ε is the expectation operator, and the random variable $Y - 1$ measures the percentage change in the stock price if the jump, modeled by a Poisson process, occurs. See Section 9.2 of Ref. 1 for more details.

We should mention that for the classical Black–Scholes model and for any other Black–Scholes models, such as models that take into account stochastic volatility, it follows that $C(S, t) \sim 0$ when $S \sim 0$ and $C(S, t) \sim S$ when S is very large. This observation will justify the boundary conditions we will be using later in this section. Namely, the boundary condition for the Black–Scholes model with stochastic volatility should be the same boundary condition used for the classical Black–Scholes model whenever the spatial domain for S is bounded and very large.

13.2.2 A GENERAL SEMILINEAR PARABOLIC PROBLEM

The generalized Black–Scholes model with stochastic volatility leads us to study a more general semilinear parabolic problem than the ones given by Equations 13.5 and 13.6.

In Ref. 6, the authors proved the existence of a strong solution to a more general problem in a parabolic domain $Q_T = \Omega \times (0, T)$, where Ω is an open, unbounded subset of $\mathbb{R}^d$, with a smooth boundary $\partial\Omega$. The fact that Ω has a boundary reflects the idea that the asset price is unbounded, whereas the volatility is assumed to be bounded. In this section, we show how the methodology used by these authors can be extended to obtain a stronger existence result.

First, we will consider the following initial-value boundary value problem in the bounded parabolic domain $V_T = U \times (0, T)$, $T > 0$:

$$\begin{aligned} u_t - Lu &= f(x, t, u) \quad \text{in} \quad V_T, \\ u(x, 0) &= u_0(x) \quad \text{on} \quad U, \\ u(x, t) &= g(x, t) \quad \text{on} \quad \partial U \times (0, T). \end{aligned} \tag{13.10}$$

Then, we will try to extend our results to the problem in an unbounded domain $Q_T = \Omega \times (0, T)$, where $\Omega \subset \mathbb{R}^d$ is open, unbounded, with a smooth boundary $\partial\Omega$.

Here, $L = L(x, t)$ is a second order elliptic operator in nondivergence form, namely,

$$L(x, t) := \sum_{i,j=1}^{d} a^{ij}(x, t)\frac{\partial^2}{\partial x_i \partial x_j} + \sum_{i=1}^{d} b^i(x, t)\frac{\partial}{\partial x_i} + c(x, t).$$

Furthermore, we impose the following assumptions in this section:

A(1) The coefficients $a^{ij}(x, t)$, $b^i(x, t)$, $c(x, t)$ belong to the Hölder space $C^{\delta,\delta/2}(\overline{V}_T)$.

A(2) For some $0 < \lambda < \Lambda$, $a^{ij}(x, t)$ satisfies the ellipticity condition

$$\lambda|v|^2 < \sum_{i,j=1}^{d} a^{ij}(x, t)v_i v_j < \Lambda|v|^2,$$

for all $(x, t) \in V_T, v \in \mathbb{R}^d$.

A(3) For all $(x, t) \in V_T$, $c(x, t) \geq 0$.

A(4) $u_0(x)$ and $g(x, t)$ belong to the Hölder spaces $C^{2+\delta}(\Omega)$ and $C^{2+\delta,1+\delta/2}(\overline{Q}_T)$, respectively, and are nonnegative. Here, $\Omega \subset \mathbb{R}^d$ is any open, unbounded set with a smooth boundary $\partial\Omega$, and $Q_T = \Omega \times (0, T)$ is the associated parabolic domain.

A(5) The two consistency conditions

$$g(x, 0) = u_0(x),$$
$$g_t(x, 0) - L(x, 0)u_0(x) = 0,$$

are satisfied for all $x \in \partial U$.

A(6) $f(x, t, z)$ belongs to $C^{\delta,\delta/2,\delta}(\overline{V}_T \times \mathbb{R})$ and $f(x, t, 0) = 0$.

A(7) The function $f(x, t, z)$ is Lipschitz continuous with respect to z. In other words, for some constant $\rho \geq 0$,

$$|f(x, t, z_1) - f(x, t, z_2)| \leq \rho|z_1 - z_2|.$$

As a direct consequence of this last assumption, the function

$$F(x, t, u) = \rho u + f(x, t, u)$$

is nondecreasing with respect to u.

We shall prove the existence of a solution to problem (Eq. 13.10) using the method of upper and lower solutions. Recall that a function $u \in C^{2,1}(V_T) \cap C(\overline{V}_T)$ is called an *upper (lower) solution* of problem (Eq. 13.10) if

$$\begin{aligned} u_t - Lu &\geq (\leq)\ f(x, t, u) && \text{in } V_T, \\ u(x, 0) &\geq (\leq)\ u_0(x) && \text{on } U, \\ u(x, t) &\geq (\leq)\ g(x, t) && \text{on } \partial U \times (0, T). \end{aligned} \tag{13.11}$$

If α is a lower solution and β is an upper solution, we say that the pair α, β is ordered if

$$\alpha(x, t) \leq \beta(x, t), \tag{13.12}$$

for all $(x, t) \in \overline{V}_T$.

We will first solve the analogous homogeneous problem, which can be thought of as a generalization of the classical Black–Scholes equation.

LEMMA 13.6

Consider the parabolic problem

$$\begin{aligned} u_t - Lu &= 0 && \text{in } V_T, \\ u(x, 0) &= u_0(x) && \text{on } U, \\ u(x, t) &= g(x, t) && \text{on } \partial U \times (0, T). \end{aligned} \tag{13.13}$$

There exists a unique solution $\varphi \in C^{2+\delta,1+\delta/2}\left(\overline{V}_T\right)$. Moreover, if β is an upper solution, then

$$0 \le \varphi(x,t) \le \beta(x,t)$$

for all $(x,t) \in V_T$. As a consequence, $\alpha = 0$ and β is an ordered lower–upper solution pair in V_T.

Proof. Using **A(4)**, it should be clear that $\alpha = 0$ is a lower solution to Equation 13.13. The existence and uniqueness of a solution to Equation 13.13 follow immediately from Theorem 10.4.1 in [4]. By the definitions of α, β, and φ, we have

$$\begin{aligned} \alpha_t - L\alpha = 0 = \partial_t\varphi - L\varphi \le \beta_t - L\beta \quad & \text{in} \quad V_T, \\ \alpha(x,0) = 0 \le u_0(x) = \varphi(x,0) \le \beta(x,0) \quad & \text{on} \quad U, \\ \alpha(x,t) = 0 \le g(x,t) = \varphi(x,t) \le \beta(x,t) \quad & \text{on} \quad \partial U \times (0,T). \end{aligned}$$

By a comparison principle, Theorem 8.1.6 in Ref. 5, we have

$$\alpha(x,t) = 0 \le \varphi(x,t) \le \beta(x,t),$$

for all $(x,t) \in V_T$. ■

Now we come to the important result of this section. This result is used later to prove our main result.

THEOREM 13.7

Suppose $\varphi \in C^{2+\delta,1+\delta/2}\left(\overline{V}_T\right)$ is defined as in Lemma 2.1. Then there exists a classical solution $u \in C^{2+\delta,1+\delta/2}(\overline{V}_T)$ to the problem

$$\begin{aligned} u_t - Lu &= f(x,t,u) \quad \text{in} \quad V_T, \\ u(x,0) &= u_0(x) \quad \text{on} \quad U, \\ u(x,t) &= \varphi(x,t) \quad \text{on} \quad \partial U \times (0,T), \end{aligned} \tag{13.14}$$

and $\alpha = 0$ is a lower solution. Assume $\beta \in C^{\delta,\delta/2}(\overline{V}_T) \cap C(\overline{V}_T)$ is an upper solution. Then

$$0 \le u(x,t) \le \beta(x,t),$$

for all $(x,t) \in V_T$.

Proof. Using A(4) and A(6), it should be clear that $\alpha = 0$ is a lower solution to Equation 13.14. We will use an iteration procedure to construct the solution to Equation 13.14. If we let $\rho \geq 0$ be the Lipschitz constant of f, then $F(x,t,u) = \rho u + f(x,t,u)$ is nondecreasing with respect to u.

For $n \geq 1$, consider the linear parabolic problem

$$\begin{aligned} \partial_t u^n - Lu^n + cu^n &= F(x,t,u^{n-1}) && \text{in } V_T, \\ u^n(x,0) &= u_0(x) && \text{on } U, \\ u^n(x,t) &= \varphi(x,t) && \text{on } \partial U \times (0,T), \end{aligned} \tag{13.15}$$

where $u^0 \in C^{\delta,\delta/2}(\overline{V}_T) \cap C(\overline{V}_T)$. Let us show that the sequence $\{u^n\}_{n=0}^{\infty}$ is well-defined. By Theorem 10.4.1 in Ref. 4, if $F(x,t,u^{n-1}(x,t)) \in C^{\delta,\delta/2}(\overline{V}_T)$, then problem (Eq. 13.15) will have a unique solution $u^n \in C^{2+\delta,1+\delta/2}(\overline{V}_T) \subset C^{\delta,\delta/2}(\overline{V}_T)$.

First, consider the case $n = 1$. Since u^0 and f are Hölder continuous in V_T, F is Hölder continuous in V_T. Also, recall that $F(x,t,z)$ is Lipschitz continuous in z, with Lipschitz constant $\rho \geq 0$. Therefore, we have

$$\begin{aligned} &|F(x,t,u^0(x,t)) - F(y,s,u^0(y,s))| \\ &\leq |F(x,t,u^0(x,t)) - F(y,s,u^0(x,t))| + |F(y,s,u^0(x,t)) - F(y,s,u^0(y,s))| \\ &\leq H_F\left(|x-y|^2 + |t-s|\right)^{\delta/2} + \rho|u^0(x,t) - u^0(y,s)| \\ &\leq (H_F + \rho H_{u^0})\left(|x-y|^2 + |t-s|\right)^{\delta/2}, \end{aligned}$$

where H_F and H_{u^0} are the Hölder constants of F and u^0, respectively. This shows $F(x,t,u^0(x,t)) \in C^{\delta,\delta/2}(\overline{V}_T)$, and so there exists a unique solution $u^1 \in C^{2+\delta,1+\delta/2}(\overline{V}_T) \subset C^{\delta,\delta/2}(\overline{V}_T)$ to Equation 13.15. By a standard induction argument, the functions $u^n \in C^{2+\delta,1+\delta/2}(\overline{V}_T) \subset C^{\delta,\delta/2}(\overline{V}_T)$ are well defined for $n \geq 1$.

For $u^0 = 0 \in C^{\delta,\delta/2}(V_T) \cap C(\overline{V}_T)$, we will refer to $\{\underline{u}^n\}_{n=0}^{\infty}$ as the lower sequence of problem (Eq. 13.15). Similarly, for $u^0 = \beta \in C^{\delta,\delta/2}(\overline{V}_T) \cap C(\overline{V}_T)$, we will refer to $\{\overline{u}^n\}_{n=0}^{\infty}$ as the upper sequence of problem (Eq. 13.15).

We claim that $\{\underline{u}^n\}_{n=0}^{\infty}$ is monotonically increasing and $\{\overline{u}^n\}_{n=0}^{\infty}$ is monotonically decreasing. In fact, we will show the more general result

$$0 \leq \underline{u}^n(x,t) \leq \underline{u}^{n+1}(x,t) \leq \overline{u}^{n+1}(x,t) \leq \overline{u}^n(x,t) \leq \beta(x,t), \tag{13.16}$$

for all $(x,t) \in \overline{V}_T$ and $n \geq 1$. Clearly, the comparison principle, Theorem 8.1.6 in Ref. 5, gives us $0 \leq \underline{u}^1$ and $\overline{u}^1 \leq \beta$.

First, let us show $\underline{u}^n \leq \underline{u}^{n+1}$ by using an induction argument. For $(x,t) \in \overline{V}_T$, let $w^1(x,t) = \underline{u}^2(x,t) - \underline{u}^1(x,t)$. From the monotonicity of F, we have

$$\begin{aligned} \partial_t w^1 - Lw^1 &= F(x,t,\underline{u}^1) - F(x,t,0) \geq 0 && \text{in } V_T, \\ w^1(x,0) &= u_0(x) - u_0(x) = 0 && \text{on } U, \\ w^1(x,t) &= \varphi(x,t) - \varphi(x,t) = 0 && \text{on } \partial U \times (0,T). \end{aligned} \tag{13.17}$$

By the maximum principle, we conclude that $w^1(x,t) \geq 0$ on $\overline{V}_T$. Therefore, $\underline{u}^1 \leq \underline{u}^2$. Next, assume $\underline{u}^n \leq \underline{u}^{n+1}$ and consider the function $w^{n+1}(x,t) = \underline{u}^{n+2}(x,t) - \underline{u}^{n+1}(x,t)$. Once again, from the monotonicity of F, we have

$$\begin{aligned} \partial_t w^{n+1} - Lw^{n+1} &= F(x,t,\underline{u}^{n+1}) - F(x,t,\underline{u}^n) \geq 0 \quad \text{in} \quad V_T, \\ w^{n+1}(x,0) &= u_0(x) - u_0(x) = 0 \qquad \text{on} \quad U, \\ w^{n+1}(x,t) &= \varphi(x,t) - \varphi(x,t) = 0 \qquad \text{on} \quad \partial U \times (0,T). \end{aligned} \tag{13.18}$$

By the maximum principle, we have $\underline{u}^{n+1} \leq \underline{u}^{n+2}$. So, we have the desired result.

Next, we show $\overline{u}^{n+1} \leq \overline{u}^n$. For $(x,t) \in \overline{V}_T$, let $w^1(x,t) = \overline{u}^2(x,t) - \overline{u}^1(x,t)$. From the monotonicity of F, we have

$$\begin{aligned} \partial_t w^1 - Lw^1 &= F(x,t,\overline{u}^1) - F(x,t,\beta) \leq 0 \quad \text{in} \quad V_T, \\ w^1(x,0) &= u_0(x) - u_0(x) = 0 \qquad \text{on} \quad U, \\ w^1(x,t) &= \varphi(x,t) - \varphi(x,t) = 0 \qquad \text{on} \quad \partial U \times (0,T). \end{aligned} \tag{13.19}$$

By the maximum principle, we conclude that $w^1(x,t) \leq 0$ on $\overline{V}_T$. Therefore, $\overline{u}^2 \leq \overline{u}^1$. As before, the remaining part follows from a standard induction argument.

Finally, we show $\underline{u}^n \leq \overline{u}^n$. For $(x,t) \in \overline{V}_T$, let $w^1(x,t) = \overline{u}^1(x,t) - \underline{u}^1(x,t)$. By the monotonicity of F, the function w^1 satisfies

$$\begin{aligned} \partial_t w^1 - Lw^1 &= F(x,t,\beta) - F(x,t,0) \geq 0 \quad \text{in} \quad V_T, \\ w^1(x,0) &= u_0(x) - u_0(x) = 0 \qquad \text{on} \quad U, \\ w^1(x,t) &= \varphi(x,t) - \varphi(x,t) = 0 \qquad \text{on} \quad \partial U \times (0,T). \end{aligned} \tag{13.20}$$

By the maximum principle, we conclude that $w^1(x,t) \geq 0$ on $\overline{V}_T$. Therefore, $\underline{u}^1 \leq \overline{u}^1$. The remaining part follows from a standard induction argument. We have just verified the inequality in Equation 13.16.

Since the lower sequence $\{\underline{u}^n\}_{n=0}^{\infty}$ is monotone nondecreasing and bounded from above, the pointwise limit

$$\lim_{n\to\infty} \underline{u}^n(x,t) = \underline{u}(x,t),$$

exists for any $(x,t) \in \overline{V}_T$. By a similar argument, the pointwise limit

$$\lim_{n\to\infty} \overline{u}^n(x,t) = \overline{u}(x,t),$$

exists for any $(x,t) \in \overline{V}_T$. Furthermore, we have

$$0 \leq \underline{u}(x,t) \leq \overline{u}(x,t) \leq \beta(x,t),$$

for any $(x,t) \in \overline{V}_T$.

Now we show $\underline{u}$ is a solution to Equation 13.15. It is well known that for each $n \geq 1$, the solution $\underline{u}^n$ to the parabolic problem (Eq. 13.15) has an integral representation given by

$$\underline{u}^n = \int_U G(x,t;y,0)\,u_0(y)\,dy + \int_0^t d\tau \int_U G(x,t;y,\tau)\,F(y,\tau,\underline{u}^{n-1}(y,\tau))\,dy$$
$$+ \int_0^t d\tau \int_{\partial U} \frac{\partial \Gamma}{\partial \nu_y}(x,t;y,\tau)\,\psi(y,\tau)\,dy,$$

where Γ is the fundamental solution to the parabolic equation in $\mathbb{R}^d \times (0,T)$, G is the Green's function to the problem, and ψ is the corresponding density function. The reader should see Ref. 20 for more details.

Since $\{\underline{u}^n\}_{n=1}^{\infty}$ is a bounded, nondecreasing sequence, $\{F(\underline{u}^n)\}_{n=1}^{\infty}$ is also bounded and nondecreasing. Therefore, by the dominated convergence theorem, we have

$$\underline{u} = \int_U G(x,t;y,0)\,u_0(y)\,dy + \int_0^t d\tau \int_U G(x,t;y,\tau)\,F(y,\tau,\underline{u}(y,\tau))\,dy$$
$$+ \int_0^t d\tau \int_{\partial U} \frac{\partial \Gamma}{\partial \nu_y}(x,t;y,\tau)\,\psi(y,\tau)\,dy.$$

By Theorem 4.2.1 of Ref. 21, the function $\underline{u}$ given by the integral representation above is a classical solution to Equation 13.14. By the same argument, we can show that $\overline{u}$ is a classical solution to Equation 13.14.

Now we show that the solution to Equation 13.14 is unique. If v is a solution to Equation 13.14 with $0 \leq v \leq \beta$, then $\alpha = 0$ and v is an ordered lower–upper solution pair. Notice that the upper sequence $\{\overline{u}^n\}_{n=0}^{\infty}$ with $\overline{u}^0 = v$ consists of the same function v for each $n \geq 0$. Because of this fact, we have $\underline{u} \leq v$.

Similarly, if v is a solution to Equation 13.14 with $0 \leq v \leq \beta$, then v and β is an ordered lower-upper solution pair. Once again, notice that the lower sequence $\{\underline{u}^n\}_{n=0}^{\infty}$ with $\underline{u}^0 = v$ consists of the same function v for each $n \geq 0$. Because of this, we have $v \leq \overline{u}$.

Combining these two results, we have that if v is a solution to Equation 13.14 with $0 \leq v \leq \beta$, then $\underline{u} \leq v \leq \overline{u}$. Therefore, to show that our solution is unique, it is enough to show that $\underline{u}(x,t) = \overline{u}(x,t)$, or equivalently that $\underline{u}(x,t) \geq \overline{u}(x,t)$ for any $(x,t) \in V_T$. Let us define the function $w(x,t) = \underline{u}(x,t) - \overline{u}(x,t)$ for any $(x,t) \in V_T$. Then w satisfies the parabolic problem

$$\begin{aligned} \partial_t w - Lw - \rho w &= f(x,t,\overline{u}) - f(x,t,\underline{u}) - \rho w \geq 0 && \text{in } V_T, \\ w(x,0) &= u_0(x) - u_0(x) = 0 && \text{on } U, \\ w(x,t) &= \varphi(x,t) - \varphi(x,t) = 0 && \text{on } \partial U \times (0,T). \end{aligned} \tag{13.21}$$

By the maximum principle, it is clear that $w \geq 0$ in V_T. Hence, the solution to Equation 13.14 is unique. ∎

Now we come to the main result of this section, which is the existence and uniqueness of the solution to the parabolic problem in an unbounded domain $Q_T = \Omega \times (0, T)$. Here, $\Omega \subset \mathbb{R}^d$ is an open and unbounded set, and has a smooth boundary $\partial\Omega$.

THEOREM 13.8

There exists a strong solution $u \in W_p^{2,1}(Q_T)$ to the problem

$$\begin{aligned} u_t - Lu &= f(x, t, u) && \text{in } Q_T, \\ u(x, 0) &= u_0(x) && \text{on } \Omega, \\ u(x, t) &= g(x, t) && \text{on } \partial\Omega \times (0, T), \end{aligned} \tag{13.22}$$

and $\alpha = 0$ is a lower solution. Moreover, if β is an upper solution, then

$$0 \leq u(x, t) \leq \beta(x, t),$$

for all $(x, t) \in Q_T$.

Proof. We approximate the domain Ω by an nondecreasing sequence $\{\Omega_N\}_{N=1}^{\infty}$ of bounded smooth subdomains of Ω, which can be chosen in such a way that $\partial\Omega \cap \partial\Omega_N \neq \emptyset$ and $\bigcup_{N=1}^{\infty} \Omega \cap \Omega_N = \Omega$. We let $V_N = \Omega_N \times (0, T)$.

By the previous theorem, let us define u^N to be the unique solution of the parabolic problem

$$\begin{aligned} Lu - u_t &= f(x, t, u) && \text{in } V_N, \\ u(x, 0) &= u_0(x) && \text{on } \Omega_N, \\ u(x, t) &= h(x, t) && \text{in } \partial\Omega_N \times (0, T), \end{aligned} \tag{13.23}$$

such that $0 < u^N < \beta$ in V_N. Let us choose $p > d$. For $M > N$, we have that

$$\begin{aligned} \|D^2(u^M)\|_{L^p(V_N)} + \|(u^M)_t\|_{L^p(V_N)} &< c\left(\|Lu^M - (u^M)_t\|_{L^p(V_N)} + \|u^M\|_{L^p(V_N)}\right) \\ &< c\left(\|f(x, t, u^M)\|_{L^p(V_N)} + \|\beta\|_{L^p(V_N)}\right) < C, \end{aligned}$$

for some constant C depending only on N. By the well known Morrey imbedding $W_p^{2,1}(V_N) \hookrightarrow C(\overline{V}_N)$, there exists a subsequence that converges uniformly on $\overline{V}_N$.

Now, we apply the well-known Cantor diagonal argument. For $N = 1$, we extract a subsequence of $u^M|_{\overline{V}_1}$ (still denoted by $\{u^M\}$) that converges uniformly to some function u_1 over $\overline{V}_1$. Next, we extract a subsequence of $u^M|_{\overline{V}_2}$ for $M > 2$ (still denoted by $\{u^M\}$) that converges uniformly to some function u_2 over $\overline{\Omega}_2 \times [0, T]$, and so on. As the families $\{\Omega_N\}$ and $\{\partial\Omega_N \cap \partial\Omega\}$ are nondecreasing, it is clear that $u_N(x, 0) = u_N(x)$ for $x \in \Omega_N$, and that $u_N(x,t) = h(x,t)$ for $x \in \partial\Omega \cap \partial\Omega_N$ and $t \in (0,T)$. Moreover, as u_{N+1} is constructed as the limit of a subsequence of $u^M|_{\overline{\Omega}_{N+1}\times[0,T]}$, which converges uniformly to some function u_N over $\overline{\Omega}_N \times [0,T]$, it follows that $u_{N+1}|_{\overline{\Omega}_N\times[0,T]} = u_N$ for every N.

Thus, the diagonal subsequence (still denoted $\{u^M\}$) converges uniformly over compact subsets of $\Omega \times (0,T)$ to the function u defined as $u = u_N$ over $\overline{\Omega}_N \times [0,T]$. For $V = U \times (0,T)$, $U \subset\subset \Omega$, taking $M, N > N_V$ for some N_V large enough, we have that

$$\|D^2(u^N - u^M)\|_{L^p(V)} + \|(u^N - u^M)_t\|_{L^p(V)}$$
$$< c\left(\|L(u^N - u^M) - (u^N - u^M)_t\|_{L^p(V)} + \|u^N - u^M\|_{L^p(V)}\right).$$

By construction,

$$L(u^N - u^M) - (u^N - u^M)_t = f(x,t,u^{N-1}) - f(x,t,u^{M-1}).$$

As before, using that $f(x,t,u)$ is continuous and that $\alpha < u^N < \beta$, by dominated convergence, it follows that $\{u^N\}_{N>N_V}$ is a Cauchy sequence in $W_p^{2,1}(V)$. Hence $u^N \to u$ over V for the $W_p^{2,1}$-norm, and then u is a strong solution in V. It follows that u satisfies the equation on $\Omega \times (0,T)$. Furthermore, it is clear that $u(x,0) = u_0(x)$. For $M > N$, we have that $u_M(x,t) = u_N(x,t) = h(x,t)$ for $x \in \partial\Omega \cap \partial\Omega_N$ and $t \in (0,T)$. Thus, u satisfies the boundary condition $u(x,t) = h(x,t)$ on $\partial\Omega \times (0,T)$. ■

13.2.3 A GENERAL INTEGRO-DIFFERENTIAL PROBLEM

The generalized Black–Scholes model with stochastic volatility and jumps leads us to study a more general integro-differential parabolic problem than the one given by Equation 13.9.

Mariani and Florescu of Ref. 7 proved the existence of a strong solution to a more general problem in an unbounded parabolic domain $Q_T = \Omega \times (0,T)$. Here, Ω is an open, unbounded subset of $\mathbb{R}^d$, with a smooth boundary $\partial\Omega$. Once again, the fact that Ω has a boundary reflects the idea that the asset price is unbounded, whereas the volatility is assumed to be bounded.

One can use the same methodology as in the previous section to obtain a stronger existence result than the result given in Ref. 7. In this section, we state the general problem, the assumptions, and the two main results. We do not give the proofs because they are essentially the same as the proofs given in the previous section.

First, we will consider the following initial-boundary value problem in the bounded parabolic domain $V_T = U \times (0,T)$, $T > 0$:

$$u_t - Lu = \mathcal{F}(x,t,u) \text{in} V_T,$$
$$u(x,0) = u_0(x) \text{ on } \Omega, \tag{13.24}$$

$$u(x,t) = g(x,t) \text{ on } \partial\Omega \times (0,T).$$

Then, we will try to extend our results to the corresponding initial-value problem in the unbounded domain $Q_T = \Omega \times (0,T)$.

As before, $L = L(x,t)$ is a second-order elliptic operator in nondivergence form, namely,

$$L(x,t) := \sum_{i,j=1}^{d} a^{ij}(x,t)\frac{\partial^2}{\partial x_i \partial x_j} + \sum_{i=1}^{d} b^i(x,t)\frac{\partial}{\partial x_i} + c(x,t).$$

The integral operator is defined by

$$\mathcal{F}(x,t,u) = \int_\Omega f(x,t,u(x,t),y)\, dy. \tag{13.25}$$

This operator will be continuous as the ones defined in Equations 13.7–13.9 modeling the jump. The case in which f is decreasing respect to u and all jumps are positive corresponds to the evolution of a call option near a crash.

Furthermore, we will impose assumptions A(1) through A(5) which were given in the previous section. Here, we change A(6) and A(7) to:

A(6) For each $y \in U$, $f(x,t,z,y)$ belongs to the space $C^{\delta,\delta/2,\delta}(\overline{V}_T \times \mathbb{R})$ and $f(x,t,0,y) = 0$.

A(7) The operator $\mathcal{F}(x,t,z)$ is nondecreasing with respect to z.

We now state an important result.

LEMMA 13.9

Suppose $\varphi \in C^{2+\delta,1+\delta/2}\left(\overline{V}_T\right)$ is defined as in Lemma 2.1. Then there exists a classical solution $u \in C^{2+\delta,1+\delta/2}(\overline{V}_T)$ to the problem

$$\begin{aligned} u_t - Lu &= \mathcal{F}(x,t,u) && \text{in } V_T, \\ u(x,0) &= u_0(x) && \text{on } U, \\ u(x,t) &= \varphi(x,t) && \text{on } \partial U \times (0,T), \end{aligned} \tag{13.26}$$

and $\alpha = 0$ is a lower solution. Moreover, if β is an upper solution, then

$$0 \le u(x,t) \le \beta(x,t),$$

for all $(x,t) \in V_T$.

Using this result and a standard diagonal argument as in the previous section, one can extend this result to the unbounded domain $Q_T = \Omega \times (0,T)$:

THEOREM 13.10

There exists a strong solution $u \in W_p^{2,1}(Q_T)$ to the problem

$$\begin{aligned} u_t - Lu &= \mathcal{F}(x,t,u) \quad \text{in} \quad Q_T, \\ u(x,0) &= u_0(x) \qquad \text{on} \quad \Omega, \\ u(x,t) &= g(x,t) \qquad \text{on} \quad \partial\Omega \times (0,T), \end{aligned} \tag{13.27}$$

and $\alpha = 0$ is a lower solution. Moreover, if β is an upper solution, then

$$0 \le u(x,t) \le \beta(x,t),$$

for all $(x,t) \in Q_T$.

13.3 Another Iterative Method

In the last part of the previous section, we discussed a Black–Scholes model with jumps, where the volatility was assumed to be stochastic. Moreover, the asset price was modeled by a Poisson process. This gave rise to a parabolic integro-differential problem, where the integral operator depended on $u(x,t)$.

In this section, we consider another Black–Scholes model with jumps. However, the asset price will now be modeled by an exponential Lévy model. Furthermore, we assume the volatility is constant. This will lead us to a parabolic integro-differential problem, where the integral operator depends on $u(x,t)$ and $u_x(x,t)$. We will then generalize the problem to an unbounded parabolic domain, just as we have done in the previous section. This will lead us to a integro-differential problem, where the integral operator depends on $u(x,t)$ and $\nabla u(x,t)$. The presence of the gradient in the integrand prevents us from being able to use the method of upper and lower solutions to analyze this class of problems. Therefore, we must use some other method to study these problems. The iterative method we will use for this problem was developed by Chadam and Yin in Ref. 22 to study a similar partial integro-differential problem.

13.3.1 STATEMENT OF THE PROBLEM

As pointed out in Ref. 17, when modeling high frequency data in applications, a Lévy-like stochastic process appears to be the best fit. When using these models, option prices are found by solving the resulting PIDE. For example, integro-differential equations appear in exponential Lévy models, where the market price of an asset is represented as the exponential of a Lévy stochastic process. These models have been discussed in several published works such as Refs 17 and 23.

In this section, we consider the following integro-differential model for a European call option

$$\frac{\partial C}{\partial t}(S,t) + rS\frac{\partial C}{\partial S}(S,t) + \frac{\sigma^2 S^2}{2}\frac{\partial^2 C}{\partial S^2}(S,t) - rC(S,t)$$
$$+ \int \nu(\mathrm{d}y)\left[C(S\mathrm{e}^y,t) - C(S,t) - S(\mathrm{e}^y - 1)\frac{\partial C}{\partial S}(S,t)\right] = 0, \qquad (13.28)$$

where the market price of an asset is represented as the exponential of a Lévy stochastic process (see Chapter 12 of Ref. 17). Also, we assume the option has the final payoff

$$C(S,T) = \max(S_T - K, 0), \qquad (13.29)$$

where $K > 0$ is the strike price. If we introduce the change of variables

$$\tau = T - t,$$
$$x = \ln\left(\frac{S}{K}\right) + r\tau,$$
$$u(x,\tau) = \frac{\mathrm{e}^{r\tau}}{K}C\left(K\mathrm{e}^{x-r\tau}, T-\tau\right),$$

then Equation 13.28 becomes

$$\frac{\partial u}{\partial \tau}(x,\tau) = \frac{\sigma^2}{2}\left[\frac{\partial^2 u}{\partial x^2}(x,\tau) - \frac{\partial u}{\partial x}(x,\tau)\right] + \mathcal{F}(u,u_x), \qquad (13.30)$$

with the initial condition

$$u(x,0) = u_0(x) \quad \text{for all } x \in \mathbb{R}. \qquad (13.31)$$

The term

$$\mathcal{F}(u,u_x) = \int \left[u(x+y,\tau) - u(x,\tau) - (\mathrm{e}^y - 1)\frac{\partial u}{\partial x}(x,\tau)\right]\nu(\mathrm{d}y) \qquad (13.32)$$

is an integro-differential operator modeling the jump.

We shall derive Equations 13.30–13.32. First, notice that to convert back to the original variables, we use the equations

$$t = T - \tau,$$
$$S = K\mathrm{e}^{x-r\tau},$$
$$C(S,t) = C\left(K\mathrm{e}^{x-r\tau}, T-\tau\right) = K\mathrm{e}^{-r\tau}u(x,\tau).$$

Next, we compute each partial derivative in Equation 13.28. We do this by using the chain and product rules repeatedly and the expression $Ke^{-r\tau}u(x,\tau)$ for $C(S,t)$:

$$\frac{\partial C}{\partial t} = \frac{\partial C}{\partial \tau}\frac{\partial \tau}{\partial t} = -\frac{\partial C}{\partial \tau} = rKe^{-r\tau}u(x,\tau) - rKe^{-r\tau}\frac{\partial u}{\partial x} - Ke^{-r\tau}\frac{\partial u}{\partial \tau},$$

$$\frac{\partial C}{\partial S} = \frac{\partial C}{\partial x}\frac{\partial x}{\partial S} = \frac{1}{S}\frac{\partial C}{\partial x} = \frac{1}{S}Ke^{-r\tau}\frac{\partial u}{\partial x},$$

$$\frac{\partial^2 C}{\partial S^2} = \frac{\partial}{\partial S}\left(\frac{1}{S}Ke^{-r\tau}\frac{\partial u}{\partial x}\right) = -\frac{1}{S^2}Ke^{-r\tau}\frac{\partial u}{\partial x} + \frac{1}{S}Ke^{-r\tau}\frac{\partial^2 u}{\partial x^2}\frac{\partial x}{\partial S},$$

$$= -\frac{1}{S^2}Ke^{-r\tau}\frac{\partial u}{\partial x} + \frac{1}{S^2}Ke^{-r\tau}\frac{\partial^2 u}{\partial x^2}.$$

Furthermore, notice that the first term in the integral operator of Equation 13.28 can be expressed as

$$C(Se^y,t) = C\left(Ke^{x+y-r\tau}, T-\tau\right) = Ke^{-r\tau}u(x+y,\tau).$$

If we substitute everything into Equation 13.28 and divide through by $Ke^{-r\tau}$, we obtain Equations 13.30 and 13.33. It is clear that $S > 0$ implies $x \in \mathbb{R}$ and $t = T$ implies $\tau = 0$. Using these two facts, Equation 13.29 becomes

$$C(S,T) = Ku(x,0) = \tilde{u}_0(x).$$

This justifies the initial condition in Equation 13.31, where $u_0(x) = \tilde{u}_0(x)/K$.

Once again, for the classical Black–Scholes model and for any other Black–Scholes model, such as models which take into account jumps, it follows that $C(S,t) \sim 0$ when $S \sim 0$ and $C(S,t) \sim S$ when S is very large. As in the previous section, this observation will justify why we will continuously be using the same boundary condition later in this section.

13.3.2 A GENERAL PARABOLIC INTEGRO-DIFFERENTIAL PROBLEM

In a more general context, the previous discussion motivates us to consider more general integro-differential parabolic problems. First, we consider the following initial-boundary value problem in the bounded parabolic domain $Q_T = \Omega \times (0,T)$, $T > 0$:

$$\begin{aligned} u_t - Lu &= \mathcal{F}(x,t,u,\nabla u) && \text{in } Q_T, \\ u(x,0) &= u_0(x) && \text{on } \Omega, \\ u(x,t) &= g(x,t) && \text{on } \partial\Omega \times (0,T). \end{aligned} \tag{13.33}$$

Then, we try to extend our results to the corresponding initial-value problem in the unbounded domain $\mathbb{R}_T^{d+1} = \mathbb{R}^d \times (0, T)$:

$$\begin{aligned} u_t - Lu &= \mathcal{F}(x, t, u, \nabla u) \text{ in } \mathbb{R}_T^{d+1}, \\ u(x, 0) &= u_0(x) \qquad\quad \text{on } \mathbb{R}^d. \end{aligned} \tag{13.34}$$

Here, $L = L(x, t)$ is a second-order elliptic operator in nondivergence form, namely,

$$L(x, t) := \sum_{i,j=1}^{d} a^{ij}(x, t)\frac{\partial^2}{\partial x_i \partial x_j} + \sum_{i=1}^{d} b^i(x, t)\frac{\partial}{\partial x_i} + c(x, t).$$

The integro-differential operator is defined by

$$\mathcal{F}(x, t, u, \nabla u) = \int_\Omega f(x, t, y, u(x, t), \nabla u(x, t))\, dy. \tag{13.35}$$

This integro-differential operator will be a continuous integral operator as the ones defined in Equations 13.28 and 13.32 modeling the jump. The case in which f is decreasing respect to u and all jumps are positive corresponds to the evolution of a call option near a crash.

Throughout this section, we impose the following assumptions:

A(1) The coefficients $a^{ij}(x, t)$, $b^i(x, t)$, $c(x, t)$ belong to the Hölder space $C^{\delta,\delta/2}(\overline{Q}_T)$.

A(2) For some $0 < \lambda < \Lambda$, $a^{ij}(x, t)$ satisfies the inequality

$$\lambda |v|^2 < \sum_{i,j=1}^{d} a^{ij}(x, t)v_i v_j < \Lambda |v|^2,$$

for all $(x, t) \in Q_T, v \in \mathbb{R}^d$.

A(3) For all $(x, t) \in Q_T$, $c(x, t) \geq 0$.

A(4) $u_0(x)$ and $g(x, t)$ belong to the Hölder spaces $C^{2+\delta}(\mathbb{R}^d)$ and $C^{2+\delta,1+\delta/2}(\overline{Q}_T)$, respectively.

A(5) The two consistency conditions

$$\begin{aligned} g(x, 0) &= u_0(x), \\ g_t(x, 0) - L(x, 0)u_0(x) &= 0, \end{aligned}$$

are satisfied for all $x \in \partial\Omega$.

A(6) $f(x, t, y, z, p)$ is nonnegative and belongs to $C^1(Q_T \times \Omega \times \mathbb{R}^{d+1})$.

A(7) For some $C_0 > 0, f$ satisfies the estimate

$$|f(x,t,y,z,p)| \leq C_0(1 + |z| + |p|),$$

for all $(x,t,y,z,p) \in \overline{Q}_T \times \overline{\Omega} \times \mathbb{R}^{d+1}$, where C_0 is independent of parameters of f.

We shall prove the existence of a solution to Equation 13.33 using an iteration argument. We will do this by proving estimates based on a Green's function. Afterward, we will use a standard argument to show that our solution can be extended to give us a solution to the initial-value problem in $\mathbb{R}^{d+1}_T$.

In this section, $Q_T = \Omega \times (0,T)$ always denotes a bounded parabolic domain, where $\Omega \subset \mathbb{R}^d$ is open and has smooth boundary $\partial\Omega$. Let us define the function space $C^{1+1,0+1}(\overline{Q}_T)$ to be the set of all $u \in C^{1,0}(\overline{Q}_T) \cap W^{2,1}_{\infty}(\overline{Q}_T)$. We will say $u \in C^{1+1,0+1}(\overline{Q}_T)$ is a strong solution to the parabolic initial-boundary value problem (Eq. 13.33) provided that u satisfies the parabolic equation almost everywhere in Q_T and the initial-boundary conditions in the classical sense. Once again, the following lemma follows immediately from Theorem 10.4.1 in Ref. 4.

LEMMA 13.11

There exists a unique solution $\varphi \in C^{2+\delta,1+\delta/2}\left(\overline{Q}_T\right)$ to the problem

$$\begin{aligned} u_t - Lu &= 0 && \text{in } Q_T, \\ u(x,0) &= u_0(x) && \text{on } \Omega, \\ u(x,t) &= g(x,t) && \text{on } \partial\Omega \times (0,T). \end{aligned} \tag{13.36}$$

As we have already mentioned in the previous section, Lemma 3.1 can be thought of as generalization of the classical Black–Scholes model where the stock price S satisfies

$$\varepsilon < S < S_{\max}.$$

In all practicality, one should not assume that S is bounded away from 0.

The problem in the next theorem can be regarded as a generalization of Equations 13.30 and 13.34, where the stock price S is bounded above and bounded below away from 0 as in Lemma 13.6. We take the same boundary condition as in Lemma 13.6, because of our earlier comment regarding the behavior of the option value when S is really small or really large for any Black–Scholes model.

THEOREM 13.12

Let φ be defined as in Lemma 13.11. Then there exists a strong solution $u \in C^{1+1,0+1}(\overline{Q}_T)$ to the problem

$$\begin{aligned} u_t - Lu &= \mathcal{F}(x,t,u,\nabla u) && \text{in } Q_T, \\ u(x,0) &= u_0(x) && \text{on } \Omega, \\ u(x,t) &= \varphi(x,t) = g(x,t) && \text{on } \partial\Omega \times (0,T). \end{aligned} \tag{13.37}$$

Proof. First, we introduce a change of variables to transform our problem into one with a zero boundary condition. If we let

$$v(x,t) = u(x,t) - \varphi(x,t),$$

$$v_0(x) = u_0(x) - \varphi(x,0) = 0,$$

then v will satisfy the initial-boundary value problem

$$\begin{aligned} v_t - Lv &= \mathcal{F}(x,t,v+\varphi,\nabla(v+\varphi)) && \text{in } Q_T, \\ v(x,0) &= 0 && \text{on } \Omega, \\ v(x,t) &= 0 && \text{on } \partial\Omega \times (0,T). \end{aligned} \tag{13.38}$$

We further change variable $\tau' = \frac{t}{A}$, where A is a constant which will be chosen later. By abuse of notation we denote ALv by Lv and $A\mathcal{F}$ by $\mathcal{F}$. Then if $T^* = \frac{T}{A}$, Equation 13.38 becomes

$$\begin{aligned} v_{\tau'} - Lv &= \mathcal{F}(x,\tau',v+\varphi,\nabla(v+\varphi)) && \text{in } Q_{T^*}, \\ v(x,0) &= 0 && \text{on } \Omega, \\ v(x,\tau') &= 0 && \text{on } \partial\Omega \times (0,T^*). \end{aligned} \tag{13.39}$$

If problem (Eq. 13.39) has a strong solution, then Equation 13.37 will have a strong solution since $u = v + \varphi$. We use an iteration procedure to construct the solution to Equation 13.39. Consider the problem

$$\begin{aligned} \beta_{\tau'} - L\beta &= \mathcal{F}(x,\tau',\alpha+\varphi,\nabla(\alpha+\varphi)) && \text{in } Q_{T^*}, \\ \beta(x,0) &= 0 && \text{on } \Omega, \\ \beta(x,\tau') &= 0 && \text{on } \partial\Omega \times (0,T^*), \end{aligned} \tag{13.40}$$

where $\alpha \in C^{2+\delta,1+\delta/2}(\overline{Q}_{T^*,U})$ is arbitrary. Using the same argument as in Section 13.2, we can show that $\mathcal{F}(x,\tau',\alpha+\varphi,\nabla(\alpha+\varphi)) \in C^{\delta,\delta/2}(\overline{Q}_{T^*})$. By Theorem 10.4.1 in Ref. 4, there exists a unique solution $\beta \in C^{2+\delta,1+\delta/2}(\overline{Q}_{T^*})$ to problem (Eq. 13.40).

Using this result, we can now define $v^n \in C^{2+\delta,1+\delta/2}(\overline{Q}_{T^*})$, $n \geq 1$, to be the unique solution to the linearized problem

$$\begin{aligned} \partial_{\tau'} v^n - Lv^n &= \mathcal{F}(x, \tau', v^{n-1} + \varphi, \nabla(v^{n-1} + \varphi)) && \text{in } \ Q_{T^*}, \\ v^n(x, 0) &= 0 && \text{on } \ \Omega, \\ v^n(x, \tau') &= 0 && \text{on } \ \partial\Omega \times (0, T^*), \end{aligned} \tag{13.41}$$

where $v^0 = v_0(x) = 0 \in C^{2+\delta,1+\delta/2}(\overline{Q}_{T^*,U})$. To prove the existence of a solution to problem (Eq. 13.39), we will show that this sequence converges.

Since the operator $\frac{\partial}{\partial t} - L$ is parabolic, therefore from Ref. 24, there exists a Green's function $G(x, y, \tau', \tau)$ for problem (Eq. 13.41). For $n \geq 1$, the solution v^n can be written as

$$\begin{aligned} v^n(x, \tau') &= \int_0^{\tau'} \int_\Omega G(x, y, \tau', \tau)\, \mathcal{F}(y, \tau, v^{n-1} + \varphi, \nabla(v^{n-1} + \varphi))\, \mathrm{d}y\, \mathrm{d}\tau \\ &\quad + \int_\Omega G(x, y, \tau', 0) v_0(y)\, \mathrm{d}y \\ &= \int_0^{\tau'} \int_\Omega G(x, y, \tau', \tau)\, \mathcal{F}(y, \tau, v^{n-1} + \varphi, \nabla(v^{n-1} + \varphi))\, \mathrm{d}y\, \mathrm{d}\tau, \end{aligned}$$

because $v_0(y) = 0$. Here,

$$\mathcal{F}(y, \tau, v^{n-1} + \varphi, \nabla(v^{n-1} + \varphi)) =$$

$$\int_\Omega \Big[f(y, \tau, z, (v^{n-1} + \varphi)(y, \tau), \nabla(v^{n-1} + \varphi)(y, \tau))\, \mathrm{d}z.$$

For convenience, we will write

$$\begin{aligned} \mathcal{F}^{n-1}(y, \tau) &= \mathcal{F}(y, \tau, v^{n-1} + \varphi, \nabla(v^{n-1} + \varphi)) \\ &= \int_\Omega f(y, \tau, z, (v^{n-1} + \varphi)(y, \tau), \nabla(v^{n-1} + \varphi)(y, \tau))\, \mathrm{d}z. \end{aligned}$$

Now we take the first and second derivatives of $v^n(x, \tau')$ with respect to x:

$$\begin{aligned} v^n_{x_i}(x, \tau') &= \int_0^{\tau'} \int_\Omega G_{x_i}(x, y, \tau', \tau)\, \mathcal{F}^{n-1}(y, \tau)\, \mathrm{d}y\, \mathrm{d}\tau, \\ v^n_{x_i x_j}(x, \tau') &= \int_0^{\tau'} \int_\Omega G_{x_i x_j}(x, y, \tau', \tau)\, \mathcal{F}^{n-1}(y, \tau)\, \mathrm{d}y\, \mathrm{d}\tau. \end{aligned}$$

For the parabolic operator, we again have from Chapter IV.16 in Ref. 24, the estimates

$$|G(x, y, \tau', \tau)| \leq c_1(\tau' - \tau)^{-\frac{d}{2}} \exp\left(-C_2 \frac{|x - y|^2}{\tau' - \tau}\right), \tag{13.42}$$

$$|G_{x_i}(x,y,\tau',\tau)| \le c_1(\tau'-\tau)^{-\frac{d+1}{2}} \exp\left(-C_2\frac{|x-y|^2}{\tau'-\tau}\right), \tag{13.43}$$

$$|G_{x_ix_j}(x,y,\tau',\tau)| \le c_1(\tau'-\tau)^{-\frac{d+2}{2}} \exp\left(-C_2\frac{|x-y|^2}{\tau'-\tau}\right), \tag{13.44}$$

where $\tau' > \tau$ and the constants c_1 and C_2 are independent of all parameters of G. If we combine everything, we get

$$\begin{aligned}
\|v^n(\cdot,\tau')\|_{W^2_\infty(\Omega)} &= \|v^n(\cdot,\tau')\|_{L^\infty(\Omega)} \\
&\quad + \sum_{i=1}^{d} \|v^n_{x_i}(\cdot,\tau')\|_{L^\infty(\Omega)} + \sum_{i,j=1}^{d} \|v^n_{x_ix_j}(\cdot,\tau')\|_{L^\infty(\Omega)} \\
&\le \int_0^{\tau'}\int_\Omega \|G(\cdot,y,\tau',\tau)\|_{L^\infty(\Omega)}\, |\mathcal{F}^{n-1}(y,\tau)|\,\mathrm{d}y\,\mathrm{d}\tau \\
&\quad + \sum_{i=1}^{d}\int_0^{\tau'}\int_\Omega \|G_{x_i}(\cdot,y,\tau',\tau)\|_{L^\infty(\Omega)}\, |\mathcal{F}^{n-1}(y,\tau)|\,\mathrm{d}y\,\mathrm{d}\tau \\
&\quad + \sum_{i,j=1}^{d}\int_0^{\tau'} \left\|\int_\Omega G_{x_ix_j}(\cdot,y,\tau',\tau)\mathcal{F}^{n-1}(y,\tau)\,\mathrm{d}y\right\|_{L^\infty(\Omega)} \mathrm{d}\tau.
\end{aligned}$$

Our goal is to show that $\|v^n(\cdot,\tau')\|_{W^2_\infty(\Omega)}$ is uniformly bounded on the interval $[0, T^*]$ so that we can use the Arzelà–Ascoli theorem and a weak compactness argument (Theorem 3 of Appendix D in Ref. 25). From A(6), we have $|\mathcal{F}^{n-1}| = \mathcal{F}^{n-1}$. We obtain the following estimates by using **A(7)**:

$$\begin{aligned}
\mathcal{F}^{n-1}(y,\tau) &\le \int_\Omega |f(y,\tau,z,(v^{n-1}+\varphi)(y,\tau),\nabla(v^{n-1}+\varphi)(y,\tau))|\,\mathrm{d}z \\
&\le \int_\Omega C_0(1+|v^{n-1}(y,\tau)| \\
&\quad + |\varphi(y,\tau)| + |\nabla v^{n-1}(y,\tau)| + |\nabla\varphi(y,\tau)|)\,\mathrm{d}z \\
&\le \int_\Omega C_0\left(\|v^{n-1}(\cdot,\tau)\|_{L^\infty(\Omega)} + \sum_{i=1}^{d}\|v^{n-1}_{y_i}(\cdot,\tau)\|_{L^\infty(\Omega)}\right) \\
&\quad + C_0\left(1+\sup_{Q_{T^*}}|\varphi(y,\tau)| + \sum_{i=1}^{d}\sup_{Q_{T^*}}|\varphi_{y_i}(y,\tau)|\right)\mathrm{d}z \\
&\le C_3\|v^{n-1}(\cdot,\tau)\|_{W^2_\infty(\Omega)} + C_{T^*},
\end{aligned}$$

where C_3 is a constant independent of T^*, whereas C_{T^*} is a constant that depends on T^*. By a direct calculation, we can easily see that (with $|x-y|^2 =$

$(x_1 - y_1)^2 + \cdots + (x_d - y_d)^2)$,

$$\begin{aligned}
&\int_{\Omega} (\tau' - \tau)^{-\frac{d}{2}} \exp\left(-C_2 \frac{|x-y|^2}{\tau' - \tau}\right) \mathrm{d}y \\
&\quad \leq \int_{\mathbb{R}^d} (\tau' - \tau)^{-\frac{d}{2}} \exp\left(-C_2 \frac{|x-y|^2}{\tau' - \tau}\right) \mathrm{d}y \\
&\quad = C_2^{-\frac{d}{2}} \int_{\mathbb{R}^d} \mathrm{e}^{-\sigma^2}\, \mathrm{d}\sigma \\
&\quad = \left(\frac{\pi}{C_2}\right)^{\frac{d}{2}}.
\end{aligned}$$

We can see this by computing the integral in one dimension:

$$\begin{aligned}
&\int_{-\infty}^{\infty} (\tau' - \tau)^{-\frac{1}{2}} \exp\left(-C_2 \frac{(x_1 - y_1)^2}{\tau' - \tau}\right) \mathrm{d}y_1 \\
&\quad = \int_{-\infty}^{\infty} (\tau' - \tau)^{-\frac{1}{2}} \sqrt{\frac{\tau' - \tau}{C_2}}\, \mathrm{e}^{-\omega_1^2}\, \mathrm{d}\omega_1 \\
&\quad = C_2^{-\frac{1}{2}} \int_{-\infty}^{\infty} \mathrm{e}^{-\omega_1^2}\, \mathrm{d}\omega_1 \\
&\quad = \left(\frac{\pi}{C_2}\right)^{\frac{1}{2}},
\end{aligned}$$

where we use

$$\omega_1 = \sqrt{\frac{C_2}{\tau' - \tau}}(x_1 - y_1).$$

The integral in $\mathbb{R}^d$ is a product of these one-dimensional integrals. This gives us the desired result.

The Green's function estimate

$$\left\| \int_{\Omega} G_{x_i x_j}(\cdot, y, \tau', \tau)\, \mathrm{d}y \right\|_{L^\infty(\Omega)} \leq C_4(\tau' - \tau)^{-\gamma}, \tag{13.45}$$

where C_4 is a constant independent of T^*, $0 < \gamma < 1$ and $\tau' > \tau$ can be found in Ref. 26. Using all of our previous estimates and Equation 13.46, we obtain

$$\begin{aligned}
\|v^n(\cdot, \tau')\|_{W^2_\infty(\Omega)} &= \|v^n(\cdot, \tau')\|_{L^\infty(\Omega)} + \sum_{i=1}^{d} \|v^n_{x_i}(\cdot, \tau')\|_{L^\infty(\Omega)} \\
&\quad + \sum_{i,j=1}^{d} \|v^n_{x_i x_j}(\cdot, \tau')\|_{L^\infty(\Omega)}
\end{aligned}$$

$$
\begin{aligned}
&\leq \int_0^{\tau'} \left(A + B(\tau' - \tau)^{-\frac{1}{2}} + D(\tau' - \tau)^{-\gamma}\right) \\
&\times \left(C_3 \|v^{n-1}(\cdot, \tau)\|_{W^2_\infty(\Omega)} + C_{T^*}\right) \mathrm{d}\tau \\
&= C_{T^*} \left(A\tau' + 2B\tau'^{1/2} + D\frac{\tau'^{1-\gamma}}{1-\gamma}\right) \\
&+ C_3 \int_0^{\tau'} \left(A + B(\tau' - \tau)^{-\frac{1}{2}} + D(\tau' - \tau)^{-\gamma}\right) \|v^{n-1}(\cdot, \tau) \\
&\|_{W^2_\infty(\Omega)} \mathrm{d}\tau \\
&\leq C(T^*, \gamma) + C \int_0^{\tau'} \left(A + B(\tau' - \tau)^{-\frac{1}{2}} + D(\tau' - \tau)^{-\gamma}\right) \\
&\|v^{n-1}(\cdot, \tau)\|_{W^2_\infty(\Omega)} \mathrm{d}\tau
\end{aligned}
$$

where the constants A, B, D, and C are independent of T^*. The constant $C(T^*, \gamma)$ depends only on T^* and γ. Therefore we have

$$
\begin{aligned}
\|v^n(\cdot, \tau')\|_{W^2_\infty(\Omega)} \leq C(T^*, \gamma) \\
&+ C \int_0^{\tau'} \left(A + B(\tau' - \tau)^{-\frac{1}{2}} + D(\tau' - \tau)^{-\gamma}\right) \\
&\|v^{n-1}(\cdot, \tau)\|_{W^2_\infty(\Omega)} \mathrm{d}\tau. \qquad (13.46)
\end{aligned}
$$

Observe that there exist an upper bound of the integral

$$
\int_0^{\tau'} \left(A + B(\tau' - \tau)^{-\frac{1}{2}} + D(\tau' - \tau)^{-\gamma}\right) \mathrm{d}\tau,
$$

for $\tau' \in [0, T^*]$. Choose A (where $\tau' = \frac{t}{A}$, as defined before) such that this upper bound is ε where $|\varepsilon C| < 1$. This is possible as C does not depend on T^*.

We observe from Equation 13.46 that

$$
\begin{aligned}
&\|v^1(\cdot, \tau')\|_{W^2_\infty(\Omega)} \leq C(T^*, \gamma), \|v^2(\cdot, \tau')\|_{W^2_\infty(\Omega)} \\
&\leq C(T^*, \gamma) + C \int_0^{\tau'} \left(A + B(\tau' - \tau)^{-\frac{1}{2}} + D(\tau' - \tau)^{-\gamma}\right) \\
&\|v^1(\cdot, \tau')\|_{W^2_\infty(\Omega)} \mathrm{d}\tau \\
&\leq C(T^*, \gamma) + C(T^*, \gamma)C\varepsilon, \|v^3(\cdot, \tau')\|_{W^2_\infty(\Omega)} \\
&\leq C(T^*, \gamma) + C \int_0^{\tau'} \left(A + B(\tau' - \tau)^{-\frac{1}{2}} + D(\tau' - \tau)^{-\gamma}\right) \\
&\|v^2(\cdot, \tau)\|_{W^2_\infty(\Omega)} \mathrm{d}\tau
\end{aligned}
$$

$$\leq C(T^*,\gamma)+C(C(T^*,\gamma)+C(T^*,\gamma)C\varepsilon)\varepsilon$$
$$= C(T^*,\gamma)+C(T^*,\gamma)C\varepsilon+C(T^*,\gamma)C^2\varepsilon^2.$$

Proceeding this way

$$\|v^n(\cdot,\tau')\|_{W^2_\infty(\Omega)} \leq C(T^*,\gamma)\left(1+C\varepsilon+\cdots+C^{n-1}\varepsilon^{n-1}\right).$$

Since $|\varepsilon C|<1$, we obtain $\|v^n(\cdot,\tau')\|_{W^2_\infty(\Omega)} \leq \frac{C(T^*,\gamma)}{1-\varepsilon C}$, where $n=0,1,2,\ldots$. Consequently $\|v^n(\cdot,\tau')\|_{W^2_\infty(\Omega)}$ is uniformly bounded on the closed interval $[0, T^*]$. Using this result along with Equation 3.11, we can easily show that $\|v^n_{\tau'}(\cdot,\tau')\|_{L^\infty(\Omega)}$ is also uniformly bounded on $[0, T^*]$.

Since $\|v^n(\cdot,\tau')\|_{W^2_\infty(\Omega)}$ and $\|v^n_{\tau'}(\cdot,\tau')\|_{L^\infty(\Omega)}$ are continuous functions of τ' on the closed interval $[0, T^*]$, it follows that $|v^n|$, $|v^n_{x_i}|$, $|v^n_{x_ix_j}|$ and $|v^n_t|$ are uniformly bounded on $\overline{Q}_{T^*}$. Thus $v^n(\cdot,\tau')$ is equicontinuous in $C(\overline{Q}_{T^*})$. By the Arzelà–Ascoli theorem, there exists a subsequence $\{v^{n_k}\}_{k=0}^\infty$ such that as $k\to\infty$,

$$v^{n_k} \to v \in C(\overline{Q}_{T^*}) \quad \text{and}$$
$$v^{n_k}_{x_i} \to v_{x_i} \in C(\overline{Q}_{T^*}),$$

where the convergence is uniform. Furthermore, by Theorem 3 in Appendix D of Ref. 25,

$$v^{n_k}_{x_ix_j} \to v_{x_ix_j} \in L^\infty(\overline{Q}_{T^*}) \quad \text{and}$$
$$v^{n_k}_{\tau'} \to v_{\tau'} \in L^\infty(\overline{Q}_{T^*}),$$

as $k\to\infty$. Here, the convergence is in the weak sense. Therefore, v^{n_k} converges uniformly on the compact set $\overline{Q}_{T^*}$ to a function $v \in C^{1+1,0+1}(\overline{Q}_{T^*})$.

By a standard argument [20], we have that v satisfies the parabolic equation in Equation 13.39 almost everywhere and the initial-boundary conditions in the classical sense. Hence, v is a strong solution to problem (Eq. 13.39). Consequently, u is a strong solution to Equation 13.37. ■

Now, we show that we can extend this solution to give us a strong solution on the unbounded domain $\mathbb{R}^{d+1}_T = \mathbb{R}^d \times (0, T)$.

THEOREM 13.13

There exists a strong solution $u \in W^{2,1}_p(\mathbb{R}^{d+1}_T)$ to the problem

$$\begin{aligned} u_t - Lu &= \mathcal{F}(x,t,u,\nabla u) \ \text{in}\ \mathbb{R}^{d+1}_T, \\ u(x,0) &= u_0(x) \qquad\quad\ \text{on}\ \mathbb{R}^d \end{aligned} \tag{13.47}$$

such that the solution $u(x,t) \to g(x,t)$ as $|x| \to \infty$.

Proof. We approximate the domain $\mathbb{R}^d$ by a nondecreasing sequence $\{\Omega_N\}_{N=1}^{\infty}$ of bounded smooth subdomains of Ω. For simplicity, we will let $\Omega_N = B(0, N)$ be the open ball in $\mathbb{R}^d$ centered at the origin with radius N. Also, we let $V_N = \Omega_N \times (0, T)$.

Using the previous theorem, we let $u_M \in C^{1+1,0+1}(\overline{V}_M)$ be a solution to the problem

$$\begin{aligned} u_t - Lu &= \mathcal{F}(x, t, u, \nabla u) \quad \text{in } V_M, \\ u(x, 0) &= u_0(x) \quad \text{on } \Omega_M, \\ u(x, t) &= g(x, t) \quad \text{on } \partial\Omega_M \times (0, T). \end{aligned} \tag{13.48}$$

Since $M \geq 1$ is arbitrary, we can use a standard diagonal argument (Theorem 13.10) to extract a subsequence that converges to a strong solution u to the problem on the whole unbounded space $\mathbb{R}_T^{d+1}$. Clearly, $u(x, 0) = u_0(x)$ and $u(x, t) \to g(x, t)$ as $|x| \to \infty$. ∎

13.4 Integro-Differential Equations in a Lévy Market

The Black–Scholes models with jumps arise from the fact that the driving Brownian motion is a continuous process, and so there are difficulties fitting the financial data presenting large fluctuations. The necessity of taking into account the large market movements, and a great amount of information arriving suddenly (i.e., a jump) has led to the study of PIDE in which the integral term is modeling the jump [1,7]. In this chapter we model the jump in such a way that it can be transformed to a convolution integral.

We assume n assets $S = (S_1, \ldots, S_n)$ and we assume $\sum_{i=1}^{n} \left(\ln \frac{S_i}{|E|}\right)^2 \leq R'^2$, for some constant R'. Let us define the region by $\mathbb{U}$. Define $\alpha_i = -\frac{1}{2}(\frac{r_i - \lambda p_i}{\sigma^2/2} - 1)$, for $i = 1, \ldots, n$ and $\Omega = \sum_{i=1}^{n} \alpha_i - 1$. We consider the constant volatility case with n independent assets. Then in Equation 13.8, $\rho_{ij} = 0$ for $i \neq j$. We consider r_i to be the riskless rate for S_i. Then Equation 13.8 becomes (if we model the jump as the integral of the following equation)

$$\begin{aligned} &\frac{\partial C}{\partial t} + \sum_{i=1}^{n} \frac{1}{2}\sigma_i^2 S_i^2 \frac{\partial^2 C}{\partial S_i^2} + \sum_{i=1}^{n} (r_i - \lambda p_i) S_i \frac{\partial C}{\partial S_i} - \sum_{i=1}^{n} r_i C \\ &+ \lambda |E|^{\Omega} \int_{\mathbb{U}} G(S, P) C(P, t) \left(\prod_{i=1}^{n} P_i^{\alpha_i + 1}\right)^{-1} \mathrm{d}P = 0, \end{aligned} \tag{13.49}$$

for some random variable $P = (P_1, \ldots, P_n) \in \mathbb{U}$, where λ is the jump intensity. We take $G(S, P) = g(\ln \frac{S_1}{P_1}, \ldots, \ln \frac{S_n}{P_n})$, where g is probability density function of its variables, $p_i = \mathbb{E}(P_i - 1)$, where $\mathbb{E}$ is the expectation operator and the random variable $P_i - 1$ measures the percentage change in the stock price for S_i if jump occurs. We assume $\sigma_i = \sigma, i = 1, \ldots, n$. So Equation 13.49 becomes

$$\frac{\partial C}{\partial t} + \frac{1}{2}\sigma^2 \sum_{i=1}^{n} S_i^2 \frac{\partial^2 C}{\partial S_i^2} + \sum_{i=1}^{n} (r_i - \lambda p_i) S_i \frac{\partial C}{\partial S_i} - \sum_{i=1}^{n} r_i C$$
$$+ \lambda |E|^{\Omega} \int_{\mathbb{U}} G(S, P) C(P, t) \left(\prod_{i=1}^{n} P_i^{\alpha_i + 1} \right)^{-1} \mathrm{d}P = 0. \qquad (13.50)$$

We set

$$S_i = |E| \mathrm{e}^{x_i}, \quad P_i = |E| \mathrm{e}^{y_i}, \quad t = T - \frac{\tau}{\sigma^2/2},$$

and

$$C(S_1, \ldots, S_n, t) = |E| \exp\left(\sum_{i=1}^{n} \alpha_i \right) u(x_1, \ldots, x_n, \tau).$$

Then we get

$$-\frac{\partial u}{\partial \tau} + \gamma u + \Delta u + \lambda \int_{\mathbb{B}(R')} g(x - Y) u(Y) \mathrm{d}Y = 0, \qquad (13.51)$$

where $\mathbb{B}(R') = \{x = (x_1, \ldots, x_n) \in \mathbb{R}^n | \sum_{i=1}^{n} x_i^2 \leq R'^2\}$ and

$$\gamma = \left[\sum_{i=1}^{n} (\alpha_i^2 + (k_i - 1)\alpha_i) - k \right], \quad k_i = \frac{r_i - \lambda p_i}{\sigma^2/2}, \quad k = \frac{\sum_{i=1}^{n} r_i}{\sigma^2/2}.$$

Clearly Equation 13.51 is the transformed version of Equation 13.49. We choose

$$g(X) = \frac{1}{N_{R'}} \frac{J_\nu(c|X|)}{(c|X|)^\nu}, \qquad (13.52)$$

where J_ν is the Bessel function for order ν, with $\nu = \frac{(n-2)}{2}$ and $N_{R'}$ is a normalizing constant such that $\int_{B(R')} g(X) \mathrm{d}X = 1$. To solve the problem (Eq. 13.51) with g given by Equation 13.52, we need the following two theorems. Proofs of them may be found in Ref. 27.

THEOREM 13.14

Suppose $\mathbf{x} = (r, \eta)$ and $\mathbf{y} = (r', \xi)$ are in $\mathbb{R}^2$ where η and ξ are angular parts of $\mathbf{x}$ and $\mathbf{y}$, respectively. Then

$$\int_{S^1} J_0(c|\mathbf{x} - \mathbf{y}|) \mathrm{e}^{ik\xi} \mathrm{d}\xi = 2\pi J_k(cr) J_k(cr') \mathrm{e}^{ik\eta}.$$

THEOREM 13.15

Suppose $\mathbf{x} = (r, \eta)$ and $\mathbf{y} = (r', \xi)$ are in $\mathbb{R}^n$, where where η and ξ are angular parts of $\mathbf{x}$ and $\mathbf{y}$, respectively, and $\nu = \frac{(n-2)}{2}$. Then

$$\int_{S^{n-1}} \frac{J_\nu(c|\mathbf{x}-\mathbf{y}|)}{(c|\mathbf{x}-\mathbf{y}|)^\nu} S_k^s(\xi)\mathrm{d}\xi = \frac{2^{3\nu+1}}{\pi^{\nu-1}} \Delta_n(\nu, cr)\Delta_n(\nu, cr')S_k^s(\eta),$$

where $\Delta_m(\nu, r) = \left(\frac{\pi}{2r}\right)^\nu J_{\nu+m}(r)$.

We consider here the case $n \geq 3$. The case $n = 2$ will be similar and simpler. We denote $\mathbf{H}_l$ as the space of degree l spherical harmonics on the n-sphere. We look for a solution of Equation 13.51 of the form

$$u(x,\tau) = \sum_{N=0}^{\infty} \sum_{l=1}^{h(N,p)} T_{Nl}(\tau) R_{Nl}(r) S_N^l(\eta), \tag{13.53}$$

where $x = (x_1, \ldots, x_n) = (r, \eta)$.

Then the integral term of Equation 13.51 becomes (with $Y = (Y_1, \ldots, Y_n) = (r', \xi)$) with the use of Theorem 13.15

$$\begin{aligned}
&\lambda \int_{\mathbb{B}(R')} g(x-Y)u(Y)\mathrm{d}Y \\
&= \frac{\lambda}{N_{R'}} \int_{\mathbb{B}(R')} \frac{J_\nu(c|x-Y|)}{(c|x-Y|)^\nu} u(Y)\mathrm{d}Y \\
&= \frac{\lambda}{N_{R'}} \sum_{N=0}^{\infty} \sum_{l=1}^{h(N,p)} \int_0^{R'} r'^{p+1}\mathrm{d}r' \int_{S^{n-1}} \frac{J_\nu(c|x-Y|)}{(c|x-Y|)^\nu} T_{Nl}(\tau)R_{Nl}(r')S_N^l(\xi)\mathrm{d}\xi \\
&= \frac{\lambda}{N_{R'}} \sum_{N=0}^{\infty} \sum_{l=1}^{h(N,p)} \int_0^{R'} r'^{p+1}\mathrm{d}r' \frac{2^{3\nu+1}}{\pi^{\nu-1}} \Delta_N(\nu, cr)\Delta_N(\nu, cr')T_{Nl}(\tau)R_{Nl}(r')S_N^l(\eta) \\
&= \sum_{N=0}^{\infty} \sum_{l=1}^{h(N,p)} \frac{2^{3\nu+1}\lambda}{\pi^{\nu-1}N_{R'}} \Delta_N(\nu, cr)T_{Nl}(\tau) \\
&\quad \left(\int_0^{R'} \Delta_N(\nu, cr')R_{Nl}(r')r'^{p+1}\mathrm{d}r'\right) S_N^l(\eta).
\end{aligned}$$

Therefore, Equation 13.15 becomes

$$-\sum_{N=0}^{\infty} \sum_{l=1}^{h(N,p)} T'_{Nl}(\tau)R_{Nl}(r)S_N^l(\eta) + \gamma \sum_{N=0}^{\infty} \sum_{l=1}^{h(N,p)} T_{Nl}(\tau)R_{Nl}(r)S_N^l(\eta)$$

$$+\sum_{N=0}^{\infty}\sum_{l=1}^{h(N,p)} T_{Nl}(\tau)r^{1-n}\frac{\partial}{\partial r}\left(r^{n-1}\frac{\partial R_{Nl}(r)}{\partial r}\right)S_N^l(\eta)$$

$$-\sum_{N=0}^{\infty}\sum_{l=1}^{h(N,p)} T_{Nl}(\tau)R_{Nl}(r)\frac{N(N+n-2)}{r^2}S_N^l(\eta)$$

$$+\sum_{N=0}^{\infty}\sum_{l=1}^{h(N,p)} \frac{2^{3\nu+1}\lambda}{\pi^{\nu-1}N_{R'}}\Delta_N(\nu,cr)T_{Nl}(\tau)$$

$$\times\left(\int_0^{R'}\Delta_N(\nu,cr')R_{Nl}(r')r'^{p+1}\mathrm{d}r'\right)S_N^l(\eta)=0.$$

Since $S_N^l(\eta)$ are linearly independent comparing the coefficients, we have the following equations for $N=0,1,\ldots$ and $l=1,\ldots,h(N,p)$.

$$T'_{Nl}(\tau)R_{Nl}(r)=\gamma T_{Nl}(\tau)R_{Nl}(r)+T_{Nl}(\tau)r^{1-n}\frac{\partial}{\partial r}\left(r^{n-1}\frac{\partial R_{Nl}(r)}{\partial r}\right)$$

$$-T_{Nl}(\tau)R_{Nl}(r)\frac{N(N+n-2)}{r^2}$$

$$+\frac{2^{3\nu+1}\lambda}{\pi^{\nu-1}N_{R'}}\Delta_N(\nu,cr)T_{Nl}(\tau)\left(\int_0^{R'}\Delta_N(\nu,cr')R_{Nl}(r')r'^{p+1}\mathrm{d}r'\right).$$

Therefore, we have the following equations

$$T'_{Nl}(\tau)=\Lambda T_{Nl}(\tau), \tag{13.54}$$

and

$$\gamma R_{Nl}(r)+r^{1-n}\frac{\partial}{\partial r}\left(r^{n-1}\frac{\partial R_{Nl}(r)}{\partial r}\right)-R_{Nl}(r)\frac{N(N+n-2)}{r^2}$$

$$+\zeta\Delta_N(\nu,cr)I=\Lambda R_{Nl}(r), \tag{13.55}$$

where Λ is a constant, $\zeta=\frac{2^{3\nu+1}\lambda}{\pi^{\nu-1}N_{R'}}$ and

$$I=\int_0^{R'}\Delta_N(\nu,cr')R_{Nl}(r')r'^{p+1}\mathrm{d}r'.$$

Initial values for $T_{Nl}(\tau)$ and the boundary values of $R(r)$ are obtained from the given problem. Solution of (13.54) is given by

$$T_{Nl}(\tau)=T_{Nl}(0)\mathrm{e}^{\Lambda\tau}.$$

Solution of Equation 13.55 can be obtained by standard techniques such as *homotopy perturbation method* [28,29]. Here we give an outline of that. Observe that Equation 13.55 can be rewritten as

$$\frac{\partial^2 R_{Nl}(r)}{\partial r^2} + \frac{(n-1)}{r}\frac{\partial R_{Nl}(r)}{\partial r} + \left(\gamma - \frac{N(N+n-2)}{r^2} - \Lambda\right) R_{Nl}(r)$$
$$+ \zeta \Delta_N(\nu, cr) \int_0^{R'} \Delta_N(\nu, cr') R_{Nl}(r') r'^{p+1} \mathrm{d}r' = 0. \tag{13.56}$$

By homotopy perturbation technique, we construct a homotopy

$$\begin{aligned} H(v,p) = & \frac{\partial^2 v(r)}{\partial r^2} - \frac{\partial^2 y_0(r)}{\partial r^2} + p\frac{\partial^2 y_0(r)}{\partial r^2} \\ & - p\left[\left(\frac{N(N+n-2)}{r^2} + \Lambda - \gamma\right) v(r) - \frac{(n-1)}{r}\frac{\partial v(r)}{\partial r} \right. \\ & \left. -\zeta \Delta_N(\nu, cr) \int_0^{R'} \Delta_N(\nu, cr') v(r') r'^{p+1} \mathrm{d}r' \right] = 0, \end{aligned} \tag{13.57}$$

where $y_0(r)$ is the initial approximation. According to homotopy perturbation theory, we can first use the embedding parameter p as a *small parameter*, and assume that the solution of Equation 13.57 can be written as a power series in p. That is

$$v(r) = v_0(r) + pv_1(r) + p^2 v_2(r) + \cdots. \tag{13.58}$$

Setting $p = 1$, we can get the solution for Equation 13.56 as

$$R_{Nl}(r) = v_0(r) + v_1(r) + v_2(r) + \cdots. \tag{13.59}$$

Substituting Equation 13.58 in Equation 13.57 and equating the coefficients of like powers of p, we obtain

$$p^0 : \frac{\partial^2 v_0(r)}{\partial r^2} - \frac{\partial^2 y_0(r)}{\partial r^2} = 0, \tag{13.60}$$

$$p^1 : \frac{\partial^2 v_1(r)}{\partial r^2} + \frac{\partial^2 y_0(r)}{\partial r^2} - [(\frac{N(N+n-2)}{r^2} + \Lambda - \gamma) v_0(r) - \frac{(n-1)}{r}\frac{\partial v_0(r)}{\partial r}$$
$$- \zeta \Delta_N(\nu, cr) \int_0^{R'} \Delta_N(\nu, cr') v_0(r') r'^{p+1} \mathrm{d}r'] = 0, \tag{13.61}$$

$$p^k : \frac{\partial^2 v_k(r)}{\partial r^2} - [(\frac{N(N+n-2)}{r^2} + \Lambda - \gamma) v_{k-1}(r) - \frac{(n-1)}{r}\frac{\partial v_{k-1}(r)}{\partial r}$$
$$- \zeta \Delta_N(\nu, cr) \int_0^{R'} \Delta_N(\nu, cr') v_{k-1}(r') r'^{p+1} \mathrm{d}r'] = 0, \quad k \geq 2. \tag{13.62}$$

Then starting with an initial approximation $y_0(r)$ and solving successively the above equations, we can find $v_k(r)$ for $k = 0, 1, 2, \ldots$. Therefore we can get the k-th approximation of the exact solution (Eq. 13.59) as $R_{Nl}^k(r) = v_0(r) + v_1(r) + \cdots + v_{k-1}(r)$. Observe that according to homotopy perturbation theory $\lim_{k \to \infty} R_{Nl}^k(r) = R_{Nl}(r)$.

REFERENCES

1. Merton RC. Continuous-time finance. Wiley-Blackwell, UK; 1992.
2. Salas M. Parabolic Problems Arising in Financial Mathematics and Semiconductor Physics. PhD Dissertation, New Mexico State University, Las Cruces, NM, August 2010.
3. Adams RA, editor. Sobolev spaces. Academic Press, Netherlands; 1975.
4. Krylov NV. Lectures on elliptic and parabolic equations in Hölder spaces. Volume 12, Graduate studies in mathematics. American Mathematical Society, Providence, Rhode Island; 1996.
5. Wang C, Wu Z, Yin J. Elliptic and parabolic equations. World Scientific Publishing, Singapore; 2006.
6. Amster P, Averbuj C, De Napoli P, Mariani MC. A parabolic problem arising on financial mathematics. Nonlinear Anal R World Appl 2010;11:759–763.
7. Florescu I, Mariani MC. Solutions to an integro-differential parabolic problem arising in the pricing of financial options in a Levy market. Electron J Differ Equat 2010;2010(62):1102010.
8. Black F, Scholes M. The valuation of options and corporate liability. J Polit Econ 1973;81:637–654.
9. Duffie D. Dynamic asset pricing theory. 3rd ed. Princeton University Press, Princeton, New Jersey; 2001.
10. Hull JC. Options, futures, and other derivatives. 7th ed. Prentice Hall, New Jersey; 2008.
11. Ikeda N. Stochastic differential equations and diffusion processes. 2nd revised ed. North Holland, Maryland Heights, Missouri; 1989.
12. Jarrow RA. Modelling fixed income securities and interest rate options. 2nd ed. Stanford Economics and Finance, California; 2002.
13. Heston SL. A closed-form solution for options with stochastic volatility with applications to bond and currency options. Rev Financ Stud 1993;6(2):327–343.
14. Avellaneda M, Zhu Y. Risk neutral stochastic volatility model. Int J Theor Appl Finance 1998;1(2):289–310.
15. Berestycki H, Busca J, Florent I. Computing the implied volatility in stochastic volatility models. Commu Pure and Appl Math 2004;57(10):1352 –1373.
16. Andersen L, Andreasen J. Jump-diffusion processes: volatility smile fitting and numerical methods for option pricing. Rev Deriv Res 2000;4:231–262.
17. Cont R, Tankov P. Financial modelling with jumps processes. CRC Financial mathematics series. Chapman & Hall, Boca Raton, Florida; 2003.

18. Florescu I. Stochastic volatility stock price: approximation and valuation using a recombining tree. sharp estimation of the almost sure lyapunov exponent estimation for the anderson model in continuous space. PhD thesis, Purdue University, West Lafayette, IN, December 2004.
19. Florescu I, Viens F. Stochastic volatility: option pricing using a multinomial recombining tree. Appl Math Finance 2008;15(2):151–181.
20. Friedman A. Partial differential equations of parabolic type. Prentice Hall, New Jersey; 1964.
21. Zheng S. Nonlinear evolution equations. Chapman & Hall, Boca Raton, Florida; 2004.
22. Chadam J, Yin HM. An iteration procedure for a class of integrodifferential equations of parabolic type. J Integr Equat 1989;2(1):31–47.
23. Geman H. Pure jump levy processes for asset pricing modeling. J Bank Finance 2002;26:1297–1316.
24. Ladyzenskaja OA, Solonikov VA, Ural'ceva NN. Linear and quasilinear equations of parabolic type. Am Math Soc 1964;23.
25. Evans LC. Partial differential equations. Volume 19, Graduate studies in mathematics. American Mathematical Society, Providence, Rhode Island; 1998.
26. Yin HM. A uniqueness theorem for a class of non-classical parabolic equations. Appl Anal 1989;34:67–78.
27. SenGupta I. Differential operator related to the generalized superradiance integral equation. J Math Anal Appl 2010;369:101–111.
28. Dehghan M, Shakeri F. Solution of an integro-differential equation arising in oscillating magnetic fields using He's homotopy perturbation method. Prog Electromagn Res 2008;78:361–376.
29. He JH. Homotopy perturbation technique. Comput Meth Appl Mech Eng 1999;178:257–262.

CHAPTER FOURTEEN

Existence of Solutions for Financial Models with Transaction Costs and Stochastic Volatility

MARIA C. MARIANI
Department of Mathematical Sciences, University of Texas at El Paso, El Paso, TX

EMMANUEL K. NCHEUGUIM
Department of Mathematical Sciences, New Mexico State University, Las Cruces, NM

INDRANIL SENGUPTA
Department of Mathematical Sciences, University of Texas at El Paso, El Paso, TX

14.1 Model with Transaction Costs

In a complete financial market without transaction costs, the celebrated Black–Scholes model [1] provides not only a rational option pricing formula, but also a hedging portfolio that replicates the contingent claim. In the Black–Scholes analysis, it is assumed that hedging takes place continuously,

Handbook of Modeling High-Frequency Data in Finance, First Edition.
Edited by Frederi G. Viens, Maria C. Mariani, and Ionuţ Florescu.

and therefore, in a market with proportional transaction costs, it tends to be infinitely expensive. So the requirement of replicating the value of the option continuously has to be relaxed. The first model in that direction was initiated by Leland (1985)[2]. He assumes that the portfolio is rebalanced at discrete time δt fixed and transaction costs are proportional to the value of the underlying; that is, the costs incurred at each step is $\kappa|\nu|S$, where ν is the number of shares of the underlying bought ($\nu > 0$) or sold ($\nu < 0$) at price S and κ is a constant depending on individual investors. Leland derived an option price formula which is the same as the Black–Scholes formula for European calls and puts with an adjusted volatility

$$\hat{\sigma} = \sigma\left(1 + \sqrt{\frac{2}{\pi}}\frac{\kappa}{\sigma\sqrt{\delta t}}\right)^{1/2}.$$

Following Leland's idea, Hoggard *et al.* [3] derive a nonlinear PDE (partial differential equation) for the option price value in the presence of transaction costs. We outline the steps used in the next section.

14.1.1 OPTION PRICE VALUATION IN THE GEOMETRIC BROWNIAN MOTION CASE WITH TRANSACTION COSTS

Let $C(S,t)$ be the value of the option and Π be the value of the hedge portfolio. The asset follows a geometric Brownian motion. Using discrete time, we assume the underlying asset follows the process

$$\delta S = \mu S \delta t + \sigma S \Phi \sqrt{\delta t}, \tag{14.1}$$

where Φ is drawn from a standard normal distribution, μ is a measure of the average rate of growth of the asset price also known as the *drift*, σ is a measure of the fluctuation (risk) in the asset prices and corresponds to the diffusion coefficient. Then the change in the value of the portfolio over the timestep δt is given by

$$\delta\Pi = \sigma S\left(\frac{\partial C}{\partial S} - \Delta\right)\Phi\sqrt{\delta t} + \left(\frac{1}{2}\sigma^2 S^2 \frac{\partial^2 C}{\partial S^2}\phi^2 + \mu S\frac{\partial C}{\partial S} + \frac{\partial C}{\partial t} - \mu\Delta S\right)\delta t - \kappa S|\nu|$$

We consider the delta-hedging strategy. Specifically, let the quantity of asset held short at time t, $\Delta = \frac{\partial C}{\partial S}(S,t)$. The timestep is assumed to be small, thus the number of assets traded after a time δt is

$$\nu = \frac{\partial C}{\partial S}(S + \delta S, t + \delta t) - \frac{\partial C}{\partial S}(S,t) = \delta S\frac{\partial^2 C}{\partial S^2} + \delta t\frac{\partial^2 C}{\partial t \partial S} + \cdots$$

Since $\delta S = \sigma S \Phi \sqrt{\delta t} + \mathcal{O}(\delta t)$, keeping only he leading term yields

$$\nu \simeq \frac{\partial^2 C}{\partial S^2} \sigma S \Phi \sqrt{\delta t}.$$

Thus, the expected transaction cost over a timestep is

$$E[\kappa S|\nu|] = \sqrt{\frac{2}{\pi}} \kappa \sigma S^2 \left| \frac{\partial^2 C}{\partial S^2} \right| \sqrt{\delta t},$$

where $\sqrt{2/\pi}$ is the expected value of $|\Phi|$. Therefore, the expected change in the value of the portfolio is

$$E(\delta \Pi) = \left(\frac{\partial C}{\partial t} \frac{1}{2} \sigma^2 S^2 \frac{\partial^2 C}{\partial S^2} - \kappa \sigma S^2 \sqrt{\frac{2}{\pi \delta t}} \left| \frac{\partial^2 C}{\partial S^2} \right| \right) \delta t.$$

If the portfolio is a hedging portfolio standard no arbitrage arguments imply that the portfolio will earn the riskfree interest rate r, and

$$E(\delta \Pi) = r \left(C - S \frac{\partial C}{\partial S} \right) \delta t.$$

Hence, Hoggard, Whalley, and Wilmott derive the model for option pricing with transaction costs as

$$\frac{\partial C}{\partial t} + \frac{1}{2} \sigma^2 S^2 \frac{\partial^2 C}{\partial^2 S} + rS \frac{\partial C}{\partial S} - rC - \kappa \sigma S^2 \sqrt{\frac{2}{\pi \delta t}} \left| \frac{\partial^2 C}{\partial S^2} \right| = 0, (S, T) \in (0, \infty) \times (0, T) \tag{14.2}$$

with the terminal condition

$$C(S, T) = \max(S - E, 0), S \in (0, \infty) \tag{14.3}$$

for European call options with strike price E, and a suitable terminal condition for European puts.

We note that Equation 14.2 contains the usual Black–Scholes terms with an additional nonlinear term that models the presence of transaction costs in the model. A related work in *quantum mechanics* has been done in Refs. 4,5.

We review some background in functional analysis useful for us in Section 14.2. In Section 14.3, we study the existence of solutions for problem (Eqs. 14.2 and 14.3) and finally in Sections 14.4 and 14.5, we extend it to the case of stochastic volatility. We prove the existence of classical solutions for the model which includes transaction cost and stochastic volatility. Our main results regarding the existence of classical solutions are given in Theorems 14.25 and 14.26.

14.2 Review of Functional Analysis

14.2.1 L^p SPACES

Let $\Omega \in \mathbb{R}^n$ be an open set and $p \geq 1$ be a real number.

DEFINITION 14.1

The space $L^p(\Omega)$ represents the class of all measurable functions on Ω such that

$$||u||_{L^p(\Omega)} = \left(\int_\Omega |u(x)|^p \mathrm{d}x \right)^{1/p} < \infty.$$

$L^p(\Omega)$ is a Banach space when endowed with the norm $||u||_{L^p(\Omega)}$.

DEFINITION 14.2

The space $L^p_{loc}(\Omega)$ represents the class of all measurable functions on Ω such that

$$\int_K |u(x)|^p \mathrm{d}x < \infty$$

for all compact subset K of Ω.

REMARK 14.3

$L^p(\Omega) \subset L^1_{loc}(\Omega)$ for all $1 \leq p < \infty$.

14.2.2 WEAK DERIVATIVES AND SOBOLEV SPACES

DEFINITION 14.4

Suppose u and $v \in L^1_{loc}(\Omega)$, and α is a multiindex. v is said to the αth-weak or distributional partial derivative of u, denoted $D^\alpha u = v$, if

$$\int_\Omega u D^\alpha \phi \mathrm{d}x = (-1)^{|\alpha|} \int_\Omega v \phi \mathrm{d}x$$

for any test function $\phi \in C^\infty(\Omega)_c$. Here $C^\infty_c(\Omega)$ represents the space of infinitely differentiable functions on Ω with compact support.

Note that the weak partial derivative of a function u, when it exits, is unique up to a set of measure zero. Weak derivatives of functions are not always functions and Sobolev spaces are particular classes of L^p functions, whose derivatives are also L^p functions.

DEFINITION 14.5

The Sobolev space

$$H^m(\Omega) = \{u \in L^2(\Omega) : D^\alpha u \in L^2(\Omega), \text{ for any multiindex } \alpha \text{ with } |\alpha| \leq m\},$$

where the derivatives are taken in the weak sense. $H^m(\Omega)$ is a Hilbert space when endowed with the inner product

$$(u, v)_{H^m(\Omega)} = \sum_{|\alpha| \leq m} (D^\alpha u, D^\alpha v)_{L^2(\Omega)}.$$

The space $H_0^1(\Omega)$ represents the closure of $C_c^\infty(\Omega)$ in $H^1(\Omega)$ and it is shown that $H_0^1(\Omega) = \{u \in H^1 \text{such that } u = 0 \text{ on } \partial\Omega\}$.
The space $H^{-1}(\Omega)$ denotes the topological dual of $H_0^1(\Omega)$ and for $f \in H^{-1}(\Omega)$, $||f||_{H^{-1}(\Omega)} = sup\{<f, u> \text{ such that } ||u||_{H_0^1(\Omega)} \leq 1 \text{ for all } u \in H_0^1(\Omega\}$. Here $<,>$ denotes the pairing between $H^{-1}(\Omega)$ and $H_0^1(\Omega)$.

REMARK 14.6

We have $H_0^1(\Omega) \subset H^1(\Omega) \subset L^2(\Omega) = H^0(\Omega) \subset H^{-1}(\Omega)$ and the embedding of $H_0^1(\Omega)$ in $L^2(\Omega)$ is compact.

14.2.3 SPACES INVOLVING TIME

Let X be a Banach space and T be a nonnegative integer.

The space $L^2(0, T; X)$ consists of all measurable functions u from $(0, T)$ to X with

$$||u||_{L^2(0,T;X)} := \left(\int_0^T ||u(t)||_X^2 \mathrm{d}t \right)^{1/2} < \infty.$$

$L^2(0, T; X)$ is a Banach space when endowed with the norm $||u||_{L^2(0,T;X)}$.

The space $C([0,T];X)$ consists of all continuous functions $u:[0,T]\longrightarrow X$ with

$$||u||_{C([0,T];X)} := \max_{0\le t\le T} ||u(t)||_X < \infty.$$

$C([0,T];X)$ is a Banach space when endowed with the norm $||u||_{C([0,T];X)}$.

THEOREM 14.7 (See Ref. 6 Theorem 3 in Section 5.9.2)

If $u\in L^2(0,T;H_0^1(B_R))$ and $\frac{\partial u}{\partial t}\in L^2(0,T;H^{-1}(B_R))$, then

(i) $u\in C([0,T];L^2(B_R))$,
(ii) the mapping $t\mapsto ||u(t)||^2_{L^2(B_R)}$ is absolutely continuous with

$$\frac{\mathrm{d}}{\mathrm{d}t}||u(t)||^2_{L^2(B_R)} = 2\int_{B_R}\frac{\partial u}{\partial t}u\mathrm{d}t \text{ for } a.e\ 0\le t\le T. \tag{14.4}$$

REMARK 14.8

For $u\in L^2(0,T;H_0^1(B_R))$ and $\frac{\partial u}{\partial t}\in L^2(0,T;H^{-1}(B_R))$, $u(0)$ is understood in the sense of the embedding $L^2(0,T;H_0^1(B_R))\hookrightarrow C([0,T];X)$.

14.2.4 HÖLDER SPACES

Next, we discuss spaces with classical derivatives, known as *Hölder spaces*. We will follow the notation and definitions given in the books [7] and [8]. We define $C^k_{loc}(\Omega)$ to be the set of all real-valued functions $u=u(x)$ with continuous classical derivatives $D^\alpha u$ in Ω, where $0\le|\alpha|\le k$. Next, we set

$$|u|_{0;\Omega} = [u]_{0;\Omega} = \sup_{\Omega}|u|,$$

$$[u]_{k;\Omega} = \max_{|\alpha|=k}\left|D^\alpha u\right|_{0;\Omega}.$$

If the seminorm

$$[u]_{\delta;\Omega} = \sup_{\substack{x,y\in\Omega\\ x\ne y}}\frac{|u(x)-u(y)|}{|x-y|^\delta}$$

is finite, then we say the real-valued function u is Hölder continuous in Ω with exponent δ. For a k-times differentiable function, we will set

$$[u]_{k+\delta;\Omega} = \max_{|\alpha|=k} \left[D^{\alpha} u\right]_{\delta;\Omega}.$$

DEFINITION 14.9

The space $C^k(\Omega)$ is the set of all functions $u \in C^k_{loc}(\Omega)$ such that the norm

$$|u|_{k;\Omega} = \sum_{j=0}^{k} [u]_{j;\Omega}$$

is finite. With this norm, it can be shown that $C^k(\Omega)$ is a Banach space.

DEFINITION 14.10

The Hölder space $C^{k+\delta}(\overline{\Omega})$ is the set of all functions $u \in C^k(\Omega)$ such that the norm

$$|u|_{k+\delta;\Omega} = |u|_{k;\Omega} + [u]_{k+\delta;\Omega}$$

is finite. With this norm, it can be shown that $C^{k+\delta}(\overline{\Omega})$ is a Banach space.

For any two points $P_1 = (x_1, t_1)$, $P_2 = (x_2, y_2) \in Q_T = \Omega \times (0, T)$, we define the parabolic distance between them as

$$d(P_1, P_2) = \left(|x_1 - x_2|^2 + |t_1 - t_2|\right)^{1/2}.$$

For a real-valued function $u = u(x, t)$ on Q_T, let us define the seminorm

$$[u]_{\delta,\delta/2;Q_T} = \sup_{\substack{P_1,P_2 \in Q_T \\ P_1 \neq P_2}} \frac{|u(x_1, t_1) - u(x_2, t_2)|}{d^{\delta}(P_1, P_2)}.$$

If this seminorm is finite for some u, then we say u is Hölder continuous with exponent δ. The maximum norm of u is given by

$$|u|_{0;Q_T} = \sup_{(x,t)\in Q_T} |u(x, t)|.$$

DEFINITION 14.11

The space $C^{\delta,\delta/2}\left(\overline{Q}_T\right)$ is the set of all functions $u \in Q_T$ such that the norm

$$|u|_{\delta,\delta/2;Q_T} = |u|_{0;Q_T} + [u]_{\delta,\delta/2;Q_T}$$

is finite. Furthermore, we define

$$C^{2k+\delta,k+\delta/2}\left(\overline{Q}_T\right) = \{u : D^\alpha \partial_t^\rho u \in C^{\delta,\delta/2}\left(\overline{Q}_T\right), 0 \leq |\alpha| + 2\rho \leq 2k\}.$$

We define a seminorm on $C^{2k+\delta,k+\delta/2}\left(\overline{Q}_T\right)$ by

$$[u]_{2k+\delta,k+\delta/2;Q_T} = \sum_{|\alpha|+2\rho=2k} [D^\alpha \partial_t^\rho u]_{\delta,\delta/2;Q_T},$$

and a norm by

$$|u|_{2k+\delta,k+\delta/2;Q_T} = \sum_{0\leq|\alpha|+2\rho\leq 2k} |D^\alpha \partial_t^\rho u|_{\delta,\delta/2;Q_T}.$$

Using this norm, it can be shown that $C^{2k+\delta,k+\delta/2}\left(\overline{Q}_T\right)$ is a Banach space.

14.2.5 INEQUALITIES

14.2.5.1 Cauchy's Inequality with ε.

$$ab \leq \varepsilon a^2 + \frac{b^2}{4\varepsilon} \qquad (a, b > 0, \varepsilon > 0).$$

14.2.5.2 Gronwall's Inequality (Integral Form). Let $\eta(t)$ be a nonnegative, absolutely continuous function on $[0, T]$ which satisfies for *a.e.* t the differential inequality

$$\eta'(t) \leq \phi(t)\eta(t) + \psi(t),$$

where $\phi(t)$ and $\psi(t)$ are nonnegative, summable functions on $[0, T]$. Then

$$\eta(t) \leq e^{\int_0^t \phi(s)ds}\left[\eta(0) + \int_0^t \psi(s)ds\right].$$

14.2.5.3 Hölder's Inequality. Assume $1 \le p, q \le \infty, \frac{1}{p} + \frac{1}{q} = 1$. Then if $u \in L^p(\Omega)$, $v \in L^q(\Omega)$, we have

$$\int_\Omega |uv| \mathrm{d}x \le ||u||_{L^p(\Omega)} ||v||_{L^q(\Omega)}.$$

14.2.5.4 Poincare's inequality. Assume Ω is a bounded open subset of $\mathbb{R}^n$. Suppose $u \in H_0^1(\Omega)$. Then

$$||u||_{L^2(\Omega)} \le C||Du||_{L^2(\Omega)}$$

where the constant C depends only on n and Ω.

14.2.6 SCHAEFER'S FIXED POINT THEOREM

X is a real Banach space.

DEFINITION 14.12

A nonlinear mapping $A : X \longrightarrow X$ is said to be compact if and only if for each bounded sequence $\{u_k\}_{k=1}^{\infty}$, the sequence $\{A[u_k]\}_{k=1}^{\infty}$ is precompact; that is there exists a subsequence $\{u_{k_j}\}_{j=1}^{\infty}$ such that $\{A[u_{k_j}]\}_{j=1}^{\infty}$ converges in X.

THEOREM 14.13 (Schaefer's Fixed Point Theorem)

Suppose $A : X \longrightarrow X$ is a continuous and compact mapping. Assume further that the set $\{u \in X$ such that $u = \lambda A[u]$ for some $0 \le \lambda \le 1\}$ is bounded. Then A has a fixed point.

Schaefer's fixed point Theorem will be useful to show the existence of solutions in a ball.

14.3 Solution of the Problem (14.2) and (14.3) in Sobolev Spaces

14.3.1 SOLUTION OF THE PROBLEM POSED IN A BALL

To begin the analysis of the problem, we set

$$x = \log(S/E), t = T - \tau / \frac{1}{2}\sigma^2, \text{ and } C = EV(X, \tau),$$

then Equation 14.2 becomes

$$-\frac{\partial V}{\partial \tau}+\frac{\partial^2 V}{\partial x^2}+(k-1)\frac{\partial V}{\partial x}-kV=\kappa^*\left|\frac{\partial^2 V}{\partial x^2}-\frac{\partial V}{\partial x}\right|,(x,\tau)\in \mathbb{R}\times(0,T^*) \tag{14.5}$$

and the initial condition

$$V(x,0)=\max(e^x-1,0),x\in\mathbb{R},$$

where $k=r/\frac{1}{2}\sigma^2$, $\kappa^*=\kappa\sqrt{\frac{8}{\pi\sigma^2\delta t}}$, and $T^*=\frac{1}{2}\sigma^2 T$.
Next set

$$V(x,\tau)=e^x U(x,\tau),$$

then Equation 14.5 yields

$$-\frac{\partial U}{\partial \tau}+\frac{\partial^2 U}{\partial x^2}+(k+1)\frac{\partial U}{\partial x}=\kappa^*\left|\frac{\partial^2 U}{\partial x^2}+\frac{\partial U}{\partial x}\right|,(x,\tau)\in \mathbb{R}\times(0,T^*) \tag{14.6}$$

and the initial condition

$$U(x,0)=\max(1-e^{-x},0).$$

The previous discussion motivates us to consider the following problem that can accommodate cost structures that go beyond proportional transaction costs:

$$-\frac{\partial U}{\partial t}+\frac{\partial^2 U}{\partial x^2}+\alpha\frac{\partial U}{\partial x}=\beta F\left(\frac{\partial U}{\partial x},\frac{\partial^2 U}{\partial x^2}\right),(x,t)\in\mathbb{R}\times(0,T) \tag{14.7}$$

and

$$U(x,0)=U_0(x),x\in\mathbb{R}, \tag{14.8}$$

where α and β are nonnegative constants.

The goal in this section is to show that the theoretical problem (Eqs. 14.7 and 14.8) has a strong solution where the derivatives are understood in the distribution sense. We assume that

(H1) $F:\mathbb{R}\times\mathbb{R}\longrightarrow\mathbb{R}^+$ is continuous,

(H2) $F(p,q)\le|p|+|q|$,

(H3) For $U\in H^2_{loc}(\mathbb{R})$, $\frac{\partial}{\partial x}F(U,\frac{\partial U}{\partial x})\in L^2(0,T;L^2_{loc}(\mathbb{R}))$. Moreover, with $B_R=\{x\in R:|x|<R\}$ if $U_k\to U$ in $L^2(0,T;H^1_0(B_R))$, then $\frac{\partial}{\partial x}F(U,\frac{\partial U_k}{\partial x})\to\frac{\partial}{\partial x}F(U,\frac{\partial U}{\partial x})$ in $L^2(0,T;L^2(B_R))$ and $U_{k0}\to U_0$ in $L^2(B_R)$,

(H4) $U_0 \in H^1_{loc}(\mathbb{R})$,
(H5) $\beta < 1$.

Let $B_R = \{x \in \mathbb{R} : |x| < R\}$ be the open ball centered at the origin with radius R. Assume that U_0 is suitable cut into bounded functions defined on B_R and such that (H1)–(H5) are satisfied in $B_R \times [0, T]$.
Set $w = \frac{\partial U}{\partial x}$ and consider an analogous problem in $B_R \times [0, T]$ with zero Dirichlet condition on the lateral boundary.

$$-\frac{\partial w}{\partial t} + \frac{\partial^2 w}{\partial x^2} + \alpha\frac{\partial w}{\partial x} = \beta\frac{\partial}{\partial x}F\left(w, \frac{\partial w}{\partial x}\right) \quad (x, t) \in B_R \times (0, T), \tag{14.9}$$

$$w(x, 0) = w_0(x) \qquad x \in B_R, \tag{14.10}$$

$$w(x, t) = 0, \qquad (x, t) \in \partial B_R \times [0, T]. \tag{14.11}$$

DEFINITION 14.14

w is said to be a weak solution of Equations 14.9–14.11 if

$$w \in L^2(0, T; H^1_0(B_R)), \frac{\partial w}{\partial t} \in L^2(0, T; H^{-1}(B_R))$$

$$\int_{B_R}\left(\frac{\partial w}{\partial t}\phi + \frac{\partial w}{\partial x}\frac{\partial \phi}{\partial x} + \alpha w\frac{\partial \phi}{\partial x}\right)\mathrm{d}x$$

$$= -\beta\int_{B_R} F\left(w, \frac{\partial w}{\partial x}\right)\frac{\partial \phi}{\partial x}\mathrm{d}x \tag{14.12}$$

for all $\phi \in H^1_0(B_R)$.

THEOREM 14.15 (A-Priori Estimates)

If w is a weak solution of Equations 14.9–14.11, then there exits a positive constant C independent of w such that

$$\max_{0\le t\le T}\|w(t)\|_{L^2(B_R)} + \|w(t)\|_{L^2(0,T;H^1_0(B_R))} + \left\|\frac{\partial w}{\partial t}\right\|_{L^2(0,T;H^{-1}(B_R))}$$
$$\le C\|w_0\|_{L^2(B_R)}. \tag{14.13}$$

Proof. Choose $w(t) \in H^1_0(B_R)$ as the test function in Equation 14.12, obtain

$$\int_{B_R}\left(\frac{\partial w}{\partial t}w + \frac{\partial w}{\partial x}\frac{\partial w}{\partial x} + \alpha w\frac{\partial w}{\partial x}\right)\mathrm{d}x = -\beta\int_{B_R} F\left(w, \frac{\partial w}{\partial x}\right)\frac{\partial w}{\partial x}\mathrm{d}x.$$

Then by Equation 14.4

$$\frac{1}{2}\frac{\mathrm{d}}{\mathrm{d}t}||w(t)||^2_{L^2(B_R)} + \left|\left|\frac{\partial w}{\partial x}\right|\right|^2_{L^2(B_R)} + \frac{1}{2}\alpha\int_{B_R}\frac{\partial}{\partial x}(w^2)\mathrm{d}x = -\beta\int_{B_R}F\left(w, \frac{\partial w}{\partial x}\right)\frac{\partial w}{\partial x}\mathrm{d}x$$

From Equation 14.11

$$\frac{1}{2}\frac{\mathrm{d}}{\mathrm{d}t}||w(t)||^2_{L^2(B_R)} + \left|\left|\frac{\partial w}{\partial x}\right|\right|^2_{L^2(B_R)} \leq \beta\int_{B_R}\left|F\left(w, \frac{\partial w}{\partial x}\right)\frac{\partial w}{\partial x}\right|\mathrm{d}x.$$

Using $(H2)$, obtain

$$\frac{1}{2}\frac{\mathrm{d}}{\mathrm{d}t}||w(t)||^2_{L^2(B_R)} + \left|\left|\frac{\partial w}{\partial x}\right|\right|^2_{L^2(B_R)} \leq \beta\int_{B_R}\left(|w|\left|\frac{\partial w}{\partial x}\right| + \left|\frac{\partial w}{\partial x}\right|^2\right)\mathrm{d}x.$$

By Cauchy inequality with $\varepsilon > 0$, we have

$$\frac{1}{2}\frac{\mathrm{d}}{\mathrm{d}t}||w(t)||^2_{L^2(B_R)} + \left|\left|\frac{\partial w}{\partial x}\right|\right|^2_{L^2(B_R)} \leq \beta\left(\int_{B_R}\left|\frac{\partial w}{\partial x}\right|^2\mathrm{d}x + \varepsilon\int_{B_R}\left|\frac{\partial w}{\partial x}\right|^2\mathrm{d}x + \frac{1}{4\varepsilon}\int_{B_R}|w|^2\,\mathrm{d}x\right).$$

Since $\beta < 1$ and choosing $\varepsilon \ll 1$ yields

$$\frac{\mathrm{d}}{\mathrm{d}t}||w(t)||^2_{L^2(B_R)} + C_1\,||w||^2_{H_0^1(B_R)} \leq C_2\|w\|^2_{L^2(B_R)} \tag{14.14}$$

for *a.e.* $0 \leq t \leq T$, and appropriate positive constants C_1 and C_2.
Next write $\eta(t) := \|w(t)\|^2_{L^2(B_R)}$, then by Equation 14.14

$$\eta'(t) \leq C_2\eta(t), \text{for } a.e.\ 0 \leq t \leq T.$$

The differential form of Gronwall inequality implies

$$\eta(t) \leq \mathrm{e}^{C_2 t}\eta(0) \text{for } a.e.\ 0 \leq t \leq T.$$

Since $\eta(0) = \|w(0)\|^2_{L^2(B_R)} = \|w_0\|^2_{L^2(B_R)}$, then

$$\|w(t)\|^2_{L^2(B_R)} \leq \mathrm{e}^{C_2 t}\|w_0\|^2_{L^2(B_R)}.$$

Hence

$$\max_{0\leq t\leq T}\|w(t)\|_{L^2(B_R)} \leq C\|w_0\|^2_{L^2(B_R)}. \tag{14.15}$$

To bound the second term, we consider Equation 3.10, and integrate from 0 to T to obtain

$$C_1 \int_0^T ||w||^2_{H_0^1(B_R)} \, dt \le C_2 \int_0^T ||w||^2_{L^2(B_R)} \, dt.$$

Use inequality (Eq. 14.15) to obtain

$$\|w\|_{L^2(0,T;H_0^1(B_R))} \le C\|w_0\|_{L^2(B_R)}. \tag{14.16}$$

Finally, to obtain a bound for the third term, fix $v \in H_0^1(B_R)$ with $\|v\|_{H_0^1(B_R)} \le 1$. By Equation 14.12, we have

$$\int_{B_R} \frac{\partial w}{\partial t} v \mathrm{d}x + \int_{B_R} \left(\frac{\partial w}{\partial x}\frac{\partial v}{\partial x} + \alpha w \frac{\partial v}{\partial x} \right) \mathrm{d}x = -\beta \int_{B_R} F\left(w, \frac{\partial w}{\partial x}\right) \frac{\partial v}{\partial x} \mathrm{d}x.$$

Thus,

$$\left| \int_{B_R} \frac{\partial w}{\partial t} v \mathrm{d}x \right| \le \left| \int_{B_R} \left(\frac{\partial w}{\partial x}\frac{\partial v}{\partial x} + \alpha w \frac{\partial v}{\partial x} \right) \mathrm{d}x \right| + \beta \left| \int_{B_R} F\left(w, \frac{\partial w}{\partial x}\right) \frac{\partial v}{\partial x} \mathrm{d}x \right|.$$

By Holder inequality, we have

$$\begin{aligned}
\left| \int_{B_R} \frac{\partial w}{\partial t} v \mathrm{d}x \right| \le & \left(\int_{B_R} \left| \frac{\partial w}{\partial x} \right|^2 \mathrm{d}x \right)^{1/2} \left(\int_{B_R} \left| \frac{\partial v}{\partial x} \right|^2 \mathrm{d}x \right)^{1/2} \\
& + \alpha \left(\int_{B_R} |w|^2 \mathrm{d}x \right)^{1/2} \left(\int_{B_R} \left| \frac{\partial v}{\partial x} \right|^2 \mathrm{d}x \right)^{1/2} \\
& + \left(\int_{B_R} \left| F\left(w, \frac{\partial w}{\partial x}\right) \right|^2 \mathrm{d}x \right)^{1/2} \left(\int_{B_R} \left| \frac{\partial v}{\partial x} \right|^2 \mathrm{d}x \right)^{1/2}.
\end{aligned}$$

Since $\|v\|_{H_0^1(B_R)} \le 1$, use $(H2)$ and Poincarre inequality to deduce

$$\left| \int_{B_R} \frac{\partial w}{\partial t} v \mathrm{d}x \right| \le C\|w(t)\|_{H_0^1(B_R)}.$$

So

$$\left\| \frac{\partial w}{\partial t}(t) \right\|_{H^{-1}(B_R)} \le C\|w(t)\|_{H_0^1(B_R)}.$$

Therefore

$$\int_0^T \left\| \frac{\partial w}{\partial t}(t) \right\|^2_{H^{-1}(B_R)} \mathrm{d}t \leq C \int_0^T \|w(t)\|^2_{H_0^1(B_R)} \mathrm{d}t$$
$$= C\|w\|^2_{L^2(0,T;H_0^1(B_R))}.$$

Then Equation 14.16 implies

$$\left\| \frac{\partial w}{\partial t} \right\|_{L^2(0,T;H^{-1}(B_R))} \leq C\|w_0\|^2_{L^2(B_R)}. \tag{14.17}$$

■

Before we prove the existence theorem in a ball, we state the following Lemma from the linear theory of parabolic PDEs. The Lemma follows directly from Ref. 6, Theorem 2, page 354.

LEMMA 14.16 (Energy Estimates)

Consider the problem

$$\begin{cases} \dfrac{\partial u}{\partial t} - L(v) = f(x,t) & \text{in} \quad B_R \times (0,T) \\ u(x,0) = u_0(x) & \text{on} \quad B_R \times \{0\} \\ u(x,t) = 0 & \text{on} \quad \partial B_R \times [0,T] \end{cases} \tag{14.18}$$

with $f \in L^2(0,T;L^2(B_R))$ and $u_0 \in L^2(B_R)$. Then there exists a unique $u \in L^2(0,T;H_0^1(B_R)) \cap C([0,T];L^2(B_R))$ solution of Equation 14.18 that satisfies

$$\max_{0\leq t\leq T} ||u(t)||_{L^2(B_R)} + \|u\|_{L^2(0,T;H_0^1(B_R))} + \left\| \frac{\partial u}{\partial t} \right\|_{L^2(0,T;H^{-1}(B_R))}$$
$$\leq C' \left(||f||_{L^2(0,T;L^2(B_R))} + ||u_0||_{L^2(B_R)} \right), \tag{14.19}$$

where C' is a positive constant depending only on B_R, T and the coefficients of the operator L.

We need another Lemma. This follows directly from Ref. 6, Theorem 5, page 360.

LEMMA 14.17 (Improved Regularity)

Consider the problem

$$\begin{cases} \dfrac{\partial u}{\partial t} - L(u) = f(x,t) & \text{in} \quad B_R \times (0,T) \\ u(x,0) = u_0(x) & \text{on} \quad B_R \times \{0\} \\ u(x,t) = 0 & \text{on} \quad \partial B_R \times [0,T] \end{cases}$$

with $f \in L^2(0,T;L^2(B_R))$ and $u_0 \in L^2(B_R)$. Then there exists a unique weak solution of the problem $u \in L^2(0,T;H_0^1(B_R)) \cap C([0,T];L^2(B_R))$, with $\frac{\partial u}{\partial t} \in L^2(0,T;H^{-1}(B_R))$. Moreover

$$u \in L^2(0,T;H^2(B_R)) \cap L^\infty(0,T;H_0^1(B_R)), \quad \frac{\partial u}{\partial t} \in L^2(0,T;L^2(B_R)).$$

We also have the estimate

$$\text{ess sup}_{0\le t\le T}\|u(t)\|_{H_0^1(B_R)} + \|u\|_{L^2(0,T;H^2(B_R))} + \left\|\frac{\partial u}{\partial t}\right\|_{L^2(0,T;L^2(B_R))} \le C''\left(\|f\|_{L^2(0,T;L^2(B_R))} + \|u_0\|_{L^2(B_R)}\right) \quad (14.20)$$

where C'' is a positive constant depending only on B_R, T, and the coefficients of the operator L.

THEOREM 14.18 (Existence Based on Schaefer's Fixed Point Theorem)

If (H1)–(H5) are satisfied, then system (Eq. 14.9–14.11) has a weak solution $w \in L^2(0,T;H_0^1(B_R)) \cap C([0,T];L^2(B_R))$.

Proof. Given $w \in L^2(0,T;H_0^1(B_R))$, set $f_w(x,t) := \beta\frac{\partial}{\partial x}F\left(w, \frac{\partial w}{\partial x}\right)$. By $(H3)$, $f_w \in L^2(0,T;L^2(B_R))$. By Lemma (14.16), there exists a unique $v \in L^2(0,T;$ $H_0^1(B_R)) \cap C([0,T];L^2(B_R))$ solution of

$$\begin{cases} \dfrac{\partial v}{\partial t} - \dfrac{\partial^2 v}{\partial x^2} - \alpha\dfrac{\partial v}{\partial x} = f_w(x,t) \text{ in } B_R \times (0,T) \\ v(x,0) = v_0(x) \text{ on } B_R \times \{0\} \\ v(x,t) = 0 \text{ on } \partial B_R \times [0,T] \end{cases} \quad (14.21)$$

Define the mapping

$$A : L^2(0, T; H_0^1(B_R)) \longrightarrow L^2(0, T; H_0^1(B_R))$$
$$w \longmapsto A(w) = v$$

where v is derived from w via Equation 14.21.
Let us show that the mapping A is continuous and compact.
⇒ Continuity
Let $\{w_k\}_k \subset L^2(0, T; H_0^1(B_R))$ be a sequence such that

$$w_k \longrightarrow w \text{ in } L^2(0, T; H_0^1(B_R)). \tag{14.22}$$

By the improved regularity (Eq. 14.20), there exists a constant C'', independent of $\{w_k\}_k$ such that

$$\sup_k ||v_k||_{L^2(0,T;H^2(B_R))} \leq C'' \left(||f_{w_k}||_{L^2(0,T;L^2(B_R))} + ||w_{k0}||_{L^2(B_R)}\right)$$

for $v_k = A[w_k]$, $k = 1, 2, \ldots$. But by (H3) as $w_k \to w$ in $L^2(0, T; H_0^1(B_R))$, we must have $f_{w_k}(x, t) \to f_w(x, t)$ in $L^2(0, T; L^2(B_R))$, $w_{k0} \to w_0$ in $L^2(B_R)$, and thus, $||f_{w_k}(x, t)||_{L^2(0,T;L^2(B_R)} \to ||f_w(x, t)||_{L^2(0,T;L^2(B_R)}$, $||w_{k0}||_{L^2(B_R)} \to ||w_0||_{L^2(B_R)}$. Therefore the sequences $\{f_{w_k}(x, t)||_{L^2(0,T;L^2(B_R)}\}_k$ and $\{||w_{k0}||_{L^2(B_R)}\}_k$ are bounded. Thus, the sequence $\{v_k\}_k$ is bounded uniformly in $L^2(0, T; H^2(B_R))$. Thus by Rellich's theorem (see Ref. 9), there exists a subsequence $\{v_{k_j}\}_j$ and a function $v \in L^2(0, T; H_0^1(B_R))$ with

$$v_{k_j} \longrightarrow v \text{ in } L^2(0, T; H_0^1(B_R)) \tag{14.23}$$

Therefore,

$$\int_{B_R} \left(\frac{\partial v_{k_j}}{\partial t}\phi + \frac{\partial v_{k_j}}{\partial x}\frac{\partial \phi}{\partial x} + \alpha v_{k_j}\frac{\partial \phi}{\partial x} \right) dx = \int_{B_R} f_{w_{k_j}}(x, t)\phi dx$$

for each $\phi \in H_0^1(B_R)$. Then using Equations 14.22 and 14.23, we see that

$$\int_{B_R} \left(\frac{\partial v}{\partial t}\phi + \frac{\partial v}{\partial x}\frac{\partial \phi}{\partial x} + \alpha v\frac{\partial \phi}{\partial x} \right) dx = \int_{B_R} f_w(x, t)\phi dx$$

Thus, $v = A[w]$. Therefore,

$$A[w_k] \longrightarrow A[w] \text{in } L^2(0, T; H_0^1(B_R)).$$

⇒ The compactness result follows from similar arguments.
Finally, to apply Schaefer's fixed point Theorem with $X = L^2(0, T; H_0^1(B_R))$, we need to show that the set $\{w \in L^2(0, T; H_0^1(B_R)) : w = \lambda A[w]$ for some

$0 \le \lambda \le 1\}$ is bounded. This follows directly from the A-priori estimates (Theorem 14.15) with $\lambda = 1$. ■

REMARK 14.19

Theorem(14.18) shows that $w = \frac{\partial U}{\partial x} \in L^2(0, T; H_0^1(B_R))$ solves problem (Eqs. 14.9–14.11). Hence $U \in L^2(0, T; H_0^1(B_R) \cap H^2(B_R))$ and is a strong solution of problem (Eqs. 14.7–14.8) in the bounded domain $B_R \times [0, T]$ with zero Dirichlet condition on the lateral boundary of the domain.

14.3.2 CONSTRUCTION OF THE SOLUTION IN THE WHOLE REAL LINE

The next step is to construct a solution of problem (Eqs. 14.9–14.11) in the whole real line. To do that, we approximate the real line by $\mathbb{R} = \cup_{N\in\mathbb{N}} B_N = \lim_{N\longrightarrow\infty} B_N$, where $B_N = \{x \in \mathbb{R} : |x| < N\}$ and w_0 by a sequence of bounded function w_{N0} defined in B_N such that $|w_{N0}| \le |w_0|$ and $w_{N0} \longrightarrow w_0$ in $L^2_{loc}(\mathbb{R})$. For $N \in \mathbb{N}$, there exists $w_N \in L^2(0, T; H_0^1(B_N)) \cap C([0, T]; L^2(B_N))$ with $\frac{\partial w_N}{\partial t} \in L^2(0, T; H^{-1}(B_N))$, weak solution of

$$-\frac{\partial w}{\partial t} + \frac{\partial^2 w}{\partial x^2} + \alpha\frac{\partial w}{\partial x} = \beta\frac{\partial}{\partial x}F\left(w, \frac{\partial w}{\partial x}\right) \quad (x, t) \in B_N \times (0, T) \tag{14.24}$$

$$w(x, 0) = w_{N0}(x) \qquad x \in B_N \tag{14.25}$$

$$w(x, t) = 0, \qquad (x, t) \in \partial B_N \times [0, T]. \tag{14.26}$$

For any given $\rho > 0$, the following sequences are bounded uniformly in $N > 2\rho$:

$$\{w_N\}_N \text{ in } L^2(0, T; H_0^1(B_\rho))$$

$$\left\{\frac{\partial w_N}{\partial t}\right\}_N \text{ in } L^2(0, T; H^{-1}(B_\rho))$$

Since these spaces are compactly embedded in $L^2(B_\rho \times (0, T))$ therefore the sequence $\{w_N\}_N$ is relatively compact in $L^2(B_\rho \times (0, T))$. Suppose we take $\rho \in \mathbb{N}$. Then using the compactness just described, we can construct a sequence consisting of diagonal elements of the converging subsequences with each $\rho \in \mathbb{N}$. Denoted this sequence also by $\{w_N\}_N$. Then there exists $w \in L^2(0, T; L^2_{loc}(\mathbb{R})) \cap L^2(0, T; H^1_{loc}(\mathbb{R}))$ with $w(x, 0) = w(x)$, so that

$$w_N \longrightarrow w \text{ } a.e \text{ and in } L^2(0, T; L^2_{loc}(\mathbb{R}))$$

and also

$$w_N \longrightarrow w \text{ weakly in } L^2(0, T; H^1_{loc}(\mathbb{R})).$$

Since F is continuous, passing to the limit in Equation 14.10 yields that w is a weak solution of the problem (Eqs. 14.7–14.8) in $\mathbb{R}$.

14.4 Model with Transaction Costs and Stochastic Volatility

In the standard Black–Scholes model, a basic assumption is that the volatility is constant. Several models proposed in recent years, however, allowed the volatility to be nonconstant or a stochastic variable. For instance, in [10] a model with stochastic volatility is proposed. In this model the underlying security S follows, as in the Black–Scholes model, a stochastic process

$$\mathrm{d}S = \mu S\,\mathrm{d}t + \sigma S\,\mathrm{d}X_1,$$

where X_1 is a standard Brownian motion.

Unlike the classical model, the variance $v(t) = \sigma^2(t)$ also follows a stochastic process given by

$$\mathrm{d}v = \kappa(\theta - v(t))\,\mathrm{d}t + \gamma\sqrt{v}\,\mathrm{d}X_2,$$

where X_2 is another standard Brownian motion. The correlation coefficient between X_1 and X_2 is denoted by ρ:

$$\mathrm{Cov}(\mathrm{d}X_1, \mathrm{d}X_2) = \rho\,\mathrm{d}t.$$

This leads to a generalized Black–Scholes equation. A similar model has been considered in Refs 11 and 12. The process used is a modified Hull–White process [13,14], to contain a mean reverting term in the volatility process. The process above may also be viewed as a generalization of the SABR process used in practice [15].

For the present chapter, we follow the model used in Ref. 16. As observed in Ref. 16, when the volatility is stochastic we may consider the process

$$\mathrm{d}S = \mu S\mathrm{d}t + \sigma S\mathrm{d}X_1, \tag{14.27}$$

$$\mathrm{d}\sigma = \alpha\sigma\,\mathrm{d}t + \beta\sigma\,\mathrm{d}X_2, \tag{14.28}$$

where the two Brownian motions X_1 and X_2 are correlated with correlation coefficient ρ:

$$\mathbb{E}[\mathrm{d}X_1\mathrm{d}X_2] = \rho\mathrm{d}t. \tag{14.29}$$

When working with stochastic volatility models the option prices are not uniquely determined by the asset price. Indeed, restated in a simple language the fundamental theorem of asset pricing [17, 18] says:

Let $M =$ the number of underlying *traded* assets in the model and let $R =$ the number of random sources in the model. Then we have

The model is arbitrage free if and only if $M \leq R$.

The model is complete if and only if $M \geq R$.

The model is complete and arbitrage free if and only if $M = R$.

We avoided using the equivalent martingale measure in the previous statement, for an exact statement we refer the reader to the original work [17, 18].

In the case of stochastic volatility models $M = 1$ and $R = 2$ thus the market is arbitrage free but not complete. This means that the derivative prices (options) are not uniquely determined by the traded asset price. The same conclusion has been reached when approximating the stochastic volatility process with a Markov chain [19]. The solution in the above citation was to fix the price of a certain derivative as a given asset and express all the other derivative prices in terms of the price of the given derivative. Next, we exemplify the choice by deriving the same nonlinear PDE in two different cases. One, when we pick the price of an option as given or two, when the volatility is a traded asset (the case of S&P500).

14.4.1 THE PDE DERIVATION WHEN WE TAKE A PARTICULAR OPTION AS A GIVEN ASSET

As we have mentioned, with the two sources of randomness, we need two contracts to hedge the option: one being the underlying assets S as usual, and the second is a particular option V_1 written on the asset S.

We consider a portfolio Π that contains the option we are trying to price with value $V(S, \sigma, t)$, a quantity Δ of the asset S and a quantity $-\Delta_1$ of the given option $V_1(S, \sigma, t)$. We have

$$\Pi = V - \Delta S - \Delta_1 V_1. \tag{14.30}$$

We apply Itô formula to get the dynamics of V and V_1, then we substitute to obtain the change in value of the portfolio Π as

$$\begin{aligned}
d\Pi = & \left(\frac{\partial V}{\partial t} + \frac{1}{2}\sigma^2 S^2 \frac{\partial^2 V}{\partial S^2} + \frac{1}{2}\beta^2\sigma^2 \frac{\partial^2 V}{\partial \sigma^2} + \rho\beta\sigma^2 S \frac{\partial^2 V}{\partial S \partial \sigma} \right) dt \\
& - \Delta_1 \left(\frac{\partial V_1}{\partial t} + \frac{1}{2}\sigma^2 S^2 \frac{\partial^2 V_1}{\partial S^2} + \frac{1}{2}\beta^2\sigma^2 \frac{\partial^2 V_1}{\partial \sigma^2} + \rho\beta\sigma^2 S \frac{\partial^2 V_1}{\partial S \partial \sigma} \right) dt \\
& + \left(\frac{\partial V}{\partial S} - \Delta_1 \frac{\partial V_1}{\partial S} - \Delta \right) dS + \left(\frac{\partial V}{\partial \sigma} - \Delta_1 \frac{\partial V_1}{\partial \sigma} \right) d\sigma \\
& - \kappa S |\nu|
\end{aligned}$$

where $\kappa S|\nu|$ represents the transaction cost for buying or selling quantity ν of the main asset S during the time step $\mathrm{d}t$. We explain in the next subsection why the portfolio rebalancing is done only through the asset S and not the option V_1 as well. To eliminate all randomness from the portfolio (terms containing $\mathrm{d}X_1$ and $\mathrm{d}X_2$), we must choose

$$\left(\frac{\partial V}{\partial S} - \Delta_1 \frac{\partial V_1}{\partial S} - \Delta\right) = 0,$$

and

$$\left(\frac{\partial V}{\partial \sigma} - \Delta_1 \frac{\partial V_1}{\partial \sigma}\right) = 0.$$

This also eliminates the drift terms (containing μ and a) and the portfolio dynamics become:

$$\begin{aligned} d\Pi = &\left(\frac{\partial V}{\partial t} + \frac{1}{2}\sigma^2 S^2 \frac{\partial^2 V}{\partial S^2} + \frac{1}{2}\beta^2\sigma^2 \frac{\partial^2 V}{\partial \sigma^2} + \rho\beta\sigma^2 S \frac{\partial^2 V}{\partial S \partial \sigma}\right)\mathrm{d}t \\ &- \Delta_1\left(\frac{\partial V_1}{\partial t} + \frac{1}{2}\sigma^2 S^2 \frac{\partial^2 V_1}{\partial S^2} + \frac{1}{2}\beta^2\sigma^2 \frac{\partial^2 V_1}{\partial \sigma^2} + \rho\beta\sigma^2 S \frac{\partial^2 V_1}{\partial S \partial \sigma}\right)\mathrm{d}t \qquad (14.31) \\ &- \kappa S|\nu| \end{aligned}$$

14.4.1.1 What is the Cost of Transaction. Note that we have two quantities that need to be rebalanced in our portfolio Δ and Δ_1. Changes in Δ represent quantities of the stock that need to be bought or sold and changes in Δ_1 represent adjustments in the option. Let us denote Δ_1 with λ and note we have

$$\lambda = \Delta_1 = \frac{\partial V}{\partial \sigma}\left(\frac{\partial V_1}{\partial \sigma}\right)^{-1} \approx \frac{V(\sigma + \delta\sigma) - V(\sigma)}{V_1(\sigma + \delta\sigma) - V_1(\sigma)}. \qquad (14.32)$$

ASSUMPTION 14.20

We assume that λ is constant in time. In other words, the variation of V with respect to σ (the vega) is at all times proportional to the variation of V_1 with respect to σ and the constant of proportionality is λ. The proportionality constant does not change in time.

If both V and V_1 represent values of two options which belong to the same option chain, the Assumption 14.20 is very realistic. This is the normal behavior of the option chain observed in practice. When the perceived instantaneous volatility changes this updates the entire option chain values not only one option. In fact the option traders quote the price of options in volatility not in dollars.

We also note an important consequence. Since $\Delta_1 = \lambda$ is a constant in time, as a result we only balance through buying and selling the underlying asset S. This is a very desirable feature since transaction costs are much more tractable and low then when only trading the asset.

Thus we only need to consider the costs associated with trading the asset. If the number of assets held short at time t is

$$\Delta_t = \frac{\partial V}{\partial S}(S,\sigma,t) - \lambda \frac{\partial V_1(S,\sigma,t)}{\partial S}(S,\sigma,t), \tag{14.33}$$

after a timestep δt and rehedging, the number of assets we hold short is

$$\Delta_{t+\delta t} = \frac{\partial V}{\partial S}(S+\delta S,\sigma+\delta\sigma,t+\delta t) - \lambda \frac{\partial V_1(S,\sigma,t)}{\partial S}(S+\delta S,\sigma+\delta\sigma,t+\delta t).$$

Since the timestep δt is assumed small, the changes in asset and the volatility are also small, and applying the Taylor's formula to expand $\Delta_{t+\delta t}$ yields

$$\begin{aligned}\Delta_{t+\delta t} \simeq{}& \frac{\partial V}{\partial S}(S,\sigma,t) - \lambda\frac{\partial V_1}{\partial S}(S,\sigma,t) + \delta t\frac{\partial^2 V}{\partial t \partial S}(S,\sigma,t) + \delta S\frac{\partial^2 V}{\partial S^2}(S,\sigma,t)\\ &+ \delta\sigma\frac{\partial^2 V}{\partial\sigma\partial S}(S,\sigma,t) - \lambda\delta t\frac{\partial^2 V_1}{\partial t\partial S}(S,\sigma,t) - \lambda\delta S\frac{\partial^2 V_1}{\partial S^2}(S,\sigma,t) - \lambda\delta\sigma\frac{\partial^2 V_1}{\partial\sigma\partial S}(S,\sigma,t) + \cdots\end{aligned}$$

Since $\delta S = \sigma S\delta X_1 + 0(\delta t)$ and $\delta\sigma = \beta\sigma\delta X_2 + 0(\delta t)$,

$$\begin{aligned}\Delta_{t+\delta t} \simeq{}& \frac{\partial V}{\partial S} - \lambda\frac{\partial V_1}{\partial S} + \sigma S\delta X_1\left(\frac{\partial^2 V}{\partial S^2} - \lambda\frac{\partial^2 V_1}{\partial S^2}\right)\\ &+ \beta\sigma\delta X_2\left(\frac{\partial^2 V}{\partial\sigma\partial S} - \lambda\frac{\partial^2 V_1}{\partial\sigma\partial S}\right)\end{aligned} \tag{14.34}$$

Subtracting Equation 14.33 from Equation 14.34, we find that the number of assets traded during a timestep is therefore

$$\nu = \sigma S\delta X_1\left(\frac{\partial^2 V}{\partial S^2} - \lambda\frac{\partial^2 V_1}{\partial S^2}\right) + \beta\sigma\delta X_2\left(\frac{\partial^2 V}{\partial\sigma\partial S} - \lambda\frac{\partial^2 V_1}{\partial\sigma\partial S}\right). \tag{14.35}$$

We do not know beforehand how many shares will be traded. However, we can compute the expected number of this variable and hence the expected transaction cost. Since X_1 and X_2 are correlated Brownian motions, we consider Z_1 and Z_2 two independent normal variables with mean 0 and variance 1 and thus we may write the distribution of X_1, X_2 as

$$\begin{aligned}\delta X_1 &= Z_1\sqrt{\delta t}\\ \delta X_2 &= \rho Z_1\sqrt{\delta t} + \sqrt{1-\rho^2}Z_2\sqrt{\delta t}.\end{aligned}$$

Substituting these expressions in ν and denoting:

$$\hat{V} = V - \lambda V_1$$
$$\varphi = \sigma S\sqrt{\delta t}\,\frac{\partial^2 \hat{V}}{\partial S^2} + \beta\sigma\rho\sqrt{\delta t}\,\frac{\partial^2 \hat{V}}{\partial\sigma\partial S} \qquad (14.36)$$
$$\psi = \beta\sigma\sqrt{1-\rho^2}\sqrt{\delta t}\,\frac{\partial^2 \hat{V}}{\partial\sigma\partial S}$$

We write the change in the number of shares over a time step δt as

$$\nu = \varphi Z_1 + \psi Z_2$$

and thus the expected transaction cost is

$$\mathbb{E}[\kappa S|\nu| \mid S] = \kappa S\,\mathbb{E}\,|\varphi Z_1 + \psi Z_2|\,.$$

Since Z_1 and Z_2 are independent normals we can calculate the expected value of the expression easily as

$$\mathbb{E}[\kappa S|\nu| \mid S] = \sqrt{\frac{2}{\pi}}\kappa S\sqrt{\varphi^2 + \psi^2}$$

Finally using Equation 14.31 and the notations in Equation 14.36, we write

$$E[\delta\Pi \mid S,\sigma] = \left(\frac{\partial \hat{V}}{\partial t} + \frac{1}{2}\sigma^2 S^2\frac{\partial^2 \hat{V}}{\partial S^2} + \frac{1}{2}\beta^2\sigma^2\frac{\partial^2 \hat{V}}{\partial\sigma^2} + \rho\beta\sigma^2 S\frac{\partial^2 \hat{V}}{\partial S\partial\sigma}\right)\delta t - \sqrt{\frac{2}{\pi}}\kappa S\sqrt{\varphi^2+\psi^2} \qquad (14.37)$$

Recall that we chose Δ and Δ_1 values to make the portfolio riskfree, thus following standard no arbitrage arguments, over the small interval δt the portfolio has expected value

$$E[\delta\Pi \mid S,\sigma] = r\Pi\delta t = r(V - \Delta S - \Delta_1 V_1)\,\delta t = \left(r\hat{V} - rS\frac{\partial \hat{V}}{\partial S}\right)\delta t$$

We equate the two expressions and we thus find an equation in $\hat{V} = V - \lambda V_1$

$$\frac{\partial \hat{V}}{\partial t} + \frac{1}{2}\sigma^2 S^2\frac{\partial^2 \hat{V}}{\partial S^2} + \frac{1}{2}\beta^2\sigma^2\frac{\partial^2 \hat{V}}{\partial\sigma^2} + \rho\beta\sigma^2 S\frac{\partial^2 \hat{V}}{\partial S\partial\sigma} + rS\frac{\partial \hat{V}}{\partial S} - r\hat{V}$$
$$-\kappa S\sqrt{\frac{2}{\pi\delta t}}\sqrt{\sigma^2 S^2\left(\frac{\partial^2 \hat{V}}{\partial S^2}\right)^2 + 2\rho\beta\sigma^2 S\frac{\partial^2 \hat{V}}{\partial S^2}\frac{\partial^2 \hat{V}}{\partial S\partial\sigma} + \beta^2\sigma^2\left(\frac{\partial^2 \hat{V}}{\partial S\partial\sigma}\right)^2} = 0. \qquad (14.38)$$

14.4.2 THE PDE DERIVATION WHEN THE VOLATILITY IS A TRADED ASSET

This case is only applicable when there exists a proxy for the stochastic volatility. Today in the financial markets there exists only one example of such a case: the Standard and Poor index (in fact, the exchange traded fund that replicates it SPX or SPY) and the volatility index VIX that is supposed to represent the associated implied volatility of an option with strike price exactly at the money and with maturity exactly one month from the current date. The VIX is calculated using an interpolating formula from the (out-of-money) options available and traded on the market, nevertheless it may be viewed as a proxy for the stochastic volatility in the model we propose here.

In the future, it is possible that more volatility indices will be traded on the market, and we denote in what follows S as the equity price and with σ the matching VIX. We are also taking σ a perfect proxy for the stochastic volatility, an in depth analysis about the appropriateness of the choice is beyond the scope of the current chapter.

We consider a portfolio Π that contains one option, with value $V(S, \sigma, t)$, and quantities Δ and Δ_1 of S and σ, respectively. That is,

$$\Pi = V - \Delta S - \Delta_1 \sigma. \tag{14.39}$$

Similarly with the previous case, we apply Itô's formula to get the dynamics of V, then we substitute to obtain the change in value of the portfolio Π as

$$\begin{aligned} d\Pi = & \left(\frac{\partial V}{\partial t} + \frac{1}{2}\sigma^2 S^2 \frac{\partial^2 V}{\partial S^2} + \frac{1}{2}\beta^2\sigma^2 \frac{\partial^2 V}{\partial \sigma^2} + \rho\sigma^2\beta S \frac{\partial^2 V}{\partial S \partial \sigma} \right) dt \\ & + \left(\frac{\partial V}{\partial S} - \Delta \right) dS + \left(\frac{\partial V}{\partial \sigma} - \Delta_1 \right) d\sigma - \kappa S|\nu| \end{aligned}$$

where $\kappa S|\nu|$ represents the transaction cost for buying or selling quantity ν of the main asset S during the time step dt. To eliminate all randomness from the portfolio (terms containing dX_1 and dX_2), we must choose

$$\left(\frac{\partial V}{\partial S} - \Delta \right) = 0,$$

and

$$\left(\frac{\partial V}{\partial \sigma} - \Delta_1 \right) = 0.$$

This also eliminates the drift terms (containing μ and α) and the portfolio dynamics is

$$d\Pi = \left(\frac{\partial V}{\partial t} + \frac{1}{2}\sigma^2 S^2 \frac{\partial^2 V}{\partial S^2} + \frac{1}{2}\beta^2\sigma^2 \frac{\partial^2 V}{\partial \sigma^2} + \rho\sigma^2\beta S \frac{\partial^2 V}{\partial S \partial \sigma} \right) dt - \kappa S|\nu|. \tag{14.40}$$

14.4.2.1 What is the Cost of Transaction. We use a simplified assumption here.

ASSUMPTION 14.21

> The price of the option is a linear function in σ and the coefficient of σ in this function does not depend on time t.

In this case changes in Δ represent changes in quantities of the stock owned and changes in Δ_1 represent changes in VIX owned. We have

$$\Delta_1 = \frac{\partial V}{\partial \sigma} \approx \frac{V(\sigma + \delta\sigma) - V(\sigma)}{\delta\sigma}. \tag{14.41}$$

An important consequence of the above assumption is Δ_1 is constant in time.

Thus, we only need to consider the costs associated with trading the asset. If the number of assets held short at time t is

$$\Delta_t = \frac{\partial V}{\partial S}(S, \sigma, t), \tag{14.42}$$

after a timestep δt and rehedging, the number of assets we hold short is

$$\Delta_{t+\delta t} = \frac{\partial V}{\partial S}(S + \delta S, \sigma + \delta\sigma, t + \delta t).$$

Since the timestep δt is assumed small, the changes in asset and the volatility are also small, and applying the Taylor's formula to expand $\Delta_{t+\delta t}$ yields

$$\Delta_{t+\delta t} \simeq \frac{\partial V}{\partial S}(S, \sigma, t) + \delta t \frac{\partial^2 V}{\partial t \partial S}(S, \sigma, t) + \delta S \frac{\partial^2 V}{\partial S^2}(S, \sigma, t)$$
$$+ \delta\sigma \frac{\partial^2 V}{\partial \sigma \partial S}(S, \sigma, t) + \cdots$$

Since $\delta S = \sigma S \delta X_1 + 0(\delta t)$ and $\delta\sigma = \beta\sigma\delta X_2 + 0(\delta t)$,

$$\Delta_{t+\delta t} \simeq \frac{\partial V}{\partial S} + \sigma S \delta X_1 \frac{\partial^2 V}{\partial S^2} + \beta\sigma\delta X_2 \frac{\partial^2 V}{\partial \sigma \partial S}. \tag{14.43}$$

Subtracting Equation 14.42 from 14.43, we found that the number of assets traded during a timestep is therefore

$$\nu = \sigma S \delta X_1 \frac{\partial^2 V}{\partial S^2} + \beta\sigma\delta X_2 \frac{\partial^2 V}{\partial \sigma \partial S}. \tag{14.44}$$

We do not know beforehand how many shares will be traded, but we can compute the expected number and hence the expected transaction cost. Since X_1 and X_2 are correlated Brownian motions, we consider Z_1 and Z_2 two independent normal variables with mean 0 and variance 1 and thus, we may write the distribution of X_1, X_2 as

$$\delta X_1 = Z_1\sqrt{\delta t}$$
$$\delta X_2 = \rho Z_1\sqrt{\delta t} + \sqrt{1-\rho^2}Z_2\sqrt{\delta t}.$$

Substituting these expressions in ν and denoting:

$$\alpha_1 = \sigma S\sqrt{\delta t}\,\frac{\partial^2 V}{\partial S^2} + \beta\sigma\rho\sqrt{\delta t}\,\frac{\partial^2 V}{\partial\sigma\partial S} \tag{14.45}$$
$$\beta_1 = \beta\sigma\sqrt{1-\rho^2}\sqrt{\delta t}\,\frac{\partial^2 V}{\partial\sigma\partial S}$$

We write the change in the number of shares over a time step δt as

$$\nu = \alpha_1 Z_1 + \beta_1 Z_2$$

and thus the expected transaction cost is

$$\mathbb{E}[\kappa S|\nu| \mid S] = \kappa S\,\mathbb{E}\left|\alpha_1 Z_1 + \beta_1 Z_2\right|.$$

Since Z_1 and Z_2 are independent normals, we can calculate the expected value of the expression easily as

$$\mathbb{E}[\kappa S|\nu| \mid S] = \sqrt{\frac{2}{\pi}}\kappa S\sqrt{\alpha_1^2 + \beta_1^2}.$$

14.4.2.2 The PDE Under Transaction Costs and Stochastic Volatility. Following Equation 14.40 and using the notations in Equations 14.45, we write

$$E[\delta\Pi \mid S,\sigma] = \left(\frac{\partial V}{\partial t} + \frac{1}{2}\sigma^2 S^2\frac{\partial^2 V}{\partial S^2} + \frac{1}{2}\beta^2\sigma^2\frac{\partial^2 V}{\partial\sigma^2} + \rho\sigma^2\beta S\frac{\partial^2 V}{\partial S\partial\sigma}\right)\delta t$$
$$-\sqrt{\frac{2}{\pi}}\kappa S\sqrt{\alpha_1^2 + \beta_1^2}. \tag{14.46}$$

Recall that we chose Δ and Δ_1 values to make the portfolio riskfree, thus following standard no arbitrage arguments, over the small interval δt the portfolio has expected value

$$E[\delta\Pi \mid S,\sigma] = r\Pi\delta t = r\left(V - \Delta S - \Delta_1\sigma\right)\delta t = \left(rV - rS\frac{\partial V}{\partial S}\right)\delta t. \tag{14.47}$$

We equate Equations 14.46 and 14.47 and we thus find an equation in V.

$$\frac{\partial V}{\partial t}+\frac{1}{2}\sigma^2S^2\frac{\partial^2 V}{\partial S^2}+\frac{1}{2}\beta^2\sigma^2\frac{\partial^2 V}{\partial\sigma^2}+\rho\sigma^2\beta S\frac{\partial^2 V}{\partial S\partial\sigma}+rS\frac{\partial V}{\partial S}-rV$$
$$-\kappa S\sqrt{\frac{2}{\pi\delta t}}\sqrt{\sigma^2S^2\left(\frac{\partial^2 V}{\partial S^2}\right)^2+2\rho\beta\sigma^2S\frac{\partial^2 V}{\partial S^2}\frac{\partial^2 V}{\partial S\partial\sigma}+\beta^2\sigma^2\left(\frac{\partial^2 V}{\partial S\partial\sigma}\right)^2}=0. \tag{14.48}$$

14.5 The Analysis of the Resulting Partial Differential Equation

We observe that the Equations 14.38 and 14.48 are identical (with the unknown functions as $\hat{V}$ and V, respectively). Therefore it is sufficient to consider any one of them for a solution procedure. We next analyze the nonlinear PDE presented in Equation 14.48. We use the following change of variables

$$S=e^x,\quad \sigma=e^y,\quad t=T-\tau,\quad V(S,\sigma,t)=Ev(x,y,\tau).$$

Since $S,\sigma\in[0,\infty)$ this gives $x,y\in(-\infty,\infty)$. Then Equation 14.48 is transformed to

$$-\frac{\partial v}{\partial\tau}+\frac{1}{2}e^{2y}\left(\frac{\partial^2 v}{\partial x^2}-\frac{\partial v}{\partial x}\right)\frac{1}{2}\beta^2\left(\frac{\partial^2 v}{\partial y^2}-\frac{\partial v}{\partial y}\right)+\rho e^y\beta\frac{\partial^2 v}{\partial x\partial y}+r\frac{\partial v}{\partial x}-rv$$
$$-\kappa\sqrt{\frac{2}{\pi\delta t}}\sqrt{e^{2y}\left(\frac{\partial^2 v}{\partial x^2}-\frac{\partial v}{\partial x}\right)^2+2\rho\beta e^y\left(\frac{\partial^2 v}{\partial x^2}-\frac{\partial v}{\partial x}\right)\frac{\partial^2 v}{\partial x\partial y}+\beta^2\left(\frac{\partial^2 v}{\partial x\partial y}\right)^2}=0.$$

that is,

$$-\frac{\partial v}{\partial\tau}+\frac{1}{2}e^{2y}\frac{\partial^2 v}{\partial x^2}+\frac{1}{2}\beta^2\frac{\partial^2 v}{\partial\sigma^2}+\rho e^y\beta\frac{\partial^2 v}{\partial x\partial\sigma}+(r-\frac{1}{2}e^{2y})\frac{\partial v}{\partial x}$$
$$-\frac{1}{2}\beta^2\frac{\partial v}{\partial y}-rv=\mathfrak{F}\left(y,\frac{\partial v}{\partial x},\frac{\partial^2 v}{\partial x^2},\frac{\partial^2 v}{\partial x\partial y}\right), \tag{14.49}$$

where

$$\mathfrak{F}\left(y,\frac{\partial v}{\partial x},\frac{\partial^2 v}{\partial x^2},\frac{\partial^2 v}{\partial x\partial y}\right)$$
$$=\kappa\sqrt{\frac{2}{\pi\delta t}}\sqrt{e^{2y}\left(\frac{\partial^2 v}{\partial x^2}-\frac{\partial v}{\partial x}\right)^2+2\rho\beta e^y\left(\frac{\partial^2 v}{\partial x^2}-\frac{\partial v}{\partial x}\right)\frac{\partial^2 v}{\partial x\partial y}+\beta^2\left(\frac{\partial^2 v}{\partial x\partial y}\right)^2}.$$

LEMMA 14.22

There exists a constant $C > 0$, independent of variables in $\mathfrak{F}$ such that

$$\left|\mathfrak{F}\left(y, \frac{\partial v}{\partial x}, \frac{\partial^2 v}{\partial x^2}, \frac{\partial^2 v}{\partial x \partial y}\right)\right| \leq C e^y \left(\left|\frac{\partial v}{\partial x}\right| + \left|\frac{\partial^2 v}{\partial x^2}\right| + \left|\frac{\partial^2 v}{\partial x \partial y}\right|\right).$$

Proof. Clearly

$$\left|\mathfrak{F}\left(y, \frac{\partial v}{\partial x}, \frac{\partial^2 v}{\partial x^2}, \frac{\partial^2 v}{\partial x \partial y}\right)\right|$$

$$= \left|\kappa\sqrt{\frac{2}{\pi\delta t}}\sqrt{e^{2y}\left(\frac{\partial^2 v}{\partial x^2} - \frac{\partial v}{\partial x}\right)^2 + 2e^y\rho\beta\left(\frac{\partial^2 v}{\partial x^2} - \frac{\partial v}{\partial x}\right)\frac{\partial^2 v}{\partial x \partial y} + \beta^2\left(\frac{\partial^2 v}{\partial x \partial y}\right)^2}\right|$$

$$\leq \left|\kappa\sqrt{\frac{2}{\pi\delta t}}\right|\sqrt{\left(e^y\left|\frac{\partial^2 v}{\partial x^2} - \frac{\partial v}{\partial x}\right| + \left|\rho\beta\frac{\partial^2 v}{\partial x \partial \sigma}\right| + \left|\beta\sqrt{1-\rho^2}\frac{\partial^2 v}{\partial x \partial \sigma}\right|\right)^2}$$

$$\leq \left|\kappa\sqrt{\frac{2}{\pi\delta t}}\right|\left(e^y\left|\frac{\partial^2 v}{\partial x^2}\right| + e^y\left|\frac{\partial v}{\partial x}\right| + (|\rho\beta| + |\beta\sqrt{1-\rho^2}|)\left|\frac{\partial^2 v}{\partial x \partial \sigma}\right|\right).$$

Therefore $\exists C > 0$ such that

$$\left|\mathfrak{F}\left(y, \frac{\partial v}{\partial x}, \frac{\partial^2 v}{\partial x^2}, \frac{\partial^2 v}{\partial x \partial y}\right)\right| \leq C e^y \left(\left|\frac{\partial v}{\partial x}\right| + \left|\frac{\partial^2 v}{\partial x^2}\right| + \left|\frac{\partial^2 v}{\partial x \partial y}\right|\right).$$

■

LEMMA 14.23

Suppose $|\rho| < 1$. Then the Equation 14.49 is of parabolic type.

Proof. For $(v_i, v_j) \in \mathbb{R}^2$ and $\theta > 0$, we have

$$(\sigma^2 - \theta)v_i v_i + (\beta^2 - \theta)v_j v_j + 2\rho\sigma\beta v_i v_j$$
$$= \left[\left(\sqrt{\sigma^2 - \theta}\, v_i + \frac{\rho\sigma\beta}{\sqrt{\sigma^2 - \theta}} v_j\right)^2 + v_j^2\left(\beta^2(1 - \frac{\rho^2\sigma^2}{\sigma^2 - \theta}) - \theta\right)\right]$$

Therefore

$$\lim_{\theta \to 0} \left(\beta^2 (1 - \frac{\rho^2 \sigma^2}{\sigma^2 - \theta}) - \theta \right) = \beta^2 (1 - \rho^2).$$

Since $|\rho| < 1$ and $\beta \neq 0$, we have

$$\lim_{\theta \to 0} \left(\beta^2 (1 - \frac{\rho^2 \sigma^2}{\sigma^2 - \theta}) - \theta \right) > 0.$$

Thus, $\exists \theta_1 > 0$ in the neighborhood of 0 such that

$$\left(\beta^2 (1 - \frac{\rho^2 \sigma^2}{\sigma^2 - \theta_1}) - \theta_1 \right) > 0.$$

Therefore with this θ_1, $\forall (v_i, v_j) \in \mathbb{R}^2$,

$$\frac{1}{2}\sigma^2 \left(\sigma^2 v_i v_i + \beta^2 v_j v_j + 2\rho\sigma\beta v_i v_j \right) > \theta_1 (|v_i|^2 + |v_j|^2).$$

Thus Equation 14.49 is parabolic. ■

14.5.1 SOLUTION OF EQUATION 14.22

In this section, we prove the existence of a classical solution for Equation 14.49. Let us denote

$$Lu = \frac{1}{2} e^{2y} \frac{\partial^2 u}{\partial x^2} + \frac{1}{2}\beta^2 \frac{\partial^2 u}{\partial \sigma^2} + \rho e^y \beta \frac{\partial^2 u}{\partial x \partial \sigma} + (r - \frac{1}{2} e^{2y}) \frac{\partial u}{\partial x} - \frac{1}{2}\beta^2 \frac{\partial u}{\partial y} - ru.$$

We first consider the following initial-boundary value problem in a bounded parabolic domain $Q_T = \Omega \times (0, T)$, $T > 0$, and Ω is a bounded domain in $\mathbb{R}^2$.

$$\begin{aligned} -u_\tau + Lu &= \mathfrak{F}\left(y, \tfrac{\partial u}{\partial x}, \tfrac{\partial^2 u}{\partial x^2}, \tfrac{\partial^2 u}{\partial x \partial y}\right) && \text{in } Q_T, \\ u(x, y, 0) &= u_0(x, y) && \text{on } \Omega, \\ u(x, y, \tau) &= g(x, y, \tau) && \text{on } \partial\Omega \times (0, T). \end{aligned} \tag{14.50}$$

Then, we try to extend our results to the corresponding initial-value problem in the unbounded domain $\mathbb{R}_T^{2+1} = \mathbb{R}^2 \times (0, T)$

$$\begin{aligned} -u_\tau + Lu &= \mathfrak{F}\left(y, \tfrac{\partial u}{\partial x}, \tfrac{\partial^2 u}{\partial x^2}, \tfrac{\partial^2 u}{\partial x \partial y}\right) && \text{in } \mathbb{R}_T^{2+1}, \\ u(x, y, 0) &= u_0(x, y) && \text{on } \mathbb{R}^2. \end{aligned} \tag{14.51}$$

Throughout this section, we impose the following assumptions:

A(1) The coefficients of L belong to the Hölder space $C^{\delta,\delta/2}(\overline{Q}_T)$;

A(2) The value of $|\rho| < 1$;

A(3) $u_0(x,y)$ and $g(x,y,t)$ belong to the Hölder spaces $C^{2+\delta}(\mathbb{R}^2)$ and $C^{2+\delta,1+\delta/2}(\overline{Q}_T)$, respectively.

A(4) The two consistency conditions

$$g(x,y,0) = u_0(x,y),$$
$$g_\tau(x,y,0) - Lu_0(x,y) = 0,$$

are satisfied for all $x \in \partial\Omega$.

We shall prove the existence of a solution to Equation 14.49 using an iteration argument. We will do this by proving estimates based on a Green's function. Afterwards, we will use a standard argument to show that our solution can be extended to give us a solution to the initial-value problem in $\mathbb{R}_T^{2+1}$.

Let us define the function space $C^{1+1,0+1}(\overline{Q}_T)$ to be the set of all $u \in C^{1,0}(\overline{Q}_T) \cap W_\infty^{2,1}(\overline{Q}_T)$. We will say $u \in C^{1+1,0+1}(\overline{Q}_T)$ is a strong solution to the parabolic initial-boundary value problem (Eq. 5.1) provided that u satisfies the parabolic equation almost everywhere in Q_T and the initial-boundary conditions in the classical sense. The following lemma follows immediately from Theorem 10.4.1 in Ref. 7.

LEMMA 14.24

There exists a unique solution $\varphi \in C^{2+\delta,1+\delta/2}\left(\overline{Q}_T\right)$ to the problem

$$\begin{aligned} -u_\tau + Lu &= 0 && \text{in } Q_T, \\ u(x,y,0) &= u_0(x,y) && \text{on } \Omega, \\ u(x,y,\tau) &= g(x,y,\tau) && \text{on } \partial\Omega \times (0,T). \end{aligned} \tag{14.52}$$

We state and prove our main theorem.

THEOREM 14.25

Let φ be defined as in Lemma 14.24. Then there exists a strong solution $u \in C^{1+1,0+1}(\overline{Q}_T)$ to the problem

$$\begin{aligned} -u_\tau + Lu &= \mathfrak{F}\left(y, \frac{\partial u}{\partial x}, \frac{\partial^2 u}{\partial x^2}, \frac{\partial^2 u}{\partial x \partial y}\right) && \text{in } Q_T, \\ u(x,y,0) &= u_0(x,y) && \text{on } \Omega, \\ u(x,y,\tau) &= \varphi(x,y,\tau) = g(x,y,\tau) && \text{on } \partial\Omega \times (0,T). \end{aligned} \tag{14.53}$$

Proof. First, we introduce a change of variables to transform our problem into one with a zero boundary condition. If we let

$$v(x,y,\tau) = u(x,y,\tau) - \varphi(x,y,\tau),$$
$$v_0(x,y) = u_0(x,y) - \varphi(x,y,0) = 0,$$

then v will satisfy the initial-boundary value problem

$$\begin{aligned} -v_\tau + Lv &= \mathfrak{F}\left(y, \frac{\partial(v+\varphi)}{\partial x}, \frac{\partial^2(v+\varphi)}{\partial x^2}, \frac{\partial^2(v+\varphi)}{\partial x \partial y}\right) && \text{in } Q_T, \\ v(x,y,0) &= 0 && \text{on } \Omega, \\ v(x,y,\tau) &= 0 && \text{on } \partial\Omega \times (0,T). \end{aligned} \tag{14.54}$$

We further change variable $\tau' = \frac{\tau}{A}$, where A is a constant which will be chosen later. By abuse of notation we denote ALv by Lv and $A\mathfrak{F}$ by $\mathfrak{F}$. Then if $T^* = \frac{T}{A}$, Equation 14.54 becomes

$$\begin{aligned} -v_{\tau'} + Lv &= \mathfrak{F}\left(y, \frac{\partial(v+\varphi)}{\partial x}, \frac{\partial^2(v+\varphi)}{\partial x^2}, \frac{\partial^2(v+\varphi)}{\partial x \partial y}\right) && \text{in } Q_{T^*}, \\ v(x,y,0) &= 0 && \text{on } \Omega, \\ v(x,y,\tau') &= 0 && \text{on } \partial\Omega \times (0,T^*). \end{aligned} \tag{14.55}$$

If problem (Eq. 14.55) has a strong solution, then Equation 14.53 will have a strong solution since $u = v + \varphi$. We use an iteration procedure to construct the solution to Equation 14.55. Consider the problem

$$\begin{aligned} -\beta_{\tau'} + L\beta &= \mathfrak{F}\left(y, \frac{\partial(\alpha+\varphi)}{\partial x}, \frac{\partial^2(\alpha+\varphi)}{\partial x^2}, \frac{\partial^2(\alpha+\varphi)}{\partial x \partial y}\right) && \text{in } Q_{T^*}, \\ \beta(x,y,0) &= 0 && \text{on } \Omega, \\ \beta(x,y,\tau') &= 0 && \text{on } \partial\Omega \times (0,T^*), \end{aligned} \tag{14.56}$$

where $\alpha \in C^{2+\delta,1+\delta/2}(\overline{Q}_{T^*,U})$ is arbitrary. We can show that

$$\mathfrak{F}\left(y, \frac{\partial(\alpha+\varphi)}{\partial x}, \frac{\partial^2(\alpha+\varphi)}{\partial x^2}, \frac{\partial^2(\alpha+\varphi)}{\partial x \partial y}\right) \in C^{\delta,\delta/2}(\overline{Q}_{T^*}).$$

By Theorem 10.4.1 in Ref. 7, there exists a unique solution $\beta \in C^{2+\delta,1+\delta/2}(\overline{Q}_{T^*})$ to problem (Eq. 14.56).

Using this result, we can now define $v^n \in C^{2+\delta,1+\delta/2}(\overline{Q}_{T^*})$, $n \geq 1$, to be the unique solution to the linearized problem

$$\begin{aligned} -\partial_{\tau'} v^n + Lv^n &= \mathfrak{F}\left(y, \frac{\partial(v^{n-1}+\varphi)}{\partial x}, \frac{\partial^2(v^{n-1}+\varphi)}{\partial x^2}, \frac{\partial^2(v^{n-1}+\varphi)}{\partial x \partial y}\right) && \text{in } Q_{T^*}, \\ v^n(x,0) &= 0 && \text{on } \Omega, \\ v^n(x,\tau') &= 0 && \text{on } \partial\Omega \times (0,T^*), \end{aligned} \tag{14.57}$$

where $v^0 = v_0(x) = 0 \in C^{2+\delta,1+\delta/2}(\overline{Q}_{T^*,U})$. To prove the existence of a solution to problem (Eq. 14.55), we will show that this sequence converges.

From Ref. 20, there exists a Green's function $G(x,y,\tau',\tau'')$ for problem (Eq. 14.57). For $n \geq 1$, the solution v^n can be written as

$$\begin{aligned}
&v^n(x,y,\tau') \\
&= \int_0^{\tau'} \int_\Omega G(x,y,z,w,\tau',\tau'')\,\mathfrak{F}\left(w, \frac{\partial(v^{n-1}+\varphi)}{\partial z}, \frac{\partial^2(v^{n-1}+\varphi)}{\partial z^2}, \frac{\partial^2(v^{n-1}+\varphi)}{\partial z\partial w}\right) \mathrm{d}z\mathrm{d}w\,\mathrm{d}\tau'' \\
&+ \int_\Omega G(x,y,z,w,\tau',0) v_0(z,w)\,\mathrm{d}z\mathrm{d}w \\
&= \int_0^{\tau'} \int_\Omega G(x,y,z,w,\tau',\tau'')\,\mathfrak{F}\left(w, \frac{\partial(v^{n-1}+\varphi)}{\partial z}, \frac{\partial^2(v^{n-1}+\varphi)}{\partial z^2}, \frac{\partial^2(v^{n-1}+\varphi)}{\partial z\partial w}\right) \mathrm{d}z\mathrm{d}w\,\mathrm{d}\tau'',
\end{aligned}$$

because $v_0(z,w) = 0$. For convenience, we will write

$$\begin{aligned}
&\mathcal{F}^{n-1}(z,w,\tau'') = \\
&\mathfrak{F}\left(w, \frac{\partial(v^{n-1}+\varphi)}{\partial z}(z,w,\tau''), \frac{\partial^2(v^{n-1}+\varphi)}{\partial z^2}(z,w,\tau''), \frac{\partial^2(v^{n-1}+\varphi)}{\partial z\partial w}(z,w,\tau'')\right).
\end{aligned}$$

Now we take the first and second derivatives of $v^n(x,y,\tau')$ with respect to x and y. Foe convenience denote $x_1 = x$ and $x_2 = y$.

$$v^n_{x_i}(x,y,\tau') = \int_0^{\tau'} \int_\Omega G_{x_i}(x,y,z,w,\tau',\tau'')\,\mathcal{F}^{n-1}(z,w,\tau'')\,\mathrm{d}z\mathrm{d}w\,\mathrm{d}\tau'',$$

$$v^n_{x_ix_j}(x,y,\tau') = \int_0^{\tau'} \int_\Omega G_{x_ix_j}(x,y,z,w,\tau',\tau'')\,\mathcal{F}^{n-1}(z,w,\tau'')\,\mathrm{d}z\mathrm{d}w\,\mathrm{d}\tau''.$$

From Chapter IV.16 in Ref. 20, we have the estimates

$$|G(x,y,z,w,\tau',\tau'')| \leq c_1(\tau'-\tau'')^{-1}\exp\left(-C_2\frac{(x-z)^2+(y-w)^2}{\tau'-\tau''}\right), \tag{14.58}$$

$$|G_{x_i}(x,y,z,w,\tau',\tau'')| \leq c_1(\tau'-\tau'')^{-\frac{3}{2}}\exp\left(-C_2\frac{(x-z)^2+(y-w)^2}{\tau'-\tau''}\right), \tag{14.59}$$

$$|G_{x_ix_j}(x,y,z,w,\tau',\tau'')| \leq c_1(\tau'-\tau'')^{-2}\exp\left(-C_2\frac{(x-z)^2+(y-w)^2}{\tau'-\tau''}\right), \tag{14.60}$$

where $\tau' > \tau''$ and the constants c_1 and C_2 are independent of all parameters of G. If we combine everything together, we get

$$
\begin{aligned}
&\|v^n(\cdot,\cdot,\tau')\|_{W^2_\infty(\Omega)} \\
&= \|v^n(\cdot,\cdot,\tau')\|_{L^\infty(\Omega)} + \sum_{i=1}^{2} \|v^n_{x_i}(\cdot,\cdot,\tau')\|_{L^\infty(\Omega)} + \sum_{i,j=1}^{2} \|v^n_{x_ix_j}(\cdot,\cdot,\tau')\|_{L^\infty(\Omega)} \\
&\leq \int_0^{\tau'} \int_\Omega \|G(\cdot,\cdot,z,w,\tau',\tau'')\|_{L^\infty(\Omega)} \, |\mathcal{F}^{n-1}(z,w,\tau'')| \, \mathrm{d}z\mathrm{d}w \, \mathrm{d}\tau'' \; + \\
&\sum_{i=1}^{2} \int_0^{\tau'} \int_\Omega \|G_{x_i}(\cdot,\cdot,z,w,\tau',\tau'')\|_{L^\infty(\Omega)} \, |\mathcal{F}^{n-1}(z,w,\tau'')| \, \mathrm{d}z\mathrm{d}w \, \mathrm{d}\tau'' \; + \\
&\sum_{i,j=1}^{2} \int_0^{\tau'} \left\| \int_\Omega G_{x_ix_j}(\cdot,\cdot,z,w,\tau',\tau'')\mathcal{F}^{n-1}(z,w,\tau'') \, \mathrm{d}z\mathrm{d}w \right\|_{L^\infty(\Omega)} \mathrm{d}\tau''.
\end{aligned}
$$

Our goal is to show that $\|v^n(\cdot,\cdot,\tau')\|_{W^2_\infty(\Omega)}$ is uniformly bounded on the interval $[0, T^*]$, so that we can use the Arzelà–Ascoli theorem and a weak compactness argument (Theorem 3 of Appendix D in Ref. 6). We obtain the following estimates by using Lemma 14.22

$$
\begin{aligned}
|\mathcal{F}^{n-1}(z,w,\tau'')| \leq C e^w &\left(\left| \frac{\partial(v^{n-1}+\varphi)}{\partial x} \right| + \left| \frac{\partial^2(v^{n-1}+\varphi)}{\partial x^2} \right| \right. \\
&\left. + \left| \frac{\partial^2(v^{n-1}+\varphi)}{\partial x \partial y} \right| \right), \leq C_3 \|v^{n-1}(\cdot,\cdot,\tau'')\|_{W^2_\infty(\Omega)} + C_{T^*},
\end{aligned}
$$

where C_3 is a constant dependent on space variable (boundedness of Ω is crucial) and independent of T^*, whereas C_{T^*} is a constant which depends on T^* (the constant comes from the upper estimate of φ in $[0, T^*]$). By a direct calculation, we can easily see that

$$
\begin{aligned}
&\int_\Omega (\tau'-\tau'')^{-1} \exp\left(-C_2 \frac{(x-z)^2+(y-w)^2}{\tau'-\tau''} \right) \mathrm{d}z\mathrm{d}w \\
&\leq \int_{\mathbb{R}^2} (\tau'-\tau'')^{-1} \exp\left(-C_2 \frac{(x-z)^2+(y-w)^2}{\tau'-\tau''} \right) \mathrm{d}z\mathrm{d}w \\
&= \left(\frac{\pi}{C_2} \right).
\end{aligned}
$$

We can see this by computing the integral in one dimension

$$
\int_{-\infty}^{\infty} (\tau'-\tau'')^{-\frac{1}{2}} \exp\left(-C_2 \frac{(x_1-y_1)^2}{\tau'-\tau''} \right) \mathrm{d}y_1
$$

$$= \int_{-\infty}^{\infty} (\tau' - \tau'')^{-\frac{1}{2}} \sqrt{\frac{\tau' - \tau''}{C_2}} e^{-\omega_1^2} d\omega_1,$$

$$= C_2^{-\frac{1}{2}} \int_{-\infty}^{\infty} e^{-\omega_1^2} d\omega_1,$$

$$= \left(\frac{\pi}{C_2}\right)^{\frac{1}{2}},$$

where we use

$$\omega_1 = \sqrt{\frac{C_2}{\tau' - \tau}} (x_1 - y_1).$$

The integral in $\mathbb{R}^2$ is a product of these one-dimensional integrals. This gives us the desired result.

The Green's function estimate

$$\left\| \int_\Omega G_{x_i x_j}(\cdot, \cdot, z, w, \tau', \tau'') \, dz dw \right\|_{L^\infty(\Omega)} \leq C_4(\tau' - \tau'')^{-\gamma}, \tag{14.61}$$

where C_4 is a constant independent of T^*, $0 < \gamma < 1$ and $\tau' > \tau''$ can be found in Lemma 2.1 of Ref. 21. Using all of our previous estimates and Equation 14.61, we obtain

$$\begin{aligned}
&\|v^n(\cdot, \cdot, \tau')\|_{W^2_\infty(\Omega)} \\
&= \|v^n(\cdot, \cdot, \tau')\|_{L^\infty(\Omega)} + \sum_{i=1}^{2} \|v^n_{x_i}(\cdot, \cdot, \tau')\|_{L^\infty(\Omega)} + \sum_{i,j=1}^{2} \|v^n_{x_i x_j}(\cdot, \cdot, \tau')\|_{L^\infty(\Omega)} \\
&\leq \int_0^{\tau'} \left(A + B(\tau' - \tau'')^{-\frac{1}{2}} + D(\tau' - \tau'')^{-\gamma}\right) \left(C_3 \|v^{n-1}(\cdot, \cdot, \tau'')\|_{W^2_\infty(\Omega)} + C_{T^*}\right) d\tau'' \\
&= C_{T^*} \left(A\tau' + 2B{\tau'}^{1/2} + D\frac{{\tau'}^{1-\gamma}}{1-\gamma}\right) \\
&+ C_3 \int_0^{\tau'} \left(A + B(\tau' - \tau'')^{-\frac{1}{2}} + D(\tau' - \tau'')^{-\gamma}\right) \|v^{n-1}(\cdot, \cdot, \tau'')\|_{W^2_\infty(\Omega)} d\tau'' \\
&\leq C(T^*, \gamma) + C \int_0^{\tau'} \left(A + B(\tau' - \tau'')^{-\frac{1}{2}} + D(\tau' - \tau'')^{-\gamma}\right) \|v^{n-1}(\cdot, \cdot, \tau'')\|_{W^2_\infty(\Omega)} d\tau'',
\end{aligned}$$

where the constants A, B, D, and C are independent of T^*. The constant $C(T^*, \gamma)$ depends only on T^* and γ. Therefore, we have

$$\begin{aligned}
&\|v^n(\cdot, \cdot, \tau')\|_{W^2_\infty(\Omega)} \\
&\leq C(T^*, \gamma) + C \int_0^{\tau'} \left(A + B(\tau' - \tau'')^{-\frac{1}{2}} + D(\tau' - \tau'')^{-\gamma}\right) \|v^{n-1}(\cdot, \cdot, \tau'')\|_{W^2_\infty(\Omega)} d\tau''.
\end{aligned} \tag{14.62}$$

Observe that there exist an upper bound of the integral

$$\int_0^{\tau'} \left(A + B(\tau' - \tau'')^{-\frac{1}{2}} + D(\tau' - \tau'')^{-\gamma}\right) d\tau'',$$

for $\tau' \in [0, T^*]$. Choose A (where $\tau' = \frac{t}{A}$, as defined before) such that this upper bound is ε where $|\varepsilon C| < 1$. This is possible as C does not depend on T^*.
We observe from Equation 14.62 that

$$\|v^1(\cdot,\cdot,\tau')\|_{W^2_\infty(\Omega)} \leq C(T^*, \gamma),$$

$$\begin{aligned}
&\|v^2(\cdot,\cdot,\tau')\|_{W^2_\infty(\Omega)} \\
&\leq C(T^*,\gamma) + C\int_0^{\tau'} \left(A + B(\tau' - \tau'')^{-\frac{1}{2}} + D(\tau' - \tau'')^{-\gamma}\right) \|v^1(\cdot,\cdot,\tau''')\|_{W^2_\infty(\Omega)}\, d\tau'' \\
&\leq C(T^*,\gamma) + C(T^*,\gamma)C\varepsilon,
\end{aligned}$$

$$\begin{aligned}
&\|v^3(\cdot,\cdot,\tau')\|_{W^2_\infty(\Omega)} \\
&\leq C(T^*,\gamma) + C\int_0^{\tau'} \left(A + B(\tau' - \tau'')^{-\frac{1}{2}} + D(\tau' - \tau'')^{-\gamma}\right) \|v^2(\cdot,\cdot,\tau'')\|_{W^2_\infty(\Omega)}\, d\tau'' \\
&\leq C(T^*,\gamma) + C(C(T^*,\gamma) + C(T^*,\gamma)C\varepsilon)\varepsilon \\
&= C(T^*,\gamma) + C(T^*,\gamma)C\varepsilon + C(T^*,\gamma)C^2\varepsilon^2.
\end{aligned}$$

Proceeding this way

$$\|v^n(\cdot,\cdot,\tau')\|_{W^2_\infty(\Omega)} \leq C(T^*,\gamma)\left(1 + C\varepsilon + \cdots + C^{n-1}\varepsilon^{n-1}\right).$$

Since $|\varepsilon C| < 1$, we obtain $\|v^n(\cdot,\cdot,\tau')\|_{W^2_\infty(\Omega)} \leq \frac{C(T^*,\gamma)}{1-\varepsilon C}$, where $n = 0, 1, 2, \ldots$. Consequently $\|v^n(\cdot,\cdot,\tau')\|_{W^2_\infty(\Omega)}$ is uniformly bounded on the closed interval $[0, T^*]$. Using this result along with Equation 5.6, we can easily show that $\|v^n_{\tau'}(\cdot,\cdot,\tau')\|_{L^\infty(\Omega)}$ is also uniformly bounded on $[0, T^*]$.

Since $\|v^n(\cdot,\cdot,\tau')\|_{W^2_\infty(\Omega)}$ and $\|v^n_{\tau'}(\cdot,\cdot,\tau')\|_{L^\infty(\Omega)}$ are continuous functions of τ' on the closed interval $[0, T^*]$, it follows that $|v^n|$, $|v^n_{x_i}|$, $|v^n_{x_ix_j}|$ and $|v^n_t|$ are uniformly bounded on $\overline{Q}_{T^*}$. Thus $v^n(\cdot,\cdot,\tau')$ is equicontinuous in $C(\overline{Q}_{T^*})$. By the Arzelà–Ascoli theorem, there exists a subsequence $\{v^{n_k}\}_{k=0}^\infty$ such that as $k \to \infty$,

$$\begin{aligned}
v^{n_k} &\to v \in C(\overline{Q}_{T^*}) \quad \text{and} \\
v^{n_k}_{x_i} &\to v_{x_i} \in C(\overline{Q}_{T^*}),
\end{aligned}$$

where the convergence is uniform. Furthermore, by Theorem 3 in Appendix D of [6],

$$v^{n_k}_{x_ix_j} \to v_{x_ix_j} \in L^\infty(\overline{Q}_{T*}) \quad \text{and}$$
$$v^{n_k}_{\tau'} \to v_{\tau'} \in L^\infty(\overline{Q}_{T*}),$$

as $k \to \infty$. Here, the convergence is in the weak sense. Therefore, v^{n_k} converges uniformly on the compact set $\overline{Q}_{T*}$ to a function $v \in C^{1+1,0+1}(\overline{Q}_{T*})$. By a standard argument Ref. 22, we have that v satisfies the parabolic equation in Equation 14.55 almost everywhere and the initial-boundary conditions in the classical sense. Hence, v is a strong solution to problem (Eq. 14.55). Consequently, u is a strong solution to Equation 14.53. ■

Now, we show that we can extend this solution to give us a classical solution on the unbounded domain $\mathbb{R}^{d+1}_T = \mathbb{R}^d \times (0, T)$.

THEOREM 14.26

There exists a classical solution $u \in C^{2,1}(\mathbb{R}^{2+1}_T)$ to the problem

$$-u_\tau + Lu = \mathfrak{F}\left(y, \frac{\partial u}{\partial x}, \frac{\partial^2 u}{\partial x^2}, \frac{\partial^2 u}{\partial x \partial y}\right) \quad \text{in} \quad \mathbb{R}^{2+1}_T$$
$$u(x, y, 0) = u_0(x, y) \quad \text{on} \quad \mathbb{R}^2 \tag{14.63}$$

such that the solution $u(x, y, t) \to g(x, y, t)$ as $\sqrt{x^2 + y^2} \to \infty$.

Proof. We approximate the domain $\mathbb{R}^2$ by a nondecreasing sequence $\{\Omega_N\}_{N=1}^\infty$ of bounded smooth subdomains of Ω. For simplicity, we will let $\Omega_N = B(0, N)$ be the open ball in $\mathbb{R}^2$ centered at the origin with radius N. Also, we let $V_N = \Omega_N \times (0, T)$.

Using the previous theorem, we let $u_M \in C^{2,1}(\overline{V}_M)$ be a solution to the problem

$$\begin{aligned} -u_\tau + Lu &= \mathfrak{F}\left(y, \tfrac{\partial u}{\partial x}, \tfrac{\partial^2 u}{\partial x^2}, \tfrac{\partial^2 u}{\partial x \partial y}\right) && \text{in } V_M, \\ u(x, y, 0) &= u_0(x, y) && \text{on } \Omega_M, \\ u(x, y, t) &= g(x, y, t) && \text{on } \partial\Omega_M \times (0, T). \end{aligned} \tag{14.64}$$

Since $M \geq 1$ is arbitrary, we can use a standard diagonal argument to extract a subsequence that converges to a solution u to the problem on the whole unbounded space $\mathbb{R}^{2+1}_T$. Clearly, $u(x, y, 0) = u_0(x, y)$ and $u(x, y, t) \to g(x, y, t)$ as $\sqrt{x^2 + y^2} \to \infty$. ■

REFERENCES

1. Black F, Scholes M. The pricing of options and corporate liabilities. J Polit Econ 1973;81:637–659.
2. Leland HE. Option pricing and replication with transaction costs. J Finance 1985;40:1283–301.
3. Hoggard T, Whalley AE, Wilmott P. Hedging option portfolios in the presence of transaction costs. Adv Fut Opt Res 1994;7: 21.
4. SenGupta I. Spectral analysis for a three-dimensional superradiance problem. J Math Anal Appl 2011;375:762–776.
5. SenGupta I. Differential operator related to the generalized superradiance integral equation. J Math Anal Appl 2010;369:101–111.
6. Evans LC. Partial differential equations. Graduate studies in Mathematics, American Mathematical Society 1998.
7. Krylov NV. Lectures on elliptic and parabolic equations in Hölder spaces. Volume 12 of Graduate studies in mathematics. American Mathematical Society, Providence, Rhode Island; 1996.
8. Wang C, Wu Z, Yin J. Elliptic and parabolic equations. World Scientific Publishing, Singapore; 2006.
9. Folland GB. Introduction to partial differential equations. 2nd ed. Princeton University Press, Princeton, New Jersey; 1995.
10. Heston SL. A closed-form solution for options with stochastic volatility with applications to bond and currency options. Rev Financ Stud 1993;6:327–344.
11. Mariani MC, Florescu I, Beccar Varela MP, Ncheuguim E. Long correlations and Levy models applied to the study of memory effects in high frequency (tick) data. Physica A 2009;388(8): 1659–1664.
12. Mariani MC, Florescu I, Beccar Varela MP, Ncheuguim E. Study of memory effects in international market indices. Physica A 2010;389(8):1653–1664.
13. Hull JC, White AD. The pricing of options on assets with stochastic volatilities. J Finance 1987;42(2):281–300.
14. Wiggins, J. B., Option values under stochastic volatility: Theory and empirical estimates, J Financ Econ *19*(2),351–372, December 1987.
15. Hagan P, Kumar D, Lesniewski A., Woodward D. Managing smile risk. Wilmott Magazine, 2002.
16. Florescu I, Mariani MC. Solutions to an integro-differential parabolic problem arising in the pricing of financial options in a Levy market. Electron J Differ Equat 2010;2010(62):1–10.
17. Harrison JM, Pliska SR. Martingales and stochastic integrals in the theory of continuous trading. Stoch Proc Appl 1981;11(3):215–260.
18. Delbaen F, Schachermayer W. A general version of the fundamental theorem of asset pricing. Math Ann 1994;300:463–520.
19. Florescu I, Viens F. Stochastic volatility: option pricing using a multinomial recombining tree. Appl Math Finance 2008;15(2):151–181.

20. Ladyzenskaja OA, Solonikov VA, Ural'ceva NN. Linear and quasilinear equations of parabolic type. Volume 23. American Mathematical Society; 1964.
21. Yin HM. A uniqueness theorem for a class of non-classical parabolic equations. Appl Anal 1989;34:67–78.
22. Friedman A. Partial differential equations of parabolic type. Prentice Hall, New Jersey; 1964.

Index

Handbook of Modeling High-Frequency Data in Finance, First Edition.
Edited by Frederi G. Viens, Maria C. Mariani, and Ionuţ Florescu.